MODEL RULES
OF PROFESSIONAL CONDUCT
and
OTHER SELECTED STANDARDS

Including California and New York Rules

on

PROFESSIONAL
RESPONSIBILITY

2019 Edition

THOMAS D. MORGAN
Oppenheim Professor Emeritus
The George Washington University Law School

 FOUNDATION
PRESS

The publisher is not engaged in rendering legal or other professional advice, and this publication is not a substitute for the advice of an attorney. If you require legal or other expert advice, you should seek the services of a competent attorney or other professional.

© 1976, 1978–1981, 1983–2004 FOUNDATION PRESS
© 2005–2013 THOMSON REUTERS/FOUNDATION PRESS
© 2014–2018 LEG, Inc. d/b/a West Academic
© 2019 LEG, Inc. d/b/a West Academic
    444 Cedar Street, Suite 700
    St. Paul, MN 55101
    1-877-888-1330

Printed in the United States of America

ISBN: 978-1-64242-089-0

In Memory of Ronald D. Rotunda
February 14, 1945–March 14, 2018

PREFACE

This 2019 Supplement reflects changes in professional standards through October 2018. The 2018 changes were even more significant than usual.

The book begins with the ABA Model Rules, whose advertising rules were amended by the ABA House of Delegates in August 2018. We then continue to include updated appendices to the Model Rules that give a state-by-state analysis of (1) rules that govern client confidences (2) rules that permit screening to avoid imputed disqualification and (3) rules that require a written fee agreement.

Next, we include the California Rules of Professional Conduct as extensively amended and reorganized by the California Supreme Court, effective November 1, 2018. The changes are the most important in California in more than a generation. We then provide expanded coverage of the related California statutes regulating lawyers.

This year's Supplement also continues to include the New York Rules of Professional Conduct, relevant federal statutes and federal rules governing lawyers.

On the subject of judicial ethics, we include the ABA Model Code of Judicial Conduct, the corresponding California Code of Judicial Ethics, the Code of Conduct for federal judges, and selected federal statutes relating to judges.

This year's editor again thanks the publishers of documents used, in particular the American Bar Association, American Law Institute and Attorneys' Liability Assurance Society, for permission to reprint their copyrighted material.

Finally, this year's Supplement continues to reflect the work of Ronald D. Rotunda, to whom this edition is dedicated. His contributions to legal ethics were enormous and his death in March 2018 is still hard to absorb.

T.D.M.

November 2018

TABLE OF CONTENTS

MODEL RULES
OF PROFESSIONAL CONDUCT
and
OTHER SELECTED STANDARDS

Including California and
New York Rules

on

PROFESSIONAL
RESPONSIBILITY

2019 Edition

THE AMERICAN BAR ASSOCIATION MODEL RULES OF PROFESSIONAL CONDUCT

The ABA House of Delegates adopted the Model Rules of Professional Conduct on August 2, 1983. They were amended over the years and were subject to substantial modifications in August, 2001, and February and August, 2002, in response to changes proposed by the ABA Commission on Evaluation of the Rules of Professional Conduct, popularly called "Ethics, 2000." Only a year later, in August, 2003, the ABA amended Rule 1.6 and Rule 1.13 in response to the Enron collapse. The ABA again amended the Model Rules in 2012, 2013, 2016 and 2018. This version reflects all of these changes.

Table of Contents

PREAMBLE: A LAWYER'S RESPONSIBILITIES

[1]   A lawyer, as a member of the legal profession, is a representative of clients, an officer of the legal system and a public citizen having special responsibility for the quality of justice.

[2]   As a representative of clients, a lawyer performs various functions. As advisor, a lawyer provides a client with an informed understanding of the client's legal rights and obligations and explains their practical implications. As advocate, a lawyer zealously asserts the client's position under the rules of the adversary system. As negotiator, a lawyer seeks a result advantageous to the client but consistent with requirements of honest dealings with others. As an evaluator, a lawyer acts by examining a client's legal affairs and reporting about them to the client or to others.

[3]   In addition to these representational functions, a lawyer may serve as a third-party neutral, a nonrepresentational role helping the parties to resolve a dispute or other matter. Some of these Rules apply directly to lawyers who are or have served as third-party neutrals. See, e.g., Rules 1.12 and 2.4. In addition, there are Rules that apply to lawyers who are not active in the practice of law or to practicing lawyers even when they are acting in a nonprofessional capacity. For example, a lawyer who commits fraud in the conduct of a business is subject to discipline for engaging in conduct involving dishonesty, fraud, deceit or misrepresentation. See Rule 8.4.

[4]   In all professional functions a lawyer should be competent, prompt and diligent. A lawyer should maintain communication with a client concerning the representation. A lawyer should keep in confidence information relating to representation of a client except so far as disclosure is required or permitted by the Rules of Professional Conduct or other law.

[5]   A lawyer's conduct should conform to the requirements of the law, both in professional service to clients and in the lawyer's business and personal affairs. A lawyer should use the law's procedures only for legitimate purposes and not to harass or intimidate others. A lawyer should demonstrate respect for the legal system and for those who serve it, including judges, other lawyers and public officials. While it is a lawyer's duty, when necessary, to challenge the rectitude of official action, it is also a lawyer's duty to uphold legal process.

[6]   As a public citizen, a lawyer should seek improvement of the law, access to the legal system, the administration of justice and the quality of service rendered by the legal profession. As a member of a learned profession, a lawyer should cultivate knowledge of the law beyond its use for clients, employ that knowledge in reform of the law and work to strengthen legal education. In addition, a lawyer should further the public's understanding of and confidence in the rule of law and the justice system because legal institutions in a constitutional democracy depend on popular participation and support to maintain their authority. A lawyer should be mindful of deficiencies in the administration of justice and of the fact that the poor, and sometimes persons who are not poor, cannot afford adequate legal assistance. Therefore, all lawyers should devote professional time and resources and use civic influence to ensure equal access to our system of justice for all those who because of economic or social barriers cannot afford or secure adequate legal counsel. A lawyer should aid the legal profession in pursuing these objectives and should help the bar regulate itself in the public interest.

[7]   Many of a lawyer's professional responsibilities are prescribed in the Rules of Professional Conduct, as well as substantive and procedural law.

However, a lawyer is also guided by personal conscience and the approbation of professional peers. A lawyer should strive to attain the highest level of skill, to improve the law and the legal profession and to exemplify the legal profession's ideals of public service.

[8] A lawyer's responsibilities as a representative of clients, an officer of the legal system and a public citizen are usually harmonious. Thus, when an opposing party is well represented, a lawyer can be a zealous advocate on behalf of a client and at the same time assume that justice is being done. So also, a lawyer can be sure that preserving client confidences ordinarily serves the public interest because people are more likely to seek legal advice, and thereby heed their legal obligations, when they know their communications will be private.

[9] In the nature of law practice, however, conflicting responsibilities are encountered. Virtually all difficult ethical problems arise from conflict between a lawyer's responsibilities to clients, to the legal system and to the lawyer's own interest in remaining an ethical person while earning a satisfactory living. The Rules of Professional Conduct often prescribe terms for resolving such conflicts. Within the framework of these Rules, however, many difficult issues of professional discretion can arise. Such issues must be resolved through the exercise of sensitive professional and moral judgment guided by the basic principles underlying the Rules. These principles include the lawyer's obligation zealously to protect and pursue a client's legitimate interests, within the bounds of the law, while maintaining a professional, courteous and civil attitude toward all persons involved in the legal system.

[10] The legal profession is largely self-governing. Although other professions also have been granted powers of self-government, the legal profession is unique in this respect because of the close relationship between the profession and the processes of government and law enforcement. This connection is manifested in the fact that ultimate authority over the legal profession is vested largely in the courts.

[11] To the extent that lawyers meet the obligations of their professional calling, the occasion for government regulation is obviated. Self-regulation also helps maintain the legal profession's independence from government domination. An independent legal profession is an important force in preserving government under law, for abuse of legal authority is more readily challenged by a profession whose members are not dependent on government for the right to practice.

[12] The legal profession's relative autonomy carries with it special responsibilities of self-government. The profession has a responsibility to assure that its regulations are conceived in the public interest and not in furtherance of parochial or self-interested concerns of the bar. Every lawyer is responsible for observance of the Rules of Professional Conduct. A lawyer should also aid in securing their observance by other lawyers. Neglect of these responsibilities compromises the independence of the profession and the public interest which it serves.

[13] Lawyers play a vital role in the preservation of society. The fulfillment of this role requires an understanding by lawyers of their relationship to our legal system. The Rules of Professional Conduct, when properly applied, serve to define that relationship.

SCOPE

[14] The Rules of Professional Conduct are rules of reason. They should be interpreted with reference to the purposes of legal representation and of

the law itself. Some of the Rules are imperatives, cast in the terms "shall" or "shall not." These define proper conduct for purposes of professional discipline. Others, generally cast in the term "may," are permissive and define areas under the Rules in which the lawyer has discretion to exercise professional judgment. No disciplinary action should be taken when the lawyer chooses not to act or acts within the bounds of such discretion. Other Rules define the nature of relationships between the lawyer and others. The Rules are thus partly obligatory and disciplinary and partly constitutive and descriptive in that they define a lawyer's professional role. Many of the Comments use the term "should." Comments do not add obligations to the Rules but provide guidance for practicing in compliance with the Rules.

[15] The Rules presuppose a larger legal context shaping the lawyer's role. That context includes court rules and statutes relating to matters of licensure, laws defining specific obligations of lawyers and substantive and procedural law in general. The Comments are sometimes used to alert lawyers to their responsibilities under such other law.

[16] Compliance with the Rules, as with all law in an open society, depends primarily upon understanding and voluntary compliance, secondarily upon reinforcement by peer and public opinion and finally, when necessary, upon enforcement through disciplinary proceedings. The Rules do not, however, exhaust the moral and ethical considerations that should inform a lawyer, for no worthwhile human activity can be completely defined by legal rules. The Rules simply provide a framework for the ethical practice of law.

[17] Furthermore, for purposes of determining the lawyer's authority and responsibility, principles of substantive law external to these Rules determine whether a client-lawyer relationship exists. Most of the duties flowing from the client-lawyer relationship attach only after the client has requested the lawyer to render legal services and the lawyer has agreed to do so. But there are some duties, such as that of confidentiality under Rule 1.6, that attach when the lawyer agrees to consider whether a client-lawyer relationship shall be established. See Rule 1.18. Whether a client-lawyer relationship exists for any specific purpose can depend on the circumstances and may be a question of fact.

[18] Under various legal provisions, including constitutional, statutory and common law, the responsibilities of government lawyers may include authority concerning legal matters that ordinarily reposes in the client in private client-lawyer relationships. For example, a lawyer for a government agency may have authority on behalf of the government to decide upon settlement or whether to appeal from an adverse judgment. Such authority in various respects is generally vested in the attorney general and the state's attorney in state government, and their federal counterparts, and the same may be true of other government law officers. Also, lawyers under the supervision of these officers may be authorized to represent several government agencies in intragovernmental legal controversies in circumstances where a private lawyer could not represent multiple private clients. These Rules do not abrogate any such authority.

[19] Failure to comply with an obligation or prohibition imposed by a Rule is a basis for invoking the disciplinary process. The Rules presuppose that disciplinary assessment of a lawyer's conduct will be made on the basis of the facts and circumstances as they existed at the time of the conduct in question and in recognition of the fact that a lawyer often has to act upon uncertain or incomplete evidence of the situation. Moreover, the Rules

presuppose that whether or not discipline should be imposed for a violation, and the severity of a sanction, depend on all the circumstances, such as the willfulness and seriousness of the violation, extenuating factors and whether there have been previous violations.

[20] Violation of a Rule should not itself give rise to a cause of action against a lawyer nor should it create any presumption in such a case that a legal duty has been breached. In addition, violation of a Rule does not necessarily warrant any other nondisciplinary remedy, such as disqualification of a lawyer in pending litigation. The Rules are designed to provide guidance to lawyers and to provide a structure for regulating conduct through disciplinary agencies. They are not designed to be a basis for civil liability. Furthermore, the purpose of the Rules can be subverted when they are invoked by opposing parties as procedural weapons. The fact that a Rule is a just basis for a lawyer's self-assessment, or for sanctioning a lawyer under the administration of a disciplinary authority, does not imply that an antagonist in a collateral proceeding or transaction has standing to seek enforcement of the Rule. Nevertheless, since the Rules do establish standards of conduct by lawyers, a lawyer's violation of a Rule may be evidence of breach of the applicable standard of conduct.

[21] The Comment accompanying each Rule explains and illustrates the meaning and purpose of the Rule. The Preamble and this note on Scope provide general orientation. The Comments are intended as guides to interpretation, but the text of each Rule is authoritative.

RULE 1.0: TERMINOLOGY

(a) "Belief" or "believes" denotes that the person involved actually supposed the fact in question to be true. A person's belief may be inferred from circumstances.

(b) "Confirmed in writing," when used in reference to the informed consent of a person, denotes informed consent that is given in writing by the person or a writing that a lawyer promptly transmits to the person confirming an oral informed consent. See paragraph (e) for the definition of "informed consent." If it is not feasible to obtain or transmit the writing at the time the person gives informed consent, then the lawyer must obtain or transmit it within a reasonable time thereafter.

(c) "Firm" or "law firm" denotes a lawyer or lawyers in a law partnership, professional corporation, sole proprietorship or other association authorized to practice law; or lawyers employed in a legal services organization or the legal department of a corporation or other organization.

(d) "Fraud" or "fraudulent" denotes conduct that is fraudulent under the substantive or procedural law of the applicable jurisdiction and has a purpose to deceive.

(e) "Informed consent" denotes the agreement by a person to a proposed course of conduct after the lawyer has communicated adequate information and explanation about the material risks of and reasonably available alternatives to the proposed course of conduct.

(f) "Knowingly," "known," or "knows" denotes actual knowledge of the fact in question. A person's knowledge may be inferred from circumstances.

(g) "Partner" denotes a member of a partnership, a shareholder in a law firm organized as a professional corporation, or a member of an association authorized to practice law.

(h) "Reasonable" or "reasonably" when used in relation to conduct by a lawyer denotes the conduct of a reasonably prudent and competent lawyer.

(i) "Reasonable belief" or "reasonably believes" when used in reference to a lawyer denotes that the lawyer believes the matter in question and that the circumstances are such that the belief is reasonable.

(j) "Reasonably should know" when used in reference to a lawyer denotes that a lawyer of reasonable prudence and competence would ascertain the matter in question.

(k) "Screened" denotes the isolation of a lawyer from any participation in a matter through the timely imposition of procedures within a firm that are reasonably adequate under the circumstances to protect information that the isolated lawyer is obligated to protect under these Rules or other law.

(*l*) "Substantial" when used in reference to degree or extent denotes a material matter of clear and weighty importance.

(m) "Tribunal" denotes a court, an arbitrator in a binding arbitration proceeding or a legislative body, administrative agency or other body acting in an adjudicative capacity. A legislative body, administrative agency or other body acts in an adjudicative capacity when a neutral official, after the presentation of evidence or legal argument by a party or parties, will render a binding legal judgment directly affecting a party's interests in a particular matter.

(n) "Writing" or "written" denotes a tangible or electronic record of a communication or representation, including handwriting, typewriting, printing, photostating, photography, audio or videorecording and electronic communications. A "signed" writing includes an electronic sound, symbol or process attached to or logically associated with a writing and executed or adopted by a person with the intent to sign the writing.

Comment

Confirmed in Writing

[1] If it is not feasible to obtain or transmit a written confirmation at the time the client gives informed consent, then the lawyer must obtain or transmit it within a reasonable time thereafter. If a lawyer has obtained a client's informed consent, the lawyer may act in reliance on that consent so long as it is confirmed in writing within a reasonable time thereafter.

Firm

[2] Whether two or more lawyers constitute a firm within paragraph (c) can depend on the specific facts. For example, two practitioners who share office space and occasionally consult or assist each other ordinarily would not be regarded as constituting a firm. However, if they present themselves to the public in a way that suggests that they are a firm or conduct themselves as a firm, they should be regarded as a firm for purposes of the Rules. The terms of any formal agreement between associated lawyers are relevant in determining whether they are a firm, as is the fact that they have mutual

access to information concerning the clients they serve. Furthermore, it is relevant in doubtful cases to consider the underlying purpose of the Rule that is involved. A group of lawyers could be regarded as a firm for purposes of the Rule that the same lawyer should not represent opposing parties in litigation, while it might not be so regarded for purposes of the Rule that information acquired by one lawyer is attributed to another.

[3] With respect to the law department of an organization, including the government, there is ordinarily no question that the members of the department constitute a firm within the meaning of the Rules of Professional Conduct. There can be uncertainty, however, as to the identity of the client. For example, it may not be clear whether the law department of a corporation represents a subsidiary or an affiliated corporation, as well as the corporation by which the members of the department are directly employed. A similar question can arise concerning an unincorporated association and its local affiliates.

[4] Similar questions can also arise with respect to lawyers in legal aid and legal services organizations. Depending upon the structure of the organization, the entire organization or different components of it may constitute a firm or firms for purposes of these Rules.

Fraud

[5] When used in these Rules, the terms "fraud" or "fraudulent" refer to conduct that is characterized as such under the substantive or procedural law of the applicable jurisdiction and has a purpose to deceive. This does not include merely negligent misrepresentation or negligent failure to apprise another of relevant information. For purposes of these Rules, it is not necessary that anyone has suffered damages or relied on the misrepresentation or failure to inform.

Informed Consent

[6] Many of the Rules of Professional Conduct require the lawyer to obtain the informed consent of a client or other person (e.g., a former client or, under certain circumstances, a prospective client) before accepting or continuing representation or pursuing a course of conduct. See, e.g., Rules 1.2(c), 1.6(a) and 1.7(b). The communication necessary to obtain such consent will vary according to the Rule involved and the circumstances giving rise to the need to obtain informed consent. The lawyer must make reasonable efforts to ensure that the client or other person possesses information reasonably adequate to make an informed decision. Ordinarily, this will require communication that includes a disclosure of the facts and circumstances giving rise to the situation, any explanation reasonably necessary to inform the client or other person of the material advantages and disadvantages of the proposed course of conduct and a discussion of the client's or other person's options and alternatives. In some circumstances it may be appropriate for a lawyer to advise a client or other person to seek the advice of other counsel. A lawyer need not inform a client or other person of facts or implications already known to the client or other person; nevertheless, a lawyer who does not personally inform the client or other person assumes the risk that the client or other person is inadequately informed and the consent is invalid. In determining whether the information and explanation provided are reasonably adequate, relevant factors include whether the client or other person is experienced in legal matters generally and in making decisions of the type involved, and whether the client or other person is independently represented by other counsel in giving the consent. Normally, such persons need less information and explanation than others,

and generally a client or other person who is independently represented by other counsel in giving the consent should be assumed to have given informed consent.

[7]   Obtaining informed consent will usually require an affirmative response by the client or other person. In general, a lawyer may not assume consent from a client's or other person's silence. Consent may be inferred, however, from the conduct of a client or other person who has reasonably adequate information about the matter. A number of Rules require that a person's consent be confirmed in writing. See Rules 1.7(b) and 1.9(a). For a definition of "writing" and "confirmed in writing," see paragraphs (n) and (b). Other Rules require that a client's consent be obtained in a writing signed by the client. See, e.g., Rules 1.8(a) and (g). For a definition of "signed," see paragraph (n).

Screened

[8]   This definition applies to situations where screening of a personally disqualified lawyer is permitted to remove imputation of a conflict of interest under Rules 1.11, 1.12 or 1.18.

[9]   The purpose of screening is to assure the affected parties that confidential information known by the personally disqualified lawyer remains protected. The personally disqualified lawyer should acknowledge the obligation not to communicate with any of the other lawyers in the firm with respect to the matter. Similarly, other lawyers in the firm who are working on the matter should be informed that the screening is in place and that they may not communicate with the personally disqualified lawyer with respect to the matter. Additional screening measures that are appropriate for the particular matter will depend on the circumstances. To implement, reinforce and remind all affected lawyers of the presence of the screening, it may be appropriate for the firm to undertake such procedures as a written undertaking by the screened lawyer to avoid any communication with other firm personnel and any contact with any firm files or other information, including information in electronic form, relating to the matter, written notice and instructions to all other firm personnel forbidding any communication with the screened lawyer relating to the matter, denial of access by the screened lawyer to firm files or other information, including information in electronic form, relating to the matter and periodic reminders of the screen to the screened lawyer and all other firm personnel.

[10] In order to be effective, screening measures must be implemented as soon as practical after a lawyer or law firm knows or reasonably should know that there is a need for screening.

CLIENT-LAWYER RELATIONSHIP

RULE 1.1: COMPETENCE

A lawyer shall provide competent representation to a client. Competent representation requires the legal knowledge, skill, thoroughness and preparation reasonably necessary for the representation.

Comment

Legal Knowledge and Skill

[1]   In determining whether a lawyer employs the requisite knowledge and skill in a particular matter, relevant factors include the relative complexity and specialized nature of the matter, the lawyer's general

experience, the lawyer's training and experience in the field in question, the preparation and study the lawyer is able to give the matter and whether it is feasible to refer the matter to, or associate or consult with, a lawyer of established competence in the field in question. In many instances, the required proficiency is that of a general practitioner. Expertise in a particular field of law may be required in some circumstances.

[2]   A lawyer need not necessarily have special training or prior experience to handle legal problems of a type with which the lawyer is unfamiliar. A newly admitted lawyer can be as competent as a practitioner with long experience. Some important legal skills, such as the analysis of precedent, the evaluation of evidence and legal drafting, are required in all legal problems. Perhaps the most fundamental legal skill consists of determining what kind of legal problems a situation may involve, a skill that necessarily transcends any particular specialized knowledge. A lawyer can provide adequate representation in a wholly novel field through necessary study. Competent representation can also be provided through the association of a lawyer of established competence in the field in question.

[3]   In an emergency a lawyer may give advice or assistance in a matter in which the lawyer does not have the skill ordinarily required where referral to or consultation or association with another lawyer would be impractical. Even in an emergency, however, assistance should be limited to that reasonably necessary in the circumstances, for ill-considered action under emergency conditions can jeopardize the client's interest.

[4]   A lawyer may accept representation where the requisite level of competence can be achieved by reasonable preparation. This applies as well to a lawyer who is appointed as counsel for an unrepresented person. See also Rule 6.2.

Thoroughness and Preparation

[5]   Competent handling of a particular matter includes inquiry into and analysis of the factual and legal elements of the problem, and use of methods and procedures meeting the standards of competent practitioners. It also includes adequate preparation. The required attention and preparation are determined in part by what is at stake; major litigation and complex transactions ordinarily require more extensive treatment than matters of lesser complexity and consequence. An agreement between the lawyer and the client regarding the scope of the representation may limit the matters for which the lawyer is responsible. See Rule 1.2(c).

Retaining or Contracting with Other Lawyers

[6]   Before a lawyer retains or contracts with other lawyers outside the lawyer's own firm to provide or assist in the provision of legal services to a client, the lawyer should ordinarily obtain informed consent from the client and must reasonably believe that the other lawyers' services will contribute to the competent and ethical representation of the client. See also Rules 1.2 (allocation of authority), 1.4 (communication with client), 1.5(e) (fee sharing), 1.6 (confidentiality), and 5.5(a) (unauthorized practice of law). The reasonableness of the decision to retain or contract with other lawyers outside the lawyer's own firm will depend upon the circumstances, including the education, experience and reputation of the nonfirm lawyers; the nature of the services assigned to the nonfirm lawyers; and the legal protections, professional conduct rules, and ethical environments of the jurisdictions in which the services will be performed, particularly relating to confidential information.

[7]   When lawyers from more than one law firm are providing legal services to the client on a particular matter, the lawyers ordinarily should consult with each other and the client about the scope of their respective representations and the allocation of responsibility among them. See Rule 1.2. When making allocations of responsibility in a matter pending before a tribunal, lawyers and parties may have additional obligations that are a matter of law beyond the scope of these Rules.

Maintaining Competence

[8]   To maintain the requisite knowledge and skill, a lawyer should keep abreast of changes in the law and its practice, including the benefits and risks associated with relevant technology, engage in continuing study and education and comply with all continuing legal education requirements to which the lawyer is subject.

RULE 1.2: SCOPE OF REPRESENTATION AND ALLOCATION OF AUTHORITY BETWEEN CLIENT AND LAWYER

(a)   Subject to paragraphs (c) and (d), a lawyer shall abide by a client's decisions concerning the objectives of representation and, as required by Rule 1.4, shall consult with the client as to the means by which they are to be pursued. A lawyer may take such action on behalf of the client as is impliedly authorized to carry out the representation. A lawyer shall abide by a client's decision whether to settle a matter. In a criminal case, the lawyer shall abide by the client's decision, after consultation with the lawyer, as to a plea to be entered, whether to waive jury trial and whether the client will testify.

(b)   A lawyer's representation of a client, including representation by appointment, does not constitute an endorsement of the client's political, economic, social or moral views or activities.

(c)   A lawyer may limit the scope of the representation if the limitation is reasonable under the circumstances and the client gives informed consent.

(d)   A lawyer shall not counsel a client to engage, or assist a client, in conduct that the lawyer knows is criminal or fraudulent, but a lawyer may discuss the legal consequences of any proposed course of conduct with a client and may counsel or assist a client to make a good faith effort to determine the validity, scope, meaning or application of the law.

Comment

Allocation of Authority between Client and Lawyer

[1]   Paragraph (a) confers upon the client the ultimate authority to determine the purposes to be served by legal representation, within the limits imposed by law and the lawyer's professional obligations. The decisions specified in paragraph (a), such as whether to settle a civil matter, must also be made by the client. See Rule 1.4(a)(1) for the lawyer's duty to communicate with the client about such decisions. With respect to the means by which the client's objectives are to be pursued, the lawyer shall consult with the client as required by Rule 1.4(a)(2) and may take such action as is impliedly authorized to carry out the representation.

[2]   On occasion, however, a lawyer and a client may disagree about the means to be used to accomplish the client's objectives. Clients normally defer to the special knowledge and skill of their lawyer with respect to the means to be used to accomplish their objectives, particularly with respect to technical, legal and tactical matters. Conversely, lawyers usually defer to the client regarding such questions as the expense to be incurred and concern for third persons who might be adversely affected. Because of the varied nature of the matters about which a lawyer and client might disagree and because the actions in question may implicate the interests of a tribunal or other persons, this Rule does not prescribe how such disagreements are to be resolved. Other law, however, may be applicable and should be consulted by the lawyer. The lawyer should also consult with the client and seek a mutually acceptable resolution of the disagreement. If such efforts are unavailing and the lawyer has a fundamental disagreement with the client, the lawyer may withdraw from the representation. See Rule 1.16(b)(4). Conversely, the client may resolve the disagreement by discharging the lawyer. See Rule 1.16(a)(3).

[3]   At the outset of a representation, the client may authorize the lawyer to take specific action on the client's behalf without further consultation. Absent a material change in circumstances and subject to Rule 1.4, a lawyer may rely on such an advance authorization. The client may, however, revoke such authority at any time.

[4]   In a case in which the client appears to be suffering diminished capacity, the lawyer's duty to abide by the client's decisions is to be guided by reference to Rule 1.14.

Independence from Client's Views or Activities

[5]   Legal representation should not be denied to people who are unable to afford legal services, or whose cause is controversial or the subject of popular disapproval. By the same token, representing a client does not constitute approval of the client's views or activities.

Agreements Limiting Scope of Representation

[6]   The scope of services to be provided by a lawyer may be limited by agreement with the client or by the terms under which the lawyer's services are made available to the client. When a lawyer has been retained by an insurer to represent an insured, for example, the representation may be limited to matters related to the insurance coverage. A limited representation may be appropriate because the client has limited objectives for the representation. In addition, the terms upon which representation is undertaken may exclude specific means that might otherwise be used to accomplish the client's objectives. Such limitations may exclude actions that the client thinks are too costly or that the lawyer regards as repugnant or imprudent.

[7]   Although this Rule affords the lawyer and client substantial latitude to limit the representation, the limitation must be reasonable under the circumstances. If, for example, a client's objective is limited to securing general information about the law the client needs in order to handle a common and typically uncomplicated legal problem, the lawyer and client may agree that the lawyer's services will be limited to a brief telephone consultation. Such a limitation, however, would not be reasonable if the time allotted was not sufficient to yield advice upon which the client could rely. Although an agreement for a limited representation does not exempt a lawyer from the duty to provide competent representation, the limitation is a factor

to be considered when determining the legal knowledge, skill, thoroughness and preparation reasonably necessary for the representation. See Rule 1.1.

[8] All agreements concerning a lawyer's representation of a client must accord with the Rules of Professional Conduct and other law. See, e.g., Rules 1.1, 1.8 and 5.6.

Criminal, Fraudulent and Prohibited Transactions

[9] Paragraph (d) prohibits a lawyer from knowingly counseling or assisting a client to commit a crime or fraud. This prohibition, however, does not preclude the lawyer from giving an honest opinion about the actual consequences that appear likely to result from a client's conduct. Nor does the fact that a client uses advice in a course of action that is criminal or fraudulent of itself make a lawyer a party to the course of action. There is a critical distinction between presenting an analysis of legal aspects of questionable conduct and recommending the means by which a crime or fraud might be committed with impunity.

[10] When the client's course of action has already begun and is continuing, the lawyer's responsibility is especially delicate. The lawyer is required to avoid assisting the client, for example, by drafting or delivering documents that the lawyer knows are fraudulent or by suggesting how the wrongdoing might be concealed. A lawyer may not continue assisting a client in conduct that the lawyer originally supposed was legally proper but then discovers is criminal or fraudulent. The lawyer must, therefore, withdraw from the representation of the client in the matter. See Rule 1.16(a). In some cases, withdrawal alone might be insufficient. It may be necessary for the lawyer to give notice of the fact of withdrawal and to disaffirm any opinion, document, affirmation or the like. See Rule 4.1.

[11] Where the client is a fiduciary, the lawyer may be charged with special obligations in dealings with a beneficiary.

[12] Paragraph (d) applies whether or not the defrauded party is a party to the transaction. Hence, a lawyer must not participate in a transaction to effectuate criminal or fraudulent avoidance of tax liability. Paragraph (d) does not preclude undertaking a criminal defense incident to a general retainer for legal services to a lawful enterprise. The last clause of paragraph (d) recognizes that determining the validity or interpretation of a statute or regulation may require a course of action involving disobedience of the statute or regulation or of the interpretation placed upon it by governmental authorities.

[13] If a lawyer comes to know or reasonably should know that a client expects assistance not permitted by the Rules of Professional Conduct or other law or if the lawyer intends to act contrary to the client's instructions, the lawyer must consult with the client regarding the limitations on the lawyer's conduct. See Rule 1.4(a)(5).

RULE 1.3: DILIGENCE

A lawyer shall act with reasonable diligence and promptness in representing a client.

Comment

[1] A lawyer should pursue a matter on behalf of a client despite opposition, obstruction or personal inconvenience to the lawyer, and take whatever lawful and ethical measures are required to vindicate a client's cause or endeavor. A lawyer must also act with commitment and dedication

to the interests of the client and with zeal in advocacy upon the client's behalf. A lawyer is not bound, however, to press for every advantage that might be realized for a client. For example, a lawyer may have authority to exercise professional discretion in determining the means by which a matter should be pursued. See Rule 1.2. The lawyer's duty to act with reasonable diligence does not require the use of offensive tactics or preclude the treating of all persons involved in the legal process with courtesy and respect.

[2]   A lawyer's work load must be controlled so that each matter can be handled competently.

[3]   Perhaps no professional shortcoming is more widely resented than procrastination. A client's interests often can be adversely affected by the passage of time or the change of conditions; in extreme instances, as when a lawyer overlooks a statute of limitations, the client's legal position may be destroyed. Even when the client's interests are not affected in substance, however, unreasonable delay can cause a client needless anxiety and undermine confidence in the lawyer's trustworthiness. A lawyer's duty to act with reasonable promptness, however, does not preclude the lawyer from agreeing to a reasonable request for a postponement that will not prejudice the lawyer's client.

[4]   Unless the relationship is terminated as provided in Rule 1.16, a lawyer should carry through to conclusion all matters undertaken for a client. If a lawyer's employment is limited to a specific matter, the relationship terminates when the matter has been resolved. If a lawyer has served a client over a substantial period in a variety of matters, the client sometimes may assume that the lawyer will continue to serve on a continuing basis unless the lawyer gives notice of withdrawal. Doubt about whether a client-lawyer relationship still exists should be clarified by the lawyer, preferably in writing, so that the client will not mistakenly suppose the lawyer is looking after the client's affairs when the lawyer has ceased to do so. For example, if a lawyer has handled a judicial or administrative proceeding that produced a result adverse to the client and the lawyer and the client have not agreed that the lawyer will handle the matter on appeal, the lawyer must consult with the client about the possibility of appeal before relinquishing responsibility for the matter. See Rule 1.4(a)(2). Whether the lawyer is obligated to prosecute the appeal for the client depends on the scope of the representation the lawyer has agreed to provide to the client. See Rule 1.2.

[5]   To prevent neglect of client matters in the event of a sole practitioner's death or disability, the duty of diligence may require that each sole practitioner prepare a plan, in conformity with applicable rules, that designates another competent lawyer to review client files, notify each client of the lawyer's death or disability, and determine whether there is a need for immediate protective action. Cf. Rule 28 of the American Bar Association Model Rules for Lawyer Disciplinary Enforcement (providing for court appointment of a lawyer to inventory files and take other protective action in absence of a plan providing for another lawyer to protect the interests of the clients of a deceased or disabled lawyer).

RULE 1.4: COMMUNICATION

(a) A lawyer shall:

(1) promptly inform the client of any decision or circumstance with respect to which the client's informed consent, as defined in Rule 1.0(e), is required by these Rules;

(2) reasonably consult with the client about the means by which the client's objectives are to be accomplished;

(3) keep the client reasonably informed about the status of the matter;

(4) promptly comply with reasonable requests for information; and

(5) consult with the client about any relevant limitation on the lawyer's conduct when the lawyer knows that the client expects assistance not permitted by the Rules of Professional Conduct or other law.

(b) A lawyer shall explain a matter to the extent reasonably necessary to permit the client to make informed decisions regarding the representation.

Comment

[1] Reasonable communication between the lawyer and the client is necessary for the client effectively to participate in the representation.

Communicating with Client

[2] If these Rules require that a particular decision about the representation be made by the client, paragraph (a)(1) requires that the lawyer promptly consult with and secure the client's consent prior to taking action unless prior discussions with the client have resolved what action the client wants the lawyer to take. For example, a lawyer who receives from opposing counsel an offer of settlement in a civil controversy or a proffered plea bargain in a criminal case must promptly inform the client of its substance unless the client has previously indicated that the proposal will be acceptable or unacceptable or has authorized the lawyer to accept or to reject the offer. See Rule 1.2(a).

[3] Paragraph (a)(2) requires the lawyer to reasonably consult with the client about the means to be used to accomplish the client's objectives. In some situations—depending on both the importance of the action under consideration and the feasibility of consulting with the client—this duty will require consultation prior to taking action. In other circumstances, such as during a trial when an immediate decision must be made, the exigency of the situation may require the lawyer to act without prior consultation. In such cases the lawyer must nonetheless act reasonably to inform the client of actions the lawyer has taken on the client's behalf. Additionally, paragraph (a)(3) requires that the lawyer keep the client reasonably informed about the status of the matter, such as significant developments affecting the timing or the substance of the representation.

[4] A lawyer's regular communication with clients will minimize the occasions on which a client will need to request information concerning the representation. When a client makes a reasonable request for information, however, paragraph (a)(4) requires prompt compliance with the request, or if a prompt response is not feasible, that the lawyer, or a member of the lawyer's staff, acknowledge receipt of the request and advise the client when a response may be expected. A lawyer should promptly respond to or acknowledge client communications.

Explaining Matters

[5] The client should have sufficient information to participate intelligently in decisions concerning the objectives of the representation and

the means by which they are to be pursued, to the extent the client is willing and able to do so. Adequacy of communication depends in part on the kind of advice or assistance that is involved. For example, when there is time to explain a proposal made in a negotiation, the lawyer should review all important provisions with the client before proceeding to an agreement. In litigation a lawyer should explain the general strategy and prospects of success and ordinarily should consult the client on tactics that are likely to result in significant expense or to injure or coerce others. On the other hand, a lawyer ordinarily will not be expected to describe trial or negotiation strategy in detail. The guiding principle is that the lawyer should fulfill reasonable client expectations for information consistent with the duty to act in the client's best interests, and the client's overall requirements as to the character of representation. In certain circumstances, such as when a lawyer asks a client to consent to a representation affected by a conflict of interest, the client must give informed consent, as defined in Rule 1.0(e).

[6]   Ordinarily, the information to be provided is that appropriate for a client who is a comprehending and responsible adult. However, fully informing the client according to this standard may be impracticable, for example, where the client is a child or suffers from diminished capacity. See Rule 1.14. When the client is an organization or group, it is often impossible or inappropriate to inform every one of its members about its legal affairs; ordinarily, the lawyer should address communications to the appropriate officials of the organization. See Rule 1.13. Where many routine matters are involved, a system of limited or occasional reporting may be arranged with the client.

Withholding Information

[7]   In some circumstances, a lawyer may be justified in delaying transmission of information when the client would be likely to react imprudently to an immediate communication. Thus, a lawyer might withhold a psychiatric diagnosis of a client when the examining psychiatrist indicates that disclosure would harm the client. A lawyer may not withhold information to serve the lawyer's own interest or convenience or the interests or convenience of another person. Rules or court orders governing litigation may provide that information supplied to a lawyer may not be disclosed to the client. Rule 3.4(c) directs compliance with such rules or orders.

RULE 1.5: FEES

(a)   **A lawyer shall not make an agreement for, charge, or collect an unreasonable fee or an unreasonable amount for expenses. The factors to be considered in determining the reasonableness of a fee include the following:**

(1)   **the time and labor required, the novelty and difficulty of the questions involved, and the skill requisite to perform the legal service properly;**

(2)   **the likelihood, if apparent to the client, that the acceptance of the particular employment will preclude other employment by the lawyer;**

(3)   **the fee customarily charged in the locality for similar legal services;**

(4)   **the amount involved and the results obtained;**

(5)   **the time limitations imposed by the client or by the circumstances;**

(6)   the nature and length of the professional relationship with the client;

(7)   the experience, reputation, and ability of the lawyer or lawyers performing the services; and

(8)   whether the fee is fixed or contingent.

(b)   The scope of the representation and the basis or rate of the fee and expenses for which the client will be responsible shall be communicated to the client, preferably in writing, before or within a reasonable time after commencing the representation, except when the lawyer will charge a regularly represented client on the same basis or rate. Any changes in the basis or rate of the fee or expenses shall also be communicated to the client.

(c)   A fee may be contingent on the outcome of the matter for which the service is rendered, except in a matter in which a contingent fee is prohibited by paragraph (d) or other law. A contingent fee agreement shall be in a writing signed by the client and shall state the method by which the fee is to be determined, including the percentage or percentages that shall accrue to the lawyer in the event of settlement, trial or appeal; litigation and other expenses to be deducted from the recovery; and whether such expenses are to be deducted before or after the contingent fee is calculated. The agreement must clearly notify the client of any expenses for which the client will be liable whether or not the client is the prevailing party. Upon conclusion of a contingent fee matter, the lawyer shall provide the client with a written statement stating the outcome of the matter and, if there is a recovery, showing the remittance to the client and the method of its determination.

(d)   A lawyer shall not enter into an arrangement for, charge, or collect:

(1)   any fee in a domestic relations matter, the payment or amount of which is contingent upon the securing of a divorce or upon the amount of alimony or support, or property settlement in lieu thereof; or

(2)   a contingent fee for representing a defendant in a criminal case.

(e)   A division of a fee between lawyers who are not in the same firm may be made only if:

(1)   the division is in proportion to the services performed by each lawyer or each lawyer assumes joint responsibility for the representation;

(2)   the client agrees to the arrangement, including the share each lawyer will receive, and the agreement is confirmed in writing; and

(3)   the total fee is reasonable.

Comment

Reasonableness of Fee and Expenses

[1]   Paragraph (a) requires that lawyers charge fees that are reasonable under the circumstances. The factors specified in (1) through (8) are not exclusive. Nor will each factor be relevant in each instance. Paragraph (a)

also requires that expenses for which the client will be charged must be reasonable. A lawyer may seek reimbursement for the cost of services performed in-house, such as copying, or for other expenses incurred in-house, such as telephone charges, either by charging a reasonable amount to which the client has agreed in advance or by charging an amount that reasonably reflects the cost incurred by the lawyer.

Basis or Rate of Fee

[2] When the lawyer has regularly represented a client, they ordinarily will have evolved an understanding concerning the basis or rate of the fee and the expenses for which the client will be responsible. In a new client-lawyer relationship, however, an understanding as to fees and expenses must be promptly established. Generally, it is desirable to furnish the client with at least a simple memorandum or copy of the lawyer's customary fee arrangements that states the general nature of the legal services to be provided, the basis, rate or total amount of the fee and whether and to what extent the client will be responsible for any costs, expenses or disbursements in the course of the representation. A written statement concerning the terms of the engagement reduces the possibility of misunderstanding.

[3] Contingent fees, like any other fees, are subject to the reasonableness standard of paragraph (a) of this Rule. In determining whether a particular contingent fee is reasonable, or whether it is reasonable to charge any form of contingent fee, a lawyer must consider the factors that are relevant under the circumstances. Applicable law may impose limitations on contingent fees, such as a ceiling on the percentage allowable, or may require a lawyer to offer clients an alternative basis for the fee. Applicable law also may apply to situations other than a contingent fee, for example, government regulations regarding fees in certain tax matters.

Terms of Payment

[4] A lawyer may require advance payment of a fee, but is obliged to return any unearned portion. See Rule 1.16(d). A lawyer may accept property in payment for services, such as an ownership interest in an enterprise, providing this does not involve acquisition of a proprietary interest in the cause of action or subject matter of the litigation contrary to Rule 1.8(i). However, a fee paid in property instead of money may be subject to the requirements of Rule 1.8(a) because such fees often have the essential qualities of a business transaction with the client.

[5] An agreement may not be made whose terms might induce the lawyer improperly to curtail services for the client or perform them in a way contrary to the client's interest. For example, a lawyer should not enter into an agreement whereby services are to be provided only up to a stated amount when it is foreseeable that more extensive services probably will be required, unless the situation is adequately explained to the client. Otherwise, the client might have to bargain for further assistance in the midst of a proceeding or transaction. However, it is proper to define the extent of services in light of the client's ability to pay. A lawyer should not exploit a fee arrangement based primarily on hourly charges by using wasteful procedures.

Prohibited Contingent Fees

[6] Paragraph (d) prohibits a lawyer from charging a contingent fee in a domestic relations matter when payment is contingent upon the securing of a divorce or upon the amount of alimony or support or property settlement

to be obtained. This provision does not preclude a contract for a contingent fee for legal representation in connection with the recovery of post-judgment balances due under support, alimony or other financial orders because such contracts do not implicate the same policy concerns.

Division of Fee

[7]   A division of fee is a single billing to a client covering the fee of two or more lawyers who are not in the same firm. A division of fee facilitates association of more than one lawyer in a matter in which neither alone could serve the client as well, and most often is used when the fee is contingent and the division is between a referring lawyer and a trial specialist. Paragraph (e) permits the lawyers to divide a fee either on the basis of the proportion of services they render or if each lawyer assumes responsibility for the representation as a whole. In addition, the client must agree to the arrangement, including the share that each lawyer is to receive, and the agreement must be confirmed in writing. Contingent fee agreements must be in a writing signed by the client and must otherwise comply with paragraph (c) of this Rule. Joint responsibility for the representation entails financial and ethical responsibility for the representation as if the lawyers were associated in a partnership. A lawyer should only refer a matter to a lawyer whom the referring lawyer reasonably believes is competent to handle the matter. See Rule 1.1.

[8]   Paragraph (e) does not prohibit or regulate division of fees to be received in the future for work done when lawyers were previously associated in a law firm.

Disputes over Fees

[9]   If a procedure has been established for resolution of fee disputes, such as an arbitration or mediation procedure established by the bar, the lawyer must comply with the procedure when it is mandatory, and, even when it is voluntary, the lawyer should conscientiously consider submitting to it. Law may prescribe a procedure for determining a lawyer's fee, for example, in representation of an executor or administrator, a class or a person entitled to a reasonable fee as part of the measure of damages. The lawyer entitled to such a fee and a lawyer representing another party concerned with the fee should comply with the prescribed procedure.

RULE 1.6: CONFIDENTIALITY OF INFORMATION

(a) A lawyer shall not reveal information relating to the representation of a client unless the client gives informed consent, the disclosure is impliedly authorized in order to carry out the representation or the disclosure is permitted by paragraph (b).

(b) A lawyer may reveal information relating to the representation of a client to the extent the lawyer reasonably believes necessary:

(1)   to prevent reasonably certain death or substantial bodily harm;

(2)   to prevent the client from committing a crime or fraud that is reasonably certain to result in substantial injury to the financial interests or property of another and in furtherance of which the client has used or is using the lawyer's services;

(3)   to prevent, mitigate or rectify substantial injury to the financial interests or property of another that is reasonably

certain to result or has resulted from the client's commission of a crime or fraud in furtherance of which the client has used the lawyer's services;

    (4) to secure legal advice about the lawyer's compliance with these Rules;

    (5) to establish a claim or defense on behalf of the lawyer in a controversy between the lawyer and the client, to establish a defense to a criminal charge or civil claim against the lawyer based upon conduct in which the client was involved, or to respond to allegations in any proceeding concerning the lawyer's representation of the client;

    (6) to comply with other law or a court order; or

    (7) to detect and resolve conflicts of interest arising from the lawyer's change of employment or from changes in the composition or ownership of a firm, but only if the revealed information would not compromise the attorney-client privilege or otherwise prejudice the client.

(c) A lawyer shall make reasonable efforts to prevent the inadvertent or unauthorized disclosure of, or unauthorized access to, information relating to the representation of a client.

Comment

[1] This Rule governs the disclosure by a lawyer of information relating to the representation of a client during the lawyer's representation of the client. See Rule 1.18 for the lawyer's duties with respect to information provided to the lawyer by a prospective client, Rule 1.9(c)(2) for the lawyer's duty not to reveal information relating to the lawyer's prior representation of a former client and Rules 1.8(b) and 1.9(c)(1) for the lawyer's duties with respect to the use of such information to the disadvantage of clients and former clients.

[2] A fundamental principle in the client-lawyer relationship is that, in the absence of the client's informed consent, the lawyer must not reveal information relating to the representation. See Rule 1.0(e) for the definition of informed consent. This contributes to the trust that is the hallmark of the client-lawyer relationship. The client is thereby encouraged to seek legal assistance and to communicate fully and frankly with the lawyer even as to embarrassing or legally damaging subject matter. The lawyer needs this information to represent the client effectively and, if necessary, to advise the client to refrain from wrongful conduct. Almost without exception, clients come to lawyers in order to determine their rights and what is, in the complex of laws and regulations, deemed to be legal and correct. Based upon experience, lawyers know that almost all clients follow the advice given, and the law is upheld.

[3] The principle of client-lawyer confidentiality is given effect by related bodies of law: the attorney-client privilege, the work product doctrine and the rule of confidentiality established in professional ethics. The attorney-client privilege and work product doctrine apply in judicial and other proceedings in which a lawyer may be called as a witness or otherwise required to produce evidence concerning a client. The rule of client-lawyer confidentiality applies in situations other than those where evidence is sought from the lawyer through compulsion of law. The confidentiality rule, for example, applies not only to matters communicated in confidence by the

client but also to all information relating to the representation, whatever its source. A lawyer may not disclose such information except as authorized or required by the Rules of Professional Conduct or other law. See also Scope.

[4]   Paragraph (a) prohibits a lawyer from revealing information relating to the representation of a client. This prohibition also applies to disclosures by a lawyer that do not in themselves reveal protected information but could reasonably lead to the discovery of such information by a third person. A lawyer's use of a hypothetical to discuss issues relating to the representation is permissible so long as there is no reasonable likelihood that the listener will be able to ascertain the identity of the client or the situation involved.

Authorized Disclosure

[5]   Except to the extent that the client's instructions or special circumstances limit that authority, a lawyer is impliedly authorized to make disclosures about a client when appropriate in carrying out the representation. In some situations, for example, a lawyer may be impliedly authorized to admit a fact that cannot properly be disputed or to make a disclosure that facilitates a satisfactory conclusion to a matter. Lawyers in a firm may, in the course of the firm's practice, disclose to each other information relating to a client of the firm, unless the client has instructed that particular information be confined to specified lawyers.

Disclosure Adverse to Client

[6]   Although the public interest is usually best served by a strict rule requiring lawyers to preserve the confidentiality of information relating to the representation of their clients, the confidentiality rule is subject to limited exceptions. Paragraph (b)(1) recognizes the overriding value of life and physical integrity and permits disclosure reasonably necessary to prevent reasonably certain death or substantial bodily harm. Such harm is reasonably certain to occur if it will be suffered imminently or if there is a present and substantial threat that a person will suffer such harm at a later date if the lawyer fails to take action necessary to eliminate the threat. Thus, a lawyer who knows that a client has accidentally discharged toxic waste into a town's water supply may reveal this information to the authorities if there is a present and substantial risk that a person who drinks the water will contract a life-threatening or debilitating disease and the lawyer's disclosure is necessary to eliminate the threat or reduce the number of victims.

[7]   Paragraph (b)(2) is a limited exception to the rule of confidentiality that permits the lawyer to reveal information to the extent necessary to enable affected persons or appropriate authorities to prevent the client from committing a crime or fraud, as defined in Rule 1.0(d), that is reasonably certain to result in substantial injury to the financial or property interests of another and in furtherance of which the client has used or is using the lawyer's services. Such a serious abuse of the client-lawyer relationship by the client forfeits the protection of this Rule. The client can, of course, prevent such disclosure by refraining from the wrongful conduct. Although paragraph (b)(2) does not require the lawyer to reveal the client's misconduct, the lawyer may not counsel or assist the client in conduct the lawyer knows is criminal or fraudulent. See Rule 1.2(d). See also Rule 1.16 with respect to the lawyer's obligation or right to withdraw from the representation of the client in such circumstances, and Rule 1.13(c), which permits the lawyer, where the client is an organization, to reveal information relating to the representation in limited circumstances.

[8]   Paragraph (b)(3) addresses the situation in which the lawyer does not learn of the client's crime or fraud until after it has been consummated. Although the client no longer has the option of preventing disclosure by refraining from the wrongful conduct, there will be situations in which the loss suffered by the affected person can be prevented, rectified or mitigated. In such situations, the lawyer may disclose information relating to the representation to the extent necessary to enable the affected persons to prevent or mitigate reasonably certain losses or to attempt to recoup their losses. Paragraph (b)(3) does not apply when a person who has committed a crime or fraud thereafter employs a lawyer for representation concerning that offense.

[9]   A lawyer's confidentiality obligations do not preclude a lawyer from securing confidential legal advice about the lawyer's personal responsibility to comply with these Rules. In most situations, disclosing information to secure such advice will be impliedly authorized for the lawyer to carry out the representation. Even when the disclosure is not impliedly authorized, paragraph (b)(4) permits such disclosure because of the importance of a lawyer's compliance with the Rules of Professional Conduct.

[10] Where a legal claim or disciplinary charge alleges complicity of the lawyer in a client's conduct or other misconduct of the lawyer involving representation of the client, the lawyer may respond to the extent the lawyer reasonably believes necessary to establish a defense. The same is true with respect to a claim involving the conduct or representation of a former client. Such a charge can arise in a civil, criminal, disciplinary or other proceeding and can be based on a wrong allegedly committed by the lawyer against the client or on a wrong alleged by a third person, for example, a person claiming to have been defrauded by the lawyer and client acting together. The lawyer's right to respond arises when an assertion of such complicity has been made. Paragraph (b)(5) does not require the lawyer to await the commencement of an action or proceeding that charges such complicity, so that the defense may be established by responding directly to a third party who has made such an assertion. The right to defend also applies, of course, where a proceeding has been commenced.

[11] A lawyer entitled to a fee is permitted by paragraph (b)(5) to prove the services rendered in an action to collect it. This aspect of the rule expresses the principle that the beneficiary of a fiduciary relationship may not exploit it to the detriment of the fiduciary.

[12] Other law may require that a lawyer disclose information about a client. Whether such a law supersedes Rule 1.6 is a question of law beyond the scope of these Rules. When disclosure of information relating to the representation appears to be required by other law, the lawyer must discuss the matter with the client to the extent required by Rule 1.4. If, however, the other law supersedes this Rule and requires disclosure, paragraph (b)(6) permits the lawyer to make such disclosures as are necessary to comply with the law.

[13] Paragraph (b)(7) recognizes that lawyers in different firms may need to disclose limited information to each other to detect and resolve conflicts of interest, such as when a lawyer is considering an association with another firm, two or more firms are considering a merger, or a lawyer is considering the purchase of a law practice. See Rule 1.17, Comment [7]. Under these circumstances, lawyers and law firms are permitted to disclose limited information, but only once substantive discussions regarding the new relationship have occurred. Any such disclosure should ordinarily include no

more than the identity of the persons and entities involved in a matter, a brief summary of the general issues involved, and information about whether the matter has terminated. Even this limited information, however should be disclosed only to the extent reasonably necessary to detect and resolve conflicts of interest that might arise from the possible new relationship. Moreover, the disclosure of any information is prohibited if it would compromise the attorney-client privilege or otherwise prejudice the client (e.g., the fact that a corporate client is seeking advice on a corporate takeover that has not been publicly announced; that a person has consulted a lawyer about the possibility of divorce before the person's intentions are known to the person's spouse; or that a person has consulted a lawyer about a criminal investigation that has not led to a public charge). Under those circumstances, paragraph (a) prohibits disclosure unless the client or former client gives informed consent. A lawyer's fiduciary duty to the lawyer's firm may also govern a lawyer's conduct when exploring an association with another firm and is beyond the scope of these Rules.

[14] Any information disclosed pursuant to paragraph (b)(7) may be used or further disclosed only to the extent necessary to detect and resolve conflicts of interest. Paragraph (b)(7) does not restrict the use of information acquired by means independent of any disclosure pursuant to paragraph (b)(7). Paragraph (b)(7) also does not affect the disclosure of information within a law firm when the disclosure is otherwise authorized, see Comment [5], such as when a lawyer in a firm discloses information to another lawyer in the same firm to detect and resolve conflicts of interest that could arise in connection with undertaking a new representation.

[15] A lawyer may be ordered to reveal information relating to the representation of a client by a court or by another tribunal or governmental entity claiming authority pursuant to other law to compel the disclosure. Absent informed consent of the client to do otherwise, the lawyer should assert on behalf of the client all nonfrivolous claims that the order is not authorized by other law or that the information sought is protected against disclosure by the attorney-client privilege or other applicable law. In the event of an adverse ruling, the lawyer must consult with the client about the possibility of appeal to the extent required by Rule 1.4. Unless review is sought, however, paragraph (b)(6) permits the lawyer to comply with the court's order.

[16] Paragraph (b) permits disclosure only to the extent the lawyer reasonably believes the disclosure is necessary to accomplish one of the purposes specified. Where practicable, the lawyer should first seek to persuade the client to take suitable action to obviate the need for disclosure. In any case, a disclosure adverse to the client's interest should be no greater than the lawyer reasonably believes necessary to accomplish the purpose. If the disclosure will be made in connection with a judicial proceeding, the disclosure should be made in a manner that limits access to the information to the tribunal or other persons having a need to know it and appropriate protective orders or other arrangements should be sought by the lawyer to the fullest extent practicable.

[17] Paragraph (b) permits but does not require the disclosure of information relating to a client's representation to accomplish the purposes specified in paragraphs (b)(1) through (b)(6). In exercising the discretion conferred by this Rule, the lawyer may consider such factors as the nature of the lawyer's relationship with the client and with those who might be injured by the client, the lawyer's own involvement in the transaction and factors that may extenuate the conduct in question. A lawyer's decision not to

disclose as permitted by paragraph (b) does not violate this Rule. Disclosure may be required, however, by other Rules. Some Rules require disclosure only if such disclosure would be permitted by paragraph (b). See Rules 1.2(d), 4.1(b), 8.1 and 8.3. Rule 3.3, on the other hand, requires disclosure in some circumstances regardless of whether such disclosure is permitted by this Rule. See Rule 3.3(c).

Acting Competently to Preserve Confidentiality

[18] Paragraph (c) requires a lawyer to act competently to safeguard information relating to the representation of a client against unauthorized access by third parties and against inadvertent or unauthorized disclosure by the lawyer or other persons who are participating in the representation of the client or who are subject to the lawyer's supervision. See Rules 1.1, 5.1 and 5.3. The unauthorized access to, or the inadvertent or unauthorized disclosure of, information relating to the representation of a client does not constitute a violation of paragraph (c) if the lawyer has made reasonable efforts to prevent the access or disclosure. Factors to be considered in determining the reasonableness of the lawyer's efforts include, but are not limited to, the sensitivity of the information, the likelihood of disclosure if additional safeguards are not employed, the cost of employing additional safeguards, the difficulty of implementing the safeguards, and the extent to which the safeguards adversely affect the lawyer's ability to represent clients (e.g., by making a device or important piece of software excessively difficult to use). A client may require the lawyer to implement special security measures not required by this Rule or may give informed consent to forgo security measures that would otherwise be required by this Rule. Whether a lawyer may be required to take additional steps to safeguard a client's information in order to comply with other law, such as state and federal laws that govern data privacy or that impose notification requirements upon the loss of, or unauthorized access to, electronic information, is beyond the scope of these Rules. For a lawyer's duties when sharing information with nonlawyers outside the lawyer's own firm, see Rule 5.3, Comments [3]–[4].

[19] When transmitting a communication that includes information relating to the representation of a client, the lawyer must take reasonable precautions to prevent the information from coming into the hands of unintended recipients. This duty, however, does not require that the lawyer use special security measures if the method of communication affords a reasonable expectation of privacy. Special circumstances, however, may warrant special precautions. Factors to be considered in determining the reasonableness of the lawyer's expectation of confidentiality include the sensitivity of the information and the extent to which the privacy of the communication is protected by law or by a confidentiality agreement. A client may require the lawyer to implement special security measures not required by this Rule or may give informed consent to the use of a means of communication that would otherwise be prohibited by this Rule. Whether a lawyer may be required to take additional steps in order to comply with other law, such as state and federal laws that govern data privacy, is beyond the scope of these Rules.

Former Client

[20] The duty of confidentiality continues after the client-lawyer relationship has terminated. See Rule 1.9(c)(2). See Rule 1.9(c)(1) for the prohibition against using such information to the disadvantage of the former client.

RULE 1.7: CONFLICT OF INTEREST: CURRENT CLIENTS

(a) Except as provided in paragraph (b), a lawyer shall not represent a client if the representation involves a concurrent conflict of interest. A concurrent conflict of interest exists if:

(1) the representation of one client will be directly adverse to another client; or

(2) there is a significant risk that the representation of one or more clients will be materially limited by the lawyer's responsibilities to another client, a former client or a third person or by a personal interest of the lawyer.

(b) Notwithstanding the existence of a concurrent conflict of interest under paragraph (a), a lawyer may represent a client if:

(1) the lawyer reasonably believes that the lawyer will be able to provide competent and diligent representation to each affected client;

(2) the representation is not prohibited by law;

(3) the representation does not involve the assertion of a claim by one client against another client represented by the lawyer in the same litigation or other proceeding before a tribunal; and

(4) each affected client gives informed consent, confirmed in writing.

Comment

General Principles

[1] Loyalty and independent judgment are essential elements in the lawyer's relationship to a client. Concurrent conflicts of interest can arise from the lawyer's responsibilities to another client, a former client or a third person or from the lawyer's own interests. For specific Rules regarding certain concurrent conflicts of interest, see Rule 1.8. For former client conflicts of interest, see Rule 1.9. For conflicts of interest involving prospective clients, see Rule 1.18. For definitions of "informed consent" and "confirmed in writing," see Rule 1.0(e) and (b).

[2] Resolution of a conflict of interest problem under this Rule requires the lawyer to: 1) clearly identify the client or clients; 2) determine whether a conflict of interest exists; 3) decide whether the representation may be undertaken despite the existence of a conflict, i.e., whether the conflict is consentable; and 4) if so, consult with the clients affected under paragraph (a) and obtain their informed consent, confirmed in writing. The clients affected under paragraph (a) include both of the clients referred to in paragraph (a)(1) and the one or more clients whose representation might be materially limited under paragraph (a)(2).

[3] A conflict of interest may exist before representation is undertaken, in which event the representation must be declined, unless the lawyer obtains the informed consent of each client under the conditions of paragraph (b). To determine whether a conflict of interest exists, a lawyer should adopt reasonable procedures, appropriate for the size and type of firm and practice, to determine in both litigation and non-litigation matters the persons and issues involved. See also Comment to Rule 5.1. Ignorance caused by a failure to institute such procedures will not excuse a lawyer's violation of this Rule.

As to whether a client-lawyer relationship exists or, having once been established, is continuing, see Comment to Rule 1.3 and Scope.

[4]   If a conflict arises after representation has been undertaken, the lawyer ordinarily must withdraw from the representation, unless the lawyer has obtained the informed consent of the client under the conditions of paragraph (b). See Rule 1.16. Where more than one client is involved, whether the lawyer may continue to represent any of the clients is determined both by the lawyer's ability to comply with duties owed to the former client and by the lawyer's ability to represent adequately the remaining client or clients, given the lawyer's duties to the former client. See Rule 1.9. See also Comments [5] and [29].

[5]   Unforeseeable developments, such as changes in corporate and other organizational affiliations or the addition or realignment of parties in litigation, might create conflicts in the midst of a representation, as when a company sued by the lawyer on behalf of one client is bought by another client represented by the lawyer in an unrelated matter. Depending on the circumstances, the lawyer may have the option to withdraw from one of the representations in order to avoid the conflict. The lawyer must seek court approval where necessary and take steps to minimize harm to the clients. See Rule 1.16. The lawyer must continue to protect the confidences of the client from whose representation the lawyer has withdrawn. See Rule 1.9(c).

Identifying Conflicts of Interest: Directly Adverse

[6]   Loyalty to a current client prohibits undertaking representation directly adverse to that client without that client's informed consent. Thus, absent consent, a lawyer may not act as an advocate in one matter against a person the lawyer represents in some other matter, even when the matters are wholly unrelated. The client as to whom the representation is directly adverse is likely to feel betrayed, and the resulting damage to the client-lawyer relationship is likely to impair the lawyer's ability to represent the client effectively. In addition, the client on whose behalf the adverse representation is undertaken reasonably may fear that the lawyer will pursue that client's case less effectively out of deference to the other client, i.e., that the representation may be materially limited by the lawyer's interest in retaining the current client. Similarly, a directly adverse conflict may arise when a lawyer is required to cross-examine a client who appears as a witness in a lawsuit involving another client, as when the testimony will be damaging to the client who is represented in the lawsuit. On the other hand, simultaneous representation in unrelated matters of clients whose interests are only economically adverse, such as representation of competing economic enterprises in unrelated litigation, does not ordinarily constitute a conflict of interest and thus may not require consent of the respective clients.

[7]   Directly adverse conflicts can also arise in transactional matters. For example, if a lawyer is asked to represent the seller of a business in negotiations with a buyer represented by the lawyer, not in the same transaction but in another, unrelated matter, the lawyer could not undertake the representation without the informed consent of each client.

Identifying Conflicts of Interest: Material Limitation

[8]   Even where there is no direct adverseness, a conflict of interest exists if there is a significant risk that a lawyer's ability to consider, recommend or carry out an appropriate course of action for the client will be materially limited as a result of the lawyer's other responsibilities or interests. For example, a lawyer asked to represent several individuals

seeking to form a joint venture is likely to be materially limited in the lawyer's ability to recommend or advocate all possible positions that each might take because of the lawyer's duty of loyalty to the others. The conflict in effect forecloses alternatives that would otherwise be available to the client. The mere possibility of subsequent harm does not itself require disclosure and consent. The critical questions are the likelihood that a difference in interests will eventuate and, if it does, whether it will materially interfere with the lawyer's independent professional judgment in considering alternatives or foreclose courses of action that reasonably should be pursued on behalf of the client.

Lawyer's Responsibilities to Former Clients and Other Third Persons

[9]   In addition to conflicts with other current clients, a lawyer's duties of loyalty and independence may be materially limited by responsibilities to former clients under Rule 1.9 or by the lawyer's responsibilities to other persons, such as fiduciary duties arising from a lawyer's service as a trustee, executor or corporate director.

Personal Interest Conflicts

[10] The lawyer's own interests should not be permitted to have an adverse effect on representation of a client. For example, if the probity of a lawyer's own conduct in a transaction is in serious question, it may be difficult or impossible for the lawyer to give a client detached advice. Similarly, when a lawyer has discussions concerning possible employment with an opponent of the lawyer's client, or with a law firm representing the opponent, such discussions could materially limit the lawyer's representation of the client. In addition, a lawyer may not allow related business interests to affect representation, for example, by referring clients to an enterprise in which the lawyer has an undisclosed financial interest. See Rule 1.8 for specific Rules pertaining to a number of personal interest conflicts, including business transactions with clients. See also Rule 1.10 (personal interest conflicts under Rule 1.7 ordinarily are not imputed to other lawyers in a law firm).

[11] When lawyers representing different clients in the same matter or in substantially related matters are closely related by blood or marriage, there may be a significant risk that client confidences will be revealed and that the lawyer's family relationship will interfere with both loyalty and independent professional judgment. As a result, each client is entitled to know of the existence and implications of the relationship between the lawyers before the lawyer agrees to undertake the representation. Thus, a lawyer related to another lawyer, e.g., as parent, child, sibling or spouse, ordinarily may not represent a client in a matter where that lawyer is representing another party, unless each client gives informed consent. The disqualification arising from a close family relationship is personal and ordinarily is not imputed to members of firms with whom the lawyers are associated. See Rule 1.10.

[12] A lawyer is prohibited from engaging in sexual relationships with a client unless the sexual relationship predates the formation of the client-lawyer relationship. See Rule 1.8(j).

Interest of Person Paying for a Lawyer's Service

[13] A lawyer may be paid from a source other than the client, including a co-client, if the client is informed of that fact and consents and the arrangement does not compromise the lawyer's duty of loyalty or independent judgment to the client. See Rule 1.8(f). If acceptance of the payment from any

other source presents a significant risk that the lawyer's representation of the client will be materially limited by the lawyer's own interest in accommodating the person paying the lawyer's fee or by the lawyer's responsibilities to a payer who is also a co-client, then the lawyer must comply with the requirements of paragraph (b) before accepting the representation, including determining whether the conflict is consentable and, if so, that the client has adequate information about the material risks of the representation.

Prohibited Representations

[14] Ordinarily, clients may consent to representation notwithstanding a conflict. However, as indicated in paragraph (b), some conflicts are nonconsentable, meaning that the lawyer involved cannot properly ask for such agreement or provide representation on the basis of the client's consent. When the lawyer is representing more than one client, the question of consentability must be resolved as to each client.

[15] Consentability is typically determined by considering whether the interests of the clients will be adequately protected if the clients are permitted to give their informed consent to representation burdened by a conflict of interest. Thus, under paragraph (b)(1), representation is prohibited if in the circumstances the lawyer cannot reasonably conclude that the lawyer will be able to provide competent and diligent representation. See Rule 1.1 (competence) and Rule 1.3 (diligence).

[16] Paragraph (b)(2) describes conflicts that are nonconsentable because the representation is prohibited by applicable law. For example, in some states substantive law provides that the same lawyer may not represent more than one defendant in a capital case, even with the consent of the clients, and under federal criminal statutes certain representations by a former government lawyer are prohibited, despite the informed consent of the former client. In addition, decisional law in some states limits the ability of a governmental client, such as a municipality, to consent to a conflict of interest.

[17] Paragraph (b)(3) describes conflicts that are nonconsentable because of the institutional interest in vigorous development of each client's position when the clients are aligned directly against each other in the same litigation or other proceeding before a tribunal. Whether clients are aligned directly against each other within the meaning of this paragraph requires examination of the context of the proceeding. Although this paragraph does not preclude a lawyer's multiple representation of adverse parties to a mediation (because mediation is not a proceeding before a "tribunal" under Rule 1.0(m)), such representation may be precluded by paragraph (b)(1).

Informed Consent

[18] Informed consent requires that each affected client be aware of the relevant circumstances and of the material and reasonably foreseeable ways that the conflict could have adverse effects on the interests of that client. See Rule 1.0(e) (informed consent). The information required depends on the nature of the conflict and the nature of the risks involved. When representation of multiple clients in a single matter is undertaken, the information must include the implications of the common representation, including possible effects on loyalty, confidentiality and the attorney-client privilege and the advantages and risks involved. See Comments [30] and [31] (effect of common representation on confidentiality).

[19] Under some circumstances it may be impossible to make the disclosure necessary to obtain consent. For example, when the lawyer represents different clients in related matters and one of the clients refuses to consent to the disclosure necessary to permit the other client to make an informed decision, the lawyer cannot properly ask the latter to consent. In some cases the alternative to common representation can be that each party may have to obtain separate representation with the possibility of incurring additional costs. These costs, along with the benefits of securing separate representation, are factors that may be considered by the affected client in determining whether common representation is in the client's interests.

Consent Confirmed in Writing

[20] Paragraph (b) requires the lawyer to obtain the informed consent of the client, confirmed in writing. Such a writing may consist of a document executed by the client or one that the lawyer promptly records and transmits to the client following an oral consent. See Rule 1.0(b). See also Rule 1.0(n) (writing includes electronic transmission). If it is not feasible to obtain or transmit the writing at the time the client gives informed consent, then the lawyer must obtain or transmit it within a reasonable time thereafter. See Rule 1.0(b). The requirement of a writing does not supplant the need in most cases for the lawyer to talk with the client, to explain the risks and advantages, if any, of representation burdened with a conflict of interest, as well as reasonably available alternatives, and to afford the client a reasonable opportunity to consider the risks and alternatives and to raise questions and concerns. Rather, the writing is required in order to impress upon clients the seriousness of the decision the client is being asked to make and to avoid disputes or ambiguities that might later occur in the absence of a writing.

Revoking Consent

[21] A client who has given consent to a conflict may revoke the consent and, like any other client, may terminate the lawyer's representation at any time. Whether revoking consent to the client's own representation precludes the lawyer from continuing to represent other clients depends on the circumstances, including the nature of the conflict, whether the client revoked consent because of a material change in circumstances, the reasonable expectations of the other clients and whether material detriment to the other clients or the lawyer would result.

Consent to Future Conflict

[22] Whether a lawyer may properly request a client to waive conflicts that might arise in the future is subject to the test of paragraph (b). The effectiveness of such waivers is generally determined by the extent to which the client reasonably understands the material risks that the waiver entails. The more comprehensive the explanation of the types of future representations that might arise and the actual and reasonably foreseeable adverse consequences of those representations, the greater the likelihood that the client will have the requisite understanding. Thus, if the client agrees to consent to a particular type of conflict with which the client is already familiar, then the consent ordinarily will be effective with regard to that type of conflict. If the consent is general and open-ended, then the consent ordinarily will be ineffective, because it is not reasonably likely that the client will have understood the material risks involved. On the other hand, if the client is an experienced user of the legal services involved and is reasonably informed regarding the risk that a conflict may arise, such consent is more likely to be effective, particularly if, e.g., the client is

independently represented by other counsel in giving consent and the consent is limited to future conflicts unrelated to the subject of the representation. In any case, advance consent cannot be effective if the circumstances that materialize in the future are such as would make the conflict nonconsentable under paragraph (b).

Conflicts in Litigation

[23] Paragraph (b)(3) prohibits representation of opposing parties in the same litigation, regardless of the clients' consent. On the other hand, simultaneous representation of parties whose interests in litigation may conflict, such as coplaintiffs or codefendants, is governed by paragraph (a)(2). A conflict may exist by reason of substantial discrepancy in the parties' testimony, incompatibility in positions in relation to an opposing party or the fact that there are substantially different possibilities of settlement of the claims or liabilities in question. Such conflicts can arise in criminal cases as well as civil. The potential for conflict of interest in representing multiple defendants in a criminal case is so grave that ordinarily a lawyer should decline to represent more than one codefendant. On the other hand, common representation of persons having similar interests in civil litigation is proper if the requirements of paragraph (b) are met.

[24] Ordinarily a lawyer may take inconsistent legal positions in different tribunals at different times on behalf of different clients. The mere fact that advocating a legal position on behalf of one client might create precedent adverse to the interests of a client represented by the lawyer in an unrelated matter does not create a conflict of interest. A conflict of interest exists, however, if there is a significant risk that a lawyer's action on behalf of one client will materially limit the lawyer's effectiveness in representing another client in a different case; for example, when a decision favoring one client will create a precedent likely to seriously weaken the position taken on behalf of the other client. Factors relevant in determining whether the clients need to be advised of the risk include: where the cases are pending, whether the issue is substantive or procedural, the temporal relationship between the matters, the significance of the issue to the immediate and long-term interests of the clients involved and the clients' reasonable expectations in retaining the lawyer. If there is significant risk of material limitation, then absent informed consent of the affected clients, the lawyer must refuse one of the representations or withdraw from one or both matters.

[25] When a lawyer represents or seeks to represent a class of plaintiffs or defendants in a class-action lawsuit, unnamed members of the class are ordinarily not considered to be clients of the lawyer for purposes of applying paragraph (a)(1) of this Rule. Thus, the lawyer does not typically need to get the consent of such a person before representing a client suing the person in an unrelated matter. Similarly, a lawyer seeking to represent an opponent in a class action does not typically need the consent of an unnamed member of the class whom the lawyer represents in an unrelated matter.

Nonlitigation Conflicts

[26] Conflicts of interest under paragraphs (a)(1) and (a)(2) arise in contexts other than litigation. For a discussion of directly adverse conflicts in transactional matters, see Comment [7]. Relevant factors in determining whether there is significant potential for material limitation include the duration and intimacy of the lawyer's relationship with the client or clients involved, the functions being performed by the lawyer, the likelihood that disagreements will arise and the likely prejudice to the client from the conflict. The question is often one of proximity and degree. See Comment [8].

[27] For example, conflict questions may arise in estate planning and estate administration. A lawyer may be called upon to prepare wills for several family members, such as husband and wife, and, depending upon the circumstances, a conflict of interest may be present. In estate administration the identity of the client may be unclear under the law of a particular jurisdiction. Under one view, the client is the fiduciary; under another view the client is the estate or trust, including its beneficiaries. In order to comply with conflict of interest rules, the lawyer should make clear the lawyer's relationship to the parties involved.

[28] Whether a conflict is consentable depends on the circumstances. For example, a lawyer may not represent multiple parties to a negotiation whose interests are fundamentally antagonistic to each other, but common representation is permissible where the clients are generally aligned in interest even though there is some difference in interest among them. Thus, a lawyer may seek to establish or adjust a relationship between clients on an amicable and mutually advantageous basis; for example, in helping to organize a business in which two or more clients are entrepreneurs, working out the financial reorganization of an enterprise in which two or more clients have an interest or arranging a property distribution in settlement of an estate. The lawyer seeks to resolve potentially adverse interests by developing the parties' mutual interests. Otherwise, each party might have to obtain separate representation, with the possibility of incurring additional cost, complication or even litigation. Given these and other relevant factors, the clients may prefer that the lawyer act for all of them.

Special Considerations in Common Representation

[29] In considering whether to represent multiple clients in the same matter, a lawyer should be mindful that if the common representation fails because the potentially adverse interests cannot be reconciled, the result can be additional cost, embarrassment and recrimination. Ordinarily, the lawyer will be forced to withdraw from representing all of the clients if the common representation fails. In some situations, the risk of failure is so great that multiple representation is plainly impossible. For example, a lawyer cannot undertake common representation of clients where contentious litigation or negotiations between them are imminent or contemplated. Moreover, because the lawyer is required to be impartial between commonly represented clients, representation of multiple clients is improper when it is unlikely that impartiality can be maintained. Generally, if the relationship between the parties has already assumed antagonism, the possibility that the clients' interests can be adequately served by common representation is not very good. Other relevant factors are whether the lawyer subsequently will represent both parties on a continuing basis and whether the situation involves creating or terminating a relationship between the parties.

[30] A particularly important factor in determining the appropriateness of common representation is the effect on client-lawyer confidentiality and the attorney-client privilege. With regard to the attorney-client privilege, the prevailing rule is that, as between commonly represented clients, the privilege does not attach. Hence, it must be assumed that if litigation eventuates between the clients, the privilege will not protect any such communications, and the clients should be so advised.

[31] As to the duty of confidentiality, continued common representation will almost certainly be inadequate if one client asks the lawyer not to disclose to the other client information relevant to the common representation. This is so because the lawyer has an equal duty of loyalty to

each client, and each client has the right to be informed of anything bearing on the representation that might affect that client's interests and the right to expect that the lawyer will use that information to that client's benefit. See Rule 1.4. The lawyer should, at the outset of the common representation and as part of the process of obtaining each client's informed consent, advise each client that information will be shared and that the lawyer will have to withdraw if one client decides that some matter material to the representation should be kept from the other. In limited circumstances, it may be appropriate for the lawyer to proceed with the representation when the clients have agreed, after being properly informed, that the lawyer will keep certain information confidential. For example, the lawyer may reasonably conclude that failure to disclose one client's trade secrets to another client will not adversely affect representation involving a joint venture between the clients and agree to keep that information confidential with the informed consent of both clients.

[32] When seeking to establish or adjust a relationship between clients, the lawyer should make clear that the lawyer's role is not that of partisanship normally expected in other circumstances and, thus, that the clients may be required to assume greater responsibility for decisions than when each client is separately represented. Any limitations on the scope of the representation made necessary as a result of the common representation should be fully explained to the clients at the outset of the representation. See Rule 1.2(c).

[33] Subject to the above limitations, each client in the common representation has the right to loyal and diligent representation and the protection of Rule 1.9 concerning the obligations to a former client. The client also has the right to discharge the lawyer as stated in Rule 1.16.

Organizational Clients

[34] A lawyer who represents a corporation or other organization does not, by virtue of that representation, necessarily represent any constituent or affiliated organization, such as a parent or subsidiary. See Rule 1.13(a). Thus, the lawyer for an organization is not barred from accepting representation adverse to an affiliate in an unrelated matter, unless the circumstances are such that the affiliate should also be considered a client of the lawyer, there is an understanding between the lawyer and the organizational client that the lawyer will avoid representation adverse to the client's affiliates, or the lawyer's obligations to either the organizational client or the new client are likely to limit materially the lawyer's representation of the other client.

[35] A lawyer for a corporation or other organization who is also a member of its board of directors should determine whether the responsibilities of the two roles may conflict. The lawyer may be called on to advise the corporation in matters involving actions of the directors. Consideration should be given to the frequency with which such situations may arise, the potential intensity of the conflict, the effect of the lawyer's resignation from the board and the possibility of the corporation's obtaining legal advice from another lawyer in such situations. If there is material risk that the dual role will compromise the lawyer's independence of professional judgment, the lawyer should not serve as a director or should cease to act as the corporation's lawyer when conflicts of interest arise. The lawyer should advise the other members of the board that in some circumstances matters discussed at board meetings while the lawyer is present in the capacity of director might not be protected by the attorney-client privilege and that conflict of interest considerations might require the lawyer's recusal as a

director or might require the lawyer and the lawyer's firm to decline representation of the corporation in a matter.

RULE 1.8: CONFLICT OF INTEREST: CURRENT CLIENTS: SPECIFIC RULES

(a) A lawyer shall not enter into a business transaction with a client or knowingly acquire an ownership, possessory, security or other pecuniary interest adverse to a client unless:

(1) the transaction and terms on which the lawyer acquires the interest are fair and reasonable to the client and are fully disclosed and transmitted in writing in a manner that can be reasonably understood by the client;

(2) the client is advised in writing of the desirability of seeking and is given a reasonable opportunity to seek the advice of independent legal counsel on the transaction; and

(3) the client gives informed consent, in a writing signed by the client, to the essential terms of the transaction and the lawyer's role in the transaction, including whether the lawyer is representing the client in the transaction.

(b) A lawyer shall not use information relating to representation of a client to the disadvantage of the client unless the client gives informed consent, except as permitted or required by these Rules.

(c) A lawyer shall not solicit any substantial gift from a client, including a testamentary gift, or prepare on behalf of a client an instrument giving the lawyer or a person related to the lawyer any substantial gift unless the lawyer or other recipient of the gift is related to the client. For purposes of this paragraph, related persons include a spouse, child, grandchild, parent, grandparent or other relative or individual with whom the lawyer or the client maintains a close, familial relationship.

(d) Prior to the conclusion of representation of a client, a lawyer shall not make or negotiate an agreement giving the lawyer literary or media rights to a portrayal or account based in substantial part on information relating to the representation.

(e) A lawyer shall not provide financial assistance to a client in connection with pending or contemplated litigation, except that:

(1) a lawyer may advance court costs and expenses of litigation, the repayment of which may be contingent on the outcome of the matter; and

(2) a lawyer representing an indigent client may pay court costs and expenses of litigation on behalf of the client.

(f) A lawyer shall not accept compensation for representing a client from one other than the client unless:

(1) the client gives informed consent;

(2) there is no interference with the lawyer's independence of professional judgment or with the client-lawyer relationship; and

(3) information relating to representation of a client is protected as required by Rule 1.6.

(g) A lawyer who represents two or more clients shall not participate in making an aggregate settlement of the claims of or against the clients, or in a criminal case an aggregated agreement as to guilty or nolo contendere pleas, unless each client gives informed consent, in a writing signed by the client. The lawyer's disclosure shall include the existence and nature of all the claims or pleas involved and of the participation of each person in the settlement.

(h) A lawyer shall not:

(1) make an agreement prospectively limiting the lawyer's liability to a client for malpractice unless the client is independently represented in making the agreement; or

(2) settle a claim or potential claim for such liability with an unrepresented client or former client unless that person is advised in writing of the desirability of seeking and is given a reasonable opportunity to seek the advice of independent legal counsel in connection therewith.

(i) A lawyer shall not acquire a proprietary interest in the cause of action or subject matter of litigation the lawyer is conducting for a client, except that the lawyer may:

(1) acquire a lien authorized by law to secure the lawyer's fee or expenses; and

(2) contract with a client for a reasonable contingent fee in a civil case.

(j) A lawyer shall not have sexual relations with a client unless a consensual sexual relationship existed between them when the client-lawyer relationship commenced.

(k) While lawyers are associated in a firm, a prohibition in the foregoing paragraphs (a) through (i) that applies to any one of them shall apply to all of them.

Comment

Business Transactions Between Client and Lawyer

[1] A lawyer's legal skill and training, together with the relationship of trust and confidence between lawyer and client, create the possibility of overreaching when the lawyer participates in a business, property or financial transaction with a client, for example, a loan or sales transaction or a lawyer investment on behalf of a client. The requirements of paragraph (a) must be met even when the transaction is not closely related to the subject matter of the representation, as when a lawyer drafting a will for a client learns that the client needs money for unrelated expenses and offers to make a loan to the client. The Rule applies to lawyers engaged in the sale of goods or services related to the practice of law, for example, the sale of title insurance or investment services to existing clients of the lawyer's legal practice. See Rule 5.7. It also applies to lawyers purchasing property from estates they represent. It does not apply to ordinary fee arrangements between client and lawyer, which are governed by Rule 1.5, although its requirements must be met when the lawyer accepts an interest in the client's business or other nonmonetary property as payment of all or part of a fee. In addition, the Rule does not apply to standard commercial transactions

between the lawyer and the client for products or services that the client generally markets to others, for example, banking or brokerage services, medical services, products manufactured or distributed by the client, and utilities' services. In such transactions, the lawyer has no advantage in dealing with the client, and the restrictions in paragraph (a) are unnecessary and impracticable.

[2]   Paragraph (a)(1) requires that the transaction itself be fair to the client and that its essential terms be communicated to the client, in writing, in a manner that can be reasonably understood. Paragraph (a)(2) requires that the client also be advised, in writing, of the desirability of seeking the advice of independent legal counsel. It also requires that the client be given a reasonable opportunity to obtain such advice. Paragraph (a)(3) requires that the lawyer obtain the client's informed consent, in a writing signed by the client, both to the essential terms of the transaction and to the lawyer's role. When necessary, the lawyer should discuss both the material risks of the proposed transaction, including any risk presented by the lawyer's involvement, and the existence of reasonably available alternatives and should explain why the advice of independent legal counsel is desirable. See Rule 1.0(e) (definition of informed consent).

[3]   The risk to a client is greatest when the client expects the lawyer to represent the client in the transaction itself or when the lawyer's financial interest otherwise poses a significant risk that the lawyer's representation of the client will be materially limited by the lawyer's financial interest in the transaction. Here the lawyer's role requires that the lawyer must comply, not only with the requirements of paragraph (a), but also with the requirements of Rule 1.7. Under that Rule, the lawyer must disclose the risks associated with the lawyer's dual role as both legal adviser and participant in the transaction, such as the risk that the lawyer will structure the transaction or give legal advice in a way that favors the lawyer's interests at the expense of the client. Moreover, the lawyer must obtain the client's informed consent. In some cases, the lawyer's interest may be such that Rule 1.7 will preclude the lawyer from seeking the client's consent to the transaction.

[4]   If the client is independently represented in the transaction, paragraph (a)(2) of this Rule is inapplicable, and the paragraph (a)(1) requirement for full disclosure is satisfied either by a written disclosure by the lawyer involved in the transaction or by the client's independent counsel. The fact that the client was independently represented in the transaction is relevant in determining whether the agreement was fair and reasonable to the client as paragraph (a)(1) further requires.

Use of Information Related to Representation

[5]   Use of information relating to the representation to the disadvantage of the client violates the lawyer's duty of loyalty. Paragraph (b) applies when the information is used to benefit either the lawyer or a third person, such as another client or business associate of the lawyer. For example, if a lawyer learns that a client intends to purchase and develop several parcels of land, the lawyer may not use that information to purchase one of the parcels in competition with the client or to recommend that another client make such a purchase. The Rule does not prohibit uses that do not disadvantage the client. For example, a lawyer who learns a government agency's interpretation of trade legislation during the representation of one client may properly use that information to benefit other clients. Paragraph (b) prohibits disadvantageous use of client information unless the client gives

informed consent, except as permitted or required by these Rules. See Rules 1.2(d), 1.6, 1.9(c), 3.3, 4.1(b), 8.1 and 8.3.

Gifts to Lawyers

[6]   A lawyer may accept a gift from a client, if the transaction meets general standards of fairness. For example, a simple gift such as a present given at a holiday or as a token of appreciation is permitted. If a client offers the lawyer a more substantial gift, paragraph (c) does not prohibit the lawyer from accepting it, although such a gift may be voidable by the client under the doctrine of undue influence, which treats client gifts as presumptively fraudulent. In any event, due to concerns about overreaching and imposition on clients, a lawyer may not suggest that a substantial gift be made to the lawyer or for the lawyer's benefit, except where the lawyer is related to the client as set forth in paragraph (c).

[7]   If effectuation of a substantial gift requires preparing a legal instrument such as a will or conveyance the client should have the detached advice that another lawyer can provide. The sole exception to this Rule is where the client is a relative of the donee.

[8]   This Rule does not prohibit a lawyer from seeking to have the lawyer or a partner or associate of the lawyer named as executor of the client's estate or to another potentially lucrative fiduciary position. Nevertheless, such appointments will be subject to the general conflict of interest provision in Rule 1.7 when there is a significant risk that the lawyer's interest in obtaining the appointment will materially limit the lawyer's independent professional judgment in advising the client concerning the choice of an executor or other fiduciary. In obtaining the client's informed consent to the conflict, the lawyer should advise the client concerning the nature and extent of the lawyer's financial interest in the appointment, as well as the availability of alternative candidates for the position.

Literary Rights

[9]   An agreement by which a lawyer acquires literary or media rights concerning the conduct of the representation creates a conflict between the interests of the client and the personal interests of the lawyer. Measures suitable in the representation of the client may detract from the publication value of an account of the representation. Paragraph (d) does not prohibit a lawyer representing a client in a transaction concerning literary property from agreeing that the lawyer's fee shall consist of a share in ownership in the property, if the arrangement conforms to Rule 1.5 and paragraphs (a) and (i).

Financial Assistance

[10] Lawyers may not subsidize lawsuits or administrative proceedings brought on behalf of their clients, including making or guaranteeing loans to their clients for living expenses, because to do so would encourage clients to pursue lawsuits that might not otherwise be brought and because such assistance gives lawyers too great a financial stake in the litigation. These dangers do not warrant a prohibition on a lawyer lending a client court costs and litigation expenses, including the expenses of medical examination and the costs of obtaining and presenting evidence, because these advances are virtually indistinguishable from contingent fees and help ensure access to the courts. Similarly, an exception allowing lawyers representing indigent clients to pay court costs and litigation expenses regardless of whether these funds will be repaid is warranted.

Person Paying for a Lawyer's Services

[11] Lawyers are frequently asked to represent a client under circumstances in which a third person will compensate the lawyer, in whole or in part. The third person might be a relative or friend, an indemnitor (such as a liability insurance company) or a co-client (such as a corporation sued along with one or more of its employees). Because third-party payers frequently have interests that differ from those of the client, including interests in minimizing the amount spent on the representation and in learning how the representation is progressing, lawyers are prohibited from accepting or continuing such representations unless the lawyer determines that there will be no interference with the lawyer's independent professional judgment and there is informed consent from the client. See also Rule 5.4(c) (prohibiting interference with a lawyer's professional judgment by one who recommends, employs or pays the lawyer to render legal services for another).

[12] Sometimes, it will be sufficient for the lawyer to obtain the client's informed consent regarding the fact of the payment and the identity of the third-party payer. If, however, the fee arrangement creates a conflict of interest for the lawyer, then the lawyer must comply with Rule. 1.7. The lawyer must also conform to the requirements of Rule 1.6 concerning confidentiality. Under Rule 1.7(a), a conflict of interest exists if there is significant risk that the lawyer's representation of the client will be materially limited by the lawyer's own interest in the fee arrangement or by the lawyer's responsibilities to the third-party payer (for example, when the third-party payer is a co-client). Under Rule 1.7(b), the lawyer may accept or continue the representation with the informed consent of each affected client, unless the conflict is nonconsentable under that paragraph. Under Rule 1.7(b), the informed consent must be confirmed in writing.

Aggregate Settlements

[13] Differences in willingness to make or accept an offer of settlement are among the risks of common representation of multiple clients by a single lawyer. Under Rule 1.7, this is one of the risks that should be discussed before undertaking the representation, as part of the process of obtaining the clients' informed consent. In addition, Rule 1.2(a) protects each client's right to have the final say in deciding whether to accept or reject an offer of settlement and in deciding whether to enter a guilty or nolo contendere plea in a criminal case. The rule stated in this paragraph is a corollary of both these Rules and provides that, before any settlement offer or plea bargain is made or accepted on behalf of multiple clients, the lawyer must inform each of them about all the material terms of the settlement, including what the other clients will receive or pay if the settlement or plea offer is accepted. See also Rule 1.0(e) (definition of informed consent). Lawyers representing a class of plaintiffs or defendants, or those proceeding derivatively, may not have a full client-lawyer relationship with each member of the class; nevertheless, such lawyers must comply with applicable rules regulating notification of class members and other procedural requirements designed to ensure adequate protection of the entire class.

Limiting Liability and Settling Malpractice Claims

[14] Agreements prospectively limiting a lawyer's liability for malpractice are prohibited unless the client is independently represented in making the agreement because they are likely to undermine competent and diligent representation. Also, many clients are unable to evaluate the desirability of making such an agreement before a dispute has arisen, particularly if they are then represented by the lawyer seeking the

agreement. This paragraph does not, however, prohibit a lawyer from entering into an agreement with the client to arbitrate legal malpractice claims, provided such agreements are enforceable and the client is fully informed of the scope and effect of the agreement. Nor does this paragraph limit the ability of lawyers to practice in the form of a limited-liability entity, where permitted by law, provided that each lawyer remains personally liable to the client for his or her own conduct and the firm complies with any conditions required by law, such as provisions requiring client notification or maintenance of adequate liability insurance. Nor does it prohibit an agreement in accordance with Rule 1.2 that defines the scope of the representation, although a definition of scope that makes the obligations of representation illusory will amount to an attempt to limit liability.

[15] Agreements settling a claim or a potential claim for malpractice are not prohibited by this Rule. Nevertheless, in view of the danger that a lawyer will take unfair advantage of an unrepresented client or former client, the lawyer must first advise such a person in writing of the appropriateness of independent representation in connection with such a settlement. In addition, the lawyer must give the client or former client a reasonable opportunity to find and consult independent counsel.

Acquiring Proprietary Interest in Litigation

[16] Paragraph (i) states the traditional general rule that lawyers are prohibited from acquiring a proprietary interest in litigation. Like paragraph (e), the general rule has its basis in common law champerty and maintenance and is designed to avoid giving the lawyer too great an interest in the representation. In addition, when the lawyer acquires an ownership interest in the subject of the representation, it will be more difficult for a client to discharge the lawyer if the client so desires. The Rule is subject to specific exceptions developed in decisional law and continued in these Rules. The exception for certain advances of the costs of litigation is set forth in paragraph (e). In addition, paragraph (i) sets forth exceptions for liens authorized by law to secure the lawyer's fees or expenses and contracts for reasonable contingent fees. The law of each jurisdiction determines which liens are authorized by law. These may include liens granted by statute, liens originating in common law and liens acquired by contract with the client. When a lawyer acquires by contract a security interest in property other than that recovered through the lawyer's efforts in the litigation, such an acquisition is a business or financial transaction with a client and is governed by the requirements of paragraph (a). Contracts for contingent fees in civil cases are governed by Rule 1.5.

Client-Lawyer Sexual Relationships

[17] The relationship between lawyer and client is a fiduciary one in which the lawyer occupies the highest position of trust and confidence. The relationship is almost always unequal; thus, a sexual relationship between lawyer and client can involve unfair exploitation of the lawyer's fiduciary role, in violation of the lawyer's basic ethical obligation not to use the trust of the client to the client's disadvantage. In addition, such a relationship presents a significant danger that, because of the lawyer's emotional involvement, the lawyer will be unable to represent the client without impairment of the exercise of independent professional judgment. Moreover, a blurred line between the professional and personal relationships may make it difficult to predict to what extent client confidences will be protected by the attorney-client evidentiary privilege, since client confidences are protected by privilege only when they are imparted in the context of the client-lawyer

relationship. Because of the significant danger of harm to client interests and because the client's own emotional involvement renders it unlikely that the client could give adequate informed consent, this Rule prohibits the lawyer from having sexual relations with a client regardless of whether the relationship is consensual and regardless of the absence of prejudice to the client.

[18] Sexual relationships that predate the client-lawyer relationship are not prohibited. Issues relating to the exploitation of the fiduciary relationship and client dependency are diminished when the sexual relationship existed prior to the commencement of the client-lawyer relationship. However, before proceeding with the representation in these circumstances, the lawyer should consider whether the lawyer's ability to represent the client will be materially limited by the relationship. See Rule 1.7(a)(2).

[19] When the client is an organization, paragraph (j) of this Rule prohibits a lawyer for the organization (whether inside counsel or outside counsel) from having a sexual relationship with a constituent of the organization who supervises, directs or regularly consults with that lawyer concerning the organization's legal matters.

Imputation of Prohibitions

[20] Under paragraph (k), a prohibition on conduct by an individual lawyer in paragraphs (a) through (i) also applies to all lawyers associated in a firm with the personally prohibited lawyer. For example, one lawyer in a firm may not enter into a business transaction with a client of another member of the firm without complying with paragraph (a), even if the first lawyer is not personally involved in the representation of the client. The prohibition set forth in paragraph (j) is personal and is not applied to associated lawyers.

RULE 1.9: DUTIES TO FORMER CLIENTS

(a) A lawyer who has formerly represented a client in a matter shall not thereafter represent another person in the same or a substantially related matter in which that person's interests are materially adverse to the interests of the former client unless the former client gives informed consent, confirmed in writing.

(b) A lawyer shall not knowingly represent a person in the same or a substantially related matter in which a firm with which the lawyer formerly was associated had previously represented a client

(1) whose interests are materially adverse to that person; and

(2) about whom the lawyer had acquired information protected by Rules 1.6 and 1.9(c) that is material to the matter;

unless the former client gives informed consent, confirmed in writing.

(c) A lawyer who has formerly represented a client in a matter or whose present or former firm has formerly represented a client in a matter shall not thereafter:

(1) use information relating to the representation to the disadvantage of the former client except as these Rules would permit or require with respect to a client, or when the information has become generally known; or

(2) reveal information relating to the representation except as these Rules would permit or require with respect to a client.

Comment

[1]   After termination of a client-lawyer relationship, a lawyer has certain continuing duties with respect to confidentiality and conflicts of interest and thus may not represent another client except in conformity with this Rule. Under this Rule, for example, a lawyer could not properly seek to rescind on behalf of a new client a contract drafted on behalf of the former client. So also a lawyer who has prosecuted an accused person could not properly represent the accused in a subsequent civil action against the government concerning the same transaction. Nor could a lawyer who has represented multiple clients in a matter represent one of the clients against the others in the same or a substantially related matter after a dispute arose among the clients in that matter, unless all affected clients give informed consent. See Comment [9]. Current and former government lawyers must comply with this Rule to the extent required by Rule 1.11.

[2]   The scope of a "matter" for purposes of this Rule depends on the facts of a particular situation or transaction. The lawyer's involvement in a matter can also be a question of degree. When a lawyer has been directly involved in a specific transaction, subsequent representation of other clients with materially adverse interests in that transaction clearly is prohibited. On the other hand, a lawyer who recurrently handled a type of problem for a former client is not precluded from later representing another client in a factually distinct problem of that type even though the subsequent representation involves a position adverse to the prior client. Similar considerations can apply to the reassignment of military lawyers between defense and prosecution functions within the same military jurisdictions. The underlying question is whether the lawyer was so involved in the matter that the subsequent representation can be justly regarded as a changing of sides in the matter in question.

[3]   Matters are "substantially related" for purposes of this Rule if they involve the same transaction or legal dispute or if there otherwise is a substantial risk that confidential factual information as would normally have been obtained in the prior representation would materially advance the client's position in the subsequent matter. For example, a lawyer who has represented a businessperson and learned extensive private financial information about that person may not then represent that person's spouse in seeking a divorce. Similarly, a lawyer who has previously represented a client in securing environmental permits to build a shopping center would be precluded from representing neighbors seeking to oppose rezoning of the property on the basis of environmental considerations; however, the lawyer would not be precluded, on the grounds of substantial relationship, from defending a tenant of the completed shopping center in resisting eviction for nonpayment of rent. Information that has been disclosed to the public or to other parties adverse to the former client ordinarily will not be disqualifying. Information acquired in a prior representation may have been rendered obsolete by the passage of time, a circumstance that may be relevant in determining whether two representations are substantially related. In the case of an organizational client, general knowledge of the client's policies and practices ordinarily will not preclude a subsequent representation; on the other hand, knowledge of specific facts gained in a prior representation that are relevant to the matter in question ordinarily will preclude such a representation. A former client is not required to reveal the confidential

information learned by the lawyer in order to establish a substantial risk that the lawyer has confidential information to use in the subsequent matter. A conclusion about the possession of such information may be based on the nature of the services the lawyer provided the former client and information that would in ordinary practice be learned by a lawyer providing such services.

Lawyers Moving Between Firms

[4]   When lawyers have been associated within a firm but then end their association, the question of whether a lawyer should undertake representation is more complicated. There are several competing considerations. First, the client previously represented by the former firm must be reasonably assured that the principle of loyalty to the client is not compromised. Second, the rule should not be so broadly cast as to preclude other persons from having reasonable choice of legal counsel. Third, the rule should not unreasonably hamper lawyers from forming new associations and taking on new clients after having left a previous association. In this connection, it should be recognized that today many lawyers practice in firms, that many lawyers to some degree limit their practice to one field or another, and that many move from one association to another several times in their careers. If the concept of imputation were applied with unqualified rigor, the result would be radical curtailment of the opportunity of lawyers to move from one practice setting to another and of the opportunity of clients to change counsel.

[5]   Paragraph (b) operates to disqualify the lawyer only when the lawyer involved has actual knowledge of information protected by Rules 1.6 and 1.9(c). Thus, if a lawyer while with one firm acquired no knowledge or information relating to a particular client of the firm, and that lawyer later joined another firm, neither the lawyer individually nor the second firm is disqualified from representing another client in the same or a related matter even though the interests of the two clients conflict. See Rule 1.10(b) for the restrictions on a firm once a lawyer has terminated association with the firm.

[6]   Application of paragraph (b) depends on a situation's particular facts, aided by inferences, deductions or working presumptions that reasonably may be made about the way in which lawyers work together. A lawyer may have general access to files of all clients of a law firm and may regularly participate in discussions of their affairs; it should be inferred that such a lawyer in fact is privy to all information about all the firm's clients. In contrast, another lawyer may have access to the files of only a limited number of clients and participate in discussions of the affairs of no other clients; in the absence of information to the contrary, it should be inferred that such a lawyer in fact is privy to information about the clients actually served but not those of other clients. In such an inquiry, the burden of proof should rest upon the firm whose disqualification is sought.

[7]   Independent of the question of disqualification of a firm, a lawyer changing professional association has a continuing duty to preserve confidentiality of information about a client formerly represented. See Rules 1.6 and 1.9(c).

[8]   Paragraph (c) provides that information acquired by the lawyer in the course of representing a client may not subsequently be used or revealed by the lawyer to the disadvantage of the client. However, the fact that a lawyer has once served a client does not preclude the lawyer from using generally known information about that client when later representing another client.

[9]   The provisions of this Rule are for the protection of former clients and can be waived if the client gives informed consent, which consent must be confirmed in writing under paragraphs (a) and (b). See Rule 1.0(e). With regard to the effectiveness of an advance waiver, see Comment [22] to Rule 1.7. With regard to disqualification of a firm with which a lawyer is or was formerly associated, see Rule 1.10.

RULE 1.10: IMPUTATION OF CONFLICTS OF INTEREST: GENERAL RULE

(a)   **While lawyers are associated in a firm, none of them shall knowingly represent a client when any one of them practicing alone would be prohibited from doing so by Rules 1.7 or 1.9, unless**

(1)   **the prohibition is based on a personal interest of the disqualified lawyer and does not present a significant risk of materially limiting the representation of the client by the remaining lawyers in the firm; or**

(2)   **the prohibition is based upon Rule 1.9(a) or (b) and arises out of the disqualified lawyer's association with a prior firm, and**

(i)   **the disqualified lawyer is timely screened from any participation in the matter and is apportioned no part of the fee therefrom;**

(ii)   **written notice is promptly given to any affected former client to enable the former client to ascertain compliance with the provisions of this Rule, which shall include a description of the screening procedures employed; a statement of the firm's and of the screened lawyer's compliance with these Rules; a statement that review may be available before a tribunal; and an agreement by the firm to respond promptly to any written inquiries or objections by the former client about the screening procedures; and**

(iii)   **certifications of compliance with these Rules and with the screening procedures are provided to the former client by the screened lawyer and by a partner of the firm, at reasonable intervals upon the former client's written request and upon termination of the screening procedures.**

(b)   **When a lawyer has terminated an association with a firm, the firm is not prohibited from thereafter representing a person with interests materially adverse to those of a client represented by the formerly associated lawyer and not currently represented by the firm, unless:**

(1)   **the matter is the same or substantially related to that in which the formerly associated lawyer represented the client; and**

(2)   **any lawyer remaining in the firm has information protected by Rules 1.6 and 1.9(c) that is material to the matter.**

(c)   **A disqualification prescribed by this rule may be waived by the affected client under the conditions stated in Rule 1.7.**

(d)   **The disqualification of lawyers associated in a firm with former or current government lawyers is governed by Rule 1.11.**

Comment

Definition of "Firm"

[1]   For purposes of the Rules of Professional Conduct, the term "firm" denotes lawyers in a law partnership, professional corporation, sole proprietorship or other association authorized to practice law; or lawyers employed in a legal services organization or the legal department of a corporation or other organization. See Rule 1.0(c). Whether two or more lawyers constitute a firm within this definition can depend on the specific facts. See Rule 1.0, Comments [2]–[4].

Principles of Imputed Disqualification

[2]   The rule of imputed disqualification stated in paragraph (a) gives effect to the principle of loyalty to the client as it applies to lawyers who practice in a law firm. Such situations can be considered from the premise that a firm of lawyers is essentially one lawyer for purposes of the rules governing loyalty to the client, or from the premise that each lawyer is vicariously bound by the obligation of loyalty owed by each lawyer with whom the lawyer is associated. Paragraph (a)(1) operates only among the lawyers currently associated in a firm. When a lawyer moves from one firm to another, the situation is governed by Rules 1.9(b) and 1.10(a)(2) and 1.10(b).

[3]   The rule in paragraph (a) does not prohibit representation where neither questions of client loyalty nor protection of confidential information are presented. Where one lawyer in a firm could not effectively represent a given client because of strong political beliefs, for example, but that lawyer will do no work on the case and the personal beliefs of the lawyer will not materially limit the representation by others in the firm, the firm should not be disqualified. On the other hand, if an opposing party in a case were owned by a lawyer in the law firm, and others in the firm would be materially limited in pursuing the matter because of loyalty to that lawyer, the personal disqualification of the lawyer would be imputed to all others in the firm.

[4]   The rule in paragraph (a) also does not prohibit representation by others in the law firm where the person prohibited from involvement in a matter is a nonlawyer, such as a paralegal or legal secretary. Nor does paragraph (a) prohibit representation if the lawyer is prohibited from acting because of events before the person became a lawyer, for example, work that the person did while a law student. Such persons, however, ordinarily must be screened from any personal participation in the matter to avoid communication to others in the firm of confidential information that both the nonlawyers and the firm have a legal duty to protect. See Rules 1.0(k) and 5.3.

[5]   Rule 1.10(b) operates to permit a law firm, under certain circumstances, to represent a person with interests directly adverse to those of a client represented by a lawyer who formerly was associated with the firm. The Rule applies regardless of when the formerly associated lawyer represented the client. However, the law firm may not represent a person with interests adverse to those of a present client of the firm, which would violate Rule 1.7. Moreover, the firm may not represent the person where the matter is the same or substantially related to that in which the formerly associated lawyer represented the client and any other lawyer currently in the firm has material information protected by Rules 1.6 and 1.9(c).

[6]   Rule 1.10(c) removes imputation with the informed consent of the affected client or former client under the conditions stated in Rule 1.7. The conditions stated in Rule 1.7 require the lawyer to determine that the

representation is not prohibited by Rule 1.7(b) and that each affected client or former client has given informed consent to the representation, confirmed in writing. In some cases, the risk may be so severe that the conflict may not be cured by client consent. For a discussion of the effectiveness of client waivers of conflicts that might arise in the future, see Rule 1.7, Comment [22]. For a definition of informed consent, see Rule 1.0(e).

[7] Rule 1.10(a)(2) similarly removes the imputation otherwise required by Rule 1.10(a), but unlike section (c), it does so without requiring that there be informed consent by the former client. Instead, it requires that the procedures laid out in sections (a)(2)(i)–(iii) be followed. A description of effective screening mechanisms appears in Rule 1.0(k). Lawyers should be aware, however, that, even where screening mechanisms have been adopted, tribunals may consider additional factors in ruling upon motions to disqualify a lawyer from pending litigation.

[8] Paragraph (a)(2)(i) does not prohibit the screened lawyer from receiving a salary or partnership share established by prior independent agreement, but that lawyer may not receive compensation directly related to the matter in which the lawyer is disqualified.

[9] The notice required by paragraph (a)(2)(ii) generally should include a description of the screened lawyer's prior representation and be given as soon as practicable after the need for screening becomes apparent. It also should include a statement by the screened lawyer and the firm that the client's material confidential information has not been disclosed or used in violation of the Rules. The notice is intended to enable the former client to evaluate and comment upon the effectiveness of the screening procedures.

[10] The certifications required by paragraph (a)(2)(iii) give the former client assurance that the client's material confidential information has not been disclosed or used inappropriately, either prior to timely implementation of a screen or thereafter. If compliance cannot be certified, the certificate must describe the failure to comply.

[11] Where a lawyer has joined a private firm after having represented the government, imputation is governed by Rule 1.11(b) and (c), not this Rule. Under Rule 1.11(d), where a lawyer represents the government after having served clients in private practice, nongovernmental employment or in another government agency, former-client conflicts are not imputed to government lawyers associated with the individually disqualified lawyer.

[12] Where a lawyer is prohibited from engaging in certain transactions under Rule 1.8, paragraph (k) of that Rule, and not this Rule, determines whether that prohibition also applies to other lawyers associated in a firm with the personally prohibited lawyer.

RULE 1.11: SPECIAL CONFLICTS OF INTEREST FOR FORMER AND CURRENT GOVERNMENT OFFICERS AND EMPLOYEES

(a) Except as law may otherwise expressly permit, a lawyer who has formerly served as a public officer or employee of the government:

(1) is subject to Rule 1.9(c); and

(2) shall not otherwise represent a client in connection with a matter in which the lawyer participated personally and substantially as a public officer or employee, unless the

appropriate government agency gives its informed consent, confirmed in writing, to the representation.

(b) When a lawyer is disqualified from representation under paragraph (a), no lawyer in a firm with which that lawyer is associated may knowingly undertake or continue representation in such a matter unless:

(1) the disqualified lawyer is timely screened from any participation in the matter and is apportioned no part of the fee therefrom; and

(2) written notice is promptly given to the appropriate government agency to enable it to ascertain compliance with the provisions of this rule.

(c) Except as law may otherwise expressly permit, a lawyer having information that the lawyer knows is confidential government information about a person acquired when the lawyer was a public officer or employee, may not represent a private client whose interests are adverse to that person in a matter in which the information could be used to the material disadvantage of that person. As used in this Rule, the term "confidential government information" means information that has been obtained under governmental authority and which, at the time this Rule is applied, the government is prohibited by law from disclosing to the public or has a legal privilege not to disclose and which is not otherwise available to the public. A firm with which that lawyer is associated may undertake or continue representation in the matter only if the disqualified lawyer is timely screened from any participation in the matter and is apportioned no part of the fee therefrom.

(d) Except as law may otherwise expressly permit, a lawyer currently serving as a public officer or employee:

(1) is subject to Rules 1.7 and 1.9; and

(2) shall not:

(i) participate in a matter in which the lawyer participated personally and substantially while in private practice or nongovernmental employment, unless the appropriate government agency gives its informed consent, confirmed in writing; or

(ii) negotiate for private employment with any person who is involved as a party or as lawyer for a party in a matter in which the lawyer is participating personally and substantially, except that a lawyer serving as a law clerk to a judge, other adjudicative officer or arbitrator may negotiate for private employment as permitted by Rule 1.12(b) and subject to the conditions stated in Rule 1.12(b).

(e) As used in this Rule, the term "matter" includes:

(1) any judicial or other proceeding, application, request for a ruling or other determination, contract, claim, controversy, investigation, charge, accusation, arrest or other particular matter involving a specific party or parties, and

(2) any other matter covered by the conflict of interest rules of the appropriate government agency.

Comment

[1]   A lawyer who has served or is currently serving as a public officer or employee is personally subject to the Rules of Professional Conduct, including the prohibition against concurrent conflicts of interest stated in Rule 1.7. In addition, such a lawyer may be subject to statutes and government regulations regarding conflict of interest. Such statutes and regulations may circumscribe the extent to which the government agency may give consent under this Rule. See Rule 1.0(e) for the definition of informed consent.

[2]   Paragraphs (a)(1) (a)(2) and (d)(1) restate the obligations of an individual lawyer who has served or is currently serving as an officer or employee of the government toward a former government or private client. Rule 1.10 is not applicable to the conflicts of interest addressed by this Rule. Rather, paragraph (b) sets forth a special imputation rule for former government lawyers that provides for screening and notice. Because of the special problems raised by imputation within a government agency, paragraph (d) does not impute the conflicts of a lawyer currently serving as an officer or employee of the government to other associated government officers or employees, although ordinarily it will be prudent to screen such lawyers.

[3]   Paragraphs (a)(2) and (d)(2) apply regardless of whether a lawyer is adverse to a former client and are thus designed not only to protect the former client, but also to prevent a lawyer from exploiting public office for the advantage of another client. For example, a lawyer who has pursued a claim on behalf of the government may not pursue the same claim on behalf of a later private client after the lawyer has left government service, except when authorized to do so by the government agency under paragraph (a). Similarly, a lawyer who has pursued a claim on behalf of a private client may not pursue the claim on behalf of the government, except when authorized to do so by paragraph (d). As with paragraphs (a)(1) and (d)(1), Rule 1.10 is not applicable to the conflicts of interest addressed by these paragraphs.

[4]   This Rule represents a balancing of interests. On the one hand, where the successive clients are a government agency and another client, public or private, the risk exists that power or discretion vested in that agency might be used for the special benefit of the other client. A lawyer should not be in a position where benefit to the other client might affect performance of the lawyer's professional functions on behalf of the government. Also, unfair advantage could accrue to the other client by reason of access to confidential government information about the client's adversary obtainable only through the lawyer's government service. On the other hand, the rules governing lawyers presently or formerly employed by a government agency should not be so restrictive as to inhibit transfer of employment to and from the government. The government has a legitimate need to attract qualified lawyers as well as to maintain high ethical standards. Thus a former government lawyer is disqualified only from particular matters in which the lawyer participated personally and substantially. The provisions for screening and waiver in paragraph (b) are necessary to prevent the disqualification rule from imposing too severe a deterrent against entering public service. The limitation of disqualification in paragraphs (a)(2) and (d)(2) to matters involving a specific party or parties, rather than extending disqualification to all substantive issues on which the lawyer worked, serves a similar function.

[5]   When a lawyer has been employed by one government agency and then moves to a second government agency, it may be appropriate to treat that second agency as another client for purposes of this Rule, as when a lawyer is employed by a city and subsequently is employed by a federal agency. However, because the conflict of interest is governed by paragraph (d), the latter agency is not required to screen the lawyer as paragraph (b) requires a law firm to do. The question of whether two government agencies should be regarded as the same or different clients for conflict of interest purposes is beyond the scope of these Rules. See Rule 1.13 Comment [9].

[6]   Paragraphs (b) and (c) contemplate a screening arrangement. See Rule 1.0(k) (requirements for screening procedures). These paragraphs do not prohibit a lawyer from receiving a salary or partnership share established by prior independent agreement, but that lawyer may not receive compensation directly relating the lawyer's compensation to the fee in the matter in which the lawyer is disqualified.

[7]   Notice, including a description of the screened lawyer's prior representation and of the screening procedures employed, generally should be given as soon as practicable after the need for screening becomes apparent.

[8]   Paragraph (c) operates only when the lawyer in question has knowledge of the information, which means actual knowledge; it does not operate with respect to information that merely could be imputed to the lawyer.

[9]   Paragraphs (a) and (d) do not prohibit a lawyer from jointly representing a private party and a government agency when doing so is permitted by Rule 1.7 and is not otherwise prohibited by law.

[10] For purposes of paragraph (e) of this Rule, a "matter" may continue in another form. In determining whether two particular matters are the same, the lawyer should consider the extent to which the matters involve the same basic facts, the same or related parties, and the time elapsed.

RULE 1.12: FORMER JUDGE, ARBITRATOR, MEDIATOR OR OTHER THIRD-PARTY NEUTRAL

(a) Except as stated in paragraph (d), a lawyer shall not represent anyone in connection with a matter in which the lawyer participated personally and substantially as a judge or other adjudicative officer or law clerk to such a person or as an arbitrator, mediator or other third-party neutral, unless all parties to the proceeding give informed consent, confirmed in writing.

(b) A lawyer shall not negotiate for employment with any person who is involved as a party or as lawyer for a party in a matter in which the lawyer is participating personally and substantially as a judge or other adjudicative officer or as an arbitrator, mediator or other third-party neutral. A lawyer serving as a law clerk to a judge or other adjudicative officer may negotiate for employment with a party or lawyer involved in a matter in which the clerk is participating personally and substantially, but only after the lawyer has notified the judge or other adjudicative officer.

(c) If a lawyer is disqualified by paragraph (a), no lawyer in a firm with which that lawyer is associated may knowingly undertake or continue representation in the matter unless:

(1) the disqualified lawyer is timely screened from any participation in the matter and is apportioned no part of the fee therefrom; and

(2) written notice is promptly given to the parties and any appropriate tribunal to enable them to ascertain compliance with the provisions of this rule.

(d) An arbitrator selected as a partisan of a party in a multimember arbitration panel is not prohibited from subsequently representing that party.

Comment

[1] This Rule generally parallels Rule 1.11. The term "personally and substantially" signifies that a judge who was a member of a multimember court, and thereafter left judicial office to practice law, is not prohibited from representing a client in a matter pending in the court, but in which the former judge did not participate. So also the fact that a former judge exercised administrative responsibility in a court does not prevent the former judge from acting as a lawyer in a matter where the judge had previously exercised remote or incidental administrative responsibility that did not affect the merits. Compare the Comment to Rule 1.11. The term "adjudicative officer" includes such officials as judges pro tempore, referees, special masters, hearing officers and other parajudicial officers, and also lawyers who serve as part-time judges. Paragraphs C(2), D(2) and E(2) of the Application Section of the Model Code of Judicial Conduct provide that a part-time judge, judge pro tempore or retired judge recalled to active service, shall not "act as a lawyer in a proceeding in which the judge has served as a judge or in any other proceeding related thereto." Although phrased differently from this Rule, those Rules correspond in meaning.

[2] Like former judges, lawyers who have served as arbitrators, mediators or other third-party neutrals may be asked to represent a client in a matter in which the lawyer participated personally and substantially. This Rule forbids such representation unless all of the parties to the proceedings give their informed consent, confirmed in writing. See Rule 1.0(e) and (b). Other law or codes of ethics governing third-party neutrals may impose more stringent standards of personal or imputed disqualification. See Rule 2.4.

[3] Although lawyers who serve as third-party neutrals do not have information concerning the parties that is protected under Rule 1.6, they typically owe the parties an obligation of confidentiality under law or codes of ethics governing third-party neutrals. Thus, paragraph (c) provides that conflicts of the personally disqualified lawyer will be imputed to other lawyers in a law firm unless the conditions of this paragraph are met.

[4] Requirements for screening procedures are stated in Rule 1.0(k). Paragraph (c)(1) does not prohibit the screened lawyer from receiving a salary or partnership share established by prior independent agreement, but that lawyer may not receive compensation directly related to the matter in which the lawyer is disqualified.

[5] Notice, including a description of the screened lawyer's prior representation and of the screening procedures employed, generally should be given as soon as practicable after the need for screening becomes apparent.

RULE 1.13: ORGANIZATION AS CLIENT

(a) A lawyer employed or retained by an organization represents the organization acting through its duly authorized constituents.

(b) If a lawyer for an organization knows that an officer, employee or other person associated with the organization is engaged in action, intends to act or refuses to act in a matter related to the representation that is a violation of a legal obligation to the organization, or a violation of law that reasonably might be imputed to the organization, and that is likely to result in substantial injury to the organization, then the lawyer shall proceed as is reasonably necessary in the best interest of the organization. Unless the lawyer reasonably believes that it is not necessary in the best interest of the organization to do so, the lawyer shall refer the matter to higher authority in the organization, including, if warranted by the circumstances, to the highest authority that can act on behalf of the organization as determined by applicable law.

(c) Except as provided in paragraph (d), if

(1) despite the lawyer's efforts in accordance with paragraph (b) the highest authority that can act on behalf of the organization insists upon or fails to address in a timely and appropriate manner an action or a refusal to act, that is clearly a violation of law, and

(2) the lawyer reasonably believes that the violation is reasonably certain to result in substantial injury to the organization,

then the lawyer may reveal information relating to the representation whether or not Rule 1.6 permits such disclosure, but only if and to the extent the lawyer reasonably believes necessary to prevent substantial injury to the organization.

(d) Paragraph (c) shall not apply with respect to information relating to a lawyer's representation of an organization to investigate an alleged violation of law, or to defend the organization or an officer, employee or other constituent associated with the organization against a claim arising out of an alleged violation of law.

(e) A lawyer who reasonably believes that he or she has been discharged because of the lawyer's actions taken pursuant to paragraphs (b) or (c), or who withdraws under circumstances that require or permit the lawyer to take action under either of those paragraphs, shall proceed as the lawyer reasonably believes necessary to assure that the organization's highest authority is informed of the lawyer's discharge or withdrawal.

(f) In dealing with an organization's directors, officers, employees, members, shareholders or other constituents, a lawyer shall explain the identity of the client when the lawyer knows or reasonably should know that the organization's interests are adverse to those of the constituents with whom the lawyer is dealing.

(g) A lawyer representing an organization may also represent any of its directors, officers, employees, members, shareholders or other constituents, subject to the provisions of Rule 1.7. If the

organization's consent to the dual representation is required by Rule 1.7, the consent shall be given by an appropriate official of the organization other than the individual who is to be represented, or by the shareholders.

Comment

The Entity as the Client

[1]   An organizational client is a legal entity, but it cannot act except through its officers, directors, employees, shareholders and other constituents. Officers, directors, employees and shareholders are the constituents of the corporate organizational client. The duties defined in this Comment apply equally to unincorporated associations. "Other constituents" as used in this Comment means the positions equivalent to officers, directors, employees and shareholders held by persons acting for organizational clients that are not corporations.

[2]   When one of the constituents of an organizational client communicates with the organization's lawyer in that person's organizational capacity, the communication is protected by Rule 1.6. Thus, by way of example, if an organizational client requests its lawyer to investigate allegations of wrongdoing, interviews made in the course of that investigation between the lawyer and the client's employees or other constituents are covered by Rule 1.6. This does not mean, however, that constituents of an organizational client are the clients of the lawyer. The lawyer may not disclose to such constituents information relating to the representation except for disclosures explicitly or impliedly authorized by the organizational client in order to carry out the representation or as otherwise permitted by Rule 1.6.

[3]   When constituents of the organization make decisions for it, the decisions ordinarily must be accepted by the lawyer even if their utility or prudence is doubtful. Decisions concerning policy and operations, including ones entailing serious risk, are not as such in the lawyer's province. Paragraph (b) makes clear, however, that when the lawyer knows that the organization is likely to be substantially injured by action of an officer or other constituent that violates a legal obligation to the organization or is in violation of law that might be imputed to the organization, the lawyer must proceed as is reasonably necessary in the best interest of the organization. As defined in Rule 1.0(f), knowledge can be inferred from circumstances, and a lawyer cannot ignore the obvious.

[4]   In determining how to proceed under paragraph (b), the lawyer should give due consideration to the seriousness of the violation and its consequences, the responsibility in the organization and the apparent motivation of the person involved, the policies of the organization concerning such matters, and any other relevant considerations. Ordinarily, referral to a higher authority would be necessary. In some circumstances, however, it may be appropriate for the lawyer to ask the constituent to reconsider the matter; for example, if the circumstances involve a constituent's innocent misunderstanding of law and subsequent acceptance of the lawyer's advice, the lawyer may reasonably conclude that the best interest of the organization does not require that the matter be referred to higher authority. If a constituent persists in conduct contrary to the lawyer's advice, it will be necessary for the lawyer to take steps to have the matter reviewed by a higher authority in the organization. If the matter is of sufficient seriousness and importance or urgency to the organization, referral to higher authority in the organization may be necessary even if the lawyer has not communicated with

the constituent. Any measures taken should, to the extent practicable, minimize the risk of revealing information relating to the representation to persons outside the organization. Even in circumstances where a lawyer is not obligated by Rule 1.13 to proceed, a lawyer may bring to the attention of an organizational client, including its highest authority, matters that the lawyer reasonably believes to be of sufficient importance to warrant doing so in the best interest of the organization.

[5] Paragraph (b) also makes clear that when it is reasonably necessary to enable the organization to address the matter in a timely and appropriate manner, the lawyer must refer the matter to higher authority, including, if warranted by the circumstances, the highest authority that can act on behalf of the organization under applicable law. The organization's highest authority to whom a matter may be referred ordinarily will be the board of directors or similar governing body. However, applicable law may prescribe that under certain conditions the highest authority reposes elsewhere, for example, in the independent directors of a corporation.

Relation to Other Rules

[6] The authority and responsibility provided in this Rule are concurrent with the authority and responsibility provided in other Rules. In particular, this Rule does not limit or expand the lawyer's responsibility under Rules 1.8, 1.16, 3.3 or 4.1. Paragraph (c) of this Rule supplements Rule 1.6(b) by providing an additional basis upon which the lawyer may reveal information relating to the representation, but does not modify, restrict, or limit the provisions of Rule 1.6(b)(1)–(6). Under paragraph (c) the lawyer may reveal such information only when the organization's highest authority insists upon or fails to address threatened or ongoing action that is clearly a violation of law, and then only to the extent the lawyer reasonably believes necessary to prevent reasonably certain substantial injury to the organization. It is not necessary that the lawyer's services be used in furtherance of the violation, but it is required that the matter be related to the lawyer's representation of the organization. If the lawyer's services are being used by an organization to further a crime or fraud by the organization, Rules 1.6(b)(2) and 1.6(b)(3) may permit the lawyer to disclose confidential information. In such circumstances Rule 1.2(d) may also be applicable, in which event, withdrawal from the representation under Rule 1.16(a)(1) may be required.

[7] Paragraph (d) makes clear that the authority of a lawyer to disclose information relating to a representation in circumstances described in paragraph (c) does not apply with respect to information relating to a lawyer's engagement by an organization to investigate an alleged violation of law or to defend the organization or an officer, employee or other person associated with the organization against a claim arising out of an alleged violation of law. This is necessary in order to enable organizational clients to enjoy the full benefits of legal counsel in conducting an investigation or defending against a claim.

[8] A lawyer who reasonably believes that he or she has been discharged because of the lawyer's actions taken pursuant to paragraph (b) or (c), or who withdraws in circumstances that require or permit the lawyer to take action under either of these paragraphs, must proceed as the lawyer reasonably believes necessary to assure that the organization's highest authority is informed of the lawyer's discharge or withdrawal.

Government Agency

[9] The duty defined in this Rule applies to governmental organizations. Defining precisely the identity of the client and prescribing the resulting obligations of such lawyers may be more difficult in the government context and is a matter beyond the scope of these Rules. See Scope [18]. Although in some circumstances the client may be a specific agency, it may also be a branch of government, such as the executive branch, or the government as a whole. For example, if the action or failure to act involves the head of a bureau, either the department of which the bureau is a part or the relevant branch of government may be the client for purposes of this Rule. Moreover, in a matter involving the conduct of government officials, a government lawyer may have authority under applicable law to question such conduct more extensively than that of a lawyer for a private organization in similar circumstances. Thus, when the client is a governmental organization, a different balance may be appropriate between maintaining confidentiality and assuring that the wrongful act is prevented or rectified, for public business is involved. In addition, duties of lawyers employed by the government or lawyers in military service may be defined by statutes and regulation. This Rule does not limit that authority. See Scope.

Clarifying the Lawyer's Role

[10] There are times when the organization's interest may be or become adverse to those of one or more of its constituents. In such circumstances the lawyer should advise any constituent, whose interest the lawyer finds adverse to that of the organization of the conflict or potential conflict of interest, that the lawyer cannot represent such constituent, and that such person may wish to obtain independent representation. Care must be taken to assure that the individual understands that, when there is such adversity of interest, the lawyer for the organization cannot provide legal representation for that constituent individual, and that discussions between the lawyer for the organization and the individual may not be privileged.

[11] Whether such a warning should be given by the lawyer for the organization to any constituent individual may turn on the facts of each case.

Dual Representation

[12] Paragraph (g) recognizes that a lawyer for an organization may also represent a principal officer or major shareholder.

Derivative Actions

[13] Under generally prevailing law, the shareholders or members of a corporation may bring suit to compel the directors to perform their legal obligations in the supervision of the organization. Members of unincorporated associations have essentially the same right. Such an action may be brought nominally by the organization, but usually is, in fact, a legal controversy over management of the organization.

[14] The question can arise whether counsel for the organization may defend such an action. The proposition that the organization is the lawyer's client does not alone resolve the issue. Most derivative actions are a normal incident of an organization's affairs, to be defended by the organization's lawyer like any other suit. However, if the claim involves serious charges of wrongdoing by those in control of the organization, a conflict may arise between the lawyer's duty to the organization and the lawyer's relationship with the board. In those circumstances, Rule 1.7 governs who should represent the directors and the organization.

RULE 1.14: CLIENT WITH DIMINISHED CAPACITY

(a) When a client's capacity to make adequately considered decisions in connection with a representation is diminished, whether because of minority, mental impairment or for some other reason, the lawyer shall, as far as reasonably possible, maintain a normal client-lawyer relationship with the client.

(b) When the lawyer reasonably believes that the client has diminished capacity, is at risk of substantial physical, financial or other harm unless action is taken and cannot adequately act in the client's own interest, the lawyer may take reasonably necessary protective action, including consulting with individuals or entities that have the ability to take action to protect the client and, in appropriate cases, seeking the appointment of a guardian ad litem, conservator or guardian.

(c) Information relating to the representation of a client with diminished capacity is protected by Rule 1.6. When taking protective action pursuant to paragraph (b), the lawyer is impliedly authorized under Rule 1.6(a) to reveal information about the client, but only to the extent reasonably necessary to protect the client's interests.

Comment

[1]   The normal client-lawyer relationship is based on the assumption that the client, when properly advised and assisted, is capable of making decisions about important matters. When the client is a minor or suffers from a diminished mental capacity, however, maintaining the ordinary client-lawyer relationship may not be possible in all respects. In particular, a severely incapacitated person may have no power to make legally binding decisions. Nevertheless, a client with diminished capacity often has the ability to understand, deliberate upon, and reach conclusions about matters affecting the client's own well-being. For example, children as young as five or six years of age, and certainly those of ten or twelve, are regarded as having opinions that are entitled to weight in legal proceedings concerning their custody. So also, it is recognized that some persons of advanced age can be quite capable of handling routine financial matters while needing special legal protection concerning major transactions.

[2]   The fact that a client suffers a disability does not diminish the lawyer's obligation to treat the client with attention and respect. Even if the person has a legal representative, the lawyer should as far as possible accord the represented person the status of client, particularly in maintaining communication.

[3]   The client may wish to have family members or other persons participate in discussions with the lawyer. When necessary to assist in the representation, the presence of such persons generally does not affect the applicability of the attorney-client evidentiary privilege. Nevertheless, the lawyer must keep the client's interests foremost and, except for protective action authorized under paragraph (b), must to look to the client, and not family members, to make decisions on the client's behalf.

[4]   If a legal representative has already been appointed for the client, the lawyer should ordinarily look to the representative for decisions on behalf of the client. In matters involving a minor, whether the lawyer should look to the parents as natural guardians may depend on the type of proceeding or matter in which the lawyer is representing the minor. If the lawyer represents the guardian as distinct from the ward, and is aware that the

guardian is acting adversely to the ward's interest, the lawyer may have an obligation to prevent or rectify the guardian's misconduct. See Rule 1.2(d).

Taking Protective Action

[5]   If a lawyer reasonably believes that a client is at risk of substantial physical, financial or other harm unless action is taken, and that a normal client-lawyer relationship cannot be maintained as provided in paragraph (a) because the client lacks sufficient capacity to communicate or to make adequately considered decisions in connection with the representation, then paragraph (b) permits the lawyer to take protective measures deemed necessary. Such measures could include: consulting with family members, using a reconsideration period to permit clarification or improvement of circumstances, using voluntary surrogate decisionmaking tools such as durable powers of attorney or consulting with support groups, professional services, adult-protective agencies or other individuals or entities that have the ability to protect the client. In taking any protective action, the lawyer should be guided by such factors as the wishes and values of the client to the extent known, the client's best interests and the goals of intruding into the client's decisionmaking autonomy to the least extent feasible, maximizing client capacities and respecting the client's family and social connections.

[6]   In determining the extent of the client's diminished capacity, the lawyer should consider and balance such factors as: the client's ability to articulate reasoning leading to a decision, variability of state of mind and ability to appreciate consequences of a decision; the substantive fairness of a decision; and the consistency of a decision with the known long-term commitments and values of the client. In appropriate circumstances, the lawyer may seek guidance from an appropriate diagnostician.

[7]   If a legal representative has not been appointed, the lawyer should consider whether appointment of a guardian ad litem, conservator or guardian is necessary to protect the client's interests. Thus, if a client with diminished capacity has substantial property that should be sold for the client's benefit, effective completion of the transaction may require appointment of a legal representative. In addition, rules of procedure in litigation sometimes provide that minors or persons with diminished capacity must be represented by a guardian or next friend if they do not have a general guardian. In many circumstances, however, appointment of a legal representative may be more expensive or traumatic for the client than circumstances in fact require. Evaluation of such circumstances is a matter entrusted to the professional judgment of the lawyer. In considering alternatives, however, the lawyer should be aware of any law that requires the lawyer to advocate the least restrictive action on behalf of the client.

Disclosure of the Client's Condition

[8]   Disclosure of the client's diminished capacity could adversely affect the client's interests. For example, raising the question of diminished capacity could, in some circumstances, lead to proceedings for involuntary commitment. Information relating to the representation is protected by Rule 1.6. Therefore, unless authorized to do so, the lawyer may not disclose such information. When taking protective action pursuant to paragraph (b), the lawyer is impliedly authorized to make the necessary disclosures, even when the client directs the lawyer to the contrary. Nevertheless, given the risks of disclosure, paragraph (c) limits what the lawyer may disclose in consulting with other individuals or entities or seeking the appointment of a legal representative. At the very least, the lawyer should determine whether it is likely that the person or entity consulted with will act adversely to the client's

interests before discussing matters related to the client. The lawyer's position in such cases is an unavoidably difficult one.

Emergency Legal Assistance

[9] In an emergency where the health, safety or a financial interest of a person with seriously diminished capacity is threatened with imminent and irreparable harm, a lawyer may take legal action on behalf of such a person even though the person is unable to establish a client-lawyer relationship or to make or express considered judgments about the matter, when the person or another acting in good faith on that person's behalf has consulted with the lawyer. Even in such an emergency, however, the lawyer should not act unless the lawyer reasonably believes that the person has no other lawyer, agent or other representative available. The lawyer should take legal action on behalf of the person only to the extent reasonably necessary to maintain the status quo or otherwise avoid imminent and irreparable harm. A lawyer who undertakes to represent a person in such an exigent situation has the same duties under these Rules as the lawyer would with respect to a client.

[10] A lawyer who acts on behalf of a person with seriously diminished capacity in an emergency should keep the confidences of the person as if dealing with a client, disclosing them only to the extent necessary to accomplish the intended protective action. The lawyer should disclose to any tribunal involved and to any other counsel involved the nature of his or her relationship with the person. The lawyer should take steps to regularize the relationship or implement other protective solutions as soon as possible. Normally, a lawyer would not seek compensation for such emergency actions taken.

RULE 1.15: SAFEKEEPING PROPERTY

(a) A lawyer shall hold property of clients or third persons that is in a lawyer's possession in connection with a representation separate from the lawyer's own property. Funds shall be kept in a separate account maintained in the state where the lawyer's office is situated, or elsewhere with the consent of the client or third person. Other property shall be identified as such and appropriately safeguarded. Complete records of such account funds and other property shall be kept by the lawyer and shall be preserved for a period of [five years] after termination of the representation.

(b) A lawyer may deposit the lawyer's own funds in a client trust account for the sole purpose of paying bank service charges on that account, but only in an amount necessary for that purpose.

(c) A lawyer shall deposit into a client trust account legal fees and expenses that have been paid in advance, to be withdrawn by the lawyer only as fees are earned or expenses incurred.

(d) Upon receiving funds or other property in which a client or third person has an interest, a lawyer shall promptly notify the client or third person. Except as stated in this rule or otherwise permitted by law or by agreement with the client, a lawyer shall promptly deliver to the client or third person any funds or other property that the client or third person is entitled to receive and, upon request by the client or third person, shall promptly render a full accounting regarding such property.

(e) When in the course of representation a lawyer is in possession of property in which two or more persons (one of whom

may be the lawyer) claim interests, the property shall be kept separate by the lawyer until the dispute is resolved. The lawyer shall promptly distribute all portions of the property as to which the interests are not in dispute.

Comment

[1]   A lawyer should hold property of others with the care required of a professional fiduciary. Securities should be kept in a safe deposit box, except when some other form of safekeeping is warranted by special circumstances. All property that is the property of clients or third persons, including prospective clients, must be kept separate from the lawyer's business and personal property and, if monies, in one or more trust accounts. Separate trust accounts may be warranted when administering estate monies or acting in similar fiduciary capacities. A lawyer should maintain on a current basis books and records in accordance with generally accepted accounting practice and comply with any recordkeeping rules established by law or court order. See, e.g., ABA Model Rules for Client Trust Account Records.

[2]   While normally it is impermissible to commingle the lawyer's own funds with client funds, paragraph (b) provides that it is permissible when necessary to pay bank service charges on that account. Accurate records must be kept regarding which part of the funds are the lawyer's.

[3]   Lawyers often receive funds from which the lawyer's fee will be paid. The lawyer is not required to remit to the client funds that the lawyer reasonably believes represent fees owed. However, a lawyer may not hold funds to coerce a client into accepting the lawyer's contention. The disputed portion of the funds must be kept in a trust account and the lawyer should suggest means for prompt resolution of the dispute, such as arbitration. The undisputed portion of the funds shall be promptly distributed.

[4]   Paragraph (e) also recognizes that third parties may have lawful claims against specific funds or other property in a lawyer's custody, such as a client's creditor who has a lien on funds recovered in a personal injury action. A lawyer may have a duty under applicable law to protect such third-party claims against wrongful interference by the client. In such cases, when the third-party claim is not frivolous under applicable law, the lawyer must refuse to surrender the property to the client until the claims are resolved. A lawyer should not unilaterally assume to arbitrate a dispute between the client and the third party, but, when there are substantial grounds for dispute as to the person entitled to the funds, the lawyer may file an action to have a court resolve the dispute.

[5]   The obligations of a lawyer under this Rule are independent of those arising from activity other than rendering legal services. For example, a lawyer who serves only as an escrow agent is governed by the applicable law relating to fiduciaries even though the lawyer does not render legal services in the transaction and is not governed by this Rule.

[6]   A lawyers' fund for client protection provides a means through the collective efforts of the bar to reimburse persons who have lost money or property as a result of dishonest conduct of a lawyer. Where such a fund has been established, a lawyer must participate where it is mandatory, and, even when it is voluntary, the lawyer should participate.

RULE 1.16: DECLINING OR
TERMINATING REPRESENTATION

(a) Except as stated in paragraph (c), a lawyer shall not represent a client or, where representation has commenced, shall withdraw from the representation of a client if:

(1) the representation will result in violation of the rules of professional conduct or other law;

(2) the lawyer's physical or mental condition materially impairs the lawyer's ability to represent the client; or

(3) the lawyer is discharged.

(b) Except as stated in paragraph (c), a lawyer may withdraw from representing a client if:

(1) withdrawal can be accomplished without material adverse effect on the interests of the client;

(2) the client persists in a course of action involving the lawyer's services that the lawyer reasonably believes is criminal or fraudulent;

(3) the client has used the lawyer's services to perpetrate a crime or fraud;

(4) the client insists upon taking action that the lawyer considers repugnant or with which the lawyer has a fundamental disagreement;

(5) the client fails substantially to fulfill an obligation to the lawyer regarding the lawyer's services and has been given reasonable warning that the lawyer will withdraw unless the obligation is fulfilled;

(6) the representation will result in an unreasonable financial burden on the lawyer or has been rendered unreasonably difficult by the client; or

(7) other good cause for withdrawal exists.

(c) A lawyer must comply with applicable law requiring notice to or permission of a tribunal when terminating a representation. When ordered to do so by a tribunal, a lawyer shall continue representation notwithstanding good cause for terminating the representation.

(d) Upon termination of representation, a lawyer shall take steps to the extent reasonably practicable to protect a client's interests, such as giving reasonable notice to the client, allowing time for employment of other counsel, surrendering papers and property to which the client is entitled and refunding any advance payment of fee or expense that has not been earned or incurred. The lawyer may retain papers relating to the client to the extent permitted by other law.

Comment

[1]   A lawyer should not accept representation in a matter unless it can be performed competently, promptly, without improper conflict of interest and to completion. Ordinarily, a representation in a matter is completed

when the agreed-upon assistance has been concluded. See Rules 1.2(c) and 6.5. See also Rule 1.3, Comment [4].

Mandatory Withdrawal

[2]   A lawyer ordinarily must decline or withdraw from representation if the client demands that the lawyer engage in conduct that is illegal or violates the Rules of Professional Conduct or other law. The lawyer is not obliged to decline or withdraw simply because the client suggests such a course of conduct; a client may make such a suggestion in the hope that a lawyer will not be constrained by a professional obligation.

[3]   When a lawyer has been appointed to represent a client, withdrawal ordinarily requires approval of the appointing authority. See also Rule 6.2. Similarly, court approval or notice to the court is often required by applicable law before a lawyer withdraws from pending litigation. Difficulty may be encountered if withdrawal is based on the client's demand that the lawyer engage in unprofessional conduct. The court may request an explanation for the withdrawal, while the lawyer may be bound to keep confidential the facts that would constitute such an explanation. The lawyer's statement that professional considerations require termination of the representation ordinarily should be accepted as sufficient. Lawyers should be mindful of their obligations to both clients and the court under Rules 1.6 and 3.3.

Discharge

[4]   A client has a right to discharge a lawyer at any time, with or without cause, subject to liability for payment for the lawyer's services. Where future dispute about the withdrawal may be anticipated, it may be advisable to prepare a written statement reciting the circumstances.

[5]   Whether a client can discharge appointed counsel may depend on applicable law. A client seeking to do so should be given a full explanation of the consequences. These consequences may include a decision by the appointing authority that appointment of successor counsel is unjustified, thus requiring self-representation by the client.

[6]   If the client has severely diminished capacity, the client may lack the legal capacity to discharge the lawyer, and in any event the discharge may be seriously adverse to the client's interests. The lawyer should make special effort to help the client consider the consequences and may take reasonably necessary protective action as provided in Rule 1.14.

Optional Withdrawal

[7]   A lawyer may withdraw from representation in some circumstances. The lawyer has the option to withdraw if it can be accomplished without material adverse effect on the client's interests. Withdrawal is also justified if the client persists in a course of action that the lawyer reasonably believes is criminal or fraudulent, for a lawyer is not required to be associated with such conduct even if the lawyer does not further it. Withdrawal is also permitted if the lawyer's services were misused in the past even if that would materially prejudice the client. The lawyer may also withdraw where the client insists on taking action that the lawyer considers repugnant or with which the lawyer has a fundamental disagreement.

[8]   A lawyer may withdraw if the client refuses to abide by the terms of an agreement relating to the representation, such as an agreement

concerning fees or court costs or an agreement limiting the objectives of the representation.

Assisting the Client upon Withdrawal

[9]   Even if the lawyer has been unfairly discharged by the client, a lawyer must take all reasonable steps to mitigate the consequences to the client. The lawyer may retain papers as security for a fee only to the extent permitted by law. See Rule 1.15.

RULE 1.17: SALE OF LAW PRACTICE

A lawyer or a law firm may sell or purchase a law practice, or an area of law practice, including good will, if the following conditions are satisfied:

(a)   The seller ceases to engage in the private practice of law, or in the area of practice that has been sold, [in the geographic area] [in the jurisdiction] (a jurisdiction may elect either version) in which the practice has been conducted;

(b)   The entire practice, or the entire area of practice, is sold to one or more lawyers or law firms;

(c)   The seller gives written notice to each of the seller's clients regarding:

(1)   the proposed sale;

(2)   the client's right to retain other counsel or to take possession of the file; and

(3)   the fact that the client's consent to the transfer of the client's files will be presumed if the client does not take any action or does not otherwise object within ninety (90) days of receipt of the notice.

If a client cannot be given notice, the representation of that client may be transferred to the purchaser only upon entry of an order so authorizing by a court having jurisdiction. The seller may disclose to the court in camera information relating to the representation only to the extent necessary to obtain an order authorizing the transfer of a file.

(d)   The fees charged clients shall not be increased by reason of the sale.

Comment

[1]   The practice of law is a profession, not merely a business. Clients are not commodities that can be purchased and sold at will. Pursuant to this Rule, when a lawyer or an entire firm ceases to practice, or ceases to practice in an area of law, and other lawyers or firms take over the representation, the selling lawyer or firm may obtain compensation for the reasonable value of the practice as may withdrawing partners of law firms. See Rules 5.4 and 5.6.

Termination of Practice by the Seller

[2]   The requirement that all of the private practice, or all of an area of practice, be sold is satisfied if the seller in good faith makes the entire practice, or the area of practice, available for sale to the purchasers. The fact that a number of the seller's clients decide not to be represented by the purchasers but take their matters elsewhere, therefore, does not result in a

violation. Return to private practice as a result of an unanticipated change in circumstances does not necessarily result in a violation. For example, a lawyer who has sold the practice to accept an appointment to judicial office does not violate the requirement that the sale be attendant to cessation of practice if the lawyer later resumes private practice upon being defeated in a contested or a retention election for the office or resigns from a judiciary position.

[3]   The requirement that the seller cease to engage in the private practice of law does not prohibit employment as a lawyer on the staff of a public agency or a legal services entity that provides legal services to the poor, or as in-house counsel to a business.

[4]   The Rule permits a sale of an entire practice attendant upon retirement from the private practice of law within the jurisdiction. Its provisions, therefore, accommodate the lawyer who sells the practice on the occasion of moving to another state. Some states are so large that a move from one locale therein to another is tantamount to leaving the jurisdiction in which the lawyer has engaged in the practice of law. To also accommodate lawyers so situated, states may permit the sale of the practice when the lawyer leaves the geographical area rather than the jurisdiction. The alternative desired should be indicated by selecting one of the two provided for in Rule 1.17(a).

[5]   This Rule also permits a lawyer or law firm to sell an area of practice. If an area of practice is sold and the lawyer remains in the active practice of law, the lawyer must cease accepting any matters in the area of practice that has been sold, either as counsel or co-counsel or by assuming joint responsibility for a matter in connection with the division of a fee with another lawyer as would otherwise be permitted by Rule 1.5(e). For example, a lawyer with a substantial number of estate planning matters and a substantial number of probate administration cases may sell the estate planning portion of the practice but remain in the practice of law by concentrating on probate administration; however, that practitioner may not thereafter accept any estate planning matters. Although a lawyer who leaves a jurisdiction or geographical area typically would sell the entire practice, this Rule permits the lawyer to limit the sale to one or more areas of the practice, thereby preserving the lawyer's right to continue practice in the areas of the practice that were not sold.

Sale of Entire Practice or Entire Area of Practice

[6]   The Rule requires that the seller's entire practice, or an entire area of practice, be sold. The prohibition against sale of less than an entire practice area protects those clients whose matters are less lucrative and who might find it difficult to secure other counsel if a sale could be limited to substantial fee-generating matters. The purchasers are required to undertake all client matters in the practice or practice area, subject to client consent. This requirement is satisfied, however, even if a purchaser is unable to undertake a particular client matter because of a conflict of interest.

Client Confidences, Consent and Notice

[7]   Negotiations between seller and prospective purchaser prior to disclosure of information relating to a specific representation of an identifiable client no more violate the confidentiality provisions of Model Rule 1.6 than do preliminary discussions concerning the possible association of another lawyer or mergers between firms, with respect to which client consent is not required. See Rule 1.6(b)(7). Providing the purchaser access to

detailed information relating to the representation, such as the client's file, however, requires client consent. The Rule provides that before such information can be disclosed by the seller to the purchaser the client must be given actual written notice of the contemplated sale, including the identity of the purchaser, and must be told that the decision to consent or make other arrangements must be made within 90 days. If nothing is heard from the client within that time, consent to the sale is presumed.

[8]   A lawyer or law firm ceasing to practice cannot be required to remain in practice because some clients cannot be given actual notice of the proposed purchase. Since these clients cannot themselves consent to the purchase or direct any other disposition of their files, the Rule requires an order from a court having jurisdiction authorizing their transfer or other disposition. The Court can be expected to determine whether reasonable efforts to locate the client have been exhausted, and whether the absent client's legitimate interests will be served by authorizing the transfer of the file so that the purchaser may continue the representation. Preservation of client confidences requires that the petition for a court order be considered in camera. (A procedure by which such an order can be obtained needs to be established in jurisdictions in which it presently does not exist).

[9]   All elements of client autonomy, including the client's absolute right to discharge a lawyer and transfer the representation to another, survive the sale of the practice or area of practice.

Fee Arrangements Between Client and Purchaser

[10] The sale may not be financed by increases in fees charged the clients of the practice. Existing arrangements between the seller and the client as to fees and the scope of the work must be honored by the purchaser.

Other Applicable Ethical Standards

[11] Lawyers participating in the sale of a law practice or a practice area are subject to the ethical standards applicable to involving another lawyer in the representation of a client. These include, for example, the seller's obligation to exercise competence in identifying a purchaser qualified to assume the practice and the purchaser's obligation to undertake the representation competently (see Rule 1.1); the obligation to avoid disqualifying conflicts, and to secure the client's informed consent for those conflicts that can be agreed to (see Rule 1.7 regarding conflicts and Rule 1.0(e) for the definition of informed consent); and the obligation to protect information relating to the representation (see Rules 1.6 and 1.9).

[12] If approval of the substitution of the purchasing lawyer for the selling lawyer is required by the rules of any tribunal in which a matter is pending, such approval must be obtained before the matter can be included in the sale (see Rule 1.16).

Applicability of the Rule

[13] This Rule applies to the sale of a law practice of a deceased, disabled or disappeared lawyer. Thus, the seller may be represented by a non-lawyer representative not subject to these Rules. Since, however, no lawyer may participate in a sale of a law practice which does not conform to the requirements of this Rule, the representatives of the seller as well as the purchasing lawyer can be expected to see to it that they are met.

[14] Admission to or retirement from a law partnership or professional association, retirement plans and similar arrangements, and a sale of

tangible assets of a law practice, do not constitute a sale or purchase governed by this Rule.

[15] This Rule does not apply to the transfers of legal representation between lawyers when such transfers are unrelated to the sale of a practice or an area of practice.

RULE 1.18: DUTIES TO PROSPECTIVE CLIENT

(a) A person who consults with a lawyer about the possibility of forming a client-lawyer relationship with respect to a matter is a prospective client.

(b) Even when no client-lawyer relationship ensues, a lawyer who has learned information from a prospective client shall not use or reveal that information, except as Rule 1.9 would permit with respect to information of a former client.

(c) A lawyer subject to paragraph (b) shall not represent a client with interests materially adverse to those of a prospective client in the same or a substantially related matter if the lawyer received information from the prospective client that could be significantly harmful to that person in the matter, except as provided in paragraph (d). If a lawyer is disqualified from representation under this paragraph, no lawyer in a firm with which that lawyer is associated may knowingly undertake or continue representation in such a matter, except as provided in paragraph (d).

(d) When the lawyer has received disqualifying information as defined in paragraph (c), representation is permissible if:

(1) both the affected client and the prospective client have given informed consent, confirmed in writing, or;

(2) the lawyer who received the information took reasonable measures to avoid exposure to more disqualifying information than was reasonably necessary to determine whether to represent the prospective client; and

(i) the disqualified lawyer is timely screened from any participation in the matter and is apportioned no part of the fee therefrom; and

(ii) written notice is promptly given to the prospective client.

Comment

[1] Prospective clients, like clients, may disclose information to a lawyer, place documents or other property in the lawyer's custody, or rely on the lawyer's advice. A lawyer's consultations with a prospective client usually are limited in time and depth and leave both the prospective client and the lawyer free (and sometimes required) to proceed no further. Hence, prospective clients should receive some but not all of the protection afforded clients.

[2] A person becomes a prospective client by consulting with a lawyer about the possibility of forming a client-lawyer relationship with respect to a matter. Whether communications, including written, oral, or electronic communications, constitute a consultation depends on the circumstances. For example, a consultation is likely to have occurred if a lawyer, either in person or through the lawyer's advertising in any medium, specifically requests or

invites the submission of information about a potential representation without clear and reasonably understandable warnings and cautionary statements that limit the lawyer's obligations, and a person provides information in response. See also Comment [4]. In contrast, a consultation does not occur if a person provides information to a lawyer in response to advertising that merely describes the lawyer's education, experience, areas of practice, and contact information, or provides legal information of general interest. Such a person communicates information unilaterally to a lawyer, without any reasonable expectation that the lawyer is willing to discuss the possibility of forming a client-lawyer relationship, and is thus not a "prospective client." Moreover, a person who communicates with a lawyer for the purpose of disqualifying the lawyer is not a "prospective client."

[3]   It is often necessary for a prospective client to reveal information to the lawyer during an initial consultation prior to the decision about formation of a client-lawyer relationship. The lawyer often must learn such information to determine whether there is a conflict of interest with an existing client and whether the matter is one that the lawyer is willing to undertake. Paragraph (b) prohibits the lawyer from using or revealing that information, except as permitted by Rule 1.9, even if the client or lawyer decides not to proceed with the representation. The duty exists regardless of how brief the initial conference may be.

[4]   In order to avoid acquiring disqualifying information from a prospective client, a lawyer considering whether or not to undertake a new matter should limit the initial consultation to only such information as reasonably appears necessary for that purpose. Where the information indicates that a conflict of interest or other reason for non-representation exists, the lawyer should so inform the prospective client or decline the representation. If the prospective client wishes to retain the lawyer, and if consent is possible under Rule 1.7, then consent from all affected present or former clients must be obtained before accepting the representation.

[5]   A lawyer may condition a consultation with a prospective client on the person's informed consent that no information disclosed during the consultation will prohibit the lawyer from representing a different client in the matter. See Rule 1.0(e) for the definition of informed consent. If the agreement expressly so provides, the prospective client may also consent to the lawyer's subsequent use of information received from the prospective client.

[6]   Even in the absence of an agreement, under paragraph (c), the lawyer is not prohibited from representing a client with interests adverse to those of the prospective client in the same or a substantially related matter unless the lawyer has received from the prospective client information that could be significantly harmful if used in the matter.

[7]   Under paragraph (c), the prohibition in this Rule is imputed to other lawyers as provided in Rule 1.10, but, under paragraph (d)(1), imputation may be avoided if the lawyer obtains the informed consent, confirmed in writing, of both the prospective and affected clients. In the alternative, imputation may be avoided if the conditions of paragraph (d)(2) are met and all disqualified lawyers are timely screened and written notice is promptly given to the prospective client. See Rule 1.0(k) (requirements for screening procedures). Paragraph (d)(2)(i) does not prohibit the screened lawyer from receiving a salary or partnership share established by prior independent agreement, but that lawyer may not receive compensation directly related to the matter in which the lawyer is disqualified.

[8]   Notice, including a general description of the subject matter about which the lawyer was consulted, and of the screening procedures employed, generally should be given as soon as practicable after the need for screening becomes apparent.

[9]   For the duty of competence of a lawyer who gives assistance on the merits of a matter to a prospective client, see Rule 1.1. For a lawyer's duties when a prospective client entrusts valuables or papers to the lawyer's care, see Rule 1.15.

COUNSELOR

RULE 2.1: ADVISOR

In representing a client, a lawyer shall exercise independent professional judgment and render candid advice. In rendering advice, a lawyer may refer not only to law but to other considerations such as moral, economic, social and political factors, that may be relevant to the client's situation.

Comment

Scope of Advice

[1]   A client is entitled to straightforward advice expressing the lawyer's honest assessment. Legal advice often involves unpleasant facts and alternatives that a client may be disinclined to confront. In presenting advice, a lawyer endeavors to sustain the client's morale and may put advice in as acceptable a form as honesty permits. However, a lawyer should not be deterred from giving candid advice by the prospect that the advice will be unpalatable to the client.

[2]   Advice couched in narrow legal terms may be of little value to a client, especially where practical considerations, such as cost or effects on other people, are predominant. Purely technical legal advice, therefore, can sometimes be inadequate. It is proper for a lawyer to refer to relevant moral and ethical considerations in giving advice. Although a lawyer is not a moral advisor as such, moral and ethical considerations impinge upon most legal questions and may decisively influence how the law will be applied.

[3]   A client may expressly or impliedly ask the lawyer for purely technical advice. When such a request is made by a client experienced in legal matters, the lawyer may accept it at face value. When such a request is made by a client inexperienced in legal matters, however, the lawyer's responsibility as advisor may include indicating that more may be involved than strictly legal considerations.

[4]   Matters that go beyond strictly legal questions may also be in the domain of another profession. Family matters can involve problems within the professional competence of psychiatry, clinical psychology or social work; business matters can involve problems within the competence of the accounting profession or of financial specialists. Where consultation with a professional in another field is itself something a competent lawyer would recommend, the lawyer should make such a recommendation. At the same time, a lawyer's advice at its best often consists of recommending a course of action in the face of conflicting recommendations of experts.

Offering Advice

[5]   In general, a lawyer is not expected to give advice until asked by the client. However, when a lawyer knows that a client proposes a course of action that is likely to result in substantial adverse legal consequences to the

client, the lawyer's duty to the client under Rule 1.4 may require that the lawyer offer advice if the client's course of action is related to the representation. Similarly, when a matter is likely to involve litigation, it may be necessary under Rule 1.4 to inform the client of forms of dispute resolution that might constitute reasonable alternatives to litigation. A lawyer ordinarily has no duty to initiate investigation of a client's affairs or to give advice that the client has indicated is unwanted, but a lawyer may initiate advice to a client when doing so appears to be in the client's interest.

RULE 2.2 (Deleted)

RULE 2.3: EVALUATION FOR USE BY THIRD PERSONS

(a) A lawyer may provide an evaluation of a matter affecting a client for the use of someone other than the client if the lawyer reasonably believes that making the evaluation is compatible with other aspects of the lawyer's relationship with the client.

(b) When the lawyer knows or reasonably should know that the evaluation is likely to affect the client's interests materially and adversely, the lawyer shall not provide the evaluation unless the client gives informed consent.

(c) Except as disclosure is authorized in connection with a report of an evaluation, information relating to the evaluation is otherwise protected by Rule 1.6.

Comment

Definition

[1] An evaluation may be performed at the client's direction or when impliedly authorized in order to carry out the representation. See Rule 1.2. Such an evaluation may be for the primary purpose of establishing information for the benefit of third parties; for example, an opinion concerning the title of property rendered at the behest of a vendor for the information of a prospective purchaser, or at the behest of a borrower for the information of a prospective lender. In some situations, the evaluation may be required by a government agency; for example, an opinion concerning the legality of the securities registered for sale under the securities laws. In other instances, the evaluation may be required by a third person, such as a purchaser of a business.

[2] A legal evaluation should be distinguished from an investigation of a person with whom the lawyer does not have a client-lawyer relationship. For example, a lawyer retained by a purchaser to analyze a vendor's title to property does not have a client-lawyer relationship with the vendor. So also, an investigation into a person's affairs by a government lawyer, or by special counsel employed by the government, is not an evaluation as that term is used in this Rule. The question is whether the lawyer is retained by the person whose affairs are being examined. When the lawyer is retained by that person, the general rules concerning loyalty to client and preservation of confidences apply, which is not the case if the lawyer is retained by someone else. For this reason, it is essential to identify the person by whom the lawyer is retained. This should be made clear not only to the person under examination, but also to others to whom the results are to be made available.

Duties Owed to Third Person and Client

[3] When the evaluation is intended for the information or use of a third person, a legal duty to that person may or may not arise. That legal

question is beyond the scope of this Rule. However, since such an evaluation involves a departure from the normal client-lawyer relationship, careful analysis of the situation is required. The lawyer must be satisfied as a matter of professional judgment that making the evaluation is compatible with other functions undertaken in behalf of the client. For example, if the lawyer is acting as advocate in defending the client against charges of fraud, it would normally be incompatible with that responsibility for the lawyer to perform an evaluation for others concerning the same or a related transaction. Assuming no such impediment is apparent, however, the lawyer should advise the client of the implications of the evaluation, particularly the lawyer's responsibilities to third persons and the duty to disseminate the findings.

Access to and Disclosure of Information

[4] The quality of an evaluation depends on the freedom and extent of the investigation upon which it is based. Ordinarily a lawyer should have whatever latitude of investigation seems necessary as a matter of professional judgment. Under some circumstances, however, the terms of the evaluation may be limited. For example, certain issues or sources may be categorically excluded, or the scope of search may be limited by time constraints or the noncooperation of persons having relevant information. Any such limitations that are material to the evaluation should be described in the report. If after a lawyer has commenced an evaluation, the client refuses to comply with the terms upon which it was understood the evaluation was to have been made, the lawyer's obligations are determined by law, having reference to the terms of the client's agreement and the surrounding circumstances. In no circumstances is the lawyer permitted to knowingly make a false statement of material fact or law in providing an evaluation under this Rule. See Rule 4.1.

Obtaining Client's Informed Consent

[5] Information relating to an evaluation is protected by Rule 1.6. In many situations, providing an evaluation to a third party poses no significant risk to the client; thus, the lawyer may be impliedly authorized to disclose information to carry out the representation. See Rule 1.6(a). Where, however, it is reasonably likely that providing the evaluation will affect the client's interests materially and adversely, the lawyer must first obtain the client's consent after the client has been adequately informed concerning the important possible effects on the client's interests. See Rules 1.6(a) and 1.0(e).

Financial Auditors' Requests for Information

[6] When a question concerning the legal situation of a client arises at the instance of the client's financial auditor and the question is referred to the lawyer, the lawyer's response may be made in accordance with procedures recognized in the legal profession. Such a procedure is set forth in the American Bar Association Statement of Policy Regarding Lawyers' Responses to Auditors' Requests for Information, adopted in 1975.

RULE 2.4: LAWYER SERVING AS THIRD-PARTY NEUTRAL

(a) A lawyer serves as a third-party neutral when the lawyer assists two or more persons who are not clients of the lawyer to reach a resolution of a dispute or other matter that has arisen between them. Service as a third-party neutral may include service as an arbitrator, a mediator or in such other capacity as will enable the lawyer to assist the parties to resolve the matter.

(b) A lawyer serving as a third-party neutral shall inform unrepresented parties that the lawyer is not representing them. When the lawyer knows or reasonably should know that a party does not understand the lawyer's role in the matter, the lawyer shall explain the difference between the lawyer's role as a third-party neutral and a lawyer's role as one who represents a client.

Comment

[1] Alternative dispute resolution has become a substantial part of the civil justice system. Aside from representing clients in dispute-resolution processes, lawyers often serve as third-party neutrals. A third-party neutral is a person, such as a mediator, arbitrator, conciliator or evaluator, who assists the parties, represented or unrepresented, in the resolution of a dispute or in the arrangement of a transaction. Whether a third-party neutral serves primarily as a facilitator, evaluator or decisionmaker depends on the particular process that is either selected by the parties or mandated by a court.

[2] The role of a third-party neutral is not unique to lawyers, although, in some court-connected contexts, only lawyers are allowed to serve in this role or to handle certain types of cases. In performing this role, the lawyer may be subject to court rules or other law that apply either to third-party neutrals generally or to lawyers serving as third-party neutrals. Lawyer-neutrals may also be subject to various codes of ethics, such as the Code of Ethics for Arbitrators in Commercial Disputes prepared by a joint committee of the American Bar Association and the American Arbitration Association or the Model Standards of Conduct for Mediators jointly prepared by the American Bar Association, the American Arbitration Association and the Society of Professionals in Dispute Resolution.

[3] Unlike nonlawyers who serve as third-party neutrals, lawyers serving in this role may experience unique problems as a result of differences between the role of a third-party neutral and a lawyer's service as a client representative. The potential for confusion is significant when the parties are unrepresented in the process. Thus, paragraph (b) requires a lawyer-neutral to inform unrepresented parties that the lawyer is not representing them. For some parties, particularly parties who frequently use dispute-resolution processes, this information will be sufficient. For others, particularly those who are using the process for the first time, more information will be required. Where appropriate, the lawyer should inform unrepresented parties of the important differences between the lawyer's role as third-party neutral and a lawyer's role as a client representative, including the inapplicability of the attorney-client evidentiary privilege. The extent of disclosure required under this paragraph will depend on the particular parties involved and the subject matter of the proceeding, as well as the particular features of the dispute-resolution process selected.

[4] A lawyer who serves as a third-party neutral subsequently may be asked to serve as a lawyer representing a client in the same matter. The conflicts of interest that arise for both the individual lawyer and the lawyer's law firm are addressed in Rule 1.12.

[5] Lawyers who represent clients in alternative dispute-resolution processes are governed by the Rules of Professional Conduct. When the dispute-resolution process takes place before a tribunal, as in binding arbitration (see Rule 1.0(m)), the lawyer's duty of candor is governed by Rule 3.3. Otherwise, the lawyer's duty of candor toward both the third-party neutral and other parties is governed by Rule 4.1.

ADVOCATE

RULE 3.1: MERITORIOUS CLAIMS AND CONTENTIONS

A lawyer shall not bring or defend a proceeding, or assert or controvert an issue therein, unless there is a basis in law and fact for doing so that is not frivolous, which includes a good faith argument for an extension, modification or reversal of existing law. A lawyer for the defendant in a criminal proceeding, or the respondent in a proceeding that could result in incarceration, may nevertheless so defend the proceeding as to require that every element of the case be established.

Comment

[1] The advocate has a duty to use legal procedure for the fullest benefit of the client's cause, but also a duty not to abuse legal procedure. The law, both procedural and substantive, establishes the limits within which an advocate may proceed. However, the law is not always clear and never is static. Accordingly, in determining the proper scope of advocacy, account must be taken of the law's ambiguities and potential for change.

[2] The filing of an action or defense or similar action taken for a client is not frivolous merely because the facts have not first been fully substantiated or because the lawyer expects to develop vital evidence only by discovery. What is required of lawyers, however, is that they inform themselves about the facts of their clients' cases and the applicable law and determine that they can make good faith arguments in support of their clients' positions. Such action is not frivolous even though the lawyer believes that the client's position ultimately will not prevail. The action is frivolous, however, if the lawyer is unable either to make a good faith argument on the merits of the action taken or to support the action taken by a good faith argument for an extension, modification or reversal of existing law.

[3] The lawyer's obligations under this Rule are subordinate to federal or state constitutional law that entitles a defendant in a criminal matter to the assistance of counsel in presenting a claim or contention that otherwise would be prohibited by this Rule.

RULE 3.2: EXPEDITING LITIGATION

A lawyer shall make reasonable efforts to expedite litigation consistent with the interests of the client.

Comment

[1] Dilatory practices bring the administration of justice into disrepute. Although there will be occasions when a lawyer may properly seek a postponement for personal reasons, it is not proper for a lawyer to routinely fail to expedite litigation solely for the convenience of the advocates. Nor will a failure to expedite be reasonable if done for the purpose of frustrating an opposing party's attempt to obtain rightful redress or repose. It is not a justification that similar conduct is often tolerated by the bench and bar. The question is whether a competent lawyer acting in good faith would regard the course of action as having some substantial purpose other than delay. Realizing financial or other benefit from otherwise improper delay in litigation is not a legitimate interest of the client.

RULE 3.3: CANDOR TOWARD THE TRIBUNAL

(a) A lawyer shall not knowingly:

(1) make a false statement of fact or law to a tribunal or fail to correct a false statement of material fact or law previously made to the tribunal by the lawyer;

(2) fail to disclose to the tribunal legal authority in the controlling jurisdiction known to the lawyer to be directly adverse to the position of the client and not disclosed by opposing counsel; or

(3) offer evidence that the lawyer knows to be false. If a lawyer, the lawyer's client, or a witness called by the lawyer, has offered material evidence and the lawyer comes to know of its falsity, the lawyer shall take reasonable remedial measures, including, if necessary, disclosure to the tribunal. A lawyer may refuse to offer evidence, other than the testimony of a defendant in a criminal matter, that the lawyer reasonably believes is false.

(b) A lawyer who represents a client in an adjudicative proceeding and who knows that a person intends to engage, is engaging or has engaged in criminal or fraudulent conduct related to the proceeding shall take reasonable remedial measures, including, if necessary, disclosure to the tribunal.

(c) The duties stated in paragraphs (a) and (b) continue to the conclusion of the proceeding, and apply even if compliance requires disclosure of information otherwise protected by Rule 1.6.

(d) In an ex parte proceeding, a lawyer shall inform the tribunal of all material facts known to the lawyer that will enable the tribunal to make an informed decision, whether or not the facts are adverse.

Comment

[1] This Rule governs the conduct of a lawyer who is representing a client in the proceedings of a tribunal. See Rule 1.0(m) for the definition of "tribunal." It also applies when the lawyer is representing a client in an ancillary proceeding conducted pursuant to the tribunal's adjudicative authority, such as a deposition. Thus, for example, paragraph (a)(3) requires a lawyer to take reasonable remedial measures if the lawyer comes to know that a client who is testifying in a deposition has offered evidence that is false.

[2] This Rule sets forth the special duties of lawyers as officers of the court to avoid conduct that undermines the integrity of the adjudicative process. A lawyer acting as an advocate in an adjudicative proceeding has an obligation to present the client's case with persuasive force. Performance of that duty while maintaining confidences of the client, however, is qualified by the advocate's duty of candor to the tribunal. Consequently, although a lawyer in an adversary proceeding is not required to present an impartial exposition of the law or to vouch for the evidence submitted in a cause, the lawyer must not allow the tribunal to be misled by false statements of law or fact or evidence that the lawyer knows to be false.

Representations by a Lawyer

[3] An advocate is responsible for pleadings and other documents prepared for litigation, but is usually not required to have personal knowledge of matters asserted therein, for litigation documents ordinarily

present assertions by the client, or by someone on the client's behalf, and not assertions by the lawyer. Compare Rule 3.1. However, an assertion purporting to be on the lawyer's own knowledge, as in an affidavit by the lawyer or in a statement in open court, may properly be made only when the lawyer knows the assertion is true or believes it to be true on the basis of a reasonably diligent inquiry. There are circumstances where failure to make a disclosure is the equivalent of an affirmative misrepresentation. The obligation prescribed in Rule 1.2(d) not to counsel a client to commit or assist the client in committing a fraud applies in litigation. Regarding compliance with Rule 1.2(d), see the Comment to that Rule. See also the Comment to Rule 8.4(b).

Legal Argument

[4]   Legal argument based on a knowingly false representation of law constitutes dishonesty toward the tribunal. A lawyer is not required to make a disinterested exposition of the law, but must recognize the existence of pertinent legal authorities. Furthermore, as stated in paragraph (a)(2), an advocate has a duty to disclose directly adverse authority in the controlling jurisdiction that has not been disclosed by the opposing party. The underlying concept is that legal argument is a discussion seeking to determine the legal premises properly applicable to the case.

Offering Evidence

[5]   Paragraph (a)(3) requires that the lawyer refuse to offer evidence that the lawyer knows to be false, regardless of the client's wishes. This duty is premised on the lawyer's obligation as an officer of the court to prevent the trier of fact from being misled by false evidence. A lawyer does not violate this Rule if the lawyer offers the evidence for the purpose of establishing its falsity.

[6]   If a lawyer knows that the client intends to testify falsely or wants the lawyer to introduce false evidence, the lawyer should seek to persuade the client that the evidence should not be offered. If the persuasion is ineffective and the lawyer continues to represent the client, the lawyer must refuse to offer the false evidence. If only a portion of a witness's testimony will be false, the lawyer may call the witness to testify but may not elicit or otherwise permit the witness to present the testimony that the lawyer knows is false.

[7]   The duties stated in paragraphs (a) and (b) apply to all lawyers, including defense counsel in criminal cases. In some jurisdictions, however, courts have required counsel to present the accused as a witness or to give a narrative statement if the accused so desires, even if counsel knows that the testimony or statement will be false. The obligation of the advocate under the Rules of Professional Conduct is subordinate to such requirements. See also Comment [9].

[8]   The prohibition against offering false evidence only applies if the lawyer knows that the evidence is false. A lawyer's reasonable belief that evidence is false does not preclude its presentation to the trier of fact. A lawyer's knowledge that evidence is false, however, can be inferred from the circumstances. See Rule 1.0(f). Thus, although a lawyer should resolve doubts about the veracity of testimony or other evidence in favor of the client, the lawyer cannot ignore an obvious falsehood.

[9]   Although paragraph (a)(3) only prohibits a lawyer from offering evidence the lawyer knows to be false, it permits the lawyer to refuse to offer testimony or other proof that the lawyer reasonably believes is false. Offering

such proof may reflect adversely on the lawyer's ability to discriminate in the quality of evidence and thus impair the lawyer's effectiveness as an advocate. Because of the special protections historically provided criminal defendants, however, this Rule does not permit a lawyer to refuse to offer the testimony of such a client where the lawyer reasonably believes but does not know that the testimony will be false. Unless the lawyer knows the testimony will be false, the lawyer must honor the client's decision to testify. See also Comment [7].

Remedial Measures

[10] Having offered material evidence in the belief that it was true, a lawyer may subsequently come to know that the evidence is false. Or, a lawyer may be surprised when the lawyer's client, or another witness called by the lawyer, offers testimony the lawyer knows to be false, either during the lawyer's direct examination or in response to cross-examination by the opposing lawyer. In such situations or if the lawyer knows of the falsity of testimony elicited from the client during a deposition, the lawyer must take reasonable remedial measures. In such situations, the advocate's proper course is to remonstrate with the client confidentially, advise the client of the lawyer's duty of candor to the tribunal and seek the client's cooperation with respect to the withdrawal or correction of the false statements or evidence. If that fails, the advocate must take further remedial action. If withdrawal from the representation is not permitted or will not undo the effect of the false evidence, the advocate must make such disclosure to the tribunal as is reasonably necessary to remedy the situation, even if doing so requires the lawyer to reveal information that otherwise would be protected by Rule 1.6. It is for the tribunal then to determine what should be done—making a statement about the matter to the trier of fact, ordering a mistrial or perhaps nothing.

[11] The disclosure of a client's false testimony can result in grave consequences to the client, including not only a sense of betrayal but also loss of the case and perhaps a prosecution for perjury. But the alternative is that the lawyer cooperate in deceiving the court, thereby subverting the truth-finding process which the adversary system is designed to implement. See Rule 1.2(d). Furthermore, unless it is clearly understood that the lawyer will act upon the duty to disclose the existence of false evidence, the client can simply reject the lawyer's advice to reveal the false evidence and insist that the lawyer keep silent. Thus the client could in effect coerce the lawyer into being a party to fraud on the court.

Preserving Integrity of Adjudicative Process

[12] Lawyers have a special obligation to protect a tribunal against criminal or fraudulent conduct that undermines the integrity of the adjudicative process, such as bribing, intimidating or otherwise unlawfully communicating with a witness, juror, court official or other participant in the proceeding, unlawfully destroying or concealing documents or other evidence or failing to disclose information to the tribunal when required by law to do so. Thus, paragraph (b) requires a lawyer to take reasonable remedial measures, including disclosure if necessary, whenever the lawyer knows that a person, including the lawyer's client, intends to engage, is engaging or has engaged in criminal or fraudulent conduct related to the proceeding.

Duration of Obligation

[13] A practical time limit on the obligation to rectify false evidence or false statements of law and fact has to be established. The conclusion of the

proceeding is a reasonably definite point for the termination of the obligation. A proceeding has concluded within the meaning of this Rule when a final judgment in the proceeding has been affirmed on appeal or the time for review has passed.

Ex Parte Proceedings

[14] Ordinarily, an advocate has the limited responsibility of presenting one side of the matters that a tribunal should consider in reaching a decision; the conflicting position is expected to be presented by the opposing party. However, in any ex parte proceeding, such as an application for a temporary restraining order, there is no balance of presentation by opposing advocates. The object of an ex parte proceeding is nevertheless to yield a substantially just result. The judge has an affirmative responsibility to accord the absent party just consideration. The lawyer for the represented party has the correlative duty to make disclosures of material facts known to the lawyer and that the lawyer reasonably believes are necessary to an informed decision.

Withdrawal

[15] Normally, a lawyer's compliance with the duty of candor imposed by this Rule does not require that the lawyer withdraw from the representation of a client whose interests will be or have been adversely affected by the lawyer's disclosure. The lawyer may, however, be required by Rule 1.16(a) to seek permission of the tribunal to withdraw if the lawyer's compliance with this Rule's duty of candor results in such an extreme deterioration of the client-lawyer relationship that the lawyer can no longer competently represent the client. Also see Rule 1.16(b) for the circumstances in which a lawyer will be permitted to seek a tribunal's permission to withdraw. In connection with a request for permission to withdraw that is premised on a client's misconduct, a lawyer may reveal information relating to the representation only to the extent reasonably necessary to comply with this Rule or as otherwise permitted by Rule 1.6.

RULE 3.4: FAIRNESS TO OPPOSING PARTY AND COUNSEL

A lawyer shall not:

(a) unlawfully obstruct another party's access to evidence or unlawfully alter, destroy or conceal a document or other material having potential evidentiary value. A lawyer shall not counsel or assist another person to do any such act;

(b) falsify evidence, counsel or assist a witness to testify falsely, or offer an inducement to a witness that is prohibited by law;

(c) knowingly disobey an obligation under the rules of a tribunal, except for an open refusal based on an assertion that no valid obligation exists;

(d) in pretrial procedure, make a frivolous discovery request or fail to make reasonably diligent effort to comply with a legally proper discovery request by an opposing party;

(e) in trial, allude to any matter that the lawyer does not reasonably believe is relevant or that will not be supported by admissible evidence, assert personal knowledge of facts in issue except when testifying as a witness, or state a personal opinion as to the justness of a cause, the credibility of a witness, the culpability of a civil litigant or the guilt or innocence of an accused; or

(f) request a person other than a client to refrain from voluntarily giving relevant information to another party unless:

(1) the person is a relative or an employee or other agent of a client; and

(2) the lawyer reasonably believes that the person's interests will not be adversely affected by refraining from giving such information.

Comment

[1] The procedure of the adversary system contemplates that the evidence in a case is to be marshalled competitively by the contending parties. Fair competition in the adversary system is secured by prohibitions against destruction or concealment of evidence, improperly influencing witnesses, obstructive tactics in discovery procedure, and the like.

[2] Documents and other items of evidence are often essential to establish a claim or defense. Subject to evidentiary privileges, the right of an opposing party, including the government, to obtain evidence through discovery or subpoena is an important procedural right. The exercise of that right can be frustrated if relevant material is altered, concealed or destroyed. Applicable law in many jurisdictions makes it an offense to destroy material for purpose of impairing its availability in a pending proceeding or one whose commencement can be foreseen. Falsifying evidence is also generally a criminal offense. Paragraph (a) applies to evidentiary material generally, including computerized information. Applicable law may permit a lawyer to take temporary possession of physical evidence of client crimes for the purpose of conducting a limited examination that will not alter or destroy material characteristics of the evidence. In such a case, applicable law may require the lawyer to turn the evidence over to the police or other prosecuting authority, depending on the circumstances.

[3] With regard to paragraph (b), it is not improper to pay a witness's expenses or to compensate an expert witness on terms permitted by law. The common law rule in most jurisdictions is that it is improper to pay an occurrence witness any fee for testifying and that it is improper to pay an expert witness a contingent fee.

[4] Paragraph (f) permits a lawyer to advise employees of a client to refrain from giving information to another party, for the employees may identify their interests with those of the client. See also Rule 4.2.

RULE 3.5: IMPARTIALITY AND DECORUM OF THE TRIBUNAL

A lawyer shall not:

(a) seek to influence a judge, juror, prospective juror or other official by means prohibited by law;

(b) communicate ex parte with such a person during the proceeding unless authorized to do so by law or court order;

(c) communicate with a juror or prospective juror after discharge of the jury if:

(1) the communication is prohibited by law or court order;

(2) the juror has made known to the lawyer a desire not to communicate; or

(3) the communication involves misrepresentation, coercion, duress or harassment; or

(d) engage in conduct intended to disrupt a tribunal.

Comment

[1] Many forms of improper influence upon a tribunal are proscribed by criminal law. Others are specified in the ABA Model Code of Judicial Conduct, with which an advocate should be familiar. A lawyer is required to avoid contributing to a violation of such provisions.

[2] During a proceeding a lawyer may not communicate ex parte with persons serving in an official capacity in the proceeding, such as judges, masters or jurors, unless authorized to do so by law or court order.

[3] A lawyer may on occasion want to communicate with a juror or prospective juror after the jury has been discharged. The lawyer may do so unless the communication is prohibited by law or a court order but must respect the desire of the juror not to talk with the lawyer. The lawyer may not engage in improper conduct during the communication.

[4] The advocate's function is to present evidence and argument so that the cause may be decided according to law. Refraining from abusive or obstreperous conduct is a corollary of the advocate's right to speak on behalf of litigants. A lawyer may stand firm against abuse by a judge but should avoid reciprocation; the judge's default is no justification for similar dereliction by an advocate. An advocate can present the cause, protect the record for subsequent review and preserve professional integrity by patient firmness no less effectively than by belligerence or theatrics.

[5] The duty to refrain from disruptive conduct applies to any proceeding of a tribunal, including a deposition. See Rule 1.0(m).

RULE 3.6: TRIAL PUBLICITY

(a) A lawyer who is participating or has participated in the investigation or litigation of a matter shall not make an extrajudicial statement that the lawyer knows or reasonably should know will be disseminated by means of public communication and will have a substantial likelihood of materially prejudicing an adjudicative proceeding in the matter.

(b) Notwithstanding paragraph (a), a lawyer may state:

(1) the claim, offense or defense involved and, except when prohibited by law, the identity of the persons involved;

(2) information contained in a public record;

(3) that an investigation of a matter is in progress;

(4) the scheduling or result of any step in litigation;

(5) a request for assistance in obtaining evidence and information necessary thereto;

(6) a warning of danger concerning the behavior of a person involved, when there is reason to believe that there exists the likelihood of substantial harm to an individual or to the public interest; and

(7) in a criminal case, in addition to subparagraphs (1) through (6):

(i) the identity, residence, occupation and family status of the accused;

(ii) if the accused has not been apprehended, information necessary to aid in apprehension of that person;

(iii) the fact, time and place of arrest; and

(iv) the identity of investigating and arresting officers or agencies and the length of the investigation.

(c) Notwithstanding paragraph (a), a lawyer may make a statement that a reasonable lawyer would believe is required to protect a client from the substantial undue prejudicial effect of recent publicity not initiated by the lawyer or the lawyer's client. A statement made pursuant to this paragraph shall be limited to such information as is necessary to mitigate the recent adverse publicity.

(d) No lawyer associated in a firm or government agency with a lawyer subject to paragraph (a) shall make a statement prohibited by paragraph (a).

Comment

[1] It is difficult to strike a balance between protecting the right to a fair trial and safeguarding the right of free expression. Preserving the right to a fair trial necessarily entails some curtailment of the information that may be disseminated about a party prior to trial, particularly where trial by jury is involved. If there were no such limits, the result would be the practical nullification of the protective effect of the rules of forensic decorum and the exclusionary rules of evidence. On the other hand, there are vital social interests served by the free dissemination of information about events having legal consequences and about legal proceedings themselves. The public has a right to know about threats to its safety and measures aimed at assuring its security. It also has a legitimate interest in the conduct of judicial proceedings, particularly in matters of general public concern. Furthermore, the subject matter of legal proceedings is often of direct significance in debate and deliberation over questions of public policy.

[2] Special rules of confidentiality may validly govern proceedings in juvenile, domestic relations and mental disability proceedings, and perhaps other types of litigation. Rule 3.4(c) requires compliance with such rules.

[3] The Rule sets forth a basic general prohibition against a lawyer's making statements that the lawyer knows or should know will have a substantial likelihood of materially prejudicing an adjudicative proceeding. Recognizing that the public value of informed commentary is great and the likelihood of prejudice to a proceeding by the commentary of a lawyer who is not involved in the proceeding is small, the rule applies only to lawyers who are, or who have been involved in the investigation or litigation of a case, and their associates.

[4] Paragraph (b) identifies specific matters about which a lawyer's statements would not ordinarily be considered to present a substantial likelihood of material prejudice, and should not in any event be considered prohibited by the general prohibition of paragraph (a). Paragraph (b) is not intended to be an exhaustive listing of the subjects upon which a lawyer may make a statement, but statements on other matters may be subject to paragraph (a).

[5]   There are, on the other hand, certain subjects that are more likely than not to have a material prejudicial effect on a proceeding, particularly when they refer to a civil matter triable to a jury, a criminal matter, or any other proceeding that could result in incarceration. These subjects relate to:

(1)   the character, credibility, reputation or criminal record of a party, suspect in a criminal investigation or witness, or the identity of a witness, or the expected testimony of a party or witness;

(2)   in a criminal case or proceeding that could result in incarceration, the possibility of a plea of guilty to the offense or the existence or contents of any confession, admission, or statement given by a defendant or suspect or that person's refusal or failure to make a statement;

(3)   the performance or results of any examination or test or the refusal or failure of a person to submit to an examination or test, or the identity or nature of physical evidence expected to be presented;

(4)   any opinion as to the guilt or innocence of a defendant or suspect in a criminal case or proceeding that could result in incarceration;

(5)   information that the lawyer knows or reasonably should know is likely to be inadmissible as evidence in a trial and that would, if disclosed, create a substantial risk of prejudicing an impartial trial; or

(6)   the fact that a defendant has been charged with a crime, unless there is included therein a statement explaining that the charge is merely an accusation and that the defendant is presumed innocent until and unless proven guilty.

[6]   Another relevant factor in determining prejudice is the nature of the proceeding involved. Criminal jury trials will be most sensitive to extrajudicial speech. Civil trials may be less sensitive. Non-jury hearings and arbitration proceedings may be even less affected. The Rule will still place limitations on prejudicial comments in these cases, but the likelihood of prejudice may be different depending on the type of proceeding.

[7]   Finally, extrajudicial statements that might otherwise raise a question under this Rule may be permissible when they are made in response to statements made publicly by another party, another party's lawyer, or third persons, where a reasonable lawyer would believe a public response is required in order to avoid prejudice to the lawyer's client. When prejudicial statements have been publicly made by others, responsive statements may have the salutary effect of lessening any resulting adverse impact on the adjudicative proceeding. Such responsive statements should be limited to contain only such information as is necessary to mitigate undue prejudice created by the statements made by others.

[8]   See Rule 3.8(f) for additional duties of prosecutors in connection with extrajudicial statements about criminal proceedings.

RULE 3.7: LAWYER AS WITNESS

(a) A lawyer shall not act as advocate at a trial in which the lawyer is likely to be a necessary witness unless:

(1)   the testimony relates to an uncontested issue;

(2)   the testimony relates to the nature and value of legal services rendered in the case; or

(3) disqualification of the lawyer would work substantial hardship on the client.

(b) A lawyer may act as advocate in a trial in which another lawyer in the lawyer's firm is likely to be called as a witness unless precluded from doing so by Rule 1.7 or Rule 1.9.

Comment

[1]   Combining the roles of advocate and witness can prejudice the tribunal and the opposing party and can also involve a conflict of interest between the lawyer and client.

Advocate-Witness Rule

[2]   The tribunal has proper objection when the trier of fact may be confused or misled by a lawyer serving as both advocate and witness. The opposing party has proper objection where the combination of roles may prejudice that party's rights in the litigation. A witness is required to testify on the basis of personal knowledge, while an advocate is expected to explain and comment on evidence given by others. It may not be clear whether a statement by an advocate-witness should be taken as proof or as an analysis of the proof.

[3]   To protect the tribunal, paragraph (a) prohibits a lawyer from simultaneously serving as advocate and necessary witness except in those circumstances specified in paragraphs (a)(1) through (a)(3). Paragraph (a)(1) recognizes that if the testimony will be uncontested, the ambiguities in the dual role are purely theoretical. Paragraph (a)(2) recognizes that where the testimony concerns the extent and value of legal services rendered in the action in which the testimony is offered, permitting the lawyers to testify avoids the need for a second trial with new counsel to resolve that issue. Moreover, in such a situation the judge has firsthand knowledge of the matter in issue; hence, there is less dependence on the adversary process to test the credibility of the testimony.

[4]   Apart from these two exceptions, paragraph (a)(3) recognizes that a balancing is required between the interests of the client and those of the tribunal and the opposing party. Whether the tribunal is likely to be misled or the opposing party is likely to suffer prejudice depends on the nature of the case, the importance and probable tenor of the lawyer's testimony, and the probability that the lawyer's testimony will conflict with that of other witnesses. Even if there is risk of such prejudice, in determining whether the lawyer should be disqualified, due regard must be given to the effect of disqualification on the lawyer's client. It is relevant that one or both parties could reasonably foresee that the lawyer would probably be a witness. The conflict of interest principles stated in Rules 1.7, 1.9 and 1.10 have no application to this aspect of the problem.

[5]   Because the tribunal is not likely to be misled when a lawyer acts as advocate in a trial in which another lawyer in the lawyer's firm will testify as a necessary witness, paragraph (b) permits the lawyer to do so except in situations involving a conflict of interest.

Conflict of Interest

[6]   In determining if it is permissible to act as advocate in a trial in which the lawyer will be a necessary witness, the lawyer must also consider that the dual role may give rise to a conflict of interest that will require compliance with Rules 1.7 or 1.9. For example, if there is likely to be substantial conflict between the testimony of the client and that of the lawyer

the representation involves a conflict of interest that requires compliance with Rule 1.7. This would be true even though the lawyer might not be prohibited by paragraph (a) from simultaneously serving as advocate and witness because the lawyer's disqualification would work a substantial hardship on the client. Similarly, a lawyer who might be permitted to simultaneously serve as an advocate and a witness by paragraph (a)(3) might be precluded from doing so by Rule 1.9. The problem can arise whether the lawyer is called as a witness on behalf of the client or is called by the opposing party. Determining whether or not such a conflict exists is primarily the responsibility of the lawyer involved. If there is a conflict of interest, the lawyer must secure the client's informed consent, confirmed in writing. In some cases, the lawyer will be precluded from seeking the client's consent. See Rule 1.7. See Rule 1.0(b) for the definition of "confirmed in writing" and Rule 1.0(e) for the definition of "informed consent."

[7] Paragraph (b) provides that a lawyer is not disqualified from serving as an advocate because a lawyer with whom the lawyer is associated in a firm is precluded from doing so by paragraph (a). If, however, the testifying lawyer would also be disqualified by Rule 1.7 or Rule 1.9 from representing the client in the matter, other lawyers in the firm will be precluded from representing the client by Rule 1.10 unless the client gives informed consent under the conditions stated in Rule 1.7.

RULE 3.8: SPECIAL RESPONSIBILITIES OF A PROSECUTOR

The prosecutor in a criminal case shall:

(a) refrain from prosecuting a charge that the prosecutor knows is not supported by probable cause;

(b) make reasonable efforts to assure that the accused has been advised of the right to, and the procedure for obtaining, counsel and has been given reasonable opportunity to obtain counsel;

(c) not seek to obtain from an unrepresented accused a waiver of important pretrial rights, such as the right to a preliminary hearing;

(d) make timely disclosure to the defense of all evidence or information known to the prosecutor that tends to negate the guilt of the accused or mitigates the offense, and, in connection with sentencing, disclose to the defense and to the tribunal all unprivileged mitigating information known to the prosecutor, except when the prosecutor is relieved of this responsibility by a protective order of the tribunal;

(e) not subpoena a lawyer in a grand jury or other criminal proceeding to present evidence about a past or present client unless the prosecutor reasonably believes:

(1) the information sought is not protected from disclosure by any applicable privilege;

(2) the evidence sought is essential to the successful completion of an ongoing investigation or prosecution; and

(3) there is no other feasible alternative to obtain the information;

(f) except for statements that are necessary to inform the public of the nature and extent of the prosecutor's action and that serve a legitimate law enforcement purpose, refrain from making extrajudicial comments that have a substantial likelihood of heightening public condemnation of the accused and exercise reasonable care to prevent investigators, law enforcement personnel, employees or other persons assisting or associated with the prosecutor in a criminal case from making an extrajudicial statement that the prosecutor would be prohibited from making under Rule 3.6 or this Rule.

(g) When a prosecutor knows of new, credible and material evidence creating a reasonable likelihood that a convicted defendant did not commit an offense of which the defendant was convicted, the prosecutor shall:

    (1) promptly disclose that evidence to an appropriate court or authority, and

    (2) if the conviction was obtained in the prosecutor's jurisdiction,

        (i) promptly disclose that evidence to the defendant unless a court authorizes delay, and

        (ii) undertake further investigation, or make reasonable efforts to cause an investigation, to determine whether the defendant was convicted of an offense that the defendant did not commit.

(h) When a prosecutor knows of clear and convincing evidence establishing that a defendant in the prosecutor's jurisdiction was convicted of an offense that the defendant did not commit, the prosecutor shall seek to remedy the conviction.

Comment

[1] A prosecutor has the responsibility of a minister of justice and not simply that of an advocate. This responsibility carries with it specific obligations to see that the defendant is accorded procedural justice, that guilt is decided upon the basis of sufficient evidence, and that special precautions are taken to prevent and to rectify the conviction of innocent persons. The extent of mandated remedial action is a matter of debate and varies in different jurisdictions. Many jurisdictions have adopted the ABA Standards of Criminal Justice Relating to the Prosecution Function, which are the product of prolonged and careful deliberation by lawyers experienced in both criminal prosecution and defense. Competent representation of the sovereignty may require a prosecutor to undertake some procedural and remedial measures as a matter of obligation. Applicable law may require other measures by the prosecutor and knowing disregard of those obligations or a systematic abuse of prosecutorial discretion could constitute a violation of Rule 8.4.

[2] In some jurisdictions, a defendant may waive a preliminary hearing and thereby lose a valuable opportunity to challenge probable cause. Accordingly, prosecutors should not seek to obtain waivers of preliminary hearings or other important pretrial rights from unrepresented accused persons. Paragraph (c) does not apply, however, to an accused appearing *pro se* with the approval of the tribunal. Nor does it forbid the lawful questioning of an uncharged suspect who has knowingly waived the rights to counsel and silence.

[3] The exception in paragraph (d) recognizes that a prosecutor may seek an appropriate protective order from the tribunal if disclosure of

information to the defense could result in substantial harm to an individual or to the public interest.

[4]   Paragraph (e) is intended to limit the issuance of lawyer subpoenas in grand jury and other criminal proceedings to those situations in which there is a genuine need to intrude into the client-lawyer relationship.

[5]   Paragraph (f) supplements Rule 3.6, which prohibits extrajudicial statements that have a substantial likelihood of prejudicing an adjudicatory proceeding. In the context of a criminal prosecution, a prosecutor's extrajudicial statement can create the additional problem of increasing public condemnation of the accused. Although the announcement of an indictment, for example, will necessarily have severe consequences for the accused, a prosecutor can, and should, avoid comments which have no legitimate law enforcement purpose and have a substantial likelihood of increasing public opprobrium of the accused. Nothing in this Comment is intended to restrict the statements which a prosecutor may make which comply with Rule 3.6(b) or 3.6(c).

[6]   Like other lawyers, prosecutors are subject to Rules 5.1 and 5.3, which relate to responsibilities regarding lawyers and nonlawyers who work for or are associated with the lawyer's office. Paragraph (f) reminds the prosecutor of the importance of these obligations in connection with the unique dangers of improper extrajudicial statements in a criminal case. In addition, paragraph (f) requires a prosecutor to exercise reasonable care to prevent persons assisting or associated with the prosecutor from making improper extrajudicial statements, even when such persons are not under the direct supervision of the prosecutor. Ordinarily, the reasonable care standard will be satisfied if the prosecutor issues the appropriate cautions to law-enforcement personnel and other relevant individuals.

[7]   When a prosecutor knows of new, credible and material evidence creating a reasonable likelihood that a person outside the prosecutor's jurisdiction was convicted of a crime that the person did not commit, paragraph (g) requires prompt disclosure to the court or other appropriate authority, such as the chief prosecutor of the jurisdiction where the conviction occurred. If the conviction was obtained in the prosecutor's jurisdiction, paragraph (g) requires the prosecutor to examine the evidence and undertake further investigation to determine whether the defendant is in fact innocent or make reasonable efforts to cause another appropriate authority to undertake the necessary investigation, and to promptly disclose the evidence to the court and, absent court-authorized delay, to the defendant. Consistent with the objectives of Rules 4.2 and 4.3, disclosure to a represented defendant must be made through the defendant's counsel, and, in the case of an unrepresented defendant, would ordinarily be accompanied by a request to a court for the appointment of counsel to assist the defendant in taking such legal measures as may be appropriate.

[8]   Under paragraph (h), once the prosecutor knows of clear and convincing evidence that the defendant was convicted of an offense that the defendant did not commit, the prosecutor must seek to remedy the conviction. Necessary steps may include disclosure of the evidence to the defendant, requesting that the court appoint counsel for an unrepresented indigent defendant and, where appropriate, notifying the court that the prosecutor has knowledge that the defendant did not commit the offense of which the defendant was convicted.

[9]   A prosecutor's independent judgment, made in good faith, that the new evidence is not of such nature as to trigger the obligations of sections (g)

and (h), though subsequently determined to have been erroneous, does not constitute a violation of this Rule.

RULE 3.9: ADVOCATE IN
NONADJUDICATIVE PROCEEDINGS

A lawyer representing a client before a legislative body or administrative agency in a nonadjudicative proceeding shall disclose that the appearance is in a representative capacity and shall conform to the provisions of Rules 3.3(a) through (c), 3.4(a) through (c), and 3.5.

Comment

[1]   In representation before bodies such as legislatures, municipal councils, and executive and administrative agencies acting in a rule-making or policy-making capacity, lawyers present facts, formulate issues and advance argument in the matters under consideration. The decision-making body, like a court, should be able to rely on the integrity of the submissions made to it. A lawyer appearing before such a body must deal with it honestly and in conformity with applicable rules of procedure. See Rules 3.3(a) through (c), 3.4(a) through (c) and 3.5.

[2]   Lawyers have no exclusive right to appear before nonadjudicative bodies, as they do before a court. The requirements of this Rule therefore may subject lawyers to regulations inapplicable to advocates who are not lawyers. However, legislatures and administrative agencies have a right to expect lawyers to deal with them as they deal with courts.

[3]   This Rule only applies when a lawyer represents a client in connection with an official hearing or meeting of a governmental agency or a legislative body to which the lawyer or the lawyer's client is presenting evidence or argument. It does not apply to representation of a client in a negotiation or other bilateral transaction with a governmental agency or in connection with an application for a license or other privilege or the client's compliance with generally applicable reporting requirements, such as the filing of income-tax returns. Nor does it apply to the representation of a client in connection with an investigation or examination of the client's affairs conducted by government investigators or examiners. Representation in such matters is governed by Rules 4.1 through 4.4.

TRANSACTIONS WITH PERSONS OTHER THAN CLIENTS

RULE 4.1: TRUTHFULNESS IN STATEMENTS TO OTHERS

In the course of representing a client a lawyer shall not knowingly:

(a) make a false statement of material fact or law to a third person; or

(b) fail to disclose a material fact when disclosure is necessary to avoid assisting a criminal or fraudulent act by a client, unless disclosure is prohibited by Rule 1.6.

Comment

Misrepresentation

[1]   A lawyer is required to be truthful when dealing with others on a client's behalf, but generally has no affirmative duty to inform an opposing party of relevant facts. A misrepresentation can occur if the lawyer incorporates or affirms a statement of another person that the lawyer knows

is false. Misrepresentations can also occur by partially true but misleading statements or omissions that are the equivalent of affirmative false statements. For dishonest conduct that does not amount to a false statement or for misrepresentations by a lawyer other than in the course of representing a client, see Rule 8.4.

Statements of Fact

[2] This Rule refers to statements of fact. Whether a particular statement should be regarded as one of fact can depend on the circumstances. Under generally accepted conventions in negotiation, certain types of statements ordinarily are not taken as statements of material fact. Estimates of price or value placed on the subject of a transaction and a party's intentions as to an acceptable settlement of a claim are ordinarily in this category, and so is the existence of an undisclosed principal except where nondisclosure of the principal would constitute fraud. Lawyers should be mindful of their obligations under applicable law to avoid criminal and tortious misrepresentation.

Crime or Fraud by Client

[3] Under Rule 1.2(d), a lawyer is prohibited from counseling or assisting a client in conduct that the lawyer knows is criminal or fraudulent. Paragraph (b) states a specific application of the principle set forth in Rule 1.2(d) and addresses the situation where a client's crime or fraud takes the form of a lie or misrepresentation. Ordinarily, a lawyer can avoid assisting a client's crime or fraud by withdrawing from the representation. Sometimes it may be necessary for the lawyer to give notice of the fact of withdrawal and to disaffirm an opinion, document, affirmation or the like. In extreme cases, substantive law may require a lawyer to disclose information relating to the representation to avoid being deemed to have assisted the client's crime or fraud. If the lawyer can avoid assisting a client's crime or fraud only by disclosing this information, then under paragraph (b) the lawyer is required to do so, unless the disclosure is prohibited by Rule 1.6.

RULE 4.2: COMMUNICATION WITH PERSON REPRESENTED BY COUNSEL

In representing a client, a lawyer shall not communicate about the subject of the representation with a person the lawyer knows to be represented by another lawyer in the matter, unless the lawyer has the consent of the other lawyer or is authorized to do so by law or a court order.

Comment

[1] This Rule contributes to the proper functioning of the legal system by protecting a person who has chosen to be represented by a lawyer in a matter against possible overreaching by other lawyers who are participating in the matter, interference by those lawyers with the client-lawyer relationship and the uncounselled disclosure of information relating to the representation.

[2] This Rule applies to communications with any person who is represented by counsel concerning the matter to which the communication relates.

[3] The Rule applies even though the represented person initiates or consents to the communication. A lawyer must immediately terminate communication with a person if, after commencing communication, the

lawyer learns that the person is one with whom communication is not permitted by this Rule.

[4]   This Rule does not prohibit communication with a represented person, or an employee or agent of such a person, concerning matters outside the representation. For example, the existence of a controversy between a government agency and a private party, or between two organizations, does not prohibit a lawyer for either from communicating with nonlawyer representatives of the other regarding a separate matter. Nor does this Rule preclude communication with a represented person who is seeking advice from a lawyer who is not otherwise representing a client in the matter. A lawyer may not make a communication prohibited by this Rule through the acts of another. See Rule 8.4(a). Parties to a matter may communicate directly with each other, and a lawyer is not prohibited from advising a client concerning a communication that the client is legally entitled to make. Also, a lawyer having independent justification or legal authorization for communicating with a represented person is permitted to do so.

[5]   Communications authorized by law may include communications by a lawyer on behalf of a client who is exercising a constitutional or other legal right to communicate with the government. Communications authorized by law may also include investigative activities of lawyers representing governmental entities, directly or through investigative agents, prior to the commencement of criminal or civil enforcement proceedings. When communicating with the accused in a criminal matter, a government lawyer must comply with this Rule in addition to honoring the constitutional rights of the accused. The fact that a communication does not violate a state or federal constitutional right is insufficient to establish that the communication is permissible under this Rule.

[6]   A lawyer who is uncertain whether a communication with a represented person is permissible may seek a court order. A lawyer may also seek a court order in exceptional circumstances to authorize a communication that would otherwise be prohibited by this Rule, for example, where communication with a person represented by counsel is necessary to avoid reasonably certain injury.

[7]   In the case of a represented organization, this Rule prohibits communications with a constituent of the organization who supervises, directs or regularly consults with the organization's lawyer concerning the matter or has authority to obligate the organization with respect to the matter or whose act or omission in connection with the matter may be imputed to the organization for purposes of civil or criminal liability. Consent of the organization's lawyer is not required for communication with a former constituent. If a constituent of the organization is represented in the matter by his or her own counsel, the consent by that counsel to a communication will be sufficient for purposes of this Rule. Compare Rule 3.4(f). In communicating with a current or former constituent of an organization, a lawyer must not use methods of obtaining evidence that violate the legal rights of the organization. See Rule 4.4.

[8]   The prohibition on communications with a represented person only applies in circumstances where the lawyer knows that the person is in fact represented in the matter to be discussed. This means that the lawyer has actual knowledge of the fact of the representation; but such actual knowledge may be inferred from the circumstances. See Rule 1.0(f). Thus, the lawyer cannot evade the requirement of obtaining the consent of counsel by closing eyes to the obvious.

[9]   In the event the person with whom the lawyer communicates is not known to be represented by counsel in the matter, the lawyer's communications are subject to Rule 4.3.

RULE 4.3: DEALING WITH UNREPRESENTED PERSON

In dealing on behalf of a client with a person who is not represented by counsel, a lawyer shall not state or imply that the lawyer is disinterested. When the lawyer knows or reasonably should know that the unrepresented person misunderstands the lawyer's role in the matter, the lawyer shall make reasonable efforts to correct the misunderstanding. The lawyer shall not give legal advice to an unrepresented person, other than the advice to secure counsel, if the lawyer knows or reasonably should know that the interests of such a person are or have a reasonable possibility of being in conflict with the interests of the client.

Comment

[1]   An unrepresented person, particularly one not experienced in dealing with legal matters, might assume that a lawyer is disinterested in loyalties or is a disinterested authority on the law even when the lawyer represents a client. In order to avoid a misunderstanding, a lawyer will typically need to identify the lawyer's client and, where necessary, explain that the client has interests opposed to those of the unrepresented person. For misunderstandings that sometimes arise when a lawyer for an organization deals with an unrepresented constituent, see Rule 1.13(f).

[2]   The Rule distinguishes between situations involving unrepresented persons whose interests may be adverse to those of the lawyer's client and those in which the person's interests are not in conflict with the client's. In the former situation, the possibility that the lawyer will compromise the unrepresented person's interests is so great that the Rule prohibits the giving of any advice, apart from the advice to obtain counsel. Whether a lawyer is giving impermissible advice may depend on the experience and sophistication of the unrepresented person, as well as the setting in which the behavior and comments occur. This Rule does not prohibit a lawyer from negotiating the terms of a transaction or settling a dispute with an unrepresented person. So long as the lawyer has explained that the lawyer represents an adverse party and is not representing the person, the lawyer may inform the person of the terms on which the lawyer's client will enter into an agreement or settle a matter, prepare documents that require the person's signature and explain the lawyer's own view of the meaning of the document or the lawyer's view of the underlying legal obligations.

RULE 4.4: RESPECT FOR RIGHTS OF THIRD PERSONS

(a)   In representing a client, a lawyer shall not use means that have no substantial purpose other than to embarrass, delay, or burden a third person, or use methods of obtaining evidence that violate the legal rights of such a person.

(b)   A lawyer who receives a document or electronically stored information relating to the representation of the lawyer's client and knows or reasonably should know that the document or electronically stored information was inadvertently sent shall promptly notify the sender.

Comment

[1] Responsibility to a client requires a lawyer to subordinate the interests of others to those of the client, but that responsibility does not imply that a lawyer may disregard the rights of third persons. It is impractical to catalogue all such rights, but they include legal restrictions on methods of obtaining evidence from third persons and unwarranted intrusions into privileged relationships, such as the client-lawyer relationship.

[2] Paragraph (b) recognizes that lawyers sometimes receive a document or electronically stored information that was mistakenly sent or produced by opposing parties or their lawyers. A document or electronically stored information is inadvertently sent when it is accidentally transmitted, such as when an email or letter is misaddressed or a document or electronically stored information is accidentally included with information that was intentionally transmitted. If a lawyer knows or reasonably should know that such a document or electronically stored information was sent inadvertently, then this Rule requires the lawyer to promptly notify the sender in order to permit that person to take protective measures. Whether the lawyer is required to take additional steps, such as returning the document or electronically stored information, is a matter of law beyond the scope of these Rules, as is the question of whether the privileged status of a document or electronically stored information has been waived. Similarly, this Rule does not address the legal duties of a lawyer who receives a document or electronically stored information that the lawyer knows or reasonably should know may have been inappropriately obtained by the sending person. For purposes of this Rule, "document or electronically stored information" includes, in addition to paper documents, email and other forms of electronically stored information, including embedded data (commonly referred to as "metadata"), that is subject to being read or put into readable form. Metadata in electronic documents creates an obligation under this Rule only if the receiving lawyer knows or reasonably should know that the metadata was inadvertently sent to the receiving lawyer.

[3] Some lawyers may choose to return a document or delete electronically stored information unread, for example, when the lawyer learns before receiving it that it was inadvertently sent. Where a lawyer is not required by applicable law to do so, the decision to voluntarily return such a document or delete electronically stored information is a matter of professional judgment ordinarily reserved to the lawyer. See Rules 1.2 and 1.4.

LAW FIRMS AND ASSOCIATIONS

RULE 5.1: RESPONSIBILITIES OF PARTNERS, MANAGERS, AND SUPERVISORY LAWYERS

(a) A partner in a law firm, and a lawyer who individually or together with other lawyers possesses comparable managerial authority in a law firm, shall make reasonable efforts to ensure that the firm has in effect measures giving reasonable assurance that all lawyers in the firm conform to the Rules of Professional Conduct.

(b) A lawyer having direct supervisory authority over another lawyer shall make reasonable efforts to ensure that the other lawyer conforms to the Rules of Professional Conduct.

(c) A lawyer shall be responsible for another lawyer's violation of the Rules of Professional Conduct if:

(1) the lawyer orders or, with knowledge of the specific conduct, ratifies the conduct involved; or

(2) the lawyer is a partner or has comparable managerial authority in the law firm in which the other lawyer practices, or has direct supervisory authority over the other lawyer, and knows of the conduct at a time when its consequences can be avoided or mitigated but fails to take reasonable remedial action.

Comment

[1] Paragraph (a) applies to lawyers who have managerial authority over the professional work of a firm. See Rule 1.0(c). This includes members of a partnership, the shareholders in a law firm organized as a professional corporation, and members of other associations authorized to practice law; lawyers having comparable managerial authority in a legal services organization or a law department of an enterprise or government agency; and lawyers who have intermediate managerial responsibilities in a firm. Paragraph (b) applies to lawyers who have supervisory authority over the work of other lawyers in a firm.

[2] Paragraph (a) requires lawyers with managerial authority within a firm to make reasonable efforts to establish internal policies and procedures designed to provide reasonable assurance that all lawyers in the firm will conform to the Rules of Professional Conduct. Such policies and procedures include those designed to detect and resolve conflicts of interest, identify dates by which actions must be taken in pending matters, account for client funds and property and ensure that inexperienced lawyers are properly supervised.

[3] Other measures that may be required to fulfill the responsibility prescribed in paragraph (a) can depend on the firm's structure and the nature of its practice. In a small firm of experienced lawyers, informal supervision and periodic review of compliance with the required systems ordinarily will suffice. In a large firm, or in practice situations in which difficult ethical problems frequently arise, more elaborate measures may be necessary. Some firms, for example, have a procedure whereby junior lawyers can make confidential referral of ethical problems directly to a designated senior partner or special committee. See Rule 5.2. Firms, whether large or small, may also rely on continuing legal education in professional ethics. In any event, the ethical atmosphere of a firm can influence the conduct of all its members, and the partners may not assume that all lawyers associated with the firm will inevitably conform to the Rules.

[4] Paragraph (c) expresses a general principle of personal responsibility for acts of another. See also Rule 8.4(a).

[5] Paragraph (c)(2) defines the duty of a partner or other lawyer having comparable managerial authority in a law firm, as well as a lawyer who has direct supervisory authority over performance of specific legal work by another lawyer. Whether a lawyer has supervisory authority in particular circumstances is a question of fact. Partners and lawyers with comparable authority have at least indirect responsibility for all work being done by the firm, while a partner or manager in charge of a particular matter ordinarily also has supervisory responsibility for the work of other firm lawyers engaged in the matter. Appropriate remedial action by a partner or managing lawyer would depend on the immediacy of that lawyer's involvement and the seriousness of the misconduct. A supervisor is required to intervene to

prevent avoidable consequences of misconduct if the supervisor knows that the misconduct occurred. Thus, if a supervising lawyer knows that a subordinate misrepresented a matter to an opposing party in negotiation, the supervisor as well as the subordinate has a duty to correct the resulting misapprehension.

[6]   Professional misconduct by a lawyer under supervision could reveal a violation of paragraph (b) on the part of the supervisory lawyer even though it does not entail a violation of paragraph (c) because there was no direction, ratification or knowledge of the violation.

[7]   Apart from this Rule and Rule 8.4(a), a lawyer does not have disciplinary liability for the conduct of a partner, associate or subordinate. Whether a lawyer may be liable civilly or criminally for another lawyer's conduct is a question of law beyond the scope of these Rules.

[8]   The duties imposed by this Rule on managing and supervising lawyers do not alter the personal duty of each lawyer in a firm to abide by the Rules of Professional Conduct. See Rule 5.2(a).

RULE 5.2: RESPONSIBILITIES OF A SUBORDINATE LAWYER

(a) A lawyer is bound by the Rules of Professional Conduct notwithstanding that the lawyer acted at the direction of another person.

(b) A subordinate lawyer does not violate the Rules of Professional Conduct if that lawyer acts in accordance with a supervisory lawyer's reasonable resolution of an arguable question of professional duty.

Comment

[1]   Although a lawyer is not relieved of responsibility for a violation by the fact that the lawyer acted at the direction of a supervisor, that fact may be relevant in determining whether a lawyer had the knowledge required to render conduct a violation of the Rules. For example, if a subordinate filed a frivolous pleading at the direction of a supervisor, the subordinate would not be guilty of a professional violation unless the subordinate knew of the document's frivolous character.

[2]   When lawyers in a supervisor-subordinate relationship encounter a matter involving professional judgment as to ethical duty, the supervisor may assume responsibility for making the judgment. Otherwise a consistent course of action or position could not be taken. If the question can reasonably be answered only one way, the duty of both lawyers is clear and they are equally responsible for fulfilling it. However, if the question is reasonably arguable, someone has to decide upon the course of action. That authority ordinarily reposes in the supervisor, and a subordinate may be guided accordingly. For example, if a question arises whether the interests of two clients conflict under Rule 1.7, the supervisor's reasonable resolution of the question should protect the subordinate professionally if the resolution is subsequently challenged.

RULE 5.3: RESPONSIBILITIES REGARDING NONLAWYER ASSISTANCE

With respect to a nonlawyer employed or retained by or associated with a lawyer:

(a) a partner, and a lawyer who individually or together with other lawyers possesses comparable managerial authority in a law

firm shall make reasonable efforts to ensure that the firm has in effect measures giving reasonable assurance that the person's conduct is compatible with the professional obligations of the lawyer;

(b) a lawyer having direct supervisory authority over the nonlawyer shall make reasonable efforts to ensure that the person's conduct is compatible with the professional obligations of the lawyer; and

(c) a lawyer shall be responsible for conduct of such a person that would be a violation of the Rules of Professional Conduct if engaged in by a lawyer if:

(1) the lawyer orders or, with the knowledge of the specific conduct, ratifies the conduct involved; or

(2) the lawyer is a partner or has comparable managerial authority in the law firm in which the person is employed, or has direct supervisory authority over the person, and knows of the conduct at a time when its consequences can be avoided or mitigated but fails to take reasonable remedial action.

Comment

[1] Paragraph (a) requires lawyers with managerial authority within a law firm to make reasonable efforts to ensure that the firm has in effect measures giving reasonable assurance that nonlawyers in the firm and nonlawyers outside the firm who work on firm matters act in a way compatible with the professional obligations of the lawyer. See Comment [6] to Rule 1.1 (retaining lawyers outside the firm) and Comment [1] to Rule 5.1 (responsibilities with respect to lawyers within a firm). Paragraph (b) applies to lawyers who have supervisory authority over such nonlawyers within or outside the firm. Paragraph (c) specifies the circumstances in which a lawyer is responsible for the conduct of such nonlawyers within or outside the firm that would be a violation of the Rules of Professional Conduct if engaged in by a lawyer.

Nonlawyers Within the Firm

[2] Lawyers generally employ assistants in their practice, including secretaries, investigators, law student interns, and paraprofessionals. Such assistants, whether employees or independent contractors, act for the lawyer in rendition of the lawyer's professional services. A lawyer must give such assistants appropriate instruction and supervision concerning the ethical aspects of their employment, particularly regarding the obligation not to disclose information relating to representation of the client, and should be responsible for their work product. The measures employed in supervising nonlawyers should take account of the fact that they do not have legal training and are not subject to professional discipline.

Nonlawyers Outside the Firm

[3] A lawyer may use nonlawyers outside the firm to assist the lawyer in rendering legal services to the client. Examples include the retention of an investigative or paraprofessional service, hiring a document management company to create and maintain a database for complex litigation, sending client documents to a third party for printing or scanning, and using an Internet-based service to store client information. When using such services outside the firm, a lawyer must make reasonable efforts to ensure that the services are provided in a manner that is compatible with the lawyer's

professional obligations. The extent of this obligation will depend upon the circumstances, including the education, experience and reputation of the nonlawyer; the nature of the services involved; the terms of any arrangements concerning the protection of client information; and the legal and ethical environments of the jurisdictions in which the services will be performed, particularly with regard to confidentiality. See also Rules 1.1 (competence), 1.2 (allocation of authority), 1.4 (communication with client), 1.6 (confidentiality), 5.4(a) (professional independence of the lawyer), and 5.5(a) (unauthorized practice of law). When retaining or directing a nonlawyer outside the firm, a lawyer should communicate directions appropriate under the circumstances to give reasonable assurance that the nonlawyer's conduct is compatible with the professional obligations of the lawyer.

[4]   Where the client directs the selection of a particular nonlawyer service provider outside the firm, the lawyer ordinarily should agree with the client concerning the allocation of responsibility for monitoring as between the client and the lawyer. See Rule 1.2. When making such an allocation in a matter pending before a tribunal, lawyers and parties may have additional obligations that are a matter of law beyond the scope of these Rules.

RULE 5.4: PROFESSIONAL INDEPENDENCE OF A LAWYER

(a) A lawyer or law firm shall not share legal fees with a nonlawyer, except that:

(1) an agreement by a lawyer with the lawyer's firm, partner, or associate may provide for the payment of money, over a reasonable period of time after the lawyer's death, to the lawyer's estate or to one or more specified persons;

(2) a lawyer who purchases the practice of a deceased, disabled, or disappeared lawyer may, pursuant to the provisions of Rule 1.17, pay to the estate or other representative of that lawyer the agreed-upon purchase price;

(3) a lawyer or law firm may include nonlawyer employees in a compensation or retirement plan, even though the plan is based in whole or in part on a profit-sharing arrangement; and

(4) a lawyer may share court-awarded legal fees with a nonprofit organization that employed, retained or recommended employment of the lawyer in the matter.

(b) A lawyer shall not form a partnership with a nonlawyer if any of the activities of the partnership consist of the practice of law.

(c) A lawyer shall not permit a person who recommends, employs, or pays the lawyer to render legal services for another to direct or regulate the lawyer's professional judgment in rendering such legal services.

(d) A lawyer shall not practice with or in the form of a professional corporation or association authorized to practice law for a profit, if:

(1) a nonlawyer owns any interest therein, except that a fiduciary representative of the estate of a lawyer may hold the stock or interest of the lawyer for a reasonable time during administration;

(2) a nonlawyer is a corporate director or officer thereof or occupies the position of similar responsibility in any form of association other than a corporation; or

(3) a nonlawyer has the right to direct or control the professional judgment of a lawyer.

Comment

[1] The provisions of this Rule express traditional limitations on sharing fees. These limitations are to protect the lawyer's professional independence of judgment. Where someone other than the client pays the lawyer's fee or salary, or recommends employment of the lawyer, that arrangement does not modify the lawyer's obligation to the client. As stated in paragraph (c), such arrangements should not interfere with the lawyer's professional judgment.

[2] This Rule also expresses traditional limitations on permitting a third party to direct or regulate the lawyer's professional judgment in rendering legal services to another. See also Rule 1.8(f) (lawyer may accept compensation from a third party as long as there is no interference with the lawyer's independent professional judgment and the client gives informed consent).

RULE 5.5: UNAUTHORIZED PRACTICE OF LAW; MULTIJURISDICTIONAL PRACTICE OF LAW

(a) A lawyer shall not practice law in a jurisdiction in violation of the regulation of the legal profession in that jurisdiction, or assist another in doing so.

(b) A lawyer who is not admitted to practice in this jurisdiction shall not:

(1) except as authorized by these Rules or other law, establish an office or other systematic and continuous presence in this jurisdiction for the practice of law; or

(2) hold out to the public or otherwise represent that the lawyer is admitted to practice law in this jurisdiction.

(c) A lawyer admitted in another United States jurisdiction, and not disbarred or suspended from practice in any jurisdiction, may provide legal services on a temporary basis in this jurisdiction that:

(1) are undertaken in association with a lawyer who is admitted to practice in this jurisdiction and who actively participates in the matter;

(2) are in or reasonably related to a pending or potential proceeding before a tribunal in this or another jurisdiction, if the lawyer, or a person the lawyer is assisting, is authorized by law or order to appear in such proceeding or reasonably expects to be so authorized;

(3) are in or reasonably related to a pending or potential arbitration, mediation, or other alternative dispute resolution proceeding in this or another jurisdiction, if the services arise out of or are reasonably related to the lawyer's practice in a jurisdiction in which the lawyer is admitted to practice and are not services for which the forum requires pro hac vice admission; or

    (4) are not within paragraphs (c)(2) or (c)(3) and arise out of or are reasonably related to the lawyer's practice in a jurisdiction in which the lawyer is admitted to practice.

(d) A lawyer admitted in another United States jurisdiction or in a foreign jurisdiction, and not disbarred or suspended from practice in any jurisdiction or the equivalent thereof, may provide legal services through an office or other systematic and continuous presence in this jurisdiction that:

    (1) are provided to the lawyer's employer or its organizational affiliates; are not services for which the forum requires pro hac vice admission; and, when performed by a foreign lawyer and requires advice on the law of this of another jurisdiction or of the United States, such advice shall be based upon the advice of a lawyer who is duly licensed and authorized by the jurisdiction to provide such advice; or

    (2) are services that the lawyer is authorized by federal or other law or rule to provide in this jurisdiction.

(e) For purposes of paragraph (d):

    (1) the foreign lawyer must be a member in good standing of a recognized legal profession in a foreign jurisdiction, the members of which are admitted to practice as lawyers or counselors at law or the equivalent, and are subject to effective regulation and discipline by a duly constituted professional body or public authority, or,

    (2) the person otherwise lawfully practicing as an in-house counsel under the laws of a foreign jurisdiction must be authorized to practice under this rule by, in the exercise of its discretion, [the highest court of this jurisdiction].

Comment

[1] A lawyer may practice law only in a jurisdiction in which the lawyer is authorized to practice. A lawyer may be admitted to practice law in a jurisdiction on a regular basis or may be authorized by court rule or order or by law to practice for a limited purpose or on a restricted basis. Paragraph (a) applies to unauthorized practice of law by a lawyer, whether through the lawyer's direct action or by the lawyer assisting another person. For example, a lawyer may not assist a person in practicing law in violation of the rules governing professional conduct in that person's jurisdiction.

[2] The definition of the practice of law is established by law and varies from one jurisdiction to another. Whatever the definition, limiting the practice of law to members of the bar protects the public against rendition of legal services by unqualified persons. This Rule does not prohibit a lawyer from employing the services of paraprofessionals and delegating functions to them, so long as the lawyer supervises the delegated work and retains responsibility for their work. See Rule 5.3.

[3] A lawyer may provide professional advice and instruction to nonlawyers whose employment requires knowledge of the law; for example, claims adjusters, employees of financial or commercial institutions, social workers, accountants and persons employed in government agencies.

Lawyers also may assist independent nonlawyers, such as paraprofessionals, who are authorized by the law of a jurisdiction to provide particular law-related services. In addition, a lawyer may counsel nonlawyers who wish to proceed pro se.

[4]   Other than as authorized by law or this Rule, a lawyer who is not admitted to practice generally in this jurisdiction violates paragraph (b)(1) if the lawyer establishes an office or other systematic and continuous presence in this jurisdiction for the practice of law. Presence may be systematic and continuous even if the lawyer is not physically present here. Such a lawyer must not hold out to the public or otherwise represent that the lawyer is admitted to practice law in this jurisdiction. See also Rule 7.1.

[5]   There are occasions in which a lawyer admitted to practice in another United States jurisdiction, and not disbarred or suspended from practice in any jurisdiction, may provide legal services on a temporary basis in this jurisdiction under circumstances that do not create an unreasonable risk to the interests of their clients, the public or the courts. Paragraph (c) identifies four such circumstances. The fact that conduct is not so identified does not imply that the conduct is or is not authorized. With the exception of paragraphs (d)(1) and (d)(2), this Rule does not authorize a U.S. or foreign lawyer to establish an office or other systematic and continuous presence in this jurisdiction without being admitted to practice generally here.

[6]   There is no single test to determine whether a lawyer's services are provided on a "temporary basis" in this jurisdiction, and may therefore be permissible under paragraph (c). Services may be "temporary" even though the lawyer provides services in this jurisdiction on a recurring basis, or for an extended period of time, as when the lawyer is representing a client in a single lengthy negotiation or litigation.

[7]   Paragraphs (c) and (d) apply to lawyers who are admitted to practice law in any United States jurisdiction, which included the District of Columbia and any state, territory or commonwealth of the United States. Paragraph (d) also applies to lawyers admitted in a foreign jurisdiction. The word "admitted" in paragraphs (c) (d) and (e) contemplates that the lawyer is authorized to practice in the jurisdiction in which the lawyer is admitted and excludes a lawyer who while technically admitted is not authorized to practice, because, for example, the lawyer is on inactive status.

[8]   Paragraph (c)(1) recognizes that the interests of clients and the public are protected if a lawyer admitted only in another jurisdiction associates with a lawyer licensed to practice in this jurisdiction. For this paragraph to apply, however, the lawyer admitted to practice in this jurisdiction must actively participate in and share responsibility for the representation of the client.

[9]   Lawyers not admitted to practice generally in a jurisdiction may be authorized by law or order of a tribunal or an administrative agency to appear before the tribunal or agency. This authority may be granted pursuant to formal rules governing admission pro hac vice or pursuant to informal practice of the tribunal or agency. Under paragraph (c)(2), a lawyer does not violate this Rule when the lawyer appears before a tribunal or agency pursuant to such authority. To the extent that a court rule or other law of this jurisdiction requires a lawyer who is not admitted to practice in this jurisdiction to obtain admission pro hac vice before appearing before a tribunal or administrative agency, this Rule requires the lawyer to obtain that authority.

[10] Paragraph (c)(2) also provides that a lawyer rendering services in this jurisdiction on a temporary basis does not violate this Rule when the lawyer engages in conduct in anticipation of a proceeding or hearing in a jurisdiction in which the lawyer is authorized to practice law or in which the lawyer reasonably expects to be admitted pro hac vice. Examples of such conduct include meetings with the client, interviews of potential witnesses, and the review of documents. Similarly, a lawyer admitted only in another jurisdiction may engage in conduct temporarily in this jurisdiction in connection with pending litigation in another jurisdiction in which the lawyer is or reasonably expects to be authorized to appear, including taking depositions in this jurisdiction.

[11] When a lawyer has been or reasonably expects to be admitted to appear before a court or administrative agency, paragraph (c)(2) also permits conduct by lawyers who are associated with that lawyer in the matter, but who do not expect to appear before the court or administrative agency. For example, subordinate lawyers may conduct research, review documents, and attend meetings with witnesses in support of the lawyer responsible for the litigation.

[12] Paragraph (c)(3) permits a lawyer admitted to practice law in another jurisdiction to perform services on a temporary basis in this jurisdiction if those services are in or reasonably related to a pending or potential arbitration, mediation, or other alternative dispute resolution proceeding in this or another jurisdiction, if the services arise out of or are reasonably related to the lawyer's practice in a jurisdiction in which the lawyer is admitted to practice. The lawyer, however, must obtain admission pro hac vice in the case of a court-annexed arbitration or mediation or otherwise if court rules or law so require.

[13] Paragraph (c)(4) permits a lawyer admitted in another jurisdiction to provide certain legal services on a temporary basis in this jurisdiction that arise out of or are reasonably related to the lawyer's practice in a jurisdiction in which the lawyer is admitted but are not within paragraphs (c)(2) or (c)(3). These services include both legal services and services that nonlawyers may perform but that are considered the practice of law when performed by lawyers.

[14] Paragraphs (c)(3) and (c)(4) require that the services arise out of or be reasonably related to the lawyer's practice in a jurisdiction in which the lawyer is admitted. A variety of factors evidence such a relationship. The lawyer's client may have been previously represented by the lawyer, or may be resident in or have substantial contacts with the jurisdiction in which the lawyer is admitted. The matter, although involving other jurisdictions, may have a significant connection with that jurisdiction. In other cases, significant aspects of the lawyer's work might be conducted in that jurisdiction or a significant aspect of the matter may involve the law of that jurisdiction. The necessary relationship might arise when the client's activities or the legal issues involve multiple jurisdictions, such as when the officers of a multinational corporation survey potential business sites and seek the services of their lawyer in assessing the relative merits of each. In addition, the services may draw on the lawyer's recognized expertise developed through the regular practice of law on behalf of clients in matters involving a particular body of federal, nationally-uniform, foreign, or international law. Lawyers desiring to provide *pro bono* legal services on a temporary basis in a jurisdiction that has been affected by a major disaster, but in which they are not otherwise authorized to practice law, as well as lawyers from the affected jurisdiction who seek to practice law temporarily in another jurisdiction, but

in which they are not otherwise authorized to practice law, should consult the [*Model Court Rule on Provision of Legal Services Following Determination of Major Disaster*].

[15] Paragraph (d) identifies two circumstances in which a lawyer who is admitted to practice in another United States or a foreign jurisdiction, and is not disbarred or suspended from practice in any jurisdiction, or the equivalent thereof, may establish an office or other systematic and continuous presence in this jurisdiction for the practice of law. Pursuant to paragraph (c) of this Rule, a lawyer admitted in any U.S. jurisdiction may also provide legal services in this jurisdiction on a temporary basis. See also *Model Rule on Temporary Practice by Foreign Lawyers*. Except as provided in paragraphs (d)(1) and (d)(2), a lawyer who is admitted to practice law in another United States or foreign jurisdiction must become admitted to practice law generally in this jurisdiction.

[16] Paragraph (d)(1) applies to a U.S. or foreign lawyer who is employed by a client to provide legal services to the client or its organizational affiliates, i.e., entities that control, are controlled by, or are under common control with the employer. This paragraph does not authorize the provision of personal legal services to the employer's officers or employees. The paragraph applies to in-house corporate lawyers, government lawyers and others who are employed to render legal services to the employer. The lawyer's ability to represent the employer outside the jurisdiction in which the lawyer is licensed generally serves the interests of the employer and does not create an unreasonable risk to the client and others because the employer is well situated to assess the lawyer's qualifications and the quality of the lawyer's work. To further decrease any risk to the client, when advising on the domestic law of a United States jurisdiction or on the law of the United States, the foreign lawyer authorized to practice under paragraph (d)(1) of this Rule needs to base that advice on the advice of a lawyer licensed and authorized by the jurisdiction to provide it.

[17] If an employed lawyer establishes an office or other systematic presence in this jurisdiction for the purpose of rendering legal services to the employer, the lawyer may be subject to registration or other requirements, including assessments for client protection funds and mandatory continuing legal education. See *Model Rule for Registration of In-House Counsel*.

[18] Paragraph (d)(2) recognizes that a U.S. or foreign lawyer may provide legal services in a jurisdiction in which the lawyer is not licensed when authorized to do so by federal or other law, which includes statute, court rule, executive regulation or judicial precedent. See, e.g., *Model Rule on Practice Pending Admission*.

[19] A lawyer who practices law in this jurisdiction pursuant to paragraphs (c) or (d) or otherwise is subject to the disciplinary authority of this jurisdiction. See Rule 8.5(a).

[20] In some circumstances, a lawyer who practices law in this jurisdiction pursuant to paragraphs (c) or (d) may have to inform the client that the lawyer is not licensed to practice law in this jurisdiction. For example, that may be required when the representation occurs primarily in this jurisdiction and requires knowledge of the law of this jurisdiction. See Rule 1.4(b).

[21] Paragraphs (c) and (d) do not authorize communications advertising legal services in this jurisdiction by lawyers who are admitted to practice in other jurisdictions. Whether and how lawyers may communicate

the availability of their services in this jurisdiction is governed by Rules 7.1 to 7.3.

RULE 5.6: RESTRICTIONS ON RIGHT TO PRACTICE

A lawyer shall not participate in offering or making:

(a) a partnership, shareholders, operating, employment, or other similar type of agreement that restricts the right of a lawyer to practice after termination of the relationship, except an agreement concerning benefits upon retirement; or

(b) an agreement in which a restriction on the lawyer's right to practice is part of the settlement of a client controversy.

Comment

[1] An agreement restricting the right of lawyers to practice after leaving a firm not only limits their professional autonomy but also limits the freedom of clients to choose a lawyer. Paragraph (a) prohibits such agreements except for restrictions incident to provisions concerning retirement benefits for service with the firm.

[2] Paragraph (b) prohibits a lawyer from agreeing not to represent other persons in connection with settling a claim on behalf of a client.

[3] This Rule does not apply to prohibit restrictions that may be included in the terms of the sale of a law practice pursuant to Rule 1.17.

RULE 5.7: RESPONSIBILITIES REGARDING LAW-RELATED SERVICES

(a) A lawyer shall be subject to the Rules of Professional Conduct with respect to the provision of law-related services, as defined in paragraph (b), if the law-related services are provided:

(1) by the lawyer in circumstances that are not distinct from the lawyer's provision of legal services to clients; or

(2) in other circumstances by an entity controlled by the lawyer individually or with others if the lawyer fails to take reasonable measures to assure that a person obtaining the law-related services knows that the services are not legal services and that the protections of the client-lawyer relationship do not exist.

(b) The term "law-related services" denotes services that might reasonably be performed in conjunction with and in substance are related to the provision of legal services, and that are not prohibited as unauthorized practice of law when provided by a nonlawyer.

Comment

[1] When a lawyer performs law-related services or controls an organization that does so, there exists the potential for ethical problems. Principal among these is the possibility that the person for whom the law-related services are performed fails to understand that the services may not carry with them the protections normally afforded as part of the client-lawyer relationship. The recipient of the law-related services may expect, for example, that the protection of client confidences, prohibitions against representation of persons with conflicting interests, and obligations of a lawyer to maintain professional independence apply to the provision of law-related services when that may not be the case.

[2]   Rule 5.7 applies to the provision of law-related services by a lawyer even when the lawyer does not provide any legal services to the person for whom the law-related services are performed and whether the law-related services are performed through a law firm or a separate entity. The Rule identifies the circumstances in which all of the Rules of Professional Conduct apply to the provision of law-related services. Even when those circumstances do not exist, however, the conduct of a lawyer involved in the provision of law-related services is subject to those Rules that apply generally to lawyer conduct, regardless of whether the conduct involves the provision of legal services. See, e.g., Rule 8.4.

[3]   When law-related services are provided by a lawyer under circumstances that are not distinct from the lawyer's provision of legal services to clients, the lawyer in providing the law-related services must adhere to the requirements of the Rules of Professional Conduct as provided in paragraph (a)(1). Even when the law-related and legal services are provided in circumstances that are distinct from each other, for example through separate entities or different support staff within the law firm, the Rules of Professional Conduct apply to the lawyer as provided in paragraph (a)(2) unless the lawyer takes reasonable measures to assure that the recipient of the law-related services knows that the services are not legal services and that the protections of the client-lawyer relationship do not apply.

[4]   Law-related services also may be provided through an entity that is distinct from that through which the lawyer provides legal services. If the lawyer individually or with others has control of such an entity's operations, the Rule requires the lawyer to take reasonable measures to assure that each person using the services of the entity knows that the services provided by the entity are not legal services and that the Rules of Professional Conduct that relate to the client-lawyer relationship do not apply. A lawyer's control of an entity extends to the ability to direct its operation. Whether a lawyer has such control will depend upon the circumstances of the particular case.

[5]   When a client-lawyer relationship exists with a person who is referred by a lawyer to a separate law-related service entity controlled by the lawyer, individually or with others, the lawyer must comply with Rule 1.8(a).

[6]   In taking the reasonable measures referred to in paragraph (a)(2) to assure that a person using law-related services understands the practical effect or significance of the inapplicability of the Rules of Professional Conduct, the lawyer should communicate to the person receiving the law-related services, in a manner sufficient to assure that the person understands the significance of the fact, that the relationship of the person to the business entity will not be a client-lawyer relationship. The communication should be made before entering into an agreement for provision of or providing law-related services, and preferably should be in writing.

[7]   The burden is upon the lawyer to show that the lawyer has taken reasonable measures under the circumstances to communicate the desired understanding. For instance, a sophisticated user of law-related services, such as a publicly held corporation, may require a lesser explanation than someone unaccustomed to making distinctions between legal services and law-related services, such as an individual seeking tax advice from a lawyer-accountant or investigative services in connection with a lawsuit.

[8]   Regardless of the sophistication of potential recipients of law-related services, a lawyer should take special care to keep separate the provision of law-related and legal services in order to minimize the risk that

the recipient will assume that the law-related services are legal services. The risk of such confusion is especially acute when the lawyer renders both types of services with respect to the same matter. Under some circumstances the legal and law-related services may be so closely entwined that they cannot be distinguished from each other, and the requirement of disclosure and consultation imposed by paragraph (a)(2) of the Rule cannot be met. In such a case a lawyer will be responsible for assuring that both the lawyer's conduct and, to the extent required by Rule 5.3, that of nonlawyer employees in the distinct entity that the lawyer controls complies in all respects with the Rules of Professional Conduct.

[9] A broad range of economic and other interests of clients may be served by lawyers' engaging in the delivery of law-related services. Examples of law-related services include providing title insurance, financial planning, accounting, trust services, real estate counseling, legislative lobbying, economic analysis, social work, psychological counseling, tax preparation, and patent, medical or environmental consulting.

[10] When a lawyer is obliged to accord the recipients of such services the protections of those Rules that apply to the client-lawyer relationship, the lawyer must take special care to heed the proscriptions of the Rules addressing conflict of interest (Rules 1.7 through 1.11, especially Rules 1.7(a)(2) and 1.8(a) (b) and (f)), and to scrupulously adhere to the requirements of Rule 1.6 relating to disclosure of confidential information. The promotion of the law-related services must also in all respects comply with Rules 7.1 through 7.3, dealing with advertising and solicitation. In that regard, lawyers should take special care to identify the obligations that may be imposed as a result of a jurisdiction's decisional law.

[11] When the full protections of all of the Rules of Professional Conduct do not apply to the provision of law-related services, principles of law external to the Rules, for example, the law of principal and agent, govern the legal duties owed to those receiving the services. Those other legal principles may establish a different degree of protection for the recipient with respect to confidentiality of information, conflicts of interest and permissible business relationships with clients. See also Rule 8.4 (Misconduct).

PUBLIC SERVICE

RULE 6.1: VOLUNTARY PRO BONO PUBLICO SERVICE

Every lawyer has a professional responsibility to provide legal services to those unable to pay. A lawyer should aspire to render at least (50) hours of pro bono publico legal services per year. In fulfilling this responsibility, the lawyer should:

(a) provide a substantial majority of the (50) hours of legal services without fee or expectation of fee to:

(1) persons of limited means or

(2) charitable, religious, civic, community, governmental and educational organizations in matters that are designed primarily to address the needs of persons of limited means; and

(b) provide any additional services through:

(1) delivery of legal services at no fee or substantially reduced fee to individuals, groups or organizations seeking to secure or protect civil rights, civil liberties or public rights, or charitable, religious, civic, community, governmental and

educational organizations in matters in furtherance of their organizational purposes, where the payment of standard legal fees would significantly deplete the organization's economic resources or would be otherwise inappropriate;

(2)   delivery of legal services at a substantially reduced fee to persons of limited means; or

(3)   participation in activities for improving the law, the legal system or the legal profession.

In addition, a lawyer should voluntarily contribute financial support to organizations that provide legal services to persons of limited means.

Comment

[1]   Every lawyer, regardless of professional prominence or professional work load, has a responsibility to provide legal services to those unable to pay, and personal involvement in the problems of the disadvantaged can be one of the most rewarding experiences in the life of a lawyer. The American Bar Association urges all lawyers to provide a minimum of 50 hours of pro bono services annually. States, however, may decide to choose a higher or lower number of hours of annual service (which may be expressed as a percentage of a lawyer's professional time) depending upon local needs and local conditions. It is recognized that in some years a lawyer may render greater or fewer hours than the annual standard specified, but during the course of his or her legal career, each lawyer should render on average per year, the number of hours set forth in this Rule. Services can be performed in civil matters or in criminal or quasi-criminal matters for which there is no government obligation to provide funds for legal representation, such as post-conviction death penalty appeal cases.

[2]   Paragraphs (a)(1) and (2) recognize the critical need for legal services that exists among persons of limited means by providing that a substantial majority of the legal services rendered annually to the disadvantaged be furnished without fee or expectation of fee. Legal services under these paragraphs consist of a full range of activities, including individual and class representation, the provision of legal advice, legislative lobbying, administrative rule making and the provision of free training or mentoring to those who represent persons of limited means. The variety of these activities should facilitate participation by government lawyers, even when restrictions exist on their engaging in the outside practice of law.

[3]   Persons eligible for legal services under paragraphs (a)(1) and (2) are those who qualify for participation in programs funded by the Legal Services Corporation and those whose incomes and financial resources are slightly above the guidelines utilized by such programs but nevertheless, cannot afford counsel. Legal services can be rendered to individuals or to organizations such as homeless shelters, battered women's centers and food pantries that serve those of limited means. The term "governmental organizations" includes, but is not limited to, public protection programs and sections of governmental or public sector agencies.

[4]   Because service must be provided without fee or expectation of fee, the intent of the lawyer to render free legal services is essential for the work performed to fall within the meaning of paragraphs (a)(1) and (2). Accordingly, services rendered cannot be considered pro bono if an anticipated fee is uncollected, but the award of statutory attorneys' fees in a case originally accepted as pro bono would not disqualify such services from

inclusion under this section. Lawyers who do receive fees in such cases are encouraged to contribute an appropriate portion of such fees to organizations or projects that benefit persons of limited means.

[5] While it is possible for a lawyer to fulfill the annual responsibility to perform pro bono services exclusively through activities described in paragraphs (a)(1) and (2), to the extent that any hours of service remained unfulfilled, the remaining commitment can be met in a variety of ways as set forth in paragraph (b). Constitutional, statutory or regulatory restrictions may prohibit or impede government and public sector lawyers and judges from performing the pro bono services outlined in paragraphs (a)(1) and (2). Accordingly, where those restrictions apply, government and public sector lawyers and judges may fulfill their pro bono responsibility by performing services outlined in paragraph (b).

[6] Paragraph (b)(1) includes the provision of certain types of legal services to those whose incomes and financial resources place them above limited means. It also permits the pro bono lawyer to accept a substantially reduced fee for services. Examples of the types of issues that may be addressed under this paragraph include First Amendment claims, Title VII claims and environmental protection claims. Additionally, a wide range of organizations may be represented, including social service, medical research, cultural and religious groups.

[7] Paragraph (b)(2) covers instances in which lawyers agree to and receive a modest fee for furnishing legal services to persons of limited means. Participation in judicare programs and acceptance of court appointments in which the fee is substantially below a lawyer's usual rate are encouraged under this section.

[8] Paragraph (b)(3) recognizes the value of lawyers engaging in activities that improve the law, the legal system or the legal profession. Serving on bar association committees, serving on boards of pro bono or legal services programs, taking part in Law Day activities, acting as a continuing legal education instructor, a mediator or an arbitrator and engaging in legislative lobbying to improve the law, the legal system or the profession are a few examples of the many activities that fall within this paragraph.

[9] Because the provision of pro bono services is a professional responsibility, it is the individual ethical commitment of each lawyer. Nevertheless, there may be times when it is not feasible for a lawyer to engage in pro bono services. At such times a lawyer may discharge the pro bono responsibility by providing financial support to organizations providing free legal services to persons of limited means. Such financial support should be reasonably equivalent to the value of the hours of service that would have otherwise been provided. In addition, at times it may be more feasible to satisfy the pro bono responsibility collectively, as by a firm's aggregate pro bono activities.

[10] Because the efforts of individual lawyers are not enough to meet the need for free legal services that exists among persons of limited means, the government and the profession have instituted additional programs to provide those services. Every lawyer should financially support such programs, in addition to either providing direct pro bono services or making financial contributions when pro bono service is not feasible.

[11] Law firms should act reasonably to enable and encourage all lawyers in the firm to provide the pro bono legal services called for by this Rule.

[12] The responsibility set forth in this Rule is not intended to be enforced through disciplinary process.

RULE 6.2: ACCEPTING APPOINTMENTS

A lawyer shall not seek to avoid appointment by a tribunal to represent a person except for good cause, such as:

(a) representing the client is likely to result in violation of the Rules of Professional Conduct or other law;

(b) representing the client is likely to result in an unreasonable financial burden on the lawyer; or

(c) the client or the cause is so repugnant to the lawyer as to be likely to impair the client-lawyer relationship or the lawyer's ability to represent the client.

Comment

[1] A lawyer ordinarily is not obliged to accept a client whose character or cause the lawyer regards as repugnant. The lawyer's freedom to select clients is, however, qualified. All lawyers have a responsibility to assist in providing pro bono publico service. See Rule 6.1. An individual lawyer fulfills this responsibility by accepting a fair share of unpopular matters or indigent or unpopular clients. A lawyer may also be subject to appointment by a court to serve unpopular clients or persons unable to afford legal services.

Appointed Counsel

[2] For good cause a lawyer may seek to decline an appointment to represent a person who cannot afford to retain counsel or whose cause is unpopular. Good cause exists if the lawyer could not handle the matter competently, see Rule 1.1, or if undertaking the representation would result in an improper conflict of interest, for example, when the client or the cause is so repugnant to the lawyer as to be likely to impair the client-lawyer relationship or the lawyer's ability to represent the client. A lawyer may also seek to decline an appointment if acceptance would be unreasonably burdensome, for example, when it would impose a financial sacrifice so great as to be unjust.

[3] An appointed lawyer has the same obligations to the client as retained counsel, including the obligations of loyalty and confidentiality, and is subject to the same limitations on the client-lawyer relationship, such as the obligation to refrain from assisting the client in violation of the Rules.

RULE 6.3: MEMBERSHIP IN LEGAL SERVICES ORGANIZATION

A lawyer may serve as a director, officer or member of a legal services organization, apart from the law firm in which the lawyer practices, notwithstanding that the organization serves persons having interests adverse to a client of the lawyer. The lawyer shall not knowingly participate in a decision or action of the organization:

(a) if participating in the decision or action would be incompatible with the lawyer's obligations to a client under Rule 1.7; or

(b) where the decision or action could have a material adverse effect on the representation of a client of the organization whose interests are adverse to a client of the lawyer.

Comment

[1]   Lawyers should be encouraged to support and participate in legal service organizations. A lawyer who is an officer or a member of such an organization does not thereby have a client-lawyer relationship with persons served by the organization. However, there is potential conflict between the interests of such persons and the interests of the lawyer's clients. If the possibility of such conflict disqualified a lawyer from serving on the board of a legal services organization, the profession's involvement in such organizations would be severely curtailed.

[2]   It may be necessary in appropriate cases to reassure a client of the organization that the representation will not be affected by conflicting loyalties of a member of the board. Established, written policies in this respect can enhance the credibility of such assurances.

RULE 6.4: LAW REFORM ACTIVITIES AFFECTING CLIENT INTERESTS

A lawyer may serve as a director, officer or member of an organization involved in reform of the law or its administration notwithstanding that the reform may affect the interests of a client of the lawyer. When the lawyer knows that the interests of a client may be materially benefitted by a decision in which the lawyer participates, the lawyer shall disclose that fact but need not identify the client.

Comment

[1]   Lawyers involved in organizations seeking law reform generally do not have a client-lawyer relationship with the organization. Otherwise, it might follow that a lawyer could not be involved in a bar association law reform program that might indirectly affect a client. See also Rule 1.2(b). For example, a lawyer specializing in antitrust litigation might be regarded as disqualified from participating in drafting revisions of rules governing that subject. In determining the nature and scope of participation in such activities, a lawyer should be mindful of obligations to clients under other Rules, particularly Rule 1.7. A lawyer is professionally obligated to protect the integrity of the program by making an appropriate disclosure within the organization when the lawyer knows a private client might be materially benefitted.

RULE 6.5: NONPROFIT AND COURT-ANNEXED LIMITED LEGAL SERVICES PROGRAMS

(a) A lawyer who, under the auspices of a program sponsored by a nonprofit organization or court, provides short-term limited legal services to a client without expectation by either the lawyer or the client that the lawyer will provide continuing representation in the matter:

(1) is subject to Rules 1.7 and 1.9(a) only if the lawyer knows that the representation of the client involves a conflict of interest; and

(2) is subject to Rule 1.10 only if the lawyer knows that another lawyer associated with the lawyer in a law firm is disqualified by Rule 1.7 or 1.9(a) with respect to the matter.

(b) Except as provided in paragraph (a)(2), Rule 1.10 is inapplicable to a representation governed by this Rule.

Comment

[1] Legal services organizations, courts and various nonprofit organizations have established programs through which lawyers provide short-term limited legal services—such as advice or the completion of legal forms—that will assist persons to address their legal problems without further representation by a lawyer. In these programs, such as legal-advice hotlines, advice-only clinics or pro se counseling programs, a client-lawyer relationship is established, but there is no expectation that the lawyer's representation of the client will continue beyond the limited consultation. Such programs are normally operated under circumstances in which it is not feasible for a lawyer to systematically screen for conflicts of interest as is generally required before undertaking a representation. See, e.g., Rules 1.7, 1.9 and 1.10.

[2] A lawyer who provides short-term limited legal services pursuant to this Rule must secure the client's informed consent to the limited scope of the representation. See Rule 1.2(c). If a short-term limited representation would not be reasonable under the circumstances, the lawyer may offer advice to the client but must also advise the client of the need for further assistance of counsel. Except as provided in this Rule, the Rules of Professional Conduct, including Rules 1.6 and 1.9(c), are applicable to the limited representation.

[3] Because a lawyer who is representing a client in the circumstances addressed by this Rule ordinarily is not able to check systematically for conflicts of interest, paragraph (a) requires compliance with Rules 1.7 or 1.9(a) only if the lawyer knows that the representation presents a conflict of interest for the lawyer, and with Rule 1.10 only if the lawyer knows that another lawyer in the lawyer's firm is disqualified by Rules 1.7 or 1.9(a) in the matter.

[4] Because the limited nature of the services significantly reduces the risk of conflicts of interest with other matters being handled by the lawyer's firm, paragraph (b) provides that Rule 1.10 is inapplicable to a representation governed by this Rule except as provided by paragraph (a)(2). Paragraph (a)(2) requires the participating lawyer to comply with Rule 1.10 when the lawyer knows that the lawyer's firm is disqualified by Rules 1.7 or 1.9(a). By virtue of paragraph (b), however, a lawyer's participation in a short-term limited legal services program will not preclude the lawyer's firm from undertaking or continuing the representation of a client with interests adverse to a client being represented under the program's auspices. Nor will the personal disqualification of a lawyer participating in the program be imputed to other lawyers participating in the program.

[5] If, after commencing a short-term limited representation in accordance with this Rule, a lawyer undertakes to represent the client in the matter on an ongoing basis, Rules 1.7, 1.9(a) and 1.10 become applicable.

INFORMATION ABOUT LEGAL SERVICES
RULE 7.1: COMMUNICATIONS CONCERNING A LAWYER'S SERVICES

A lawyer shall not make a false or misleading communication about the lawyer or the lawyer's services. A communication is false or misleading if it contains a material misrepresentation of fact or law, or omits a fact necessary to make the statement considered as a whole not materially misleading.

Comment

[1]   This Rule governs all communications about a lawyer's services, including advertising. Whatever means are used to make known a lawyer's services, statements about them must be truthful.

[2]   Misleading truthful statements are also prohibited by this Rule. A truthful statement is misleading if it omits a fact necessary to make the lawyer's communication considered as a whole not materially misleading. A truthful statement is misleading if a substantial likelihood exists that it will lead a reasonable person to formulate a specific conclusion about the lawyer or the lawyer's services for which there is no reasonable factual foundation. A truthful statement is also misleading if presented in a way that creates a substantial likelihood that a reasonable person would believe the lawyer's communication requires that person to take further action when, in fact, no action is required.

[3]   A communication that truthfully reports a lawyer's achievements on behalf of clients or former clients may be misleading if presented so as to lead a reasonable person to form an unjustified expectation that the same results could be obtained for other clients in similar matters without reference to the specific factual and legal circumstances of each client's case. Similarly, an unsubstantiated claim about a lawyer's or law firm's services or fees, or an unsubstantiated comparison of the lawyer's or law firm's services or fees with those of other lawyers or law firms, may be misleading if presented with such specificity as would lead a reasonable person to conclude that the comparison or claim can be substantiated. The inclusion of an appropriate disclaimer or qualifying language may preclude a finding that a statement is likely to create unjustified expectations or otherwise mislead the public.

[4]   It is professional misconduct for a lawyer to engage in conduct involving dishonesty, fraud, deceit or misrepresentation. Rule 8.4(c). See also Rule 8.4(e) for the prohibition against stating or implying an ability to influence improperly a government agency or official or to achieve results by means that violate the Rules of Professional Conduct or other law.

[5]   Firm names, letterhead and professional designations are communications concerning a lawyer's services. A firm may be designated by the names of all or some of its current members, by the names of deceased members where there has been a succession in the firm's identity or by a trade name if it is not false or misleading. A lawyer or law firm also may be designated by a distinctive website address, social media username or comparable professional designation that is not misleading. A law firm name or designation is misleading if it implies a connection with a government agency, with a deceased lawyer who was not a former member of the firm, with a lawyer not associated with the firm or a predecessor firm, with a nonlawyer or with a public or charitable legal services organization. If a firm uses a trade name that includes a geographical name such as "Springfield Legal Clinic," an express statement explaining that it is not a public legal aid organization may be required to avoid a misleading implication.

[6]   A law firm with offices in more than one jurisdiction may use the same name or other professional designation in each jurisdiction

[7]   Lawyers may not imply or hold themselves out as practicing together in one firm when they are not a firm, as defined in Rule 1.0(c), because to do so would be false and misleading.

[8]   It is misleading to use the name of a lawyer holding a public office in the name of a law firm, or in communications on the law firm's behalf, during any substantial period in which the lawyer is not actively and regularly practicing with the firm.

RULE 7.2: COMMUNICATIONS CONCERNING A LAWYER'S SERVICES: SPECIFIC RULES

(a) A lawyer may communicate information regarding the lawyer's services through any media.

(b) A lawyer shall not compensate, give or promise anything of value to a person for recommending the lawyer's services except that a lawyer may:

(1) pay the reasonable costs of advertisements or communications permitted by this Rule;

(2) pay the usual charges of a legal service plan or a not-for-profit or qualified lawyer referral service.

(3) pay for a law practice in accordance with Rule 1.17; and

(4) refer clients to another lawyer or a nonlawyer professional pursuant to an agreement not otherwise prohibited under these Rules that provides for the other person to refer clients or customers to the lawyer, if

(i)   the reciprocal referral agreement is not exclusive, and

(ii) the client is informed of the existence and nature of the agreement; and

(5)   give nominal gifts as an expression of appreciation that are neither intended nor reasonably expected to be a form of compensation for recommending a lawyer's services.

(c) A lawyer shall not state or imply that a lawyer is certified as a specialist in a particular field of law, unless:

(1) the lawyer has been certified as a specialist by an organization that has been approved by an appropriate authority of the state or the District of Columbia or a U.S. Territory or that has been accredited by the American Bar Association; and

(2) the name of the certifying organization is clearly identified in the communication.

(d) Any communication made under this rule must include the name and contact information of at least one lawyer or law firm responsible for its content.

Comment

[1]   This Rule permits public dissemination of information concerning a lawyer's or law firm's name, address, email address, website, and telephone number; the kinds of services the lawyer will undertake; the basis on which the lawyer's fees are determined, including prices for specific services and payment and credit arrangements; a lawyer's foreign language ability; names of references and, with their consent, names of clients regularly represented; and other information that might invite the attention of those seeking legal assistance.

Paying Others to Recommend a Lawyer

[2]   Except as permitted under paragraphs (b)(1)–(b)(5), lawyers are not permitted to pay others for recommending the lawyer's services. A communication contains a recommendation if it endorses or vouches for a lawyer's credentials, abilities, competence, character, or other professional qualities. Directory listings and group advertisements that list lawyers by practice area, without more, do not constitute impermissible "recommendations."

[3]   Paragraph (b)(1) allows a lawyer to pay for advertising and communications permitted by this Rule, including the costs of print directory listings, on-line directory listings, newspaper ads, television and radio airtime, domain-name registrations, sponsorship fees, Internet-based advertisements, and group advertising. A lawyer may compensate employees, agents and vendors who are engaged to provide marketing or client development services, such as publicists, public-relations personnel, business development staff, television and radio station employees or spokespersons and website designers.

[4]   Paragraph (b)(5) permits lawyers to give nominal gifts as an expression or appreciation to a person for recommending the lawyer's services or referring a prospective client. The gift may not be more than a token item as might be given for holidays, or other ordinary social hospitality. A gift is prohibited if offered or given in consideration of any promise, agreement or understanding that such a gift would be forthcoming or that referrals would be made or encouraged in the future.

[5]   A lawyer may pay others for generating client leads, such as Internet-based client leads, as long as the lead generator does not recommend the lawyer, any payment to the lead generator is consistent with Rules 1.5(e) (division of fees) and 5.4 (professional independence of the lawyer), and the lead generator's communications are consistent with Rule 7.1 (communications concerning a lawyer's services). To comply with Rule 7.1, a lawyer must not pay a lead generator that states, implies, or creates a reasonable impression that it is recommending the lawyer, is making the referral without payment from the lawyer, or has analyzed a person's legal problems when determining which lawyer should receive the referral. See Comment [2] (definition of "recommendation"). See also Rule 5.3 (duties of lawyers and law firms with respect to the conduct of nonlawyers); Rule 8.4(a) (duty to avoid violating the Rules through the acts of another).

[6]   A lawyer may pay the usual charges of a legal service plan or a not-for-profit or qualified lawyer referral service. A legal service plan is a prepaid or group legal service plan or a similar delivery system that assists people who seek to secure legal representation. A lawyer referral service, on the other hand, is any organization that holds itself out to the public as a lawyer referral service. Qualified referral services are consumer-oriented organizations that provide unbiased referrals to lawyers with appropriate experience in the subject matter of the representation and afford other client protections, such as complaint procedures or malpractice insurance requirements. Consequently, this Rule only permits a lawyer to pay the usual charges of a not-for-profit or qualified lawyer referral service. A qualified lawyer referral service is one that is approved by an appropriate regulatory authority as affording adequate protections for the public. See, e.g., the American Bar Association's Model Supreme Court Rules Governing Lawyer Referral Services and Model Lawyer Referral and Information Service Quality Assurance Act.

[7]   A lawyer who accepts assignments or referrals from a legal service plan or referrals from a lawyer referral service must act reasonably to assure that the activities of the plan or service are compatible with the lawyer's professional obligations. Legal service plans and lawyer referral services may communicate with the public, but such communication must be in conformity with these Rules. Thus, advertising must not be false or misleading, as would be the case if the communications of a group advertising program or a group legal services plan would mislead the public to think that it was a lawyer referral service sponsored by a state agency or bar association.

[8]   A lawyer also may agree to refer clients to another lawyer or a nonlawyer professional, in return for the undertaking of that person to refer clients or customers to the lawyer. Such reciprocal referral arrangements must not interfere with the lawyer's professional judgment as to making referrals or as to providing substantive legal services. See Rules 2.1 and 5.4(c). Except as provided in Rule 1.5(e), a lawyer who receives referrals from a lawyer or nonlawyer professional must not pay anything solely for the referral, but the lawyer does not violate paragraph (b) of this Rule by agreeing to refer clients to the other lawyer or nonlawyer professional, so long as the reciprocal referral agreement is not exclusive and the client is informed of the referral agreement. Conflicts of interest created by such arrangements are governed by Rule 1.7. Reciprocal referral agreements should not be of indefinite duration and should be reviewed periodically to determine whether they comply with these Rules. This Rule does not restrict referrals or divisions of revenues or net income among lawyers within firms comprised of multiple entities.

Communications about Fields of Practice

[9]   Paragraph (a) of this Rule permits a lawyer to communicate that the lawyer does or does not practice in particular areas of law. A lawyer is generally permitted to state that the lawyer "concentrates in" or is a "specialist," practices a "specialty," or "specializes in" particular fields, but such communications are subject to the "false and misleading" standard applied in Rule 7.1 to communications concerning a lawyer's services.

[10] The Patent and Trademark Office has a long-established policy of designating lawyers practicing before the Office. The designation of Admiralty practice also has a long historical tradition associated with maritime commerce and the federal courts. A lawyer's communications about these practice areas are not prohibited by this Rule.

[11] This Rule permits a lawyer to state that the lawyer is certified as a specialist in a field of law if such certification is granted by an organization approved by an appropriate authority of a state, the District of Columbia or a U.S. Territory or accredited by the American Bar Association or another organization, such as a state supreme court or state bar association, that has been approved by the authority of the state, the District of Columbia or a U.S. Territory to accredit organizations that certify lawyers as specialists. Certification signifies that an objective entity has recognized an advanced degree of knowledge and experience in the specialty area greater than is suggested by general licensure to practice law. Certifying organizations may be expected to apply standards of experience, knowledge and proficiency to ensure that a lawyer's recognition as a specialist is meaningful and reliable. To ensure that consumers can obtain access to useful information about an organization granting certification, the name of the certifying organization must be included in any communication regarding the certification.

Required Contact Information

[12] This Rule requires that any communication about a lawyer or law firm's services include the name of, and contact information for, the lawyer or law firm. Contact information includes a website address, a telephone number, an email address or a physical office location.

RULE 7.3: SOLICITATION OF CLIENTS

(a) "Solicitation" or "solicit" denotes a communication initiated by or on behalf of a lawyer or law firm that is directed to a specific person the lawyer knows or reasonably should know needs legal services in a particular matter and that offers to provide, or reasonably can be understood as offering to provide, legal services for that matter.

(b) A lawyer shall not solicit professional employment by live person-to-person contact when a significant motive for the lawyer's doing so is the lawyer's or law firm's pecuniary gain, unless the contact is with a:

(1) lawyer;

(2) person who has a family, close personal, or prior business or professional relationship with the lawyer or law firm; or

(3) person who routinely uses for business purposes the type of legal services offered by the lawyer.

(c) A lawyer shall not solicit professional employment even when not otherwise prohibited by paragraph (a), if:

(1) the target of the solicitation has made known to the lawyer a desire not to be solicited by the lawyer; or

(2) the solicitation involves coercion, duress or harassment.

(d) This Rule does not prohibit communications authorized by law or ordered by a court or other tribunal.

(e) Notwithstanding the prohibitions in this Rule, a lawyer may participate with a prepaid or group legal service plan operated by an organization not owned or directed by the lawyer that uses live person-to-person contact to enroll members or sell subscriptions for the plan from persons who are not known to need legal services in a particular matter covered by the plan.

Comment

[1] Paragraph (b) prohibits a lawyer from soliciting professional employment by live person-to-person contact when a significant motive for the lawyer's doing so is the lawyer's or the law firm's pecuniary gain. A lawyer's communication is not a solicitation if it is directed to the general public, such as through a billboard, an Internet banner advertisement, a website or a television commercial, or if it is in response to a request for information or is automatically generated in response to electronic searches.

[2] "Live person-to-person contact" means in-person, face-to-face, live telephone and other real-time visual or auditory person-to-person communications where the person is subject to a direct personal encounter without time for reflection. Such person-to-person contact does not include

chat rooms, text messages or other written communications that recipients may easily disregard. A potential for overreaching exists when a lawyer, seeking pecuniary gain, solicits a person known to be in need of legal services. This form of contact subjects a person to the private importuning of the trained advocate in a direct interpersonal encounter. The person, who may already feel overwhelmed by the circumstances giving rise to the need for legal services, may find it difficult to fully evaluate all available alternatives with reasoned judgment and appropriate self-interest in the face of the lawyer's presence and insistence upon an immediate response. The situation is fraught with the possibility of undue influence, intimidation, and over-reaching.

[3]   The potential for overreaching inherent in live person-to-person contact justifies its prohibition, since lawyers have alternative means of conveying necessary information. In particular, communications can be mailed or transmitted by email or other electronic means that do not violate other laws. These forms of communications make it possible for the public to be informed about the need for legal services, and about the qualifications of available lawyers and law firms, without subjecting the public to live person-to-person persuasion that may overwhelm a person's judgment.

[4]   The contents of live person-to-person contact can be disputed and may not be subject to third-party scrutiny. Consequently, they are much more likely to approach (and occasionally cross) the dividing line between accurate representations and those that are false and misleading.

[5]   There is far less likelihood that a lawyer would engage in overreaching against a former client, or a person with whom the lawyer has a close personal, family, business or professional relationship, or in situations in which the lawyer is motivated by considerations other than the lawyer's pecuniary gain. Nor is there a serious potential for overreaching when the person contacted is a lawyer or is known to routinely use the type of legal services involved for business purposes. Examples include persons who routinely hire outside counsel to represent the entity; entrepreneurs who regularly engage business, employment law or intellectual property lawyers; small business proprietors who routinely hire lawyers for lease or contract issues; and other people who routinely retain lawyers for business transactions or formations. Paragraph (a) is not intended to prohibit a lawyer from participating in constitutionally protected activities of public or charitable legal-service organizations or bona fide political, social, civic, fraternal, employee or trade organizations whose purposes include providing or recommending legal services to their members or beneficiaries.

[6]   A solicitation that contains false or misleading information within the meaning of Rule 7.1, that involves coercion, duress or harassment within the meaning of Rule 7.3(c)(2), or that involves contact with someone who has made known to the lawyer a desire not to be solicited by the lawyer within the meaning of Rule 7.3(c)(1) is prohibited. Live, person-to-person contact of individuals who may be especially vulnerable to coercion or duress is ordinarily not appropriate, for example, the elderly, those whose first language is not English, or the disabled.

[7]   This Rule does not prohibit a lawyer from contacting representatives of organizations or groups that may be interested in establishing a group or prepaid legal plan for their members, insureds, beneficiaries or other third parties for the purpose of informing such entities of the availability of and details concerning the plan or arrangement which the lawyer or lawyer's firm is willing to offer. This form of communication is

not directed to people who are seeking legal services for themselves. Rather, it is usually addressed to an individual acting in a fiduciary capacity seeking a supplier of legal services for others who may, if they choose, become prospective clients of the lawyer. Under these circumstances, the activity which the lawyer undertakes in communicating with such representatives and the type of information transmitted to the individual are functionally similar to and serve the same purpose as advertising permitted under Rule 7.2.

[8] Communications authorized by law or ordered by a court or tribunal include a notice to potential members of a class in class action litigation.

[9] Paragraph (e) of this Rule permits a lawyer to participate with an organization which uses personal contact to enroll members for its group or prepaid legal service plan, provided that the personal contact is not undertaken by any lawyer who would be a provider of legal services through the plan. The organization must not be owned by or directed (whether as manager or otherwise) by any lawyer or law firm that participates in the plan. For example, paragraph (e) would not permit a lawyer to create an organization controlled directly or indirectly by the lawyer and use the organization for the person-to-person solicitation of legal employment of the lawyer through memberships in the plan or otherwise. The communication permitted by these organizations also must not be directed to a person known to need legal services in a particular matter, but must be designed to inform potential plan members generally of another means of affordable legal services. Lawyers who participate in a legal service plan must reasonably assure that the plan sponsors are in compliance with Rules 7.1, 7.2 and 7.3(c).

RULE 7.4 (Deleted)

RULE 7.5 (Deleted)

RULE 7.6: POLITICAL CONTRIBUTIONS TO OBTAIN GOVERNMENT LEGAL ENGAGEMENTS OR APPOINTMENTS BY JUDGES

A lawyer or law firm shall not accept a government legal engagement or an appointment by a judge if the lawyer or law firm makes a political contribution or solicits political contributions for the purpose of obtaining or being considered for that type of legal engagement or appointment.

Comment

[1] Lawyers have a right to participate fully in the political process, which includes making and soliciting political contributions to candidates for judicial and other public office. Nevertheless, when lawyers make or solicit political contributions in order to obtain an engagement for legal work awarded by a government agency, or to obtain appointment by a judge, the public may legitimately question whether the lawyers engaged to perform the work are selected on the basis of competence and merit. In such a circumstance, the integrity of the profession is undermined.

[2] The term "political contribution" denotes any gift, subscription, loan, advance or deposit of anything of value made directly or indirectly to a candidate, incumbent, political party or campaign committee to influence or provide financial support for election to or retention in judicial or other government office. Political contributions in initiative and referendum

elections are not included. For purposes of this Rule, the term "political contribution" does not include uncompensated services.

[3]   Subject to the exceptions below (i) the term "government legal engagement" denotes any engagement to provide legal services that a public official has the direct or indirect power to award; and (ii) the term "appointment by a judge" denotes an appointment to a position such as referee, commissioner, special master, receiver, guardian or other similar position that is made by a judge. Those terms do not, however, include (a) substantially uncompensated services; (b) engagements or appointments made on the basis of experience, expertise, professional qualifications and cost following a request for proposal or other process that is free from influence based upon political contributions; and (c) engagements or appointments made on a rotational basis from a list compiled without regard to political contributions.

[4]   The term "lawyer or law firm" includes a political action committee or other entity owned or controlled by a lawyer or law firm.

[5]   Political contributions are for the purpose of obtaining or being considered for a government legal engagement or appointment by a judge if, but for the desire to be considered for the legal engagement or appointment, the lawyer or law firm would not have made or solicited the contributions. The purpose may be determined by an examination of the circumstances in which the contributions occur. For example, one or more contributions that in the aggregate are substantial in relation to other contributions by lawyers or law firms, made for the benefit of an official in a position to influence award of a government legal engagement, and followed by an award of the legal engagement to the contributing or soliciting lawyer or the lawyer's firm would support an inference that the purpose of the contributions was to obtain the engagement, absent other factors that weigh against existence of the proscribed purpose. Those factors may include among others that the contribution or solicitation was made to further a political, social, or economic interest or because of an existing personal, family, or professional relationship with a candidate.

[6]   If a lawyer makes or solicits a political contribution under circumstances that constitute bribery or another crime, Rule 8.4(b) is implicated.

MAINTAINING THE INTEGRITY OF THE PROFESSION

RULE 8.1: BAR ADMISSION AND DISCIPLINARY MATTERS

An applicant for admission to the bar, or a lawyer in connection with a bar admission application or in connection with a disciplinary matter, shall not:

(a)   knowingly make a false statement of material fact; or

(b) fail to disclose a fact necessary to correct a misapprehension known by the person to have arisen in the matter, or knowingly fail to respond to a lawful demand for information from an admissions or disciplinary authority, except that this rule does not require disclosure of information otherwise protected by Rule 1.6.

Comment

[1]   The duty imposed by this Rule extends to persons seeking admission to the bar as well as to lawyers. Hence, if a person makes a

material false statement in connection with an application for admission, it may be the basis for subsequent disciplinary action if the person is admitted, and in any event may be relevant in a subsequent admission application. The duty imposed by this Rule applies to a lawyer's own admission or discipline as well as that of others. Thus, it is a separate professional offense for a lawyer to knowingly make a misrepresentation or omission in connection with a disciplinary investigation of the lawyer's own conduct. Paragraph (b) of this Rule also requires correction of any prior misstatement in the matter that the applicant or lawyer may have made and affirmative clarification of any misunderstanding on the part of the admissions or disciplinary authority of which the person involved becomes aware.

[2] This Rule is subject to the provisions of the Fifth Amendment of the United States Constitution and corresponding provisions of state constitutions. A person relying on such a provision in response to a question, however, should do so openly and not use the right of nondisclosure as a justification for failure to comply with this Rule.

[3] A lawyer representing an applicant for admission to the bar, or representing a lawyer who is the subject of a disciplinary inquiry or proceeding, is governed by the rules applicable to the client-lawyer relationship, including Rule 1.6 and, in some cases, Rule 3.3.

RULE 8.2: JUDICIAL AND LEGAL OFFICIALS

(a) A lawyer shall not make a statement that the lawyer knows to be false or with reckless disregard as to its truth or falsity concerning the qualifications or integrity of a judge, adjudicatory officer or public legal officer, or of a candidate for election or appointment to judicial or legal office.

(b) A lawyer who is a candidate for judicial office shall comply with the applicable provisions of the Code of Judicial Conduct.

Comment

[1] Assessments by lawyers are relied on in evaluating the professional or personal fitness of persons being considered for election or appointment to judicial office and to public legal offices, such as attorney general, prosecuting attorney and public defender. Expressing honest and candid opinions on such matters contributes to improving the administration of justice. Conversely, false statements by a lawyer can unfairly undermine public confidence in the administration of justice.

[2] When a lawyer seeks judicial office, the lawyer should be bound by applicable limitations on political activity.

[3] To maintain the fair and independent administration of justice, lawyers are encouraged to continue traditional efforts to defend judges and courts unjustly criticized.

RULE 8.3: REPORTING PROFESSIONAL MISCONDUCT

(a) A lawyer who knows that another lawyer has committed a violation of the Rules of Professional Conduct that raises a substantial question as to that lawyer's honesty, trustworthiness or fitness as a lawyer in other respects, shall inform the appropriate professional authority.

(b) A lawyer who knows that a judge has committed a violation of applicable rules of judicial conduct that raises a substantial

question as to the judge's fitness for office shall inform the appropriate authority.

(c) This Rule does not require disclosure of information otherwise protected by Rule 1.6 or information gained by a lawyer or judge while participating in an approved lawyers assistance program.

Comment

[1]   Self-regulation of the legal profession requires that members of the profession initiate disciplinary investigation when they know of a violation of the Rules of Professional Conduct. Lawyers have a similar obligation with respect to judicial misconduct. An apparently isolated violation may indicate a pattern of misconduct that only a disciplinary investigation can uncover. Reporting a violation is especially important where the victim is unlikely to discover the offense.

[2]   A report about misconduct is not required where it would involve violation of Rule 1.6. However, a lawyer should encourage a client to consent to disclosure where prosecution would not substantially prejudice the client's interests.

[3]   If a lawyer were obliged to report every violation of the Rules, the failure to report any violation would itself be a professional offense. Such a requirement existed in many jurisdictions but proved to be unenforceable. This Rule limits the reporting obligation to those offenses that a self-regulating profession must vigorously endeavor to prevent. A measure of judgment is, therefore, required in complying with the provisions of this Rule. The term "substantial" refers to the seriousness of the possible offense and not the quantum of evidence of which the lawyer is aware. A report should be made to the bar disciplinary agency unless some other agency, such as a peer review agency, is more appropriate in the circumstances. Similar considerations apply to the reporting of judicial misconduct.

[4]   The duty to report professional misconduct does not apply to a lawyer retained to represent a lawyer whose professional conduct is in question. Such a situation is governed by the Rules applicable to the client-lawyer relationship.

[5]   Information about a lawyer's or judge's misconduct or fitness may be received by a lawyer in the course of that lawyer's participation in an approved lawyers or judges assistance program. In that circumstance, providing for an exception to the reporting requirements of paragraphs (a) and (b) of this Rule encourages lawyers and judges to seek treatment through such a program. Conversely, without such an exception, lawyers and judges may hesitate to seek assistance from these programs, which may then result in additional harm to their professional careers and additional injury to the welfare of clients and the public. These Rules do not otherwise address the confidentiality of information received by a lawyer or judge participating in an approved lawyers assistance program; such an obligation, however, may be imposed by the rules of the program or other law.

RULE 8.4: MISCONDUCT

It is professional misconduct for a lawyer to:

(a) violate or attempt to violate the Rules of Professional Conduct, knowingly assist or induce another to do so, or do so through the acts of another;

(b) commit a criminal act that reflects adversely on the lawyer's honesty, trustworthiness or fitness as a lawyer in other respects;

(c) engage in conduct involving dishonesty, fraud, deceit or misrepresentation;

(d) engage in conduct that is prejudicial to the administration of justice;

(e) state or imply an ability to influence improperly a government agency or official or to achieve results by means that violate the Rules of Professional Conduct or other law; or

(f) knowingly assist a judge or judicial officer in conduct that is a violation of applicable rules of judicial conduct or other law.

(g) engage in a conduct that the lawyer knows or reasonably should know is harassment or discrimination on the basis of race, sex, religion, national origin, ethnicity, disability, age, sexual orientation, gender identity, marital status or socioeconomic status in conduct related to the practice of law. This paragraph does not limit the ability of a lawyer to accept, decline or withdraw from a representation in accordance with Rule 1.16. This paragraph does not preclude legitimate advice or advocacy consistent with these Rules.

Comment

[1] Lawyers are subject to discipline when they violate or attempt to violate the Rules of Professional Conduct, knowingly assist or induce another to do so or do so through the acts of another, as when they request or instruct an agent to do so on the lawyer's behalf. Paragraph (a), however, does not prohibit a lawyer from advising a client concerning action the client is legally entitled to take.

[2] Many kinds of illegal conduct reflect adversely on fitness to practice law, such as offenses involving fraud and the offense of willful failure to file an income tax return. However, some kinds of offenses carry no such implication. Traditionally, the distinction was drawn in terms of offenses involving "moral turpitude." That concept can be construed to include offenses concerning some matters of personal morality, such as adultery and comparable offenses, that have no specific connection to fitness for the practice of law. Although a lawyer is personally answerable to the entire criminal law, a lawyer should be professionally answerable only for offenses that indicate lack of those characteristics relevant to law practice. Offenses involving violence, dishonesty, breach of trust, or serious interference with the administration of justice are in that category. A pattern of repeated offenses, even ones of minor significance when considered separately, can indicate indifference to legal obligation.

[3] Discrimination and harassment by lawyers in violation of paragraph (g) undermine confidence in the legal profession and the legal system. Such discrimination includes harmful verbal or physical conduct that manifests bias or prejudice towards others. Harassment includes sexual harassment and derogatory or demeaning verbal or physical conduct. Sexual harassment includes unwelcome sexual advances, requests for sexual favors, and other unwelcome verbal or physical conduct of a sexual nature. The substantive law of antidiscrimination and anti-harassment statutes and case law may guide application of paragraph (g).

[4]   Conduct related to the practice of law includes representing clients; interacting with witnesses, coworkers, court personnel, lawyers and others while engaged in the practice of law; operating or managing a law firm or law practice; and participating in bar association, business or social activities in connection with the practice of law. Lawyers may engage in conduct undertaken to promote diversity and inclusion without violating this Rule by, for example, implementing initiatives aimed at recruiting, hiring, retaining and advancing diverse employees or sponsoring diverse law student organizations.

[5]   A trial judge's finding that peremptory challenges were exercised on a discriminatory basis does not alone establish a violation of paragraph (g). A lawyer does not violate paragraph (g) by limiting the scope or subject matter of the lawyer's practice or by limiting the lawyer's practice to members of underserved populations in accordance with these Rules and other law. A lawyer may charge and collect reasonable fees and expenses for a representation. Rule 1.5(a). Lawyers also should be mindful of their professional obligations under Rule 6.2 not to avoid appointments from a tribunal except for good cause. See Rule 6.2(a), (b) and (c). A lawyer's representation of a client does not constitute an endorsement by the lawyer of the client's views or activities. See Rule 1.2(b).

[6]   A lawyer may refuse to comply with an obligation imposed by law upon a good faith belief that no valid obligation exists. The provisions of Rule 1.2(d) concerning a good faith challenge to the validity, scope, meaning or application of the law apply to challenges of legal regulation of the practice of law.

[7]   Lawyers holding public office assume legal responsibilities going beyond those of other citizens. A lawyer's abuse of public office can suggest an inability to fulfill the professional role of lawyers. The same is true of abuse of positions of private trust such as trustee, executor, administrator, guardian, agent and officer, director or manager of a corporation or other organization.

RULE 8.5: DISCIPLINARY AUTHORITY; CHOICE OF LAW

(a)   Disciplinary Authority. A lawyer admitted to practice in this jurisdiction is subject to the disciplinary authority of this jurisdiction, regardless of where the lawyer's conduct occurs. A lawyer not admitted in this jurisdiction is also subject to the disciplinary authority of this jurisdiction if the lawyer provides or offers to provide any legal services in this jurisdiction. A lawyer may be subject to the disciplinary authority of both this jurisdiction and another jurisdiction for the same conduct.

(b)   Choice of Law. In any exercise of the disciplinary authority of this jurisdiction, the rules of professional conduct to be applied shall be as follows:

(1)   for conduct in connection with a matter pending before a tribunal, the rules of the jurisdiction in which the tribunal sits, unless the rules of the tribunal provide otherwise; and

(2)   for any other conduct, the rules of the jurisdiction in which the lawyer's conduct occurred, or, if the predominant effect of the conduct is in a different jurisdiction, the rules of that jurisdiction shall be applied to the conduct. A lawyer shall not be subject to discipline if the lawyer's conduct conforms to the rules of a jurisdiction in which the lawyer reasonably

believes the predominant effect of the lawyer's conduct will occur.

Comment

Disciplinary Authority

[1]   It is longstanding law that the conduct of a lawyer admitted to practice in this jurisdiction is subject to the disciplinary authority of this jurisdiction. Extension of the disciplinary authority of this jurisdiction to other lawyers who provide or offer to provide legal services in this jurisdiction is for the protection of the citizens of this jurisdiction. Reciprocal enforcement of a jurisdiction's disciplinary findings and sanctions will further advance the purposes of this Rule. See, Rules 6 and 22, ABA *Model Rules for Lawyer Disciplinary Enforcement.* A lawyer who is subject to the disciplinary authority of this jurisdiction under Rule 8.5(a) appoints an official to be designated by this Court to receive service of process in this jurisdiction. The fact that the lawyer is subject to the disciplinary authority of this jurisdiction may be a factor in determining whether personal jurisdiction may be asserted over the lawyer for civil matters.

Choice of Law

[2]   A lawyer may be potentially subject to more than one set of rules of professional conduct which impose different obligations. The lawyer may be licensed to practice in more than one jurisdiction with differing rules, or may be admitted to practice before a particular court with rules that differ from those of the jurisdiction or jurisdictions in which the lawyer is licensed to practice. Additionally, the lawyer's conduct may involve significant contacts with more than one jurisdiction.

[3]   Paragraph (b) seeks to resolve such potential conflicts. Its premise is that minimizing conflicts between rules, as well as uncertainty about which rules are applicable, is in the best interest of both clients and the profession (as well as the bodies having authority to regulate the profession). Accordingly, it takes the approach of (i) providing that any particular conduct of a lawyer shall be subject to only one set of rules of professional conduct (ii) making the determination of which set of rules applies to particular conduct as straightforward as possible, consistent with recognition of appropriate regulatory interests of relevant jurisdictions, and (iii) providing protection from discipline for lawyers who act reasonably in the face of uncertainty.

[4]   Paragraph (b)(1) provides that as to a lawyer's conduct relating to a proceeding pending before a tribunal, the lawyer shall be subject only to the rules of professional conduct of that tribunal. As to all other conduct, including conduct in anticipation of a proceeding not yet pending before a tribunal, paragraph (b)(2) provides that a lawyer shall be subject to the rules of the jurisdiction in which the lawyer's conduct occurred, or, if the predominant effect of the conduct is in another jurisdiction, the rules of that jurisdiction shall be applied to the conduct. In the case of conduct in anticipation of a proceeding that is likely to be before a tribunal, the predominant effect of such conduct could be where the conduct occurred, where the tribunal sits or in another jurisdiction.

[5]   When a lawyer's conduct involves significant contacts with more than one jurisdiction, it may not be clear whether the predominant effect of the lawyer's conduct will occur in a jurisdiction other than the one in which the conduct occurred. So long as the lawyer's conduct conforms to the rules of a jurisdiction in which the lawyer reasonably believes the predominant effect will occur, the lawyer shall not be subject to discipline under this Rule. With

respect to conflicts of interest, in determining a lawyer's reasonable belief under paragraph (b)(2), a written agreement between the lawyer and client that reasonably specifies a particular jurisdiction as within the scope of that paragraph may be considered if the agreement was obtained with the client's informed consent confirmed in the agreement.

[6] If two admitting jurisdictions were to proceed against a lawyer for the same conduct, they should, applying this rule, identify the same governing ethics rules. They should take all appropriate steps to see that they do apply the same rule to the same conduct, and in all events should avoid proceeding against a lawyer on the basis of two inconsistent rules.

[7] The choice of law provision applies to lawyers engaged in transnational practice, unless international law, treaties or other agreements between competent regulatory authorities in the affected jurisdictions provide otherwise.

INDEX TO MODEL RULES

A

Appointed counsel,
    Accepting appointments, Rule 6.2
    Endorsement of client's views, Rule 1.2(b)
    Requirement of competence, Rule 1.1
    Withdrawal by, Rule 1.16 (Comment)

Arbitrator,
    Disqualification of, Rule 1.12
    Former arbitrator negotiating for private employment, Rule 1.12(b)
    Serving as, Rule 2.4

Attorney-client privilege,
    Distinguished from confidentiality rule, Rule 1.6 (Comment)

Attorney General,
    Authority of, Scope

Authority of lawyer,
    Decisionmaking authority, Rule 1.2(a)
    Government lawyer, Scope

Autonomy of legal profession, Preamble

B

Belief,
    Defined, Rule 1.0(a)

Believes,
    Defined, Rule 1.0(a)

Business affairs of lawyer,
    Duty to conduct in compliance with law, Preamble
    Transaction with client, Rule 1.8(a)

C

Candor toward the tribunal,
    Requirements of, Rule 3.3

Cause of action,
    Violation of Rules as basis for, Scope

Choice of Law, Rule 8.5(b)

Civil disobedience,
    To test validity of statute, Rule 1.2 (Comment)

Civil liability,
    Violation of Rules as basis for, Scope

Class actions,
    Notice to members, Rule 7.2 (Comment)

Client-lawyer relationship,
    Existence of, defined by substantive law, Scope

Client's security fund,
    Participation in, Rule 1.15 (Comment)

F

G

Gender identity discrimination, Rule 8.4(g)

Gift,
    To lawyer by client, Rule 1.8(c)

Government agency,
    Representation of, Rule 1.13 (Comment)

Government lawyer,
    Authority established by constitution, statutes and common law, Scope
    Conflict of interest, Rule 1.7 (Comment)
    Representing multiple clients, Scope
    Subject to rules, Rule 1.11 (Comment)

H

Harass,
    Law's procedures used to, Preamble

I

Impartiality and decorum of the tribunal, Rule 3.5

Imputed disqualification,
    General rule, Rule 1.10
    Government lawyers, Rule 1.11 (Comment)
    Witness, when member of firm serves as, Rule 3.7(b)

Incompetent client,
    Appointment of guardian for, Rule 1.14(b)
    Representation of, Rule 1.14(a)

Independence of the legal profession, Preamble

Independent professional judgment,
    Duty to exercise, Rule 2.1; Rule 5.4

Indigent client,
    Paying court costs and expenses on behalf of, Rule 1.8(e)(2)

Informed Consent,
    Affecting conflict of interest, Rule 1.7 (Comment)
    Defined as, Terminology
    Required for evaluation, Rule 2.3(b)
    Required if former judge, arbitrator, mediator, or third-party neutral, Rule 1.12(a)
    Required to inform client on basis of, Rule 1.42(a)(1)
    That of former clients, Rule 1.9(a)

Insurance representation,
    Conflict of interest, Rule 1.8(f) (Comment 11)

Intermediary,
    Lawyer as, Preamble

Intimidate,
    Law's procedures used to, Preamble

J

Judges,
    Appointments by judges and political contributions, Rule 7.6
    Duty to show respect for, Preamble
    Ex parte communication with, Rule 3.5(b)
    Former judge, disqualification, Rule 1.12
    Improper influence on, Rule 3.5(a)
    Reporting misconduct by, Rule 8.3(b)
    Statements about, Rule 8.2

Juror,
    Improper influence on, Rule 3.5(a)

Jury trial,
    Client's right to waive, Rule 1.2(a)

K

Know, Knows, Knowingly,
    Defined as, Rule 1.0(f)
    Legal knowledge required for competence, Rule 1.1

L

Law clerk,
    Negotiating for private employment, Rule 1.12(b)

Law firm,
    Ancillary services, Rule 5.7
    Defined, Terminology
    Nonlawyer assistants, responsibility for, Rule 5.3
    Responsibility of partner or supervisory lawyer, Rule 5.1
    Subordinate lawyer, responsibility of, Rule 5.2

Law reform activities,
    Affecting clients' interests, Rule 6.4

Law-related services, Rule 5.7

Lawyer referral service,
    Advertising by way of, Rule 7.2(c)(2)
    Financial support of, Rule 6.1 (Comment)
    Legal aid and, Rule 6.1 (Comment)

Legal education,
    Duty to work to strengthen, Preamble

Legislature,
    Appearance before on behalf of client, Rule 3.9

Letterheads,
    False or misleading, Rule 7.1 (Comment)
    Jurisdictional limitations of members, Rule 7.1 (Comment)
    Public officials, Rule 7.1 (Comment)

Liability to client,
    Agreements limiting, Rule 1.8(h)

O

Objectives of the representation,
    Client's right to determine, Rule 1.2(a)
    Lawyer's right to limit, Rule 1.2(c)

Opposing party,
    Communications with represented party, Rule 4.2
    Duty of fairness to, Rule 3.4

Organization, representation of,
    Board of directors, lawyer for serving on, Rule 1.7 (Comment)
    Communication with, Rule 1.4 (Comment)
    Conflict of interest, Rule 1.7 (Comment)
    Conflicting interests among officers and employees, Rule 1.7 (Comment)
    Constituents, representing, Rule 1.13(e)
    Identity of client, Rule 1.13(a); Rule 1.13(d)
    Misconduct, client engaged in, Rule 1.13(b)

P

Partner,
    Defined, Rule 1.0(g)

Patent practice,
    Advertising, Rule 7.2 (Comment)

Perjury,
    Criminal defendant, Rule 3.3 (Comment)
    Disclosure of, Rule 3.3(b)

Personal affairs of lawyer,
    Duty to conduct in compliance with law, Preamble

Plea bargain,
    Client's right to accept or reject, Rule 1.2(a)

Pleadings,
    Verification of, Rule 3.3 (Comment)

Peremptory challenges, Rule 8.4 (Comment)

Political contributions to secure legal work, Rule 7.6

Positional conflicts, Rule 1.7 (Comment)

Precedent,
    Failure to disclose to court, Rule 3.3(a)(2)

Prepaid legal services,
    Advertising for, Rule 7.2 (Comment)

Pro bono publico service, Rule 6.1

Procedural law,
    Lawyer's professional responsibilities proscribed by, Preamble

Professional corporation,
    Ownership in, Rule 5.4(d)

Prompt,
    Lawyer's duty to be, Preamble

S

T

Trust accounts,
    Maintain for client funds, Rule 1.15 (Comment)

U

Unauthorized practice of law,
    Assisting in, Rule 5.5(a)
    Engaging in, Rule 5.5(a)
    Foreign lawyers, Rule 5.5(d)

W

Waiver,
    Prosecutor obtaining from criminal defendant, Rule 3.8(c)

Withdrawal,
    Conflict of interest, Rule 1.7 (Comment)
    Discharge, Rule 1.16(a)(3)
    Giving notice of fact of, Rule 1.2, Comment 10; Rule 4.1, Comment 3
    Incapacity, Rule 1.16(a)(2)
    Property of client, Rule 1.16(d)
    When client persists in criminal or fraudulent conduct, Rule 1.2
        (Comment); Rule 1.16(b)(2); Rule 1.13(c); Rule 4.1 Comment

Witness,
    Bribing, Rule 3.4(b)
    Client's right to decide whether to testify, Rule 1.2(a)
    Expenses, payment of, Rule 3.4 (Comment)
    Expert, payment of, Rule 3.4 (Comment)
    Lawyer as, Rule 3.7

Writing,
    Defined as, Rule 1.0(n)

Work product privilege,
    Rule 1.6 (Comment 3); Rule 5.3 (Comment 1)

Z

Zealous representation,
    Opposing party well-represented, Preamble
    Requirement of, Rule 1.3 (Comment)

APPENDIX A

Disclosure of Client Confidences*

One of the most vexing professional liability questions that can confront a lawyer is whether the lawyer may, must, or must not reveal confidential client information. This section focuses on a lawyer's obligations in three key situations: (1) disclosure of client misconduct, (2) disclosure of confidential client information to comply with other law or a court order, and (3) disclosure under Rule 1.13 of an organizational client's confidential information outside the organization. Disclosures that are required or permitted by specific laws—such as money-laundering statutes and directives applicable in the United Kingdom, Europe, or elsewhere—are beyond the scope of this Appendix. In addition, it should be noted that this Appendix does not address other circumstances in which disclosure may be permitted (such as when necessary to litigate a fee dispute, seek legal advice about the lawyer's ethical obligations, or defend a malpractice claim), nor does it discuss inadvertent disclosures.

In general, when a lawyer invokes an exception to the general prohibition against disclosing client confidences, the burden of proof to show that the exception applies may rest with the lawyer. After noting the paucity of authority on this issue from other jurisdictions, the New Hampshire Supreme Court ruled that under Rule 1.6, the lawyer bears the burden of proof to establish that disclosure was necessary to prevent a former client from stealing money from his father's estate. *See In re Lane's Case*, 889 A.2d 3 (N.H. 2005). The court reasoned that putting the burden of proof on the lawyer properly balances the public interest in ensuring the integrity of lawyers with a lawyer's right to avoid discipline when there is justification for making a disclosure not authorized by the client. Maryland has by rule put the burden of establishing a defense on the lawyer in disciplinary proceedings. *See id.* at 12 (citing Md. Rule 16–757(b)). Cases in other jurisdictions have reached the same result, albeit not in cases involving disclosure of confidential information. *See Beery v. State Bar of Cal.*, 739 P.2d 1289, 1294 (Cal. 1987) (lawyer had burden of proving an exception to professional conduct charge for entering into prohibited business transaction with client); *Rodgers v. Comm'n for Lawyer Discip.*, 151 S.W.3d 602, 615 (Tex. App. 2004) (lawyer had burden of proving applicability of exception to disciplinary rule requiring lawyers to file advertisements); *In re Cohen*, 82 P.3d 224, 230 (Wash. 2004) (en banc) (lawyer had burden of proving applicability of exception to disciplinary rule forbidding prejudicial withdrawals).

2.1 Disclosure of Client Misconduct

The chart in Section 2.2 below summarizes key authorities regarding disclosure of client misconduct, including: the relevant provisions of the ABA Model Rules of Professional Conduct; the pertinent state professional conduct rules; and related comments, ethics opinions, and case law. The chart reflects amendments to the Model Rules and the relevant state rules of which we are aware as of early 2018. We have not undertaken to determine the existence or effect of amendments effective after February 1, 2018.

The chart indicates, with citations, whether a lawyer may, must, or must not disclose confidential client information or take some other action, when faced with the following situations:

A. client's intention to commit any crime;

B. client's or other's intention to commit a crime or other act likely to result in death or substantial bodily harm;

C. client's intention to commit a criminal fraud;

D. client's intention to commit a noncriminal fraud (some states interpret criminal statutes broadly, such that virtually any fraud likely to result in injury to the financial interest or property of another would be a crime);

E. client's prior commission of a crime or fraud using the lawyer's services, resulting in injury to the financial interest or property of another party;

F. client's prior or contemporaneous commission of perjury or other fraud on a tribunal; and

G. client's ongoing criminal or fraudulent act.

It must be emphasized that the chart in Section 2.2 below is intended only as a tool to alert lawyers to situations giving rise to questions about disclosure of confidential client information and to direct the reader to the relevant provisions and language in the Model Rules and related authorities. There is no substitute for reading the relevant rule and related authorities. The reader also should consider whether to consult case law from other jurisdictions, as the scarcity of case law in a particular jurisdiction may lead a court to look to cases decided elsewhere.

We recommend using the chart in conjunction with the accompanying notes contained in Section 2.3 below. The notes point out situations in which the applicable rules, relevant ethics opinions, and case law are ambiguous. The notes also mention several subtle distinctions and refinements that emerge when one compares the Model Rules, the rules of any particular state, the local rules of federal district courts, a state's comments and ethics opinions, and case law. For example, the Model Rules permit a lawyer to disclose confidential information to prevent a client crime or fraud that threatens substantial financial harm to others, but only when the lawyer's services are used in connection with the threatened conduct. Several states permit such disclosure without requiring any nexus between the lawyer's services and the potential crime or fraud, however, and many of those states do not require the crime or fraud to threaten "substantial" financial harm. The accompanying notes identify these and many other distinctions.

In general, the *Restatement Third, The Law Governing Lawyers* (2000) supports disclosures of client wrongdoing in the same range of circumstances as do the Model Rules. *See Restatement*, §§ 59–67 (addressing client confidential information and its disclosure), § 120 (discussing disclosure as potential "remedial measure" when lawyer has offered evidence to court, administrative agency, arbitrator, or similar body acting in adjudicative capacity and "comes to know" that evidence is false).

2.2   Chart on Disclosure of Client Misconduct

A.   Client's intention to commit any crime.

B.   Client's or other's intention to commit a crime or other act likely to result in death or substantial bodily harm.*

C.   Client's intention to commit a criminal fraud.

D.   Client's intention to commit a noncriminal fraud.

E.   Client's prior commission of a financial crime or fraud using the lawyer's services.

F.   Client's prior or contemporaneous commission of perjury or other fraud on a tribunal.

G.   Client's ongoing criminal or fraudulent act.

* In certain states, whether a lawyer must, may, or must not disclose depends on whether a crime is involved. If so, some of these states require that the lawyer must disclose, while others provide that the lawyer may disclose. In contrast, if no crime is involved, some of these states provide that the lawyer may disclose, while others provide that the lawyer must not disclose.

	INTENT TO COMMIT/PREVENTION				RECTIFICATION		
	A	B	C	D	E	F	G
ABA Model Rule (2010)	Must Not 1.6(a)	May 1.6(b)(1)	May 1.6(b)(2)[1]	May 1.6(b)(2)[1]	May 1.6(b)(3)[2]	Must 3.3(a)(1), (a)(3) and (b)[3]	Must 4.1(b)[4] *See also* 1.2(d)
Alabama	Must Not 1.6(a)	May, if crime 1.6(b)(1) Must Not, if no crime 1.6(a)	Must Not 1.6(a)	Must Not 1.6(a)	Must Not 1.6(a)	Must 3.3(a)(3) and (b)	Must 4.1(b)[4] *See also* 1.2(d)
Alaska	Must Not 1.6(a)	May 1.6(b)(1)	May 1.6(b)(2)[1]	May 1.6(b)(2)[1]	May 1.6(b)(3)[2]	Must 3.3(a)(3) and (b)[3]	Must 4.1(b)[4] *See also* 1.2(d)
Arizona	May 1.6(c)	Must, if crime 1.6(b) May, if no crime 1.6(d)(6)	May 1.6(d)(1)	May 1.6(d)(1)	May 1.6(d)(2)[2]	Must 3.3(a)(3) and (b)[5]	Must 4.1(b)[4] *See also* 1.2(d)
Arkansas	May 1.6(b)(1)	May, if crime 1.6(b)(1) Must Not, if no crime 1.6(a)	May 1.6(b)(1)	May 1.6(b)(2)	May 1.6(b)(3)	Must 3.3(a)(1), (a)(3) and (b)[3]	Must 4.1(b)[4] *See also* 1.2(d)

A.   Client's intention to commit any crime.

B.   Client's or other's intention to commit a crime or other act likely to result in death or substantial bodily harm.*

C.   Client's intention to commit a criminal fraud.

D.   Client's intention to commit a noncriminal fraud.

E.   Client's prior commission of a financial crime or fraud using the lawyer's services.

F.   Client's prior or contemporaneous commission of perjury or other fraud on a tribunal.

G.   Client's ongoing criminal or fraudulent act.

* In certain states, whether a lawyer must, may, or must not disclose depends on whether a crime is involved. If so, some of these states require that the lawyer must disclose, while others provide that the lawyer may disclose. In contrast, if no crime is involved, some of these states provide that the lawyer may disclose, while others provide that the lawyer must not disclose.

	INTENT TO COMMIT/PREVENTION				RECTIFICATION		
	A	**B**	**C**	**D**	**E**	**F**	**G**
California	Must Not 3–100(A) § 6068(e) Business and Professions Code[6]	May, if crime 3–100(B) § 6068(e)(2) Business and Professions Code[6] Must Not, if no crime 3–100(A)	Must Not 3–100(A) § 6068(e) Business and Professions Code[6]	Must Not 3–100(A) § 6068(e) Business and Professions Code[6]	Must Not 3–100(A) § 6068(e) Business and Professions Code[6]	Must Not 3–100(A) § 6068(e) Business and Professions Code[6]	Must Not 3–100(A) § 6068(e) Business and Professions Code[6]
Colorado	May 1.6(b)(2)	May 1.6(b)(1)	May 1.6(b)(2)	May 1.6(b)(3)	May 1.6(b)(4)	Must 3.3(a)(3)[3] and (b)	Must 4.1(b)[4] *See also* 1.2(d)
Connecticut	Must Not 1.6(a)	Must 1.6(b)	May 1.6(c)(1)	May 1.6(c)(1)	May 1.6(c)(2)	Must 3.3(a)(3)[7] and (b)	Must 4.1(2)[4] *See also* 1.2(d)
Delaware	Must Not 1.6(a)	May 1.6(b)(1)	May 1.6(b)(2)	May 1.6(b)(2)	May 1.6(b)(3)[2]	Must 3.3(a)(3) and (b)	Must 4.1(b)[4] *See also* 1.2(d)
District of Columbia	Must Not 1.6(a)(1)[8]	May, if crime 1.6(c)(1) Must Not, if no crime 1.6(a)	May 1.6(d)(1)	May 1.6(d)(1)	May 1.6(d)(2)	May 3.3(a)(1) and (d); 1.6(c)(2) and (d)[8]	Must 1.6(d), 4.1(b)[4] *See also* 1.2(e)
Florida	Must 4–1.6(b)(1)	Must 4–1.6(b)(2)[9]	Must 4–1.6(b)(1)	Must Not 4–1.6(a)	Must Not 4–1.6(a)[10]	Must 4–3.3(a)(2) and (b)	Must 4–4.1(b)[4] *See also* 4–1.2(d)
Georgia	May 1.6(b)(1)(i) [11]	May 1.6(b)(1)(ii) [11]	May 1.6(b)(1)(i) [11]	Must Not 1.6(a)	Must Not 1.6(a)	Must 3.3(a)(2) and (b)	Must 4.1(b)[4] *See also* 1.2(d)

A. Client's intention to commit any crime.
B. Client's or other's intention to commit a crime or other act likely to result in death or substantial bodily harm.*
C. Client's intention to commit a criminal fraud.
D. Client's intention to commit a noncriminal fraud.
E. Client's prior commission of a financial crime or fraud using the lawyer's services.
F. Client's prior or contemporaneous commission of perjury or other fraud on a tribunal.
G. Client's ongoing criminal or fraudulent act.

* In certain states, whether a lawyer must, may, or must not disclose depends on whether a crime is involved. If so, some of these states require that the lawyer must disclose, while others provide that the lawyer may disclose. In contrast, if no crime is involved, some of these states provide that the lawyer may disclose, while others provide that the lawyer must not disclose.

	INTENT TO COMMIT/PREVENTION				RECTIFICATION		
	A	**B**	**C**	**D**	**E**	**F**	**G**
Hawaii	Must Not 1.6(a)	May, if crime 1.6(b)(1) Must Not, if no crime 1.6(a)	May 1.6(b)(1)	May 1.6(b)(1)	May 1.6(b)(3)	Must 3.3(a)(2) and (b)	Must 4.1(b)[12] *See also* 1.2(d)
Idaho	May 1.6(b)(1)	May 1.6(b)(2)	May 1.6(b)(1)	Must Not 1.6(a)	May 1.6(b)(3)[2]	Must 3.3(a)(3) and (b)	Must 4.1(b)[4] *See also* 1.2(d)
Illinois	May 1.6(b)(1)	Must 1.6(c)	May 1.6(b)(2)	May 1.6(b)(2)	May 1.6(b)(3)[13]	Must 3.3(a)(1), (a)(3), and (b)[12]	Must 4.1(b)[4] *See also* 1.2(d)
Indiana	Must Not 1.6(a)	May 1.6(b)(1)[14]	May 1.6(b)(2)	May 1.6(b)(2)	May 1.6(b)(3)[2]	Must 3.3(a)(3) and (b)	Must 4.1(b)[4] *See also* 1.2(d)
Iowa	Must Not 32:1.6(a)	Must 32:1.6(c)	May 32:1.6(b)(2)	May 32:1.6(b)(2)	May 32:1.6(b)(3)[2]	Must 32:3.3(a)(3)[3] and (b)	Must 32:4.1(b)[4] *See also* 32:1.2(d)
Kansas	May 1.6(b)(1)	May, if crime 1.6(b)(1) Must Not, if no crime 1.6(a)	May 1.6(b)(1)	Must Not 1.6(a)	Must Not 1.6(a)	Must 3.3(a)(3)[3] and (b)	Must 4.1(b)[4] *See also* 1.2(d)
Kentucky	Must Not SCR 3.130 (1.6(a))	May SCR 3.130 (1.6(b))	Must Not SCR 3.130 (1.6(a))	Must Not SCR 3.130 (1.6(a))	Must Not SCR 3.130 (1.6(a))	Must SCR 3.130 (3.3(a)(3) and (b))	Must SCR 3.130 (4.1(b)) *See also* 1.2(d)[15]
Louisiana	Must Not 1.6(a)	May 1.6(b)(1)	May 1.6(b)(2)	May 1.6(b)(2)	May 1.6(b)(3)[2]	Must 3.3(a)(3) and (b)[3]	Must 4.1(b)[4] *See also* 1.2(d)

A. Client's intention to commit any crime.

B. Client's or other's intention to commit a crime or other act likely to result in death or substantial bodily harm.*

C. Client's intention to commit a criminal fraud.

D. Client's intention to commit a noncriminal fraud.

E. Client's prior commission of a financial crime or fraud using the lawyer's services.

F. Client's prior or contemporaneous commission of perjury or other fraud on a tribunal.

G. Client's ongoing criminal or fraudulent act.

* In certain states, whether a lawyer must, may, or must not disclose depends on whether a crime is involved. If so, some of these states require that the lawyer must disclose, while others provide that the lawyer may disclose. In contrast, if no crime is involved, some of these states provide that the lawyer may disclose, while others provide that the lawyer must not disclose.

	INTENT TO COMMIT/PREVENTION				RECTIFICATION		
	A	B	C	D	E	F	G
Maine	Must Not 1.6(a)	May 1.6(b)(1)	May 1.6(b)(2)	May 1.6(b)(2)	May 1.6(b)(3)[2, 16]	Must 3.3(a)(3) and (b)[3]	Must 4.1(b)[4] See also 1.2(e)
Maryland	Must Not 1.6(a)	May 1.6(b)(1)	May 1.6(b)(2)	May 1.6(b)(2)	May 1.6(b)(3)[2]	Must 3.3(a)(2) [17] and (b)	Must 4.1(a)(2) and (b)[12] See also 1.2(d)
Massachusetts	Must Not 1.6(a)	May 1.6(b)(1)[18]	May 1.6(b)(2)	May 1.6(b)(2)	May 1.6(b)(3)	Must 3.3(a)(2)[19] and (b)	Must 4.1(b)[4] See also 1.2(d)
Michigan	May 1.6(c)(4)	May, if crime 1.6(c)(4) Must Not, if no crime 1.6(b)(1)	May 1.6(c)(4)	Must Not 1.6(b)(1)	May 1.6(c)(3)	Must 3.3(a)(1)[20] (a)(3) and (b)	May 1.6(c)(3) See also 1.2(c)
Minnesota	May 1.6(b)(4)	May 1.6(b)(6)	May 1.6(b)(4)	May 1.6(b)(4)	May 1.6(b)(5)	Must 3.3(a)(3) and (b)	May 1.6(b)(4) See also 1.2(d)
Mississippi	Must Not 1.6(a)	May 1.6(b)(1)	May 1.6(b)(2)	May 1.6(b)(2)	May 1.6(b)(3)	Must 3.3(a)(2) and (b)	Must 4.1(b)[4] See also 1.2(d)
Missouri	Must Not 1.6(a)	May 1.6(b)(1)	Must Not 1.6(a)	Must Not 1.6(a)	Must Not 1.6(a)	Must 3.3(a)(3) and (b)[3]	Must 4.1(b)[4] See also 1.2(d)
Montana	Must Not 1.6(a)	May 1.6(b)(1)	Must Not 1.6(a)	Must Not 1.6(a)	Must Not 1.6(a)	Must 3.3(a)(3) and (b)[21]	Must 4.1(b)[4] See also 1.2(d)

A.	Client's intention to commit any crime.
B.	Client's or other's intention to commit a crime or other act likely to result in death or substantial bodily harm.*
C.	Client's intention to commit a criminal fraud.
D.	Client's intention to commit a noncriminal fraud.
E.	Client's prior commission of a financial crime or fraud using the lawyer's services.
F.	Client's prior or contemporaneous commission of perjury or other fraud on a tribunal.
G.	Client's ongoing criminal or fraudulent act.

* In certain states, whether a lawyer must, may, or must not disclose depends on whether a crime is involved. If so, some of these states require that the lawyer must disclose, while others provide that the lawyer may disclose. In contrast, if no crime is involved, some of these states provide that the lawyer may disclose, while others provide that the lawyer must not disclose.

	INTENT TO COMMIT/PREVENTION				RECTIFICATION		
	A	**B**	**C**	**D**	**E**	**F**	**G**
Nebraska	May 1.6(b)(1)	May 1.6(b)(1)	May 1.6(b)(1)	Must Not 1.6(a)	Must Not 1.6(a)	Must 3.3(a)(3) and (b)	Must 4.1(b)[4] *See also* 1.2(f)
Nevada	May 1.6(b)(2)	Must, if crime 1.6(d) May, if no crime 1.6(b)(1)	May 1.6(b)(2)	May 1.6(b)(2)	May 1.6(b)(3)	Must 3.3(a)(3) and (b)	Must Rule 4.1(b)[4] *See also* 1.2(d)
New Hampshire	Must Not 1.6(a)	May 1.6(b)(1)[22]	May 1.6(b)(1)	Must Not 1.6(a)	Must Not 1.6(a)	Must 3.3(a)(3) and (b)[23]	Must 4.1(b)[4] *See also* 1.2(d)
New Jersey	Must Not 1.6(a)	Must, if crime or fraud 1.6(b)(1)[24] May, if harm to client 1.6(d)(3) Must Not, if no crime or fraud or harm to client 1.6(a)	Must 1.6(b)(1)[24]	Must 1.6(b)(1)[24]	May 1.6(d)[38] (1)[24]	Must 3.3(a)(2)[25] and (b)	Must 4.1(a) and (b)[12] *See also* 1.2(d)
New Mexico	Must Not 16–106(A)	May 16–106(B)(1)	May 16–106(B)(2)	May 16–106(B)(2)	May 16–106(B)(3)	Must 16–303(A)(3) and (B)	Must 16–401(B)[4] *See also* 16–102(D)
New York	May 1.6(b)(2)	May 1.6(b)(1)	May 1.6(b)(2)	Must Not 1.6(a)	May 1.6(b)(3)[26]	Must 3.3(a)(3)[26] and (b)	May 1.6(b)(3)[26] *See also* 1.2(d)

A.	Client's intention to commit any crime.	
B.	Client's or other's intention to commit a crime or other act likely to result in death or substantial bodily harm.*	
C.	Client's intention to commit a criminal fraud.	
D.	Client's intention to commit a noncriminal fraud.	
E.	Client's prior commission of a financial crime or fraud using the lawyer's services.	
F.	Client's prior or contemporaneous commission of perjury or other fraud on a tribunal.	
G.	Client's ongoing criminal or fraudulent act.	

* In certain states, whether a lawyer must, may, or must not disclose depends on whether a crime is involved. If so, some of these states require that the lawyer must disclose, while others provide that the lawyer may disclose. In contrast, if no crime is involved, some of these states provide that the lawyer may disclose, while others provide that the lawyer must not disclose.

	INTENT TO COMMIT/PREVENTION				RECTIFICATION		
	A	B	C	D	E	F	G
North Carolina	May 1.6(b)(2)	May 1.6(b)(3)	May 1.6(b)(4)[27]	May 1.6(b)(4)[27]	May 1.6(b)(4)[27]	Must 3.3(a)(3) and (b)	May 1.6(b)(4)[27] *See also* 1.2(d)
North Dakota	Must Not 1.6(a)	Must 1.6(b)	May 1.6(c)(1)	May 1.6(c)(1)	May 1.6(c)(2)	Must Not 1.6(a) and 3.3(a)(3)	May 1.6(c)(2) *See also* 1.2(d)
Ohio	May 1.6(b)(2)	May 1.6(b)(1)	May 1.6(b)(2)	Must Not 1.6(a)	May 1.6(b)(3)	Must 3.3(a)(3) and (b)[28]	Must 4.1(b)[4] *See also* 1.2(d) and 1.6(c)
Oklahoma	May 1.6(b)(2)(i)	May 1.6(b)(1)	May 1.6(b)(2)(i)	May 1.6(b)(2)(ii)	May 1.6(b)(3)	Must 3.3(a)(3) and (b)[3]	Must 4.1(b)[4] *See also* 1.2(d)
Oregon	May 1.6(b)(1)	May 1.6(b)(2)	May 1.6(b)(1)	Must Not 1.6(a)	Must Not 1.6(a)	Must 3.3(a)(3) and (b)	Must 4.1(b)[4] *See also* 1.2(c)
Pennsylvania	May 1.6(c)(3)[28]	May 1.6(c)(1)	May 1.6(c)(2)	May 1.6(c)(3)	May 1.6(c)(3)	Must 3.3(a)(3)[29] and (b) *See also* 1.6(b)	Must 4.1(b)[4] *See also* 1.2(d)
Rhode Island	Must Not 1.6(a)	May, if crime 1.6(b)(1) Must Not, if no crime 1.6(a)	Must Not 1.6(a)	Must Not 1.6(a)	Must Not 1.6(a)	Must 3.3(a)(3) and (b)[3]	Must 4.1(b)[4] *See also* 1.2(d)
South Carolina	May 1.6(b)(1)	May 1.6(b)(2)	May 1.6(b)(3)	May 1.6(b)(3)	May 1.6(b)(4)	Must 3.3(a)(3) and (b)	Must 4.1(b)[4] *See also* 1.2(d)

A. Client's intention to commit any crime.
B. Client's or other's intention to commit a crime or other act likely to result in death or substantial bodily harm.*
C. Client's intention to commit a criminal fraud.
D. Client's intention to commit a noncriminal fraud.
E. Client's prior commission of a financial crime or fraud using the lawyer's services.
F. Client's prior or contemporaneous commission of perjury or other fraud on a tribunal.
G. Client's ongoing criminal or fraudulent act.

* In certain states, whether a lawyer must, may, or must not disclose depends on whether a crime is involved. If so, some of these states require that the lawyer must disclose, while others provide that the lawyer may disclose. In contrast, if no crime is involved, some of these states provide that the lawyer may disclose, while others provide that the lawyer must not disclose.

	INTENT TO COMMIT/PREVENTION				RECTIFICATION		
	A	B	C	D	E	F	G
South Dakota	Must Not 1.6(a)	May, if crime 1.6(b)(1) Must Not, if no crime 1.6(a)	Must Not 1.6(a)	Must Not 1.6(a)	May 1.6(b)(4)	Must 3.3(a)(2) and (b)	Must 4.1(b)[4] *See also* 1.2(d) and 1.6(b)(4)
Tennessee	May 1.6(b)(1)[31]	Must 1.6(c)(1)	May 1.6(b)(1)[31]	Must Withdraw 4.1(b)	Must Withdraw 4.1(c)[31]	Must Seek Withdrawal 3.3(f)[31]	Must Withdraw 4.1(b)[31]
Texas	May 1.05(c)(7)	Must, if crime or fraud 1.05(e) Must Not, if no crime or fraud 1.05(b)	May 1.05(c)(7)	May 1.05(c)(7)	May 1.05(c)(8)	Must 3.03(b)[32]	Must 4.01(b) *See also* 1.02(c)
Utah	Must Not 1.6(a)	May 1.6(b)(1)	May 1.6(b)(2)	May 1.6(b)(2)	May 1.6(b)(3)	Must 3.3(a)(3) and (b)	Must 4.1(b)[4] *See also* 1.2(d)
Vermont	May 1.6(c)(1)	Must, if crime 1.6(b)(1) May, if no crime 1.6(c)(1)	Must 1.6(b)(2)	Must 1.6(b)(2)	Must See 1.6(b)(3)	Must 3.3(a)(3) and (b)	Must 1.6(b)(2)[33]
Virginia	Must 1.6(c)(1) 34	Must, if crime 1.6(c)(1) Must Not, if no crime 1.6(a)	Must 1.6(c)(1) 34	Must Not 1.6(a)	May 1.6(b)(3)	Must 1.6(c)(2) and 3.3(a)(2), (4)	Must 4.1(b)[4] *See also* 1.2(c)

A.   Client's intention to commit any crime.

B.   Client's or other's intention to commit a crime or other act likely to result in death or substantial bodily harm.*

C.   Client's intention to commit a criminal fraud.

D.   Client's intention to commit a noncriminal fraud.

E.   Client's prior commission of a financial crime or fraud using the lawyer's services.

F.   Client's prior or contemporaneous commission of perjury or other fraud on a tribunal.

G.   Client's ongoing criminal or fraudulent act.

* In certain states, whether a lawyer must, may, or must not disclose depends on whether a crime is involved. If so, some of these states require that the lawyer must disclose, while others provide that the lawyer may disclose. In contrast, if no crime is involved, some of these states provide that the lawyer may disclose, while others provide that the lawyer must not disclose.

	INTENT TO COMMIT/PREVENTION				RECTIFICATION		
	A	B	C	D	E	F	G
Washington	May 1.6(b)(2)	Must 1.6(b)(1)	May 1.6(b)(2)	May 1.6(b)(3)	May 1.6(b)(3) and 1.6(b)(7)[35]	Must Not 3.3(a)(2)[36]	Must 4.1(b)[4] *See also* 1.2(d)
West Virginia	Must Not 1.6(a)[37]	May 1.6(b)(1)[37]	May 1.6(b)(2)[37]	May 1.6(b)(2)[37]	May 1.6(b)(3)[37]	Must 3.3(a)(4) and (b)	Must 4.1(b)[4] *See also* 1.2(d)
Wisconsin	Must Not 20:1.6(a)	Must, if crime 20:1.6(b) May, if no crime 20:1.6(c)(1)	Must 20:1.6(b)	Must 20:1.6(b)	May 20:1.6(c)(2)	Must 20:3.3(a)(3) and (b)	Must 20:4.1(a)(2)[4] *See also* 20:1.2(d)
Wyoming	May 1.6(b)(1)	May, if crime 1.6(b)(1) Must Not, if no crime 1.6(a)	May 1.6(b)(1)	May 1.6(b)(2)[38]	May 1.6(b)(2)[38]	Must 3.3(a)(4) and (b)	Must 4.1(b)[4] *See also* 1.2(d)
TOTALS	Must: 2 May: 23 Must Not: 27	Must: 7 May: 28 Must Not: 0 Combin-ation: 17	Must: 5 May: 40 Must Not: 7	Must: 3 May: 30 Must Not: 18 Must With-draw: 1	Must: 1 May: 38 Must Not: 12 Must With-draw: 1	Must: 47 May: 1 Must Not: 3 Must Seek With-drawal: 1	Must: 45 May: 5 Must Not: 1 Must With-draw: 1

2.3   Explanatory Notes to Chart in Section 2.2

(1)   **Model Rule 1.6 and Disclosures to Prevent Client Crimes or Frauds.** Model Rule 1.6(b)(2) permits a lawyer to disclose confidential information to prevent a threatened client crime or fraud that is likely to result in substantial financial harm to others, but only when the lawyer's services are used in connection with the threatened conduct. Some states that permit disclosure of a client's threatened crime or fraud do not require this nexus between the lawyer's services and the threatened conduct.

(2) **Model Rule 1.6 and Disclosures Regarding Prior Client Crimes or Frauds.** Model Rule 1.6(b)(3) permits a lawyer to disclose confidential information to mitigate or rectify the consequences of prior client crimes or frauds that threaten substantial financial harm to others and in which the lawyer's services were used. When "substantial" financial harm is not threatened, however, Model Rule 1.6 prohibits a lawyer from revealing client confidences with respect to a prior crime or fraud. Nevertheless, Comment [16] to the 1983 version of Model Rule 1.6, Comment [10] to Model Rule 1.2, and Comment [3] to Model Rule 4.1, as well as the comments to many state versions of Model Rule 1.6, permit, under some circumstances, what has been referred to as a "noisy withdrawal" from the representation. The idea is that, although the lawyer is prohibited from disclosing any specifics about the client's conduct, the lawyer's resignation, accompanied by the "withdrawal" or "disaffirmance" of the lawyer's previous "opinion, document, affirmation, or the like," will, in most instances, signal the other parties involved in the transaction that the client may be engaged in wrongdoing. The 2003 version of the Model Rules inexplicably omits "noisy withdrawal" from the comments to Model Rule 1.6, but the inclusion of the "noisy withdrawal" comments to the 2003 version of Model Rule 1.2, Comment [10], and Model Rule 4.1, Comment [3], indicates the continued vitality of this concept. *See* ABA Formal Opinion 92–366 (Aug. 8, 1992) (analyzing "noisy withdrawal" concept). Citing the Model Rules, in *United States ex rel. Holmes v. Northrup Grumman*, 642 Fed. Appx. 373 (5th Cir. 2016), the court dismissed a False Claims Act suit initiated by a lawyer and disqualified him from pursuing the claims because he used confidential client information covered by a protective order.

(3) **Disclosing Confidential Client Information to Avoid Perjury or Fraud on a Tribunal under Model Rule 3.3.** The disclosure obligations under Model Rule 3.3 were strengthened in a 2002 amendment to the Rule. Rules 3.3(a) and (b) support the "must disclose" obligation. Model Rule 3.3(c) provides that the duties stated in Model Rules 3.3(a) and (b) apply even if compliance requires disclosure of information otherwise protected by Model Rule 1.6. *See* ABA Formal Opinion 87–353 (Apr. 20, 1987); *see also* ABA Formal Opinion 93–376 (Aug. 6, 1993) (discussing application of Model Rule 3.3(a) to client perjury in pretrial deposition). This obligation continues to "the conclusion of the proceeding." Model Rule 3.3(c), Comment [13] defines the conclusion of the proceeding as a final judgment "affirmed on appeal or the time for review has passed."

(4) **Disclosing Ongoing Crime or Fraud and the Relationship of Model Rules 4.1(b) and 1.6.** The permissive reporting provisions of Model Rule 1.6 become mandatory if Model Rule 4.1(b) applies, which is why we classify the ongoing crime or fraud situation as one the lawyer "must" disclose. The starting point of our analysis is Model Rule 4.1(b), which provides that:

> In the course of representing a client a lawyer shall not knowingly: . . . (b) fail to disclose a material fact . . . when disclosure is necessary to avoid assisting a criminal or fraudulent act by a client, *unless disclosure is prohibited by Rule 1.6.*

Model Rule 4.1(b) (emphasis added). The italicized clause was a last-minute addition during the final drafting process in 1983 to make Model

Rule 4.1(b) consistent with the 1983 version of Model Rule 1.6. Some suggested that this effectively negated the entire paragraph (b) of Model Rule 4.1. We think that is incorrect.

The 2003 amendments to Model Rule 1.6 permit disclosure of client crimes and frauds involving substantial financial interests. If disclosure of a client's intent to commit a crime or fraud is permitted under the current version of Model Rule 1.6, then such disclosure becomes mandatory under the "shall not knowingly . . . fail to disclose" language of Model Rule 4.1(b) if the situation also meets the requirements of that rule. Even under the 1983 version of Model Rule 1.6, a lawyer prohibited by the final clause of Model Rule 4.1(b) from explicitly disclosing that the client is concealing or misrepresenting material facts was nevertheless required by Model Rules 1.2(d) and 1.16(a)(1) to resign immediately as counsel if the client cannot be persuaded to correct the record. Further, under Comment [10] to Model Rule 1.2 and Comment [3] to Model Rule 4.1, discussed in Note 2 above, after resigning the lawyer also may noisily "withdraw or disaffirm" any fraudulent statement of the client with which the lawyer might be deemed to be associated by reason of the lawyer's prior presence as the client's counsel. *See* Geoffrey C. Hazard, Jr. & W. William Hodes, *The Law of Lawyering* §§ 9.30–31 (3d ed. 2001); *see also* ABA Formal Opinion 93–375 (Aug. 6, 1993) (analyzing lawyer's disclosure obligations in context of representing financial institution in connection with statutory examination of institution by regulators). For these reasons, we believe that the ongoing crime or fraud situation is a "must" disclose case.

(5) **Arizona.** Arizona Opinion 2000–02 (Mar. 2000) concluded that constitutional concerns might call for a different standard in criminal cases. Specifically, the committee decided that a lawyer is not required to disclose a client's factual misrepresentations to the court in connection with a plea bargain. The committee cautioned, however, that the lawyer cannot become a party to or endorse any misrepresentation under any circumstances.

(6) **California.** The duty of confidentiality is interpreted broadly in California. As California Opinion 2016–195 (undated) explained, a lawyer may not disclose his client's secrets, which include not only confidential information communicated between the client and the lawyer, but also publicly available information that the lawyer obtained during the professional relationship that the client requested to be kept secret or the disclosure of which is likely to be embarrassing or detrimental to the client. The opinion stated that even after termination of the attorney-client relationship, the lawyer may not disclose potentially embarrassing or detrimental information about the former client if that information was acquired by virtue of the lawyer's prior representation.

Unlike all other states, however, California does not base its duty of confidentiality on Model Rule 1.6. The obligation to maintain client confidences in California is governed by Section 6068(e) of the California Business and Professions Code, as well as by the Rule 3–100 of the California Rules of Professional Conduct. Section 6068(e)(2) permits, but does not require, a lawyer to disclose confidential information to prevent a criminal act that the lawyer believes is likely to result in death or substantial bodily harm. *See* Cal. Bus. & Prof. Code § 6068(e)(2) (West 2014). Section 6068(e)(2) closely tracks the 1983 version of Model Rule

1.6(b)(1), except that the potential death or bodily harm does not have to be "imminent" as required by the 1983 version of Model Rule 1.6.

Rule 3–100[1] also addresses a lawyer's duty of confidentiality. Like Section 6068(e)(2), Rule 3–100(B) provides that a lawyer may, but is not required to, disclose confidential client information "to prevent a criminal act that the [lawyer] reasonably believes is likely to result in death of, or substantial bodily harm to, an individual." Although narrower than Model Rule 1.6(b)(1) because it applies only to a future or ongoing "criminal act," Rule 3–100 is broader than the 1983 version of Model Rule 1.6 because it does not require that the criminal act be committed by the client, or that the death or injury be "imminent." Also, Rule 3–100(C) requires the lawyer, before revealing confidential information, to attempt, if reasonable under the circumstances, to dissuade the client from the criminal act or to pursue a course of conduct that will prevent any injury or both, and inform the client of the lawyer's ability or decision to reveal the information. The limited relaxation of the lawyer's duty to maintain client confidentiality does not extend to financial crimes or frauds. California Opinion 1996–146 (undated) reiterated the duty of confidentiality in the context of a case in which a lawyer learns that a general contractor client is using inferior piping in violation of contractual warranties. The opinion discusses steps a lawyer might take when faced with such conduct, but allows no room for disclosure.

California lawyers who "blow the whistle" to prevent their clients from causing financial harm may find themselves facing a lawsuit. The day after being fired from his job as in-house counsel, a lawyer told authorities about his former employer's alleged plan to sell assets of an insolvent affiliate. When the lawyer brought a wrongful termination suit, his former employer/client filed a cross-complaint alleging breach of fiduciary duty, breach of confidence, violation of a conflicts rule, and equitable indemnity. In *Fremont Reorganizing Corp. v. Faigin*, 198 Cal. App. 4th 1153, 1175–76 (2011), the court permitted the breach of fiduciary duty and breach of confidence claims to proceed, finding that the former employer/client had established a probability of prevailing.

In *Biller v. Toyota Motor Corp.*, 668 F.3d 655 (9th Cir. 2012), the Ninth Circuit upheld a $2.6 million arbitration award against a fired in-house lawyer who disclosed confidential information about his former employer's alleged misconduct in products liability litigation. Although the lawyer contended that he posted the information to his website to disclose the employer's continuing misconduct, the court noted that some of his disclosures "bore no relationship to [his] stated goal and instead appeared to stem from [his] desire to advance his career." 668 F.3d at 668.

Los Angeles County Opinion 519 (Feb. 26, 2007) concluded that there is no "self-defense" exception to a lawyer's confidentiality obligations when a third party complains about a lawyer's conduct. The inquiring lawyer was a defendant in two actions: a legal malpractice claim asserted by the former client's bankruptcy trustee and a class action brought by purchasers of notes issued by the client. After a thorough discussion of

---

[1] Editor's note. The tables for this year were prepared before the California Supreme Court issued the new California Rules included in this Supplement. The corresponding provision in the new California Rules is Rule 1.6. It remains to be seen whether the new rule will change any of the principles asserted in the analysis in this table.

California and federal law on this subject, the opinion concluded that even if the lawyer were permitted or compelled to disclose confidential information in the legal malpractice case under California Evidence Code § 958 (permitting disclosure where client accuses lawyer of wrongdoing), she still could not use that information to defend herself in the investors' class action because: (1) Section 958 was limited to disputes with clients, and (2) no California authority permitted lawyers to disclose privileged or confidential information to defend attacks from someone other than the client.

San Diego County Opinion 2011–01 (undated) decided that although the Model Rules may compel a different result, under certain circumstances, the California Rules of Professional Conduct and the State Bar Act preclude a lawyer from answering a judge's questions about the client's whereabouts. The opinion involved a defense lawyer scheduled to appear in court to represent a client on a drug charge. The night before the appearance, the client's mother called the lawyer and said not to expect the client in court, as "he just left the house high as a kite." When the client failed to appear, the judge asked, "Do you have any idea why your client isn't here?" According to the opinion, the lawyer must respectfully decline to answer, citing his or her ethical duty of confidentiality. The opinion explained that although Comment [2] to Model Rule 3.3 states that a lawyer's duty to the client is qualified by the duty of candor to the court, in California the duty of confidentiality is not qualified by the duty of candor.

(7) **Connecticut.** The Connecticut Supreme Court affirmed a decision accepting defense counsel's representation of the necessity to invoke Rule 3.3(a)(3) in a criminal case, finding that it was the minimum disclosure necessary to satisfy the lawyer's obligation under that rule against offering evidence known to be false. *See State v. Chambers*, 994 A.2d 1248, 1265 (Conn. 2010).

(8) **District of Columbia.** A lawyer may reveal client confidences and secrets to prevent bribery or intimidation of witnesses, jurors, court officials, or others in proceedings before a tribunal. *See* D.C. Rule 1.6(c)(2). *See also* Maryland Opinion 86–28 (undated); Note 17 below (discussing Maryland Opinion 86–28).

(9) **Florida.** In *R.L.R. v. The State of Florida*, 116 So. 3d 570 (Fla. 2013), the court held that even though a juvenile may have been a danger to himself, this was not an exception justifying disclosure of his communications with his court-appointed lawyer about his location.

(10) **Florida.** In *Florida Bar v. Knowles*, 99 So. 3d 918, 922 (Fla. 2012), the court held that the crime-fraud exception did not apply when a lawyer told the Assistant State Attorney that she "had reason to believe" her former client would lie to the Immigration Court at an upcoming hearing and sent the prosecutor an anonymous mailing containing confidential documents regarding the former client's political asylum case. The lawyer testified that she believed the former client would lie because the client had stated she "would do anything, including lying in court, to avoid deportation." According to the court, that testimony failed to establish a sufficient basis for the lawyer to reasonably believe that her client would commit a crime by lying at the hearing.

In *TransPetrol, Ltd. v. Radulovic*, 764 So. 2d 878, 880–81 (Fla. Dist. Ct. App. 2000), the court dismissed a claim against lawyers and accountants who allegedly failed to disclose a client's fraudulent scheme to avoid paying a debt. The court held that there was no duty of disclosure to a third party. The court also rejected RICO and aiding and abetting claims. The opinion does not mention Florida Rule 4–1.6. The May 2006 revisions to the Florida rules did not change the substance of Rule 4–1.6.

(11) **Georgia.** Georgia Rule 1.6(b)(1)(i) also permits disclosure to avoid or prevent harm or substantial financial loss to another as a result of third-party criminal conduct.

(12) **Disclosing Ongoing Client Fraud under Model Rule 4.1.** Some state versions of Model Rule 4.1(b) do not contain the ABA's confusing limiting clause at the end ("unless disclosure is prohibited by Rule 1.6") referred to in Note 4 above. Therefore, in the context of an ongoing transaction where the lawyer's client has committed a criminal or fraudulent act by concealing or misrepresenting a material fact, the lawyer must disclose the full truth to the affected third parties. As a general proposition, the lawyer should first remonstrate with the client if practicable, then act affirmatively to reveal the client's deceit only after the client has refused to rectify the situation. In *Davin, L.L.C. v. Daham*, 746 A.2d 1034 (N.J. Super. Ct. App. Div. 2000), the court reversed a summary judgment in favor of a landlord's lawyer on a claim asserted by a tenant against the lawyer based on the lawyer's failure to disclose (or urge his client to disclose) during lease negotiations that the property was in foreclosure. The court cited New Jersey Rule 4.1 in holding that the lawyer might have a duty of disclosure on the facts presented. *Id.* at 1045. The court's opinion includes some rather broad language about a lawyer's duty of candor.

(13) **Illinois.** Since January 1, 2010, Illinois Rule 1.6(b)(3) has permitted disclosure to rectify the consequences of a client's crime or fraud in which the lawyer's services were used.

(14) **Indiana.** Indiana Opinion 2 (2015) concluded that although state law mandates that anyone who suspects child abuse must report it, a lawyer's duty of confidentiality "is generally paramount over the general duty to report." Absent client consent, the lawyer must not report the suspected abuse unless the lawyer believes it necessary to prevent reasonably certain death or substantial bodily harm, in which case the lawyer must report it.

(15) **Kentucky.** Kentucky's counterpart to Model Rule 4.1(b) permits "reasonable remedial measures to avoid assisting a fraudulent or criminal act by a client including, if necessary, disclosure of a material fact, unless prohibited by Rule 1.6."

(16) **Maine.** Maine Opinion 209 (May 20, 2014) concluded that a lawyer whose client pleaded guilty to a crime in exchange for a "deferred disposition" and promise of reduced charges may not disclose voluntarily that the client later engaged in criminal conduct that violated the conditions of his deferred disposition, making him ineligible for the earlier bargain. At the same time, the opinion noted that the lawyer could not knowingly allow the client to make false statements to the court as part of the deferred disposition process. If the client does make false statements to the court, the lawyer must disavow them, which may require advising the court that the client's testimony was false. Maine Opinion 213 (Apr. 6, 2016) concluded that a law firm may not donate old, inactive client files to a library or university despite the passage of time and the materials' potential historical significance, unless the firm

147

determines that the files do not contain confidential information or the client consents to the donation.

(17) **Maryland.** In Maryland Opinion No. 86–28, the inquiring lawyer was a member of the Maryland and District of Columbia Bars. The lawyer had introduced evidence in a court proceeding in the District of Columbia and subsequently learned that his client had forged the documents. The Maryland rules required disclosure, while the D.C. rules prohibited it. The Maryland opinion concluded that when a Maryland lawyer acts in accordance with a foreign jurisdiction's ethics rules, the conduct is per se ethical.

(18) **Massachusetts.** As amended in 2015, Massachusetts Rule 1.6 now follows the Model Rule in most ways, while maintaining some differences. For example, the amended Rule permits disclosure of confidential information to prevent "reasonably certain" death or bodily harm whether or not a crime is involved, but maintains the old Rule's provision allowing lawyers to reveal confidential information to prevent the wrongful execution or incarceration of another. An earlier ethics opinion, Massachusetts Opinion 01–02 (undated), concluded that a lawyer may disclose a client's believable threat of suicide to family members or appropriate authorities.

(19) **Massachusetts.** Massachusetts Rule 3.3(e) provides an exception to Rule 3.3(a) that applies only in criminal cases.

(20) **Michigan.** Although similar to Model Rule 3.3(b), Michigan Rule 3.3(b) does not include the introductory phrase, "[a] lawyer who represents a client in an adjudicative proceeding," which suggests the remedial obligations of the rule may apply to a lawyer who does not represent a litigant in the proceeding. New Rule 3.3(e) requires a lawyer to seek to withdraw if necessary to remedy the introduction of material evidence that the lawyer ascertains is false.

(21) **Montana.** The Montana Supreme Court censured a lawyer for not disclosing, at his client's direction, facts that would have clarified a litigation opponent's misunderstanding regarding the value of a settlement, holding that the lawyer should have withdrawn pursuant to Rule 1.16. *See In re Potts*, 158 P.3d 418, 431 (Mont. 2007). The court acknowledged that Rule 1.6 prohibited disclosure, but further stated that Rule 1.6 "does not stand alone," and must be read in conjunction with Rule 1.2(d). Moreover, the court also stated that the obligation of candor to the court under the Montana version of 1983 Model Rule 3.3(a)(2) "superseded [any] duty of confidentiality under Rule 1.6," 158 P.3d at 424. The court applied Rule 3.3(a)(2) because the settlement resulted in a stipulation that was filed with the court.

(22) **New Hampshire.** According to New Hampshire Opinion 2014–15/5 (undated), when a lawyer believes a client is the victim of elder abuse, the lawyer should gather "sufficient evidence" to support those concerns before disclosing the suspected abuse over the client's objections.

(23) **New Hampshire.** In *Feld's Case*, 815 A.2d 383, 392 (N.H. 2002), the New Hampshire Supreme Court suspended a lawyer from the practice of law for one year for failing to advise his client to correct false testimony in a civil deposition.

(24) **New Jersey.** New Jersey Rule 1.6(b)(1) requires disclosure to prevent the client or another person from committing a crime, fraud, or "illegal act" that is likely to result in death or substantial bodily harm or

substantial financial injury, and Rule 1.6(b)(2) contains the same requirement regarding conduct that is likely to perpetrate a fraud on a tribunal. New Jersey Rule 1.6(d)(1) permits disclosure to rectify the consequences of a client's crime, fraud, or "illegal act" in which the lawyer's services were used.

New Jersey Opinion 677 (Oct. 17, 1994) opined that a supervisory and regulatory "department of the state of New Jersey" is a "tribunal" within the meaning of New Jersey Rule 1.6. If the lawyer reveals the information pursuant to New Jersey Rule 1.6, the lawyer also may reveal the information to the person threatened to the extent reasonably necessary to protect that person from substantial bodily harm, substantial financial injury, or substantial property loss.

(25) **New Jersey.** In *In re Forrest*, 730 A.2d 340, 343 (N.J. 1999), the New Jersey Supreme Court held that withholding a material fact from an arbitrator violates the duty of candor to a "tribunal" under New Jersey Rule 3.3(a).

(26) **New York.** New York Rule 1.6(b)(3) permits a lawyer to withdraw a written or oral representation if the lawyer believes it was materially inaccurate or is being used to further a crime or fraud. But New York did not adopt Model Rule 4.1(b), so New York is designated "may" disclose in columns E and G.

New York City Opinion 1994–10 (Oct. 21, 1994) held that a lawyer who represents a limited partnership and the general partner on partnership and other matters must disclose wrongdoing by the general partner to the limited partners.

New York State Opinion 945 (Nov. 7, 2012) concluded that a lawyer in a matrimonial matter may not disclose that the lawyer's client had been reading emails between his or her spouse and the spouse's lawyer unless the lawyer knows that the client is committing a crime or fraud and no other remedial measures will prevent harm to the opposing party; governing judicial decisions require disclosure; or other law requires disclosure. The opinion did not decide whether the client's conduct constituted a crime or fraud or whether other authorities required disclosure, as those issues fall outside the committee's purview of interpreting the rules of professional conduct. The opinion also noted that the client had not provided the emails to the lawyer, although the client might have been using knowledge of their contents to make decisions about the litigation.

Disclosure may be permissive, not mandatory, if the threatened misconduct remains unexecuted when the representation ends. In Nassau County, New York Opinion 01–07 (undated), the client advised his lawyer of his intention to omit a half-sibling from the list of potential distributees in a probate proceeding. When the lawyer advised that this would be improper, the client discharged the lawyer before proceeding so he could do it anyway. The opinion stated that the lawyer may disclose the fraud, but was not obligated to do so because the lawyer had not assisted in the fraud. In contrast, New York State Opinion 982 (Oct. 2, 2013) concluded that a lawyer who has not appeared before a tribunal is not permitted to disclose confidential information to correct a prior false statement the lawyer made to opposing counsel before any proceeding began unless the lawyer reasonably believes that opposing counsel is continuing to rely on the false statement.

New York State Opinion 837 (Mar. 6, 2010) considered what constitutes reasonable remedial measures under New York Rule 3.3, when a lawyer discovers a document previously entered into evidence was forged. The opinion concluded that offering to withdraw the document was sufficient and disclosure to the tribunal was not necessary. New York City Opinion 2013–2 (undated) addressed a lawyer's obligations if, after the conclusion of a proceeding, the lawyer discovers that material evidence offered by the lawyer, the lawyer's client, or a witness called by the lawyer was false. The opinion concluded that the obligation to take remedial action survives the conclusion of the proceeding and ends only when a reasonable remedial measure is no longer available.

New York County Opinion 746 (Oct. 7, 2013) concluded that a lawyer may not collect a bounty for "blowing the whistle" on a client pursuant to the Dodd-Frank Wall Street Reform and Consumer Protection Act of 2010. The opinion reasoned that such bounties pose an inherent conflict of interest.

New York State Opinion 1084 (Jan. 22, 2016) concluded that a lawyer whose client died in prison may not reveal the client's exculpatory statements about a co-defendant unless the client somehow authorized the disclosure, even if doing so would exonerate the co-defendant. If the co-defendant had been charged with a capital crime, however, the exception in Rule 1.6(b)(1), which permits disclosure "to prevent reasonably certain death or substantial bodily harm," would apply.

New York State Opinion 1088 (Mar. 31, 2016) concluded that lawyers may reveal the names of current or past clients without asking their permission if the information is publicly known or the lawyer is certain the disclosure will not embarrass or harm the client. Lawyers may not, however, use the client's name in advertising without the client's written consent or disclose it if the client has requested secrecy.

(27) **North Carolina.** Similar to Model Rule 1.6, North Carolina Rule 1.6(b)(4) permits, but does not require, disclosure "to prevent, mitigate, or rectify the consequences of a client's criminal or fraudulent act in the commission of which the lawyer's services were used." North Carolina is thus listed as a "may" disclose state in columns C, D, and E. North Carolina did not, however, adopt Model Rule 4.1(b), which requires disclosure to avoid assisting a client crime or fraud if such disclosure is not prohibited by Rule 1.6. Therefore, North Carolina also is designated "may" disclose in column G. *See also* North Carolina Opinion 2005–09 (addressing "safe harbor" in Sarbanes-Oxley's reporting-out provision). In 2017, North Carolina adopted Rule 8.6, which extends the obligation to report information about a possible wrongful conviction to all lawyers, not just prosecutors. It applies when a lawyer has credible evidence that the defendant did not commit the offense for which he was convicted, even if that evidence is protected by Rule 1.6. Rule 8.6 contains several exceptions, however, such as when the evidence is protected from disclosure by law or court order, when disclosure would criminally incriminate a client or former client, or when disclosure would violate the attorney-client privilege.

(28) **Ohio.** Ohio Rule 3.3(c) defines the duration of the lawyer's duty under Rule 3.3 to rectify false evidence or false statements of law or fact as lasting only "until the issue to which the duty relates is determined by the highest *tribunal* that may consider the issue, or the time has expired for such determination." To the extent that *Office of Disciplinary*

Counsel v. Heffernan, 569 N.E.2d 1027 (Ohio 1991), could be read as imposing a duty to disclose that was not limited in time, Comment [13] to Rule 3.3(c) modifies that interpretation. In *Heffernan*, the Ohio Supreme Court suspended a lawyer for six months for failing to inform a lower court that the lawyer's client had perpetrated a fraud upon that court, even though the lawyer learned of the client's fraud "a few months" after the fact. *Id.* at 1027.

(29) **Pennsylvania.** Disclosure is authorized "to prevent, mitigate or rectify . . . a client's criminal or fraudulent act in the commission of which the lawyer's services are being or had been used." Pennsylvania Rule 1.6(c)(3). In Philadelphia Opinion 2014–7 (Oct. 2014), the committee concluded that it was permissible for a lawyer who submitted a claim for unpaid fees in a former client's bankruptcy proceeding to tell the bankruptcy trustee that the former client owned property not listed in his bankruptcy petition. The committee reasoned that disclosure was allowed to prevent the former client's possible bankruptcy fraud, as well as to help the lawyer collect his fee.

(30) **Pennsylvania.** Philadelphia Opinion 2001–02 (Mar. 2001) concluded that on the facts presented, the inquiring lawyer was not required to disclose that he had filed pleadings containing false statements because the lawyer did not learn of the falsity until after the proceeding ended. In contrast, Philadelphia Opinion 2013–5 (June 2013) concerned a lawyer who verified and filed a complaint, only to learn weeks later that it contained false, material information provided by the lawyers' clients. The lawyer also forwarded documents containing the same false information to the clients' insurer. The opinion concluded that the lawyer must advise the clients about the options for rectifying their misstatement and, if the clients refuse to rectify the misstatement, the lawyer must take corrective action.

(31) **Tennessee.** Tennessee Rule 1.6(b)(1) permits disclosure to prevent a client or another person from committing a crime unless disclosure is prohibited by Rule 3.3. Effective January 1, 2011, Tennessee modified its rules to incorporate Model Rules 1.6(b)(2) and (3). In matters pending before a tribunal, new Rule 3.3(f) requires a lawyer to seek permission to withdraw when the lawyer is unable to dissuade a client from perpetrating a fraud on a tribunal or to convince the client to rectify a prior fraud on a tribunal. A lawyer seeking permission to withdraw "shall inform the tribunal, without further disclosure of information protected by [Rule] 1.6," that the lawyer's request to withdraw is required by the rules of professional conduct.

For nonadjudicative matters, Rule 4.1(b) requires a lawyer who learns that a client intends to perpetrate a crime or fraud to consult with the client about the consequences of the client's conduct. If the consultation fails to change the client's intent, the lawyer must withdraw and give notice of the withdrawal to those likely to be injured, as well as disaffirm any existing written materials prepared by the lawyer that may be used by the client in furtherance of the crime or fraud. If the client's intended conduct is a crime relating to a nonadjudicative matter, disclosure by the lawyer is permitted by Rule 1.6(b)(1), but not required by Rule 4.1(b). If the client's crime or fraud relating to a nonadjudicative matter has been completed before the lawyer learns of the misconduct, Rule 4.1(c) requires the lawyer to advise the client to rectify the crime or fraud and consult with the client about the consequences of the client's failure to do so. If the client refuses or is unable to rectify the crime or fraud, the lawyer must withdraw, give notice of the withdrawal to those likely to be injured, and disaffirm any written materials prepared by the lawyer that may be used by the client in furtherance of the crime or fraud.

(32) **Texas.** Texas Disciplinary Rule 3.03(b) requires disclosure of "true facts" after offering material evidence the lawyer later knows to be false, but only after attempting to persuade the client to authorize the lawyer to correct or withdraw the false evidence. Texas Opinion 589 (Sept. 2009) considered whether a lawyer may or must report possibly illegal activity by an adverse party or witness when the lawyer learns about the activity in the course of representing the client. The opinion concluded that the lawyer must not report the activity if it would be contrary to the client's best interest, or if prohibited by the Texas version of the Model Rule 1.6. Otherwise, the lawyer may disclose the illegal activity unless the report was made for an improper purpose under Texas Rule 4.04.

(33) **Vermont.** The Reporter's Note to Vermont Rule 4.1 states that the substance of Model Rule 4.1(b) was incorporated into Vermont Rule 1.6(b)(2) to make the disclosure mandatory.

(34) **Virginia.** Virginia Rule 1.6(c)(1), in addition to requiring disclosure of a client's intent to commit a crime, also directs the lawyer to "seek to withdraw as counsel" if the crime involves client perjury.

(35) **Washington.** Washington Rule 1.6(b)(7) permits a lawyer to reveal to the tribunal confidences or secrets which disclose "any breach of fiduciary responsibility when the client is serving as a court appointed fiduciary such as a guardian, personal representative, or receiver."

(36) **Washington.** Washington Rule 3.3(a)(2) differs from the Model Rule. The Washington rule provides that a lawyer shall not knowingly "fail to disclose a material fact to a tribunal when disclosure is necessary to avoid assisting a criminal or fraudulent act by the client unless such disclosure is prohibited by Rule 1.6." The Washington rules do not have a provision equivalent to Model Rule 3.3(b). Therefore, Washington is designated as "Must Not" disclose in column F.

(37) **West Virginia.** Effective January 1, 2015, West Virginia amended its Rule 1.6 to conform to the Model Rule regarding the issues summarized in the chart above.

In *In re Christina W.*, 639 S.E.2d 770 (W. Va. 2006), the West Virginia Supreme Court addressed the issue of whether a guardian ad litem appointed in an abuse case owes her child client a duty of confidentiality that prohibits the lawyer from disclosing confidential information regarding abuse to the court. The 14-year-old client initially told officers who responded to a domestic disturbance call that her mother's boyfriend touched her inappropriately. She later recanted. When the lawyer was appointed for the girl, however, she sought assurances that the lawyer would not reveal the client's confidences. Upon receiving those assurances, the girl told the lawyer that the boyfriend had in fact sexually abused her. The lawyer kept that disclosure in confidence, but when the client later told caseworkers, they asked the court to remove the lawyer as guardian. On appeal from the denial of that motion, the court cited West Virginia Rules 1.6 and 1.14 (client under a disability) in disapproving the lawyer's conduct. *Id.* at 777–78. The court held that a guardian ad litem's duty of confidentiality to the children he or she represents in child abuse and neglect proceedings "is not absolute," and that when honoring that duty of confidentiality would expose the clients to a "high risk of probable harm," then the guardian must make a disclosure to the presiding court in order to safeguard the child's best interests. *Id.* at 778.

(38) **Wyoming.** Effective October 6, 2014, Wyoming amended its Rule 1.6 to permit, under certain circumstances, (1) disclosures intended to prevent a client from committing a crime or fraud, and (2) disclosures of past crimes or frauds. Note that in both instances Wyoming follows the Model Rule in that it allows disclosure only if the client has used or is using the lawyer's services in connection with the client's threatened or actual misconduct.

2.4 Disclosure to Comply with Law

The chart in Section 2.5 below sets forth, by jurisdiction, whether a lawyer is permitted to disclose confidential client information to comply with other law. Comment [21] to Model Rule 1.6 of the 1983 version of the Model Rules (described in the chart as 1983 Model Rule 1.6) acknowledged that other provisions of law might obligate or permit a lawyer to disclose confidential client information, but cautioned, "Whether another provision of law supersedes Rule 1.6 is a matter of interpretation beyond the scope of these Rules, but a presumption should exist against such a supersession." The current version of Model Rule 1.6(b)(6) expressly provides that a lawyer may reveal information relating to the representation of a client "to comply with other law or a court order." Comments [5] and [12] to Model Rule 1.6 remind lawyers that they must discuss the matter with the affected client to the extent required by Model Rule 1.4. *See also* ABA Formal Opinion 473 (Feb. 17, 2016) (addressing lawyer's duty of confidentiality when responding to subpoena for client documents). As shown by the chart below, most, but not all, states permit disclosure to comply with other law, such as the permissive reporting-out provisions of the Sarbanes-Oxley Act. *See* Section 2.6 below.

2.5 Chart on Disclosure to Comply with Law

State	Permit Lawyer Disclosure to Comply with Law?
Alabama	No, but has former Comment [21] to 1983 Model Rule 1.6
Alaska	Yes, Alaska RPC 1.6(b)(6)
Arizona	Yes, Arizona ER 1.6(d)(5)
Arkansas	Yes, Arkansas RPC 1.6(b)(6)
California	No
Colorado	Yes, Colorado RPC 1.6(b)(7)
Connecticut	Yes, Connecticut RPC 1.6(c)(4)
Delaware	Yes, Delaware RPC 1.6(b)(6)
District of Columbia	Yes, District of Columbia RPC 1.6(e)(2)(A)
Florida	No, but has former Comment [21] to 1983 Model Rule 1.6
Georgia	No, but has former Comment [21] to 1983 Model Rule 1.6 as Comment [18]
Hawaii	Yes, Hawaii RPC 1.6(b)(7)

Idaho	Yes, Idaho RPC 1.6(b)(6)
Illinois	Yes, Illinois RPC 1.6(b)(6)
Indiana	Yes, Indiana RPC 1.6(b)(6)
Iowa	Yes, Iowa RPC 32:1.6(b)(6)
Kansas	Yes, Kansas RPC 1.6(b)(4)
Kentucky	Yes, Kentucky RPC 3.130 (1.6(b)(4))
Louisiana	Yes, Louisiana RPC 1.6(b)(6)
Maine	Yes, Maine RPC 1.6(b)(6)
Maryland	Yes, Maryland RPC 1.6(b)(6)
Massachusetts	Yes, Massachusetts RPC 1.6(b)(4)
Michigan	Yes, Michigan RPC 1.6(c)(2)
Minnesota	Yes, Minnesota RPC 1.6(b)(9)
Mississippi	Yes, Mississippi RPC 1.6(e)
Missouri	Yes, Missouri RPC 4–1.6(b)(4)
Montana	Yes, Montana RPC 1.6(b)(4)
Nebraska	Yes, Nebraska RPC 1.6(b)(4)
Nevada	Yes, Nevada RPC 1.6(b)(6)
New Hampshire	Yes, New Hampshire RPC 1.6(b)(4)
New Jersey	Yes, New Jersey RPC 1.6(d)(4)
New Mexico	Yes, New Mexico RPC 1.6(b)(6)
New York	Yes, New York RPC 1.6(b)(6)
North Carolina	Yes, North Carolina RPC 1.6(b)(1)
North Dakota	Yes, North Dakota RPC 1.6(c)(5)
Ohio	Yes, Ohio RPC 1.6(b)(6)
Oklahoma	Yes, Oklahoma RPC 1.6(b)(6)
Oregon	Yes, Oregon CPC 1.6(b)(5)
Pennsylvania	No, *but see* Comments [18] and [19] to RPC 1.6
Rhode Island	Yes, Rhode Island RPC 1.6(b)(4)
South Carolina	Yes, South Carolina RPC 1.6(b)(7)
South Dakota	Yes, South Dakota RPC 1.6(b)(5)
Tennessee	Yes, Tennessee RPC 1.6(c)(3)
Texas	Yes, Texas RPC 1.05(c)(4)
Utah	Yes, Utah RPC 1.6(b)(6)
Vermont	Yes, Vermont RPC 1.6(c)
Virginia	Yes, Virginia RPC 1.6(b)(1)
Washington	No, but may reveal to comply with "court order," Washington RPC 1.6(b)(6)
West Virginia	Yes, West Virginia RPC 1.6(b)(6)

| Wisconsin | Yes, Wisconsin RPC 1.6(c)(5) |
| Wyoming | Yes, Wyoming RPC 1.6(b)(6) |

2.6   Disclosure Outside an Organization

The chart in Section 2.7 below sets forth, by jurisdiction, whether a lawyer is permitted to disclose confidential information of an organizational client outside the organization under the applicable version of Model Rule 1.13. In determining whether disclosure is permitted or required, lawyers also need to consider the applicable versions of Model Rules 1.6, 3.3, and 4.1.

Model Rule 1.13 of the 1983 version of the Model Rules (described in the chart as "1983 Model Rule 1.13") provided that a lawyer who "knows" that an officer or other agent of an organizational client is engaged in misconduct that will cause substantial injury to the organization must "proceed as is reasonably necessary in the best interest of the organization." That rule required no particular course of action of the lawyer, but identified up-the-line reporting of the misconduct, including reporting to the entity's board of directors, as a potential option.

Model Rule 1.13 was amended in 2002 (described in the chart as "Ethics 2000") to require a lawyer to explain to constituents the identity of the client as the organization when the lawyer "knows or reasonably should know" of a conflict between the organization and its constituents. *See* 2002 version of Model Rule 1.13(f). The 1983 version of Model Rule 1.13(d) required an explanation only when the conflict was "apparent."

Model Rule 1.13 was amended again in August 2003. The August 2003 version of Model Rule 1.13 (described in the chart as "Aug. 2003") requires a lawyer who knows of corporate misconduct to report such misconduct up the line, to the organization's board of directors if necessary, unless "the lawyer reasonably believes that it is not necessary in the best interest of the organization to do so." As noted above, such up-the-line reporting was formerly just one option that the lawyer could consider.

Paragraph (c) of the August 2003 version of Model Rule 1.13 further provides that when a lawyer has reported corporate misconduct to the organization's highest authority, and the organization fails to take timely remedial action, the lawyer may reveal client confidences outside the organization to the extent necessary to prevent substantial injury to the organizational client, whether or not Model Rule 1.6 permits such disclosure. Paragraph (e) of the August 2003 rule also provides that a lawyer who reasonably believes that he or she has been discharged because of reporting up the line, or making an authorized outside report, or who withdraws under circumstances that would permit such reporting, must inform the organization's board of the discharge or withdrawal, and what the lawyer reasonably believes to be the basis for the discharge or withdrawal.

The up-the-line reporting obligations imposed by Section 307 of the Sarbanes-Oxley Act of 2002, 15 U.S.C. § 7245, implementing regulation, SEC Rule 205 (17 C.F.R. § 205 (2011)), are similar to those imposed by Model Rule 1.13. Model Rule 1.13, however, requires up-the-line reporting with respect to all organizational clients, not just the public companies covered by Sarbanes-Oxley.

Another important distinction between SEC Rule 205 and the Model Rules is that SEC Rule 205 permits disclosure of confidential information in certain cases of client misconduct even though the rules in the lawyer's home state forbid disclosure. SEC Rule 205.3(d)(2) permits a lawyer to disclose to the SEC, without the client-issuer's consent, confidential information related to the representation that the lawyer reasonably believes is necessary: (1) to prevent the issuer from committing a material violation that is likely to cause substantial injury to the financial interest or property of the issuer or investors; (2) to prevent the issuer from committing or suborning perjury in a SEC investigation or administrative proceeding or otherwise perpetrating a fraud upon the SEC; or (3) to rectify the consequences of the issuer's material violation in the furtherance of which the lawyer's services were used that caused, or may cause, substantial injury to the financial interest or property of the issuer or investors. 17 C.F.R. § 205.3(d).

The chart in Section 2.7 below shows that several states forbid such disclosures. Yet, SEC Rule 205, in theory, provides a safe harbor for lawyers who make disclosures in violation of state professional conduct rules, stating: "An attorney who complies in good faith with the provisions of this part shall not be subject to discipline or otherwise liable under inconsistent standards imposed by any state or other United States jurisdiction where the attorney is admitted or practices." SEC Rule 205.6(c). The California Bar, however, has cautioned its lawyers against making disclosures permitted by the SEC but forbidden by California law unless and until a court of competent jurisdiction decides whether SEC Rule 205 could and properly did preempt state professional conduct rules. *See* California Bar Association, *The New SEC Attorney Conduct Rules v. California's Duty of Confidentiality*, Ethics Hotliner (Spring 2004). In *Wadler v. Bio-Rad Labs., Inc.*, 2016 U.S. Dist. LEXIS 176166, 2016 WL 7369246 (N.D. Cal. Dec. 20, 2016), however, the court held that, to the extent the two conflict, Sarbanes-Oxley preempts California lawyers' ethical obligations regarding the disclosure of privileged and confidential information.

North Carolina has assured lawyers that the SEC safe harbor should protect them. Without citing the California ethics alert discussed above, the North Carolina State Bar concluded that "unless and until the Fourth Circuit Court of Appeals or the U.S. Supreme Court determines that [SEC] Rule 205 was not validly promulgated . . . a North Carolina attorney may, without violating the North Carolina Rules of Professional Conduct, disclose confidential information as permitted by [SEC] Rule 205 although such disclosure would not otherwise be permitted by . . . [North Carolina] Rule [1.6]," North Carolina Opinion 2005–09 (Jan. 20, 2006). A 2005 amendment to North Carolina Rule 1.13(c), which permits "reporting out" in specified circumstances, received final approval on March 2, 2006, a few months after the ethics opinion was issued.

Even if a jurisdiction allows reporting out to the SEC, lawyers probably should not attempt to collect a bounty for blowing the whistle on a client. New York County Opinion 746 (Oct. 7, 2013) concluded that New York's professional conduct rules do not allow lawyers to participate in the SEC's bounty program because doing so gives rise to a conflict between the lawyers' interests and those of their clients. Lawyers also should be aware that whistleblower protections may be interpreted narrowly, as illustrated by a matter involving an in-house lawyer at General Electric who disclosed company documents to support her whistleblower retaliation claim under SOX. The documents allegedly showed that the company had engaged in tax fraud regarding sales in Brazil and then fired the lawyer for raising concerns about it with her supervisors. She provided the documents to the SEC, the Department of Labor, federal prosecutors, Brazilian law enforcement, and the press. The lawyer retained counsel, who assisted her with some of those disclosures, including the press leaks. The District of Columbia Court of Appeals Board on Professional Responsibility found that disciplinary counsel had established a prima facie case that the lawyer's disclosures violated Rule 1.6. The board also found that because the lawyer had refused to participate in the disciplinary process, she had not produced evidence showing that an exception applied under SOX or other otherwise and thus had not met her burden of presenting some evidence to rebut the disciplinary counsel's showing. In addition, the board found that one of her lawyers violated Rule 8.4 by knowingly assisting in her disclosure to the press. Accordingly, the board recommended that the lawyer be suspended for 60 days and that that her counsel be admonished informally. *See In re Koeck*, Report, Recommendation, and Order, D.C. Ct. of App. Bd. on Prof. Responsibility (Aug. 30, 2017).

2.7   Chart on Disclosure Outside an Organization under Rule 1.13

State	Permit Lawyer Disclosure Outside the Organization?	Corresponding Version of ABA Model Rule 1.13
Alabama	No, Alabama RPC 1.13	1983 Model Rule 1.13
Alaska	Yes, Alaska RPC 1.13(c)	Modified Aug. 2003
Arizona	Yes, Arizona ER 1.13(c)	Aug. 2003
Arkansas	Yes, Arkansas RPC 1.13(c)	Aug. 2003
California	No, California RPC 3–600	Modified 1983 Model Rule 1.13
Colorado	Yes, Colorado RPC 1.13(c)	Aug. 2003
Connecticut	Yes, Connecticut RPC 1.13(c)	Aug. 2003
Delaware	No, Delaware RPC 1.13(c)	Ethics 2000
District of Columbia	No, District of Columbia RPC 1.13	Modified 1983 Model Rule 1.13
Florida	No, Florida RPC 4–1.13	Ethics 2000
Georgia	Yes, Georgia RPC 1.13	Aug. 2003
Hawaii	Yes, Hawaii RPC 1.13	Aug. 2003
Idaho	Yes, Idaho RPC 1.13(c)	Aug. 2003
Illinois	Yes, Illinois RPC 1.13(c)	Modified Aug. 2003
Indiana	Yes, Indiana RPC 1.13(c)	Aug. 2003
Iowa	Yes, Iowa RPC 32:1.13(c)	Aug. 2003
Kansas	No, Kansas RPC 1.13	1983 Model Rule 1.13
Kentucky	Yes, Kentucky SCR 3.130 (1.13(c))	Aug. 2003
Louisiana	Yes, Louisiana RPC 1.13(c)	Aug. 2003

Maine	Yes, Maine RPC 1.13(c)	Modified Aug. 2003
Maryland	Yes, Maryland RPC 1.13(c)	Modified Aug. 2003
Massachusetts	Yes, Massachusetts RPC 1.13(c)	Aug. 2003
Michigan	Yes, Michigan RPC 1.13(c)	Modified 1983 Model Rule 1.13
Minnesota	Yes, Minnesota RPC 1.13(c)	Modified Aug. 2003
Mississippi	No, Mississippi RPC 1.13	1983 Model Rule 1.13
Missouri	No, Missouri RPC 4–1.13	Ethics 2000
Montana	No, Montana RPC 1.13	Ethics 2000
Nebraska	Yes, Nebraska RPC 1.13(c)	Aug. 2003
Nevada	Yes, Nevada RPC 1.13(c)	Modified Aug. 2003
New Hampshire	Yes, New Hampshire RPC 1.13(c)	Aug. 2003
New Jersey	Yes, New Jersey RPC 1.13(c)	Modified 1983 Model Rule 1.13
New Mexico	Yes, New Mexico RPC 16–113 (c)	Modified Aug. 2003
New York	Yes, New York RPC 1.13(c)	Modified Aug. 2003
North Carolina	Yes, North Carolina RPC 1.13(c)	Modified Aug. 2003
North Dakota	Yes, North Dakota RPC 1.13(c)	Aug. 2003
Ohio	Yes, Ohio RPC 1.13(c)	Modified Aug. 2003
Oklahoma	Yes, Oklahoma RPC 1.13(c)	Aug. 2003
Oregon	Yes, Oregon CPC 1.13(c)	Modified Aug. 2003
Pennsylvania	No, Pennsylvania RPC 1.13	Ethics 2000
Rhode Island	Yes, Rhode Island RPC 1.13(c)	Aug. 2003
South Carolina	Yes, South Carolina RPC 1.13(c)	Aug. 2003
South Dakota	No, South Dakota RPC 1.13	Ethics 2000
Tennessee	No, Tennessee RPC 1.13	Modified 1983 Model Rule 1.13
Texas	No, Texas RPC 1.12	Modified 1983 Model Rule 1.13

DISCLOSURE OF CLIENT CONFIDENCES

Utah	Yes, Utah RPC 1.13(c)	Aug. 2003
Vermont	Yes, Vermont RPC 1.13(c)	Modified Aug. 2003
Virginia	No, Virginia RPC 1.13	1983 Model Rule 1.13
Washington	Yes, Washington RPC 1.13(c)	Aug. 2003
West Virginia	Yes, West Virginia RPC 1.13(c)	Aug. 2003
Wisconsin	Yes, Wisconsin RPC 1.13(c)	Aug. 2003
Wyoming	Yes, Wyoming RPC 1.13(c)	Aug. 2003

APPENDIX B

Chart on Lateral Lawyer Screening*

The following chart indicates whether, under the Model Rules, the *Restatement*, and the various state professional conduct rules, a firm can avoid imputed disqualification by constructing an effective screen when it hires a lateral lawyer who is personally disqualified from a matter because of a representation at a previous firm.

A "No" answer on the chart means that an ethical screen is not sufficient by itself, and that, in addition to the ethical screen, the lawyer's new firm must obtain the consent of the previous firm's client if the new firm is acting as counsel in the matter adverse to the previous firm's client. This must be done before the disqualified lawyer begins work at the new firm. Failure to obtain consent of the previous firm's client ordinarily will subject the new firm to disqualification. If that happens, a malpractice claim by the new firm's client is possible. As the chart shows, numerous jurisdictions still do not recognize screening as a cure for imputed disqualification. As mentioned above, and referenced in the notes to the chart, federal courts may differ with state courts and ethics committees in the same jurisdiction on this issue.

This chart and the subsequent notes deal only with lawyer movement from one private firm to another. In the case of a new lawyer who formerly worked for the executive or judicial branch of government, some form of effective screening is usually acceptable.

Lateral Lawyer Screening

Jurisdiction	Applicable Rules	Screening by Rule?	Screening Rule	Note
	ABA Model Rules of Professional Conduct	Yes	1.10(a)	
	Restatement	Limited	§ 124(2)	
AL	Rules of Professional Conduct	No		1
AK	Rules of Professional Conduct	No		2
AZ	Rules of Professional Conduct	Limited	1.10(d)	3
AR	Rules of Professional Conduct	No		4
CA	Rules of Professional Conduct	No		5
CO	Rules of Professional Conduct	Yes	1.10(a)	6
CT	Rules of Professional Conduct	Yes	1.10(a)	7

Jurisdiction	Applicable Rules	Screening by Rule?	Screening Rule	Note
DE	Lawyers' Rules of Professional Conduct	Yes	1.10(b)	8
DC	Rules of Professional Conduct	Yes	1.10(b)	9
FL	Rules of Professional Conduct	No		10
GA	Rules of Professional Conduct	No		11
HI	Rules of Professional Conduct	Limited	1.10(c)	12
ID	Rules of Professional Conduct	Yes	1.10(a)	
IL	Rules of Professional Conduct	Yes	1.10(e)	13
IN	Rules of Professional Conduct	Limited	1.10(c)	14
IA	Rules of Professional Conduct	Yes	32:1.10(a)	15
KS	Rules of Professional Conduct	No		16
KY	Rules of Professional Conduct	Yes	SCR 3.130(1.10)(d)	17
LA	Rules of Professional Conduct	No		18
ME	Rules of Professional Conduct	No		19
MD	Lawyer's Rules of Professional Conduct	Yes	1.10(c)	20
MA	Rules of Professional Conduct	Limited	1.10(d)	21
MI	Rules of Professional Conduct	Yes	1.10(b)	22
MN	Rules of Professional Conduct	Limited	1.10(b)	23
MS	Rules of Professional Conduct	No		24
MO	Rules of Professional Conduct	No		25
MT	Rules of Professional Conduct	Yes	1.10(c)	
NE	Rules of Professional Conduct	No		26
NV	Rules of Professional Conduct	Limited	1.10(e)	

Jurisdiction	Applicable Rules	Screening by Rule?	Screening Rule	Note
NH	Rules of Professional Conduct	No		
NJ	Rules of Professional Conduct	Limited	1.10(c)	27
NM	Rules of Professional Conduct	Limited	16–110(B)	28
NY	Rules of Professional Conduct	No		29
NC	Rules of Professional Conduct	Yes	1.10(c)	
ND	Rules of Professional Conduct	Limited	1.10(b)	
OH	Rules of Professional Conduct	Limited	1.10(d)	30
OK	Rules of Professional Conduct	No		
OR	Rules of Professional Conduct	Yes	1.10(c)	31
PA	Rules of Professional Conduct	Yes	1.10(b)	32
RI	Disciplinary Rules of Professional Conduct	Yes	1.10(c)	33
SC	Rules of Professional Conduct	No		34
SD	Rules of Professional Conduct	No		
TN	Rules of Professional Conduct	Limited	1.10(c) and (d)	35
TX	Disciplinary Rules of Professional Conduct	No		36
UT	Rules of Professional Conduct	Yes	1.10(c)	37
VT	Rules of Professional Conduct	Limited	1.10(a)	38
VA	Rules of Professional Conduct	No		39
WA	Rules of Professional Conduct	Yes	1.10(e)	
WV	Rules of Professional Conduct	No		40
WI	Rules of Professional Conduct for Attorneys	Limited	SCR 20:1.10(a)(2)	41
WY	Rules of Professional Conduct for Attorneys at Law	Yes	1.10(a)	

Notes for Chart

1. *See Roberts v. Hutchins*, 572 So. 2d 1231, 1234 (Ala. 1990).

2. *See Richard B. v. State*, 71 P.3d 811, 822–23 (Alaska 2003) (screen does not prevent disqualification).

3. *See Eberle Design, Inc.*, 354 F. Supp. 2d at 1096.

4. *See generally Burnette v. Morgan*, 794 S.W.2d 145 (Ark. 1990).

5. Although the California Supreme Court has not decided this issue, it opened the door to screening in *SpeeDee Oil Change Sys., Inc.*, 980 P.2d at 382, by discussing and not rejecting the idea. In *Kirk v. First Am. Title Ins. Co.*, 183 Cal. App. 4th 776, 802–10 (2010), the Second District Court of Appeals issued a thoughtful and well-reasoned opinion in which it approved of screening. Other California decisions (state and federal) are mixed. In *Panther v. Park*, 101 Cal. App. 4th 69, 71 (2002), the Fourth District Court of Appeal found that a "firm may rebut a presumption of shared confidences and avoid vicarious disqualification by showing that effective screening methods were in place," but that order was vacated without opinion by the California Supreme Court. *Panther v. Park*, 63 P.3d 215 (Cal. 2003). Some California decisions have been hostile to screening. *See generally Beltran*, 867 F. Supp. 2d 1068; *Hitachi, Ltd. v. Tatung Co.*, 419 F. Supp. 2d 1158 (N.D. Cal. 2006); *Andric v. State*, 55 F. Supp. 2d 1056 (C.D. Cal. 1999); *Emp'rs. Ins. of Wausau v. Albert D. Seeno Const. Co.*, 692 F. Supp. 1150 (N.D. Cal. 1988); *In re Mortg. & Realty Trust*, 195 B.R. 740; *Henriksen v. Great Am. Sav. & Loan*, 11 Cal. App. 4th 109 (1992). Others have been more receptive. *See generally In re Cty. of Los Angeles*, 223 F.3d 990 (9th Cir. 2000) (approved screen but in context of federal magistrate judge moving to private practice); *Nat'l Grange of Order of Patrons of Husbandry v. Cal. Guild*, 2017 U.S. Dist. LEXIS 72884, 2017 WL 2021731 (E.D. Cal. May 11, 2017) (screen effective; no disqualification); *Openwave Sys. Inc.*, 2011 U.S. Dist. LEXIS 35526, 2011 WL 1225987 (presumption that lateral lawyer had shared confidential information was rebutted, in part, because firm had screened lawyer); *All Am. Semiconductor, Inc.*, 2008 U.S. Dist. LEXIS 106619, at *29, 2008 WL 5484552, at *9 (disapproved screen, but indicated law in California "might well be headed" toward approval in some circumstances); *City of Santa Barbara v. Superior Court of Santa Barbara Cnty.*, 122 Cal. App. 4th 17 (2004) (court approved screening for government lawyers); *Klein v. Superior Court of Santa Clara Cnty.*, 198 Cal. App. 3d 894 (1988) (court implied that California courts might approve ethical walls provided new lawyer had not actually worked on affected client's matter while at previous firm); *cf. Castaneda v. Superior Court*, 237 Cal. App. 4th 1434, 1449 (2015) (screening will not cure conflict if lawyer learned confidential information while serving as settlement officer); *In re Charlisse C.*, 194 P.3d 330 (Cal. 2008) (firm might be able to cure conflict by erecting screen); *City & Cnty. of S.F. v. Cobra Solutions, Inc.*, 135 P.3d 20 (Cal. 2006) (California Supreme Court rejected screening with respect to city government law office).

6. *See also Hunter Douglas, Inc. v. Home Fashions, Inc.*, 811 F. Supp. 566, 569–70 (D. Colo. 1992) (applying Illinois professional conduct rules, federal court found lateral lawyer had been effectively screened); Colorado Opinion 88 (May 18, 1991) (predating Colorado Rule 1.10(a) that permits screening).

7. Several authorities addressed the issue before the amendment to Rule 1.10(a) that permits screening. *See* Connecticut Informal Opinion 01–16 (Dec. 28, 2001) (screening not allowed). *But see Horch v. United of Omaha Life Ins. Co.*, 1999 Conn. Super. LEXIS 1792, at *5–6, 1999 WL 511165, at *2 (July 1, 1999) (refusing to disqualify firm that hired lawyer who had worked on other side because lawyer had been effectively screened from matter); *Wellner v. Carroll*, 1995 Conn. Super. LEXIS 359, at *16–18, 1995 WL 55048, at *6–7 (Jan. 6, 1995) (suggesting screen might have avoided disqualification).

8. *See generally* Delaware Opinion 1986–1 (undated). The opinion relates specifically to nonlawyers; however, it relies, in part, on a case that extended Rule 1.11(b) screening provisions to private lawyers, *Nemours Found. v. Gilbane, Aetna, Fed. Ins. Co.*, 632 F. Supp. 418, 425–27 (D. Del. 1986).

9. Under D.C. Rule 1.10(b)(2), the conflict of a new lawyer who was tainted because of work at a previous firm as a summer associate, law clerk, paralegal, or other similar capacity before becoming a lawyer is not imputed to the firm. Of course, the second firm would be expected to take steps to ensure that the new lawyer does not have any involvement with, or make any improper disclosure regarding, any case in which he or she was previously involved (similar to the traditional requirement applicable to former judicial clerks). *See* District of Columbia Opinion 279 (Mar. 18, 1998); D.C. Rule 1.10 cmt. [18].

10. *See generally Nissan Motor Corp. in U.S.A. v. Orozco*, 595 So. 2d 240 (Fla. Dist. Ct. App. 1992); *Birdsall v. Crowngap, Ltd.*, 575 So. 2d 231 (Fla. Dist. Ct. App. 1991); *Edward J. DeBartolo Corp. v. Petrin*, 516 So. 2d 6 (Fla. Dist. Ct. App. 1987) (discussing Florida rules on screening and disqualification).

11. We are not aware of any Georgia court or ethics committee squarely deciding the screening issue. In *Georgia Baptist Health Care Sys., Inc. v. Hanafi*, 559 S.E.2d 746, 749 (Ga. Ct. App. 2002), however, the court in dicta noted the conflict was of the type that could be "managed and ameliorated" through screening. A Georgia federal court declared in dicta that it would reject screening measures in *Amoco Chems. Corp. v. MacArthur*, 568 F. Supp. 42, 47 (N.D. Ga. 1983).

12. *Reading Int'l, Inc. v. Malulani Grp., Ltd.*, 814 F.3d 1185 (9th Cir. 2016) (screening lateral lawyer with confidential information did not prevent disqualification under Hawaii's restrictive screening rule). Hawaii Rule of Professional Conduct 1.10(c) allows screening only when "the disqualified lawyer did not participate in the matter and has no confidential information regarding the matter."

13. The language of the Illinois screening rule (Rule 1.10(e)) differs from the Model Rule on Screening. Construing Illinois Rule 1.10(e) narrowly, Illinois Opinion 18-02 said screening is available only at the time a lateral lawyer becomes associated with a firm, not subsequent to that time. Illinois Opinion 18-02 (Jan. 2018). *See generally Cromley v. Bd. of Educ. of Lockport Twp. High Sch. Dist. 205*, 17 F.3d 1059 (7th Cir. 1994); *Hyatt Franchising, LLC v. Shen Zhen New World I, LLC*, 2017 U.S. Dist. LEXIS 594554, 2017 WL 1397553 (N.D. Ill. Apr. 19, 2017); *Amurol Confections Co. v. Morris Nat'l, Inc.*, 2003 U.S. Dist. LEXIS 9544, 2003 WL 21321344 (N.D. Ill. June 4, 2003); *Van Jackson v. Check 'N Go of Ill., Inc.*, 114 F. Supp. 2d 731 (N.D. Ill. 2000) (recognized screening but

nevertheless disqualified firm because screen ineffective); *Miller v. Chi. & Nw. Transp. Co.*, 938 F. Supp. 503 (N.D. Ill. 1996).

14. *See generally XYZ, D.O. v. Sykes*, 20 N.E.3d 582 (Ind. Ct. App. 2014) (screen does not cure conflict where lateral lawyer had primary responsibility for prior related matters); *Gerald v. Turnock Plumbing, Heating & Cooling, LLC*, 768 N.E.2d 498, 503–04 (Ind. Ct. App. 2002) (court approved of screening, but the screen at issue was implemented too late). In *Chapman v. Chrysler Corp.*, 54 F. Supp. 2d 864, 866 (S.D. Ind. 1999), and *Speedy v. Rexnord Corp.*, 54 F. Supp. 2d 867, 869 (S.D. Ind. 1999), Indiana federal district courts found screening measures effective and, following Seventh Circuit precedent, refused to disqualify the firms with alleged conflicts.

15. Before the Iowa Rules of Professional Conduct were amended to approve screening, the Iowa Supreme Court had rejected the concept. *See Doe v. Perry Cmty. Sch. Dist.*, 650 N.W.2d 594, 600 (Iowa 2002).

16. *See generally Graham v. Wyeth Labs. Div. of Am. Home Prods. Corp.*, 906 F.2d 1419 (10th Cir. 1990); *Pac. Emp'rs Ins. Co.*, 789 F. Supp. 1112; *Lansing-Del. Water Dist. v. Oak Lane Park, Inc.*, 808 P.2d 1369 (Kan. 1991); *Parker v. Volkswagenwerk Aktiengesellschaft*, 781 P.2d 1099 (Kan. 1989).

17. A literal reading of the Kentucky screening rule permits screening of any lawyer who has a conflict because of a former client, not just lateral lawyers. It seems highly questionable, however, whether any court would interpret the rule this broadly.

18. The Louisiana Rules of Professional Conduct do not permit screening, but *Petrovich v. Petrovich*, 556 So. 2d 281, 282 (La. Ct. App. 1990), upheld a trial court's finding that the lawyers had established a "cone of silence," and therefore, there was no disqualification. Federal courts in Louisiana follow Fifth Circuit precedent and refuse to allow the use of a screen to cure an imputed disqualification. *See, e.g., Green v. Adm'rs of Tulane Educ. Fund*, 1998 U.S. Dist. LEXIS 769, at *3, 1998 WL 24424, at *9 (E.D. La. Jan. 22, 1998).

19. *See generally Casco N. Bank v. JBI Assocs., Ltd.*, 667 A.2d 856 (Me. 1995).

20. *See generally Compass Mktg., Inc. v. Schering-Plough Corp.*, 2006 U.S. Dist. LEXIS 49311, 2006 WL 1892405 (D. Md. July 6, 2006).

21. *See U.S. Filter Corp. v. Ionics, Inc.*, 189 F.R.D. 26, 31 (D. Mass. 1999) (refusing to approve screen because Massachusetts Rule 1.10(d)(2) screening requirements were not satisfied). At least one decision decided prior to the 1998 rule change allowed limited screening. *See Thomalen v. Marriott Corp.*, 1994 U.S. Dist. LEXIS 13650, at *5, 1994 WL 524123, at *2 (D. Mass. Sept. 19, 1994).

22. *See generally Nat'l Union Fire Ins. Co. of Pittsburgh*, 472 F.3d 436, discussed in Section 7.6.3 above and "The Wild Card in Analyzing Conflicts or Other Legal Ethics Issues—'Questionable' Judicial Decisions," *Journal* (Winter 2007). *See also Cobb Publ'g, Inc. v. Hearst Corp.*, 907 F. Supp. 1038 (E.D. Mich. 1995); Michigan Informal Opinion RI-115 (Jan. 31, 1992); Michigan Formal Opinion R-4 (Sept. 22, 1989).

23. Under Minnesota Rule of Professional Conduct 1.10(b), a lateral lawyer's conflict will not be imputed to others in the firm if: (1) the lawyer does not have "significant" confidential information, (2) the

lawyer is screened, and (3) affected clients receive timely and adequate notice of the screen. In *Lennartson v. Anoka-Hennepin Indep. Sch. Dist. No. 11*, 662 N.W.2d 125, 130–31 (Minn. 2003), the Minnesota Supreme Court held Rule 1.10(b) should be read literally so that a conflict will be imputed unless all of the rule's subparts are satisfied.

24. *But see Aldridge v. State*, 583 So. 2d 203, 205–06 (Miss. 1991) (in criminal case, when deciding motion to disqualify counsel, court should consider whether conflicted lawyer was screened).

25. *See* Missouri Informal Opinions 20050030 (undated) and 20030007 (undated) (screening will not avoid disqualification). *But see Sch. Dist. of Kan. City v. ACandS, Inc.*, 1989 U.S. Dist. LEXIS 10009, at *3, 1989 WL 99138, at *3 (W.D. Mo. Aug. 23, 1989); *Hallmark Cards, Inc. v. Hallmark Dodge, Inc.*, 616 F. Supp. 516 (W.D. Mo. 1985).

26. *See generally State ex rel. FirsTier Bank, N.A. v. Buckley*, 503 N.W.2d 838 (Neb. 1993).

27. *See Ford Motor Co.*, 2011 U.S. Dist. LEXIS 123348, at *35–37, 2011 WL 5080347, at *8–9 (lawyer had "primary responsibility"; screening not available); *Martin*, 2011 U.S. Dist. LEXIS 122987, at *11–13, 2011 WL 5080255, at *4 (even though not supervising lawyer, associate had "primary responsibility" and could not be screened). The following opinions were issued before New Jersey Rule 1.10 was amended to allow limited screening: *Cardona*, 942 F. Supp. 968, 976–77 (court noted that in New Jersey ethics screens had not been approved to preclude imputed disqualification); New Jersey Opinion 667 (required consent as condition precedent to screening).

28. *See Mercer, LLC v. Reynolds*, 292 P.3d 466, 471 (N.M. 2012) (imputed conflict could not be cured by screening because lateral had played "substantial role" in matter at prior firm).

29. *See Alicea v. Bencivenga*, 704 N.Y.S.2d 578, 579 (App. Div. 2000); *Cummin v. Cummin*, 695 N.Y.S.2d 346, 347 (App. Div. 1999) (screen around lawyer with preliminary consultation conflict provided adequate safeguard); *Kassis v. Teacher's Ins. & Annuity Ass'n*, 717 N.E.2d 674, 678 (N.Y. 1999) (if moving lawyer has information that is either "significant" or "material," screen will not work); *Trustco Bank N.Y. v. Melino*, 625 N.Y.S.2d 803, 808 (Sup. Ct. 1995) (rejected screening). New York federal courts approved of screening measures or de facto barriers in *Arista Records LLC*, 2011 U.S. Dist. LEXIS 17434, at *31–32, 2011 WL 672254, at *7–8; *Reilly v. Computer Assocs. Long-Term Disability Plan*, 423 F. Supp. 2d 5, 11 (E.D.N.Y. 2006); *Papyrus Tech. Corp.*, 325 F. Supp. 2d at 282; *G.D. Searle & Co.*, 1999 U.S. Dist. LEXIS 5963, at *7, 1999 WL 249725, at *3; *Schwed v. Gen. Elec. Co.*, 990 F. Supp. 113, 118–19 (N.D.N.Y. 1998); *In re Del-Val Fin. Corp. Sec. Litig.*, 158 F.R.D. at 275. *But see United States v. Salvagno*, 2003 U.S. Dist. LEXIS 4145, at *26–27, 2003 WL 21939629, at *7 (N.D.N.Y. Feb. 28, 2003) (screen will not work in two-lawyer office); *Decora Inc. v. DW Wallcovering, Inc.*, 899 F. Supp. 132, 139–40 (S.D.N.Y. 1995) (new firm too small and screen erected too late).

30. *See Dickens v. J&E Custom Homes, Inc.*, 933 N.E.2d 291, 293 (Ohio Ct. App. 2010) (discussing Ohio Rule of Professional Conduct 1.10 and *Kala v. Aluminum Smelting & Refining Co.*, 688 N.E.2d 258, 266 (Ohio 1998)).

31. Oregon Rule of Professional Conduct 1.10(c) approves of screening provided the disqualified lawyer and his or her firm take certain steps

prescribed by the rule. In *Portland Gen. Elec. Co. v. Duncan, Weinberg, Miller & Pembroke, P.C.*, 986 P.2d 35, 49 (Or. Ct. App. 1999), the court held that a screen could prevent imputation of a conflict, provided it was approved either by the lower court or by the ethics experts who testified in the matter.

32. Philadelphia Opinion 91–18 (July 1991) confirms that consent is not required where screening is used. The court applied that rule in *Dworkin v. Gen. Motors Corp.*, 906 F. Supp. 273 (E.D. Pa. 1995); *see also Norfolk S. Ry. Co.*, 397 F. Supp. 2d at 555 (screen ineffective because, among other reasons, it failed to provide sanctions for violation); *James v. Teleflex, Inc.*, 1999 U.S. Dist. LEXIS 1961, at *15–16, 1999 WL 98559, at *6 (E.D. Pa. Feb. 24, 1999) (screen inadequate).

33. *See Fedora*, 84 A.3d at 814 (court assumed lawyer screening rule applied to paralegal).

34. *See generally H & C Corp. v Puka*, 2013 U.S. Dist. LEXIS 147174, 2013 WL 5597180 (D.S.C. Oct. 11, 2013); South Carolina Opinion 92–23 (1992). The South Carolina Rules of Professional Conduct, however, provide that a lawyer in a "program serving indigent clients shall not be disqualified under [Rule 1.10] because of the program's representation of another client in the same or a substantially related matter if . . . the lawyer is [timely] screened." South Carolina Rule of Prof'l Conduct 1.10(e).

35. Before the new Tennessee Rules of Professional Conduct, the Tennessee Supreme Court held that screening procedures adequately rebutted the presumption of shared confidences, but nevertheless disqualified the firm involved because of an appearance of impropriety. *See Clinard v. Blackwood*, 46 S.W.3d 177, 184–85 (Tenn. 2001). The Sixth Circuit and Tennessee federal district courts also have approved of screening. *See generally Manning v. Waring, Cox, James, Sklar & Allen*, 849 F.2d 222 (6th Cir. 1988); *Vergos v. Timber Creek, Inc.*, 200 B.R. 624 (W.D. Tenn. 1996). *But see Penn. Mut. Life Ins. Co. v. Cleveland Mall Assocs.*, 841 F. Supp. 815, 819 (E.D. Tenn. 1993), where on facts similar to those in *Club Income Properties*, a district court ruled that the firm should be disqualified.

36. *See generally Henderson v. Floyd*, 891 S.W.2d 252 (Tex. 1995); *Phoenix Founders, Inc. v. Marshall*, 887 S.W.2d 831 (Tex. 1994). *But see COC Servs., Ltd. v. CompUSA, Inc.*, 2002 Tex. App. LEXIS 5687, at *6–9, 2002 WL 1792479, at *3 (Aug. 6, 2002) (defendant's firm not disqualified even though it hired lawyer who had worked on matter for plaintiff, because moving lawyer's work was minimal and equities weighed against disqualification). *See also Nat'l Oilwell Varco, L.P.*, 60 F. Supp. 3d at 751 (in Fifth Circuit, federal courts allow screening); Texas Opinion 644 (July 2016) (replacing Texas Opinion 644 (Aug. 2014)) (firm does not have to withdraw provided it screens lawyer who had worked for opposing party while working as a law student clerk at another firm).

37. *See Lutron Elecs. Co., Inc.*, 2010 U.S. Dist. LEXIS 120864, at *17, 2010 WL 4720693, at *5 (screen was timely because it was erected as soon as firm became aware of conflict).

38. *See generally* Vermont Opinion 87–07 (undated).

39. *See Audio MPEG, Inc. v. Dell, Inc.*, 2016 U.S. Dist. LEXIS 147920, 2016 WL 6246772 (E.D. Va. Oct. 25, 2016) (screen does not cure imputation

of lateral conflict); Virginia Opinion 1428 (Feb. 22, 1992) (disapproves of screening without consent).

40. *Burgess-Lester*, 643 F. Supp. 2d at 813–14, recognized that screening might be effective in a particular case but noted that all doubts should be resolved in favor of disqualification. The court found the screen at issue ineffective because the tainted lawyer was unsure of its precise parameters. Other federal courts in West Virginia have rejected screening. *See generally CSX Transp., Inc. v. Gilkison*, 2006 U.S. Dist. LEXIS 81019, 2006 WL 3203419 (N.D. W. Va. Nov. 3, 2006); *Healthnet, Inc.*, 289 F. Supp. 2d at 755; *Roberts & Schaefer Co. v. San-Con, Inc.*, 898 F. Supp. 356 (S.D.W. Va. 1995).

41. Although the Wisconsin Rules of Professional Conduct only permit limited screening, several Wisconsin federal courts have taken a broader view. *See Silicon Graphics*, 741 F. Supp. 2d 982–83 (federal court denied disqualification motion because tainted lawyer had been effectively screened); *Nelson*, 823 F. Supp. at 1449 (court indicated that timely screen would have prevented disqualification in broader context). In *Nelson*, the court found that the firm's screen was too late when it was not erected until after the other side raised conflicts concerns.

APPENDIX C

Chart on Written Fee Agreements*

Model Rule 1.5(c) requires a written fee agreement in contingent fee matters, and Model Rule 1.5(b) recommends one in all other matters except when the lawyer will charge a regularly represented client on the same basis or rate. Changes in the basis or rate of fees or expenses are also to be communicated to the client. A chart summarizing each state's rules appears below, although a firm should always check the rules in each applicable jurisdiction. As the chart shows, most states follow the Model Rules pattern, but some jurisdictions require written fee agreements for all new clients. Generally, but not always, the "Others" column in the chart cites a provision that refers to a new client, noncontingent fee situation. States impose many additional requirements for the content and terms of fee agreements that are not included in the chart below. The chart should also not obscure that the Model Rules usually require lawyers, at a minimum, to orally communicate their fees and other charges. *See* Model Rule 1.5(b).

The jurisdictions that require written fee agreements for all new clients are Arizona, Colorado, Connecticut, District of Columbia, Georgia, New Jersey, Pennsylvania, Rhode Island, and Wisconsin. As noted in the chart below, some states require written fee agreements if the fees will exceed a de minimus amount. Connecticut Rule 1.5(b) has been construed to require a written "statement" of noncontingent fees, costs, and expenses, but not a written fee "agreement." *See* Connecticut Informal Opinion 01–09 (June 26, 2001) (distinguishing written contingent fee "agreement" required by Rule 1.5(c)). Even where a client is "regularly represented" by a lawyer, the lawyer still must provide "appropriate written communication" to that client setting out noncontingent fees and costs for a new matter "if the evolved past understanding [from prior engagements] provides insufficient basis for the fee in the new matter."

Several states have no provision relating to the need for written fee agreements in the rules of professional conduct, but deal with the issue elsewhere in court rules or statutes. We have included the appropriate references where we are aware of them.

The consequences of not having a written fee agreement where one is required can range from troublesome to disastrous. In *Starkey, Kelly, Blaney & White v. Estate of Nicolaysen*, 796 A.2d 238 (N.J. 2002), the court invalidated a contingent fee agreement that was not reduced to writing until 33 months after the engagement began, but allowed the lawyer to recover in quantum meruit. *See also Alioto v. Hoiles*, 531 F. App'x 842, 857 (10th Cir. 2013) (allowing quantum meruit recovery where written contingent fee invalidated due to incomplete description of scope of engagement); *Nabi v. Sells*, 892 N.Y.S.2d 41, 45 (App. Div. 2009) (firm could recover reasonable value of its services despite failure to provide written contingent fee agreement). In *Statewide Grievance Comm. v. Dixon*, 772 A.2d 160, 166 (Conn. App. Ct. 2001), however, the court affirmed the imposition of a nine-month suspension against a lawyer who did not put his contingent fee agreement in writing. *See also Eng v. Cummings, McClorey, Davis & Acho, PLC*, 611 F.3d 428, 435 (8th Cir. 2010) (barring claim by lawyer to enforce contingent fee agreement not reduced to writing); *Strong v. Beydoun*, 166 Cal. App. 4th 1398, 1404–05 (2008) (rejecting any recovery from clients by lawyer with invalid fee sharing agreement, including in quantum meruit).

Chart on Written Fee Agreements

Jurisdiction	Applicable Rules	Contingent	Others
	Model Rules of Professional Conduct	Must: 1.5(c)	Preferred: 1.5(b) (unless lawyer regularly represents client on same basis or rate)
AL	Rules of Professional Conduct	Must: 1.5(c)	Preferred (if lawyer has not regularly represented client): 1.5(b)
AK	Rules of Professional Conduct	Must: 1.5(c)	Must (if over $1,000): 1.5(b)
AZ	Rules of Professional Conduct	Must: 1.5(c)	Must (unless lawyer regularly represents client on same basis or rate): 1.5(b)
AR	Rules of Professional Conduct	Must: 1.5(c)	Preferred (unless lawyer regularly represents client on same basis or rate): 1.5(b)
CA	Statutory Provisions	Must: Cal. Bus. & Prof. Code § 6147	Must (if not a corporation and over $1,000 unless facts imply agreement based on fees previously paid for same kind of services rendered): § 6148 of Business and Professions Code
CO	Rules of Professional Conduct, Rules of Civil Procedure, and Court Rules	Must: Ch. 23.3 Col. Civ. P. R. 1 Court Rule 4(b)	Must (if lawyer has not regularly represented client): 1.5(b)
CT	Rules of Professional Conduct	Must: 1.5(c)	Must (unless lawyer regularly represents client on same basis or rate): 1.5(b)
DE	Lawyers' Rules of Professional Conduct	Must: 1.5(c)	Preferred (unless lawyer regularly represents client on same basis or rate): 1.5(b)

CHART ON WRITTEN FEE AGREEMENTS

Jurisdiction	Applicable Rules	Contingent	Others
DC	Rules of Professional Conduct	Must: 1.5(c)	Must (if lawyer has not regularly represented client): 1.5(b)
FL	Rules of Professional Conduct	Must: 4–1.5(f)	Preferred (if lawyer has not regularly represented client); Must (if any part of legal fee is nonrefundable): 4–1.5(e)
GA	Rules of Professional Conduct	Must: 1.5(c)	Preferred (unless lawyer regularly represents client on same basis or rate): 1.5(b)
HI	Rules of Professional Conduct	Must: 1.5(c)	Preferred (if lawyer has not regularly represented client): 1.5(b)
ID	Rules of Professional Conduct	Must: 1.5(c)	Preferred (if lawyer has not regularly represented client on same basis or rate): 1.5(b)
IL	Rules of Professional Conduct	Must: 1.5(c)	Preferred (unless lawyer regularly represents client on same basis or rate): 1.5(b)
IN	Rules of Professional Conduct	Must: 1.5(c)	Preferred (unless lawyer regularly represents client on same basis or rate): 1.5(b)
IA	Rules of Professional Conduct	Must: 32: 1.5(c)	Preferred (unless lawyer regularly represents client on same basis or rate): 32: 1.5(b)
KS	Rules of Professional Conduct	Must: 1.5(d)	Preferred (if lawyer has not regularly represented client): 1.5(b)
KY	Rules of Professional Conduct	Must: 1.5(c)	Preferred (if lawyer has not regularly represented client on same basis or rate): 1.5(b)

Jurisdiction	Applicable Rules	Contingent	Others
LA	Rules of Professional Conduct	Must: 1.5(c)	Preferred (unless lawyer regularly represents client on same basis or rate): 1.5(b)
ME	Rules of Professional Conduct	Must: 1.5(c)	Preferred (unless lawyer regularly represents client on same basis or rate): 1.5(b)
MD	Lawyers' Rules of Professional Conduct	Must: 1.5(c)	Preferred (unless lawyer regularly represents client on same basis or rate): 1.5(b)
MA	Rules of Professional Conduct	Must: 1.5(c) (except in collections of commercial accounts and in insurance company subrogation claims)	Must (unless lawyer regularly represents client on same basis or rate, if it is single session consultation, or if less than $500): 1.5(b)
MI	Rules of Professional Conduct	Must: 1.5(c)	Preferred (if lawyer has not regularly represented client): 1.5(b)
MN	Rules of Professional Conduct	Must: 1.5(c)	Preferred (unless lawyer regularly represents client on same basis or rate): 1.5(b)
MS	Rules of Professional Conduct	Must: 1.5(c)	Preferred (if lawyer has not regularly represented client): 1.5(b)
MO	Rules of Professional Conduct	Must: 1.5(c)	Preferred (unless lawyer regularly represents client on same basis or rate): 1.5(b)
MT	Rules of Professional Conduct	Must: 1.5(c)	Must (unless lawyer regularly represents client on same basis or rate, or if less than $500): 1.5(b)

Jurisdiction	Applicable Rules	Contingent	Others
NE	Rules of Professional Conduct	Must: 3–501.5(c)	Preferred (unless lawyer regularly represents client on same basis or rate): 3–501.5(b)
NV	Rules of Professional Conduct	Must: 1.5(c)	Preferred (unless lawyer regularly represents client on same basis or rate): 1.5(b)
NH	Rules of Professional Conduct	Must: 1.5(c)	Preferred (if lawyer has not regularly represented client): 1.5(b)
NJ	Rules of Professional Conduct	Must: 1.5(c)	Must (if lawyer has not regularly represented client): 1.5(b)
NM	Rules of Professional Conduct	Must: 16–105(C)	Must (unless lawyer regularly represents client on same basis or rate or public service representation): 16–105(B)
NY	Rules of Professional Conduct N.Y. Comp. Codes R. & Regs. tit. 22, § 1200 (2014)	Must: 1.5(c)	Must where required by statute or court rule (unless lawyer regularly performs same general kind of services for client on same basis or rate): 1.5(b); Must in domestic relations matters: 1.5(d)(5)(ii) (Must unless fee is expected to be less than $3,000)
NC	Revised Rules of Professional Conduct	Must: 1.5(c)	Preferred (if lawyer has not regularly represented client): 1.5(b)
ND	Rules of Professional Conduct	Must: 1.5(c)	Preferred (if lawyer has not regularly represented client): 1.5(b)
OH	Rules of Professional Conduct	Must: 1.5(c)(1)	Preferred (unless lawyer regularly represents client on same basis or rate): 1.5(b)

Jurisdiction	Applicable Rules	Contingent	Others
OK	Rules of Professional Conduct	Must: 1.5(c)	Preferred (unless lawyer regularly represents client on same basis or rate): 1.5(b)
OR	Rules of Professional Conduct; Oregon Revised Statutes	Must for personal injury and property damage claims: Ore. Rev. Stat. § 20.340	Must (if nonrefundable fee): 1.5(c)(3)
PA	Rules of Professional Conduct	Must: 1.5(c)	Must (if lawyer has not regularly represented client): 1.5(b)
RI	Disciplinary Rules of Professional Conduct	Must: 1.5(c)	Must (unless lawyer regularly represents client on same basis or rate): 1.5(b)
SC	Rules of Professional Conduct	Must: 1.5(c)	Preferred (unless lawyer regularly represents client on same basis or rate): 1.5(b)
SD	Rules of Professional Conduct	Must: 1.5(c)	Preferred (unless lawyer regularly represents client on same basis or rate): 1.5(b), (f)
TN	Rules of Professional Conduct	Must: 1.5(c)	Preferred (unless lawyer regularly represents client on same basis or rate): 1.5(b)
TX	Disciplinary Rules of Professional Conduct	Must: 1.04(d)	Preferred (if lawyer has not regularly represented client): 1.04(c)
UT	Rules of Professional Conduct	Must: 1.5(c)	Preferred (unless lawyer regularly represents client on same basis or rate): 1.5(b)
VT	Rules of Professional Conduct	Must: 1.5(c)	Preferred (unless lawyer regularly represented client on same basis or rate); Must (if nonrefundable):1.5(b)

CHART ON WRITTEN FEE AGREEMENTS

Jurisdiction	Applicable Rules	Contingent	Others
VA	Rules of Professional Conduct	Must: 1.5(c)	Preferred (if lawyer has not regularly represented client): 1.5(b)
WA	Rules of Professional Conduct	Must: 1.5(c)(1)	Preferred (unless lawyer regularly represents client on same basis or rate): 1.5(b)
WV	Rules of Professional Conduct	Must: 1.5(c)	Must (unless lawyer regularly represents client on same basis or rate): 1.5(b)
WI	Rules of Professional Conduct for Attorneys	Must: 20:1.5(c)	Must (unless lawyer regularly represents client on same basis or rate, or if less than $1,000): 20:1.5(b)
WY	Rules of Professional Conduct for Attorneys at Law	Must: 1.5(c)	Preferred (unless lawyer regularly represents client on same basis or rate): 1.5(b)

AMERICAN BAR ASSOCIATION MODEL CODE OF PROFESSIONAL RESPONSIBILITY

As Amended

PREAMBLE AND PRELIMINARY STATEMENT

Preamble

The continued existence of a free and democratic society depends upon recognition of the concept that justice is based upon the rule of law grounded in respect for the dignity of the individual and his capacity through reason for enlightened self-government. Law so grounded makes justice possible, for only through such law does the dignity of the individual attain respect and protection. Without it, individual rights become subject to unrestrained power, respect for law is destroyed, and rational self-government is impossible.

Lawyers, as guardians of the law, play a vital role in the preservation of society. The fulfillment of this role requires an understanding by lawyers of their relationship with and function in our legal system. A consequent obligation of lawyers is to maintain the highest standards of ethical conduct.

In fulfilling his professional responsibilities, a lawyer necessarily assumes various roles that require the performance of many difficult tasks. Not every situation which he may encounter can be foreseen, but fundamental ethical principles are always present to guide him. Within the framework of these principles, a lawyer must with courage and foresight be able and ready to shape the body of the law to the ever-changing relationships of society.

The Code of Professional Responsibility points the way to the aspiring and provides standards by which to judge the transgressor. Each lawyer must find within his own conscience the touchstone against which to test the extent to which his actions should rise above minimum standards. But in the last analysis it is the desire for the respect and confidence of the members of his profession and of the society which he serves that should provide to a lawyer the incentive for the highest possible degree of ethical conduct. The possible loss of that respect and confidence is the ultimate sanction. So long as its practitioners are guided by these principles, the law will continue to be a noble profession. This is its greatness and its strength, which permit of no compromise.

Preliminary Statement

In furtherance of the principles stated in the Preamble, the American Bar Association has promulgated this Model Code of Professional Responsibility, consisting of three separate but interrelated parts: Canons, Ethical Considerations, and Disciplinary Rules. The Code is designed to be adopted by appropriate agencies both as an inspirational guide to the members of the profession and as a basis for disciplinary action when the conduct of a lawyer falls below the required minimum standards stated in the Disciplinary Rules.

Obviously the Canons, Ethical Considerations, and Disciplinary Rules cannot apply to non-lawyers; however, they do define the type of ethical conduct that the public has a right to expect not only of lawyers but also of their non-professional employees and associates in all matters pertaining to professional employment. A lawyer should ultimately be responsible for the conduct of his employees and associates in the course of the professional representation of the client.

The Canons are statements of axiomatic norms, expressing in general terms the standards of professional conduct expected of lawyers in their relationships with the public, with the legal system, and with the legal profession. They embody the general concepts from which the Ethical Considerations and the Disciplinary Rules are derived.

The Ethical Considerations are aspirational in character and represent the objectives toward which every member of the profession should strive. They constitute a body of principles upon which the lawyer can rely for guidance in many specific situations.

The Disciplinary Rules, unlike the Ethical Considerations, are mandatory in character. The Disciplinary Rules state the minimum level of conduct below which no lawyer can fall without being subject to disciplinary action. Within the framework of fair trial, the Disciplinary Rules should be uniformly applied to all lawyers, regardless of the nature of their professional activities. The Code makes no attempt to prescribe either disciplinary procedures or penalties for violation of a Disciplinary Rule, nor does it undertake to define standards for civil liability of lawyers for professional conduct. The severity of judgment against one found guilty of violating a Disciplinary Rule should be determined by the character of the offense and the attendant circumstances. An enforcing agency, in applying the Disciplinary Rules, may find interpretive guidance in the basic principles embodied in the Canons and in the objectives reflected in the Ethical Considerations.

CANON 1

A Lawyer Should Assist in Maintaining the Integrity and Competence of the Legal Profession

ETHICAL CONSIDERATIONS

EC 1–1 A basic tenet of the professional responsibility of lawyers is that every person in our society should have ready access to the independent professional services of a lawyer of integrity and competence. Maintaining the integrity and improving the competence of the bar to meet the highest standards is the ethical responsibility of every lawyer.

EC 1–2 The public should be protected from those who are not qualified to be lawyers by reason of a deficiency in education or moral standards or of other relevant factors but who nevertheless seek to practice law. To assure the maintenance of high moral and educational standards of the legal profession, lawyers should affirmatively assist courts and other appropriate bodies in promulgating, enforcing, and improving requirements for admission to the bar. In like manner, the bar has a positive obligation to aid in the continued improvement of all phases of pre-admission and post-admission legal education.

EC 1–3 Before recommending an applicant for admission, a lawyer should satisfy himself that the applicant is of good moral character. Although a lawyer should not become a self-appointed investigator or judge of applicants for admission, he should report to proper officials all unfavorable information he possesses relating to the character or other qualifications of an applicant.

EC 1–4 The integrity of the profession can be maintained only if conduct of lawyers in violation of the Disciplinary Rules is brought to the attention of the proper officials. A lawyer should reveal voluntarily to those officials all unprivileged knowledge of conduct of lawyers which he believes clearly to be in violation of the Disciplinary Rules. A lawyer should, upon request, serve on and assist committees and boards having responsibility for the administration of the Disciplinary Rules.

EC 1–5 A lawyer should maintain high standards of professional conduct and should encourage fellow lawyers to do likewise. He should be temperate and dignified, and he should refrain from all illegal and morally reprehensible conduct. Because of his position in society, even minor violations of law by a lawyer may tend to lessen public confidence in the legal profession. Obedience to law exemplifies respect for law. To lawyers especially, respect for the law should be more than a platitude.

EC 1–6 An applicant for admission to the bar or a lawyer may be unqualified, temporarily or permanently, for other than moral and educational reasons, such as mental or emotional instability. Lawyers should be diligent in taking steps to see that during a period of disqualification such person is not granted a license or, if licensed, is not permitted to practice. In like manner, when the disqualification has terminated, members of the bar should assist such person in being licensed, or, if licensed, in being restored to his full right to practice.

DISCIPLINARY RULES

DR 1–101 **Maintaining Integrity and Competence of the Legal Profession.**

(A) A lawyer is subject to discipline if he has made a materially false statement in, or if he has deliberately failed to disclose a material fact requested in connection with, his application for admission to the bar.

(B) A lawyer shall not further the application for admission to the bar of another person known by him to be unqualified in respect to character, education, or other relevant attribute.

DR 1–102 **Misconduct.**

(A) A lawyer shall not:

    (1) Violate a Disciplinary Rule.

    (2) Circumvent a Disciplinary Rule through actions of another.

    (3) Engage in illegal conduct involving moral turpitude.

    (4) Engage in conduct involving dishonesty, fraud, deceit, or misrepresentation.

    (5) Engage in conduct that is prejudicial to the administration of justice.

    (6) Engage in any other conduct that adversely reflects on his fitness to practice law.

DR 1–103   Disclosure of Information to Authorities.

(A) A lawyer possessing unprivileged knowledge of a violation of DR 1–102 shall report such knowledge to a tribunal or other authority empowered to investigate or act upon such violation.

(B) A lawyer possessing unprivileged knowledge or evidence concerning another lawyer or a judge shall reveal fully such knowledge or evidence upon proper request of a tribunal or other authority empowered to investigate or act upon the conduct of lawyers or judges.

CANON 2

A Lawyer Should Assist the Legal Profession in Fulfilling Its Duty to Make Legal Counsel Available

ETHICAL CONSIDERATIONS

EC 2–1   The need of members of the public for legal services is met only if they recognize their legal problems, appreciate the importance of seeking assistance, and are able to obtain the services of acceptable legal counsel. Hence, important functions of the legal profession are to educate laymen to recognize their problems, to facilitate the process of intelligent selection of lawyers, and to assist in making legal services fully available.

Recognition of Legal Problems

EC 2–2   The legal profession should assist lay-persons to recognize legal problems because such problems may not be self-revealing and often are not timely noticed. Therefore, lawyers should encourage and participate in educational and public relations programs concerning our legal system with particular reference to legal problems that frequently arise. Preparation of advertisements and professional articles for lay publications and participation in seminars, lectures, and civic programs should be motivated by a desire to educate the public to an awareness of legal needs and to provide information relevant to the selection of the most appropriate counsel rather than to obtain publicity for particular lawyers. The problems of advertising on television require special consideration, due to the style, cost, and transitory nature of such media. If the interests of laypersons in receiving relevant lawyer advertising are not adequately served by print media and radio advertising, and if adequate safeguards to protect the public can reasonably be formulated, television advertising may serve a public interest.

EC 2–3   Whether a lawyer acts properly in volunteering in-person advice to a layperson to seek legal services depends upon the circumstances. The giving of advice that one should take legal action could well be in fulfillment of the duty of the legal profession to assist laypersons in recognizing legal problems. The advice is proper only if motivated by a desire to protect one who does not recognize that he may have legal problems or who is ignorant of his legal rights or obligations. It is improper if motivated by a desire to obtain personal benefit, secure personal publicity, or cause legal action to be taken merely to harass or injure another. A lawyer should not initiate an in-person contact with a non-client, personally or through a representative, for the purpose of being retained to represent him for compensation.

EC 2–4   Since motivation is subjective and often difficult to judge, the motives of a lawyer who volunteers in-person advice likely to produce legal controversy may well be suspect if he receives professional employment or other benefits as a result. A lawyer who volunteers in-person advice that one should obtain the services of a lawyer generally should not himself accept employment, compensation, or other benefit in connection with that matter. However, it is not improper for a lawyer to volunteer such advice and render resulting legal services to close friends, relatives, former clients (in regard to matters germane to former employment), and regular clients.

EC 2–5   A lawyer who writes or speaks for the purpose of educating members of the public to recognize their legal problems should carefully refrain from giving or appearing to give a general solution applicable to all apparently similar individual problems, since slight changes in fact situations may require a material variance in the applicable advice; otherwise, the public may be misled and misadvised. Talks and writings by lawyers for laypersons should caution them not to attempt to solve individual problems upon the basis of the information contained therein.

Selection of a Lawyer

EC 2–6   Formerly a potential client usually knew the reputations of local lawyers for competency and integrity and therefore could select a practitioner in whom he had confidence. This traditional selection process worked well because it was initiated by the client and the choice was an informed one.

EC 2–7   Changed conditions, however, have seriously restricted the effectiveness of the traditional selection process. Often the reputations of lawyers are not sufficiently known to enable laypersons to make intelligent choices. The law has become increasingly complex and specialized. Few lawyers are willing and competent to deal with every kind of legal matter, and many laypersons have difficulty in determining the competence of lawyers to render different types of legal services. The selection of legal counsel is particularly difficult for transients, persons moving into new areas, persons of limited education or means, and others who have little or no contact with lawyers. Lack of information about the availability of lawyers, the qualifications of particular lawyers, and the expense of legal representation leads laypersons to avoid seeking legal advice.

EC 2–8   Selection of a lawyer by a layperson should be made on an informed basis. Advice and recommendation of third parties—relatives, friends, acquaintances, business associates, or other lawyers—and disclosure of relevant information about the lawyer and his practice may be helpful. A layperson is best served if the recommendation is disinterested and informed. In order that the recommendation be disinterested, a lawyer should not seek to influence another to recommend his employment. A lawyer should not compensate another person for recommending him, for influencing a prospective client to employ him, or to encourage future recommendations. Advertisements and public communications, whether in law lists, telephone directories, newspapers, other forms of print media, television or radio, should be formulated to convey only information that is necessary to make an appropriate selection. Such information includes: (1) office information, such as, name, including name of law firm and names of professional associates; addresses; telephone numbers; credit card acceptability; fluency in foreign languages; and office hours; (2) relevant biographical information; (3) description of the practice, but only by using designations and definitions authorized by [the agency having jurisdiction of the subject under state law], for example, one or more fields of law in which the lawyer or law firm practices; a statement that practice is limited to one or more fields of law; and/or a statement that the lawyer or law firm specializes in a particular field of law practice, but only by using designations, definitions and standards authorized by [the agency having jurisdiction of the subject under state law]; and (4) permitted fee information. Self-laudation should be avoided.

183

Selection of a Lawyer: Lawyer Advertising

EC 2–9 The lack of sophistication on the part of many members of the public concerning legal services, the importance of the interests affected by the choice of a lawyer and prior experience with unrestricted lawyer advertising, require that special care be taken by lawyers to avoid misleading the public and to assure that the information set forth in any advertising is relevant to the selection of a lawyer. The lawyer must be mindful that the benefits of lawyer advertising depend upon its reliability and accuracy. Examples of information in lawyer advertising that would be deceptive include misstatements of fact, suggestions that the ingenuity or prior record of a lawyer rather than the justice of the claim are the principal factors likely to determine the result, inclusion of information irrelevant to selecting a lawyer, and representations concerning the quality of service, which cannot be measured or verified. Since lawyer advertising is calculated and not spontaneous, reasonable regulation of lawyer advertising designed to foster compliance with appropriate standards serves the public interest without impeding the flow of useful, meaningful, and relevant information to the public.

EC 2–10 A lawyer should ensure that the information contained in any advertising which the lawyer publishes, broadcasts or causes to be published or broadcast is relevant, is disseminated in an objective and understandable fashion, and would facilitate the prospective client's ability to compare the qualifications of the lawyers available to represent him. A lawyer should strive to communicate such information without undue emphasis upon style and advertising stratagems which serve to hinder rather than to facilitate intelligent selection of counsel. Because technological change is a recurrent feature of communications forms, and because perceptions of what is relevant in lawyer selection may change, lawyer advertising regulations should not be cast in rigid, unchangeable terms. Machinery is therefore available to advertisers and consumers for prompt consideration of proposals to change the rules governing lawyer advertising. The determination of any request for such change should depend upon whether the proposal is necessary in light of existing Code provisions, whether the proposal accords with standards of accuracy, reliability and truthfulness, and whether the proposal would facilitate informed selection of lawyers by potential consumers of legal services. Representatives of lawyers and consumers should be heard in addition to the applicant concerning any proposed change. Any change which is approved should be promulgated in the form of an amendment to the Code so that all lawyers practicing in the jurisdiction may avail themselves of its provisions.

EC 2–11 The name under which a lawyer conducts his practice may be a factor in the selection process. The use of a trade name or an assumed name could mislead laypersons concerning the identity, responsibility, and status of those practicing thereunder. Accordingly, a lawyer in private practice should practice only under a designation containing his own name, the name of a lawyer employing him, the name of one or more of the lawyers practicing in a partnership, or, if permitted by law, the name of a professional legal corporation, which should be clearly designated as such. For many years some law firms have used a firm name retaining one or more names of deceased or retired partners and such practice is not improper if the firm is a bona fide successor of a firm in which the deceased or retired person was a member, if the use of the name is authorized by law or by contract, and if the public is not misled thereby. However, the name of a partner who withdraws from a firm but continues to practice law should be omitted from the firm name in order to avoid misleading the public.

EC 2–12 A lawyer occupying a judicial, legislative, or public executive or administrative position who has the right to practice law concurrently may allow his name to remain in the name of the firm if he actively continues to practice law as a member thereof. Otherwise, his name should be removed from the firm name, and he should not be identified as a past or present member of the firm; and he should not hold himself out as being a practicing lawyer.

EC 2–13 In order to avoid the possibility of misleading persons with whom he deals, a lawyer should be scrupulous in the representation of his professional status. He should not hold himself out as being a partner or associate of a law firm if he is not one in fact, and thus should not hold himself out as partner or associate if he only shares offices with another lawyer.

EC 2–14 In some instances a lawyer confines his practice to a particular field of law. In the absence of state controls to insure the existence of special competence, a lawyer should not be permitted to hold himself out as a specialist or as having official recognition as a specialist, other than in the fields of admiralty, trademark, and patent law where a holding out as a specialist historically has been permitted. A lawyer may, however, indicate in permitted advertising, if it is factual, a limitation of his practice or one or more particular areas or fields of law in which he practices using designations and definitions authorized for that purpose by [the state agency having jurisdiction]. A lawyer practicing in a jurisdiction which certifies specialists must also be careful not to confuse laypersons as to his status. If a lawyer discloses areas of law in which he practices or to which he limits his practice, but is not certified in [the jurisdiction], he, and the designation authorized in [the jurisdiction], should avoid any implication that he is in fact certified.

EC 2–15 The legal profession has developed lawyer referral systems designed to aid individuals who are able to pay fees but need assistance in locating lawyers competent to handle their particular problems. Use of a lawyer referral system enables a layman to avoid an uninformed selection of a lawyer because such a system makes possible the employment of competent lawyers who have indicated an interest in the subject matter involved. Lawyers should support the principle of lawyer referral systems and should encourage the evolution of other ethical plans which aid in the selection of qualified counsel.

Financial Ability to Employ Counsel: Generally

EC 2–16 The legal profession cannot remain a viable force in fulfilling its role in our society unless its members receive adequate compensation for services rendered, and reasonable fees should be charged in appropriate cases to clients able to pay them. Nevertheless, persons unable to pay all or a portion of a reasonable fee should be able to obtain necessary legal services, and lawyers should support and participate in ethical activities designed to achieve that objective.

Financial Ability to Employ Counsel: Persons Able to Pay Reasonable Fees

EC 2–17 The determination of a proper fee requires consideration of the interests of both client and lawyer. A lawyer should not charge more than a reasonable fee, for excessive cost of legal service would deter laymen from utilizing the legal system in protection of their rights. Furthermore, an excessive charge abuses the professional relationship between lawyer and client. On the other hand, adequate compensation is necessary in order to enable the lawyer to serve his client effectively and to preserve the integrity and independence of the profession.

EC 2–18 The determination of the reasonableness of a fee requires consideration of all relevant circumstances, including those stated in the Disciplinary Rules. The fees of a lawyer will vary according to many factors, including the time required, his experience, ability, and reputation, the nature of the employment, the responsibility involved, and the results obtained. It is a commendable and long-standing tradition of the bar that special consideration is given in the fixing of any fee for services rendered a brother lawyer or a member of his immediate family.

EC 2–19 As soon as feasible after a lawyer has been employed, it is desirable that he reach a clear agreement with his client as to the basis of the fee charges to be made. Such a course will not only prevent later misunderstanding but will also work for good relations between the lawyer and the client. It is usually beneficial to reduce to writing the understanding of the parties regarding the fee, particularly when it is contingent. A lawyer should be mindful that many persons who desire to employ him may have had little or no experience with fee charges of lawyers, and for this reason he should explain fully to such persons the reasons for the particular fee arrangement he proposes.

EC 2–20 Contingent fee arrangements in civil cases have long been commonly accepted in the United States in proceedings to enforce claims. The historical bases of their acceptance are that (1) they often, and in a variety of circumstances, provide the only practical means by which one having a claim against another can economically afford, finance, and obtain the services of a competent lawyer to prosecute his claim, and (2) a successful prosecution of the claim produces a *res* out of which the fee can be paid. Although a lawyer generally should decline to accept employment on a contingent fee basis by one who is able to pay a reasonable fixed fee, it is not necessarily improper for a lawyer, where justified by the particular circumstances of a case, to enter into a contingent fee contract in a civil case with any client who, after being fully informed of all relevant factors, desires that arrangement. Because of the human relationships involved and the unique character of the proceedings, contingent fee arrangements in domestic relation cases are rarely justified. In administrative agency proceedings contingent fee contracts should be governed by the same consideration as in other civil cases. Public policy properly condemns contingent fee arrangements in criminal cases, largely on the ground that legal services in criminal cases do not produce a *res* with which to pay the fee.

EC 2–21 A lawyer should not accept compensation or any thing of value incident to his employment or services from one other than his client without the knowledge and consent of his client after full disclosure.

EC 2–22 Without the consent of his client, a lawyer should not associate in a particular matter another lawyer outside his firm. A fee may properly be divided between lawyers properly associated if the division is in proportion to the services performed and the responsibility assumed by each lawyer and if the total fee is reasonable.

EC 2–23 A lawyer should be zealous in his efforts to avoid controversies over fees with clients and should attempt to resolve amicably any differences on the subject. He should not sue a client for a fee unless necessary to prevent fraud or gross imposition by the client.

Financial Ability to Employ Counsel: Persons Unable to Pay Reasonable Fees

EC 2–24 A layman whose financial ability is not sufficient to permit payment of any fee cannot obtain legal services, other than in cases where a contingent fee is appropriate, unless the services are provided for him. Even a person of moderate means may be unable to pay a reasonable fee which is large because of the complexity, novelty, or difficulty of the problem or similar factors.

EC 2–25 Historically, the need for legal services of those unable to pay reasonable fees has been met in part by lawyers who donated their services or accepted court appointments on behalf of such individuals. The basic responsibility for providing legal services for those unable to pay ultimately rests upon the individual lawyer, and personal involvement in the problems of the disadvantaged can be one of the most rewarding experiences in the life of a lawyer. Every lawyer, regardless of professional prominence or professional workload, should find time to participate in serving the disadvantaged. The rendition of free legal services to those unable to pay reasonable fees continues to be an obligation of each lawyer, but the efforts of individual lawyers are often not enough to meet the need. Thus it has been necessary for the profession to institute additional programs to provide legal services. Accordingly, legal aid offices, lawyer referral services, and other related programs have been developed, and others will be developed, by the profession. Every lawyer should support all proper efforts to meet this need for legal services.

Acceptance and Retention of Employment

EC 2–26 A lawyer is under no obligation to act as advisor or advocate for every person who may wish to become his client; but in furtherance of the objective of the bar to make legal services fully available, a lawyer should not lightly decline proffered employment. The fulfillment of this objective requires acceptance by a lawyer of his share of tendered employment which may be unattractive both to him and the bar generally.

EC 2–27 History is replete with instances of distinguished and sacrificial services by lawyers who have represented unpopular clients and causes. Regardless of his personal feelings, a lawyer should not decline representation because a client or a cause is unpopular or community reaction is adverse.

EC 2–28 The personal preference of a lawyer to avoid adversary alignment against judges, other lawyers, public officials, or influential members of the community does not justify his rejection of tendered employment.

EC 2–29 When a lawyer is appointed by a court or requested by a bar association to undertake representation of a person unable to obtain counsel, whether for financial or other reasons, he should not seek to be excused from undertaking the representation except for compelling reasons. Compelling reasons do not include such factors as the repugnance of the subject matter of the proceeding, the identity or position of a person involved in the case, the belief of the lawyer that the defendant in a criminal proceeding is guilty, or the belief of the lawyer regarding the merits of the civil case.

EC 2–30 Employment should not be accepted by a lawyer when he is unable to render competent service or when he knows or it is obvious that the person seeking to employ him desires to institute or maintain an action merely for the purpose of harassing or maliciously injuring another. Likewise, a lawyer should decline employment if the intensity of his personal feeling, as distinguished from a community attitude, may impair his effective representation of a prospective client. If a lawyer knows a client has previously obtained counsel, he should not accept employment in the matter unless the other counsel approves or withdraws, or the client terminates the prior employment.

EC 2–31 Full availability of legal counsel requires both that persons be able to obtain counsel and that lawyers who undertake representation complete the work involved. Trial counsel for a convicted defendant should continue to represent his client by advising whether to take an appeal and, if the appeal is prosecuted, by representing him through the appeal unless new counsel is substituted or withdrawal is permitted by the appropriate court.

EC 2–32 A decision by a lawyer to withdraw should be made only on the basis of compelling circumstances, and in a matter pending before a tribunal he must comply with the rules of the tribunal regarding withdrawal. A lawyer should not withdraw without considering carefully and endeavoring to minimize the possible adverse effect on the rights of his client and the possibility of prejudice to his client as a result of his withdrawal. Even when he justifiably withdraws, a lawyer should protect the welfare of his client by giving due notice of his withdrawal, suggesting employment of other counsel, delivering to the client all papers and property to which the client is entitled, cooperating with counsel subsequently employed, and otherwise endeavoring to minimize the possibility of harm. Further, he should refund to the client any compensation not earned during the employment.

EC 2–33 As a part of the legal profession's commitment to the principle that high quality legal services should be available to all, attorneys are encouraged to cooperate with qualified legal assistance organizations providing prepaid legal services. Such participation should at all times be in accordance with the basic tenets of the profession: independence, integrity, competence and devotion to the interests of individual clients. An attorney so participating should make certain that his relationship with a qualified legal assistance organization in no way interferes with his independent, professional representation of the interests of the individual client. An attorney should avoid situations in which officials of the organization who are not lawyers attempt to direct attorneys concerning the manner in which legal services are performed for individual members, and should also avoid situations in which considerations of economy are given undue weight in determining the attorneys employed by an organization or the legal services to be performed for the member or beneficiary rather than competence and quality of service. An attorney interested in maintaining the historic traditions of the profession and preserving the function of a lawyer as a trusted and independent advisor to individual members of society should carefully assess such factors when accepting employment by, or otherwise participating in, a particular qualified legal assistance organization, and while so participating should adhere to the highest professional standards of effort and competence.

DISCIPLINARY RULES

DR 2–101   **Publicity.**

(A) **A lawyer shall not, on behalf of himself, his partner, associate or any other lawyer affiliated with him or his firm, use or participate in the use of any form of public communication containing a false, fraudulent, misleading, deceptive, self-laudatory or unfair statement or claim.**

(B) In order to facilitate the process of informed selection of a lawyer by potential consumers of legal services, a lawyer may publish or broadcast, subject to DR 2–103, the following information in print media distributed or over television or radio broadcast in the geographic area or areas in which the lawyer resides or maintains offices or in which a significant part of the lawyer's clientele resides, provided that the information disclosed by the lawyer in such publication or broadcast complies with DR 2–101(A), and is presented in a dignified manner:

   (1) Name, including name of law firm and names of professional associates; addresses and telephone numbers;

   (2) One or more fields of law in which the lawyer or law firm practices, a statement that practice is limited to one or more fields of law, or a statement that the lawyer or law firm specializes in a particular field of law practice, to the extent authorized under DR 2–105;

   (3) Date and place of birth;

   (4) Date and place of admission to the bar of state and federal courts;

   (5) Schools attended, with dates of graduation, degrees and other scholastic distinctions;

   (6) Public or quasi-public offices;

   (7) Military service;

   (8) Legal authorships;

   (9) Legal teaching positions;

   (10) Memberships, offices, and committee assignments, in bar associations;

   (11) Membership and offices in legal fraternities and legal societies;

   (12) Technical and professional licenses;

   (13) Memberships in scientific, technical and professional associations and societies;

   (14) Foreign language ability;

   (15) Names and addresses of bank references;

   (16) With their written consent, names of clients regularly represented;

   (17) Prepaid or group legal services programs in which the lawyer participates;

   (18) Whether credit cards or other credit arrangements are accepted;

   (19) Office and telephone answering service hours;

   (20) Fee for an initial consultation;

(21) Availability upon request of a written schedule of fees and/or an estimate of the fee to be charged for specific services;

(22) Contingent fee rates subject to DR 2–106(C), provided that the statement discloses whether percentages are computed before or after deduction of costs;

(23) Range of fees for services, provided that the statement discloses that the specific fee within the range which will be charged will vary depending upon the particular matter to be handled for each client and the client is entitled without obligation to an estimate of the fee within the range likely to be charged, in print size equivalent to the largest print used in setting forth the fee information;

(24) Hourly rate, provided that the statement discloses that the total fee charged will depend upon the number of hours which must be devoted to the particular matter to be handled for each client and the client is entitled to without obligation an estimate of the fee likely to be charged, in print size at least equivalent to the largest print used in setting forth the fee information;

(25) Fixed fees for specific legal services, the description of which would not be misunderstood or be deceptive, provided that the statement discloses that the quoted fee will be available only to clients whose matters fall into the services described and that the client is entitled without obligation to a specific estimate of the fee likely to be charged in print size at least equivalent to the largest print used in setting forth the fee information.

(C) Any person desiring to expand the information authorized for disclosure in DR 2–101(B), or to provide for its dissemination through other forums may apply to [the agency having jurisdiction under state law]. Any such application shall be served upon [the agencies having jurisdiction under state law over the regulation of the legal profession and consumer matters] who shall be heard, together with the applicant, on the issue of whether the proposal is necessary in light of the existing provisions of the Code, accords with standards of accuracy, reliability and truthfulness, and would facilitate the process of informed selection of lawyers by potential consumers of legal services. The relief granted in response to any such application shall be promulgated as an amendment to DR 2–101(B), universally applicable to all lawyers.

(D) If the advertisement is communicated to the public over television or radio, it shall be prerecorded, approved for broadcast by the lawyer, and a recording of the actual transmission shall be retained by the lawyer.

(E) If a lawyer advertises a fee for a service, the lawyer must render that service for no more than the fee advertised.

(F) Unless otherwise specified in the advertisement if a lawyer publishes any fee information authorized under DR 2–101(B) in a publication that is published more frequently than one time per month, the lawyer shall be bound by any representation made therein for a period of not less than 30 days after such publication. If a lawyer publishes any fee information authorized under DR 2–101(B) in a publication that is published once a month or less frequently, he shall be bound by any representation made therein until the publication of the succeeding issue. If a lawyer publishes any fee information authorized under DR 2–101(B) in a publication which has no fixed date for publication of a succeeding issue, the lawyer shall be bound by any representation made therein for a reasonable period of time after publication but in no event less than one year.

(G) Unless otherwise specified, if a lawyer broadcasts any fee information authorized under DR 2–101(B), the lawyer shall be bound by any representation made therein for a period of not less than 30 days after such broadcast.

(H) This rule does not prohibit limited and dignified identification of a lawyer as a lawyer as well as by name:

(1) In political advertisements when his professional status is germane to the political campaign or to a political issue.

(2) In public notices when the name and profession of a lawyer are required or authorized by law or are reasonably pertinent for a purpose other than the attraction of potential clients.

(3) In routine reports and announcements of a bona fide business, civic, professional, or political organization in which he serves as a director or officer.

(4) In and on legal documents prepared by him.

(5) In and on legal textbooks, treatises, and other legal publications, and in dignified advertisements thereof.

(I) A lawyer shall not compensate or give any thing of value to representatives of the press, radio, television, or other communication medium in anticipation of or in return for professional publicity in a news item.

DR 2–102 Professional Notices, Letterheads and Offices.

(A) A lawyer or law firm shall not use or participate in the use of professional cards, professional announcement cards, office signs, letterheads, or similar professional notices or devices, except that the following may be used if they are in dignified form:

(1) A professional card of a lawyer identifying him by name and as a lawyer, and giving his addresses, telephone numbers, the name of his law firm, and any information permitted under DR 2–105. A professional card of a law firm may also give the names of members and associates. Such cards may be used for identification.

(2) A brief professional announcement card stating new or changed associations or addresses, change of firm name, or similar matters pertaining to the professional offices of a lawyer or law firm, which may be mailed to lawyers, clients, former clients, personal friends, and relatives. It shall not

state biographical data except to the extent reasonably necessary to identify the lawyer or to explain the change in his association, but it may state the immediate past position of the lawyer. It may give the names and dates of predecessor firms in a continuing line of succession. It shall not state the nature of the practice except as permitted under DR 2–105.

(3) A sign on or near the door of the office and in the building directory identifying the law office. The sign shall not state the nature of the practice, except as permitted under DR 2–105.

(4) A letter head of a lawyer identifying him by name and as a lawyer, and giving his addresses, telephone numbers, the name of his law firm, associates and any information permitted under DR 2–105. A letterhead of a law firm may also give the names of members and associates, and names and dates relating to deceased and retired members. A lawyer may be designated "Of Counsel" on a letterhead if he has a continuing relationship with a lawyer or law firm, other than as a partner or associate. A lawyer or law firm may be designated as "General Counsel" or by similar professional reference on stationary of a client if he or the firm devotes a substantial amount of professional time in the representation of that client. The letterhead of a law firm may give the names and dates of predecessor firms in a continuing line of succession.

(B) A lawyer in private practice shall not practice under a trade name, a name that is misleading as to the identity of the lawyer or lawyers practicing under such name, or a firm name containing names other than those of one or more of the lawyers in the firm, except that the name of a professional corporation or professional association may contain "P.C." or "P.A." or similar symbols indicating the nature of the organization, and if otherwise lawful a firm may use as, or continue to include in, its name the name or names of one or more deceased or retired members of the firm or of a predecessor firm in a continuing line of succession. A lawyer who assumes a judicial, legislative, or public executive or administrative post or office shall not permit his name to remain in the name of a law firm or to be used in professional notices of the firm during any significant period in which he is not actively and regularly practicing law as a member of the firm, and during such period other members of the firm shall not use his name in the firm name or in professional notices of the firm.

(C) A lawyer shall not hold himself out as having a partnership with one or more other lawyers or professional corporations unless they are in fact partners.

(D) A partnership shall not be formed or continued between or among lawyers licensed in different jurisdictions unless all enumerations of the members and associates of the firm on its letterhead and in other permissible listings make clear the jurisdictional limitations on those members and associates of the firm not licensed to practice in all listed jurisdictions; however, the same firm name may be used in each jurisdiction.

(E) Nothing contained herein shall prohibit a lawyer from using or permitting the use of, in connection with his name, an earned degree or title derived therefrom indicating his training in the law.

DR 2–103   Recommendation of Professional Employment.

(A) A lawyer shall not, except as authorized in DR 2–101(B), recommend employment as a private practitioner, of himself, his partner, or associate to a layperson who has not sought his advice regarding employment of a lawyer.

(B) A lawyer shall not compensate or give anything of value to a person or organization to recommend or secure his employment by a client, or as a reward for having made a recommendation resulting in his employment by a client, except that he may pay the usual and reasonable fees or dues charged by any of the organizations listed in DR 2–103(D).

(C) A lawyer shall not request a person or organization to recommend or promote the use of his services or those of his partner or associate, or any other lawyer affiliated with him or his firm, as a private practitioner, except as authorized in DR 2–101, and except that

 (1) He may request referrals from a lawyer referral service operated, sponsored, or approved by a bar association and may pay its fees incident thereto.

 (2) He may cooperate with the legal service activities of any of the offices or organizations enumerated in DR 2–103(D)(1) through (4) and may perform legal services for those to whom he was recommended by it to do such work if:

 (a) The person to whom the recommendation is made is a member or beneficiary of such office or organization; and

 (b) The lawyer remains free to exercise his independent professional judgment on behalf of his client.

(D) A lawyer or his partner or associate or any other lawyer affiliated with him or his firm may be recommended, employed or paid by, or may cooperate with, one of the following offices or organizations that promote the use of his services or those of his partner or associate or any other lawyer affiliated with him or his firm if there is no interference with the exercise of independent professional judgment in behalf of his client:

 (1) A legal aid office or public defender office:

 (a) Operated or sponsored by a duly accredited law school.

 (b) Operated or sponsored by a bona fide nonprofit community organization.

 (c) Operated or sponsored by a governmental agency.

 (d) Operated, sponsored, or approved by a bar association.

 (2) A military legal assistance office.

(3) A lawyer referral service operated, sponsored, or approved by a bar association.

(4) Any bona fide organization that recommends, furnishes or pays for legal services to its members or beneficiaries provided the following conditions are satisfied:

(a) Such organization, including any affiliate, is so organized and operated that no profit is derived by it from the rendition of legal services by lawyers, and that, if the organization is organized for profit, the legal services are not rendered by lawyers employed, directed, supervised or selected by it except in connection with matters where such organization bears ultimate liability of its member or beneficiary.

(b) Neither the lawyer, nor his partner, nor associate, nor any other lawyer affiliated with him or his firm, nor any non-lawyer, shall have initiated or promoted such organization for the primary purpose of providing financial or other benefit to such lawyer, partner, associate or affiliated lawyer.

(c) Such organization is not operated for the purpose of procuring legal work or financial benefit for any lawyer as a private practitioner outside of the legal services program of the organization.

(d) The member or beneficiary to whom the legal services are furnished, and not such organization, is recognized as the client of the lawyer in the matter.

(e) Any member or beneficiary who is entitled to have legal services furnished or paid for by the organization may, if such member or beneficiary so desires, select counsel other than that furnished, selected or approved by the organization for the particular matter involved; and the legal service plan of such organization provides appropriate relief for any member or beneficiary who asserts a claim that representation by counsel furnished, selected or approved would be unethical, improper or inadequate under the circumstances of the matter involved and the plan provides an appropriate procedure for seeking such relief.

(f) The lawyer does not know or have cause to know that such organization is in violation of applicable laws, rules of court and other legal requirements that govern its legal service operations.

(g) Such organization has filed with the appropriate disciplinary authority at least annually a report with respect to its legal service plan, if any, showing its terms, its schedule of benefits, its subscription charges, agreements with counsel, and financial results of its legal service activities or, if it has failed to do so, the lawyer does not know or have cause to know of such failure.

(E) A lawyer shall not accept employment when he knows or it is obvious that the person who seeks his services does so as a result of conduct prohibited under this Disciplinary Rule.

DR 2–104   Suggestion of Need of Legal Services.

(A) A lawyer who has given in-person unsolicited advice to a layperson that he should obtain counsel or take legal action shall not accept employment resulting from that advice, except that:

> (1) A lawyer may accept employment by a close friend, relative, former client (if the advice is germane to the former employment), or one whom the lawyer reasonably believes to be a client.
>
> (2) A lawyer may accept employment that results from his participation in activities designed to educate laypersons to recognize legal problems, to make intelligent selection of counsel, or to utilize available legal services if such activities are conducted or sponsored by a qualified legal assistance organization.
>
> (3) A lawyer who is recommended, furnished or paid by a qualified legal assistance organization enumerated in DR 2–103(D)(1) through (4) may represent a member or beneficiary thereof, to the extent and under the conditions prescribed therein.
>
> (4) Without affecting his right to accept employment, a lawyer may speak publicly or write for publication on legal topics so long as he does not emphasize his own professional experience or reputation and does not undertake to give individual advice.
>
> (5) If success in asserting rights or defenses of his client in litigation in the nature of a class action is dependent upon the joinder of others, a lawyer may accept, but shall not seek, employment from those contacted for the purpose of obtaining their joinder.

DR 2–105   Limitation of Practice.

(A) A lawyer shall not hold himself out publicly as a specialist, as practicing in certain areas of law or as limiting his practice permitted under DR 2–101(B), except as follows:

> (1) A lawyer admitted to practice before the United States Patent and Trademark Office may use the designation "Patents," "Patent Attorney," "Patent Lawyer," or "Registered Patent Attorney" or any combination of those terms, on his letterhead and office sign.
>
> (2) A lawyer who publicly discloses fields of law in which the lawyer or the law firm practices or states that his practice is limited to one or more fields of law shall do so by using designations and definitions authorized and approved by [the agency having jurisdiction of the subject under state law].
>
> (3) A lawyer who is certified as a specialist in a particular field of law or law practice by [the authority having jurisdiction

under state law over the subject of specialization by lawyers] may hold himself out as such, but only in accordance with the rules prescribed by that authority.

DR 2–106   Fees for Legal Services.

(A) A lawyer shall not enter into an agreement for, charge, or collect an illegal or clearly excessive fee.

(B) A fee is clearly excessive when, after a review of the facts, a lawyer of ordinary prudence would be left with a definite and firm conviction that the fee is in excess of a reasonable fee. Factors to be considered as guides in determining the reasonableness of a fee include the following:

   (1) The time and labor required, the novelty and difficulty of the questions involved, and the skill requisite to perform the legal service properly.

   (2) The likelihood, if apparent to the client, that the acceptance of the particular employment will preclude other employment by the lawyer.

   (3) The fee customarily charged in the locality for similar legal services.

   (4) The amount involved and the results obtained.

   (5) The time limitations imposed by the client or by the circumstances.

   (6) The nature and length of the professional relationship with the client.

   (7) The experience, reputation, and ability of the lawyer or lawyers performing the services.

   (8) Whether the fee is fixed or contingent.

(C) A lawyer shall not enter into an arrangement for, charge, or collect a contingent fee for representing a defendant in a criminal case.

DR 2–107   Division of Fees Among Lawyers.

(A) A lawyer shall not divide a fee for legal services with another lawyer who is not a partner in or associate of his law firm or law office, unless:

   (1) The client consents to employment of the other lawyer after a full disclosure that a division of fees will be made.

   (2) The division is made in proportion to the services performed and responsibility assumed by each.

   (3) The total fee of the lawyers does not clearly exceed reasonable compensation for all legal services they rendered the client.

(B) This Disciplinary Rule does not prohibit payment to a former partner or associate pursuant to a separation or retirement agreement.

DR 2–108   Agreements Restricting the Practice of a Lawyer.

(A) A lawyer shall not be a party to or participate in a partnership or employment agreement with another lawyer that restricts the right of a lawyer to practice law after the termination of a relationship created by the agreement, except as a condition to payment of retirement benefits.

(B) In connection with the settlement of a controversy or suit, a lawyer shall not enter into an agreement that restricts his right to practice law.

DR 2–109   Acceptance of Employment.

(A) A lawyer shall not accept employment on behalf of a person if he knows or it is obvious that such person wishes to:

> (1) Bring a legal action, conduct a defense, or assert a position in litigation, or otherwise have steps taken for him, merely for the purpose of harassing or maliciously injuring any person.

> (2) Present a claim or defense in litigation that is not warranted under existing law, unless it can be supported by good faith argument for an extension, modification, or reversal of existing law.

DR 2–110   Withdrawal from Employment.

(A) In general.

> (1) If permission for withdrawal from employment is required by the rules of a tribunal, a lawyer shall not withdraw from employment in a proceeding before that tribunal without its permission.

> (2) In any event, a lawyer shall not withdraw from employment until he has taken reasonable steps to avoid foreseeable prejudice to the rights of his client, including giving due notice to his client, allowing time for employment of other counsel, delivering to the client all papers and property to which the client is entitled, and complying with applicable laws and rules.

> (3) A lawyer who withdraws from employment shall refund promptly any part of a fee paid in advance that has not been earned.

(B) Mandatory Withdrawal.

A lawyer representing a client before a tribunal, with its permission if required by its rules, shall withdraw from employment, and a lawyer representing a client in other matters shall withdraw from employment, if:

> (1) He knows or it is obvious that his client is bringing the legal action, conducting the defense, or asserting a position in the litigation, or is otherwise having steps taken for him, merely for the purpose of harassing or maliciously injuring any person.

> (2) He knows or it is obvious that his continued employment will result in violation of a Disciplinary Rule.

(3) His mental or physical condition renders it unreasonably difficult for him to carry out the employment effectively.

(4) He is discharged by his client.

(C) Permissive withdrawal.

If DR 2–110(B) is not applicable, a lawyer may not request permission to withdraw in matters pending before a tribunal, and may not withdraw in other matters, unless such request or such withdrawal is because:

(1) His client:

(a) Insists upon presenting a claim or defense that is not warranted under existing law and cannot be supported by good faith argument for an extension, modification, or reversal of existing law.

(b) Personally seeks to pursue an illegal course of conduct.

(c) Insists that the lawyer pursue a course of conduct that is illegal or that is prohibited under the Disciplinary Rules.

(d) By other conduct renders it unreasonably difficult for the lawyer to carry out his employment effectively.

(e) Insists, in a matter not pending before a tribunal, that the lawyer engage in conduct that is contrary to the judgment and advice of the lawyer but not prohibited under the Disciplinary Rules.

(f) Deliberately disregards an agreement or obligation to the lawyer as to expenses or fees.

(2) His continued employment is likely to result in a violation of a Disciplinary Rule.

(3) His inability to work with co-counsel indicates that the best interests of the client likely will be served by withdrawal.

(4) His mental or physical condition renders it difficult for him to carry out the employment effectively.

(5) His client knowingly and freely assents to termination of his employment.

(6) He believes in good faith, in a proceeding pending before a tribunal, that the tribunal will find the existence of other good cause for withdrawal.

CANON 3

A Lawyer Should Assist in Preventing the Unauthorized Practice of Law

ETHICAL CONSIDERATIONS

EC 3–1 The prohibition against the practice of law by a layman is grounded in the need of the public for integrity and competence of those who undertake to render legal services. Because of the fiduciary and personal character of the lawyer-client relationship and the inherently complex nature of our legal system, the public can better be assured of the requisite responsibility and competence if the practice of law is confined to those who are subject to the requirements and regulations imposed upon members of the legal profession.

EC 3–2 The sensitive variations in the considerations that bear on legal determinations often make it difficult even for a lawyer to exercise appropriate professional judgment, and it is therefore essential that the personal nature of the relationship of client and lawyer be preserved. Competent professional judgment is the product of a trained familiarity with law and legal processes, a disciplined, analytical approach to legal problems, and a firm ethical commitment.

EC 3–3 A non-lawyer who undertakes to handle legal matters is not governed as to integrity or legal competence by the same rules that govern the conduct of a lawyer. A lawyer is not only subject to that regulation but also is committed to high standards of ethical conduct. The public interest is best served in legal matters by a regulated profession committed to such standards. The Disciplinary Rules protect the public in that they prohibit a lawyer from seeking employment by improper overtures, from acting in cases of divided loyalties, and from submitting to the control of others in the exercise of his judgment. Moreover, a person who entrusts legal matters to a lawyer is protected by the attorney-client privilege and by the duty of the lawyer to hold inviolate the confidences and secrets of his client.

EC 3–4 A layman who seeks legal services often is not in a position to judge whether he will receive proper professional attention. The entrustment of a legal matter may well involve the confidences, the reputation, the property, the freedom, or even the life of the client. Proper protection of members of the public demands that no person be permitted to act in the confidential and demanding capacity of a lawyer unless he is subject to the regulations of the legal profession.

EC 3–5 It is neither necessary nor desirable to attempt the formulation of a single, specific definition of what constitutes the practice of law. Functionally, the practice of law relates to the rendition of services for others that call for the professional judgment of a lawyer. The essence of the professional judgment of the lawyer is his educated ability to relate the general body and philosophy of law to a specific legal problem of a client; and thus, the public interest will be better served if only lawyers are permitted to act in matters involving professional judgment. Where this professional judgment is not involved, non-lawyers, such as court clerks, police officers, abstracters, and many governmental employees, may engage in occupations that require a special knowledge of law in certain areas. But the services of a lawyer are essential in the public interest whenever the exercise of professional legal judgment is required.

EC 3–6 A lawyer often delegates tasks to clerks, secretaries, and other lay persons. Such delegation is proper if the lawyer maintains a direct relationship with his client, supervises the delegated work, and has complete professional responsibility for the work product. This delegation enables a lawyer to render legal service more economically and efficiently.

EC 3–7 The prohibition against a non-lawyer practicing law does not prevent a layman from representing himself, for then he is ordinarily exposing only himself to possible injury. The purpose of the legal profession is to make educated legal representation available to the public; but anyone who does not wish to avail himself of such representation is not required to do so. Even so, the legal profession should help members of the public to recognize legal problems and to understand why it may be unwise for them to act for themselves in matters having legal consequences.

EC 3–8   Since a lawyer should not aid or encourage a layman to practice law, he should not practice law in association with a layman or otherwise share legal fees with a layman. This does not mean, however, that the pecuniary value of the interest of a deceased lawyer in his firm or practice may not be paid to his estate or specified persons such as his widow or heirs. In like manner, profit-sharing retirement plans of a lawyer or law firm which include non-lawyer office employees are not improper. These limited exceptions to the rule against sharing legal fees with laymen are permissible since they do not aid or encourage laymen to practice law.

EC 3–9   Regulation of the practice of law is accomplished principally by the respective states. Authority to engage in the practice of law conferred in any jurisdiction is not per se a grant of the right to practice elsewhere, and it is improper for a lawyer to engage in practice where he is not permitted by law or by court order to do so. However, the demands of business and the mobility of our society pose distinct problems in the regulation of the practice of law by the states. In furtherance of the public interest, the legal profession should discourage regulation that unreasonably imposes territorial limitations upon the right of a lawyer to handle the legal affairs of his client or upon the opportunity of a client to obtain the services of a lawyer of his choice in all matters including the presentation of a contested matter in a tribunal before which the lawyer is not permanently admitted to practice.

DISCIPLINARY RULES

DR 3–101   **Aiding Unauthorized Practice of Law.**

(A) A lawyer shall not aid a non-lawyer in the unauthorized practice of law.

(B) A lawyer shall not practice law in a jurisdiction where to do so would be in violation of regulations of the profession in that jurisdiction.

DR 3–102   **Dividing Legal Fees with a Non-Lawyer.**

(A) A lawyer or law firm shall not share legal fees with a non-lawyer, except that:

    (1) An agreement by a lawyer with his firm, partner, or associate may provide for the payment of money, over a reasonable period of time after his death, to his estate or to one or more specified persons.

    (2) A lawyer who undertakes to complete unfinished legal business of a deceased lawyer may pay to the estate of the deceased lawyer that proportion of the total compensation which fairly represents the services rendered by the deceased lawyer.

    (3) A lawyer or law firm may include non-lawyer employees in a compensation or retirement plan, even though the plan is based in whole or in part on a profit-sharing arrangement providing such plan does not circumvent another disciplinary rule.

DR 3–103   **Forming a Partnership with a Non-Lawyer.**

(A) A lawyer shall not form a partnership with a non-lawyer if any of the activities of the partnership consist of the practice of law.

CANON 4

A Lawyer Should Preserve the Confidences and Secrets of a Client

ETHICAL CONSIDERATIONS

EC 4–1 Both the fiduciary relationship existing between lawyer and client and the proper functioning of the legal system require the preservation by the lawyer of confidences and secrets of one who has employed or sought to employ him. A client must feel free to discuss whatever he wishes with his lawyer and a lawyer must be equally free to obtain information beyond that volunteered by his client. A lawyer should be fully informed of all the facts of the matter he is handling in order for his client to obtain the full advantage of our legal system. It is for the lawyer in the exercise of his independent professional judgment to separate the relevant and important from the irrelevant and unimportant. The observance of the ethical obligation of a lawyer to hold inviolate the confidences and secrets of his client not only facilitates the full development of facts essential to proper representation of the client but also encourages laymen to seek early legal assistance.

EC 4–2 The obligation to protect confidences and secrets obviously does not preclude a lawyer from revealing information when his client consents after full disclosure, when necessary to perform his professional employment, when permitted by a Disciplinary Rule, or when required by law. Unless the client otherwise directs, a lawyer may disclose the affairs of his client to partners or associates of his firm. It is a matter of common knowledge that the normal operation of a law office exposes confidential professional information to non-lawyer employees of the office, particularly secretaries and those having access to the files; and this obligates a lawyer to exercise care in selecting and training his employees so that the sanctity of all confidences and secrets of his clients may be preserved. If the obligation extends to two or more clients as to the same information, a lawyer should obtain the permission of all before revealing the information. A lawyer must always be sensitive to the rights and wishes of his client and act scrupulously in the making of decisions which may involve the disclosure of information obtained in his professional relationship. Thus, in the absence of consent of his client after full disclosure, a lawyer should not associate another lawyer in the handling of a matter; nor should he, in the absence of consent, seek counsel from another lawyer if there is a reasonable possibility that the identity of the client or his confidences or secrets would be revealed to such lawyer. Both social amenities and professional duty should cause a lawyer to shun indiscreet conversations concerning his clients.

EC 4–3 Unless the client otherwise directs, it is not improper for a lawyer to give limited information from his files to an outside agency necessary for statistical, bookkeeping, accounting, data processing, banking, printing, or other legitimate purposes, provided he exercises due care in the selection of the agency and warns the agency that the information must be kept confidential.

EC 4–4 The attorney-client privilege is more limited than the ethical obligation of a lawyer to guard the confidences and secrets of his client. This ethical precept, unlike the evidentiary privilege, exists without regard to the nature or source of information or the fact that others share the knowledge. A lawyer should endeavor to act in a manner which preserves the evidentiary privilege; for example, he should avoid professional discussions in the presence of persons to whom the privilege does not extend. A lawyer owes an obligation to advise the client of the attorney-client privilege and timely to assert the privilege unless it is waived by the client.

EC 4–5   A lawyer should not use information acquired in the course of the representation of a client to the disadvantage of the client and a lawyer should not use, except with the consent of his client after full disclosure, such information for his own purposes. Likewise, a lawyer should be diligent in his efforts to prevent the misuse of such information by his employees and associates. Care should be exercised by a lawyer to prevent the disclosure of the confidences and secrets of one client to another, and no employment should be accepted that might require such disclosure.

EC 4–6   The obligation of a lawyer to preserve the confidences and secrets of his client continues after the termination of his employment. Thus a lawyer should not attempt to sell a law practice as a going business because, among other reasons, to do so would involve the disclosure of confidences and secrets. A lawyer should also provide for the protection of the confidences and secrets of his client following the termination of the practice of the lawyer, whether termination is due to death, disability, or retirement. For example, a lawyer might provide for the personal papers of the client to be returned to him and for the papers of the lawyer to be delivered to another lawyer or to be destroyed. In determining the method of disposition, the instructions and wishes of the client should be a dominant consideration.

DISCIPLINARY RULES

DR 4–101   Preservation of Confidences and Secrets of a Client.

(A) **"Confidence" refers to information protected by the attorney-client privilege under applicable law, and "secret" refers to other information gained in the professional relationship that the client has requested be held inviolate or the disclosure of which would be embarrassing or would be likely to be detrimental to the client.**

(B) **Except when permitted under DR 4–101(C), a lawyer shall not knowingly:**

　　(1) **Reveal a confidence or secret of his client.**

　　(2) **Use a confidence or secret of his client to the disadvantage of the client.**

　　(3) **Use a confidence or secret of his client for the advantage of himself or of a third person, unless the client consents after full disclosure.**

(C) **A lawyer may reveal:**

　　(1) **Confidences or secrets with the consent of the client or clients affected, but only after a full disclosure to them.**

　　(2) **Confidences or secrets when permitted under Disciplinary Rules or required by law or court order.**

　　(3) **The intention of his client to commit a crime and the information necessary to prevent the crime.**

　　(4) **Confidences or secrets necessary to establish or collect his fee or to defend himself or his employees or associates against an accusation of wrongful conduct.**

(D) A lawyer shall exercise reasonable care to prevent his employees, associates, and others whose services are utilized by him from disclosing or using confidences or secrets of a client, except that a lawyer may reveal the information allowed by DR 4–101(C) through an employee.

CANON 5

A Lawyer Should Exercise Independent Professional Judgment on Behalf of a Client

ETHICAL CONSIDERATIONS

EC 5–1 The professional judgment of a lawyer should be exercised, within the bounds of the law, solely for the benefit of his client and free of compromising influences and loyalties. Neither his personal interests, the interests of other clients, nor the desires of third persons should be permitted to dilute his loyalty to his client.

Interests of a Lawyer That May Affect His Judgment

EC 5–2 A lawyer should not accept proffered employment if his personal interests or desires will, or there is a reasonable probability that they will, affect adversely the advice to be given or services to be rendered the prospective client. After accepting employment, a lawyer carefully should refrain from acquiring a property right or assuming a position that would tend to make his judgment less protective of the interests of his client.

EC 5–3 The self-interest of a lawyer resulting from his ownership of property in which his client also has an interest or which may affect property of his client may interfere with the exercise of free judgment on behalf of his client. If such interference would occur with respect to a prospective client, a lawyer should decline employment proffered by him. After accepting employment, a lawyer should not acquire property rights that would adversely affect his professional judgment in the representation of his client. Even if the property interests of a lawyer do not presently interfere with the exercise of his independent judgment, but the likelihood of interference can reasonably be foreseen by him, a lawyer should explain the situation to his client and should decline employment or withdraw unless the client consents to the continuance of the relationship after full disclosure. A lawyer should not seek to persuade his client to permit him to invest in an undertaking of his client nor make improper use of his professional relationship to influence his client to invest in an enterprise in which the lawyer is interested.

EC 5–4 If, in the course of his representation of a client, a lawyer is permitted to receive from his client a beneficial ownership in publication rights relating to the subject matter of the employment, he may be tempted to subordinate the interests of his client to his own anticipated pecuniary gain. For example, a lawyer in a criminal case who obtains from his client television, radio, motion picture, newspaper, magazine, book, or other publication rights with respect to the case may be influenced, consciously or unconsciously, to a course of conduct that will enhance the value of his publication rights to the prejudice of his client. To prevent these potentially differing interests, such arrangements should be scrupulously avoided prior to the termination of all aspects of the matter giving rise to the employment, even though his employment has previously ended.

EC 5–5 A lawyer should not suggest to his client that a gift be made to himself or for his benefit. If a lawyer accepts a gift from his client, he is peculiarly susceptible to the charge that he unduly influenced or over-reached the client. If a client voluntarily offers to make a gift to his lawyer, the lawyer may accept the gift, but before doing so, he should urge that his client secure disinterested advice from an independent, competent person who is cognizant of all the circumstances. Other than in exceptional circumstances, a lawyer should insist that an instrument in which his client desires to name him beneficially be prepared by another lawyer selected by the client.

EC 5–6 A lawyer should not consciously influence a client to name him as executor, trustee, or lawyer in an instrument. In those cases where a client wishes to name his lawyer as such, care should be taken by the lawyer to avoid even the appearance of impropriety.

EC 5–7 The possibility of an adverse effect upon the exercise of free judgment by a lawyer on behalf of his client during litigation generally makes it undesirable for the lawyer to acquire a proprietary interest in the cause of his client or otherwise to become financially interested in the outcome of the litigation. However, it is not improper for a lawyer to protect his right to collect a fee for his services by the assertion of legally permissible liens, even though by doing so he may acquire an interest in the outcome of litigation. Although a contingent fee arrangement gives a lawyer a financial interest in the outcome of litigation, a reasonable contingent fee is permissible in civil cases because it may be the only means by which a layman can obtain the services of a lawyer of his choice. But a lawyer, because he is in a better position to evaluate a cause of action, should enter into a contingent fee arrangement only in those instances where the arrangement will be beneficial to the client.

EC 5–8 A financial interest in the outcome of litigation also results if monetary advances are made by the lawyer to his client. Although this assistance generally is not encouraged, there are instances when it is not improper to make loans to a client. For example, the advancing or guaranteeing of payment of the costs and expenses of litigation by a lawyer may be the only way a client can enforce his cause of action, but the ultimate liability for such costs and expenses must be that of the client.

EC 5–9 Occasionally a lawyer is called upon to decide in a particular case whether he will be a witness or an advocate. If a lawyer is both counsel and witness, he becomes more easily impeachable for interest and thus may be a less effective witness. Conversely, the opposing counsel may be handicapped in challenging the credibility of the lawyer when the lawyer also appears as an advocate in the case. An advocate who becomes a witness is in the unseemly and ineffective position of arguing his own credibility. The roles of an advocate and of a witness are inconsistent; the function of an advocate is to advance or argue the cause of another, while that of a witness is to state facts objectively.

EC 5–10 Problems incident to the lawyer-witness relationship arise at different stages; they relate either to whether a lawyer should accept employment or should withdraw from employment. Regardless of when the problem arises, his decision is to be governed by the same basic considerations. It is not objectionable for a lawyer who is a potential witness to be an advocate if it is unlikely that he will be called as a witness because his testimony would be merely cumulative or if his testimony will relate only to an uncontested issue. In the exceptional situation where it will be manifestly unfair to the client for the lawyer to refuse employment or to withdraw when he will likely be a witness on a contested issue, he may serve as advocate even though he may be a witness. In making such decision, he should determine the personal or financial sacrifice of the client that may result from his refusal of employment or withdrawal therefrom, the materiality of his testimony, and the effectiveness of his representation in view of his personal involvement. In weighing these factors, it should be clear that refusal or withdrawal will impose an unreasonable hardship upon the client before the lawyer accepts or continues the employment. Where the question arises, doubts should be resolved in favor of the lawyer testifying and against his becoming or continuing as an advocate.

EC 5–11 A lawyer should not permit his personal interests to influence his advice relative to a suggestion by his client that additional counsel be employed. In like manner, his personal interests should not deter him from suggesting that additional counsel be employed; on the contrary, he should be alert to the desirability of recommending additional counsel when, in his judgment, the proper representation of his client requires it. However, a lawyer should advise his client not to employ additional counsel suggested by the client if the lawyer believes that such employment would be a disservice to the client, and he should disclose the reasons for his belief.

EC 5–12 Inability of co-counsel to agree on a matter vital to the representation of their client requires that their disagreement be submitted by them jointly to their client for his resolution, and the decision of the client shall control the action to be taken.

EC 5–13 A lawyer should not maintain membership in or be influenced by any organization of employees that undertakes to prescribe, direct, or suggest when or how he should fulfill his professional obligations to a person or organization that employs him as a lawyer. Although it is not necessarily improper for a lawyer employed by a corporation or similar entity to be a member of an organization of employees, he should be vigilant to safeguard his fidelity as a lawyer to his employer, free from outside influences.

Interests of Multiple Clients

EC 5–14 Maintaining the independence of professional judgment required of a lawyer precludes his acceptance or continuation of employment that will adversely affect his judgment on behalf of or dilute his loyalty to a client. This problem arises whenever a lawyer is asked to represent two or more clients who may have differing interests, whether such interests be conflicting, inconsistent, diverse, or otherwise discordant.

EC 5–15 If a lawyer is requested to undertake or to continue representation of multiple clients having potentially differing interests, he must weigh carefully the possibility that his judgment may be impaired or his loyalty divided if he accepts or continues the employment. He should resolve all doubts against the propriety of the representation. A lawyer should never represent in litigation multiple clients with differing interests; and there are few situations in which he would be justified in representing in litigation multiple clients with potentially differing interests. If a lawyer accepted such employment and the interests did become actually differing, he would have to withdraw from employment with likelihood of resulting hardship on the clients; and for this reason it is preferable that he refuse the employment initially. On the other hand, there are many instances in which a lawyer may properly serve multiple clients having potentially differing interests in matters not involving litigation. If the interests vary only slightly, it is generally likely that the lawyer will not be subjected to an adverse influence and that he can retain his independent judgment on behalf of each client; and if the interests become differing, withdrawal is less likely to have a disruptive effect upon the causes of his clients.

EC 5–16 In those instances in which a lawyer is justified in representing two or more clients having differing interests, it is nevertheless essential that each client be given the opportunity to evaluate his need for representation free of any potential conflict and to obtain other counsel if he so desires. Thus before a lawyer may represent multiple clients, he should explain fully to each client the implications of the common representation and should accept or continue employment only if the clients consent. If there are present other circumstances that might cause any of the multiple clients to question the undivided loyalty of the lawyer, he should also advise all of the clients of those circumstances.

EC 5–17 Typically recurring situations involving potentially differing interests are those in which a lawyer is asked to represent co-defendants in a criminal case, co-plaintiffs in a personal injury case, an insured and his insurer, and beneficiaries of the estate of a decedent. Whether a lawyer can fairly and adequately protect the interests of multiple clients in these and similar situations depends upon an analysis of each case. In certain circumstances, there may exist little chance of the judgment of the lawyer being adversely affected by the slight possibility that the interests will become actually differing; in other circumstances, the chance of adverse effect upon his judgment is not unlikely.

EC 5–18 A lawyer employed or retained by a corporation or similar entity owes his allegiance to the entity and not to a stockholder, director, officer, employee, representative, or other person connected with the entity. In advising the entity, a lawyer should keep paramount its interests and his professional judgment should not be influenced by the personal desires of any person or organization. Occasionally a lawyer for an entity is requested by a stockholder, director, officer, employee, representative, or other person connected with the entity to represent him in an individual capacity; in such case the lawyer may serve the individual only if the lawyer is convinced that differing interests are not present.

EC 5–19 A lawyer may represent several clients whose interests are not actually or potentially differing. Nevertheless, he should explain any circumstances that might cause a client to question his undivided loyalty. Regardless of the belief of a lawyer that he may properly represent multiple clients, he must defer to a client who holds the contrary belief and withdraw from representation of that client.

EC 5–20 A lawyer is often asked to serve as an impartial arbitrator or mediator in matters which involve present or former clients. He may serve in either capacity if he first discloses such present or former relationships. After a lawyer has undertaken to act as an impartial arbitrator or mediator, he should not thereafter represent in the dispute any of the parties involved.

Desires of Third Persons

EC 5–21 The obligation of a lawyer to exercise professional judgment solely on behalf of his client requires that he disregard the desires of others that might impair his free judgment. The desires of a third person will seldom adversely affect a lawyer unless that person is in a position to exert strong economic, political, or social pressures upon the lawyer. These influences are often subtle, and a lawyer must be alert to their existence. A lawyer subjected to outside pressures should make full disclosure of them to his client; and if he or his client believes that the effectiveness of his representation has been or will be impaired thereby, the lawyer should take proper steps to withdraw from representation of his client.

EC 5–22 Economic, political, or social pressures by third persons are less likely to impinge upon the independent judgment of a lawyer in a matter in which he is compensated directly by his client and his professional work is exclusively with his client. On the other hand, if a lawyer is compensated from a source other than his client, he may feel a sense of responsibility to someone other than his client.

EC 5–23 A person or organization that pays or furnishes lawyers to represent others possesses a potential power to exert strong pressures against the independent judgment of those lawyers. Some employers may be interested in furthering their own economic, political, or social goals without regard to the professional responsibility of the lawyer to his individual client. Others may be far more concerned with establishment or extension of legal principles than in the immediate protection of the rights of the lawyer's individual client. On some occasions, decisions on priority of work may be made by the employer rather than the lawyer with the result that prosecution of work already undertaken for clients is postponed to their detriment. Similarly, an employer may seek, consciously or unconsciously, to further its own economic interests through the action of the lawyers employed by it. Since a lawyer must always be free to exercise his professional judgment without regard to the interests or motives of a third person, the lawyer who is employed by one to represent another must constantly guard against erosion of his professional freedom.

EC 5–24 To assist a lawyer in preserving his professional independence, a number of courses are available to him. For example, a lawyer should not practice with or in the form of a professional legal corporation, even though the corporate form is permitted by law, if any director, officer, or stockholder of it is a non-lawyer. Although a lawyer may be employed by a business corporation with non-lawyers serving as directors or officers, and they necessarily have the right to make decisions of business policy, a lawyer must decline to accept direction of his professional judgment from any layman. Various types of legal aid offices are administered by boards of directors composed of lawyers and laymen. A lawyer should not accept employment from such an organization unless the board sets only broad policies and there is no interference in the relationship of the lawyer and the individual client he serves. Where a lawyer is employed by an organization, a written agreement that defines the relationship between him and the organization and provides for his independence is desirable since it may serve to prevent misunderstanding as to their respective roles. Although other innovations in the means of supplying legal counsel may develop, the responsibility of the lawyer to maintain his professional independence remains constant, and the legal profession must insure that changing circumstances do not result in loss of the professional independence of the lawyer.

DISCIPLINARY RULES

DR 5–101   Refusing Employment When the Interests of the Lawyer May Impair His Independent Professional Judgment.

(A) Except with the consent of his client after full disclosure, a lawyer shall not accept employment if the exercise of his professional judgment on behalf of his client will be or reasonably may be affected by his own financial, business, property, or personal interests.

(B) A lawyer shall not accept employment in contemplated or pending litigation if he knows or it is obvious that he or a lawyer in his firm ought to be called as a witness, except that he may undertake the employment and he or a lawyer in his firm may testify:

(1) If the testimony will relate solely to an uncontested matter.

(2) If the testimony will relate solely to a matter of formality and there is no reason to believe that substantial evidence will be offered in opposition to the testimony.

(3) If the testimony will relate solely to the nature and value of legal services rendered in the case by the lawyer or his firm to the client.

(4) As to any matter, if refusal would work a substantial hardship on the client because of the distinctive value of the lawyer or his firm as counsel in the particular case.

DR 5–102   Withdrawal as Counsel When the Lawyer Becomes a Witness.

(A) If, after undertaking employment in contemplated or pending litigation, a lawyer learns or it is obvious that he or a lawyer in his firm ought to be called as a witness on behalf of his client, he shall withdraw from the conduct of the trial and his firm, if any, shall not continue representation in the trial, except that he may continue the representation and he or a lawyer in his firm may testify in the circumstances enumerated in DR 5–101(B)(1) through (4).

(B) If, after undertaking employment in contemplated or pending litigation, a lawyer learns or it is obvious that he or a lawyer in his firm may be called as a witness other than on behalf of his client, he may continue the representation until it is apparent that his testimony is or may be prejudicial to his client.

DR 5–103   Avoiding Acquisition of Interest in Litigation.

(A) A lawyer shall not acquire a proprietary interest in the cause of action or subject matter of litigation he is conducting for a client, except that he may:

(1) Acquire a lien granted by law to secure his fee or expenses.

(2) Contract with a client for a reasonable contingent fee in a civil case.

(B) While representing a client in connection with contemplated or pending litigation, a lawyer shall not advance or guarantee financial assistance to his client, except that a lawyer may advance or guarantee the expenses of litigation, including court costs, expenses of investigation, expenses of medical examination, and costs of obtaining and presenting evidence, provided the client remains ultimately liable for such expenses.

DR 5–104   Limiting Business Relations With a Client.

(A) A lawyer shall not enter into a business transaction with a client if they have differing interests therein and if the client expects the lawyer to exercise his professional judgment therein for the protection of the client, unless the client has consented after full disclosure.

(B)   Prior to conclusion of all aspects of the matter giving rise to his employment, a lawyer shall not enter into any arrangement or understanding with a client or a prospective client by which he acquires an interest in publication rights with respect to the subject matter of his employment or proposed employment.

DR 5–105   Refusing to Accept or Continue Employment if the Interests of Another Client May Impair the Independent Professional Judgment of the Lawyer.

(A)   A lawyer shall decline proffered employment if the exercise of his independent professional judgment in behalf of a client will be or is likely to be adversely affected by the acceptance of the proffered employment, or if it would be likely to involve him in representing differing interests, except to the extent permitted under DR 5–105(C).

(B)   A lawyer shall not continue multiple employment if the exercise of his independent professional judgment in behalf of a client will be or is likely to be adversely affected by his representation of another client, or if it would be likely to involve him in representing differing interests, except to the extent permitted under DR 5–105(C).

(C)   In the situations covered by DR 5–105(A) and (B), a lawyer may represent multiple clients if it is obvious that he can adequately represent the interest of each and if each consents to the representation after full disclosure of the possible effect of such representation on the exercise of his independent professional judgment on behalf of each.

(D)   If a lawyer is required to decline employment or to withdraw from employment under a Disciplinary Rule, no partner or associate, or any other lawyer affiliated with him or his firm may accept or continue such employment.

DR 5–106   Settling Similar Claims of Clients.

(A)   A lawyer who represents two or more clients shall not make or participate in the making of an aggregate settlement of the claims of or against his clients, unless each client has consented to the settlement after being advised of the existence and nature of all the claims involved in the proposed settlement, of the total amount of the settlement, and of the participation of each person in the settlement.

DR 5–107   Avoiding Influence by Others Than the Client.

(A)   Except with the consent of his client after full disclosure, a lawyer shall not:

   (1)   Accept compensation for his legal services from one other than his client.

   (2)   Accept from one other than his client any thing of value related to his representation of or his employment by his client.

(B)   A lawyer shall not permit a person who recommends, employs, or pays him to render legal services for another to direct or regulate his professional judgment in rendering such legal services.

(C) A lawyer shall not practice with or in the form of a professional corporation or association authorized to practice law for a profit, if:

   (1) A non-lawyer owns any interest therein, except that a fiduciary representative of the estate of a lawyer may hold the stock or interest of the lawyer for a reasonable time during administration;

   (2) A non-lawyer is a corporate director or officer thereof; or

   (3) A non-lawyer has the right to direct or control the professional judgment of a lawyer.

CANON 6

A Lawyer Should Represent a Client Competently

ETHICAL CONSIDERATIONS

EC 6–1   Because of his vital role in the legal process, a lawyer should act with competence and proper care in representing clients. He should strive to become and remain proficient in his practice and should accept employment only in matters which he is or intends to become competent to handle.

EC 6–2   A lawyer is aided in attaining and maintaining his competence by keeping abreast of current legal literature and developments, participating in continuing legal education programs, concentrating in particular areas of the law, and by utilizing other available means. He has the additional ethical obligation to assist in improving the legal profession, and he may do so by participating in bar activities intended to advance the quality and standards of members of the profession. Of particular importance is the careful training of his younger associates and the giving of sound guidance to all lawyers who consult him. In short, a lawyer should strive at all levels to aid the legal profession in advancing the highest possible standards of integrity and competence and to meet those standards himself.

EC 6–3   While the licensing of a lawyer is evidence that he has met the standards then prevailing for admission to the bar, a lawyer generally should not accept employment in any area of the law in which he is not qualified. However, he may accept such employment if in good faith he expects to become qualified through study and investigation, as long as such preparation would not result in unreasonable delay or expense to his client. Proper preparation and representation may require the association by the lawyer of professionals in other disciplines. A lawyer offered employment in a matter in which he is not and does not expect to become so qualified should either decline the employment or, with the consent of his client, accept the employment and associate a lawyer who is competent in the matter.

EC 6–4   Having undertaken representation, a lawyer should use proper care to safeguard the interests of his client. If a lawyer has accepted employment in a matter beyond his competence but in which he expected to become competent, he should diligently undertake the work and study necessary to qualify himself. In addition to being qualified to handle a particular matter, his obligation to his client requires him to prepare adequately for and give appropriate attention to his legal work.

EC 6–5   A lawyer should have pride in his professional endeavors. His obligation to act competently calls for higher motivation than that arising from fear of civil liability or disciplinary penalty.

EC 6–6 A lawyer should not seek, by contract or other means, to limit his individual liability to his client for his malpractice. A lawyer who handles the affairs of his client properly has no need to attempt to limit his liability for his professional activities and one who does not handle the affairs of his client properly should not be permitted to do so. A lawyer who is a stockholder in or is associated with a professional legal corporation may, however, limit his liability for malpractice of his associates in the corporation, but only to the extent permitted by law.

DISCIPLINARY RULES

DR 6–101   Failing to Act Competently.

(A) A lawyer shall not:

   (1) Handle a legal matter which he knows or should know that he is not competent to handle, without associating with him a lawyer who is competent to handle it.

   (2) Handle a legal matter without preparation adequate in the circumstances.

   (3) Neglect a legal matter entrusted to him.

DR 6–102   Limiting Liability to Client.

(A) A lawyer shall not attempt to exonerate himself from or limit his liability to his client for his personal malpractice.

CANON 7

A Lawyer Should Represent a Client Zealously Within the Bounds of the Law

ETHICAL CONSIDERATIONS

EC 7–1 The duty of a lawyer, both to his client and to the legal system, is to represent his client zealously within the bounds of the law, which includes Disciplinary Rules and enforceable professional regulations. The professional responsibility of a lawyer derives from his membership in a profession which has the duty of assisting members of the public to secure and protect available legal rights and benefits. In our government of laws and not of men, each member of our society is entitled to have his conduct judged and regulated in accordance with the law; to seek any lawful objective through legally permissible means; and to present for adjudication any lawful claim, issue, or defense.

EC 7–2 The bounds of the law in a given case are often difficult to ascertain. The language of legislative enactments and judicial opinions may be uncertain as applied to varying factual situations. The limits and specific meaning of apparently relevant law may be made doubtful by changing or developing constitutional interpretations, inadequately expressed statutes or judicial opinions, and changing public and judicial attitudes. Certainty of law ranges from well-settled rules through areas of conflicting authority to areas without precedent.

EC 7–3 Where the bounds of law are uncertain, the action of a lawyer may depend on whether he is serving as advocate or adviser. A lawyer may serve simultaneously as both advocate and adviser, but the two roles are essentially different. In asserting a position on behalf of his client, an advocate for the most part deals with past conduct and must take the facts as he finds them. By contrast, a lawyer serving as adviser primarily assists his client in determining the course of future conduct and relationships. While serving as advocate, a lawyer should resolve in favor of his client doubts as to the bounds of the law. In serving a client as adviser, a lawyer in appropriate circumstances should give his professional opinion as to what the ultimate decisions of the courts would likely be as to the applicable law.

Duty of the Lawyer to a Client

EC 7–4   The advocate may urge any permissible construction of the law favorable to his client, without regard to his professional opinion as to the likelihood that the construction will ultimately prevail. His conduct is within the bounds of the law, and therefore permissible, if the position taken is supported by the law or is supportable by a good faith argument for an extension, modification, or reversal of the law. However, a lawyer is not justified in asserting a position in litigation that is frivolous.

EC 7–5   A lawyer as adviser furthers the interest of his client by giving his professional opinion as to what he believes would likely be the ultimate decision of the courts on the matter at hand and by informing his client of the practical effect of such decision. He may continue in the representation of his client even though his client has elected to pursue a course of conduct contrary to the advice of the lawyer so long as he does not thereby knowingly assist the client to engage in illegal conduct or to take a frivolous legal position. A lawyer should never encourage or aid his client to commit criminal acts or counsel his client on how to violate the law and avoid punishment therefor.

EC 7–6   Whether the proposed action of a lawyer is within the bounds of the law may be a perplexing question when his client is contemplating a course of conduct having legal consequences that vary according to the client's intent, motive, or desires at the time of the action. Often a lawyer is asked to assist his client in developing evidence relevant to the state of mind of the client at a particular time. He may properly assist his client in the development and preservation of evidence of existing motive, intent, or desire; obviously, he may not do anything furthering the creation or preservation of false evidence. In many cases a lawyer may not be certain as to the state of mind of his client, and in those situations he should resolve reasonable doubts in favor of his client.

EC 7–7   In certain areas of legal representation not affecting the merits of the cause or substantially prejudicing the rights of a client, a lawyer is entitled to make decisions on his own. But otherwise the authority to make decisions is exclusively that of the client and, if made within the framework of the law, such decisions are binding on his lawyer. As typical examples in civil cases, it is for the client to decide whether he will accept a settlement offer or whether he will waive his right to plead an affirmative defense. A defense lawyer in a criminal case has the duty to advise his client fully on whether a particular plea to a charge appears to be desirable and as to the prospects of success on appeal, but it is for the client to decide what plea should be entered and whether an appeal should be taken.

EC 7–8   A lawyer should exert his best efforts to insure that decisions of his client are made only after the client has been informed of relevant considerations. A lawyer ought to initiate this decision-making process if the client does not do so. Advice of a lawyer to his client need not be confined to purely legal considerations. A lawyer should advise his client of the possible effect of each legal alternative. A lawyer should bring to bear upon this decision-making process the fullness of his experience as well as his objective viewpoint. In assisting his client to reach a proper decision, it is often desirable for a lawyer to point out those factors which may lead to a decision that is morally just as well as legally permissible. He may emphasize the possibility of harsh consequences that might result from assertion of legally permissible positions. In the final analysis, however, the lawyer should always remember that the decision whether to forego legally available objectives or methods because of non-legal factors is ultimately for the client and not for himself. In the event that the client in a non-adjudicatory matter insists upon a course of conduct that is contrary to the judgment and advice of the lawyer but not prohibited by Disciplinary Rules, the lawyer may withdraw from the employment.

EC 7–9 In the exercise of his professional judgment on those decisions which are for his determination in the handling of a legal matter, a lawyer should always act in a manner consistent with the best interests of his client. However, when an action in the best interest of his client seems to him to be unjust, he may ask his client for permission to forego such action.

EC 7–10 The duty of a lawyer to represent his client with zeal does not militate against his concurrent obligation to treat with consideration all persons involved in the legal process and to avoid the infliction of needless harm.

EC 7–11 The responsibilities of a lawyer may vary according to the intelligence, experience, mental condition or age of a client, the obligation of a public officer, or the nature of a particular proceeding. Examples include the representation of an illiterate or an incompetent, service as a public prosecutor or other government lawyer, and appearances before administrative and legislative bodies.

EC 7–12 Any mental or physical condition of a client that renders him incapable of making a considered judgment on his own behalf casts additional responsibilities upon his lawyer. Where an incompetent is acting through a guardian or other legal representative, a lawyer must look to such representative for those decisions which are normally the prerogative of the client to make. If a client under disability has no legal representative, his lawyer may be compelled in court proceedings to make decisions on behalf of the client. If the client is capable of understanding the matter in question or of contributing to the advancement of his interests, regardless of whether he is legally disqualified from performing certain acts, the lawyer should obtain from him all possible aid. If the disability of a client and the lack of a legal representative compel the lawyer to make decisions for his client, the lawyer should consider all circumstances then prevailing and act with care to safeguard and advance the interests of his client. But obviously a lawyer cannot perform any act or make any decision which the law requires his client to perform or make, either acting for himself if competent, or by a duly constituted representative if legally incompetent.

EC 7–13 The responsibility of a public prosecutor differs from that of the usual advocate; his duty is to seek justice, not merely to convict. This special duty exists because: (1) the prosecutor represents the sovereign and therefore should use restraint in the discretionary exercise of governmental powers, such as in the selection of cases to prosecute; (2) during trial the prosecutor is not only an advocate but he also may make decisions normally made by an individual client, and those affecting the public interest should be fair to all; and (3) in our system of criminal justice the accused is to be given the benefit of all reasonable doubts. With respect to evidence and witnesses, the prosecutor has responsibilities different from those of a lawyer in private practice; the prosecutor should make timely disclosure to the defense of available evidence, known to him, that tends to negate the guilt of the accused, mitigate the degree of the offense, or reduce the punishment. Further, a prosecutor should not intentionally avoid pursuit of evidence merely because he believes it will damage the prosecutor's case or aid the accused.

EC 7–14 A government lawyer who has discretionary power relative to litigation should refrain from instituting or continuing litigation that is obviously unfair. A government lawyer not having such discretionary power who believes there is lack of merit in a controversy submitted to him should so advise his superiors and recommend the avoidance of unfair litigation. A government lawyer in a civil action or administrative proceeding has the responsibility to seek justice and to develop a full and fair record, and he should not use his position or the economic power of the government to harass parties or to bring about unjust settlements or results.

EC 7–15 The nature and purpose of proceedings before administrative agencies vary widely. The proceedings may be legislative or quasi-judicial, or a combination of both. They may be *ex parte* in character, in which event they may originate either at the instance of the agency or upon motion of an interested party. The scope of an inquiry may be purely investigative or it may be truly adversary looking toward the adjudication of specific rights of a party or of classes of parties. The foregoing are but examples of some of the types of proceedings conducted by administrative agencies. A lawyer appearing before an administrative agency, regardless of the nature of the proceeding it is conducting, has the continuing duty to advance the cause of his client within the bounds of the law. Where the applicable rules of the agency impose specific obligations upon a lawyer, it is his duty to comply therewith, unless the lawyer has a legitimate basis for challenging the validity thereof. In all appearances before administrative agencies, a lawyer should identify himself, his client if identity of his client is not privileged, and the representative nature of his appearance. It is not improper, however, for a lawyer to seek from an agency information available to the public without identifying his client.

EC 7–16 The primary business of a legislative body is to enact laws rather than to adjudicate controversies, although on occasion the activities of a legislative body may take on the characteristics of an adversary proceeding, particularly in investigative and impeachment matters. The role of a lawyer supporting or opposing proposed legislation normally is quite different from his role in representing a person under investigation or on trial by a legislative body. When a lawyer appears in connection with proposed legislation, he seeks to affect the lawmaking process, but when he appears on behalf of a client in investigatory or impeachment proceedings, he is concerned with the protection of the rights of his client. In either event, he should identify himself and his client, if identity of his client is not privileged, and should comply with applicable laws and legislative rules.

EC 7–17 The obligation of loyalty to his client applies only to a lawyer in the discharge of his professional duties and implies no obligation to adopt a personal viewpoint favorable to the interests or desires of his client. While a lawyer must act always with circumspection in order that his conduct will not adversely affect the rights of a client in a matter he is then handling, he may take positions on public issues and espouse legal reforms he favors without regard to the individual views of any client.

EC 7–18 The legal system in its broadest sense functions best when persons in need of legal advice or assistance are represented by their own counsel. For this reason a lawyer should not communicate on the subject matter of the representation of his client with a person he knows to be represented in the matter by a lawyer, unless pursuant to law or rule of court or unless he has the consent of the lawyer for that person. If one is not represented by counsel, a lawyer representing another may have to deal directly with the unrepresented person; in such an instance, a lawyer should not undertake to give advice to the person who is attempting to represent himself, except that he may advise him to obtain a lawyer.

Duty of the Lawyer to the Adversary System of Justice

EC 7–19 Our legal system provides for the adjudication of disputes governed by the rules of substantive, evidentiary, and procedural law. An adversary presentation counters the natural human tendency to judge too swiftly in terms of the familiar that which is not yet fully known; the advocate, by his zealous preparation and presentation of facts and law, enables the tribunal to come to the hearing with an open and neutral mind and to render impartial judgments. The duty of a lawyer to his client and his duty to the legal system are the same: to represent his client zealously within the bounds of the law.

EC 7–20 In order to function properly, our adjudicative process requires an informed, impartial tribunal capable of administering justice promptly and efficiently according to procedures that command public confidence and respect. Not only must there be competent, adverse presentation of evidence and issues, but a tribunal must be aided by rules appropriate to an effective and dignified process. The procedures under which tribunals operate in our adversary system have been prescribed largely by legislative enactments, court rules and decisions, and administrative rules. Through the years certain concepts of proper professional conduct have become rules of law applicable to the adversary adjudicative process. Many of these concepts are the bases for standards of professional conduct set forth in the Disciplinary Rules.

EC 7–21 The civil adjudicative process is primarily designed for the settlement of disputes between parties, while the criminal process is designed for the protection of society as a whole. Threatening to use, or using, the criminal process to coerce adjustment of private civil claims or controversies is a subversion of that process; further, the person against whom the criminal process is so misused may be deterred from asserting his legal rights and thus the usefulness of the civil process in settling private disputes is impaired. As in all cases of abuse of judicial process, the improper use of criminal process tends to diminish public confidence in our legal system.

EC 7–22 Respect for judicial rulings is essential to the proper administration of justice; however, a litigant or his lawyer may, in good faith and within the framework of the law, take steps to test the correctness of a ruling of a tribunal.

EC 7–23 The complexity of law often makes it difficult for a tribunal to be fully informed unless the pertinent law is presented by the lawyers in the cause. A tribunal that is fully informed on the applicable law is better able to make a fair and accurate determination of the matter before it. The adversary system contemplates that each lawyer will present and argue the existing law in the light most favorable to his client. Where a lawyer knows of legal authority in the controlling jurisdiction directly adverse to the position of his client, he should inform the tribunal of its existence unless his adversary has done so; but, having made such disclosure, he may challenge its soundness in whole or in part.

EC 7–24 In order to bring about just and informed decisions, evidentiary and procedural rules have been established by tribunals to permit the inclusion of relevant evidence and argument and the exclusion of all other considerations. The expression by a lawyer of his personal opinion as to the justness of a cause, as to the credibility of a witness, as to the culpability of a civil litigant, or as to the guilt or innocence of an accused is not a proper subject for argument to the trier of fact. It is improper as to factual matters because admissible evidence possessed by a lawyer should be presented only as sworn testimony. It is improper as to all other matters because, were the rule otherwise, the silence of a lawyer on a given occasion could be construed unfavorably to his client. However, a lawyer may argue, on his analysis of the evidence, for any position or conclusion with respect to any of the foregoing matters.

EC 7–25 Rules of evidence and procedure are designed to lead to just decisions and are part of the framework of the law. Thus while a lawyer may take steps in good faith and within the framework of the law to test the validity of rules, he is not justified in consciously violating such rules and he should be diligent in his efforts to guard against his unintentional violation of them. As examples, a lawyer should subscribe to or verify only those pleadings that he believes are in compliance with applicable law and rules; a lawyer should not make any prefatory statement before a tribunal in regard to the purported facts of the case on trial unless he believes that his statement will be supported by admissible evidence; a lawyer should not ask a witness a question solely for the purpose of harassing or embarrassing him; and a lawyer should not by subterfuge put before a jury matters which it cannot properly consider.

EC 7–26 The law and Disciplinary Rules prohibit the use of fraudulent, false, or perjured testimony or evidence. A lawyer who knowingly participates in introduction of such testimony or evidence is subject to discipline. A lawyer should, however, present any admissible evidence his client desires to have presented unless he knows, or from facts within his knowledge should know, that such testimony or evidence is false, fraudulent, or perjured.

EC 7–27 Because it interferes with the proper administration of justice, a lawyer should not suppress evidence that he or his client has a legal obligation to reveal or produce. In like manner, a lawyer should not advise or cause a person to secrete himself or to leave the jurisdiction of a tribunal for the purpose of making him unavailable as a witness therein.

EC 7–28 Witnesses should always testify truthfully and should be free from any financial inducements that might tempt them to do otherwise. A lawyer should not pay or agree to pay a non-expert witness an amount in excess of reimbursement for expenses and financial loss incident to his being a witness; however, a lawyer may pay or agree to pay an expert witness a reasonable fee for his services as an expert. But in no event should a lawyer pay or agree to pay a contingent fee to any witness. A lawyer should exercise reasonable diligence to see that his client and lay associates conform to these standards.

EC 7–29 To safeguard the impartiality that is essential to the judicial process, veniremen and jurors should be protected against extraneous influences. When impartiality is present, public confidence in the judicial system is enhanced. There should be no extrajudicial communication with veniremen prior to trial or with jurors during trial by or on behalf of a lawyer connected with the case. Furthermore, a lawyer who is not connected with the case should not communicate with or cause another to communicate with a venireman or a juror about the case. After the trial, communication by a lawyer with jurors is permitted so long as he refrains from asking questions or making comments that tend to harass or embarrass the juror or to influence actions of the juror in future cases. Were a lawyer to be prohibited from communicating after a trial with a juror, he could not ascertain if the verdict might be subject to legal challenge, in which event the invalidity of a verdict might go undetected. When an extrajudicial communication by a lawyer with a juror is permitted by law, it should be made considerately and with deference to the personal feelings of the juror.

EC 7–30 Vexatious or harassing investigations of veniremen or jurors seriously impair the effectiveness of our jury system. For this reason, a lawyer or anyone on his behalf who conducts an investigation of veniremen or jurors should act with circumspection and restraint.

EC 7–31 Communications with or investigations of members of families of veniremen or jurors by a lawyer or by anyone on his behalf are subject to the restrictions imposed upon the lawyer with respect to his communications with or investigations of veniremen and jurors.

EC 7–32 Because of his duty to aid in preserving the integrity of the jury system, a lawyer who learns of improper conduct by or towards a venireman, a juror, or a member of the family of either should make a prompt report to the court regarding such conduct.

EC 7–33 A goal of our legal system is that each party shall have his case, criminal or civil, adjudicated by an impartial tribunal. The attainment of this goal may be defeated by dissemination of news or comments which tend to influence judge or jury. Such news or comments may prevent prospective jurors from being impartial at the outset of the trial and may also interfere with the obligation of jurors to base their verdict solely upon the evidence admitted in the trial. The release by a lawyer of out-of-court statements regarding an anticipated or pending trial may improperly affect the impartiality of the tribunal. For these reasons, standards for permissible and prohibited conduct of a lawyer with respect to trial publicity have been established.

EC 7–34 The impartiality of a public servant in our legal system may be impaired by the receipt of gifts or loans. A lawyer, therefore, is never justified in making a gift or a loan to a judge, a hearing officer, or an official or employee of a tribunal, except as permitted by Section C(4) of Canon 5 of the Code of Judicial Conduct, but a lawyer may make a contribution to the campaign fund of a candidate for judicial office in conformity with Section B(2) under Canon 7 of the Code of Judicial Conduct.

EC 7–35 All litigants and lawyers should have access to tribunals on an equal basis. Generally, in adversary proceedings a lawyer should not communicate with a judge relative to a matter pending before, or which is to be brought before, a tribunal over which he presides in circumstances which might have the effect or give the appearance of granting undue advantage to one party. For example, a lawyer should not communicate with a tribunal by a writing unless a copy thereof is promptly delivered to opposing counsel or to the adverse party if he is not represented by a lawyer. Ordinarily an oral communication by a lawyer with a judge or hearing officer should be made only upon adequate notice to opposing counsel, or, if there is none, to the opposing party. A lawyer should not condone or lend himself to private importunities by another with a judge or hearing officer on behalf of himself or his client.

EC 7–36 Judicial hearings ought to be conducted through dignified and orderly procedures designed to protect the rights of all parties. Although a lawyer has the duty to represent his client zealously, he should not engage in any conduct that offends the dignity and decorum of proceedings. While maintaining his independence, a lawyer should be respectful, courteous, and above-board in his relations with a judge or hearing officer before whom he appears. He should avoid undue solicitude for the comfort or convenience of judge or jury and should avoid any other conduct calculated to gain special consideration.

EC 7–37 In adversary proceedings, clients are litigants and though ill feeling may exist between clients, such ill feeling should not influence a lawyer in his conduct, attitude, and demeanor towards opposing lawyers. A lawyer should not make unfair or derogatory personal reference to opposing counsel. Haranguing and offensive tactics by lawyers interfere with the orderly administration of justice and have no proper place in our legal system.

EC 7–38 A lawyer should be courteous to opposing counsel and should accede to reasonable requests regarding court proceedings, settings, continuances, waiver of procedural formalities, and similar matters which do not prejudice the rights of his client. He should follow local customs of courtesy or practice, unless he gives timely notice to opposing counsel of his intention not to do so. A lawyer should be punctual in fulfilling all professional commitments.

EC 7–39 In the final analysis, proper functioning of the adversary system depends upon cooperation between lawyers and tribunals in utilizing procedures which will preserve the impartiality of tribunals and make their decisional processes prompt and just, without impinging upon the obligation of lawyers to represent their clients zealously within the framework of the law.

DISCIPLINARY RULES

DR 7–101   **Representing a Client Zealously.**

(A) A lawyer shall not intentionally:

    (1) Fail to seek the lawful objectives of his client through reasonably available means permitted by law and the Disciplinary Rules, except as provided by DR 7–101(B). A lawyer does not violate this Disciplinary Rule, however, by acceding to reasonable requests of opposing counsel which do not prejudice the rights of his client, by being punctual in fulfilling all professional commitments, by avoiding offensive tactics, or by treating with courtesy and consideration all persons involved in the legal process.

    (2) Fail to carry out a contract of employment entered into with a client for professional services, but he may withdraw as permitted under DR 2–110, DR 5–102, and DR 5–105.

    (3) Prejudice or damage his client during the course of the professional relationship except as required under DR 7–102(B).

(B) In his representation of a client, a lawyer may:

    (1) Where permissible, exercise his professional judgment to waive or fail to assert a right or position of his client.

    (2) Refuse to aid or participate in conduct that he believes to be unlawful, even though there is some support for an argument that the conduct is legal.

DR 7–102   Representing a Client Within the Bounds of the Law.

(A) In his representation of a client, a lawyer shall not:

    (1) File a suit, assert a position, conduct a defense, delay a trial, or take other action on behalf of his client when he knows or when it is obvious that such action would serve merely to harass or maliciously injure another.

    (2) Knowingly advance a claim or defense that is unwarranted under existing law, except that he may advance such claim or defense if it can be supported by good faith argument for an extension, modification, or reversal of existing law.

    (3) Conceal or knowingly fail to disclose that which he is required by law to reveal.

    (4) Knowingly use perjured testimony or false evidence.

    (5) Knowingly make a false statement of law or fact.

    (6) Participate in the creation or preservation of evidence when he knows or it is obvious that the evidence is false.

    (7) Counsel or assist his client in conduct that the lawyer knows to be illegal or fraudulent.

    (8) Knowingly engage in other illegal conduct or conduct contrary to a Disciplinary Rule.

(B) A lawyer who receives information clearly establishing that:

    (1) His client has, in the course of the representation, perpetrated a fraud upon a person or tribunal shall promptly call upon his client to rectify the same, and if his client refuses or is unable to do so, he shall reveal the fraud to the affected person or tribunal, except when the information is protected as a privileged communication.

    (2) A person other than his client has perpetrated a fraud upon a tribunal shall promptly reveal the fraud to the tribunal.

DR 7–103   Performing the Duty of Public Prosecutor or Other Government Lawyer.

(A) A public prosecutor or other government lawyer shall not institute or cause to be instituted criminal charges when he knows or it is obvious that the charges are not supported by probable cause.

(B) A public prosecutor or other government lawyer in criminal litigation shall make timely disclosure to counsel for the defendant, or to the defendant if he has no counsel, of the existence of evidence, known to the prosecutor or other government lawyer, that tends to negate the guilt of the accused, mitigate the degree of the offense, or reduce the punishment.

DR 7–104   Communicating With One of Adverse Interest.

(A) During the course of his representation of a client a lawyer shall not:

   (1) Communicate or cause another to communicate on the subject of the representation with a party he knows to be represented by a lawyer in that matter unless he has the prior consent of the lawyer representing such other party or is authorized by law to do so.

   (2) Give advice to a person who is not represented by a lawyer, other than the advice to secure counsel, if the interests of such person are or have a reasonable possibility of being in conflict with the interests of his client.

DR 7–105   Threatening Criminal Prosecution.

(A) A lawyer shall not present, participate in presenting, or threaten to present criminal charges solely to obtain an advantage in a civil matter.

DR 7–106   Trial Conduct.

(A) A lawyer shall not disregard or advise his client to disregard a standing rule of a tribunal or a ruling of a tribunal made in the course of a proceeding, but he may take appropriate steps in good faith to test the validity of such rule or ruling.

(B) In presenting a matter to a tribunal, a lawyer shall disclose:

   (1) Legal authority in the controlling jurisdiction known to him to be directly adverse to the position of his client and which is not disclosed by opposing counsel.

   (2) Unless privileged or irrelevant, the identities of the clients he represents and of the persons who employed him.

(C) In appearing in his professional capacity before a tribunal, a lawyer shall not:

   (1) State or allude to any matter that he has no reasonable basis to believe is relevant to the case or that will not be supported by admissible evidence.

   (2) Ask any question that he has no reasonable basis to believe is relevant to the case and that is intended to degrade a witness or other person.

   (3) Assert his personal knowledge of the facts in issue, except when testifying as a witness.

   (4) Assert his personal opinion as to the justness of a cause, as to the credibility of a witness, as to the culpability of a civil litigant, or as to the guilt or innocence of an accused; but he may argue, on his analysis of the evidence, for any position or conclusion with respect to the matters stated herein.

   (5) Fail to comply with known local customs of courtesy or practice of the bar or a particular tribunal without giving to opposing counsel timely notice of his intent not to comply.

   (6) Engage in undignified or discourteous conduct which is degrading to a tribunal.

   (7) Intentionally or habitually violate any established rule of procedure or of evidence.

DR 7–107   Trial Publicity.

(A) A lawyer participating in or associated with the investigation of a criminal matter shall not make or participate in making an extrajudicial statement that a reasonable person would expect to be disseminated by means of public communication and that does more than state without elaboration:

    (1) Information contained in a public record.

    (2) That the investigation is in progress.

    (3) The general scope of the investigation including a description of the offense and, if permitted by law, the identity of the victim.

    (4) A request for assistance in apprehending a suspect or assistance in other matters and the information necessary thereto.

    (5) A warning to the public of any dangers.

(B) A lawyer or law firm associated with the prosecution or defense of a criminal matter shall not, from the time of the filing of a complaint, information, or indictment, the issuance of an arrest warrant, or arrest until the commencement of the trial or disposition without trial, make or participate in making an extrajudicial statement that a reasonable person would expect to be disseminated by means of public communication and that relates to:

    (1) The character, reputation, or prior criminal record (including arrests, indictments, or other charges of crime) of the accused.

    (2) The possibility of a plea of guilty to the offense charged or to a lesser offense.

    (3) The existence or contents of any confession, admission, or statement given by the accused or his refusal or failure to make a statement.

    (4) The performance or results of any examinations or tests or the refusal or failure of the accused to submit to examinations or tests.

    (5) The identity, testimony, or credibility of a prospective witness.

    (6) Any opinion as to the guilt or innocence of the accused, the evidence, or the merits of the case.

(C) DR 7–107(B) does not preclude a lawyer during such period from announcing:

    (1) The name, age, residence, occupation, and family status of the accused.

    (2) If the accused has not been apprehended, any information necessary to aid in his apprehension or to warn the public of any dangers he may present.

    (3) A request for assistance in obtaining evidence.

    (4) The identity of the victim of the crime.

(5) The fact, time, and place of arrest, resistance, pursuit, and use of weapons.

(6) The identity of investigating and arresting officers or agencies and the length of the investigation.

(7) At the time of seizure, a description of the physical evidence seized, other than a confession, admission, or statement.

(8) The nature, substance, or text of the charge.

(9) Quotations from or references to public records of the court in the case.

(10) The scheduling or result of any step in the judicial proceedings.

(11) That the accused denies the charges made against him.

(D) During the selection of a jury or the trial of a criminal matter, a lawyer or law firm associated with the prosecution or defense of a criminal matter shall not make or participate in making an extra-judicial statement that a reasonable person would expect to be disseminated by means of public communication and that relates to the trial, parties, or issues in the trial or other matters that are reasonably likely to interfere with a fair trial, except that he may quote from or refer without comment to public records of the court in the case.

(E) After the completion of a trial or disposition without trial of a criminal matter and prior to the imposition of sentence, a lawyer or law firm associated with the prosecution or defense shall not make or participate in making an extra-judicial statement that a reasonable person would expect to be disseminated by public communication and that is reasonably likely to affect the imposition of sentence.

(F) The foregoing provisions of DR 7–107 also apply to professional disciplinary proceedings and juvenile disciplinary proceedings when pertinent and consistent with other law applicable to such proceedings.

(G) A lawyer or law firm associated with a civil action shall not during its investigation or litigation make or participate in making an extra-judicial statement, other than a quotation from or reference to public records, that a reasonable person would expect to be disseminated by means of public communication and that relates to:

(1) Evidence regarding the occurrence or transaction involved.

(2) The character, credibility, or criminal record of a party, witness, or prospective witness.

(3) The performance or results of any examinations or tests or the refusal or failure of a party to submit to such.

(4) His opinion as to the merits of the claims or defenses of a party, except as required by law or administrative rule.

(5) Any other matter reasonably likely to interfere with a fair trial of the action.

(H) During the pendency of an administrative proceeding, a lawyer or law firm associated therewith shall not make or participate in making a statement, other than a quotation from or reference to public records, that a reasonable person would expect to be disseminated by means of public communication if it is made outside the official course of the proceeding and relates to:

    (1) Evidence regarding the occurrence or transaction involved.

    (2) The character, credibility, or criminal record of a party, witness, or prospective witness.

    (3) Physical evidence or the performance or results of any examinations or tests or the refusal or failure of a party to submit to such.

    (4) His opinion as to the merits of the claims, defenses, or positions of an interested person.

    (5) Any other matter reasonably likely to interfere with a fair hearing.

(I) The foregoing provisions of DR 7–107 do not preclude a lawyer from replying to charges of misconduct publicly made against him or from participating in the proceedings of legislative, administrative, or other investigative bodies.

(J) A lawyer shall exercise reasonable care to prevent his employees and associates from making an extra-judicial statement that he would be prohibited from making under DR 7–107.

DR 7–108   Communication with or Investigation of Jurors.

(A) Before the trial of a case a lawyer connected therewith shall not communicate with or cause another to communicate with anyone he knows to be a member of the venire from which the jury will be selected for the trial of the case.

(B) During the trial of a case:

    (1) A lawyer connected therewith shall not communicate with or cause another to communicate with any member of the jury.

    (2) A lawyer who is not connected therewith shall not communicate with or cause another to communicate with a juror concerning the case.

(C) DR 7–108(A) and (B) do not prohibit a lawyer from communicating with veniremen or jurors in the course of official proceedings.

(D) After discharge of the jury from further consideration of a case with which the lawyer was connected, the lawyer shall not ask questions of or make comments to a member of that jury that are calculated merely to harass or embarrass the juror or to influence his actions in future jury service.

(E) A lawyer shall not conduct or cause, by financial support or otherwise, another to conduct a vexatious or harassing investigation of either a venireman or a juror.

(F) All restrictions imposed by DR 7–108 upon a lawyer also apply to communications with or investigations of members of a family of a venireman or a juror.

(G) A lawyer shall reveal promptly to the court improper conduct by a venireman or a juror, or by another toward a venireman or a juror or a member of his family, of which the lawyer has knowledge.

DR 7–109   Contact With Witnesses.

(A) A lawyer shall not suppress any evidence that he or his client has a legal obligation to reveal or produce.

(B) A lawyer shall not advise or cause a person to secrete himself or to leave the jurisdiction of a tribunal for the purpose of making him unavailable as a witness therein.

(C) A lawyer shall not pay, offer to pay, or acquiesce in the payment of compensation to a witness contingent upon the content of his testimony or the outcome of the case. But a lawyer may advance, guarantee, or acquiesce in the payment of:

   (1) Expenses reasonably incurred by a witness in attending or testifying.

   (2) Reasonable compensation to a witness for his loss of time in attending or testifying.

   (3) A reasonable fee for the professional services of an expert witness.

DR 7–110   Contact With Officials.

(A) A lawyer shall not give or lend any thing of value to a judge, official, or employee of a tribunal, except as permitted by Section C(4) of Canon 5 of the Code of Judicial Conduct, but a lawyer may make a contribution to the campaign fund of a candidate for judicial office in conformity with Section B(2) under Canon 7 of the Code of Judicial Conduct.

(B) In an adversary proceeding, a lawyer shall not communicate, or cause another to communicate, as to the merits of the cause with a judge or an official before whom the proceeding is pending, except:

   (1) In the course of official proceedings in the cause.

   (2) In writing if he promptly delivers a copy of the writing to opposing counsel or to the adverse party if he is not represented by a lawyer.

   (3) Orally upon adequate notice to opposing counsel or to the adverse party if he is not represented by a lawyer.

   (4) As otherwise authorized by law, or by Section A(4) under Canon 3 of the Code of Judicial Conduct.

CANON 8

A Lawyer Should Assist in Improving the Legal System

ETHICAL CONSIDERATIONS

EC 8-1   Changes in human affairs and imperfections in human institutions make necessary constant efforts to maintain and improve our legal system. This system should function in a manner that commands public respect and fosters the use of legal remedies to achieve redress of grievances. By reason of education and experience, lawyers are especially qualified to recognize deficiencies in the legal system and to initiate corrective measures therein. Thus they should participate in proposing and supporting legislation and programs to improve the system, without regard to the general interests or desires of clients or former clients.

EC 8-2   Rules of law are deficient if they are not just, understandable, and responsive to the needs of society. If a lawyer believes that the existence or absence of a rule of law, substantive or procedural, causes or contributes to an unjust result, he should endeavor by lawful means to obtain appropriate changes in the law. He should encourage the simplification of laws and the repeal or amendment of laws that are outmoded. Likewise, legal procedures should be improved whenever experience indicates a change is needed.

EC 8-3   The fair administration of justice requires the availability of competent lawyers. Members of the public should be educated to recognize the existence of legal problems and the resultant need for legal services, and should be provided methods for intelligent selection of counsel. Those persons unable to pay for legal services should be provided needed services. Clients and lawyers should not be penalized by undue geographical restraints upon representation in legal matters, and the bar should address itself to improvements in licensing, reciprocity, and admission procedures consistent with the needs of modern commerce.

EC 8-4   Whenever a lawyer seeks legislative or administrative changes, he should identify the capacity in which he appears, whether on behalf of himself, a client, or the public. A lawyer may advocate such changes on behalf of a client even though he does not agree with them. But when a lawyer purports to act on behalf of the public, he should espouse only those changes which he conscientiously believes to be in the public interest.

EC 8-5   Fraudulent, deceptive, or otherwise illegal conduct by a participant in a proceeding before a tribunal or legislative body is inconsistent with fair administration of justice, and it should never be participated in or condoned by lawyers. Unless constrained by his obligation to preserve the confidences and secrets of his client, a lawyer should reveal to appropriate authorities any knowledge he may have of such improper conduct.

EC 8-6   Judges and administrative officials having adjudicatory powers ought to be persons of integrity, competence, and suitable temperament. Generally, lawyers are qualified, by personal observation or investigation, to evaluate the qualifications of persons seeking or being considered for such public offices, and for this reason they have a special responsibility to aid in the selection of only those who are qualified. It is the duty of lawyers to endeavor to prevent political considerations from outweighing judicial fitness in the selection of judges. Lawyers should protest earnestly against the appointment or election of those who are unsuited for the bench and should strive to have elected or appointed thereto only those who are willing to forego pursuits, whether of a business, political, or other nature, that may interfere with the free and fair consideration of questions presented for adjudication.

Adjudicatory officials, not being wholly free to defend themselves, are entitled to receive the support of the bar against unjust criticism. While a lawyer as a citizen has a right to criticize such officials publicly, he should be certain of the merit of his complaint, use appropriate language, and avoid petty criticisms, for unrestrained and intemperate statements tend to lessen public confidence in our legal system. Criticisms motivated by reasons other than a desire to improve the legal system are not justified.

EC 8–7 Since lawyers are a vital part of the legal system, they should be persons of integrity, of professional skill, and of dedication to the improvement of the system. Thus a lawyer should aid in establishing, as well as enforcing, standards of conduct adequate to protect the public by insuring that those who practice law are qualified to do so.

EC 8–8 Lawyers often serve as legislators or as holders of other public offices. This is highly desirable, as lawyers are uniquely qualified to make significant contributions to the improvement of the legal system. A lawyer who is a public officer, whether full or part-time, should not engage in activities in which his personal or professional interests are or foreseeably may be in conflict with his official duties.

EC 8–9 The advancement of our legal system is of vital importance in maintaining the rule of law and in facilitating orderly changes; therefore, lawyers should encourage, and should aid in making, needed changes and improvements.

DISCIPLINARY RULES

DR 8–101   **Action as a Public Official.**

(A) A lawyer who holds public office shall not:

    (1) Use his public position to obtain, or attempt to obtain, a special advantage in legislative matters for himself or for a client under circumstances where he knows or it is obvious that such action is not in the public interest.

    (2) Use his public position to influence, or attempt to influence, a tribunal to act in favor of himself or of a client.

    (3) Accept any thing of value from any person when the lawyer knows or it is obvious that the offer is for the purpose of influencing his action as a public official.

DR 8–102   **Statements Concerning Judges and Other Adjudicatory Officers.**

(A) A lawyer shall not knowingly make false statements of fact concerning the qualifications of a candidate for election or appointment to a judicial office.

(B) A lawyer shall not knowingly make false accusations against a judge or other adjudicatory officer.

DR 8–103   **Lawyer Candidate for Judicial Office.**

(A) A lawyer who is a candidate for judicial office shall comply with the applicable provisions of Canon 7 of the Code of Judicial Conduct.

CANON 9

A Lawyer Should Avoid Even the Appearance of Professional Impropriety

ETHICAL CONSIDERATIONS

EC 9-1 Continuation of the American concept that we are to be governed by rules of law requires that the people have faith that justice can be obtained through our legal system. A lawyer should promote public confidence in our system and in the legal profession.

EC 9-2 Public confidence in law and lawyers may be eroded by irresponsible or improper conduct of a lawyer. On occasion, ethical conduct of a lawyer may appear to laymen to be unethical. In order to avoid misunderstandings and hence to maintain confidence, a lawyer should fully and promptly inform his client of material developments in the matters being handled for the client. While a lawyer should guard against otherwise proper conduct that has a tendency to diminish public confidence in the legal system or in the legal profession, his duty to clients or to the public should never be subordinate merely because the full discharge of his obligation may be misunderstood or may tend to subject him or the legal profession to criticism. When explicit ethical guidance does not exist, a lawyer should determine his conduct by acting in a manner that promotes public confidence in the integrity and efficiency of the legal system and the legal profession.

EC 9-3 After a lawyer leaves judicial office or other public employment, he should not accept employment in connection with any matter in which he had substantial responsibility prior to his leaving, since to accept employment would give the appearance of impropriety even if none exists.

EC 9-4 Because the very essence of the legal system is to provide procedures by which matters can be presented in an impartial manner so that they may be decided solely upon the merits, any statement or suggestion by a lawyer that he can or would attempt to circumvent those procedures is detrimental to the legal system and tends to undermine public confidence in it.

EC 9-5 Separation of the funds of a client from those of his lawyer not only serves to protect the client but also avoids even the appearance of impropriety, and therefore commingling of such funds should be avoided.

EC 9-6 Every lawyer owes a solemn duty to uphold the integrity and honor of his profession; to encourage respect for the law and for the courts and the judges thereof; to observe the Code of Professional Responsibility; to act as a member of a learned profession, one dedicated to public service; to cooperate with his brother lawyers in supporting the organized bar through the devoting of his time, efforts, and financial support as his professional standing and ability reasonably permit; to conduct himself so as to reflect credit on the legal profession and to inspire the confidence, respect, and trust of his clients and of the public; and to strive to avoid not only professional impropriety but also the appearance of impropriety.

EC 9-7 A lawyer has an obligation to the public to participate in collective efforts of the bar to reimburse persons who have lost money or property as a result of the misappropriation or defalcation of another lawyer, and contribution to a clients' security fund is an acceptable method of meeting this obligation.

DISCIPLINARY RULES

DR 9–101   Avoiding Even the Appearance of Impropriety.

(A) A lawyer shall not accept private employment in a matter upon the merits of which he has acted in a judicial capacity.

(B) A lawyer shall not accept private employment in a matter in which he had substantial responsibility while he was a public employee.

(C) A lawyer shall not state or imply that he is able to influence improperly or upon irrelevant grounds any tribunal, legislative body, or public official.

DR 9–102   Preserving Identity of Funds and Property of a Client.

(A) All funds of clients paid to a lawyer or law firm, other than advances for costs and expenses, shall be deposited in one or more identifiable bank accounts maintained in the state in which the law office is situated and no funds belonging to the lawyer or law firm shall be deposited therein except as follows:

    (1) Funds reasonably sufficient to pay bank charges may be deposited therein.

    (2) Funds belonging in part to a client and in part presently or potentially to the lawyer or law firm must be deposited therein, but the portion belonging to the lawyer or law firm may be withdrawn when due unless the right of the lawyer or law firm to receive it is disputed by the client, in which event the disputed portion shall not be withdrawn until the dispute is finally resolved.

(B) A lawyer shall:

    (1) Promptly notify a client of the receipt of his funds, securities, or other properties.

    (2) Identify and label securities and properties of a client promptly upon receipt and place them in a safe deposit box or other place of safekeeping as soon as practicable.

    (3) Maintain complete records of all funds, securities, and other properties of a client coming into the possession of the lawyer and render appropriate accounts to his client regarding them.

    (4) Promptly pay or deliver to the client as requested by a client the funds, securities, or other properties in the possession of the lawyer which the client is entitled to receive.

DEFINITIONS

As used in the Disciplinary Rules of the Code of Professional Responsibility:

    (1) "Differing interests" include every interest that will adversely affect either the judgment or the loyalty of a lawyer to a client, whether it be a conflicting, inconsistent, diverse, or other interest.

    (2) "Law firm" includes a professional legal corporation.

(3) "Person" includes a corporation, an association, a trust, a partnership, and any other organization or legal entity.

(4) "Professional legal corporation" means a corporation, or an association treated as a corporation, authorized by law to practice law for profit.

(5) "State" includes the District of Columbia, Puerto Rico, and other federal territories and possessions.

(6) "Tribunal" includes all courts and all other adjudicatory bodies.

(7) "A Bar association" includes a bar association of specialists as referred to in DR 2–105(A)(1) or (3).

(8) "Qualified legal assistance organization" means an office or organization of one of the four types listed in DR 2–103(D)(1)–(4), inclusive that meets all the requirements thereof.

INDEX TO MODEL CODE

A

Circumvention of disciplinary rule, DR 1–102(A)(2)

Class action. *See* Advice by lawyer to secure legal services

Clients,
> *See also* Employment; Adverse effect on professional judgment; Fee for legal services; Indigents, representation of; Mental competence of client; Unpopular party, representation of

Appearance as witness for, EC 5–9, 5–10, DR 5–101(B), 5–102
Attorney-client privilege, EC 3–3, Canon 4
Commingling of funds of, EC 9–5, DR 9–102
> Confidences of, Canon 4
> Counseling, EC 7–3, 7–5 to 7–9, 7–12, DR 7–102(A)(7) (B)(1), 7–106(A), 7–109(B)
> Decisions of, EC 5–12, 7–7, 7–8, 7–12
> Property, protection of, DR 9–102
> Secrets of, EC 3–3, Canon 4

Co-counsel,
> *See also* Association of counsel

Disagreements with, EC 5–12
Division of fee with, DR 2–107(A)
Inability to work with, DR 2–110(C)(3)

Commercial publicity. *See* Advertising, commercial publicity

Commingling of funds, EC 9–5, DR 9–102

Communications with,
> Judicial officers, EC 7–34, 7–35, 7–36, DR 7–110(B)
> Jurors, EC 7–29 to 7–32, DR 7–108
> One of adverse interests, EC 7–18, DR 7–104
> Opposing party, EC 7–21, DR 7–104
> Veniremen, EC 7–29 to 7–32, DR 7–108
> Witnesses, EC 7–27, 7–28, DR 7–109

Compensation for recommendation of employment, prohibition against, EC 2–8, DR 2–103(B)

Competence, mental. *See* Mental competence of bar applicant; Mental competence of client, effect on representation; Mental competence of lawyer

Competence, professional, EC 2–30, Canon 6

Confidences of client, EC 3–3, 3–4, Canon 4

Conflicting interests. *See* Adverse effect on professional judgment

Consent of client, requirement of,
> Acceptance of employment though interests conflict, EC 5–3, 5–14 to 5–20, DR 5–101(A), 5–104(A), 5–105(C)
> Acceptance of value from third person, EC 2–21, 5–22, 5–23, DR 5–107(A) (B)
> Advice requested from another lawyer, EC 4–2
> Aggregate settlement of claims, DR 5–106
> Association of lawyer, EC 2–22, DR 2–107(A)(1)
> Division of legal fees, DR 2–107(A)(1)
> Foregoing legal action, EC 7–7, 7–8, 7–9
> Multiple representation, EC 5–16, DR 5–105(C)
> Revelation of client's confidences and secrets, EC 4–2, 4–4, 4–5, DR 4–101(B)(3) (C)

Use of client's confidences and secrets, EC 4–2, 4–5, DR 4–101(B)(3) (C)
Withdrawal from employment, EC 2–32, DR 2–110(A)(2) (C)(5)

Consent of tribunal to lawyer's withdrawal, requirement of, EC 2–32, DR 2–110(A)(1) (C)

Contingent fee, propriety of,
In administrative actions, EC 2–20
In civil actions, EC 2–20, 5–7, DR 5–103(A)(2)
In criminal actions, EC 2–20, DR 2–106(C)
In domestic relation actions, EC 2–20

Continuing legal education programs, EC 1–2, 6–2

Contract of employment,
Fee provisions, desirability of writing, EC 2–19
Restrictive covenant in, DR 2–108

Controversy over fee, avoiding, EC 2–19, 2–23

Corporation,
Lawyer employed by, EC 5–18, 5–24, DR 5–107(C)
Professional legal, EC 2–11, 5–24, DR 5–107(C), definitions (4)

Counsel, designation as,
"General Counsel" designation, DR 2–102(A)(4)
"Of Counsel" designation, DR 2–102(A)(4)

Counseling, client, EC 7–3, 7–5 to 7–8, DR 7–102(A)(7) (B)(1), 7–106(A)

Courts,
See also Consent of tribunal to lawyer's withdrawal, requirement of; Evidence, conduct regarding; Trial tactics
Appointment of lawyer as counsel, EC 2–29
Courtesy, known customs of, EC 7–36, 7–38, DR 7–106(C)(5) (6)
Personal influence, prohibitions against exerting, EC 7–34 to 7–36, DR 7–110
Representation of client before, Canon 7

Criminal conduct,
As basis for discipline of lawyer, EC 1–5, DR 1–102(A)(3), 7–102(A)

Criticism of judges and administrative officials, EC 8–6, DR 8–102

Cross-examination of witness. See Witnesses, questioning of
Duty to reveal information as to, EC 1–4, DR 1–103
Providing counsel for those accused of, EC 2–26 to 2–31

D

De facto specialization, EC 2–8, 2–14, DR 2–101(B)(2), 2–105(A)(2)

Deceased lawyer,
Payment to estate of, EC 3–8, DR 3–102(A)(1) (2)
Use of name by law firm, EC 2–11, DR 2–102(A)(4) (B)

Defender, public, working with. See Public defender office, working with

Defense against accusation by client, privilege to disclose confidences and secrets, DR 4–101(C)(4)

Defense of those accused of crime, EC 2–26 to 2–31

Definitions, following Canon 9
  A bar association, Definitions (7)
  Differing interests, Definitions (1), EC 5–14
  Law firm, Definitions (2)
  Person, Definitions (3)
  Professional legal corporation, Definitions (4)
  Qualified legal assistance organization, Definitions (8)
  State, Definitions (5)
  Tribunal, Definitions (6)

Delegation of tasks to lay employees, EC 3–6

Desires of third parties, duty to avoid influence of, EC 5–21 to 5–24, DR 5–107

Differing interests, Definitions (1), EC 5–14
  See also Adverse effect on professional judgment

Disciplinary procedures, Preliminary statement

Disciplinary rules, Preliminary statement,
  Application of, Preliminary statement
  Fair trial, requirement of, Preliminary statement
  Penalties imposed, Preliminary statement
  Purpose and function of, Preliminary statement

Disciplinary sanction, Preliminary statement

Discipline of lawyer, grounds for,
  Advertising, improper, DR 1–102, 2–101(A), 2–102
  Associates, failure to exercise reasonable care toward, DR 4–101(D)
  Bribery of legal officials, DR 7–110(A)
  Circumvention of disciplinary rule, DR 1–102(A)(2)
  Clients' funds, mismanagement of, DR 9–102
  Communication with adverse party, improper, DR 7–104
  Communication with jurors, improper, DR 7–108
  Communication with tribunal, improper, DR 7–110(B)
  Compensation, accepting from third party, DR 5–107
  Confidences, improper use of, DR 4–101(B) (D)
  Confidential information, disclosure of, DR 4–101(B) (D)
  Conflict of interest with clients, disregard of duty to avoid, DR 5–101 to 5–107
  Conflicting interests, representation of, DR 5–105, 5–106, 5–107
  Crime of moral turpitude, DR 1–102(A)(3)
  Criminal conduct, DR 1–102, DR 7–102, 7–109(A)
  Criminal prosecution threatening, DR 7–105
  Differing interests, improper representation of, DR 5–105, 5–106
  Disregard of tribunal ruling, DR 7–106(A)
  Division of fee, improper, DR 2–107(A), 3–102
  Employees, failure to exercise reasonable care toward, DR 3–102, 4–101(D)
  Evidence,
    False or misleading, use of, DR 7–102(A)(4) (6)
    Suppression of, DR 7–103(B), 7–109(A)
  Extra-judicial statement, improper, DR 7–107
  Failure to act competently, DR 6–101
  Failure to act zealously, DR 7–101(A)
  Failure to disclose information concerning another lawyer or judge, DR 1–103

With associated lawyer, EC 2–22, DR 2–107
With estate of deceased lawyer, EC 3–8, DR 3–102(A)(1) (2) (3)
With laymen, EC 3–8, DR 3–102

E

Education,
Continuing legal education programs, EC 6–2
Elections, DR 2–101(H)(1), 8–102(A)
Of laymen to recognize legal problems, EC 2–1 to 2–5, 8–1, 8–3, DR 2–104
Of laymen to select lawyers, EC 2–6 to 2–15, 18–1, DR 2–104(A)(2)
Requirement of education for bar applicant, EC 1–2

Emotional instability. *See* Mental competence of lawyer

Employees of lawyer,
Delegation of tasks, EC 3–6
Duty of lawyer to control, EC 3–6, 4–2, 4–3, DR 4–101(D), 7–107(J)

Employment,
See also Advice by lawyer to secure legal services; Recommendation of professional employment
Acceptance of,
Generally, EC 2–26 to 2–33
Indigent client, on behalf of, EC 2–25, 2–29
Instances when improper, EC 2–3, 2–4, 2–30, 4–6, 5–2, 5–3, 5–10, 5–14 to 5–16, 5–20, 5–24, 6–1, 6–3, 9–3, DR 2–103(E), 2–104, 2–109, 5–101, 5–105, 6–101(A)(1), 9–101(A) (B)
Multiple clients, on behalf of, EC 5–14 to 5–19, DR 5–105(A) (C)
Unpopular cause, on behalf of, EC 2–26 to 2–30
Unpopular client, on behalf of, EC 2–26 to 2–30
When able to render competent service, EC 2–30, 6–1, 6–3, DR 6–101
Arbitrator, in capacity as, EC 5–20
Contract,
Desirability of, EC 2–19
Restrictive covenant in, DR 2–108
Mediator, in capacity as, EC 5–20
Public, retirement from, EC 9–3, DR 9–101(A) (B)
Rejection of, EC 2–26 to 2–33, 4–5, 6–1, 6–3, 9–3, DR 2–103, 2–104, 2–109, 2–110, 6–101, 9–101(A) (B)
Withdrawal from,
Generally, EC 2–32, 5–3, 5–10, 5–14 to 5–16, 5–19, 7–8, DR 2–110, 5–102, 5–105, 7–101(A)(2)
Harm to client, avoidance of, EC 2–32, 4–6, 5–10, 5–15, DR 2–110(A)(2), 5–102(B), 5–105(B)
Mandatory withdrawal, DR 2–110(B), 5–102, 5–105(B) (D)
Permissive withdrawal, EC 7–8, DR 2–110(C)
Refund of unearned fee paid in advance, requirement of, EC 2–32, DR 2–110(A)(3)
Tribunal, consent to, EC 2–32, DR 2–110(A)(1)
When arbitrator or mediator, EC 5–20

Estate of deceased lawyer, EC 3–8, DR 3–102(A)(1) (2)

Ethical considerations, purpose and function of, Preliminary statement

F

Explanation of, EC 2–17, 2–18, 2–19
Illegal fee, prohibition against, DR 2–106(A)
Persons able to pay reasonable fee, EC 2–17 to 2–23
Persons only able to pay a partial fee, EC 2–16
Persons without means to pay a fee, EC 2–24, 2–25
Reasonable fee, EC 2–17, 2–18, DR 2–106(B)
Rebate, propriety of accepting, EC 2–21, 22, DR 2–107, 5–107(A)
Refund of unearned portion to client, EC 2–32, DR 2–110(A)(3)

Fee of lawyer referral service, propriety of paying, DR 2–103(C)(1)

Felony. *See* Criminal conduct; Discipline of lawyer, grounds for, illegal conduct

Firm name. *See* Name, use of, firm name

Framework of law. *See* Bounds of law

Fraud, duty to reveal, EC 8–5, DR 7–102(B)

Frivolous position avoiding, EC 7–4, DR 7–102(A)(1) (2), 7–106(C)(1)

Funds of client, protection of, EC 9–5, DR 9–102

Future conduct of client, counseling as to. *See* Clients, counseling

G

"General counsel" designation, DR 2–102(A)(4)

Gift to lawyer by client, EC 5–5

Gifts to tribunal officer or employee by lawyer, EC 7–34, 7–110(A)

Government, employment in,
 Civil cases, EC 7–14
 Criminal cases, EC 7–11, 7–13, 7–14, DR 7–103
  Name in partnership name, EC 2–12, DR 2–102(B)
  Retirement from government service, EC 9–3, DR 9–101(B)

Government legal assistance agencies, working with, DR 2–103(C)(2)(D)(1)(c)

Grievance committee. *See* Bar applicant, disciplinary authority, assisting

Guaranteeing payment of client's costs and expenses, EC 5–8, DR 5–103(B)

H

Harassment, duty to avoid litigation involving, EC 2–30, DR 2–109(A)(1), 2–110(B)(1), 7–102(A)(1)

Holding out,
 As being engaged in both law and another field, DR 2–102(E)
 As limiting practice, EC 2–8, 2–14, DR 2–101(B)(2), 2–105
 As partnership, EC 2–13, DR 2–102(C)
 As specialist, EC 2–8, 2–14, DR 2–101(B)(2), 2–105

I

Identity of client, duty to reveal, EC 7–15, 7–16, 8–4, 8–5, DR 7–106(B)(2)

Illegal conduct, as cause for discipline, EC 1–5, 7–26, DR 1–102(A)(3), 7–102(A)

Impartiality of tribunal, aiding in the, EC 7–34, 7–35, DR 7–110

Improper influences,
    Gift or loan to judicial officer, EC 7–34, DR 7–110(A)
    On judgment of lawyer. *See* Adverse effect on professional judgment

Improvement of legal system, Canon 8

Incompetence,
    Mental. *See* Mental competence of bar applicant; Mental competence of
        client; Mental competence of lawyer
    Professional. *See* Competence, professional

Independent professional judgment, duty to preserve, Canon 5

Indigents,
    Provision of legal services to, EC 2–16, 2–24, 2–25, 8–3, DR 2–103(D)(1)
    Representation of, EC 2–24, 2–25, 2–29

Integrity of legal profession, maintaining, Canon 1, EC 1–1, 1–4, 8–7, 9–1, 9–2, 9–6, DR 1–101

Intent of client, as factor in giving advice, EC 7–5, 7–6, DR 7–102(A)(7)

Interests of lawyer. *See* Adverse effect on professional judgment, interests of lawyer

Interests of other client. *See* Adverse effect on professional judgment, interests of other clients

Interests of third person. *See* Adverse effect on professional judgment, desires of third persons

Intermediary, prohibition against use of, EC 5–21 to 5–24, DR 5–107

Interview,
    With opposing party, EC 7–18, DR 7–104
    With news media, EC 7–33, DR 7–107
    With witness, EC 7–27, 7–28, DR 7–109

Investigation expenses, advancing or guaranteeing payment, EC 5–8, DR 5–103(B)

J

Judges,
    False statements concerning, DR 8–102
    Improper influences on,
        Gifts or loans to, EC 7–34, 7–110(A)
        Private communication with, EC 7–35, 7–39, DR 7–110(B)
    Misconduct toward,
        Criticisms of, EC 8–6, DR 8–102
        Disobedience of orders, EC 7–36, DR 7–106(A)
        False statement regarding, DR 8–102
    Name in partnership name, EC 2–12, DR 2–102(B)
    Retirement from bench, EC 9–3, DR 9–101
    Selection of, EC 8–6, DR 8–102, 8–103

Judgment of lawyer, EC 3–2
    See also Adverse effect on professional judgment

Judicial rulings, EC 7–22, DR 7–106(A)

Jury,
> Arguments before, EC 7–24, 7–25, 7–37, DR 7–102(A), 7–106(C)
> Communications with,
>> After dismissal, EC 7–29, DR 7–108(D)
>> Before trial, EC 7–29, 7–31, 7–33, DR 7–108(A), 7–108(C)
>> During trial, EC 7–29, 7–31, 7–33, DR 7–108(B), 7–108(C)
> Improper influences on,
>> Extra judicial statements, EC 7–29, 7–31, 7–33, DR 7–108
>> Undue solicitude for, EC 7–36
> Investigation of members, EC 7–30, 7–31, DR 7–108(E) (F)
> Misconduct of, duty to reveal, EC 7–32, DR 7–108(G)
> Misconduct toward, EC 7–30, 7–31, DR 7–108(E) (G)
> Questioning members of after their dismissal, EC 7–29, DR 7–108(D)

K

Knowledge of intended crime, revealing, DR 4–101(C)(3)

L

Law firm, Definitions (2)

Law lists. *See* Advertising law lists

Law office. *See* Partnership

Law school, working with legal aid office or public defender office sponsored by, DR 2–103(D)(1)(a)

Lawyer-client privilege. *See* Attorney-client privilege

Lawyer referral services, EC 2–15
> Fee for listing, propriety of paying, DR 2–103(C)(1)
> Listing of type referrals accepted, propriety of, DR 2–105(A)(2)
> Request for referrals, propriety of, DR 2–103(C)(1) (D)
> Working with, DR 2–103(C) (D)

Laypersons,
> *See also* Unauthorized practice of law
> Need to legal services, EC 2–1 to 2–3, 2–6 to 2–8, 3–3, DR 2–104
> Recognition of legal problems, need to improve, EC 2–1 to 2–3, 8–3
> Selection of lawyer, need to facilitate, EC 2–7 to 2–10, 8–3

Legal aid offices, working with, EC 2–25, DR 2–103(D)(1)

Legal corporation. *See* Professional legal corporation

Legal directory. *See* Advertising, law lists

Legal documents of clients, duty to safeguard, EC 4–2, 4–3

Legal education programs. *See* Continuing legal education programs

Legal problems, recognition of by laymen, EC 2–1 to 2–3, 8–3, DR 2–104

Legal system, duty to improve, Canon 8

Legislature,
> Improper influence upon, EC 9–2, 9–3, 9–4, DR 8–101(A)(1), 9–101(B)
> (C)

Representation of client before, EC 7–16, 7–17, 8–4, 8–5
Serving as member of, EC 8–8, DR 8–101

Letterhead. *See* Advertising, letterheads

Liability to client, limiting, EC 6–6, DR 6–102

Licensing of lawyers,
As evidence of competence, EC 6–3
Control of, EC 3–1, 3–3 to 3–6, 3–9, DR 3–101
Modernization of, EC 3–5, 3–9, 8–3

Liens, attorneys', EC 5–7, DR 5–103(A)(1)

Limited practice, holding out as having, EC 2–8, 2–14, DR 2–101(B)(2), 2–105(A)(2)

Litigation,
Acquiring an interest in, EC 5–7, 5–8, DR 5–103
Expenses of, advancing or guaranteeing payment of, EC 5–7, 5–8, DR 5–103(B)
Pending, media discussion of, EC 7–33, DR 7–107(A) to (D) (F) (G) (I) (J)
Responsibility of lawyer for conduct of, EC 7–4, 7–5, 7–7, 7–10, 7–13, 7–14, 7–20, 7–22 to 7–25, DR 7–102, 7–103, 7–106
To harass or maliciously harm another, duty to avoid, EC 2–30, 7–10, 7–14, DR 2–109, 2–110(B)(1), 7–102(A)(1), 7–103(A)(1)

Living expenses of client, advances to client of, EC 5–8, DR 5–103(B)

Loan to judicial officer, EC 7–34, DR 7–110(A)

Loyalty to client. *See* Zeal

Lump-sum settlements, DR 5–106

M

Malpractice, Canon 6

Mandatory withdrawal. *See* Employment, withdrawal from, mandatory

Mediator, lawyer as, EC 5–20

Medical expenses, EC 5–8, DR 5–103(B)

Mental competence of bar applicant, EC 1–6

Mental competence of client, effect on representation, EC 7–11, 7–12

Mental competence of lawyer,
Generally, EC 1–6, DR 2–110(B)(3) (C)(4)
Recognition of rehabilitation, EC 1–6

Military legal service office, working with, DR 2–103(D)(2)

Misappropriation,
Confidences or secrets of client, EC 4–1, 4–5, 4–6, DR 4–101(B)(3) (D)
Property of client, EC 9–5, 9–6, DR 9–102

Misconduct,
See also Discipline of lawyer
Of client, EC 2–23, 2–30, 7–5 to 7–10, 7–26, DR 2–109, 2–110(B)(1) (C), 4–101(C)(3), 7–101(B)(2), 7–102
Of juror, EC 7–32, DR 7–108(D) (F) (G)
Of lawyer, duty to reveal to proper officials, EC 1–4, DR 1–103

Misleading advertisement or professional notice, prohibition of, EC 2–9, 2–11, 2–13, 2–14, DR 2–101, 2–102(B) (C)

Moral character, requirement of, Canon 1, EC 1–2, 1–3, 1–5, DR 1–102

Moral factors, considered in counseling, EC 7–3, 7–5, 7–8, 7–9

Moral turpitude, crime of as ground for discipline, DR 1–102(A)(3)

Multiple clients, representation of, EC 5–14 to 5–20, DR 5–105, 5–106

N

Name, use of,
    Assumed name, EC 2–11, DR 2–102(B)
    Deceased partner's, EC 2–11, DR 2–102(A)(4) (B)
    Firm name, EC 2–11 to 2–13, DR 2–102(B)
    Misleading name, EC 2–11, 2–13, DR 2–102(B) (C)
    Partners who hold public office, EC 2–12, DR 2–102(B)
    Predecessor firms, EC 2–11, DR 2–102(A)(4) (B)
    Proper for law firm, EC 2–11, DR 2–102(B)
    Proper for lawyer in law practice, EC 2–11, DR 2–102(B)
    Retired partner, EC 2–11, DR 2–102(A)(4) (B)
    Trade name, EC 2–11, DR 2–102(B)
    Withdrawn partner's, EC 2–11, 2–12, DR 2–102(B)

Need for legal services, suggestion of. *See* Advice by lawyer to secure legal services

Negligence of lawyer, Canon 6

Negotiations with opposite party, EC 7–18, 7–20, DR 7–104, 7–105

Neighborhood law offices, working with, EC 2–6, 2–7, 2–25, DR 2–103(D)(1)(b)

Newspapers,
    Advertising in, EC 2–8 to 2–10, DR 2–101(A) to (C) (E) (F) (I)
    News releases in, during or pending trial, EC 7–33, DR 7–107
    News stories in, DR 2–101(I)

Non-meritorious position, duty to avoid, EC 7–4, 7–5, 7–14, DR 2–109, 2–110(B)(1), 7–102(A)(1) (2), 7–103(A), 7–106(C)(1)

Non-profit organization, legal aid services of, EC 2–24, 2–25, DR 2–103(D)(1)(4)(a), 2–104(A)(2) (3)

Notices. *See* Advertising

O

Objectives of client, duty to seek, EC 7–1, 7–10, DR 7–101(A)(1), 7–102

"Of Counsel" designation, DR 2–102(A)(4)

Offensive tactics by lawyer, EC 7–4, 7–5, 7–10, DR 7–101, 7–102, 7–104, 7–105

Office building directory. *See* Advertising, building directory

Office sign, DR 2–102(A)(3)

Opposing counsel, EC 5–9, 7–20, 7–23, 7–35, 7–37, 7–38, DR 7–101(A)(1), 7–104(A)(1), 7–106(C)(5), 7–110(B)(2) (3)

Opposing party, communications with, EC 7–18, DR 7–104

P

Partnership,
    Advertising. *See* Advertising
    Conflicts of interest, DR 5–105(D)
    Deceased member,
        Payments to estate of, EC 3–8, DR 3–102(A)(1) (2)
        Use of name, EC 2–11, DR 2–102(A)(4) (B)
    Dissolved, use of name of, EC 2–11 to 2–13, DR 2–102(A)(4) (B) (C)
    Holding out as, falsely, EC 2–13, DR 2–102(B) (C)
    Imputed disability of partner and associates, DR 5–105(D)
    Layperson, partnership with, EC 3–8, DR 3–103
    Members licensed in different jurisdictions, DR 2–102(D)
    Name, EC 2–11, 2–12, 2–13, DR 2–102(B)
    Nonexistent, holding out falsely, EC 2–13, DR 2–102(B) (C)

Partnership with, DR 2–102(C)

Patent practitioner, EC 2–14, DR 2–105(A)(1)

Payment to obtain recommendation of employment, prohibition against, EC 2–8, DR 2–103(B) (D)

Pending litigation, discussion of in media, EC 7–33, DR 7–107

Perjury, EC 7–5, 7–6, 7–26, 7–28, DR 7–102(A)(4) (6) (7), 7–102(B)

Person, definitions (3)

Personal interests of lawyer. *See* Adverse effect on professional judgment, interests of lawyer

Personal opinion of client's cause, EC 2–27 to 2–30, 7–24, DR 7–106(C)(4)

Phone directory, listing in. *See* Advertising, telephone directory

Political activity, EC 8–6, 8–8, DR 2–101(H)(1), 8–101, 8–102, 8–103

Political considerations in selection of judges, EC 8–6, DR 8–103

Potentially differing interest. *See* Adverse effect on professional judgment

Prejudice to right of client, duty to avoid, EC 2–32, DR 2–110(A)(2) (C)(3) (C)(4), 7–101(A)(3)

Prepaid legal services, EC 2–33, 5–23, DR 2–101(B)(17), 2–103(D)(4)

Preservation of confidences and secrets of client, EC 3–3, Canon 4

Pressure on lawyer by third person. *See* Adverse effect on professional judgment of lawyer

Privilege, attorney-client. *See* Attorney-client privilege

Procedures, duty to help improve, EC 8–1, 8–2, 8–9

Professional card of lawyer. *See* Advertising cards, professional

Professional impropriety, avoiding appearance of, EC 5–1, 5–6, Canon 9

Professional judgment, duty to protect independence of, EC 2–33, Canon 5

Professional legal corporations, EC 2–11, 5–24, DR 2–102(B)(C), 5–107(C), definitions (4)

Professional notices. *See* Advertising

Professional status, responsibility not to mislead concerning, EC 2–11 to 2–14, DR 2–102(B) to (D)

Profit-sharing with lay employees, authorization of, EC 3–8, DR 3–102(A)(3)

Property of client, handling, EC 9–5, DR 9–102

Prosecuting attorney, duty of, EC 7–13, 7–14, DR 7–103

Public defender office, working with, DR 2–103(C)(2) (D)(1)

Public employment, retirement from, EC 9–3, DR 9–101(A) (B)

Public office, duty of holder, EC 8–8, DR 8–101

Public opinion, irrelevant to acceptance of employment, EC 2–26 to 2–29

Public prosecutor. *See* Prosecuting attorney, duty of

Publication of articles for lay press, EC 2–2, 2–5, DR 2–104(A)(4)
Publication rights of lawyer, relating to subject matter of employment, EC 5–4, DR 5–104(B)
Publicity,
Commercial. *See* Advertising, commercial publicity
Trial. *See* Trial publicity

Q

Qualified legal assistance organization, EC 2–33, DR 2–103(C)(2) (D), 2–104(A)(2) (3), definitions (8)

Quasi-judicial proceedings, EC 7–15, 7–16, 8–4, DR 7–107(H)

R

Radio, broadcasting. *See* Advertising, radio

Reasonable fee. *See* Fee for legal services, amount of

Rebate, propriety of accepting, EC 2–21, 2–22, 5–22, DR 2–107, 5–107

Recognition of legal problems, aiding laymen in, EC 2–1 to 2–5, 8–3, DR 2–104

Recommendation of bar applicant, duty of lawyer to satisfy himself that applicant is qualified, EC 1–3, DR 1–101(B)

Recommendation of professional employment, EC 2–8, 2–15, DR 2–103

Records of funds, securities, and properties of clients, EC 9–5, DR 9–102(B)(3)

Referral service. *See* Lawyer referral services

Refund of unearned fee when withdrawing, duty to give to client, EC 2–32, DR 2–110(A)(3)

Regulation of legal profession, EC 3–1, 3–3, 3–9, 8–3, 8–7, DR 3–101(B)

Rehabilitation of bar applicant or lawyer, recognition of, EC 1–6

Representation of multiple clients. *See* Adverse effect on professional judgment, interests of other clients

Reputation of lawyer, EC 2–6, 2–7

Requests for recommendation for employment, EC 2–8, DR 2–103(C)

Requirements for bar admission, EC 1–2, 1–6, DR 1–101(B)

Respect for law, EC 1–5, 9–6

Restrictive covenant, DR 2–108

Retention of employment. *See* Employment

Retirement,
> *See also* Name, use of, retired partner
> From judicial office, EC 9–3, DR 9–101(A)
> From public employment, EC 9–3, DR 9–101(B)
> Plan for laymen employees', EC 3–8, DR 3–102(A)(3)

Revealing of confidences, Canon 4

Revealing of secrets, Canon 4

Revealing to tribunal,
> Jury misconduct, EC 7–32, DR 7–108(G)
> Representative capacity in which appearing, EC 7–15, 7–16, DR 7–106(B)(2)

Runner, prohibition against use of. *See* Recommendation of professional employment

S

Sanction for violating disciplinary rules, Preliminary statement

Secrets of client, Canon 4

Selection of judges, duty of lawyers, EC 8–6, DR 8–102

Selection of lawyer. EC 2–6 to 2–15, DR 2–101 to 2–105

Self-interest of lawyer. *See* Adverse effect on professional judgment, interests of lawyer

Self-representation, privilege of, EC 3–7

Settlement agreement. EC 7–7, DR 5–106

Solicitation of business. *See* Advertising; Advice by lawyer to secure legal services; Recommendation of professional employment

Specialist, holding out as, EC 2–8, 2–14, DR 2–101(B)(2), 2–105

Specialization, EC 2–8, 2–14, DR 2–101(B)(2), 2–105
> Admiralty, EC 2–14
> Holding out as having, EC 2–8, 2–14, DR 2–101(B)(2), 2–105
> Patents, EC 2–14, DR 2–105(A)(1)
> Trademark, EC 2–14, DR 2–105(A)(1)

Speeches to lay groups, EC 2–2, 2–5, DR 2–104(A)(4)

State, Definitions (5)

State of mind of client, effect of in advising him, EC 7–6, 7–11, 7–12

State's attorney. *See* Prosecuting attorney

"Stirring up litigation." *See* Advertising; Advice by lawyer to secure legal services; Recommendation of; professional employment

Stockholders of corporation, corporate counsel's allegiance to, EC 5–18

Suggestion of need for legal services. *See* Advice by lawyer to secure legal services

Suit to harass or maliciously harm another, duty to avoid, EC 2–30, 7–10, 7–14, DR 2–109, 2–110(B)(1), 7–102(A)(1)

Suppression of evidence, EC 7–27, DR 7–102(A)(3), 7–103(B), 7–106(C)(7), 7–109(A)

T

Technical and professional licenses. *See* Advertising, technical and professional licenses

Telephone directory. *See* Advertising, telephone directory

Television. *See* Advertising, television

Termination of employment. *See* Confidences of client; Employment, withdrawal from

Third persons, desires of. *See* Adverse effect on professional judgment, desires of third persons

Threatening criminal process, EC 7–21, DR 7–105

Trade name, EC 2–11, DR 2–102(B)

Trademark practitioner, EC 2–14, DR 2–105(A)(1)

Trial publicity, EC 7–33, DR 7–107

Trial tactics, EC 7–19 to 7–39, DR 7–101(A)(1), 7–102, 7–103(B), 7–105 to 7–110

Tribunal,
Definitions (6)
Representation of client before, Canon 7

Trustee, client naming lawyer as, EC 5–6

U

Unauthorized practice of law, Canon 3
See also Division of legal fees, with laymen; Partnership, laypersons with
Aiding a layman in the prohibited, EC 3–8, DR 3–101
Distinguished from delegation of tasks to subprofessionals, EC 3–5, 3–6, DR 3–102(A)(3)
Functional meaning of, EC 3–5, 3–9
Self-representation by layman not included in, EC 3–7

Undignified conduct, duty to avoid, EC 7–36 to 7–38, DR 7–106(C)(6)

Unions, lawyers as members of, EC 5–13

Unlawful conduct, aiding client in, EC 7–5, 7–6, DR 7–102(A)(6) (7) (B)(1)

Unpopular party, representation of, EC 2–27, 2–29 to 2–31

Unreasonable fees. *See* Fee for legal services, amount of, excessive

Unsolicited advice. *See* Advice by lawyer to secure legal services

V

Varying interests of clients. *See* Adverse effect on professional judgment, interests of other clients

Veniremen. *See* Communications with, venireman; Jury

Violation of disciplinary rule as cause for discipline, DR 1–102(A)(1) (2)

Violation of law as cause for discipline, EC 1–5, 7–6, DR 1–102(A)(3) (A)(4), 7–102(A)(3) to (A)(8)

Voluntary gifts by client to lawyer, EC 5–5

Volunteered advice to secure legal services. *See* Advice by lawyer to secure legal services

W

Waiver of position of client, DR 7–101(B)(1)

Will of client, gift to lawyer in, EC 5–5

Withdrawal. *See* Employment, withdrawal from

Witness,
    Communications with. *See* Communications with, witnesses
    Expert, EC 7–28, DR 7–109(C)(3)
    False testimony by, EC 7–26, 7–28, DR 7–102(A)(4) (B)(2)
    Lawyer acting as, EC 5–9, 5–10, DR 5–101(B), 5–102
    Member of lawyer's firm acting as, DR 5–101(B), 5–102
    Payment to, EC 7–28, DR 7–109(C)
    Questioning of, EC 7–25, DR 7–106(C)(2)
    Secreting of, EC 7–27, DR 7–109(B)

Writing for lay publication, avoiding appearance of giving general solution, EC 2–2, 2–5, DR 2–104(4)

Z

Zeal,
    General duty of, EC 7–1, 7–8 to 7–10, DR 7–101(A)
    Limitations upon, Canon 7

RESTATEMENT OF LAW GOVERNING LAWYERS

In 1986 the American Law Institute ("ALI"), a prestigious group of practicing lawyers, judges, and academics, began drafting a *Restatement of the Law Governing Lawyers*. Unlike the ABA's Model Rules, the ALI has not proposed a code of regulations that it expects state courts to adopt as rules of court. Instead, it has drafted a series of principles, also called "black letter rules," followed by commentary and examples. Because the Restatement analyzes and systematizes the law governing the practice of law, it goes beyond the ethics rules to cover other areas that affect the practice of law, such as tort doctrines relating to malpractice, vicarious liability, the work-product doctrine, the attorney-client evidentiary privilege, the agent-principal relationship, and related areas. The Restatement of the Law Governing Lawyers follows in the tradition of the other Restatements that the ALI has drafted over many years.

In 1998, the ALI completed this project and approved the Restatement, which it labeled "Restatement of the Law, Third," to signify that the American Law Institute is now working on a third major series of Restatements. The ALI published the final version of its Restatement in 2000.

Table of Contents

Restatement of the Law (Third): The Law Governing Lawyers

§ 1.   Regulation of Lawyers—In General

Upon admission to the bar of any jurisdiction, a person becomes a lawyer and is subject to applicable law governing such matters as professional discipline, procedure and evidence, civil remedies, and criminal sanctions.

§ 2.   Admission to Practice Law

In order to become a lawyer and qualify to practice law in a jurisdiction of admission, a prospective lawyer must comply with requirements of the jurisdiction relating to such matters as education, other demonstration of competence such as success in a bar examination, and character.

§ 3.   Jurisdictional Scope of the Practice of Law by a Lawyer

A lawyer currently admitted to practice in a jurisdiction may provide legal services to a client:

(1)   at any place within the admitting jurisdiction;

(2)   before a tribunal or administrative agency of another jurisdiction or the federal government in compliance with requirements

for temporary or regular admission to practice before that tribunal or agency; and

(3) at a place within a jurisdiction in which the lawyer is not admitted to the extent that the lawyer's activities arise out of or are otherwise reasonably related to the lawyer's practice under Subsection (1) or (2).

§ 4.   Unauthorized Practice by a Nonlawyer

A person not admitted to practice as a lawyer (see § 2) may not engage in the unauthorized practice of law, and a lawyer may not assist a person to do so.

§ 5.   Professional Discipline

(1) A lawyer is subject to professional discipline for violating any provision of an applicable lawyer code.

(2) A lawyer is also subject to professional discipline under Subsection (1) for attempting to commit a violation, knowingly assisting or inducing another to do so, or knowingly doing so through the acts of another.

(3) A lawyer who knows of another lawyer's violation of applicable rules of professional conduct raising a substantial question of the lawyer's honesty or trustworthiness or the lawyer's fitness as a lawyer in some other respect must report that information to appropriate disciplinary authorities.

§ 6.   Judicial Remedies Available to a Client or Nonclient for Lawyer Wrongs

For a lawyer's breach of a duty owed to the lawyer's client or to a nonclient, judicial remedies may be available through judgment or order entered in accordance with the standards applicable to the remedy awarded, including standards concerning limitation of remedies. Judicial remedies include the following:

(1) awarding a sum of money as damages;

(2) providing injunctive relief, including requiring specific performance of a contract or enjoining its nonperformance;

(3) requiring restoration of a specific thing or awarding a sum of money to prevent unjust enrichment;

(4) ordering cancellation or reformation of a contract, deed, or similar instrument;

(5) declaring the rights of the parties, such as determining that an obligation claimed by the lawyer to be owed to the lawyer is not enforceable;

(6) punishing the lawyer for contempt;

(7) enforcing an arbitration award;

(8) disqualifying a lawyer from a representation;

(9) forfeiting a lawyer's fee (see § 37);

(10) denying the admission of evidence wrongfully obtained;

(11) dismissing the claim or defense of a litigant represented by the lawyer;

(12) granting a new trial; and

(13) entering a procedural or other sanction.

§ 7.   Judicial Remedies Available to a Lawyer for Client Wrongs

A lawyer may obtain a remedy based on a present or former client's breach of a duty to the lawyer if the remedy:

(1) is appropriate under applicable law governing the remedy; and

(2) does not put the lawyer in a position prohibited by an applicable lawyer code.

§ 8.   Lawyer Criminal Offenses

The traditional and appropriate activities of a lawyer in representing a client in accordance with the requirements of the applicable lawyer code are relevant factors for the tribunal in assessing the propriety of the lawyer's conduct under the criminal law. In other respects, a lawyer is guilty of an offense for an act committed in the course of representing a client to the same extent and on the same basis as would a nonlawyer acting similarly.

§ 9.   Law-Practice Organizations—In General

(1) A lawyer may practice as a solo practitioner, as an employee of another lawyer or law firm, or as a member of a law firm constituted as a partnership, professional corporation, or similar entity.

(2) A lawyer employed by an entity described in Subsection (1) is subject to applicable law governing the creation, operation, management, and dissolution of the entity.

(3) Absent an agreement with the firm providing a more permissive rule, a lawyer leaving a law firm may solicit firm clients:

(a) prior to leaving the firm:

(i) only with respect to firm clients on whose matters the lawyer is actively and substantially working; and

(ii) only after the lawyer has adequately and timely informed the firm of the lawyer's intent to contact firm clients for that purpose; and

(b) after ceasing employment in the firm, to the same extent as any other nonfirm lawyer.

§ 10.   Limitations on Nonlawyer Involvement in a Law Firm

(1) A nonlawyer may not own any interest in a law firm, and a nonlawyer may not be empowered to or actually direct or control the professional activities of a lawyer in the firm.

(2) A lawyer may not form a partnership or other business enterprise with a nonlawyer if any of the activities of the enterprise consist of the practice of law.

(3) A lawyer or law firm may not share legal fees with a person not admitted to practice as a lawyer, except that:

(a) an agreement by a lawyer with the lawyer's firm or another lawyer in the firm may provide for payment, over a reasonable period of time after the lawyer's death, to the lawyer's estate or to one or more specified persons;

(b) a lawyer who undertakes to complete unfinished legal business of a deceased lawyer may pay to the estate of the deceased lawyer a portion of the total compensation that fairly represents services rendered by the deceased lawyer; and

(c) a lawyer or law firm may include nonlawyer employees in a compensation or retirement plan, even though the plan is based in whole or in part on a profit-sharing arrangement.

§ 11. A Lawyer's Duty of Supervision

(1) A lawyer who is a partner in a law-firm partnership or a principal in a law firm organized as a corporation or similar entity is subject to professional discipline for failing to make reasonable efforts to ensure that the firm has in effect measures giving reasonable assurance that all lawyers in the firm conform to applicable lawyer-code requirements.

(2) A lawyer who has direct supervisory authority over another lawyer is subject to professional discipline for failing to make reasonable efforts to ensure that the other lawyer conforms to applicable lawyer-code requirements.

(3) A lawyer is subject to professional discipline for another lawyer's violation of the rules of professional conduct if:

(a) the lawyer orders or, with knowledge of the specific conduct, ratifies the conduct involved; or

(b) the lawyer is a partner or principal in the law firm, or has direct supervisory authority over the other lawyer, and knows of the conduct at a time when its consequences can be avoided or mitigated but fails to take reasonable remedial measures.

(4) With respect to a nonlawyer employee of a law firm, the lawyer is subject to professional discipline if either:

(a) the lawyer fails to make reasonable efforts to ensure:

(i) that the firm in which the lawyer practices has in effect measures giving reasonable assurance that the nonlawyer's conduct is compatible with the professional obligations of the lawyer; and

(ii) that conduct of a nonlawyer over whom the lawyer has direct supervisory authority is compatible with the professional obligations of the lawyer; or

(b) the nonlawyer's conduct would be a violation of the applicable lawyer code if engaged in by a lawyer, and

(i) the lawyer orders or, with knowledge of the specific conduct, ratifies the conduct; or

(ii) the lawyer is a partner or principal in the law firm, or has direct supervisory authority over the nonlawyer, and knows of the conduct at a time when its consequences can be avoided or mitigated but fails to take reasonable remedial measures.

§ 12. Duty of a Lawyer Subject to Supervision

(1) For purposes of professional discipline, a lawyer must conform to the requirements of an applicable lawyer code even if the lawyer acted at the direction of another lawyer or other person.

(2)   For purposes of professional discipline, a lawyer under the direct supervisory authority of another lawyer does not violate an applicable lawyer code by acting in accordance with the supervisory lawyer's direction based on a reasonable resolution of an arguable question of professional duty.

§ 13.   Restrictions on the Right to Practice Law

(1)   A lawyer may not offer or enter into a law-firm agreement that restricts the right of the lawyer to practice law after terminating the relationship, except for a restriction incident to the lawyer's retirement from the practice of law.

(2)   In settling a client claim, a lawyer may not offer or enter into an agreement that restricts the right of the lawyer to practice law, including the right to represent or take particular action on behalf of other clients.

§ 14.   Formation of a Client-Lawyer Relationship

A relationship of client and lawyer arises when:

(1)   a person manifests to a lawyer the person's intent that the lawyer provide legal services for the person; and either

(a)   the lawyer manifests to the person consent to do so; or

(b)   the lawyer fails to manifest lack of consent to do so, and the lawyer knows or reasonably should know that the person reasonably relies on the lawyer to provide the services; or

(2)   a tribunal with power to do so appoints the lawyer to provide the services.

§ 15.   A Lawyer's Duties to a Prospective Client

(1)   When a person discusses with a lawyer the possibility of their forming a client-lawyer relationship for a matter and no such relationship ensues, the lawyer must:

(a)   not subsequently use or disclose confidential information learned in the consultation, except to the extent permitted with respect to confidential information of a client or former client as stated in §§ 61–67;

(b)   protect the person's property in the lawyer's custody as stated in §§ 44–46; and

(c)   use reasonable care to the extent the lawyer provides the person legal services.

(2)   A lawyer subject to Subsection (1) may not represent a client whose interests are materially adverse to those of a former prospective client in the same or a substantially related matter when the lawyer or another lawyer whose disqualification is imputed to the lawyer under §§ 123 and 124 has received from the prospective client confidential information that could be significantly harmful to the prospective client in the matter, except that such a representation is permissible if:

(a)   (i) any personally prohibited lawyer takes reasonable steps to avoid exposure to confidential information other than information appropriate to determine whether to represent the prospective client, and (ii) such lawyer is screened as stated in § 124(2)(b) and (c); or

    (b) both the affected client and the prospective client give informed consent to the representation under the limitations and conditions provided in § 122.

§ 16.   A Lawyer's Duties to a Client—In General

To the extent consistent with the lawyer's other legal duties and subject to the other provisions of this Restatement, a lawyer must, in matters within the scope of the representation:

    (1) proceed in a manner reasonably calculated to advance a client's lawful objectives, as defined by the client after consultation;

    (2) act with reasonable competence and diligence;

    (3) comply with obligations concerning the client's confidences and property, avoid impermissible conflicting interests, deal honestly with the client, and not employ advantages arising from the client-lawyer relationship in a manner adverse to the client; and

    (4) fulfill valid contractual obligations to the client.

§ 17.   A Client's Duties to a Lawyer

Subject to the other provisions of this Restatement, in matters covered by the representation a client must:

    (1) compensate a lawyer for services and expenses as stated in Chapter 3;

    (2) indemnify the lawyer for liability to which the client has exposed the lawyer without the lawyer's fault; and

    (3) fulfill any valid contractual obligations to the lawyer.

§ 18.   Client-Lawyer Contracts

    (1) A contract between a lawyer and client concerning the client-lawyer relationship, including a contract modifying an existing contract, may be enforced by either party if the contract meets other applicable requirements, except that:

    (a) if the contract or modification is made beyond a reasonable time after the lawyer has begun to represent the client in the matter (see § 38(1)), the client may avoid it unless the lawyer shows that the contract and the circumstances of its formation were fair and reasonable to the client; and

    (b) if the contract is made after the lawyer has finished providing services, the client may avoid it if the client was not informed of facts needed to evaluate the appropriateness of the lawyer's compensation or other benefits conferred on the lawyer by the contract.

    (2) A tribunal should construe a contract between client and lawyer as a reasonable person in the circumstances of the client would have construed it.

§ 19.   Agreements Limiting Client or Lawyer Duties

    (1) Subject to other requirements stated in this Restatement, a client and lawyer may agree to limit a duty that a lawyer would otherwise owe to the client if:

    (a) the client is adequately informed and consents; and

(b) the terms of the limitation are reasonable in the circumstances.

(2)   A lawyer may agree to waive a client's duty to pay or other duty owed to the lawyer.

§ 20.   A Lawyer's Duty to Inform and Consult with a Client

(1)   A lawyer must keep a client reasonably informed about the matter and must consult with a client to a reasonable extent concerning decisions to be made by the lawyer under §§ 21–23.

(2)   A lawyer must promptly comply with a client's reasonable requests for information.

(3)   A lawyer must notify a client of decisions to be made by the client under §§ 21–23 and must explain a matter to the extent reasonably necessary to permit the client to make informed decisions regarding the representation.

§ 21.   Allocating the Authority to Decide Between a Client and a Lawyer

As between client and lawyer:

(1)   A client and lawyer may agree which of them will make specified decisions, subject to the requirements stated in §§ 18, 19, 22, 23, and other provisions of this Restatement. The agreement may be superseded by another valid agreement.

(2)   A client may instruct a lawyer during the representation, subject to the requirements stated in §§ 22, 23, and other provisions of this Restatement.

(3)   Subject to Subsections (1) and (2) a lawyer may take any lawful measure within the scope of representation that is reasonably calculated to advance a client's objectives as defined by the client, consulting with the client as required by § 20.

(4)   A client may ratify an act of a lawyer that was not previously authorized.

§ 22.   Authority Reserved to a Client

(1)   As between client and lawyer, subject to Subsection (2) and § 23, the following and comparable decisions are reserved to the client except when the client has validly authorized the lawyer to make the particular decision: whether and on what terms to settle a claim; how a criminal defendant should plead; whether a criminal defendant should waive jury trial; whether a criminal defendant should testify; and whether to appeal in a civil proceeding or criminal prosecution.

(2)   A client may not validly authorize a lawyer to make the decisions described in Subsection (1) when other law (such as criminal-procedure rules governing pleas, jury-trial waiver, and defendant testimony) requires the client's personal participation or approval.

(3)   Regardless of any contrary contract with a lawyer, a client may revoke a lawyer's authority to make the decisions described in Subsection (1).

§ 23.   Authority Reserved to a Lawyer

As between client and lawyer, a lawyer retains authority that may not be overridden by a contract with or an instruction from the client:

(1)   to refuse to perform, counsel, or assist future or ongoing acts in the representation that the lawyer reasonably believes to be unlawful;

(2)   to make decisions or take actions in the representation that the lawyer reasonably believes to be required by law or an order of a tribunal.

§ 24.   A Client with Diminished Capacity

(1)   When a client's capacity to make adequately considered decisions in connection with the representation is diminished, whether because of minority, physical illness, mental disability, or other cause, the lawyer must, as far as reasonably possible, maintain a normal client-lawyer relationship with the client and act in the best interests of the client as stated in Subsection (2).

(2)   A lawyer representing a client with diminished capacity as described in Subsection (1) and for whom no guardian or other representative is available to act, must, with respect to a matter within the scope of the representation, pursue the lawyer's reasonable view of the client's objectives or interests as the client would define them if able to make adequately considered decisions on the matter, even if the client expresses no wishes or gives contrary instructions.

(3)   If a client with diminished capacity as described in Subsection (1) has a guardian or other person legally entitled to act for the client, the client's lawyer must treat that person as entitled to act with respect to the client's interests in the matter, unless:

(a)   the lawyer represents the client in a matter against the interests of that person; or

(b)   that person instructs the lawyer to act in a manner that the lawyer knows will violate the person's legal duties toward the client.

(4)   A lawyer representing a client with diminished capacity as described in Subsection (1) may seek the appointment of a guardian or take other protective action within the scope of the representation when doing so is practical and will advance the client's objectives or interests, determined as stated in Subsection (2).

§ 25.   Appearance Before a Tribunal

A lawyer who enters an appearance before a tribunal on behalf of a person is presumed to represent that person as a client. The presumption may be rebutted.

§ 26.   A Lawyer's Actual Authority

A lawyer's act is considered to be that of a client in proceedings before a tribunal or in dealings with third persons when:

(1)   the client has expressly or impliedly authorized the act;

(2)   authority concerning the act is reserved to the lawyer as stated in § 23; or

(3)   the client ratifies the act.

§ 27.   A Lawyer's Apparent Authority

A lawyer's act is considered to be that of the client in proceedings before a tribunal or in dealings with a third person if the tribunal or third person reasonably assumes that the lawyer is authorized to do the act on the basis of the client's (and not the lawyer's) manifestations of such authorization.

§ 28.   A Lawyer's Knowledge; Notification to a Lawyer; and Statements of a Lawyer

(1)   Information imparted to a lawyer during and relating to the representation of a client is attributed to the client for the purpose of determining the client's rights and liabilities in matters in which the lawyer represents the client, unless those rights or liabilities require proof of the client's personal knowledge or intentions or the lawyer's legal duties preclude disclosure of the information to the client.

(2)   Unless applicable law otherwise provides, a third person may give notification to a client, in a matter in which the client is represented by a lawyer, by giving notification to the client's lawyer, unless the third person knows of circumstances reasonably indicating that the lawyer's authority to receive notification has been abrogated.

(3)   A lawyer's unprivileged statement is admissible in evidence against a client as if it were the client's statement if either:

(a)   the client authorized the lawyer to make a statement concerning the subject; or

(b)   the statement concerns a matter within the scope of the representation and was made by the lawyer during it.

§ 29.   A Lawyer's Act or Advice as Mitigating or Avoiding a Client's Responsibility

(1)   When a client's intent or mental state is in issue, a tribunal may consider otherwise admissible evidence of a lawyer's advice to the client.

(2)   In deciding whether to impose a sanction on a person or to relieve a person from a criminal or civil ruling, default, or judgment, a tribunal may consider otherwise admissible evidence to prove or disprove that the lawyer who represented the person did so inadequately or contrary to the client's instructions.

§ 30.   A Lawyer's Liability to a Third Person for Conduct on Behalf of a Client

(1)   For improper conduct while representing a client, a lawyer is subject to professional discipline as stated in § 5, to civil liability as stated in Chapter 4, and to prosecution as provided in the criminal law (see § 7).

(2)   Unless at the time of contracting the lawyer or third person disclaimed such liability, a lawyer is subject to liability to third persons on contracts the lawyer entered into on behalf of a client if:

(a)   the client's existence or identity was not disclosed to the third person; or

(b)   the contract is between the lawyer and a third person who provides goods or services used by lawyers and who, as the lawyer knows or reasonably should know, relies on the lawyer's credit.

(3)   A lawyer is subject to liability to a third person for damages for loss proximately caused by the lawyer's acting without authority from a client under § 26 if:

(a)   the lawyer tortiously misrepresents to the third person that the lawyer has authority to make a contract, conveyance, or affirmation on behalf of the client and the third person reasonably relies on the misrepresentation; or

(b) the lawyer purports to make a contract, conveyance, or affirmation on behalf of the client, unless the lawyer manifests that the lawyer does not warrant that the lawyer is authorized to act or the other party knows that the lawyer is not authorized to act.

§ 31. Termination of a Lawyer's Authority

(1) A lawyer must comply with applicable law requiring notice to or permission of a tribunal when terminating a representation and with an order of a tribunal requiring the representation to continue.

(2) Subject to Subsection (1) and § 33, a lawyer's actual authority to represent a client ends when:

(a) the client discharges the lawyer;

(b) the client dies or, in the case of a corporation or similar organization, loses its capacity to function as such;

(c) the lawyer withdraws;

(d) the lawyer dies or becomes physically or mentally incapable of providing representation, is disbarred or suspended from practicing law, or is ordered by a tribunal to cease representing a client; or

(e) the representation ends as provided by contract or because the lawyer has completed the contemplated services.

(3) A lawyer's apparent authority to act for a client with respect to another person ends when the other person knows or should know of facts from which it can be reasonably inferred that the lawyer lacks actual authority, including knowledge of any event described in Subsection (2).

§ 32. Discharge by a Client and Withdrawal by a Lawyer

(1) Subject to Subsection (5), a client may discharge a lawyer at any time.

(2) Subject to Subsection (5), a lawyer may not represent a client or, where representation has commenced, must withdraw from the representation of a client if:

(a) the representation will result in the lawyer's violating rules of professional conduct or other law;

(b) the lawyer's physical or mental condition materially impairs the lawyer's ability to represent the client; or

(c) the client discharges the lawyer.

(3) Subject to Subsections (4) and (5), a lawyer may withdraw from representing a client if:

(a) withdrawal can be accomplished without material adverse effect on the interests of the client;

(b) the lawyer reasonably believes withdrawal is required in circumstances stated in Subsection (2);

(c) the client gives informed consent;

(d)   the client persists in a course of action involving the lawyer's services that the lawyer reasonably believes is criminal, fraudulent, or in breach of the client's fiduciary duty;

(e)   the lawyer reasonably believes the client has used or threatens to use the lawyer's services to perpetrate a crime or fraud;

(f)   the client insists on taking action that the lawyer considers repugnant or imprudent;

(g)   the client fails to fulfill a substantial financial or other obligation to the lawyer regarding the lawyer's services and the lawyer has given the client reasonable warning that the lawyer will withdraw unless the client fulfills the obligation;

(h)   the representation has been rendered unreasonably difficult by the client or by the irreparable breakdown of the client-lawyer relationship; or

(i)   other good cause for withdrawal exists.

(4)   In the case of permissive withdrawal under Subsections (3)(f)–(i), a lawyer may not withdraw if the harm that withdrawal would cause significantly exceeds the harm to the lawyer or others in not withdrawing.

(5)   Notwithstanding Subsections (1)–(4), a lawyer must comply with applicable law requiring notice to or permission of a tribunal when terminating a representation and with a valid order of a tribunal requiring the representation to continue.

§ 33.   A Lawyer's Duties When a Representation Terminates

(1)   In terminating a representation, a lawyer must take steps to the extent reasonably practicable to protect the client's interests, such as giving notice to the client of the termination, allowing time for employment of other counsel, surrendering papers and property to which the client is entitled, and refunding any advance payment of fee the lawyer has not earned.

(2)   Following termination of a representation, a lawyer must:

(a)   observe obligations to a former client such as those dealing with client confidences (see Chapter 5), conflicts of interest (see Chapter 8), client property and documents (see §§ 44–46), and fee collection (see § 41);

(b)   take no action on behalf of a former client without new authorization and give reasonable notice, to those who might otherwise be misled, that the lawyer lacks authority to act for the client;

(c)   take reasonable steps to convey to the former client any material communication the lawyer receives relating to the matter involved in the representation; and

(d)   take no unfair advantage of a former client by abusing knowledge or trust acquired by means of the representation.

§ 34.   Reasonable and Lawful Fees

A lawyer may not charge a fee larger than is reasonable in the circumstances or that is prohibited by law.

§ 35.   Contingent-Fee Arrangements

(1)   A lawyer may contract with a client for a fee the size or payment of which is contingent on the outcome of a matter, unless the contract violates

§ 34 or another provision of this Restatement or the size or payment of the fee is:

    (a) contingent on success in prosecuting or defending a criminal proceeding; or

    (b) contingent on a specified result in a divorce proceeding or a proceeding concerning custody of a child.

    (2) Unless the contract construed in the circumstances indicates otherwise, when a lawyer has contracted for a contingent fee, the lawyer is entitled to receive the specified fee only when and to the extent the client receives payment.

§ 36.   Forbidden Client-Lawyer Financial Arrangements

    (1) A lawyer may not acquire a proprietary interest in the cause of action or subject matter of litigation that the lawyer is conducting for a client, except that the lawyer may:

    (a) acquire a lien as provided by § 43 to secure the lawyer's fee or expenses; and

    (b) contract with a client for a contingent fee in a civil case except when prohibited as stated in § 35.

    (2) A lawyer may not make or guarantee a loan to a client in connection with pending or contemplated litigation that the lawyer is conducting for the client, except that the lawyer may make or guarantee a loan covering court costs and expenses of litigation, the repayment of which to the lawyer may be contingent on the outcome of the matter.

    (3) A lawyer may not, before the lawyer ceases to represent a client, make an agreement giving the lawyer literary or media rights to a portrayal or account based in substantial part on information relating to the representation.

§ 37.   Partial or Complete Forfeiture of a Lawyer's Compensation

    A lawyer engaging in clear and serious violation of duty to a client may be required to forfeit some or all of the lawyer's compensation for the matter. Considerations relevant to the question of forfeiture include the gravity and timing of the violation, its willfulness, its effect on the value of the lawyer's work for the client, any other threatened or actual harm to the client, and the adequacy of other remedies.

§ 38.   Client-Lawyer Fee Contracts

    (1) Before or within a reasonable time after beginning to represent a client in a matter, a lawyer must communicate to the client, in writing when applicable rules so provide, the basis or rate of the fee, unless the communication is unnecessary for the client because the lawyer has previously represented that client on the same basis or at the same rate.

    (2) The validity and construction of a contract between a client and a lawyer concerning the lawyer's fees are governed by § 18.

    (3) Unless a contract construed in the circumstances indicates otherwise:

    (a) a lawyer may not charge separately for the lawyer's general office and overhead expenses;

(b)   payments that the law requires an opposing party or that party's lawyer to pay as attorney-fee awards or sanctions are credited to the client, not the client's lawyer, absent a contrary statute or court order; and

(c)   when a lawyer requests and receives a fee payment that is not for services already rendered, that payment is to be credited against whatever fee the lawyer is entitled to collect.

§ 39.   A Lawyer's Fee in the Absence of a Contract

If a client and lawyer have not made a valid contract providing for another measure of compensation, a client owes a lawyer who has performed legal services for the client the fair value of the lawyer's services.

§ 40.   Fees on Termination

If a client-lawyer relationship ends before the lawyer has completed the services due for a matter and the lawyer's fee has not been forfeited under § 37:

(1)   a lawyer who has been discharged or withdraws may recover the lesser of the fair value of the lawyer's services as determined under § 39 and the ratable proportion of the compensation provided by any otherwise enforceable contract between lawyer and client for the services performed; except that

(2)   the tribunal may allow such a lawyer to recover the ratable proportion of the compensation provided by such a contract if:

(a)   the discharge or withdrawal is not attributable to misconduct of the lawyer;

(b)   the lawyer has performed severable services; and

(c)   allowing contractual compensation would not burden the client's choice of counsel or the client's ability to replace counsel.

§ 41.   Fee-Collection Methods

In seeking compensation claimed from a client or former client, a lawyer may not employ collection methods forbidden by law, use confidential information (as defined in Chapter 5) when not permitted under § 65, or harass the client.

§ 42.   Remedies and the Burden of Persuasion

(1)   A fee dispute between a lawyer and a client may be adjudicated in any appropriate proceeding, including a suit by the lawyer to recover an unpaid fee, a suit for a refund by a client, an arbitration to which both parties consent unless applicable law renders the lawyer's consent unnecessary, or in the court's discretion a proceeding ancillary to a pending suit in which the lawyer performed the services in question.

(2)   In any such proceeding the lawyer has the burden of persuading the trier of fact, when relevant, of the existence and terms of any fee contract, the making of any disclosures to the client required to render a contract enforceable, and the extent and value of the lawyer's services.

§ 43.   Lawyer Liens

(1)   Except as provided in Subsection (2) or by statute or rule, a lawyer does not acquire a lien entitling the lawyer to retain the client's property in the lawyer's possession in order to secure payment of the lawyer's fees and

disbursements. A lawyer may decline to deliver to a client or former client an original or copy of any document prepared by the lawyer or at the lawyer's expense if the client or former client has not paid all fees and disbursements due for the lawyer's work in preparing the document and nondelivery would not unreasonably harm the client or former client.

(2) Unless otherwise provided by statute or rule, client and lawyer may agree that the lawyer shall have a security interest in property of the client recovered for the client through the lawyer's efforts, as follows:

(a) the lawyer may contract in writing with the client for a lien on the proceeds of the representation to secure payment for the lawyer's services and disbursements in that matter;

(b) the lien becomes binding on a third party when the party has notice of the lien;

(c) the lien applies only to the amount of fees and disbursements claimed reasonably and in good faith for the lawyer's services performed in the representation; and

(d) the lawyer may not unreasonably impede the speedy and inexpensive resolution of any dispute concerning those fees and disbursements or the lien.

(3) A tribunal where an action is pending may in its discretion adjudicate any fee or other dispute concerning a lien asserted by a lawyer on property of a party to the action, provide for custody of the property, release all or part of the property to the client or lawyer, and grant such other relief as justice may require.

(4) With respect to property neither in the lawyer's possession nor recovered by the client through the lawyer's efforts, the lawyer may obtain a security interest on property of a client only as provided by other law and consistent with §§ 18 and 126. Acquisition of such a security interest is a business or financial transaction with a client within the meaning of § 126.

§ 44. Safeguarding and Segregating Property

(1) A lawyer holding funds or other property of a client in connection with a representation, or such funds or other property in which a client claims an interest, must take reasonable steps to safeguard the funds or property. A similar obligation may be imposed by law on funds or other property so held and owned or claimed by a third person. In particular, the lawyer must hold such property separate from the lawyer's property, keep records of it, deposit funds in an account separate from the lawyer's own funds, identify tangible objects, and comply with related requirements imposed by regulatory authorities.

(2) Upon receiving funds or other property in a professional capacity and in which a client or third person owns or claims an interest, a lawyer must promptly notify the client or third person. The lawyer must promptly render a full accounting regarding such property upon request by the client or third person.

§ 45. Surrendering Possession of Property

(1) Except as provided in Subsection (2), a lawyer must promptly deliver, to the client or nonclient so entitled, funds or other property in the lawyer's possession belonging to a client or nonclient.

(2)   A lawyer may retain possession of funds or other property of a client or nonclient if:

(a)   the client or nonclient consents;

(b)   the lawyer's client is entitled to the property, the lawyer appropriately possesses the property for purposes of the representation, and the client has not asked for delivery of the property;

(c)   the lawyer has a valid lien on the property (see § 43);

(d)   there are substantial grounds for dispute as to the person entitled to the property; or

(e)   delivering the property to the client or nonclient would violate a court order or other legal obligation of the lawyer.

§ 46.   Documents Relating to a Representation

(1)   A lawyer must take reasonable steps to safeguard documents in the lawyer's possession relating to the representation of a client or former client.

(2)   On request, a lawyer must allow a client or former client to inspect and copy any document possessed by the lawyer relating to the representation, unless substantial grounds exist to refuse.

(3)   Unless a client or former client consents to nondelivery or substantial grounds exist for refusing to make delivery, a lawyer must deliver to the client or former client, at an appropriate time and in any event promptly after the representation ends, such originals and copies of other documents possessed by the lawyer relating to the representation as the client or former client reasonably needs.

(4)   Notwithstanding Subsections (2) and (3), a lawyer may decline to deliver to a client or former client an original or copy of any document under circumstances permitted by § 43(1).

§ 47.   Fee-Splitting Between Lawyers Not in the Same Firm

A division of fees between lawyers who are not in the same firm may be made only if:

(1)   (a) the division is in proportion to the services performed by each lawyer or (b) by agreement with the client, the lawyers assume joint responsibility for the representation;

(2)   the client is informed of and does not object to the fact of division, the terms of the division, and the participation of the lawyers involved; and

(3)   the total fee is reasonable (see § 34).

§ 48.   Professional Negligence—Elements and Defenses Generally

In addition to the other possible bases of civil liability described in §§ 49, 55, and 56, a lawyer is civilly liable for professional negligence to a person to whom the lawyer owes a duty of care within the meaning of § 50 or § 51, if the lawyer fails to exercise care within the meaning of § 52 and if that failure is a legal cause of injury within the meaning of § 53, unless the lawyer has a defense within the meaning of § 54.

§ 49.   Breach of Fiduciary Duty—Generally

In addition to the other possible bases of civil liability described in §§ 48, 55, and 56, a lawyer is civilly liable to a client if the lawyer breaches a fiduciary duty to the client set forth in § 16(3) and if that failure is a legal cause of injury within the meaning of § 53, unless the lawyer has a defense within the meaning of § 54.

§ 50.   Duty of Care to a Client

For purposes of liability under § 48, a lawyer owes a client the duty to exercise care within the meaning of § 52 in pursuing the client's lawful objectives in matters covered by the representation.

§ 51.   Duty of Care to Certain Nonclients

For purposes of liability under § 48, a lawyer owes a duty to use care within the meaning of § 52 in each of the following circumstances:

(1)   to a prospective client, as stated in § 15;

(2)   to a nonclient when and to the extent that:

(a)   the lawyer or (with the lawyer's acquiescence) the lawyer's client invites the nonclient to rely on the lawyer's opinion or provision of other legal services, and the nonclient so relies; and

(b)   the nonclient is not, under applicable tort law, too remote from the lawyer to be entitled to protection;

(3)   to a nonclient when and to the extent that:

(a)   the lawyer knows that a client intends as one of the primary objectives of the representation that the lawyer's services benefit the nonclient;

(b)   such a duty would not significantly impair the lawyer's performance of obligations to the client; and

(c)   the absence of such a duty would make enforcement of those obligations to the client unlikely; and

(4)   to a nonclient when and to the extent that:

(a)   the lawyer's client is a trustee, guardian, executor, or fiduciary acting primarily to perform similar functions for the nonclient;

(b)   the lawyer knows that appropriate action by the lawyer is necessary with respect to a matter within the scope of the representation to prevent or rectify the breach of a fiduciary duty owed by the client to the nonclient, where (i) the breach is a crime or fraud or (ii) the lawyer has assisted or is assisting the breach;

(c)   the nonclient is not reasonably able to protect its rights; and

(d)   such a duty would not significantly impair the performance of the lawyer's obligations to the client.

§ 52.   The Standard of Care

(1)   For purposes of liability under §§ 48 and 49, a lawyer who owes a duty of care must exercise the competence and diligence normally exercised by lawyers in similar circumstances.

(2)   Proof of a violation of a rule or statute regulating the conduct of lawyers:

(a)   does not give rise to an implied cause of action for professional negligence or breach of fiduciary duty;

(b)   does not preclude other proof concerning the duty of care in Subsection (1) or the fiduciary duty; and

(c)   may be considered by a trier of fact as an aid in understanding and applying the standard of Subsection (1) or § 49 to the extent that (i) the rule or statute was designed for the protection of persons in the position of the claimant and (ii) proof of the content and construction of such a rule or statute is relevant to the claimant's claim.

§ 53.   Causation and Damages

A lawyer is liable under § 48 or § 49 only if the lawyer's breach of a duty of care or breach of fiduciary duty was a legal cause of injury, as determined under generally applicable principles of causation and damages.

§ 54.   Defenses; Prospective Liability Waiver; Settlement with a Client

(1)   Except as otherwise provided in this Section, liability under §§ 48 and 49 is subject to the defenses available under generally applicable principles of law governing respectively actions for professional negligence and breach of fiduciary duty. A lawyer is not liable under § 48 or § 49 for any action or inaction the lawyer reasonably believed to be required by law, including a professional rule.

(2)   An agreement prospectively limiting a lawyer's liability to a client for malpractice is unenforceable.

(3)   The client or former client may rescind an agreement settling a claim by the client or former client against the person's lawyer if:

(a)   the client or former client was subjected to improper pressure by the lawyer in reaching the settlement; or

(b)   (i) the client or former client was not independently represented in negotiating the settlement, and (ii) the settlement was not fair and reasonable to the client or former client.

(4)   For purposes of professional discipline, a lawyer may not:

(a)   make an agreement prospectively limiting the lawyer's liability to a client for malpractice; or

(b)   settle a claim for such liability with an unrepresented client or former client without first advising that person in writing that independent representation is appropriate in connection therewith.

§ 55.   Civil Remedies of a Client Other Than for Malpractice

(1)   A lawyer is subject to liability to a client for injury caused by breach of contract in the circumstances and to the extent provided by contract law.

(2)   A client is entitled to restitutionary, injunctive, or declaratory remedies against a lawyer in the circumstances and to the extent provided by generally applicable law governing such remedies.

§ 56.   Liability to a Client or Nonclient Under General Law

Except as provided in § 57 and in addition to liability under §§ 48–55, a lawyer is subject to liability to a client or nonclient when a nonlawyer would be in similar circumstances.

§ 57.   Nonclient Claims—Certain Defenses and Exceptions to Liability

(1)   In addition to other absolute or conditional privileges, a lawyer is absolutely privileged to publish matter concerning a nonclient if:

   (a)   the publication occurs in communications preliminary to a reasonably anticipated proceeding before a tribunal or in the institution or during the course and as a part of such a proceeding;

   (b)   the lawyer participates as counsel in that proceeding; and

   (c)   the matter is published to a person who may be involved in the proceeding, and the publication has some relation to the proceeding.

(2)   A lawyer representing a client in a civil proceeding or procuring the institution of criminal proceedings by a client is not liable to a nonclient for wrongful use of civil proceedings or for malicious prosecution if the lawyer has probable cause for acting, or if the lawyer acts primarily to help the client obtain a proper adjudication of the client's claim in that proceeding.

(3)   A lawyer who advises or assists a client to make or break a contract, to enter or dissolve a legal relationship, or to enter or not enter a contractual relation, is not liable to a nonclient for interference with contract or with prospective contractual relations or with a legal relationship, if the lawyer acts to advance the client's objectives without using wrongful means.

§ 58.   Vicarious Liability

(1)   A law firm is subject to civil liability for injury legally caused to a person by any wrongful act or omission of any principal or employee of the firm who was acting in the ordinary course of the firm's business or with actual or apparent authority.

(2)   Each of the principals of a law firm organized as a general partnership without limited liability is liable jointly and severally with the firm.

(3)   A principal of a law firm organized other than as a general partnership without limited liability as authorized by law is vicariously liable for the acts of another principal or employee of the firm to the extent provided by law.

§ 59.   Definition of "Confidential Client Information"

Confidential client information consists of information relating to representation of a client, other than information that is generally known.

§ 60.   A Lawyer's Duty to Safeguard Confidential Client Information

(1)   Except as provided in §§ 61–67, during and after representation of a client:

   (a)   the lawyer may not use or disclose confidential client information as defined in § 59 if there is a reasonable prospect that doing so will adversely affect a material interest of the client or if the client has instructed the lawyer not to use or disclose such information;

   (b)   the lawyer must take steps reasonable in the circumstances to protect confidential client information against impermissible use or disclosure by the lawyer's associates or agents that may adversely affect a material interest of the client or otherwise than as instructed by the client.

(2)   Except as stated in § 62, a lawyer who uses confidential information of a client for the lawyer's pecuniary gain other than in the practice of law must account to the client for any profits made.

§ 61.   Using or Disclosing Information to Advance Client Interests

A lawyer may use or disclose confidential client information when the lawyer reasonably believes that doing so will advance the interests of the client in the representation.

§ 62.   Using or Disclosing Information with Client Consent

A lawyer may use or disclose confidential client information when the client consents after being adequately informed concerning the use or disclosure.

§ 63.   Using or Disclosing Information When Required by Law

A lawyer may use or disclose confidential client information when required by law, after the lawyer takes reasonably appropriate steps to assert that the information is privileged or otherwise protected against disclosure.

§ 64.   Using or Disclosing Information in a Lawyer's Self-Defense

A lawyer may use or disclose confidential client information when and to the extent that the lawyer reasonably believes necessary to defend the lawyer or the lawyer's associate or agent against a charge or threatened charge by any person that the lawyer or such associate or agent acted wrongfully in the course of representing a client.

§ 65.   Using or Disclosing Information in a Compensation Dispute

A lawyer may use or disclose confidential client information when and to the extent that the lawyer reasonably believes necessary to permit the lawyer to resolve a dispute with the client concerning compensation or reimbursement that the lawyer reasonably claims the client owes the lawyer.

§ 66.   Using or Disclosing Information to Prevent Death or Serious Bodily Harm

(1)   A lawyer may use or disclose confidential client information when the lawyer reasonably believes that its use or disclosure is necessary to prevent reasonably certain death or serious bodily harm to a person.

(2)   Before using or disclosing information under this Section, the lawyer must, if feasible, make a good-faith effort to persuade the client not to act. If the client or another person has already acted, the lawyer must, if feasible, advise the client to warn the victim or to take other action to prevent the harm and advise the client of the lawyer's ability to use or disclose information as provided in this Section and the consequences thereof.

(3)   A lawyer who takes action or decides not to take action permitted under this Section is not, solely by reason of such action or inaction, subject to professional discipline, liable for damages to the lawyer's client or any third person, or barred from recovery against a client or third person.

§ 67.   Using or Disclosing Information to Prevent, Rectify, or Mitigate Substantial Financial Loss

(1)   A lawyer may use or disclose confidential client information when the lawyer reasonably believes that its use or disclosure is necessary to prevent a crime or fraud, and:

(a)   the crime or fraud threatens substantial financial loss;

(b) the loss has not yet occurred;

(c) the lawyer's client intends to commit the crime or fraud either personally or through a third person; and

(d) the client has employed or is employing the lawyer's services in the matter in which the crime or fraud is committed.

(2) If a crime or fraud described in Subsection (1) has already occurred, a lawyer may use or disclose confidential client information when the lawyer reasonably believes its use or disclosure is necessary to prevent, rectify, or mitigate the loss.

(3) Before using or disclosing information under this Section, the lawyer must, if feasible, make a good-faith effort to persuade the client not to act. If the client or another person has already acted, the lawyer must, if feasible, advise the client to warn the victim or to take other action to prevent, rectify, or mitigate the loss. The lawyer must, if feasible, also advise the client of the lawyer's ability to use or disclose information as provided in this Section and the consequences thereof.

(4) A lawyer who takes action or decides not to take action permitted under this Section is not, solely by reason of such action or inaction, subject to professional discipline, liable for damages to the lawyer's client or any third person, or barred from recovery against a client or third person.

§ 68. Attorney-Client Privilege

Except as otherwise provided in this Restatement, the attorney-client privilege may be invoked as provided in § 86 with respect to:

(1) a communication

(2) made between privileged persons

(3) in confidence

(4) for the purpose of obtaining or providing legal assistance for the client.

§ 69. Attorney-Client Privilege—"Communication"

A communication within the meaning of § 68 is any expression through which a privileged person, as defined in § 70, undertakes to convey information to another privileged person and any document or other record revealing such an expression.

§ 70. Attorney-Client Privilege—"Privileged Persons"

Privileged persons within the meaning of § 68 are the client (including a prospective client), the client's lawyer, agents of either who facilitate communications between them, and agents of the lawyer who facilitate the representation.

§ 71. Attorney-Client Privilege—"In Confidence"

A communication is in confidence within the meaning of § 68 if, at the time and in the circumstances of the communication, the communicating person reasonably believes that no one will learn the contents of the communication except a privileged person as defined in § 70 or another person with whom communications are protected under a similar privilege.

§ 72.   Attorney-Client Privilege—Legal Assistance as the Object of a Privileged Communication

A communication is made for the purpose of obtaining or providing legal assistance within the meaning of § 68 if it is made to or to assist a person:

(1)   who is a lawyer or who the client or prospective client reasonably believes to be a lawyer; and

(2)   whom the client or prospective client consults for the purpose of obtaining legal assistance.

§ 73.   The Privilege for an Organizational Client

When a client is a corporation, unincorporated association, partnership, trust, estate, sole proprietorship, or other for-profit or not-for-profit organization, the attorney-client privilege extends to a communication that:

(1)   otherwise qualifies as privileged under §§ 68–72;

(2)   is between an agent of the organization and a privileged person as defined in § 70;

(3)   concerns a legal matter of interest to the organization; and

(4)   is disclosed only to:

(a)   privileged persons as defined in § 70; and

(b)   other agents of the organization who reasonably need to know of the communication in order to act for the organization.

§ 74.   The Privilege for a Governmental Client

Unless applicable law otherwise provides, the attorney-client privilege extends to a communication of a governmental organization as stated in § 73 and of an individual employee or other agent of a governmental organization as a client with respect to his or her personal interest as stated in §§ 68–72.

§ 75.   The Privilege of Co-Clients

(1)   If two or more persons are jointly represented by the same lawyer in a matter, a communication of either co-client that otherwise qualifies as privileged under §§ 68–72 and relates to matters of common interest is privileged as against third persons, and any co-client may invoke the privilege, unless it has been waived by the client who made the communication.

(2)   Unless the co-clients have agreed otherwise, a communication described in Subsection (1) is not privileged as between the co-clients in a subsequent adverse proceeding between them.

§ 76.   The Privilege in Common-Interest Arrangements

(1)   If two or more clients with a common interest in a litigated or nonlitigated matter are represented by separate lawyers and they agree to exchange information concerning the matter, a communication of any such client that otherwise qualifies as privileged under §§ 68–72 that relates to the matter is privileged as against third persons. Any such client may invoke the privilege, unless it has been waived by the client who made the communication.

(2)   Unless the clients have agreed otherwise, a communication described in Subsection (1) is not privileged as between clients described in Subsection (1) in a subsequent adverse proceeding between them.

§ 77. Duration of the Privilege

Unless waived (see §§ 78–80) or subject to exception (see §§ 81–85), the attorney-client privilege may be invoked as provided in § 86 at any time during or after termination of the relationship between client or prospective client and lawyer.

§ 78. Agreement, Disclaimer, or Failure to Object

The attorney-client privilege is waived if the client, the client's lawyer, or another authorized agent of the client:

    (1)   agrees to waive the privilege;

    (2)   disclaims protection of the privilege and

        (a)   another person reasonably relies on the disclaimer to that person's detriment; or

        (b)   reasons of judicial administration require that the client not be permitted to revoke the disclaimer; or

    (3)   in a proceeding before a tribunal, fails to object properly to an attempt by another person to give or exact testimony or other evidence of a privileged communication.

§ 79. Subsequent Disclosure

The attorney-client privilege is waived if the client, the client's lawyer, or another authorized agent of the client voluntarily discloses the communication in a nonprivileged communication.

§ 80. Putting Assistance or a Communication in Issue

(1)   The attorney-client privilege is waived for any relevant communication if the client asserts as to a material issue in a proceeding that:

    (a)   the client acted upon the advice of a lawyer or that the advice was otherwise relevant to the legal significance of the client's conduct; or

    (b)   a lawyer's assistance was ineffective, negligent, or otherwise wrongful.

(2)   The attorney-client privilege is waived for a recorded communication if a witness:

    (a)   employs the communication to aid the witness while testifying; or

    (b)   employed the communication in preparing to testify, and the tribunal finds that disclosure is required in the interests of justice.

§ 81. A Dispute Concerning a Decedent's Disposition of Property

The attorney-client privilege does not apply to a communication from or to a decedent relevant to an issue between parties who claim an interest through the same deceased client, either by testate or intestate succession or by an inter vivos transaction.

§ 82. Client Crime or Fraud

The attorney-client privilege does not apply to a communication occurring when a client:

(a)   consults a lawyer for the purpose, later accomplished, of obtaining assistance to engage in a crime or fraud or aiding a third person to do so, or

(b)   regardless of the client's purpose at the time of consultation, uses the lawyer's advice or other services to engage in or assist a crime or fraud.

§ 83.   Lawyer Self-Protection

The attorney-client privilege does not apply to a communication that is relevant and reasonably necessary for a lawyer to employ in a proceeding:

(1)   to resolve a dispute with a client concerning compensation or reimbursement that the lawyer reasonably claims the client owes the lawyer; or

(2)   to defend the lawyer or the lawyer's associate or agent against a charge by any person that the lawyer, associate, or agent acted wrongfully during the course of representing a client.

§ 84.   Fiduciary-Lawyer Communications

In a proceeding in which a trustee of an express trust or similar fiduciary is charged with breach of fiduciary duties by a beneficiary, a communication otherwise within § 68 is nonetheless not privileged if the communication:

(a)   is relevant to the claimed breach; and

(b)   was between the trustee and a lawyer (or other privileged person within the meaning of § 70) who was retained to advise the trustee concerning the administration of the trust.

§ 85.   Communications Involving a Fiduciary Within an Organization

In a proceeding involving a dispute between an organizational client and shareholders, members, or other constituents of the organization toward whom the directors, officers, or similar persons managing the organization bear fiduciary responsibilities, the attorney-client privilege of the organization may be withheld from a communication otherwise within § 68 if the tribunal finds that:

(a)   those managing the organization are charged with breach of their obligations toward the shareholders, members, or other constituents or toward the organization itself;

(b)   the communication occurred prior to the assertion of the charges and relates directly to those charges; and

(c)   the need of the requesting party to discover or introduce the communication is sufficiently compelling and the threat to confidentiality sufficiently confined to justify setting the privilege aside.

§ 86.   Invoking the Privilege and Its Exceptions

(1)   When an attempt is made to introduce in evidence or obtain discovery of a communication privileged under § 68:

(a)   A client, a personal representative of an incompetent or deceased client, or a person succeeding to the interest of a client may invoke or waive the privilege, either personally or through counsel or another authorized agent.

(b)   A lawyer, an agent of the lawyer, or an agent of a client from whom a privileged communication is sought must invoke the privilege when doing so appears reasonably appropriate, unless the client:

(i)   has waived the privilege; or

(ii)   has authorized the lawyer or agent to waive it.

(c)   Notwithstanding failure to invoke the privilege as specified in Subsections (1)(a) and (1)(b), the tribunal has discretion to invoke the privilege.

(2)   A person invoking the privilege must ordinarily object contemporaneously to an attempt to disclose the communication and, if the objection is contested, demonstrate each element of the privilege under § 68.

(3)   A person invoking a waiver of or exception to the privilege (§§ 78–85) must assert it and, if the assertion is contested, demonstrate each element of the waiver or exception.

§ 87.   Lawyer Work-Product Immunity

(1)   Work product consists of tangible material or its intangible equivalent in unwritten or oral form, other than underlying facts, prepared by a lawyer for litigation then in progress or in reasonable anticipation of future litigation.

(2)   Opinion work product consists of the opinions or mental impressions of a lawyer; all other work product is ordinary work product.

(3)   Except for material which by applicable law is not so protected, work product is immune from discovery or other compelled disclosure to the extent stated in §§ 88 (ordinary work product) and 89 (opinion work product) when the immunity is invoked as described in § 90.

§ 88.   Ordinary Work Product

When work product protection is invoked as described in § 90, ordinary work product (§ 87(2)) is immune from discovery or other compelled disclosure unless either an exception recognized in §§ 91–93 applies or the inquiring party:

(1)   has a substantial need for the material in order to prepare for trial; and

(2)   is unable without undue hardship to obtain the substantial equivalent of the material by other means.

§ 89.   Opinion Work Product

When work product protection is invoked as described in § 90, opinion work product (§ 87(2)) is immune from discovery or other compelled disclosure unless either the immunity is waived or an exception applies (§§ 91–93) or extraordinary circumstances justify disclosure.

§ 90.   Invoking the Lawyer Work-Product Immunity and Its Exceptions

(1)   Work-product immunity may be invoked by or for a person on whose behalf the work product was prepared.

(2)   The person invoking work-product immunity must object and, if the objection is contested, demonstrate each element of the immunity.

(3)   Once a claim of work product has been adequately supported, a person entitled to invoke a waiver or exception must assert it and, if the assertion is contested, demonstrate each element of the waiver or exception.

§ 91.   Voluntary Acts

Work-product immunity is waived if the client, the client's lawyer, or another authorized agent of the client:

(1)   agrees to waive the immunity;

(2)   disclaims protection of the immunity and:

(a)   another person reasonably relies on the disclaimer to that person's detriment; or

(b)   reasons of judicial administration require that the client not be permitted to revoke the disclaimer; or

(3)   in a proceeding before a tribunal, fails to object properly to an attempt by another person to give or exact testimony or other evidence of work product; or

(4)   discloses the material to third persons in circumstances in which there is a significant likelihood that an adversary or potential adversary in anticipated litigation will obtain it.

§ 92.   Use of Lawyer Work Product in Litigation

(1)   Work-product immunity is waived for any relevant material if the client asserts as to a material issue in a proceeding that:

(a)   the client acted upon the advice of a lawyer or that the advice was otherwise relevant to the legal significance of the client's conduct; or

(b)   a lawyer's assistance was ineffective, negligent, or otherwise wrongful.

(2)   The work-product immunity is waived for recorded material if a witness

(a)   employs the material to aid the witness while testifying, or

(b)   employed the material in preparing to testify, and the tribunal finds that disclosure is required in the interests of justice.

§ 93.   Client Crime or Fraud

Work-product immunity does not apply to materials prepared when a client consults a lawyer for the purpose, later accomplished, of obtaining assistance to engage in a crime or fraud or to aid a third person to do so or uses the materials for such a purpose.

§ 94.   Advising and Assisting a Client—In General

(1)   A lawyer who counsels or assists a client to engage in conduct that violates the rights of a third person is subject to liability:

(a)   to the third person to the extent stated in §§ 51 and 56–57; and

(b)   to the client to the extent stated in §§ 50, 55, and 56.

(2)   For purposes of professional discipline, a lawyer may not counsel or assist a client in conduct that the lawyer knows to be criminal or fraudulent or in violation of a court order with the intent of facilitating or encouraging

the conduct, but the lawyer may counsel or assist a client in conduct when the lawyer reasonably believes:

 (a) that the client's conduct constitutes a good-faith effort to determine the validity, scope, meaning, or application of a law or court order; or

 (b) that the client can assert a nonfrivolous argument that the client's conduct will not constitute a crime or fraud or violate a court order.

 (3) In counseling a client, a lawyer may address nonlegal aspects of a proposed course of conduct, including moral, reputational, economic, social, political, and business aspects.

§ 95. An Evaluation Undertaken for a Third Person

 (1) In furtherance of the objectives of a client in a representation, a lawyer may provide to a nonclient the results of the lawyer's investigation and analysis of facts or the lawyer's professional evaluation or opinion on the matter.

 (2) When providing the information, evaluation, or opinion under Subsection (1) is reasonably likely to affect the client's interests materially and adversely, the lawyer must first obtain the client's consent after the client is adequately informed concerning important possible effects on the client's interests.

 (3) In providing the information, evaluation, or opinion under Subsection (1), the lawyer must exercise care with respect to the nonclient to the extent stated in § 51(2) and not make false statements prohibited under § 98.

§ 96. Representing an Organization as Client

 (1) When a lawyer is employed or retained to represent an organization:

 (a) the lawyer represents the interests of the organization as defined by its responsible agents acting pursuant to the organization's decision-making procedures; and

 (b) subject to Subsection (2), the lawyer must follow instructions in the representation, as stated in § 21(2), given by persons authorized so to act on behalf of the organization.

 (2) If a lawyer representing an organization knows of circumstances indicating that a constituent of the organization has engaged in action or intends to act in a way that violates a legal obligation to the organization that will likely cause substantial injury to it, or that reasonably can be foreseen to be imputable to the organization and likely to result in substantial injury to it, the lawyer must proceed in what the lawyer reasonably believes to be the best interests of the organization.

 (3) In the circumstances described in Subsection (2), the lawyer may, in circumstances warranting such steps, ask the constituent to reconsider the matter, recommend that a second legal opinion be sought, and seek review by appropriate supervisory authority within the organization, including referring the matter to the highest authority that can act in behalf of the organization.

§ 97.   Representing a Governmental Client

A lawyer representing a governmental client must proceed in the representation as stated in § 96, except that the lawyer:

(1)   possesses such rights and responsibilities as may be defined by law to make decisions on behalf of the governmental client that are within the authority of a client under §§ 22 and 21(2);

(2)   except as otherwise provided by law, must proceed as stated in §§ 96(2) and 96(3) with respect to an act of a constituent of the governmental client that violates a legal obligation that will likely cause substantial public or private injury or that reasonably can be foreseen to be imputable to and thus likely result in substantial injury to the client;

(3)   if a prosecutor or similar lawyer determining whether to file criminal proceedings or take other steps in such proceedings, must do so only when based on probable cause and the lawyer's belief, formed after due investigation, that there are good factual and legal grounds to support the step taken; and

(4)   must observe other applicable restrictions imposed by law on those similarly functioning for the governmental client.

§ 98.   Statements to a Nonclient

A lawyer communicating on behalf of a client with a nonclient may not:

(1)   knowingly make a false statement of material fact or law to the nonclient,

(2)   make other statements prohibited by law; or

(3)   fail to make a disclosure of information required by law.

§ 99.   A Represented Nonclient—The General Anti-Contact Rule

(1)   A lawyer representing a client in a matter may not communicate about the subject of the representation with a nonclient whom the lawyer knows to be represented in the matter by another lawyer or with a representative of an organizational nonclient so represented as defined in § 100, unless:

(a)   the communication is with a public officer or agency to the extent stated in § 101;

(b)   the lawyer is a party and represents no other client in the matter;

(c)   the communication is authorized by law;

(d)   the communication reasonably responds to an emergency; or

(e)   the other lawyer consents.

(2)   Subsection (1) does not prohibit the lawyer from assisting the client in otherwise proper communication by the lawyer's client with a represented nonclient.

§ 100.   Definition of a Represented Nonclient

Within the meaning of § 99, a represented nonclient includes:

(1)   a natural person represented by a lawyer; and:

(2)   a current employee or other agent of an organization represented by a lawyer:

>   (a)   if the employee or other agent supervises, directs, or regularly consults with the lawyer concerning the matter or if the agent has power to compromise or settle the matter;

>   (b)   if the acts or omissions of the employee or other agent may be imputed to the organization for purposes of civil or criminal liability in the matter; or

>   (c)   if a statement of the employee or other agent, under applicable rules of evidence, would have the effect of binding the organization with respect to proof of the matter.

§ 101.   A Represented Governmental Agency or Officer

(1)   Unless otherwise provided by law (see § 99(1)(c)) and except as provided in Subsection (2), the prohibition stated in § 99 against contact with a represented nonclient does not apply to communications with employees of a represented governmental agency or with a governmental officer being represented in the officer's official capacity.

(2)   In negotiation or litigation by a lawyer of a specific claim of a client against a governmental agency or against a governmental officer in the officer's official capacity, the prohibition stated in § 99 applies, except that the lawyer may contact any officer of the government if permitted by the agency or with respect to an issue of general policy.

§ 102.   Information of a Nonclient Known to be Legally Protected

A lawyer communicating with a nonclient in a situation permitted under § 99 may not seek to obtain information that the lawyer reasonably should know the nonclient may not reveal without violating a duty of confidentiality to another imposed by law.

§ 103.   Dealings with an Unrepresented Nonclient

In the course of representing a client and dealing with a nonclient who is not represented by a lawyer:

>   (1)   the lawyer may not mislead the nonclient, to the prejudice of the nonclient, concerning the identity and interests of the person the lawyer represents; and

>   (2)   when the lawyer knows or reasonably should know that the unrepresented nonclient misunderstands the lawyer's role in the matter, the lawyer must make reasonable efforts to correct the misunderstanding when failure to do so would materially prejudice the nonclient.

§ 104.   Representing a Client in Legislative and Administrative Matters

A lawyer representing a client before a legislature or administrative agency:

>   (1)   must disclose that the appearance is in a representative capacity and not misrepresent the capacity in which the lawyer appears;

>   (2)   must comply with applicable law and regulations governing such representations; and

>   (3)   except as applicable law otherwise provides:

(a) in an adjudicative proceeding before a government agency or involving such an agency as a participant, has the legal rights and responsibilities of an advocate in a proceeding before a judicial tribunal; and

(b) in other types of proceedings and matters, has the legal rights and responsibilities applicable in the lawyer's dealings with a private person.

§ 105. Complying with Law and Tribunal Rulings

In representing a client in a matter before a tribunal, a lawyer must comply with applicable law, including rules of procedure and evidence and specific tribunal rulings.

§ 106. Dealing with Other Participants in Proceedings

In representing a client in a matter before a tribunal, a lawyer may not use means that have no substantial purpose other than to embarrass, delay, or burden a third person or use methods of obtaining evidence that are prohibited by law.

§ 107. Prohibited Forensic Tactics

In representing a client in a matter before a tribunal, a lawyer may not, in the presence of the trier of fact:

(1) state a personal opinion about the justness of a cause, the credibility of a witness, the culpability of a civil litigant, or the guilt or innocence of an accused, but the lawyer may argue any position or conclusion adequately supported by the lawyer's analysis of the evidence; or

(2) allude to any matter that the lawyer does not reasonably believe is relevant or that will not be supported by admissible evidence.

§ 108. An Advocate as a Witness

(1) Except as provided in Subsection (2), a lawyer may not represent a client in a contested hearing or trial of a matter in which:

(a) the lawyer is expected to testify for the lawyer's client; or

(b) the lawyer does not intend to testify but (i) the lawyer's testimony would be material to establishing a claim or defense of the client, and (ii) the client has not consented as stated in § 122 to the lawyer's intention not to testify.

(2) A lawyer may represent a client when the lawyer will testify as stated in Subsection (1)(a) if:

(a) the lawyer's testimony relates to an issue that the lawyer reasonably believes will not be contested or to the nature and value of legal services rendered in the proceeding;

(b) deprivation of the lawyer's services as advocate would work a substantial hardship on the client; or

(c) consent has been given by (i) opposing parties who would be adversely affected by the lawyer's testimony and (ii) if relevant, the lawyer's client, as stated in § 122 with respect to any conflict of interest between lawyer and client (see § 125) that the lawyer's testimony would create.

(3)   A lawyer may not represent a client in a litigated matter pending before a tribunal when the lawyer or a lawyer in the lawyer's firm will give testimony materially adverse to the position of the lawyer's client or materially adverse to a former client of any such lawyer with respect to a matter substantially related to the earlier representation, unless the affected client has consented as stated in § 122 with respect to any conflict of interest between lawyer and client (see § 125) that the testimony would create.

(4)   A tribunal should not permit a lawyer to call opposing trial counsel as a witness unless there is a compelling need for the lawyer's testimony.

§ 109.   An Advocate's Public Comment on Pending Litigation

(1)   In representing a client in a matter before a tribunal, a lawyer may not make a statement outside the proceeding that a reasonable person would expect to be disseminated by means of public communication when the lawyer knows or reasonably should know that the statement will have a substantial likelihood of materially prejudicing a juror or influencing or intimidating a prospective witness in the proceeding. However, a lawyer may in any event make a statement that is reasonably necessary to mitigate the impact on the lawyer's client of substantial, undue, and prejudicial publicity recently initiated by one other than the lawyer or the lawyer's client.

(2)   A prosecutor must, except for statements necessary to inform the public of the nature and extent of the prosecutor's action and that serve a legitimate law-enforcement purpose, refrain from making extrajudicial comments that have a substantial likelihood of heightening public condemnation of the accused.

§ 110.   Frivolous Advocacy

(1)   A lawyer may not bring or defend a proceeding or assert or controvert an issue therein, unless there is a basis for doing so that is not frivolous, which includes a good-faith argument for an extension, modification, or reversal of existing law.

(2)   Notwithstanding Subsection (1), a lawyer for the defendant in a criminal proceeding or the respondent in a proceeding that could result in incarceration may so defend the proceeding as to require that the prosecutor establish every necessary element.

(3)   A lawyer may not make a frivolous discovery request, fail to make a reasonably diligent effort to comply with a proper discovery request of another party, or intentionally fail otherwise to comply with applicable procedural requirements concerning discovery.

§ 111.   Disclosure of Legal Authority

In representing a client in a matter before a tribunal, a lawyer may not knowingly:

(1)   make a false statement of a material proposition of law to the tribunal; or

(2)   fail to disclose to the tribunal legal authority in the controlling jurisdiction known to the lawyer to be directly adverse to the position asserted by the client and not disclosed by opposing counsel.

§ 112.   Advocacy in Ex Parte and Other Proceedings

In representing a client in a matter before a tribunal, a lawyer applying for ex parte relief or appearing in another proceeding in which similar special requirements of candor apply must comply with the requirements of § 110 and §§ 118–120 and further:

>　(1)　must not present evidence the lawyer reasonably believes is false;

>　(2)　must disclose all material and relevant facts known to the lawyer that will enable the tribunal to reach an informed decision; and

>　(3)　must comply with any other applicable special requirements of candor imposed by law.

§ 113.　Improperly Influencing a Judicial Officer

>　(1)　A lawyer may not knowingly communicate ex parte with a judicial officer before whom a proceeding is pending concerning the matter, except as authorized by law.

>　(2)　A lawyer may not make a gift or loan prohibited by law to a judicial officer, attempt to influence the officer otherwise than by legally proper procedures, or state or imply an ability so to influence a judicial officer.

§ 114.　A Lawyer's Statements Concerning a Judicial Officer

A lawyer may not knowingly or recklessly make publicly a false statement of fact concerning the qualifications or integrity of an incumbent of a judicial office or a candidate for election to such an office.

§ 115.　Lawyer Contact with a Juror

A lawyer may not:

>　(1)　except as allowed by law, communicate with or seek to influence a person known by the lawyer to be a member of a jury pool from which the jury will be drawn;

>　(2)　except as allowed by law, communicate with or seek to influence a member of a jury; or

>　(3)　communicate with a juror who has been excused from further service:

>>　(a)　when that would harass the juror or constitute an attempt to influence the juror's actions as a juror in future cases; or

>>　(b)　when otherwise prohibited by law.

§ 116.　Interviewing and Preparing a Prospective Witness

>　(1)　A lawyer may interview a witness for the purpose of preparing the witness to testify.

>　(2)　A lawyer may not unlawfully obstruct another party's access to a witness.

>　(3)　A lawyer may not unlawfully induce or assist a prospective witness to evade or ignore process obliging the witness to appear to testify.

>　(4)　A lawyer may not request a person to refrain from voluntarily giving relevant testimony or information to another party, unless:

>>　(a)　the person is the lawyer's client in the matter; or

>>　(b)　(i) the person is not the lawyer's client but is a relative or employee or other agent of the lawyer or the lawyer's client, and (ii) the

lawyer reasonably believes compliance will not materially and adversely affect the person's interests.

§ 117. Compensating a Witness

A lawyer may not offer or pay to a witness any consideration:

(1) in excess of the reasonable expenses of the witness incurred and the reasonable value of the witness's time spent in providing evidence, except that an expert witness may be offered and paid a noncontingent fee;

(2) contingent on the content of the witness's testimony or the outcome of the litigation; or

(3) otherwise prohibited by law.

§ 118. Falsifying or Destroying Evidence

(1) A lawyer may not falsify documentary or other evidence.

(2) A lawyer may not destroy or obstruct another party's access to documentary or other evidence when doing so would violate a court order or other legal requirements, or counsel or assist a client to do so.

§ 119. Physical Evidence of a Client Crime

With respect to physical evidence of a client crime, a lawyer:

(1) may, when reasonably necessary for purposes of the representation, take possession of the evidence and retain it for the time reasonably necessary to examine it and subject it to tests that do not alter or destroy material characteristics of the evidence; but

(2) following possession under Subsection (1), the lawyer must notify prosecuting authorities of the lawyer's possession of the evidence or turn the evidence over to them.

§ 120. False Testimony or Evidence

(1) A lawyer may not:

(a) knowingly counsel or assist a witness to testify falsely or otherwise to offer false evidence;

(b) knowingly make a false statement of fact to the tribunal;

(c) offer testimony or other evidence as to an issue of fact known by the lawyer to be false.

(2) If a lawyer has offered testimony or other evidence as to a material issue of fact and comes to know of its falsity, the lawyer must take reasonable remedial measures and may disclose confidential client information when necessary to take such a measure.

(3) A lawyer may refuse to offer testimony or other evidence that the lawyer reasonably believes is false, even if the lawyer does not know it to be false.

§ 121. The Basic Prohibition of Conflicts of Interest

Unless all affected clients and other necessary persons consent to the representation under the limitations and conditions provided in § 122, a lawyer may not represent a client if the representation would involve a conflict of interest. A conflict of interest is involved if there is a substantial risk that the lawyer's representation of the client would be materially and adversely affected by the lawyer's own interests or by the lawyer's duties to another current client, a former client, or a third person.

§ 122.   Client Consent to a Conflict of Interest

(1)   A lawyer may represent a client notwithstanding a conflict of interest prohibited by § 121 if each affected client or former client gives informed consent to the lawyer's representation. Informed consent requires that the client or former client have reasonably adequate information about the material risks of such representation to that client or former client.

(2)   Notwithstanding the informed consent of each affected client or former client, a lawyer may not represent a client if:

(a)   the representation is prohibited by law;

(b)   one client will assert a claim against the other in the same litigation; or

(c)   in the circumstances, it is not reasonably likely that the lawyer will be able to provide adequate representation to one or more of the clients.

§ 123.   Imputation of a Conflict of Interest to an Affiliated Lawyer

Unless all affected clients consent to the representation under the limitations and conditions provided in § 122 or unless imputation hereunder is removed as provided in § 124, the restrictions upon a lawyer imposed by §§ 125–135 also restrict other affiliated lawyers who:

(1)   are associated with that lawyer in rendering legal services to others through a law partnership, professional corporation, sole proprietorship, or similar association;

(2)   are employed with that lawyer by an organization to render legal services either to that organization or to others to advance the interests or objectives of the organization; or

(3)   share office facilities without reasonably adequate measures to protect confidential client information so that it will not be available to other lawyers in the shared office.

§ 124.   Removing Imputation

(1)   Imputation specified in § 123 does not restrict an affiliated lawyer when the affiliation between the affiliated lawyer and the personally prohibited lawyer that required the imputation has been terminated, and no material confidential information of the client, relevant to the matter, has been communicated by the personally prohibited lawyer to the affiliated lawyer or that lawyer's firm.

(2)   Imputation specified in § 123 does not restrict an affiliated lawyer with respect to a former-client conflict under § 132, when there is no substantial risk that confidential information of the former client will be used with material adverse effect on the former client because:

(a)   any confidential client information communicated to the personally prohibited lawyer is unlikely to be significant in the subsequent matter;

(b)   the personally prohibited lawyer is subject to screening measures adequate to eliminate participation by that lawyer in the representation; and

(c)   timely and adequate notice of the screening has been provided to all affected clients.

(3)   Imputation specified in § 123 does not restrict a lawyer affiliated with a former government lawyer with respect to a conflict under § 133 if:

(a)   the personally prohibited lawyer is subject to screening measures adequate to eliminate involvement by that lawyer in the representation; and

(b)   timely and adequate notice of the screening has been provided to the appropriate government agency and to affected clients.

§ 125.   A Lawyer's Personal Interest Affecting the Representation of a Client

Unless the affected client consents to the representation under the limitations and conditions provided in § 122, a lawyer may not represent a client if there is a substantial risk that the lawyer's representation of the client would be materially and adversely affected by the lawyer's financial or other personal interests.

§ 126.   Business Transactions Between a Lawyer and a Client

A lawyer may not participate in a business or financial transaction with a client, except a standard commercial transaction in which the lawyer does not render legal services, unless:

(1)   the client has adequate information about the terms of the transaction and the risks presented by the lawyer's involvement in it;

(2)   the terms and circumstances of the transaction are fair and reasonable to the client; and

(3)   the client consents to the lawyer's role in the transaction under the limitations and conditions provided in § 122 after being encouraged, and given a reasonable opportunity, to seek independent legal advice concerning the transaction.

§ 127.   A Client Gift to a Lawyer

(1)   A lawyer may not prepare any instrument effecting any gift from a client to the lawyer, including a testamentary gift, unless the lawyer is a relative or other natural object of the client's generosity and the gift is not significantly disproportionate to those given other donees similarly related to the donor.

(2)   A lawyer may not accept a gift from a client, including a testamentary gift, unless:

(a)   the lawyer is a relative or other natural object of the client's generosity;

(b)   the value conferred by the client and the benefit to the lawyer are insubstantial in amount; or

(c)   the client, before making the gift, has received independent advice or has been encouraged, and given a reasonable opportunity, to seek such advice.

§ 128.   **Representing Clients with Conflicting Interests in Civil Litigation**

Unless all affected clients consent to the representation under the limitations and conditions provided in § 122, a lawyer in civil litigation may not:

(1)   represent two or more clients in a matter if there is a substantial risk that the lawyer's representation of one client would be materially and adversely affected by the lawyer's duties to another client in the matter; or

(2)   represent one client to assert or defend a claim against or brought by another client currently represented by the lawyer, even if the matters are not related.

§ 129.   **Conflicts of Interest in Criminal Litigation**

Unless all affected clients consent to the representation under the limitations and conditions provided in § 122, a lawyer in a criminal matter may not represent:

(1)   two or more defendants or potential defendants in the same matter; or

(2)   a single defendant, if the representation would involve a conflict of interest as defined in § 121.

§ 130.   **Multiple Representation in a Nonlitigated Matter**

Unless all affected clients consent to the representation under the limitations and conditions provided in § 122, a lawyer may not represent two or more clients in a matter not involving litigation if there is a substantial risk that the lawyer's representation of one or more of the clients would be materially and adversely affected by the lawyer's duties to one or more of the other clients.

§ 131.   **Conflicts of Interest in Representing an Organization**

Unless all affected clients consent to the representation under the limitations and conditions provided in § 122, a lawyer may not represent both an organization and a director, officer, employee, shareholder, owner, partner, member, or other individual or organization associated with the organization if there is a substantial risk that the lawyer's representation of either would be materially and adversely affected by the lawyer's duties to the other.

§ 132.   **A Representation Adverse to the Interests of a Former Client**

Unless both the affected present and former clients consent to the representation under the limitations and conditions provided in § 122, a lawyer who has represented a client in a matter may not thereafter represent another client in the same or a substantially related matter in which the interests of the former client are materially adverse. The current matter is substantially related to the earlier matter if:

(1)   the current matter involves the work the lawyer performed for the former client; or

(2)   there is a substantial risk that representation of the present client will involve the use of information acquired in the course of

representing the former client, unless that information has become generally known.

§ 133.   A Former Government Lawyer or Officer

(1)   A lawyer may not act on behalf of a client with respect to a matter in which the lawyer participated personally and substantially while acting as a government lawyer or officer unless both the government and the client consent to the representation under the limitations and conditions provided in § 122.

(2)   A lawyer who acquires confidential information while acting as a government lawyer or officer may not:

(a)   if the information concerns a person, represent a client whose interests are materially adverse to that person in a matter in which the information could be used to the material disadvantage of that person; or

(b)   if the information concerns the governmental client or employer, represent another public or private client in circumstances described in § 132(2).

§ 134.   Compensation or Direction of a Lawyer by a Third Person

(1)   A lawyer may not represent a client if someone other than the client will wholly or partly compensate the lawyer for the representation, unless the client consents under the limitations and conditions provided in § 122 and knows of the circumstances and conditions of the payment.

(2)   A lawyer's professional conduct on behalf of a client may be directed by someone other than the client if:

(a)   the direction does not interfere with the lawyer's independence of professional judgment;

(b)   the direction is reasonable in scope and character, such as by reflecting obligations borne by the person directing the lawyer; and

(c)   the client consents to the direction under the limitations and conditions provided in § 122.

§ 135.   A Lawyer with a Fiduciary or Other Legal Obligation to a Nonclient

Unless the affected client consents to the representation under the limitations and conditions provided in § 122, a lawyer may not represent a client in any matter with respect to which the lawyer has a fiduciary or other legal obligation to another if there is a substantial risk that the lawyer's representation of the client would be materially and adversely affected by the lawyer's obligation.

CALIFORNIA RULES OF PROFESSIONAL CONDUCT

(Effective November 1, 2018)*

TABLE OF CONTENTS

CLIENT-LAWYER RELATIONSHIP

Rule

---

* Editor's Note. California was long the state with Rules of Professional Conduct that most significantly departed from the format of the ABA Model Rules. On May 10, 2018, the California Supreme Court issued an order approving new Rules of Professional Conduct, which became effective on November 1, 2018. The court's adoption of these 2018 rules overcomes much of the format difference, although as is true in most states, the rules reflect some substantive differences from the ABA Model Rules.

PUBLIC SERVICE

INFORMATION ABOUT LEGAL SERVICES

MAINTAINING THE INTEGRITY OF THE PROFESSION

CALIFORNIA RULES OF PROFESSIONAL CONDUCT

CLIENT-LAWYER RELATIONSHIP

Rule 1.0   Purpose and Function of the Rules of Professional Conduct

(a)   Purpose.

The following rules are intended to regulate professional conduct of lawyers through discipline. They have been adopted by the Board of Trustees of the State Bar of California and approved by the Supreme Court of California pursuant to Business and Professions Code sections 6076 and 6077 to protect the public, the courts, and the legal profession; protect the integrity of the legal system; and promote the administration of justice and confidence in the legal profession. These rules together with any standards adopted by the Board of Trustees pursuant to these rules shall be binding upon all lawyers.

(b)   Function.

(1)   A willful violation of any of these rules is a basis for discipline.

(2)   The prohibition of certain conduct in these rules is not exclusive. Lawyers are also bound by applicable law including the State Bar Act (Bus. & Prof. Code, § 6000 et seq.) and opinions of California courts.

(3)   A violation of a rule does not itself give rise to a cause of action for damages caused by failure to comply with the rule. Nothing in these

293

rules or the Comments to the rules is intended to enlarge or to restrict the law regarding the liability of lawyers to others.

(c)   Purpose of Comments.

The comments are not a basis for imposing discipline but are intended only to provide guidance for interpreting and practicing in compliance with the rules.

(d)   These rules may be cited and referred to as the "California Rules of Professional Conduct."

Comment

[1]   The Rules of Professional Conduct are intended to establish the standards for lawyers for purposes of discipline. (See *Ames v. State Bar* (1973) 8 Cal.3d 910, 917 [106 Cal.Rptr. 489].) Therefore, failure to comply with an obligation or prohibition imposed by a rule is a basis for invoking the disciplinary process. Because the rules are not designed to be a basis for civil liability, a violation of a rule does not itself give rise to a cause of action for enforcement of a rule or for damages caused by failure to comply with the rule. (*Stanley v. Richmond* (1995) 35 Cal.App.4th 1070, 1097 [41 Cal.Rptr.2d 768].) Nevertheless, a lawyer's violation of a rule may be evidence of breach of a lawyer's fiduciary or other substantive legal duty in a non-disciplinary context. (*Ibid.*; see also *Mirabito v. Liccardo* (1992) 4 Cal.App.4th 41, 44 [5 Cal.Rptr.2d 571].) A violation of a rule may have other non-disciplinary consequences. (See, e.g., *Fletcher v. Davis* (2004) 33 Cal.4th 61, 71–72 [14 Cal.Rptr.3d 58] [enforcement of attorney's lien]; *Chambers v. Kay* (2002) 29 Cal.4th 142, 161 [126 Cal.Rptr.2d 536] [enforcement of fee sharing agreement].)

[2]   While the rules are intended to regulate professional conduct of lawyers, a violation of a rule can occur when a lawyer is not practicing law or acting in a professional capacity.

[3]   A willful violation of a rule does not require that the lawyer intend to violate the rule. (*Phillips v. State Bar* (1989) 49 Cal.3d 944, 952 [264 Cal.Rptr. 346]; and see Bus. & Prof. Code, § 6077.)

[4]   In addition to the authorities identified in paragraph (b)(2), opinions of ethics committees in California, although not binding, should be consulted for guidance on proper professional conduct. Ethics opinions and rules and standards promulgated by other jurisdictions and bar associations may also be considered.

[5]   The disciplinary standards created by these rules are not intended to address all aspects of a lawyer's professional obligations. A lawyer, as a member of the legal profession, is a representative and advisor of clients, an officer of the legal system and a public citizen having special responsibilities for the quality of justice. A lawyer should be aware of deficiencies in the administration of justice and of the fact that the poor, and sometimes persons* who are not poor cannot afford adequate legal assistance. Therefore, all lawyers are encouraged to devote professional time and resources and use civic influence to ensure equal access to the system of justice for those who because of economic or social barriers cannot afford or secure adequate legal counsel. In meeting this responsibility of the profession, every lawyer should aspire to render at least fifty hours of pro bono publico legal services per year. The lawyer should aim to provide a substantial* majority of such hours to

---

*   An asterisk (*) identifies a word or phrase defined in the terminology rule, rule 1.0.1.

indigent individuals or to nonprofit organizations with a primary purpose of providing services to the poor or on behalf of the poor or disadvantaged. Lawyers may also provide financial support to organizations providing free legal services. (See Bus. & Prof. Code, § 6073.)

Rule 1.0.1   Terminology

(a) "Belief" or "believes" means that the person* involved actually supposes the fact in question to be true. A person's* belief may be inferred from circumstances.

(b) [Reserved]

(c) "Firm" or "law firm" means a law partnership; a professional law corporation; a lawyer acting as a sole proprietorship; an association authorized to practice law; or lawyers employed in a legal services organization or in the legal department, division or office of a corporation, of a government organization, or of another organization.

(d) "Fraud" or "fraudulent" means conduct that is fraudulent under the law of the applicable jurisdiction and has a purpose to deceive.

(e) "Informed consent" means a person's* agreement to a proposed course of conduct after the lawyer has communicated and explained (i) the relevant circumstances and (ii) the material risks, including any actual and reasonably* foreseeable adverse consequences of the proposed course of conduct.

(e-1) "Informed written consent" means that the disclosures and the consent required by paragraph (e) must be in writing.*

(f) "Knowingly," "known," or "knows" means actual knowledge of the fact in question. A person's* knowledge may be inferred from circumstances.

(g) "Partner" means a member of a partnership, a shareholder in a law firm* organized as a professional corporation, or a member of an association authorized to practice law.

(g-1) "Person" has the meaning stated in Evidence Code section 175.

(h) "Reasonable" or "reasonably" when used in relation to conduct by a lawyer means the conduct of a reasonably prudent and competent lawyer.

(i) "Reasonable belief" or "reasonably believes" when used in reference to a lawyer means that the lawyer believes the matter in question and that the circumstances are such that the belief is reasonable.

(j) "Reasonably should know" when used in reference to a lawyer means that a lawyer of reasonable prudence and competence would ascertain the matter in question.

(k) "Screened" means the isolation of a lawyer from any participation in a matter, including the timely imposition of procedures within a law firm* that are adequate under the circumstances (i) to protect information that the isolated lawyer is obligated to protect under these rules or other law; and (ii) to protect against other law firm* lawyers and nonlawyer personnel communicating with the lawyer with respect to the matter.

(l) "Substantial" when used in reference to degree or extent means a material matter of clear and weighty importance.

---

*   An asterisk (*) identifies a word or phrase defined in the terminology rule, rule 1.0.1.

(m) "Tribunal" means: (i) a court, an arbitrator, an administrative law judge, or an administrative body acting in an adjudicative capacity and authorized to make a decision that can be binding on the parties involved; or (ii) a special master or other person* to whom a court refers one or more issues and whose decision or recommendation can be binding on the parties if approved by the court.

(n) "Writing" or "written" has the meaning stated in Evidence Code section 250. A "signed" writing includes an electronic sound, symbol, or process attached to or logically associated with a writing and executed, inserted, or adopted by or at the direction of a person* with the intent to sign the writing.

Comment

Firm or Law Firm**

[1] Practitioners who share office space and occasionally consult or assist each other ordinarily would not be regarded as constituting a law firm.* However, if they present themselves to the public in a way that suggests that they are a law firm* or conduct themselves as a law firm,* they may be regarded as a law firm* for purposes of these rules. The terms of any formal agreement between associated lawyers are relevant in determining whether they are a firm,* as is the fact that they have mutual access to information concerning the clients they serve.

[2] The term "of counsel" implies that the lawyer so designated has a relationship with the law firm,* other than as a partner* or associate, or officer or shareholder, that is close, personal, continuous, and regular. Whether a lawyer who is denominated as "of counsel" or by a similar term should be deemed a member of a law firm* for purposes of these rules will also depend on the specific facts. (Compare *People ex rel. Department of Corporations v. Speedee Oil Change Systems, Inc.* (1999) 20 Cal.4th 1135 [86 Cal.Rptr.2d 816] with *Chambers v. Kay* (2002) 29 Cal.4th 142 [126 Cal.Rptr.2d 536].)

*Fraud**

[3] When the terms "fraud"* or "fraudulent"* are used in these rules, it is not necessary that anyone has suffered damages or relied on the misrepresentation or failure to inform because requiring the proof of those elements of fraud* would impede the purpose of certain rules to prevent fraud* or avoid a lawyer assisting in the perpetration of a fraud,* or otherwise frustrate the imposition of discipline on lawyers who engage in fraudulent* conduct. The term "fraud"* or "fraudulent"* when used in these rules does not include merely negligent misrepresentation or negligent failure to apprise another of relevant information.

Informed Consent and Informed Written Consent**

[4] The communication necessary to obtain informed consent* or informed written consent* will vary according to the rule involved and the circumstances giving rise to the need to obtain consent.

*Screened**

[5] The purpose of screening* is to assure the affected client, former client, or prospective client that confidential information known* by the personally prohibited lawyer is neither disclosed to other law firm* lawyers or nonlawyer personnel nor used to the detriment of the person* to whom the

---

*   An asterisk (*) identifies a word or phrase defined in the terminology rule, rule 1.0.1.

duty of confidentiality is owed. The personally prohibited lawyer shall acknowledge the obligation not to communicate with any of the other lawyers and nonlawyer personnel in the law firm* with respect to the matter. Similarly, other lawyers and nonlawyer personnel in the law firm* who are working on the matter promptly shall be informed that the screening* is in place and that they may not communicate with the personally prohibited lawyer with respect to the matter. Additional screening* measures that are appropriate for the particular matter will depend on the circumstances. To implement, reinforce and remind all affected law firm* personnel of the presence of the screening,* it may be appropriate for the law firm* to undertake such procedures as a written* undertaking by the personally prohibited lawyer to avoid any communication with other law firm* personnel and any contact with any law firm* files or other materials relating to the matter, written* notice and instructions to all other law firm* personnel forbidding any communication with the personally prohibited lawyer relating to the matter, denial of access by that lawyer to law firm* files or other materials relating to the matter, and periodic reminders of the screen* to the personally prohibited lawyer and all other law firm* personnel.

[6] In order to be effective, screening* measures must be implemented as soon as practical after a lawyer or law firm* knows* or reasonably should know* that there is a need for screening.*

Rule 1.1   Competence

(a) A lawyer shall not intentionally, recklessly, with gross negligence, or repeatedly fail to perform legal services with competence.

(b) For purposes of this rule, "competence" in any legal service shall mean to apply the (i) learning and skill, and (ii) mental, emotional, and physical ability reasonably* necessary for the performance of such service.

(c) If a lawyer does not have sufficient learning and skill when the legal services are undertaken, the lawyer nonetheless may provide competent representation by (i) associating with or, where appropriate, professionally consulting another lawyer whom the lawyer reasonably believes* to be competent, (ii) acquiring sufficient learning and skill before performance is required, or (iii) referring the matter to another lawyer whom the lawyer reasonably believes* to be competent.

(d) In an emergency a lawyer may give advice or assistance in a matter in which the lawyer does not have the skill ordinarily required if referral to, or association or consultation with, another lawyer would be impractical. Assistance in an emergency must be limited to that reasonably* necessary in the circumstances.

Comment

[1] This rule addresses only a lawyer's responsibility for his or her own professional competence. See rules 5.1 and 5.3 with respect to a lawyer's disciplinary responsibility for supervising subordinate lawyers and nonlawyers.

[2] See rule 1.3 with respect to a lawyer's duty to act with reasonable* diligence.

---

*   An asterisk (*) identifies a word or phrase defined in the terminology rule, rule 1.0.1.

Rule 1.2   Scope of Representation and Allocation of Authority

(a) Subject to rule 1.2.1, a lawyer shall abide by a client's decisions concerning the objectives of representation and, as required by rule 1.4, shall reasonably* consult with the client as to the means by which they are to be pursued. Subject to Business and Professions Code section 6068, subdivision (e)(1) and rule 1.6, a lawyer may take such action on behalf of the client as is impliedly authorized to carry out the representation. A lawyer shall abide by a client's decision whether to settle a matter. Except as otherwise provided by law in a criminal case, the lawyer shall abide by the client's decision, after consultation with the lawyer, as to a plea to be entered, whether to waive jury trial and whether the client will testify.

(b) A lawyer may limit the scope of the representation if the limitation is reasonable* under the circumstances, is not otherwise prohibited by law, and the client gives informed consent.*

Comment

Allocation of Authority between Client and Lawyer

[1] Paragraph (a) confers upon the client the ultimate authority to determine the purposes to be served by legal representation, within the limits imposed by law and the lawyer's professional obligations. (See, e.g., Cal. Const., art. I, § 16; Pen. Code, § 1018.) A lawyer retained to represent a client is authorized to act on behalf of the client, such as in procedural matters and in making certain tactical decisions. A lawyer is not authorized merely by virtue of the lawyer's retention to impair the client's substantive rights or the client's claim itself. (*Blanton v. Womancare, Inc.* (1985) 38 Cal.3d 396, 404 [212 Cal.Rptr. 151, 156].)

[2] At the outset of, or during a representation, the client may authorize the lawyer to take specific action on the client's behalf without further consultation. Absent a material change in circumstances and subject to rule 1.4, a lawyer may rely on such an advance authorization. The client may revoke such authority at any time.

Independence from Client's Views or Activities

[3] A lawyer's representation of a client, including representation by appointment, does not constitute an endorsement of the client's political, economic, social or moral views or activities.

Agreements Limiting Scope of Representation

[4] All agreements concerning a lawyer's representation of a client must accord with the Rules of Professional Conduct and other law. (See, e.g., rules 1.1, 1.8.1, 5.6; see also Cal. Rules of Court, rules 3.35–3.37 [limited scope rules applicable in civil matters generally], 5.425 [limited scope rule applicable in family law matters].)

Rule 1.2.1   Advising or Assisting the Violation of Law

(a) A lawyer shall not counsel a client to engage, or assist a client in conduct that the lawyer knows* is criminal, fraudulent,* or a violation of any law. rule, or ruling of a tribunal.*

(b) Notwithstanding paragraph (a), a lawyer may:

---

*   An asterisk (*) identifies a word or phrase defined in the terminology rule, rule 1.0.1.

(1)   discuss the legal consequences of any proposed course of conduct with a client, and

(2)   counsel or assist a client to make a good faith effort to determine the validity, scope, meaning, or application of a law, rule, or ruling of a tribunal.*

Comment

[1]   There is a critical distinction under this rule between presenting an analysis of legal aspects of questionable conduct and recommending the means by which a crime or fraud* might be committed with impunity. The fact that a client uses a lawyer's advice in a course of action that is criminal or fraudulent* does not of itself make a lawyer a party to the course of action.

[2]   Paragraphs (a) and (b) apply whether or not the client's conduct has already begun and is continuing. In complying with this rule, a lawyer shall not violate the lawyer's duty under Business and Professions Code section 6068, subdivision (a) to uphold the Constitution and laws of the United States and California or the duty of confidentiality as provided in Business and Professions Code section 6068, subdivision (c)(1) and rule 1.6. In some cases, the lawyer's response is limited to the lawyer's right and, where appropriate, duty to resign or withdraw in accordance with rules 1.13 and 1.16.

[3]   Paragraph (b) authorizes a lawyer to advise a client in good faith regarding the validity, scope, meaning or application of a law, rule, or ruling of a tribunal* or of the meaning placed upon it by governmental authorities, and of potential consequences to disobedience of the law, rule, or ruling of a tribunal* that the lawyer concludes in good faith to be invalid, as well as legal procedures that may be invoked to obtain a determination of invalidity.

[4]   Paragraph (b) also authorizes a lawyer to advise a client on the consequences of violating a law, rule, or ruling of a tribunal* that the client does not contend is unenforceable or unjust in itself, as a means or protesting a law or policy the client finds objectionable. For example, a lawyer may properly advise a client about the consequences of blocking the entrance to a public building as a means of protesting a law or policy the client believes* to be unjust or invalid.

[5]   If a lawyer comes to know or reasonably should know that a client expects assistance not permitted by these rules or other law or if the lawyer intends to act contrary to the client's instructions, the lawyer must advise the client regarding the limitations on the lawyer's conduct. (See rule 1.4(a)(4).)

[6]   Paragraph (b) permits a lawyer to advise a client regarding the validity, scope, and meaning of California laws that might conflict with federal or tribal law. In the event of such a conflict, the lawyer may assist a client in drafting or administering, or interpreting or complying with California laws, including statutes, regulations, orders, and other state or local provisions, even if the client's actions might violate the conflicting federal or tribal law. If California law conflicts with federal or tribal law, the lawyer must inform the client about related federal or tribal law and policy and under certain circumstances may also be required to provide legal advice to the client regarding the conflict. (See rules 1.1 and 1.4.).

---

*   An asterisk (*) identifies a word or phrase defined in the terminology rule, rule 1.0.1.

Rule 1.3   Diligence

(a)   A lawyer shall not intentionally, repeatedly, recklessly or with gross negligence fail to act with reasonable diligence in representing a client.

(b)   For purposes of this rule, "reasonable diligence" shall mean that a lawyer acts with commitment and dedication to the interests of the client and does not neglect or disregard, or unduly delay a legal matter entrusted to the lawyer.

Comment

[1]   This rule addresses only a lawyer's responsibility for his or her own professional diligence. See rules 5.1 and 5.3 with respect to a lawyer's disciplinary responsibility for supervising subordinate lawyers and nonlawyers.

[2]   See rule 1.1 with respect to a lawyer's duty to perform legal services with competence.

Rule 1.4   Communication with Clients

(a)   A lawyer shall:

(1)   promptly inform the client of any decision or circumstance with respect to which disclosure or the client's informed consent* is required by these rules or the State Bar Act;

(2)   reasonably* consult with the client about the means by which to accomplish the client's objectives in the representation;

(3)   keep the client reasonably* informed about significant developments relating to the representation, including promptly complying with reasonable* requests for information and copies of significant documents when necessary to keep the client so informed; and

(4)   advise the client about any relevant limitation on the lawyer's conduct when the lawyer knows* that the client expects assistance not permitted by the Rules of Professional Conduct or other law.

(b)   A lawyer shall explain a matter to the extent reasonably* necessary to permit the client to make informed decisions regarding the representation.

(c)   A lawyer may delay transmission of information to a client if the lawyer reasonably believes* that the client would be likely to react in a way that may cause imminent harm to the client or others.

(d)   A lawyer's obligation under this rule to provide information and documents is subject to any applicable protective order, non-disclosure agreement, or limitation under statutory or decisional law.

Comment

[1]   A lawyer will not be subject to discipline under paragraph (a)(3) of this rule for failing to communicate insignificant or irrelevant information. (See Bus. & Prof. Code, § 6068, subd. (m).) Whether a particular development is significant will generally depend on the surrounding facts and circumstances.

[2]   A lawyer may comply with paragraph (a)(3) by providing to the client copies of significant documents by electronic or other means. This rule does

---

*   An asterisk (*) identifies a word or phrase defined in the terminology rule, rule 1.0.1.

not prohibit a lawyer from seeking recovery of the lawyer's expense in any subsequent legal proceeding.

[3] Paragraph (c) applies during a representation and does not alter the obligations applicable at termination of a representation. (See rule 1.16(e)(1).)

[4] This rule is not intended to create, augment, diminish, or eliminate any application of the work product rule. The obligation of the lawyer to provide work product to the client shall be governed by relevant statutory and decisional law.

Rule 1.4.1   Communication of Settlement Offers

(a) A lawyer shall promptly communicate to the lawyer's client:

(1) all terms and conditions of a proposed plea bargain or other dispositive offer made to the client in a criminal matter; and

(2) all amounts, terms, and conditions of any written* offer of settlement made to the client in all other matters.

(b) As used in this rule, "client" includes a person* who possesses the authority to accept an offer of settlement or plea, or, in a class action, all the named representatives of the class.

Comment

An oral offer of settlement made to the client in a civil matter must also be communicated if it is a "significant development" under rule 1.4.

Rule 1.4.2   Disclosure of Professional Liability Insurance

(a) A lawyer who knows* or reasonably should know* that the lawyer does not have professional liability insurance shall inform a client in writing,* at the time of the client's engagement of the lawyer, that the lawyer does not have professional liability insurance.

(b) If notice under paragraph (a) has not been provided at the time of a client's engagement of the lawyer, the lawyer shall inform the client in writing* within thirty days of the date the lawyer knows* or reasonably should know* that the lawyer no longer has professional liability insurance during the representation of the client.

(c) This rule does not apply to:

(1) a lawyer who knows* or reasonably should know* at the time of the client's engagement of the lawyer that the lawyer's legal representation of the client in the matter will not exceed four hours; provided that if the representation subsequently exceeds four hours, the lawyer must comply with paragraphs (a) and (b);

(2) a lawyer who is employed as a government lawyer or in-house counsel when that lawyer is representing or providing legal advice to a client in that capacity;

(3) a lawyer who is rendering legal services in an emergency to avoid foreseeable prejudice to the rights or interests of the client;

(4) a lawyer who has previously advised the client in writing* under paragraph (a) or (b) that the lawyer does not have professional liability insurance.

---

* An asterisk (*) identifies a word or phrase defined in the terminology rule, rule 1.0.1.

Comment

[1] The disclosure obligation imposed by paragraph (a) applies with respect to new clients and new engagements with returning clients.

[2] A lawyer may use the following language in making the disclosure required by paragraph (a), and may include that language in a written* fee agreement with the client or in a separate writing:

> *"Pursuant to rule 1.4.2 of the California Rules of Professional Conduct, I am informing you in writing that I do not have professional liability insurance."*

[3] A lawyer may use the following language in making the disclosure required by paragraph (b):

> *"Pursuant to rule 1.4.2 of the California Rules of Professional Conduct, I am informing you in writing that I no longer have professional liability insurance."*

[4] The exception in paragraph (c)(2) for government lawyers and in-house counsels is limited to situations involving direct employment and representation, and does not, for example, apply to outside counsel for a private or governmental entity, or to counsel retained by an insurer to represent an insured. If a lawyer is employed by and provides legal services directly for a private entity or a federal, state or local governmental entity, that entity is presumed to know* whether the lawyer is or is not covered by professional liability insurance.

Rule 1.5   Fees for Legal Services

(a) A lawyer shall not make an agreement for, charge, or collect an unconscionable or illegal fee.

(b) Unconscionability of a fee shall be determined on the basis of all the facts and circumstances existing at the time the agreement is entered into except where the parties contemplate that the fee will be affected by later events. The factors to be considered in determining the unconscionability of a fee include without limitation the following:

(1) whether the lawyer engaged in fraud* or overreaching in negotiating or setting the fee;

(2) whether the lawyer has failed to disclose material facts;

(3) the amount of the fee in proportion to the value of the services performed;

(4) the relative sophistication of the lawyer and the client;

(5) the novelty and difficulty of the questions involved, and the skill requisite to perform the legal service properly;

(6) the likelihood, if apparent to the client, that the acceptance of the particular employment will preclude other employment by the lawyer;

(7) the amount involved and the results obtained;

(8) the time limitations imposed by the client or by the circumstances;

(9) the nature and length of the professional relationship with the client;

---

*   An asterisk (*) identifies a word or phrase defined in the terminology rule, rule 1.0.1.

(10) the experience, reputation, and ability of the lawyer or lawyers performing the services;

(11) whether the fee is fixed or contingent;

(12) the time and labor required; and

(13) whether the client gave informed consent* to the fee.

(c) A lawyer shall not make an agreement for, charge, or collect:

(1) any fee in a family law matter, the payment or amount of which is contingent upon the securing of a dissolution or declaration of nullity of a marriage or upon the amount of spousal or child support, or property settlement in lieu thereof; or

(2) a contingent fee for representing a defendant in a criminal case.

(d) A lawyer may make an agreement for, charge, or collect a fee that is denominated as "earned on receipt" or "non-refundable," or in similar terms, only if the fee is a true retainer and the client agrees in writing* after disclosure that the client will not be entitled to a refund of all or part of the fee charged. A true retainer is a fee that a client pays to a lawyer to ensure the lawyer's availability to the client during a specified period or on a specified matter, but not to any extent as compensation for legal services performed or to be performed.

(e) A lawyer may make an agreement for, charge, or collect a flat fee for specified legal services. A flat fee is a fixed amount that constitutes complete payment for the performance of described services regardless of the amount of work ultimately involved, and which may be paid in whole or in part in advance of the lawyer providing those services.

Comment

Prohibited Contingent Fees

[1] Paragraph (c)(1) does not preclude a contract for a contingent fee for legal representation in connection with the recovery of post-judgment balances due under child or spousal support or other financial orders.

Payment of Fees in Advance of Services

[2] Rule 1.15(a) and (b) govern whether a lawyer must deposit in a trust account a fee paid in advance.

[3] When a lawyer-client relationship terminates, the lawyer must refund the unearned portion of a fee. (See rule 1.16(e)(2).)

Division of Fee

[4] A division of fees among lawyers is governed by rule 1.5.1.

Written* Fee Agreements

[5] Some fee agreements must be in writing* to be enforceable. (See, e.g., Bus. & Prof. Code, §§ 6147 and 6148.)

Rule 1.5.1   Fee Divisions Among Lawyers

(a) Lawyers who are not in the same law firm* shall not divide a fee for legal services unless:

(1) the lawyers enter into a written* agreement to divide the fee;

---

*   An asterisk (*) identifies a word or phrase defined in the terminology rule, rule 1.0.1.

(2)   the client has consented in writing,* either at the time the lawyers enter into the agreement to divide the fee or as soon thereafter as reasonably* practicable, after a full written* disclosure to the client of: (i) the fact that a division of fees will be made; (ii) the identity of the lawyers or law firms* that are parties to the division; and (iii) the terms of the division; and

(3)   the total fee charged by all lawyers is not increased solely by reason of the agreement to divide fees.

(b)   This rule does not apply to a division of fees pursuant to court order.

Comment

The writing* requirements of paragraphs (a)(1) and (a)(2) may be satisfied by one or more writings.*

Rule 1.6   Confidential Information of a Client

(a)   A lawyer shall not reveal information protected from disclosure by Business and Professions Code section 6068, subdivision (e)(1) unless the client gives informed consent,* or the disclosure is permitted by paragraph (b) of this rule.

(b)   A lawyer may, but is not required to, reveal information protected by Business and Professions Code section 6068, subdivision (e)(1) to the extent that the lawyer reasonably believes* the disclosure is necessary to prevent a criminal act that the lawyer reasonably believes* is likely to result in death of, or substantial* bodily harm to, an individual, as provided in paragraph (c).

(c)   Before revealing information protected by Business and Professions Code section 6068, subdivision (e)(1) to prevent a criminal act as provided in paragraph (b), a lawyer shall, if reasonable* under the circumstances:

(1)   make a good faith effort to persuade the client: (i) not to commit or to continue the criminal act; or (ii) to pursue a course of conduct that will prevent the threatened death or substantial* bodily harm; or do both (i) and (ii); and

(2)   inform the client, at an appropriate time, of the lawyer's ability or decision to reveal information protected by Business and Professions Code section 6068, subdivision (e)(1) as provided in paragraph (b).

(d)   In revealing information protected by Business and Professions Code section 6068, subdivision (e)(1) as provided in paragraph (b), the lawyer's disclosure must be no more than is necessary to prevent the criminal act, given the information known* to the lawyer at the time of the disclosure.

(e)   A lawyer who does not reveal information permitted by paragraph (b) does not violate this rule.

Comment

Duty of confidentiality

[1]   Paragraph (a) relates to a lawyer's obligations under Business and Professions Code section 6068, subdivision (e)(1), which provides it is a duty of a lawyer: "To maintain inviolate the confidence, and at every peril to himself or herself to preserve the secrets, of his or her client." A lawyer's duty to preserve the confidentiality of client information involves public policies of

---

* An asterisk (*) identifies a word or phrase defined in the terminology rule, rule 1.0.1.

paramount importance. (*In Re Jordan* (1974) 12 Cal.3d 575, 580 [116 Cal.Rptr. 371].) Preserving the confidentiality of client information contributes to the trust that is the hallmark of the lawyer-client relationship. The client is thereby encouraged to seek legal assistance and to communicate fully and frankly with the lawyer even as to embarrassing or detrimental subjects. The lawyer needs this information to represent the client effectively and, if necessary, to advise the client to refrain from wrongful conduct. Almost without exception, clients come to lawyers in order to determine their rights and what is, in the complex of laws and regulations, deemed to be legal and correct. Based upon experience, lawyers know* that almost all clients follow the advice given, and the law is upheld. Paragraph (a) thus recognizes a fundamental principle in the lawyer-client relationship, that, in the absence of the client's informed consent,* a lawyer must not reveal information protected by Business and Professions Code section 6068, subdivision (e)(1). (See, e.g., *Commercial Standard Title Co. v. Superior Court* (1979) 92 Cal.App.3d 934, 945 [155 Cal.Rptr.393].)

Lawyer-client confidentiality encompasses the lawyer-client privilege, the work-product doctrine and ethical standards of confidentiality

[2]   The principle of lawyer-client confidentiality applies to information a lawyer acquires by virtue of the representation, whatever its source, and encompasses matters communicated in confidence by the client, and therefore protected by the lawyer-client privilege, matters protected by the work product doctrine, and matters protected under ethical standards of confidentiality, all as established in law, rule and policy. (See *In the Matter of Johnson* (Rev. Dept. 2000) 4 Cal. State Bar Ct. Rptr. 179; *Goldstein v. Lees* (1975) 46 Cal.App.3d 614, 621 [120 Cal.Rptr. 253].) The lawyer-client privilege and work-product doctrine apply in judicial and other proceedings in which a lawyer may be called as a witness or be otherwise compelled to produce evidence concerning a client. A lawyer's ethical duty of confidentiality is not so limited in its scope of protection for the lawyer-client relationship of trust and prevents a lawyer from revealing the client's information even when not subjected to such compulsion. Thus, a lawyer may not reveal such information except with the informed consent* of the client or as authorized or required by the State Bar Act, these rules, or other law.

Narrow exception to duty of confidentiality under this rule

[3]   Notwithstanding the important public policies promoted by lawyers adhering to the core duty of confidentiality, the overriding value of life permits disclosures otherwise prohibited by Business and Professions Code section 6068, subdivision (e)(1). Paragraph (b) is based on Business and Professions Code section 6068, subdivision (e)(2), which narrowly permits a lawyer to disclose information protected by Business and Professions Code section 6068, subdivision (e)(1) even without client consent. Evidence Code section 956.5, which relates to the evidentiary lawyer-client privilege, sets forth a similar express exception. Although a lawyer is not permitted to reveal information protected by section 6068, subdivision (e)(1) concerning a client's past, completed criminal acts, the policy favoring the preservation of human life that underlies this exception to the duty of confidentiality and the evidentiary privilege permits disclosure to prevent a future or ongoing criminal act.

---

*   An asterisk (*) identifies a word or phrase defined in the terminology rule, rule 1.0.1.

Lawyer not subject to discipline for revealing information protected by Business and Professions Code section 6068, subdivision (e)(1) as permitted under this rule

[4]   Paragraph (b) reflects a balancing between the interests of preserving client confidentiality and of preventing a criminal act that a lawyer reasonably believes* is likely to result in death or substantial* bodily harm to an individual. A lawyer who reveals information protected by Business and Professions Code section 6068, subdivision (e)(1) as permitted under this rule is not subject to discipline.

No duty to reveal information protected by Business and Professions Code section 6068, subdivision (e)(1)

[5]   Neither Business and Professions Code section 6068, subdivision (e)(2) nor paragraph (b) imposes an affirmative obligation on a lawyer to reveal information protected by Business and Professions Code section 6068, subdivision (e)(1) in order to prevent harm. A lawyer may decide not to reveal such information. Whether a lawyer chooses to reveal information protected by section 6068, subdivision (e)(1) as permitted under this rule is a matter for the individual lawyer to decide, based on all the facts and circumstances, such as those discussed in Comment [6] of this rule.

Whether to reveal information protected by Business and Professions Code section 6068, subdivision (e) as permitted under paragraph (b)

[6]   Disclosure permitted under paragraph (b) is ordinarily a last resort, when no other available action is reasonably* likely to prevent the criminal act. Prior to revealing information protected by Business and Professions Code section 6068, subdivision (e)(1) as permitted by paragraph (b), the lawyer must, if reasonable* under the circumstances, make a good faith effort to persuade the client to take steps to avoid the criminal act or threatened harm. Among the factors to be considered in determining whether to disclose information protected by section 6068, subdivision (e)(1) are the following:

  (1)   the amount of time that the lawyer has to make a decision about disclosure;

  (2)   whether the client or a third-party has made similar threats before and whether they have ever acted or attempted to act upon them;

  (3)   whether the lawyer believes* the lawyer's efforts to persuade the client or a third person* not to engage in the criminal conduct have or have not been successful;

  (4)   the extent of adverse effect to the client's rights under the Fifth, Sixth and Fourteenth Amendments of the United States Constitution and analogous rights and privacy rights under Article I of the Constitution of the State of California that may result from disclosure contemplated by the lawyer;

  (5)   the extent of other adverse effects to the client that may result from disclosure contemplated by the lawyer; and

  (6)   the nature and extent of information that must be disclosed to prevent the criminal act or threatened harm.

A lawyer may also consider whether the prospective harm to the victim or victims is imminent in deciding whether to disclose the information protected by section 6068, subdivision (e)(1). However, the imminence of the harm is

---

  *   An asterisk (*) identifies a word or phrase defined in the terminology rule, rule 1.0.1.

not a prerequisite to disclosure and a lawyer may disclose the information protected by section 6068, subdivision (e)(1) without waiting until immediately before the harm is likely to occur.

Whether to counsel client or third person* not to commit a criminal act reasonably* likely to result in death or substantial* bodily harm

[7] Subparagraph (c)(1) provides that before a lawyer may reveal information protected by Business and Professions Code section 6068, subdivision (e)(1), the lawyer must, if reasonable* under the circumstances, make a good faith effort to persuade the client not to commit or to continue the criminal act, or to persuade the client to otherwise pursue a course of conduct that will prevent the threatened death or substantial* bodily harm, including persuading the client to take action to prevent a third person* from committing or continuing a criminal act. If necessary, the client may be persuaded to do both. The interests protected by such counseling are the client's interests in limiting disclosure of information protected by section 6068, subdivision (e) and in taking responsible action to deal with situations attributable to the client. If a client, whether in response to the lawyer's counseling or otherwise, takes corrective action—such as by ceasing the client's own criminal act or by dissuading a third person* from committing or continuing a criminal act before harm is caused—the option for permissive disclosure by the lawyer would cease because the threat posed by the criminal act would no longer be present. When the actor is a nonclient or when the act is deliberate or malicious, the lawyer who contemplates making adverse disclosure of protected information may reasonably* conclude that the compelling interests of the lawyer or others in their own personal safety preclude personal contact with the actor. Before counseling an actor who is a nonclient, the lawyer should, if reasonable* under the circumstances, first advise the client of the lawyer's intended course of action. If a client or another person* has already acted but the intended harm has not yet occurred, the lawyer should consider, if reasonable* under the circumstances, efforts to persuade the client or third person* to warn the victim or consider other appropriate action to prevent the harm. Even when the lawyer has concluded that paragraph (b) does not permit the lawyer to reveal information protected by section 6068, subdivision (e)(1), the lawyer nevertheless is permitted to counsel the client as to why it may be in the client's best interest to consent to the attorney's disclosure of that information.

Disclosure of information protected by Business and Professions Code section 6068, subdivision (e)(1) must be no more than is reasonably* necessary to prevent the criminal act

[8] Paragraph (d) requires that disclosure of information protected by Business and Professions Code section 6068, subdivision (e) as permitted by paragraph (b), when made, must be no more extensive than is necessary to prevent the criminal act. Disclosure should allow access to the information to only those persons* who the lawyer reasonably believes* can act to prevent the harm. Under some circumstances, a lawyer may determine that the best course to pursue is to make an anonymous disclosure to the potential victim or relevant law-enforcement authorities. What particular measures are reasonable* depends on the circumstances known* to the lawyer. Relevant circumstances include the time available, whether the victim might be unaware of the threat, the lawyer's prior course of dealings with the client,

---

*   An asterisk (*) identifies a word or phrase defined in the terminology rule, rule 1.0.1.

and the extent of the adverse effect on the client that may result from the disclosure contemplated by the lawyer.

Informing client pursuant to subparagraph (c)(2) of lawyer's ability or decision to reveal information protected by Business and Professions Code section 6068, subdivision (e)(1)

[9] A lawyer is required to keep a client reasonably* informed about significant developments regarding the representation. (See rule 1.4; Bus. & Prof. Code, § 6068, subd. (m).) Paragraph (c)(2), however, recognizes that under certain circumstances, informing a client of the lawyer's ability or decision to reveal information protected by section 6068, subdivision (e)(1) as permitted in paragraph (b) would likely increase the risk of death or substantial* bodily harm, not only to the originally-intended victims of the criminal act, but also to the client or members of the client's family, or to the lawyer or the lawyer's family or associates. Therefore, paragraph (c)(2) requires a lawyer to inform the client of the lawyer's ability or decision to reveal information protected by section 6068, subdivision (e)(1) as permitted in paragraph (b) only if it is reasonable* to do so under the circumstances. Paragraph (c)(2) further recognizes that the appropriate time for the lawyer to inform the client may vary depending upon the circumstances. (See Comment [10] of this rule.) Among the factors to be considered in determining an appropriate time, if any, to inform a client are:

(1) whether the client is an experienced user of legal services;

(2) the frequency of the lawyer's contact with the client;

(3) the nature and length of the professional relationship with the client;

(4) whether the lawyer and client have discussed the lawyer's duty of confidentiality or any exceptions to that duty;

(5) the likelihood that the client's matter will involve information within paragraph (b);

(6) the lawyer's belief,* if applicable, that so informing the client is likely to increase the likelihood that a criminal act likely to result in the death of, or substantial* bodily harm to, an individual; and

(7) the lawyer's belief,* if applicable, that good faith efforts to persuade a client not to act on a threat have failed.

Avoiding a chilling effect on the lawyer-client relationship

[10] The foregoing flexible approach to the lawyer's informing a client of his or her ability or decision to reveal information protected by Business and Professions Code section 6068, subdivision (e)(1) recognizes the concern that informing a client about limits on confidentiality may have a chilling effect on client communication. (See Comment [1].) To avoid that chilling effect, one lawyer may choose to inform the client of the lawyer's ability to reveal information protected by section 6068, subdivision (e)(1) as early as the outset of the representation, while another lawyer may choose to inform a client only at a point when that client has imparted information that comes within paragraph (b), or even choose not to inform a client until such time as the lawyer attempts to counsel the client as contemplated in Comment [7]. In each situation, the lawyer will have satisfied the lawyer's obligation under paragraph (c)(2), and will not be subject to discipline.

---

* An asterisk (*) identifies a word or phrase defined in the terminology rule, rule 1.0.1.

Informing client that disclosure has been made; termination of the lawyer-client relationship

[11] When a lawyer has revealed information protected by Business and Professions Code section 6068, subdivision (e) as permitted in paragraph (b), in all but extraordinary cases the relationship between lawyer and client that is based on trust and confidence will have deteriorated so as to make the lawyer's representation of the client impossible. Therefore, when the relationship has deteriorated because of the lawyer's disclosure, the lawyer is required to seek to withdraw from the representation, unless the client has given informed consent* to the lawyer's continued representation. The lawyer normally must inform the client of the fact of the lawyer's disclosure. If the lawyer has a compelling interest in not informing the client, such as to protect the lawyer, the lawyer's family or a third person* from the risk of death or substantial* bodily harm, the lawyer must withdraw from the representation. (See rule 1.16.)

Other consequences of the lawyer's disclosure

[12] Depending upon the circumstances of a lawyer's disclosure of information protected by Business and Professions Code section 6068, subdivision (e)(1) as permitted by this rule, there may be other important issues that a lawyer must address. For example, a lawyer who is likely to testify as a witness in a matter involving a client must comply with rule. 3.7. Similarly, the lawyer must also consider his or her duties of loyalty and competence. (See rules 1.7 and 1.1.)

Other exceptions to confidentiality under California law

[13] This rule is not intended to augment, diminish, or preclude any other exceptions to the duty to preserve information protected by Business and Professions Code section 6068, subdivision (e)(1) recognized under California law.

Rule 1.7   Conflict of Interest: Current Clients

(a)   A lawyer shall not, without informed written consent* from each client and compliance with paragraph (d), represent a client if the representation is directly adverse to another client in the same or a separate matter.

(b)   A lawyer shall not, without informed written consent* from each affected client and compliance with paragraph (d), represent a client if there is a significant risk the lawyer's representation of the client will be materially limited by the lawyer's responsibilities to or relationships with another client, a former client or a third person,* or by the lawyer's own interests.

(c)   Even when a significant risk requiring a lawyer to comply with paragraph (b) is not present, a lawyer shall not represent a client without written* disclosure of the relationship to the client and compliance with paragraph (d) where:

(1)   the lawyer has, or knows* that another lawyer in the lawyer's firm* has, a legal, business, financial, professional, or personal relationship with or responsibility to a party or witness in the same matter; or

(2)   the lawyer knows* or reasonably should know* that another party's lawyer is a spouse, parent, child, or sibling of the lawyer, lives with the lawyer, is a client of the lawyer or another lawyer in the lawyer's firm,* or has an intimate personal relationship with the lawyer.

---

*   An asterisk (*) identifies a word or phrase defined in the terminology rule, rule 1.0.1.

(d)   Representation is permitted under this rule only if the lawyer complies with paragraphs (a), (b), and (c), and:

(1)   the lawyer reasonably believes* that the lawyer will be able to provide competent and diligent representation to each affected client;

(2)   the representation is not prohibited by law; and

(3)   the representation does not involve the assertion of a claim by one client against another client represented by the lawyer in the same litigation or other proceeding before a tribunal.

(e)   For purposes of this rule, "matter" includes any judicial or other proceeding, application, request for a ruling or other determination, contract, transaction, claim, controversy, investigation, charge, accusation, arrest, or other deliberation, decision, or action that is focused on the interests of specific persons,* or a discrete and identifiable class of persons.*

Comment

[1]   Loyalty and independent judgment are essential elements in the lawyer's relationship to a client. The duty of undivided loyalty to a current client prohibits undertaking representation directly adverse to that client without that client's informed written consent.* Thus, absent consent, a lawyer may not act as an advocate in one matter against a person* the lawyer represents in some other matter, even when the matters are wholly unrelated. (See *Flatt v. Superior Court* (1994) 9 Cal.4th 275 [36 Cal.Rptr.2d 537].) A directly adverse conflict under paragraph (a) can arise in a number of ways, for example, when: (i) a lawyer accepts representation of more than one client in a matter in which the interests of the clients actually conflict; (ii) a lawyer, while representing a client, accepts in another matter the representation of a person* who, in the first matter, is directly adverse to the lawyer's client; or (iii) a lawyer accepts representation of a person* in a matter in which an opposing party is a client of the lawyer or the lawyer's law firm.* Similarly, direct adversity can arise when a lawyer cross-examines a nonparty witness who is the lawyer's client in another matter, if the examination is likely to harm or embarrass the witness. On the other hand, simultaneous representation in unrelated matters of clients whose interests are only economically adverse, such as representation of competing economic enterprises in unrelated litigation, does not ordinarily constitute a conflict of interest and thus may not require informed written consent* of the respective clients.

[2]   Paragraphs (a) and (b) apply to all types of legal representations, including the concurrent representation of multiple parties in litigation or in a single transaction or in some other common enterprise or legal relationship. Examples of the latter include the formation of a partnership for several partners* or a corporation for several shareholders, the preparation of a pre-nuptial agreement, or joint or reciprocal wills for a husband and wife, or the resolution of an "uncontested" marital dissolution. If a lawyer initially represents multiple clients with the informed written consent* as required under paragraph (b), and circumstances later develop indicating that direct adversity exists between the clients, the lawyer must obtain further informed written consent* of the clients under paragraph (a).

[3]   In *State Farm Mutual Automobile Insurance Company v. Federal Insurance Company* (1999) 72 Cal.App.4th 1422 [86 Cal.Rptr.2d 20], the court held that subparagraph (C)(3) of predecessor rule 3–310 was violated when a

---

*   An asterisk (*) identifies a word or phrase defined in the terminology rule, rule 1.0.1.

lawyer, retained by an insurer to defend one suit, and while that suit was still pending, filed a direct action against the same insurer in an unrelated action without securing the insurer's consent. Notwithstanding *State Farm*, paragraph (a) does not apply with respect to the relationship between an insurer and a lawyer when, in each matter, the insurer's interest is only as an indemnity provider and not as a direct party to the action.

[4] Even where there is no direct adversity, a conflict of interest requiring informed written consent* under paragraph (b) exists if there is a significant risk that a lawyer's ability to consider, recommend or carry out an appropriate course of action for the client will be materially limited as a result of the lawyer's other responsibilities, interests, or relationships, whether legal, business, financial, professional, or personal. For example, a lawyer's obligations to two or more clients in the same matter, such as several individuals seeking to form a joint venture, may materially limit the lawyer's ability to recommend or advocate all possible positions that each might take because of the lawyer's duty of loyalty to the other clients. The risk is that the lawyer may not be able to offer alternatives that would otherwise be available to each of the clients. The mere possibility of subsequent harm does not itself require disclosure and informed written consent.* The critical questions are the likelihood that a difference in interests exists or will eventuate and, if it does, whether it will materially interfere with the lawyer's independent professional judgment in considering alternatives or foreclose courses of action that reasonably* should be pursued on behalf of each client. The risk that the lawyer's representation may be materially limited may also arise from present or past relationships between the lawyer, or another member of the lawyer's firm*, with a party, a witness, or another person* who may be affected substantially by the resolution of the matter.

[5] Paragraph (c) requires written* disclosure of any of the specified relationships even if there is not a significant risk the relationship will materially limit the lawyer's representation of the client. However, if the particular circumstances present a significant risk the relationship will materially limit the lawyer's representation of the client, informed written consent* is required under paragraph (b).

[6] Ordinarily paragraphs (a) and (b) will not require informed written consent* simply because a lawyer takes inconsistent legal positions in different tribunals* at different times on behalf of different clients. Advocating a legal position on behalf of a client that might create precedent adverse to the interests of another client represented by a lawyer in an unrelated matter is not sufficient, standing alone, to create a conflict of interest requiring informed written consent.* Informed written consent* may be required, however, if there is a significant risk that: (i) the lawyer may temper the lawyer's advocacy on behalf of one client out of concern about creating precedent adverse to the interest of another client; or (ii) the lawyer's action on behalf of one client will materially limit the lawyer's effectiveness in representing another client in a different case, for example, when a decision favoring one client will create a precedent likely to seriously weaken the position taken on behalf of the other client. Factors relevant in determining whether the clients' informed written consent* is required include: the courts and jurisdictions where the different cases are pending, whether a ruling in one case would have a precedential effect on the other case, whether the legal question is substantive or procedural, the temporal relationship between the matters, the significance of the legal question to the

---

* An asterisk (*) identifies a word or phrase defined in the terminology rule, rule 1.0.1.

immediate and long-term interests of the clients involved, and the clients' reasonable* expectations in retaining the lawyer.

[7]   Other rules and laws may preclude the disclosures necessary to obtain the informed written consent* or provide the information required to permit representation under this rule. (See, e.g., Bus. & Prof. Code, § 6068, subd. (e)(1) and rule 1.6.) If such disclosure is precluded, representation subject to paragraph (a), (b), or (c) of this rule is likewise precluded.

[8]   Paragraph (d) imposes conditions that must be satisfied even if informed written consent* is obtained as required by paragraphs (a) or (b) or the lawyer has informed the client in writing* as required by paragraph (c). There are some matters in which the conflicts are such that even informed written consent* may not suffice to permit representation. (See *Woods v. Superior Court* (1983) 149 Cal.App.3d 931 [197 Cal.Rptr. 185]; *Klemm v. Superior Court* (1977) 75 Cal.App.3d 893 [142 Cal.Rptr. 509]; *Ishmael v. Millington* (1966) 241 Cal.App.2d 520 [50 Cal.Rptr. 592].)

[9]   This rule does not preclude an informed written consent* to a future conflict in compliance with applicable case law. The effectiveness of an advance consent is generally determined by the extent to which the client reasonably* understands the material risks that the consent entails. The more comprehensive the explanation of the types of future representations that might arise and the actual and reasonably* foreseeable adverse consequences to the client of those representations, the greater the likelihood that the client will have the requisite understanding. The experience and sophistication of the client giving consent, as well as whether the client is independently represented in connection with giving consent, are also relevant in determining whether the client reasonably* understands the risks involved in giving consent. An advance consent cannot be effective if the circumstances that materialize in the future make the conflict nonconsentable under paragraph (d). A lawyer who obtains from a client an advance consent that complies with this rule will have all the duties of a lawyer to that client except as expressly limited by the consent. A lawyer cannot obtain an advance consent to incompetent representation. (See rule 1.8.8.)

[10] A material change in circumstances relevant to application of this rule may trigger a requirement to make new disclosures and, where applicable, obtain new informed written consents.* In the absence of such consents, depending on the circumstances, the lawyer may have the option to withdraw from one or more of the representations in order to avoid the conflict. The lawyer must seek court approval where necessary and take steps to minimize harm to the clients. See rule 1.16. The lawyer must continue to protect the confidences of the clients from whose representation the lawyer has withdrawn. (See rule 1.9(c).)

[11] For special rules governing membership in a legal service organization, see rule 6.3; and for work in conjunction with certain limited legal services programs, see rule 6.5.

Rule 1.8.1   Business Transactions with a Client and Pecuniary Interests Adverse to a Client

A lawyer shall not enter into a business transaction with a client, or knowingly* acquire an ownership, possessory, security or other pecuniary

---

*   An asterisk (*) identifies a word or phrase defined in the terminology rule, rule 1.0.1.

interest adverse to a client, unless each of the following requirements has been satisfied:

(a)   the transaction or acquisition and its terms are fair and reasonable* to the client and the terms and the lawyer's role in the transaction or acquisition are fully disclosed and transmitted in writing* to the client in a manner that should reasonably* have been understood by the client;

(b)   the client either is represented in the transaction or acquisition by an independent lawyer of the client's choice or the client is advised in writing* to seek the advice of an independent lawyer of the client's choice and is given a reasonable* opportunity to seek that advice; and

(c)   the client thereafter provides informed written consent* to the terms of the transaction or acquisition, and to the lawyer's role in it.

Comment

[1]   A lawyer has an "other pecuniary interest adverse to a client" within the meaning of this rule when the lawyer possesses a legal right to significantly impair or prejudice the client's rights or interests without court action. (See *Fletcher v. Davis* (2004) 33 Cal.4th 61, 68 [14 Cal.Rptr.3d 58]; see also Bus. & Prof. Code, § 6175.3 [Sale of financial products to elder or dependent adult clients; Disclosure]; Fam. Code, §§ 2033–2034 [Attorney lien on community real property].) However, this rule does not apply to a charging lien given to secure payment of a contingency fee. (See *Plummer v. Day/Eisenberg, LLP* (2010) 184 Cal.App.4th 38 [108 Cal.Rptr.3d 455].)

[2]   For purposes of this rule, factors that can be considered in determining whether a lawyer is independent include whether the lawyer: (i) has a financial interest in the transaction or acquisition; and (ii) has a close legal, business, financial, professional or personal relationship with the lawyer seeking the client's consent.

[3]   Fairness and reasonableness under paragraph (a) are measured at the time of the transaction or acquisition based on the facts that then exist.

[4]   In some circumstances, this rule may apply to a transaction entered into with a former client. (Compare *Hunniecutt v. State Bar* (1988) 44 Cal.3d 362, 370–71 ["[W]hen an attorney enters into a transaction with a former client regarding a fund which resulted from the attorney's representation, it is reasonable to examine the relationship between the parties for indications of special trust resulting therefrom. We conclude that if there is evidence that the client placed his trust in the attorney because of the representation, an attorney-client relationship exists for the purposes of [the predecessor rule) even if the representation has otherwise ended [and] It appears that [the client] became a target of [the lawyer's] solicitation because he knew, through his representation of her, that she had recently received the settlement fund [and the court also found the client to be unsophisticated]."] with *Wallis v. State Bar* (1942) 21 Cal.2d 322 [finding lawyer not subject to discipline for entering into business transaction with a former client where the former client was a sophisticated businesswoman who had actively negotiated for terms she thought desirable, and the transaction was not connected with the matter on which the lawyer previously represented her].)

[5]   This rule does not apply to the agreement by which the lawyer is retained by the client, unless the agreement confers on the lawyer an ownership, possessory, security, or other pecuniary interest adverse to the

---

*   An asterisk (*) identifies a word or phrase defined in the terminology rule, rule 1.0.1.

client. Such an agreement is governed, in part, by rule 1.5. This rule also does not apply to an agreement to advance to or deposit with a lawyer a sum to be applied to fees, or costs or other expenses, to be incurred in the future. Such agreements are governed, in part, by rules 1.5 and 1.15.

[6]   This rule does not apply: (i) where a lawyer and client each make an investment on terms offered by a third person* to the general public or a significant portion thereof; or (ii) to standard commercial transactions for products or services that a lawyer acquires from a client on the same terms that the client generally markets them to others, where the lawyer has no advantage in dealing with the client.

Rule 1.8.2   Use of Current Client's Information

A lawyer shall not use a client's information protected by Business and Professions Code section 6068, subdivision (e)(1) to the disadvantage of the client unless the client gives informed consent,* except as permitted by these rules or the State Bar Act.

Comment

A lawyer violates the duty of loyalty by using information protected by Business and Professions Code section 6068, subdivision (e)(1) to the disadvantage of a current client.

Rule 1.8.3   Gifts From Client

(a)   A lawyer shall not:

(1)   solicit a client to make a substantial* gift, including a testamentary gift, to the lawyer or a person* related to the lawyer, unless the lawyer or other recipient of the gift is related to the client, or

(2)   prepare on behalf of a client an instrument giving the lawyer or a person* related to the lawyer any substantial* gift, unless (i) the lawyer or other recipient of the gift is related to the client, or (ii) the client has been advised by an independent lawyer who has provided a certificate of independent review that complies with the requirements of Probate Code section 21384.

(b)   For purposes of this rule, related persons* include a person* who is "related by blood or affinity" as that term is defined in California Probate Code section 21374, subdivision (a).

Comment

[1]   A lawyer or a person* related to a lawyer may accept a gift from the lawyer's client, subject to general standards of fairness and absence of undue influence. A lawyer also does not violate this rule merely by engaging in conduct that might result in a client making a gift, such as by sending the client a wedding announcement. Discipline is appropriate where impermissible influence occurs. (See *Magee v. State Bar* (1962) 58 Cal.2d 423 [24 Cal.Rptr. 839].)

[2]   This rule does not prohibit a lawyer from seeking to have the lawyer or a partner* or associate of the lawyer named as executor of the client's estate or to another potentially lucrative fiduciary position. Such appointments, however, will be subject to rule 1.7(b) and (c).

---

*   An asterisk (*) identifies a word or phrase defined in the terminology rule, rule 1.0.1.

Rule 1.8.4   [Reserved]

Rule 1.8.5   Payment of Personal or Business Expenses Incurred by or for a Client

(a)   A lawyer shall not directly or indirectly pay or agree to pay, guarantee, or represent that the lawyer or lawyer's law firm* will pay the personal or business expenses of a prospective or existing client.

(b)   Notwithstanding paragraph (a), a lawyer may:

(1)   pay or agree to pay such expenses to third persons,* from funds collected or to be collected for the client as a result of the representation, with the consent of the client;

(2)   after the lawyer is retained by the client, agree to lend money to the client based on the client's written* promise to repay the loan, provided the lawyer complies with rules 1.7(b), 1.7(c), and 1.8.1 before making the loan or agreeing to do so;

(3)   advance the costs of prosecuting or defending a claim or action, or of otherwise protecting or promoting the client's interests, the repayment of which may be contingent on the outcome of the matter; and

(4)   pay the costs of prosecuting or defending a claim or action, or of otherwise protecting or promoting the interests of an indigent person* in a matter in which the lawyer represents the client.

(c)   "Costs" within the meaning of paragraphs (b)(3) and (b)(4) are not limited to those costs that are taxable or recoverable under any applicable statute or rule of court but may include any reasonable* expenses of litigation, including court costs, and reasonable* expenses in preparing for litigation or in providing other legal services to the client.

(d)   Nothing in this rule shall be deemed to limit the application of rule 1.8.9.

Rule 1.8.6   Compensation from One Other Than Client

A lawyer shall not enter into an agreement for, charge, or accept compensation for representing a client from one other than the client unless:

(a)   there is no interference with the lawyer's independent professional judgment or with the lawyer-client relationship;

(b)   information is protected as required by Business and Professions Code section 6068, subdivision (e)(1) and rule 1.6; and

(c)   the lawyer obtains the client's informed written consent* at or before the time the lawyer has entered into the agreement for, charged, or accepted the compensation, or as soon thereafter as reasonably* practicable, provided that no disclosure or consent is required if:

(1)   nondisclosure or the compensation is otherwise authorized by law or a court order; or

(2)   the lawyer is rendering legal services on behalf of any public agency or nonprofit organization that provides legal services to other public agencies or the public.

---

*   An asterisk (*) identifies a word or phrase defined in the terminology rule, rule 1.0.1.

Comment

[1]   A lawyer's responsibilities in a matter are owed only to the client except where the lawyer also represents the payor in the same matter. With respect to the lawyer's additional duties when representing both the client and the payor in the same matter, see rule 1.7.

[2]   A lawyer who is exempt from disclosure and consent requirements under paragraph (c) nevertheless must comply with paragraphs (a) and (b).

[3]   This rule is not intended to abrogate existing relationships between insurers and insureds whereby the insurer has the contractual right to unilaterally select counsel for the insured, where there is no conflict of interest. (See *San Diego Navy Federal Credit Union v. Cumis Insurance Society* (1984) 162 Cal.App.3d 358 [208 Cal.Rptr. 494].).

[4]   In some limited circumstances, a lawyer might not be able to obtain client consent before the lawyer has entered into an agreement for, charged, or accepted compensation, as required by this rule. This might happen, for example, when a lawyer is retained or paid by a family member on behalf of an incarcerated client or in certain commercial settings, such as when a lawyer is retained by a creditors' committee involved in a corporate debt restructuring and agrees to be compensated for any services to be provided to other similarly situated creditors who have not yet been identified. In such limited situations, paragraph (c) permits the lawyer to comply with this rule as soon thereafter as is reasonably* practicable.

[5]   This rule is not intended to alter or diminish a lawyer's obligations under rule 5.4(c).

Rule 1.8.7   Aggregate Settlements

(a)   A lawyer who represents two or more clients shall not enter into an aggregate settlement of the claims of or against the clients, or in a criminal case an aggregate agreement as to guilty or nolo contendere pleas, unless each client gives informed written consent.* The lawyer's disclosure shall include the existence and nature of all the claims or pleas involved and of the participation of each person* in the settlement.

(b)   This rule does not apply to class action settlements subject to court approval.

Rule 1.8.8   Limiting Liability to Client

A lawyer shall not:

(a)   Contract with a client prospectively limiting the lawyer's liability to the client for the lawyer's professional malpractice; or

(b)   Settle a claim or potential claim for the lawyer's liability to a client or former client for the lawyer's professional malpractice, unless the client or former client is either:

   (1)   represented by an independent lawyer concerning the settlement; or

   (2)   advised in writing* by the lawyer to seek the advice of an independent lawyer of the client's choice regarding the settlement and given a reasonable* opportunity to seek that advice.

---

*   An asterisk (*) identifies a word or phrase defined in the terminology rule, rule 1.0.1.

Comment

[1]   Paragraph (b) does not absolve the lawyer of the obligation to comply with other law. (See, e.g., Bus. & Prof. Code, § 6090.5.)

[2]   This rule does not apply to customary qualifications and limitations in legal opinions and memoranda, nor does it prevent a lawyer from reasonably* limiting the scope of the lawyer's representation. (See rule 1.2(b).)

Rule 1.8.9   Purchasing Property at a Foreclosure or a Sale Subject to Judicial Review

(a)   A lawyer shall not directly or indirectly purchase property at a probate, foreclosure, receiver's, trustee's, or judicial sale in an action or proceeding in which such lawyer or any lawyer affiliated by reason of personal, business, or professional relationship with that lawyer or with that lawyer's law firm* is acting as a lawyer for a party or as executor, receiver, trustee, administrator, guardian, or conservator.

(b)   A lawyer shall not represent the seller at a probate, foreclosure, receiver, trustee, or judicial sale in an action or proceeding in which the purchaser is a spouse or relative of the lawyer or of another lawyer in the lawyer's law firm* or is an employee of the lawyer or the lawyer's law firm.*

(c)   This rule does not prohibit a lawyer's participation in transactions that are specifically authorized by and comply with Probate Code sections 9880 through 9885, but such transactions remain subject to the provisions of rules 1.8.1 and 1.7.

Comment

A lawyer may lawfully participate in a transaction involving a probate proceeding which concerns a client by following the process described in Probate Code sections 9880–9885. These provisions, which permit what would otherwise be impermissible self-dealing by specific submissions to and approval by the courts, must be strictly followed in order to avoid violation of this rule.

Rule 1.8.10   Sexual Relations With Current Client

(a)   A lawyer shall not engage in sexual relations with a current client who is not the lawyer's spouse or registered domestic partner, unless a consensual sexual relationship existed between them when the lawyer-client relationship commenced.

(b)   For purposes of this rule, "sexual relations" means sexual intercourse or the touching of an intimate part of another person* for the purpose of sexual arousal, gratification, or abuse.

(c)   If a person* other than the client alleges a violation of this rule, no Notice of Disciplinary Charges may be filed by the State Bar against a lawyer under this rule until the State Bar has attempted to obtain the client's statement regarding, and has considered, whether the client would be unduly burdened by further investigation or a charge.

Comment

[1]   Although this rule does not apply to a consensual sexual relationship that exists when a lawyer-client relationship commences, the lawyer

---

*   An asterisk (*) identifies a word or phrase defined in the terminology rule, rule 1.0.1.

nevertheless must comply with all other applicable rules. (See, e.g., rules 1.1, 1.7, and 2.1.)

[2]   When the client is an organization, this rule applies to a lawyer for the organization (whether inside counsel or outside counsel) who has sexual relations with a constituent of the organization who supervises, directs or regularly consults with that lawyer concerning the organization's legal matters. (See rule 1.13.)

[3]   Business and Professions Code section 6106.9, including the requirement that the complaint be verified, applies to charges under subdivision (a) of that section. This rule and the statute impose different obligations.

Rule 1.8.11   Imputation of Prohibitions Under Rules 1.8.1 to 1.8.9

While lawyers are associated in a law firm,* a prohibition in rules 1.8.1 through 1.8.9 that applies to any one of them shall apply to all of them.

Comment

A prohibition on conduct by an individual lawyer in rules 1.8.1 through 1.8.9 also applies to all lawyers associated in a law firm* with the personally prohibited lawyer. For example, one lawyer in a law firm* may not enter into a business transaction with a client of another lawyer associated in the law firm* without complying with rule 1.8.1, even if the first lawyer is not personally involved in the representation of the client. This rule does not apply to rule 1.8.10 since the prohibition in that rule is personal and is not applied to associated lawyers.

Rule 1.9   Duties to Former Clients

(a)   A lawyer who has formerly represented a client in a matter shall not thereafter represent another person* in the same or a substantially related matter in which that person's* interests are materially adverse to the interests of the former client unless the former client gives informed written consent.*

(b)   A lawyer shall not knowingly* represent a person* in the same or a substantially related matter in which a firm* with which the lawyer formerly was associated had previously represented a client

> (1)   whose interests are materially adverse to that person;* and
>
> (2)   about whom the lawyer had acquired information protected by Business and Professions Code section 6068, subdivision (e) and rules 1.6 and 1.9(c) that is material to the matter; unless the former client gives informed written consent.*

(c)   A lawyer who has formerly represented a client in a matter or whose present or former firm* has formerly represented a client in a matter shall not thereafter:

> (1)   use information protected by Business and Professions Code section 6068, subdivision (e) and rule 1.6 acquired by virtue of the representation of the former client to the disadvantage of the former client except as these rules or the State Bar Act would permit with respect to a current client, or when the information has become generally known;* or

---

*   An asterisk (*) identifies a word or phrase defined in the terminology rule, rule 1.0.1.

(2)   reveal information protected by Business and Professions Code section 6068, subdivision (e) and rule 1.6 acquired by virtue of the representation of the former client except as these rules or the State Bar Act permit with respect to a current client.

Comment

[1]   After termination of a lawyer-client relationship, the lawyer owes two duties to a former client. The lawyer may not (i) do anything that will injuriously affect the former client in any matter in which the lawyer represented the former client, or (ii) at any time use against the former client knowledge or information acquired by virtue of the previous relationship. (See *Oasis West Realty, LLC v. Goldman* (2011) 51 Cal.4th 811 [124 Cal.Rptr.3d 256]; *Wutchumna Water Co. v. Bailey* (1932) 216 Cal. 564 [15 P.2d 505].) For example, (i) a lawyer could not properly seek to rescind on behalf of a new client a contract drafted on behalf of the former client and (ii) a lawyer who has prosecuted an accused person* could not represent the accused in a subsequent civil action against the government concerning the same matter. (See also Bus. & Prof. Code, § 6131; 18 U.S.C. § 207(a).) These duties exist to preserve a client's trust in the lawyer and to encourage the client's candor in communications with the lawyer.

[2]   For what constitutes a "matter" for purposes of this rule, see rule 1.7(e).

[3]   Two matters are "the same or substantially related" for purposes of this rule if they involve a substantial* risk of a violation of one of the two duties to a former client described above in Comment [1]. For example, this will occur: (i) if the matters involve the same transaction or legal dispute or other work performed by the lawyer for the former client; or (ii) if the lawyer normally would have obtained information in the prior representation that is protected by Business and Professions Code section 6068, subdivision (e) and rule 1.6, and the lawyer would be expected to use or disclose that information in the subsequent representation because it is material to the subsequent representation.

[4]   Paragraph (b) addresses a lawyer's duties to a client who has become a former client because the lawyer no longer is associated with the law firm* that represents or represented the client. In that situation, the lawyer has a conflict of interest only when the lawyer involved has actual knowledge of information protected by Business and Professions Code section 6068, subdivision (e) and rules 1.6 and 1.9(c). Thus, if a lawyer while with one firm* acquired no knowledge or information relating to a particular client of the firm,* and that lawyer later joined another firm,* neither the lawyer individually nor lawyers in the second firm* would violate this rule by representing another client in the same or a related matter even though the interests of the two clients conflict. See rule 1.10(b) for the restrictions on lawyers in a firm* once a lawyer has terminated association with the firm.*

[5]   The fact that information can be discovered in a public record does not, by itself, render that information generally known* under paragraph (c). (See, e.g., *In the Matter of Johnson* (Review Dept. 2000) 4 Cal. State Bar Ct. Rptr. 179.)

[6]   With regard to the effectiveness of an advance consent, see rule 1.7, Comment [9]. With regard to imputation of conflicts to lawyers in a firm* with which a lawyer is or was formerly associated, see rule 1.10. Current and

---

*   An asterisk (*) identifies a word or phrase defined in the terminology rule, rule 1.0.1.

former government lawyers must comply with this rule to the extent required by rule 1.11.

Rule 1.10   Imputation Of Conflicts Of Interest: General Rule

(a)   While lawyers are associated in a firm,* none of them shall knowingly* represent a client when any one of them practicing alone would be prohibited from doing so by rules 1.7 or 1.9, unless

(1)   the prohibition is based on a personal interest of the prohibited lawyer and does not present a significant risk of materially limiting the representation of the client by the remaining lawyers in the firm;* or

(2)   the prohibition is based upon rule 1.9(a) or (b) and arises out of the prohibited lawyer's association with a prior firm,* and

(i)   the prohibited lawyer did not substantially participate in the same or a substantially related matter;

(ii)   the prohibited lawyer is timely screened* from any participation in the matter and is apportioned no part of the fee therefrom; and

(iii)   written* notice is promptly given to any affected former client to enable the former client to ascertain compliance with the provisions of this rule, which shall include a description of the screening* procedures employed; and an agreement by the firm* to respond promptly to any written* inquiries or objections by the former client about the screening* procedures.

(b)   When a lawyer has terminated an association with a firm,* the firm* is not prohibited from thereafter representing a person* with interests materially adverse to those of a client represented by the formerly associated lawyer and not currently represented by the firm,* unless:

(1)   the matter is the same or substantially related to that in which the formerly associated lawyer represented the client; and

(2)   any lawyer remaining in the firm* has information protected by Business and Professions Code section 6068, subdivision (e) and rules 1.6 and 1.9(c) that is material to the matter.

(c)   A prohibition under this rule may be waived by each affected client under the conditions stated in rule 1.7.

(d)   The imputation of a conflict of interest to lawyers associated in a firm* with former or current government lawyers is governed by rule 1.11.

Comment

[1]   In determining whether a prohibited lawyer's previously participation was substantial,* a number of factors should be considered, such as the lawyer's level of responsibility in the prior matter, the duration of the lawyer's participation, the extent to which the lawyer advised or had personal contact with the former client, and the extent to which the lawyer was exposed to confidential information of the former client likely to be material in the current matter.

[2]   Paragraph (a) does not prohibit representation by others in the law firm* where the person* prohibited from involvement in a matter is a nonlawyer, such as a paralegal or legal secretary. Nor does paragraph (a)

---

*   An asterisk (*) identifies a word or phrase defined in the terminology rule, rule 1.0.1.

prohibit representation if the lawyer is prohibited from acting because of events before the person* became a lawyer, for example, work that the person* did as a law student. Such persons,* however, ordinarily must be screened* from any personal participation in the matter. (See rules 1.0.1(k) and 5.3.)

[3]   Paragraph (a)(2)(ii) does not prohibit the screened* lawyer from receiving a salary or partnership share established by prior independent agreement, but that lawyer may not receive compensation directly related to the matter in which the lawyer is prohibited.

[4]   Where a lawyer is prohibited from engaging in certain transactions under rules 1.8.1 through 1.8.9, rule 1.8.11, and not this rule, determines whether that prohibition also applies to other lawyers associated in a firm* with the personally prohibited lawyer.

[5]   The responsibilities of managerial and supervisory lawyers prescribed by rules 5.1 and 5.3 apply to screening* arrangements implemented under this rule.

[6]   Standards for disqualification, and whether in a particular matter (1) a lawyer's conflict will be imputed to other lawyers in the same firm,* or (2) the use of a timely screen* is effective to avoid that imputation, are also the subject of statutes and case law. (See, e.g., Code Civ. Proc., § 128, subd. (a)(5); Pen. Code, § 1424; *In re Charlisse C.* (2008) 45 Cal.4th 145 [84 Cal.Rptr.3d 597]; *Rhaburn v. Superior Court* (2006) 140 Cal.App.4th 1566 [45 Cal.Rptr.3d 464]; *Kirk v. First American Title Ins. Co.* (2010) 183 Cal.App.4th 776 [108 Cal.Rptr.3d 620].)

Rule 1.11   Special Conflicts of Interest for Former and Current Government Officials and Employees

(a)   Except as law may otherwise expressly permit, a lawyer who has formerly served as a public official or employee of the government:

(1)   is subject to rule 1.9(c); and

(2)   shall not otherwise represent a client in connection with a matter in which the lawyer participated personally and substantially as a public official or employee, unless the appropriate government agency gives its informed written consent* to the representation. This paragraph shall not apply to matters governed by rule 1.12(a).

(b)   When a lawyer is prohibited from representation under paragraph (a), no lawyer in a firm* with which that lawyer is associated may knowingly* undertake or continue representation in such a matter unless:

(1)   the personally prohibited lawyer is timely screened* from any participation in the matter and is apportioned no part of the fee therefrom; and

(2)   written* notice is promptly given to the appropriate government agency to enable it to ascertain compliance with the provisions of this rule

(c)   Except as law may otherwise expressly permit, a lawyer who was a public official or employee and, during that employment, acquired information that the lawyer knows* is confidential government information about a person,* may not represent a private client whose interests are adverse to that person* in a matter in which the information could be used to

---

the material disadvantage of that person.* As used in this rule, the term "confidential government information" means information that has been obtained under governmental authority, that, at the time this rule is applied, the government is prohibited by law from disclosing to the public, or has a legal privilege not to disclose, and that is not otherwise available to the public. A firm* with which that lawyer is associated may undertake or continue representation in the matter only if the personally prohibited lawyer is timely screened* from any participation in the matter and is apportioned no part of the fee therefrom.

(d)   Except as law may otherwise expressly permit, a lawyer currently serving as a public official or employee:

(1)   is subject to rules 1.7 and 1.9; and

(2)   shall not:

(i)   participate in a matter in which the lawyer participated personally and substantially while in private practice or nongovernmental employment, unless the appropriate government agency gives its informed written consent;* or

(ii)   negotiate for private employment with any person* who is involved as a party, or as a lawyer for a party, or with a law firm* for a party, in a matter in which the lawyer is participating personally and substantially, except that a lawyer serving as a law clerk to a judge, other adjudicative officer or arbitrator may negotiate for private employment as permitted by rule 1.12(b) and subject to the conditions stated in rule 1.12(b).

Comment

[1]   Rule 1.10 is not applicable to the conflicts of interest addressed by this rule.

[2]   For what constitutes a "matter" for purposes of this rule, see rule 1.7(e).

[3]   Paragraphs (a)(2) and (d)(2) apply regardless of whether a lawyer is adverse to a former client. Both provisions apply when the former public official or employee of the government has personally and substantially participated in the matter. Personal participation includes both direct participation and the supervision of a subordinate's participation. Substantial* participation requires that the lawyer's involvement be of significance to the matter. Participation may be substantial* even though it is not determinative of the outcome of a particular matter. However, it requires more than official responsibility, knowledge, perfunctory involvement, or involvement on an administrative or peripheral issue. A finding of substantiality should be based not only on the effort devoted to the matter, but also on the importance of the effort. Personal and substantial* participation may occur when, for example, a lawyer participates through decision, approval, disapproval, recommendation, investigation or the rendering of advice in a particular matter.

[4]   By requiring a former government lawyer to comply with rule 1.9(c), paragraph (a)(1) protects information obtained while working for the government to the same extent as information learned while representing a private client. This provision applies regardless of whether the lawyer was working in a "legal" capacity. Thus, information learned by the lawyer while

---

*   An asterisk (*) identifies a word or phrase defined in the terminology rule, rule 1.0.1.

in public service in an administrative, policy, or advisory position also is covered by paragraph (a)(1).

[5]   Paragraph (c) operates only when the lawyer in question has actual knowledge of the information; it does not operate with respect to information that merely could be imputed to the lawyer.

[6]   When a lawyer has been employed by one government agency and then moves to a second government agency, it may be appropriate to treat that second agency as another client for purposes of this rule, as when a lawyer is employed by a city and subsequently is employed by a federal agency. Because conflicts of interest are governed by paragraphs (a) and (b), the latter agency is required to screen* the lawyer. Whether two government agencies should be regarded as the same or different clients for conflict of interest purposes is beyond the scope of these rules. (See rule 1.13, Comment [6]; see also *Civil Service Commission v. Superior Court* (1984) 163 Cal.App.3d 70, 76–78 [209 Cal.Rptr. 159].)

[7]   Paragraphs (b) and (c) do not prohibit a lawyer from receiving a salary or partnership share established by prior independent agreement, but that lawyer may not receive compensation directly relating the lawyer's compensation to the fee in the matter in which the lawyer is personally prohibited from participating.

[8]   Paragraphs (a) and (d) do not prohibit a lawyer from jointly representing a private party and a government agency when doing so is permitted by rule 1.7 and is not otherwise prohibited by law.

[9]   A lawyer serving as a public official or employee of the government may participate in a matter in which the lawyer participated substantially while in private practice or non-governmental employment only if: (i) the government agency gives its informed written consent* as required by paragraph (d)(2)(i); and (ii) the former client gives its informed written consent* as required by rule 1.9, to which the lawyer is subject by paragraph (d)(1).

[10] This rule is not intended to address whether in a particular matter: (i) a lawyer's conflict under paragraph (d) will be imputed to other lawyers serving in the same governmental agency; or (ii) the use of a timely screen* will avoid that imputation. The imputation and screening* rules for lawyers moving from private practice into government service under paragraph (d) are left to be addressed by case law and its development. (See *City & County of San Francisco v. Cobra Solutions, Inc.* (2006) 38 Cal.4th 839, 847, 851–54 [43 Cal.Rptr.3d 776]; *City of Santa Barbara v. Superior Court* (2004) 122 Cal.App.4th 17, 26–27 [18 Cal.Rptr.3d 403].) Regarding the standards for recusals of prosecutors in criminal matters, see Penal Code section 1424; *Haraguchi v. Superior Court* (2008) 43 Cal. 4th 706, 711–20 [76 Cal.Rptr.3d 250]; and *Hollywood v. Superior Court* (2008) 43 Cal.4th 721, 727–35 [76 Cal.Rptr.3d 264]. Concerning prohibitions against former prosecutors participating in matters in which they served or participated in as prosecutor, see, e.g., Business and Professions Code section 6131 and 18 United States Code section 207(a).

Rule 1.12   Former Judge, Arbitrator, Mediator, Or Other Third-Party Neutral

(a)   Except as stated in paragraph (d), a lawyer shall not represent anyone in connection with a matter in which the lawyer participated personally and

---

*   An asterisk (*) identifies a word or phrase defined in the terminology rule, rule 1.0.1.

substantially as a judge or other adjudicative officer, judicial staff attorney or law clerk to such a person* or as an arbitrator, mediator, or other third-party neutral, unless all parties to the proceeding give informed written consent.*

(b)   A lawyer shall not seek employment from any person* who is involved as a party or as lawyer for a party, or with a law firm* for a party, in a matter in which the lawyer is participating personally and substantially as a judge or other adjudicative officer or as an arbitrator, mediator, or other third party neutral. A lawyer serving as a judicial staff attorney or law clerk to a judge or other adjudicative officer may seek employment from a party, or with a lawyer or a law firm* for a party, in a matter in which the staff attorney or clerk is participating personally and substantially, but only with the approval of the court.

(c)   If a lawyer is prohibited from representation by paragraph (a), other lawyers in a firm* with which that lawyer is associated may knowingly* undertake or continue representation in the matter only if:

(1)   the prohibition does not arise from the lawyer's service as a mediator or settlement judge;

(2)   the prohibited lawyer is timely screened* from any participation in the matter and is apportioned no part of the fee therefrom; and

(3)   written* notice is promptly given to the parties and any appropriate tribunal* to enable them to ascertain compliance with the provisions of this rule.

(d)   An arbitrator selected as a partisan of a party in a multimember arbitration panel is not prohibited from subsequently representing that party.

Comment

[1]   Paragraphs (a) and (b) apply when a former judge or other adjudicative officer, or a judicial staff attorney or law clerk to such a person,* or an arbitrator, mediator, or other third-party neutral, has personally and substantially participated in the matter. Personal participation includes both direct participation and the supervision of a subordinate's participation, as may occur in a chambers with several staff attorneys or law clerks. Substantial* participation requires that the lawyer's involvement was of significance to the matter. Participation may be substantial* even though it was not determinative of the outcome of a particular case or matter. A finding of substantiality should be based not only on the effort devoted to the matter, but also on the importance of the effort. Personal and substantial* participation may occur when, for example, the lawyer participated through decision, recommendation, or the rendering of advice on a particular case or matter. However, a judge who was a member of a multi-member court, and thereafter left judicial office to practice law, is not prohibited from representing a client in a matter pending in the court, but in which the former judge did not participate, or acquire material confidential information. The fact that a former judge exercised administrative responsibility in a court also does not prevent the former judge from acting as a lawyer in a matter where the judge had previously exercised remote or incidental administrative responsibility that did not affect the merits, such as uncontested procedural duties typically performed by a presiding or supervising judge or justice. The

---

*   An asterisk (*) identifies a word or phrase defined in the terminology rule, rule 1.0.1.

term "adjudicative officer" includes such officials as judges pro tempore, referees, and special masters.

[2]   Other law or codes of ethics governing third-party neutrals may impose more stringent standards of personal or imputed disqualification. (See rule 2.4.)

[3]   Paragraph (c)(2) does not prohibit the screened* lawyer from receiving a salary or partnership share established by prior independent agreement, but that lawyer may not receive compensation directly related to the matter in which the lawyer is personally prohibited from participating.

Rule 1.13   Organization as Client

(a)   A lawyer employed or retained by an organization shall conform his or her representation to the concept that the client is the organization itself, acting through its duly authorized directors, officers, employees, members, shareholders, or other constituents overseeing the particular engagement.

(b)   If a lawyer representing an organization knows* that a constituent is acting, intends to act or refuses to act in a matter related to the representation in a manner that the lawyer knows* or reasonably should know* is (i) a violation of a legal obligation to the organization or a violation of law reasonably* imputable to the organization, and (ii) likely to result in substantial* injury to the organization, the lawyer shall proceed as is reasonably* necessary in the best lawful interest of the organization. Unless the lawyer reasonably believes* that it is not necessary in the best lawful interest of the organization to do so, the lawyer shall refer the matter to higher authority in the organization, including, if warranted by the circumstances, to the highest authority that can act on behalf of the organization as determined by applicable law.

(c)   In taking any action pursuant to paragraph (b), the lawyer shall not reveal information protected by Business and Professions Code section 6068, subdivision (e).

(d)   If, despite the lawyer's actions in accordance with paragraph (b), the highest authority that can act on behalf of the organization insists upon action, or fails to act, in a manner that is a violation of a legal obligation to the organization or a violation of law reasonably* imputable to the organization, and is likely to result in substantial* injury to the organization, the lawyer shall continue to proceed as is reasonably* necessary in the best lawful interests of the organization. The lawyer's response may include the lawyer's right and, where appropriate, duty to resign or withdraw in accordance with rule 1.16.

(e)   A lawyer who reasonably believes* that he or she has been discharged because of the lawyer's actions taken pursuant to paragraph (b), or who resigns or withdraws under circumstances described in paragraph (d), shall proceed as the lawyer reasonably believes* necessary to assure that the organization's highest authority is informed of the lawyer's discharge, resignation, or withdrawal.

(f)   In dealing with an organization's constituents, a lawyer representing the organization shall explain the identity of the lawyer's client whenever the lawyer knows* or reasonably should know* that the organization's interests are adverse to those of the constituent(s) with whom the lawyer is dealing.

---

*   An asterisk (*) identifies a word or phrase defined in the terminology rule, rule 1.0.1.

(g) A lawyer representing an organization may also represent any of its constituents, subject to the provisions of rules 1.7, 1.8.2, 1.8.6, and 1.8.7. If the organization's consent to the dual representation is required by any of these rules, the consent shall be given by an appropriate official, constituent, or body of the organization other than the individual who is to be represented, or by the shareholders.

Comment

The Entity as the Client

[1] This rule applies to all forms of private, public and governmental organizations. (See Comment [6].) An organizational client can only act through individuals who are authorized to conduct its affairs. The identity of an organization's constituents will depend on its form, structure, and chosen terminology. For example, in the case of a corporation, constituents include officers, directors, employees and shareholders. In the case of other organizational forms, constituents include the equivalents of officers, directors, employees, and shareholders. For purposes of this rule, any agent or fiduciary authorized to act on behalf of an organization is a constituent of the organization.

[2] A lawyer ordinarily must accept decisions an organization's constituents make on behalf of the organization, even if the lawyer questions their utility or prudence. It is not within the lawyer's province to make decisions on behalf of the organization concerning policy and operations, including ones entailing serious risk. A lawyer, however, has a duty to inform the client of significant developments related to the representation under Business and Professions Code section 6068, subdivision (m) and rule 1.4. Even when a lawyer is not obligated to proceed in accordance with paragraph (b), the lawyer may refer to higher authority, including the organization's highest authority, matters that the lawyer reasonably believes* are sufficiently important to refer in the best interest of the organization subject to Business and Professions Code section 6068, subdivision (e) and rule 1.6.

[3] Paragraph (b) distinguishes between knowledge of the conduct and knowledge of the consequences of that conduct. When a lawyer knows* of the conduct, the lawyer's obligations under paragraph (b) are triggered when the lawyer knows* or reasonably should know* that the conduct is (i) a violation of a legal obligation to the organization, or a violation of law reasonably* imputable to the organization, and (ii) likely to result in substantial* injury to the organization.

[4] In determining how to proceed under paragraph (b), the lawyer should consider the seriousness of the violation and its potential consequences, the responsibility in the organization and the apparent motivation of the person* involved, the policies of the organization concerning such matters, and any other relevant considerations. Ordinarily, referral to a higher authority would be necessary. In some circumstances, however, the lawyer may ask the constituent to reconsider the matter. For example, if the circumstances involve a constituent's innocent misunderstanding of law and subsequent acceptance of the lawyer's advice, the lawyer may reasonably* conclude that the best interest of the organization does not require that the matter be referred to higher authority. If a constituent persists in conduct contrary to the lawyer's advice, it will be necessary for the lawyer to take steps to have the matter reviewed by a higher authority in the organization. If the matter is of sufficient seriousness and importance or urgency to the organization,

---

* An asterisk (*) identifies a word or phrase defined in the terminology rule, rule 1.0.1.

referral to higher authority in the organization may be necessary even if the lawyer has not communicated with the constituent. For the responsibility of a subordinate lawyer in representing an organization, see rule 5.2.

[5]   In determining how to proceed in the best lawful interests of the organization, a lawyer should consider the extent to which the organization should be informed of the circumstances, the actions taken by the organization with respect to the matter and the direction the lawyer has received from the organizational client.

Governmental Organizations

[6]   It is beyond the scope of this rule to define precisely the identity of the client and the lawyer's obligations when representing a governmental agency. Although in some circumstances the client may be a specific agency, it may also be a branch of government or the government as a whole. In a matter involving the conduct of government officials, a government lawyer may have authority under applicable law to question such conduct more extensively than that of a lawyer for a private organization in similar circumstances. Duties of lawyers employed by the government or lawyers in military service may be defined by statutes and regulations. In addition, a governmental organization may establish internal organizational rules and procedures that identify an official, agency, organization, or other person* to serve as the designated recipient of whistle-blower reports from the organization's lawyers, consistent with Business and Professions Code section 6068, subdivision (e) and rule 1.6. This rule is not intended to limit that authority.

Rule 1.14   [Reserved]

Rule 1.15   Safekeeping Funds and Property of Clients and Other Persons*

(a)   All funds received or held by a lawyer or law firm* for the benefit of a client, or other person* to whom the lawyer owes a contractual, statutory, or other legal duty, including advances for fees, costs and expenses, shall be deposited in one or more identifiable bank accounts labeled "Trust Account" or words of similar import, maintained in the State of California, or, with written* consent of the client, in any other jurisdiction where there is a substantial* relationship between the client or the client's business and the other jurisdiction.

(b)   Notwithstanding paragraph (a), a flat fee paid in advance for legal services may be deposited in a lawyer's or law firm's operating account, provided:

(1)   the lawyer or law firm* discloses to the client in writing* (i) that the client has a right under paragraph (a) to require that the flat fee be deposited in an identified trust account until the fee is earned, and (ii) that the client is entitled to a refund of any amount of the fee that has not been earned in the event the representation is terminated or the services for which the fee has been paid are not completed; and

(2)   if the flat fee exceeds $1,000.00, the client's agreement to deposit the flat fee in the lawyer's operating account and the disclosures required by paragraph (b)(1) are set forth in a writing* signed by the client.

---

*   An asterisk (*) identifies a word or phrase defined in the terminology rule, rule 1.0.1.

(c)   Funds belonging to the lawyer or the law firm* shall not be deposited or otherwise commingled with funds held in a trust account except:

    (1)   funds reasonably* sufficient to pay bank charges; and

    (2)   funds belonging in part to a client or other person* and in part presently or potentially to the lawyer or the law firm,* in which case the portion belonging to the lawyer or law firm* must be withdrawn at the earliest reasonable* time after the lawyer or law firm's interest in that portion becomes fixed. However, if a client or other person* disputes the lawyer or law firm's right to receive a portion of trust funds, the disputed portion shall not be withdrawn until the dispute is finally resolved.

(d)   A lawyer shall:

    (1)   promptly notify a client or other person* of the receipt of funds, securities, or other property in which the lawyer knows* or reasonably should know* the client or other person* has an interest;

    (2)   identify and label securities and properties of a client or other person* promptly upon receipt and place them in a safe deposit box or other place of safekeeping as soon as practicable;

    (3)   maintain complete records of all funds, securities, and other property of a client or other person* coming into the possession of the lawyer or law firm;*

    (4)   promptly account in writing* to the client or other person* for whom the lawyer holds funds or property;

    (5)   preserve records of all funds and property held by a lawyer or law firm* under this rule for a period of no less than five years after final appropriate distribution of such funds or property;

    (6)   comply with any order for an audit of such records issued pursuant to the Rules of Procedure of the State Bar; and

    (7)   promptly distribute, as requested by the client or other person,* any undisputed funds or property in the possession of the lawyer or law firm* that the client or other person* is entitled to receive.

(e)   The Board of Trustees of the State Bar shall have the authority to formulate and adopt standards as to what "records" shall be maintained by lawyers and law firms* in accordance with subparagraph (d)(3). The standards formulated and adopted by the Board, as from time to time amended, shall be effective and binding on all lawyers.

Standards:

Pursuant to this rule, the Board of Trustees of the State Bar adopted the following standards, effective November 1, 2018, as to what "records" shall be maintained by lawyers and law firms* in accordance with paragraph (d)(3).

    (1)   A lawyer shall, from the date of receipt of funds of the client or other person* through the period ending five years from the date of appropriate disbursement of such funds, maintain:

        (a)   a written* ledger for each client or other person* on whose behalf funds are held that sets forth:

---

* An asterisk (*) identifies a word or phrase defined in the terminology rule, rule 1.0.1.

(i)   the name of such client or other person;*

(ii)   the date, amount and source of all funds received on behalf of such client or other person;*

(iii) the date, amount, payee and purpose of each disbursement made on behalf of such client or other person;* and

(iv)   the current balance for such client or other person;*

(b)   a written* journal for each bank account that sets forth:

(i)   the name of such account;

(ii)   the date, amount and client or other person* affected by each debit and credit; and

(iii) the current balance in such account;

(c)   all bank statements and cancelled checks for each bank account; and

(d)   each monthly reconciliation (balancing) of (a), (b), and (c).

(2)   A lawyer shall, from the date of receipt of all securities and other properties held for the benefit of client or other person* through the period ending five years from the date of appropriate disbursement of such securities and other properties, maintain a written* journal that specifies:

(a)   each item of security and property held;

(b)   the person* on whose behalf the security or property is held;

(c)   the date of receipt of the security or property;

(d)   the date of distribution of the security or property; and

(e)   person* to whom the security or property was distributed.

Comment

[1]   Whether a lawyer owes a contractual, statutory or other legal duty under paragraph (a) to hold funds on behalf of a person* other than a client in situations where client funds are subject to a third-party lien will depend on the relationship between the lawyer and the third-party, whether the lawyer has assumed a contractual obligation to the third person* and whether the lawyer has an independent obligation to honor the lien under a statute or other law. In certain circumstances, a lawyer may be civilly liable when the lawyer has notice of a lien and disburses funds in contravention of the lien. (See *Kaiser Foundation Health Plan, Inc. v. Aguiluz* (1996) 47 Cal.App.4th 302 [54 Cal.Rptr.2d 665].) However, civil liability by itself does not establish a violation of this rule. (Compare *Johnstone v. State Bar of California* (1966) 64 Cal.2d 153, 155–156 [49 Cal.Rptr. 97] [" 'When an attorney assumes a fiduciary relationship and violates his duty in a manner that would justify disciplinary action if the relationship had been that of attorney and client, he may properly be disciplined for his misconduct.' "] with *Crooks v. State Bar* (1970) 3 Cal.3d 346, 358 [90 Cal.Rptr. 600] [lawyer who agrees to act as escrow or stakeholder for a client and a third-party owes a duty to the nonclient with regard to held funds].)

---

*   An asterisk (*) identifies a word or phrase defined in the terminology rule, rule 1.0.1.

[2]   As used in this rule, "advances for fees" means a payment intended by the client as an advance payment for some or all of the services that the lawyer is expected to perform on the client's behalf. With respect to the difference between a true retainer and a flat fee, which is one type of advance fee, see rule 1.5(d) and (e). Subject to rule 1.5, a lawyer or law firm* may enter into an agreement that defines when or how an advance fee is earned and may be withdrawn from the client trust account.

[3]   Absent written* disclosure and the client's agreement in a writing* signed by the client as provided in paragraph (b), a lawyer must deposit a flat fee paid in advance of legal services in the lawyer's trust account. Paragraph (b) does not apply to advance payment for costs and expenses. Paragraph (b) does not alter the lawyer's obligations under paragraph (d) or the lawyer's burden to establish that the fee has been earned.

Rule 1.16   Declining Or Terminating Representation

(a)   Except as stated in paragraph (c), a lawyer shall not represent a client or, where representation has commenced, shall withdraw from the representation of a client if:

(1)   the lawyer knows* or reasonably should know* that the client is bringing an action, conducting a defense, asserting a position in litigation, or taking an appeal, without probable cause and for the purpose of harassing or maliciously injuring any person;*

(2)   the lawyer knows* or reasonably should know* that the representation will result in violation of these rules or of the State Bar Act;

(3)   the lawyer's mental or physical condition renders it unreasonably difficult to carry out the representation effectively; or

(4)   the client discharges the lawyer.

(b)   Except as stated in paragraph (c), a lawyer may withdraw from representing a client if:

(1)   the client insists upon presenting a claim or defense in litigation, or asserting a position or making a demand in a non-litigation matter, that is not warranted under existing law and cannot be supported by good faith argument for an extension, modification, or reversal of existing law;

(2)   the client either seeks to pursue a criminal or fraudulent* course of conduct or has used the lawyer's services to advance a course of conduct that the lawyer reasonably believes* was a crime or fraud;*

(3)   the client insists that the lawyer pursue a course of conduct that is criminal or fraudulent;*

(4)   the client by other conduct renders it unreasonably difficult for the lawyer to carry out the representation effectively;

(5)   the client breaches a material term of an agreement with, or obligation, to the lawyer relating to the representation, and the lawyer has given the client a reasonable* warning after the breach that the lawyer will withdraw unless the client fulfills the agreement or performs the obligation;

---

*   An asterisk (*) identifies a word or phrase defined in the terminology rule, rule 1.0.1.

(6)   the client knowingly* and freely assents to termination of the representation;

(7)   the inability to work with co-counsel indicates that the best interests of the client likely will be served by withdrawal;

(8)   the lawyer's mental or physical condition renders it difficult for the lawyer to carry out the representation effectively;

(9)   a continuation of the representation is likely to result in a violation of these rules or the State Bar Act; or

(10) the lawyer believes* in good faith, in a proceeding pending before a tribunal,* that the tribunal* will find the existence of other good cause for withdrawal.

(c)   If permission for termination of a representation is required by the rules of a tribunal,* a lawyer shall not terminate a representation before that tribunal* without its permission.

(d)   A lawyer shall not terminate a representation until the lawyer has taken reasonable* steps to avoid reasonably* foreseeable prejudice to the rights of the client, such as giving the client sufficient notice to permit the client to retain other counsel, and complying with paragraph (e).

(e)   Upon the termination of a representation for any reason:

(1)   subject to any applicable protective order, nondisclosure agreement, statute or regulation, the lawyer promptly shall release to the client, at the request of the client, all client materials and property. "Client materials and property" includes correspondence, pleadings, deposition transcripts, experts' reports and other writings,* exhibits, and physical evidence, whether in tangible, electronic or other form, and other items reasonably* necessary to the client's representation, whether the client has paid for them or not; and

(2)   the lawyer promptly shall refund any part of a fee or expense paid in advance that the lawyer has not earned or incurred. This provision is not applicable to a true retainer fee paid solely for the purpose of ensuring the availability of the lawyer for the matter.

Comment

[1]   This rule applies, without limitation, to a sale of a law practice under rule 1.17. A lawyer can be subject to discipline for improperly threatening to terminate a representation. (See *In the Matter of Shalant* (Review Dept. 2005) 4 Cal. State Bar Ct. Rptr. 829, 837.)

[2]   When a lawyer withdraws from the representation of a client in a particular matter under paragraph (a) or (b), the lawyer might not be obligated to withdraw from the representation of the same client in other matters. For example, a lawyer might be obligated under paragraph (a)(1) to withdraw from representing a client because the lawyer has a conflict of interest under rule 1.7, but that conflict might not arise in other representations of the client.

[3]   Withdrawal under paragraph (a)(1) is not mandated where a lawyer for the defendant in a criminal proceeding, or the respondent in a proceeding that could result in incarceration, or involuntary commitment or

---

*   An asterisk (*) identifies a word or phrase defined in the terminology rule, rule 1.0.1.

confinement, defends the proceeding by requiring that every element of the case be established. (See rule 3.1(b).)

[4]   Lawyers must comply with their obligations to their clients under Business and Professions Code section 6068, subdivision (e) and rule 1.6, and to the courts under rule 3.3 when seeking permission to withdraw under paragraph (c). If a tribunal* denies a lawyer permission to withdraw, the lawyer is obligated to comply with the tribunal's* order. (See Bus. & Prof. Code, §§ 6068, subd. (b) and 6103.) This duty applies even if the lawyer sought permission to withdraw because of a conflict of interest. Regarding withdrawal from limited scope representations that involve court appearances, compliance with applicable California Rules of Court concerning limited scope representation satisfies paragraph (c).

[5]   Statutes may prohibit a lawyer from releasing information in the client materials and property under certain circumstances. (See, e.g., Pen. Code, §§ 1054.2 and 1054.10.)

[6]   Paragraph (e)(1) does not prohibit a lawyer from making, at the lawyer's own expense, and retaining copies of papers released to the client, or to prohibit a claim for the recovery of the lawyer's expense in any subsequent legal proceeding.

Rule 1.17   Sale of a Law Practice

All or substantially* all of the law practice of a lawyer, living or deceased, including goodwill, may be sold to another lawyer or law firm* subject to all the following conditions:

(a)   Fees charged to clients shall not be increased solely by reason of the sale.

(b)   If the sale contemplates the transfer of responsibility for work not yet completed or responsibility for client files or information protected by Business and Professions Code section 6068, subdivision (e)(1), then;

  (1)   if the seller is deceased, or has a conservator or other person* acting in a representative capacity, and no lawyer has been appointed to act for the seller pursuant to Business and Professions Code section 6180.5, then prior to the transfer;

    (i)   the purchaser shall cause a written* notice to be given to each client whose matter is included in the sale, stating that the interest in the law practice is being transferred to the purchaser; that the client has the right to retain other counsel; that the client may take possession of any client materials and property, as required by rule 1.16(e)(1); and that if no response is received to the notice within 90 days after it is sent, or if the client's rights would be prejudiced by a failure of the purchaser to act during that time, the purchaser may act on behalf of the client until otherwise notified by the client, and

    (ii)   the purchaser shall obtain the written* consent of the client. If reasonable* efforts have been made to locate the client and no response to the paragraph (b)(1)(i) notice is received within 90 days, consent shall be presumed until otherwise notified by the client.

  (2)   in all other circumstances, not less than 90 days prior to the transfer;

---

*   An asterisk (*) identifies a word or phrase defined in the terminology rule, rule 1.0.1.

(i)   the seller, or the lawyer appointed to act for the seller pursuant to Business and Professions Code section 6180.5, shall cause a written* notice to be given to each client whose matter is included in the sale, stating that the interest in the law practice is being transferred to the purchaser; that the client has the right to retain other counsel; that the client may take possession of any client materials and property, as required by rule 1.16(e)(1); and that if no response is received to the notice within 90 days after it is sent, or if the client's rights would be prejudiced by a failure of the purchaser to act during that time, the purchaser may act on behalf of the client until otherwise notified by the client, and

(ii)   the seller, or the lawyer appointed to act for the seller pursuant to Business and Professions Code section 6180.5, shall obtain the written* consent of the client prior to the transfer. If reasonable* efforts have been made to locate the client and no response to the paragraph (b)(2)(i) notice is received within 90 days, consent shall be presumed until otherwise notified by the client.

(c)   If substitution is required by the rules of a tribunal* in which a matter is pending, all steps necessary to substitute a lawyer shall be taken.

(d)   The purchaser shall comply with the applicable requirements of rules 1.7 and 1.9.

(e)   Confidential information shall not be disclosed to a nonlawyer in connection with a sale under this rule.

(f)   This rule does not apply to the admission to or retirement from a law firm,* retirement plans and similar arrangements, or sale of tangible assets of a law practice.

Comment

[1]   The requirement that the sale be of "all or substantially* all of the law practice of a lawyer" prohibits the sale of only a field or area of practice or the seller's practice in a geographical area or in a particular jurisdiction. The prohibition against the sale of less than all or substantially* all of a practice protects those clients whose matters are less lucrative and who might find it difficult to secure other counsel if a sale could be limited to substantial* fee-generating matters. The purchasers are required to undertake all client matters sold in the transaction, subject to client consent. This requirement is satisfied, however, even if a purchaser is unable to undertake a particular client matter because of a conflict of interest.

[2]   Under paragraph (a), the purchaser must honor existing arrangements between the seller and the client as to fees and scope of work and the sale may not be financed by increasing fees charged for client matters transferred through the sale. However, fee increases or other changes to the fee arrangements might be justified by other factors, such as modifications of the purchaser's responsibilities, the passage of time, or reasonable* costs that were not addressed in the original agreement. Any such modifications must comply with rules 1.4 and 1.5 and other relevant provisions of these rules and the State Bar Act.

[3]   Transfer of individual client matters, where permitted, is governed by rule 1.5.1. Payment of a fee to a nonlawyer broker for arranging the sale or purchase of a law practice is governed by rule 5.4(a).

---

*   An asterisk (*) identifies a word or phrase defined in the terminology rule, rule 1.0.1.

Rule 1.18   Duties To Prospective Client

(a) A person* who, directly or through an authorized representative, consults a lawyer for the purpose of retaining the lawyer or securing legal service or advice from the lawyer in the lawyer's professional capacity, is a prospective client.

(b) Even when no lawyer-client relationship ensues, a lawyer who has communicated with a prospective client shall not use or reveal information protected by Business and Professions Code section 6068, subdivision (e) and rule 1.6 that the lawyer learned as a result of the consultation, except as rule 1.9 would permit with respect to information of a former client.

(c) A lawyer subject to paragraph (b) shall not represent a client with interests materially adverse to those of a prospective client in the same or a substantially related matter if the lawyer received from the prospective client information protected by Business and Professions Code section 6068, subdivision (e) and rule 1.6 that is material to the matter, except as provided in paragraph (d). If a lawyer is prohibited from representation under this paragraph, no lawyer in a firm* with which that lawyer is associated may knowingly* undertake or continue representation in such a matter, except as provided in paragraph (d).

(d) When the lawyer has received information that prohibits representation as provided in paragraph (c), representation of the affected client is permissible if:

> (1) both the affected client and the prospective client have given informed written consent,* or

> (2) the lawyer who received the information took reasonable* measures to avoid exposure to more information than was reasonably* necessary to determine whether to represent the prospective client; and

>> (i) the prohibited lawyer is timely screened* from any participation in the matter and is apportioned no part of the fee therefrom; and

>> (ii) written* notice is promptly given to the prospective client to enable the prospective client to ascertain compliance with the provisions of this rule.

Comment

[1] As used in this rule, a prospective client includes a person's* authorized representative. A lawyer's discussions with a prospective client can be limited in time and depth and leave both the prospective client and the lawyer free, and sometimes required, to proceed no further. Although a prospective client's information is protected by Business and Professions Code section 6068, subdivision (e) and rule 1.6 the same as that of a client, in limited circumstances provided under paragraph (d), a law firm* is permitted to accept or continue representation of a client with interests adverse to the prospective client. This rule is not intended to limit the application of Evidence Code section 951 (defining "client" within the meaning of the Evidence Code).

[2] Not all persons* who communicate information to a lawyer are entitled to protection under this rule. A person* who by any means communicates information unilaterally to a lawyer, without reasonable* expectation that

---

*   An asterisk (*) identifies a word or phrase defined in the terminology rule, rule 1.0.1.

the lawyer is willing to discuss the possibility of forming a lawyer-client relationship or provide legal advice is not a "prospective client" within the meaning of paragraph (a). In addition, a person* who discloses information to a lawyer after the lawyer has stated his or her unwillingness or inability to consult with the person* (*People v. Gionis* (1995) 9 Cal.4th 1196 [40 Cal.Rptr.2d 456]), or who communicates information to a lawyer without a good faith intention to seek legal advice or representation, is not a prospective client within the meaning of paragraph (a).

[3]   In order to avoid acquiring information from a prospective client that would prohibit representation as provided in paragraph (c), a lawyer considering whether or not to undertake a new matter must limit the initial interview to only such information as reasonably* appears necessary for that purpose.

[4]   Under paragraph (c), the prohibition in this rule is imputed to other lawyers in a law firm* as provided in rule 1.10. However, under paragraph (d)(1), the consequences of imputation may be avoided if the informed written consent* of both the prospective and affected clients is obtained. (See rule 1.0.1(e-1) [informed written consent].) In the alternative, imputation may be avoided if the conditions of paragraph (d)(2) are met and all prohibited lawyers are timely screened* and written* notice is promptly given to the prospective client. Paragraph (d)(2)(i) does not prohibit the screened* lawyer from receiving a salary or partnership share established by prior independent agreement, but that lawyer may not receive compensation directly related to the matter in which the lawyer is prohibited.

[5]   Notice under paragraph (d)(2)(ii) must include a general description of the subject matter about which the lawyer was consulted, and the screening* procedures employed.

COUNSELOR

Rule 2.1   Advisor

In representing a client, a lawyer shall exercise independent professional judgment and render candid advice.

Comment

[1]   A lawyer ordinarily has no duty to initiate investigation of a client's affairs or to give advice that the client has indicated is unwanted, but a lawyer may initiate advice to a client when doing so appears to be in the client's interest.

[2]   This rule does not preclude a lawyer who renders advice from referring to considerations other than the law, such as moral, economic, social and political factors that may be relevant to the client's situation.

Rule 2.2   [Reserved]

Rule 2.3   [Reserved]

Rule 2.4   Lawyer as Third-Party Neutral

(a)   A lawyer serves as a third-party neutral when the lawyer assists two or more persons* who are not clients of the lawyer to reach a resolution of a dispute, or other matter, that has arisen between them. Service as a third-party neutral may include service as an arbitrator, a mediator or in such

---

*   An asterisk (*) identifies a word or phrase defined in the terminology rule, rule 1.0.1.

other capacity as will enable the lawyer to assist the parties to resolve the matter.

(b)   A lawyer serving as a third-party neutral shall inform unrepresented parties that the lawyer is not representing them. When the lawyer knows* or reasonably should know* that a party does not understand the lawyer's role in the matter, the lawyer shall explain the difference between the lawyer's role as a third-party neutral and a lawyer's role as one who represents a client.

Comment

[1]   In serving as a third-party neutral, the lawyer may be subject to court rules or other law that apply either to third-party neutrals generally or to lawyers serving as third-party neutrals. Lawyer neutrals may also be subject to various codes of ethics, such as the Judicial Council Standards for Mediators in Court Connected Mediation Programs or the Judicial Council Ethics Standards for Neutral Arbitrators in Contractual Arbitration.

[2]   A lawyer who serves as a third-party neutral subsequently may be asked to serve as a lawyer representing a client in the same matter. The conflicts of interest that arise for both the individual lawyer and the lawyer's law firm* are addressed in rule 1.12.

[3]   This rule is not intended to apply to temporary judges, referees or court-appointed arbitrators. (See rule 2.4.1.)

Rule 2.4.1   Lawyer as Temporary Judge, Referee, or Court-Appointed Arbitrator

A lawyer who is serving as a temporary judge, referee, or court-appointed arbitrator, and is subject to canon 6D of the California Code of Judicial Ethics, shall comply with the terms of that canon.

Comment

[1]   This rule is intended to permit the State Bar to discipline lawyers who violate applicable portions of the California Code of Judicial Ethics while acting in a judicial capacity pursuant to an order or appointment by a court.

[2]   This rule is not intended to apply to a lawyer serving as a third-party neutral in a mediation or a settlement conference, or as a neutral arbitrator pursuant to an arbitration agreement. (See rule 2.4.)

ADVOCATE

Rule 3.1   Meritorious Claims and Contentions

(a)   A lawyer shall not:

(1)   bring or continue an action, conduct a defense, assert a position in litigation, or take an appeal, without probable cause and for the purpose of harassing or maliciously injuring any person;* or

(2)   present a claim or defense in litigation that is not warranted under existing law, unless it can be supported by a good faith argument for an extension, modification, or reversal of the existing law.

(b)   A lawyer for the defendant in a criminal proceeding, or the respondent in a proceeding that could result in incarceration, or involuntary commitment

---

*   An asterisk (*) identifies a word or phrase defined in the terminology rule, rule 1.0.1.

or confinement, may nevertheless defend the proceeding by requiring that every element of the case be established.

Rule 3.2 Delay of Litigation

In representing a client, a lawyer shall not use means that have no substantial* purpose other than to delay or prolong the proceeding or to cause needless expense.

Comment

See rule 1.3 with respect to a lawyer's duty to act with reasonable* diligence and rule 3.1(b) with respect to a lawyer's representation of a defendant in a criminal proceeding. See also Business and Professions Code section 6128, subdivision (b).

Rule 3.3 Candor Toward The Tribunal*

(a) A lawyer shall not:

(1) knowingly* make a false statement of fact or law to a tribunal* or fail to correct a false statement of material fact or law previously made to the tribunal* by the lawyer;

(2) fail to disclose to the tribunal* legal authority in the controlling jurisdiction known* to the lawyer to be directly adverse to the position of the client and not disclosed by opposing counsel, or knowingly* misquote to a tribunal* the language of a book, statute, decision or other authority; or

(3) offer evidence that the lawyer knows* to be false. If a lawyer, the lawyer's client, or a witness called by the lawyer, has offered material evidence, and the lawyer comes to know* of its falsity, the lawyer shall take reasonable* remedial measures, including, if necessary, disclosure to the tribunal,* unless disclosure is prohibited by Business and Professions Code section 6068, subdivision (e) and rule 1.6. A lawyer may refuse to offer evidence, other than the testimony of a defendant in a criminal matter, that the lawyer reasonably believes* is false.

(b) A lawyer who represents a client in a proceeding before a tribunal* and who knows* that a person* intends to engage, is engaging or has engaged in criminal or fraudulent* conduct related to the proceeding shall take reasonable* remedial measures to the extent permitted by Business and Professions Code section 6068, subdivision (e) and rule 1.6.

(c) The duties stated in paragraphs (a) and (b) continue to the conclusion of the proceeding.

(d) In an ex parte proceeding where notice to the opposing party in the proceeding is not required or given and the opposing party is not present, a lawyer shall inform the tribunal* of all material facts known* to the lawyer that will enable the tribunal* to make an informed decision, whether or not the facts are adverse to the position of the client.

Comment

[1] This rule governs the conduct of a lawyer in proceedings of a tribunal,* including ancillary proceedings such as a deposition conducted pursuant to a tribunal's* authority. See rule 1.0.1(m) for the definition of "tribunal."

---

*   An asterisk (*) identifies a word or phrase defined in the terminology rule, rule 1.0.1.

[2]   The prohibition in paragraph (a)(1) against making false statements of law or failing to correct a material misstatement of law includes citing as authority a decision that has been overruled or a statute that has been repealed or declared unconstitutional, or failing to correct such a citation previously made to the tribunal* by the lawyer.

Legal Argument

[3]   Legal authority in the controlling jurisdiction may include legal authority outside the jurisdiction in which the tribunal* sits, such as a federal statute or case that is determinative of an issue in a state court proceeding or a Supreme Court decision that is binding on a lower court.

[4]   The duties stated in paragraphs (a) and (b) apply to all lawyers, including defense counsel in criminal cases. If a lawyer knows* that a client intends to testify falsely or wants the lawyer to introduce false evidence, the lawyer should seek to persuade the client that the evidence should not be offered and, if unsuccessful, must refuse to offer the false evidence. If a criminal defendant insists on testifying, and the lawyer knows* that the testimony will be false, the lawyer may offer the testimony in a narrative form if the lawyer made reasonable* efforts to dissuade the client from the unlawful course of conduct and the lawyer has sought permission from the court to withdraw as required by rule 1.16. (See, e.g., *People v. Johnson* (1998) 62 Cal.App.4th 608 [72 Cal.Rptr.2d 805]; *People v. Jennings* (1999) 70 Cal.App.4th 899 [83 Cal.Rptr.2d 33].) The obligations of a lawyer under these rules and the State Bar Act are subordinate to applicable constitutional provisions.

Remedial Measures

[5]   Reasonable* remedial measures under paragraphs (a)(3) and (b) refer to measures that are available under these rules and the State Bar Act, and which a reasonable* lawyer would consider appropriate under the circumstances to comply with the lawyer's duty of candor to the tribunal.* (See, e.g., rules 1.2.1, 1.4(a)(4), 1.16(a), 8.4; Bus. & Prof. Code, §§ 6068, subd. (d), 6128.) Remedial measures also include explaining to the client the lawyer's obligations under this rule and, where applicable, the reasons for the lawyer's decision to seek permission from the tribunal* to withdraw, and remonstrating further with the client to take corrective action that would eliminate the need for the lawyer to withdraw. If the client is an organization, the lawyer should also consider the provisions of rule 1.13. Remedial measures do not include disclosure of client confidential information, which the lawyer is required to protect under Business and Professions Code section 6068, subdivision (e) and rule 1.6.

Duration of Obligation

[6]   A proceeding has concluded within the meaning of this rule when a final judgment in the proceeding has been affirmed on appeal or the time for review has passed. A prosecutor may have obligations that go beyond the scope of this rule. (See, e.g., rule 3.8(f) and (g).)

Ex Parte Communications

[7]   Paragraph (d) does not apply to ex parte communications that are not otherwise prohibited by law or the tribunal.*

---

*   An asterisk (*) identifies a word or phrase defined in the terminology rule, rule 1.0.1.

Withdrawal

[8]   A lawyer's compliance with the duty of candor imposed by this rule does not require that the lawyer withdraw from the representation. The lawyer may, however, be required by rule 1.16 to seek permission of the tribunal* to withdraw if the lawyer's compliance with this rule results in a deterioration of the lawyer-client relationship such that the lawyer can no longer competently and diligently represent the client, or where continued employment will result in a violation of these rules. A lawyer must comply with Business and Professions Code section 6068, subdivision (e) and rule 1.6 with respect to a request to withdraw that is premised on a client's misconduct.

[9]   In addition to this rule, lawyers remain bound by Business and Professions Code sections 6068, subdivision (d) and 6106.

Rule 3.4   Fairness to Opposing Party and Counsel

A lawyer shall not:

(a)   unlawfully obstruct another party's access to evidence, including a witness, or unlawfully alter, destroy or conceal a document or other material having potential evidentiary value. A lawyer shall not counsel or assist another person* to do any such act;

(b)   suppress any evidence that the lawyer or the lawyer's client has a legal obligation to reveal or to produce;

(c)   falsify evidence, counsel or assist a witness to testify falsely, or offer an inducement to a witness that is prohibited by law;

(d)   directly or indirectly pay, offer to pay, or acquiesce in the payment of compensation to a witness contingent upon the content of the witness's testimony or the outcome of the case. Except where prohibited by law, a lawyer may advance, guarantee, or acquiesce in the payment of:

>   (1)   expenses reasonably* incurred by a witness in attending or testifying;

>   (2)   reasonable* compensation to a witness for loss of time in attending or testifying; or

>   (3)   a reasonable* fee for the professional services of an expert witness;

(e)   advise or directly or indirectly cause a person* to secrete himself or herself or to leave the jurisdiction of a tribunal* for the purpose of making that person* unavailable as a witness therein;

(f)   knowingly* disobey an obligation under the rules of a tribunal* except for an open refusal based on an assertion that no valid obligation exists; or

(g)   in trial, assert personal knowledge of facts in issue except when testifying as a witness, or state a personal opinion as to the guilt or innocence of an accused.

Comment

[1]   Paragraph (a) applies to evidentiary material generally, including computerized information. It is a criminal offense to destroy material for purpose of impairing its availability in a pending proceeding or one whose commencement can be foreseen. (See, e.g., Pen. Code, § 135; 18 U.S.C. §§ 1501–1520.) Falsifying evidence is also generally a criminal offense. (See,

---

  *   An asterisk (*) identifies a word or phrase defined in the terminology rule, rule 1.0.1.

e.g., Pen. Code, § 132; 18 U.S.C. § 1519.) Applicable law may permit a lawyer to take temporary possession of physical evidence of client crimes for the purpose of conducting a limited examination that will not alter or destroy material characteristics of the evidence. Applicable law may require a lawyer to turn evidence over to the police or other prosecuting authorities, depending on the circumstances. (See *People v. Lee* (1970) 3 Cal.App.3d 514, 526 [83 Cal.Rptr. 715]; *People v. Meredith* (1981) 29 Cal.3d 682 [175 Cal.Rptr. 612].)

[2]   A violation of a civil or criminal discovery rule or statute does not by itself establish a violation of this rule. See rule 3.8 for special disclosure responsibilities of a prosecutor.

Rule 3.5   Contact With Judges, Officials, Employees, and Jurors

(a)   Except as permitted by statute, an applicable code of judicial ethics or code of judicial conduct, or standards governing employees of a tribunal,* a lawyer shall not directly or indirectly give or lend anything of value to a judge, official, or employee of a tribunal.* This rule does not prohibit a lawyer from contributing to the campaign fund of a judge or judicial officer running for election or confirmation pursuant to applicable law pertaining to such contributions.

(b)   Unless permitted to do so by law, an applicable code of judicial ethics or code of judicial conduct, a rule or ruling of a tribunal,* or a court order, a lawyer shall not directly or indirectly communicate with or argue to a judge or judicial officer upon the merits of a contested matter pending before the judge or judicial officer, except:

   (1)   in open court;

   (2)   with the consent of all other counsel and any unrepresented parties in the matter;

   (3)   in the presence of all other counsel and any unrepresented parties in the matter;

   (4)   in writing* with a copy thereof furnished to all other counsel and any unrepresented parties in the matter; or

   (5)   in ex parte matters.

(c)   As used in this rule, "judge" and "judicial officer" shall also include: (i) administrative law judges; (ii) neutral arbitrators; (iii) State Bar Court judges; (iv) members of an administrative body acting in an adjudicative capacity; and (v) law clerks, research attorneys, or other court personnel who participate in the decision-making process, including referees, special masters, or other persons* to whom a court refers one or more issues and whose decision or recommendation can be binding on the parties if approved by the court.

(d)   A lawyer connected with a case shall not communicate directly or indirectly with anyone the lawyer knows* to be a member of the venire from which the jury will be selected for trial of that case.

(e)   During trial, a lawyer connected with the case shall not communicate directly or indirectly with any juror.

(f)   During trial, a lawyer who is not connected with the case shall not communicate directly or indirectly concerning the case with anyone the lawyer knows* is a juror in the case.

---

*   An asterisk (*) identifies a word or phrase defined in the terminology rule, rule 1.0.1.

(g)   After discharge of the jury from further consideration of a case a lawyer shall not communicate directly or indirectly with a juror if:

    (1)   the communication is prohibited by law or court order;

    (2)   the juror has made known* to the lawyer a desire not to communicate; or

    (3)   the communication involves misrepresentation, coercion, or duress, or is intended to harass or embarrass the juror or to influence the juror's actions in future jury service.

(h)   A lawyer shall not directly or indirectly conduct an out of court investigation of a person* who is either a member of a venire or a juror in a manner likely to influence the state of mind of such person* in connection with present or future jury service.

(i)   All restrictions imposed by this rule also apply to communications with, or investigations of, members of the family of a person* who is either a member of a venire or a juror.

(j)   A lawyer shall reveal promptly to the court improper conduct by a person* who is either a member of a venire or a juror, or by another toward a person* who is either a member of a venire or a juror or a member of his or her family, of which the lawyer has knowledge.

(k)   This rule does not prohibit a lawyer from communicating with persons* who are members of a venire or jurors as a part of the official proceedings.

(l)   For purposes of this rule, "juror" means any empaneled, discharged, or excused juror.

Comment

[1]   An applicable code of judicial ethics or code of judicial conduct under this rule includes the California Code of Judicial Ethics and the Code of Conduct for United States Judges. Regarding employees of a tribunal* not subject to judicial ethics or conduct codes, applicable standards include the Code of Ethics for the Court Employees of California and 5 United States Code section 7353 (Gifts to Federal employees). The statutes applicable to adjudicatory proceedings of state agencies generally are contained in the Administrative Procedure Act (Gov. Code, § 11340 et seq.; see Gov. Code, § 11370 [listing statutes with the act].) State and local agencies also may adopt their own regulations and rules governing communications with members or employees of a tribunal.*

[2]   For guidance on permissible communications with a juror in a criminal action after discharge of the jury, see Code of Civil Procedure section 206.

[3]   It is improper for a lawyer to communicate with a juror who has been removed, discharged, or excused from an empaneled jury, regardless of whether notice is given to other counsel, until such time as the entire jury has been discharged from further service or unless the communication is part of the official proceedings of the case.

Rule 3.6   Trial Publicity

(a)   A lawyer who is participating or has participated in the investigation or litigation of a matter shall not make an extrajudicial statement that the lawyer knows* or reasonably should know* will (i) be disseminated by means

---

*   An asterisk (*) identifies a word or phrase defined in the terminology rule, rule 1.0.1.

of public communication and (ii) have a substantial* likelihood of materially prejudicing an adjudicative proceeding in the matter.

(b) Notwithstanding paragraph (a), but only to the extent permitted by Business and Professions Code section 6068, subdivision (e) and rule 1.6, lawyer may state:

(1) the claim, offense or defense involved and, except when prohibited by law, the identity of the persons* involved;

(2) information contained in a public record;

(3) that an investigation of a matter is in progress;

(4) the scheduling or result of any step in litigation;

(5) a request for assistance in obtaining evidence and information necessary thereto;

(6) a warning of danger concerning the behavior of a person* involved, when there is reason to believe* that there exists the likelihood of substantial* harm to an individual or to the public but only to the extent that dissemination by public communication is reasonably* necessary to protect the individual or the public; and

(7) in a criminal case, in addition to subparagraphs (1) through (6):

(i) the identity, general area of residence, and occupation of the accused;

(ii) if the accused has not been apprehended, the information necessary to aid in apprehension of that person;*

(iii) the fact, time, and place of arrest; and

(iv) the identity of investigating and arresting officers or agencies and the length of the investigation.

(c) Notwithstanding paragraph (a), a lawyer may make a statement that a reasonable* lawyer would believe* is required to protect a client from the substantial* undue prejudicial effect of recent publicity not initiated by the lawyer or the lawyer's client. A statement made pursuant to this paragraph shall be limited to such information as is necessary to mitigate the recent adverse publicity.

(d) No lawyer associated in a law firm* or government agency with a lawyer subject to paragraph (a) shall make a statement prohibited by paragraph (a).

Comment

[1] Whether an extrajudicial statement violates this rule depends on many factors, including: (i) whether the extrajudicial statement presents information clearly inadmissible as evidence in the matter for the purpose of proving or disproving a material fact in issue; (ii) whether the extrajudicial statement presents information the lawyer knows* is false, deceptive, or the use of which would violate Business and Professions Code section 6068, subdivision (d) or rule 3.3; (iii) whether the extrajudicial statement violates a lawful "gag" order, or protective order, statute, rule of court, or special rule of confidentiality, for example, in juvenile, domestic, mental disability, and certain criminal proceedings, (see Bus. & Prof. Code, § 6068, subd. (a) and

---

*   An asterisk (*) identifies a word or phrase defined in the terminology rule, rule 1.0.1.

rule 3.4(f), which require compliance with such obligations); and (iv) the timing of the statement.

[2]   This rule applies to prosecutors and criminal defense counsel. See rule 3.8(e) for additional duties of prosecutors in connection with extrajudicial statements about criminal proceedings.

Rule 3.7   Lawyer as Witness

(a)   A lawyer shall not act as an advocate in a trial in which the lawyer is likely to be a witness unless:

(1)   the lawyer's testimony relates to an uncontested issue or matter;

(2)   the lawyer's testimony relates to the nature and value of legal services rendered in the case; or

(3)   the lawyer has obtained informed written consent* from the client. If the lawyer represents the People or a governmental entity, the consent shall be obtained from the head of the office or a designee of the head of the office by which the lawyer is employed.

(b)   A lawyer may act as advocate in a trial in which another lawyer in the lawyer's firm* is likely to be called as a witness unless precluded from doing so by rule 1.7 or rule 1.9.

Comment

[1]   This rule applies to a trial before a jury, judge, administrative law judge or arbitrator. This rule does not apply to other adversarial proceedings. This rule also does not apply in non-adversarial proceedings, as where a lawyer testifies on behalf of a client in a hearing before a legislative body.

[2]   A lawyer's obligation to obtain informed written consent* may be satisfied when the lawyer makes the required disclosure, and the client gives informed consent* on the record in court before a licensed court reporter or court recorder who prepares a transcript or recording of the disclosure and consent. See definition of "written" in rule 1.0.1(n).

[3]   Notwithstanding a client's informed written consent,* courts retain discretion to take action, up to and including disqualification of a lawyer who seeks to both testify and serve as an advocate, to protect the trier of fact from being misled or the opposing party from being prejudiced. (See, e.g., *Lyle v. Superior Court* (1981) 122 Cal.App.3d 470 [175 Cal.Rptr. 918].)

Rule 3.8   Special Responsibilities of a Prosecutor

The prosecutor in a criminal case shall:

(a)   not institute or continue to prosecute a charge that the prosecutor knows* is not supported by probable cause;

(b)   make reasonable* efforts to assure that the accused has been advised of the right to, and the procedure for obtaining, counsel and has been given reasonable* opportunity to obtain counsel;

(c)   not seek to obtain from an unrepresented accused a waiver of important pretrial rights unless the tribunal* has approved the appearance of the accused in propria persona;

(d)   make timely disclosure to the defense of all evidence or information known* to the prosecutor that the prosecutor knows* or reasonably should

---

*   An asterisk (*) identifies a word or phrase defined in the terminology rule, rule 1.0.1.

know* tends to negate the guilt of the accused, mitigate the offense, or mitigate the sentence, except when the prosecutor is relieved of this responsibility by a protective order of the tribunal;* and

(e)   exercise reasonable* care to prevent persons* under the supervision or direction of the prosecutor, including investigators, law enforcement personnel, employees or other persons* assisting or associated with the prosecutor in a criminal case from making an extrajudicial statement that the prosecutor would be prohibited from making under rule 3.6.

(f)   When a prosecutor knows* of new, credible and material evidence creating a reasonable* likelihood that a convicted defendant did not commit an offense of which the defendant was convicted, the prosecutor shall:

> (1)   promptly disclose that evidence to an appropriate court or authority, and

> (2)   if the conviction was obtained in the prosecutor's jurisdiction,

>> (i)   promptly disclose that evidence to the defendant unless a court authorizes delay, and

>> (ii)   undertake further investigation, or make reasonable* efforts to cause an investigation, to determine whether the defendant was convicted of an offense that the defendant did not commit.

(g)   When a prosecutor knows* of clear and convincing evidence establishing that a defendant in the prosecutor's jurisdiction was convicted of an offense that the defendant did not commit, the prosecutor shall seek to remedy the conviction.

Comment

[1]   A prosecutor has the responsibility of a minister of justice and not simply that of an advocate. This responsibility carries with it specific obligations to see that the defendant is accorded procedural justice, that guilt is decided upon the basis of sufficient evidence, and that special precautions are taken to prevent and to rectify the conviction of innocent persons.* This rule is intended to achieve those results. All lawyers in government service remain bound by rules 3.1 and 3.4.

[2]   Paragraph (c) does not forbid the lawful questioning of an uncharged suspect who has knowingly* waived the right to counsel and the right to remain silent. Paragraph (c) also does not forbid prosecutors from seeking from an unrepresented accused a reasonable* waiver of time for initial appearance or preliminary hearing as a means of facilitating the accused's voluntary cooperation in an ongoing law enforcement investigation.

[3]   The disclosure obligations in paragraph (d) are not limited to evidence or information that is material as defined by *Brady v. Maryland* (1963) 373 U.S. 83 [83 S.Ct. 1194] and its progeny. For example, these obligations include, at a minimum, the duty to disclose impeachment evidence or information that a prosecutor knows* or reasonably should know* casts significant doubt on the accuracy or admissibility of witness testimony on which the prosecution intends to rely. Paragraph (d) does not require disclosure of information protected from disclosure by federal or California laws and rules, as interpreted by case law or court orders. Nothing in this rule is intended to be applied in a manner inconsistent with statutory and constitutional provisions governing discovery in California courts. A

---

*   An asterisk (*) identifies a word or phrase defined in the terminology rule, rule 1.0.1.

disclosure's timeliness will vary with the circumstances, and paragraph (d) is not intended to impose timing requirements different from those established by statutes, procedural rules, court orders, and case law interpreting those authorities and the California and federal constitutions.

[4]   The exception in paragraph (d) recognizes that a prosecutor may seek an appropriate protective order from the tribunal* if disclosure of information to the defense could result in substantial* harm to an individual or to the public interest.

[5]   Paragraph (e) supplements rule 3.6, which prohibits extrajudicial statements that have a substantial* likelihood of prejudicing an adjudicatory proceeding. Paragraph (e) is not intended to restrict the statements which a prosecutor may make which comply with rule 3.6(b) or 3.6(c).

[6]   Prosecutors have a duty to supervise the work of subordinate lawyers and nonlawyer employees or agents. (See rules 5.1 and 5.3.) Ordinarily, the reasonable* care standard of paragraph (e) will be satisfied if the prosecutor issues the appropriate cautions to law enforcement personnel and other relevant individuals.

[7]   When a prosecutor knows* of new, credible and material evidence creating a reasonable* likelihood that a person* outside the prosecutor's jurisdiction was convicted of a crime that the person* did not commit, paragraph (f) requires prompt disclosure to the court or other appropriate authority, such as the chief prosecutor of the jurisdiction where the conviction occurred. If the conviction was obtained in the prosecutor's jurisdiction, paragraph (f) requires the prosecutor to examine the evidence and undertake further investigation to determine whether the defendant is in fact innocent or make reasonable* efforts to cause another appropriate authority to undertake the necessary investigation, and to promptly disclose the evidence to the court and, absent court authorized delay, to the defendant. Disclosure to a represented defendant must be made through the defendant's counsel, and, in the case of an unrepresented defendant, would ordinarily be accompanied by a request to a court for the appointment of counsel to assist the defendant in taking such legal measures as may be appropriate. (See rule 4.2.)

[8]   Under paragraph (g), once the prosecutor knows* of clear and convincing evidence that the defendant was convicted of an offense that the defendant did not commit, the prosecutor must seek to remedy the conviction. Depending upon the circumstances, steps to remedy the conviction could include disclosure of the evidence to the defendant, requesting that the court appoint counsel for an unrepresented indigent defendant and, where appropriate, notifying the court that the prosecutor has knowledge that the defendant did not commit the offense of which the defendant was convicted.

[9]   A prosecutor's independent judgment, made in good faith, that the new evidence is not of such nature as to trigger the obligations of paragraphs (f) and (g), though subsequently determined to have been erroneous, does not constitute a violation of this rule.

Rule 3.9   Advocate in Nonadjudicative Proceedings

A lawyer representing a client before a legislative body or administrative agency in connection with a pending nonadjudicative matter or proceeding shall disclose that the appearance is in a representative capacity, except

---

*   An asterisk (*) identifies a word or phrase defined in the terminology rule, rule 1.0.1.

when the lawyer seeks information from an agency that is available to the public.

Comment

This rule only applies when a lawyer represents a client in connection with an official hearing or meeting of a governmental agency or a legislative body to which the lawyer or the lawyer's client is presenting evidence or argument. It does not apply to representation of a client in a negotiation or other bilateral transaction with a governmental agency or in connection with an application for a license or other privilege or the client's compliance with generally applicable reporting requirements, such as the filing of income-tax returns. This rule also does not apply to the representation of a client in connection with an investigation or examination of the client's affairs conducted by government investigators or examiners. Representation in such matters is governed by rules 4.1 through 4.4. This rule does not require a lawyer to disclose a client's identity.

Rule 3.10 Threatening Criminal, Administrative, or Disciplinary Charges

(a) A lawyer shall not threaten to present criminal, administrative, or disciplinary charges to obtain an advantage in a civil dispute.

(b) As used in paragraph (a) of this rule, the term "administrative charges" means the filing or lodging of a complaint with any governmental organization that may order or recommend the loss or suspension of a license, or may impose or recommend the imposition of a fine, pecuniary sanction, or other sanction of a quasi-criminal nature but does not include filing charges with an administrative entity required by law as a condition precedent to maintaining a civil action.

(c) As used in this rule, the term "civil dispute" means a controversy or potential controversy over the rights and duties of two or more persons* under civil law, whether or not an action has been commenced, and includes an administrative proceeding of a quasi-civil nature pending before a federal, state, or local governmental entity.

Comment

[1] Paragraph (a) does not prohibit a statement by a lawyer that the lawyer will present criminal, administrative, or disciplinary charges, unless the statement is made to obtain an advantage in a civil dispute. For example, if a lawyer believes* in good faith that the conduct of the opposing lawyer or party violates criminal or other laws, the lawyer may state that if the conduct continues the lawyer will report it to criminal or administrative authorities. On the other hand, a lawyer could not state or imply that a criminal or administrative action will be pursued unless the opposing party agrees to settle the civil dispute.

[2] This rule does not apply to a threat to bring a civil action. It also does not prohibit actually presenting criminal, administrative or disciplinary charges, even if doing so creates an advantage in a civil dispute. Whether a lawyer's statement violates this rule depends on the specific facts. (See, e.g., *Crane v. State Bar* (1981) 30 Cal.3d 117 [177 Cal.Rptr. 670].) A statement that the lawyer will pursue "all available legal remedies," or words of similar import, does not by itself violate this rule.

---

* An asterisk (*) identifies a word or phrase defined in the terminology rule, rule 1.0.1.

[3]   This rule does not apply to: (i) a threat to initiate contempt proceedings for a failure to comply with a court order; or (ii) the offer of a civil compromise in accordance with a statute such as Penal Code sections 1377 and 1378.

[4]   This rule does not prohibit a government lawyer from offering a global settlement or release-dismissal agreement in connection with related criminal, civil or administrative matters. The government lawyer must have probable cause for initiating or continuing criminal charges. (See rule 3.8(a).)

[5]   As used in paragraph (b), "governmental organizations" includes any federal, state, local, and foreign governmental organizations. Paragraph (b) exempts the threat of filing an administrative charge that is a prerequisite to filing a civil complaint on the same transaction or occurrence.

TRANSACTIONS WITH PERSONS* OTHER THAN CLIENTS

Rule 4.1   Truthfulness in Statements to Others

In the course of representing a client a lawyer shall not knowingly:*

(a)   make a false statement of material fact or law to a third person;* or

(b)   fail to disclose a material fact to a third person* when disclosure is necessary to avoid assisting a criminal or fraudulent* act by a client, unless disclosure is prohibited by Business and Professions Code section 6068, subdivision (e)(1) or rule 1.6.

Comment

[1]   A lawyer is required to be truthful when dealing with others on a client's behalf, but generally has no affirmative duty to inform an opposing party of relevant facts. A misrepresentation can occur if the lawyer incorporates or affirms the truth of a statement of another person* that the lawyer knows* is false. However, in drafting an agreement or other document on behalf of a client, a lawyer does not necessarily affirm or vouch for the truthfulness of representations made by the client in the agreement or document. A nondisclosure can be the equivalent of a false statement of material fact or law under paragraph (a) where a lawyer makes a partially true but misleading material statement or material omission. In addition to this rule, lawyers remain bound by Business and Professions Code section 6106 and rule 8.4.

[2]   This rule refers to statements of fact. Whether a particular statement should be regarded as one of fact can depend on the circumstances. For example, in negotiation, certain types of statements ordinarily are not taken as statements of material fact. Estimates of price or value placed on the subject of a transaction and a party's intentions as to an acceptable settlement of a claim are ordinarily in this category, and so is the existence of an undisclosed principal except where nondisclosure of the principal would constitute fraud.*

[3]   Under rule 1.2.1, a lawyer is prohibited from counseling or assisting a client in conduct that the lawyer knows* is criminal or fraudulent.* See rule 1.4(a)(4) regarding a lawyer's obligation to consult with the client about limitations on the lawyer's conduct. In some circumstances, a lawyer can avoid assisting a client's crime or fraud* by withdrawing from the representation in compliance with rule 1.16.

---

*   An asterisk (*) identifies a word or phrase defined in the terminology rule, rule 1.0.1.

[4]   Regarding a lawyer's involvement in lawful covert activity in the investigation of violations of law, see rule 8.4, Comment [5].

Rule 4.2   Communication With a Represented Person*

(a)   In representing a client, a lawyer shall not communicate directly or indirectly about the subject of the representation with a person* the lawyer knows* to be represented by another lawyer in the matter, unless the lawyer has the consent of the other lawyer.

(b)   In the case of a represented corporation, partnership, association, or other private or governmental organization, this rule prohibits communications with:

> (1)   A current officer, director, partner,*or managing agent of the organization; or
>
> (2)   A current employee, member, agent, or other constituent of the organization, if the subject of the communication is any act or omission of such person* in connection with the matter which may be binding upon or imputed to the organization for purposes of civil or criminal liability.

(c)   This rule shall not prohibit:

> (1)   communications with a public official, board, committee, or body; or
>
> (2)   communications otherwise authorized by law or a court order.

(d)   For purposes of this rule:

> (1)   "Managing agent" means an employee, member, agent, or other constituent of an organization with substantial* discretionary authority over decisions that determine organizational policy.
>
> (2)   "Public official" means a public officer of the United States government, or of a state, county, city, town, political subdivision, or other governmental organization, with the comparable decision-making authority and responsibilities as the organizational constituents described in paragraph (b)(1).

Comment

[1]   This rule applies even though the represented person* initiates or consents to the communication. A lawyer must immediately terminate communication with a person* if, after commencing communication, the lawyer learns that the person* is one with whom communication is not permitted by this rule.

[2]   "Subject of the representation," "matter," and "person" are not limited to a litigation context. This rule applies to communications with any person,* whether or not a party to a formal adjudicative proceeding, contract, or negotiation, who is represented by counsel concerning the matter to which the communication relates.

[3]   The prohibition against communicating "indirectly" with a person* represented by counsel in paragraph (a) is intended to address situations where a lawyer seeks to communicate with a represented person* through an intermediary such as an agent, investigator or the lawyer's client. This rule, however, does not prevent represented persons* from communicating directly

---

*   An asterisk (*) identifies a word or phrase defined in the terminology rule, rule 1.0.1.

with one another with respect to the subject of the representation, nor does it prohibit a lawyer from advising a client concerning such a communication. A lawyer may also advise a client not to accept or engage in such communications. The rule also does not prohibit a lawyer who is a party to a legal matter from communicating on his or her own behalf with a represented person* in that matter.

[4]   This rule does not prohibit communications with a represented person* concerning matters outside the representation. Similarly, a lawyer who knows* that a person* is being provided with limited scope representation is not prohibited from communicating with that person* with respect to matters that are outside the scope of the limited representation. (See, e.g., Cal. Rules of Court, rules 3.35–3.37, 5.425 [Limited Scope Representation].)

[5]   This rule does not prohibit communications initiated by a represented person* seeking advice or representation from an independent lawyer of the person's* choice.

[6]   If a current constituent of the organization is represented in the matter by his or her own counsel, the consent by that counsel to a communication is sufficient for purposes of this rule.

[7]   This rule applies to all forms of governmental and private organizations, such as cities, counties, corporations, partnerships, limited liability companies, and unincorporated associations. When a lawyer communicates on behalf of a client with a governmental organization, or certain employees, members, agents, or other constituents of a governmental organization, however, special considerations exist as a result of the right to petition conferred by the First Amendment of the United States Constitution and article I, section 3 of the California Constitution. Paragraph (c)(1) recognizes these special considerations by generally exempting from application of this rule communications with public boards, committees, and bodies, and with public officials as defined in paragraph (d)(2) of this rule. Communications with a governmental organization constituent who is not a public official, however, will remain subject to this rule when the lawyer knows* the governmental organization is represented in the matter and the communication with that constituent falls within paragraph (b)(2).

[8]   Paragraph (c)(2) recognizes that statutory schemes, case law, and court orders may authorize communications between a lawyer and a person* that would otherwise be subject to this rule. Examples of such statutory schemes include those protecting the right of employees to organize and engage in collective bargaining, employee health and safety, and equal employment opportunity. The law also recognizes that prosecutors and other government lawyers are authorized to contact represented persons,* either directly or through investigative agents and informants, in the context of investigative activities, as limited by relevant federal and state constitutions, statutes, rules, and case law. (See, e.g., *United States v. Carona* (9th Cir. 2011) 630 F.3d 917; *United States v. Talao* (9th Cir. 2000) 222 F.3d 1133.) The rule is not intended to preclude communications with represented persons* in the course of such legitimate investigative activities as authorized by law. This rule also is not intended to preclude communications with represented persons* in the course of legitimate investigative activities engaged in, directly or indirectly, by lawyers representing persons* whom the government has accused of or is investigating for crimes, to the extent those investigative activities are authorized by law.

---

*   An asterisk (*) identifies a word or phrase defined in the terminology rule, rule 1.0.1.

[9]   A lawyer who communicates with a represented person* pursuant to paragraph (c) is subject to other restrictions in communicating with the person.* (See, e.g. Bus. & Prof. Code, § 6106; *Snider v. Superior Court* (2003) 113 Cal.App.4th 1187, 1213 [7 Cal.Rptr.3d 119]; *In the Matter of Dale* (2005) 4 Cal. State Bar Ct. Rptr. 798.)

Rule 4.3   Communicating with an Unrepresented Person*

(a)   In communicating on behalf of a client with a person* who is not represented by counsel, a lawyer shall not state or imply that the lawyer is disinterested. When the lawyer knows* or reasonably should know* that the unrepresented person* incorrectly believes* the lawyer is disinterested in the matter, the lawyer shall make reasonable* efforts to correct the misunderstanding. If the lawyer knows* or reasonably should know* that the interests of the unrepresented person* are in conflict with the interests of the client, the lawyer shall not give legal advice to that person,* except that the lawyer may, but is not required to, advise the person* to secure counsel.

(b)   In communicating on behalf of a client with a person* who is not represented by counsel, a lawyer shall not seek to obtain privileged or other confidential information the lawyer knows* or reasonably should know* the person* may not reveal without violating a duty to another or which the lawyer is not otherwise entitled to receive.

Comment

[1]   This rule is intended to protect unrepresented persons,* whatever their interests, from being misled when communicating with a lawyer who is acting for a client.

[2]   Paragraph (a) distinguishes between situations in which a lawyer knows* or reasonably should know* that the interests of an unrepresented person* are in conflict with the interests of the lawyer's client and situations in which the lawyer does not. In the former situation, the possibility that the lawyer will compromise the unrepresented person's* interests is so great that the rule prohibits the giving of any legal advice, apart from the advice to obtain counsel. A lawyer does not give legal advice merely by stating a legal position on behalf of the lawyer's client. This rule does not prohibit a lawyer from negotiating the terms of a transaction or settling a dispute with an unrepresented person.* So long as the lawyer discloses that the lawyer represents an adverse party and not the person,* the lawyer may inform the person* of the terms on which the lawyer's client will enter into the agreement or settle the matter, prepare documents that require the person's* signature, and explain the lawyer's own view of the meaning of the document and the underlying legal obligations.

[3]   Regarding a lawyer's involvement in lawful covert activity in the investigation of violations of law, see rule 8.4, Comment [5].

Rule 4.4   Duties Concerning Inadvertently Transmitted Writings*

Where it is reasonably* apparent to a lawyer who receives a writing* relating to a lawyer's representation of a client that the writing* was inadvertently sent or produced, and the lawyer knows* or reasonably should know* that the writing* is privileged or subject to the work product doctrine, the lawyer shall:

---

*   An asterisk (*) identifies a word or phrase defined in the terminology rule, rule 1.0.1.

(a)   refrain from examining the writing* any more than is necessary to determine that it is privileged or subject to the work product doctrine, and

(b)   promptly notify the sender.

Comment

[1]   If a lawyer determines this rule applies to a transmitted writing,* the lawyer should return the writing* to the sender, seek to reach agreement with the sender regarding the disposition of the writing,* or seek guidance from a tribunal.* (See *Rico v. Mitsubishi* (2007) 42 Cal.4th 807, 817 [68 Cal.Rptr.3d 758].) In providing notice required by this rule, the lawyer shall comply with rule 4.2.

[2]   This rule does not address the legal duties of a lawyer who receives a writing* that the lawyer knows* or reasonably should know* may have been inappropriately disclosed by the sending person.* (See *Clark v. Superior Court* (2011) 196 Cal.App.4th 37 [125 Cal.Rptr.3d 361].)

LAW FIRMS AND ASSOCIATIONS

Rule 5.1   Responsibilities   of   Managerial   and   Supervisory   Lawyers

(a)   A lawyer who individually or together with other lawyers possesses managerial authority in a law firm,* shall make reasonable* efforts to ensure that the firm* has in effect measures giving reasonable* assurance that all lawyers in the firm* comply with these rules and the State Bar Act.

(b)   A lawyer having direct supervisory authority over another lawyer, whether or not a member or employee of the same law firm,* shall make reasonable* efforts to ensure that the other lawyer complies with these rules and the State Bar Act.

(c)   A lawyer shall be responsible for another lawyer's violation of these rules and the State Bar Act if:

   (1)   the lawyer orders or, with knowledge of the relevant facts and of the specific conduct, ratifies the conduct involved; or

   (2)   the lawyer, individually or together with other lawyers, possesses managerial authority in the law firm* in which the other lawyer practices, or has direct supervisory authority over the other lawyer, whether or not a member or employee of the same law firm,* and knows* of the conduct at a time when its consequences can be avoided or mitigated but fails to take reasonable* remedial action.

Comment

Paragraph (a)—Duties Of Managerial Lawyers To Reasonably Assure Compliance with the Rules*

[1]   Paragraph (a) requires lawyers with managerial authority within a law firm* to make reasonable* efforts to establish internal policies and procedures designed, for example, to detect and resolve conflicts of interest, identify dates by which actions must be taken in pending matters, account for client funds and property, and ensure that inexperienced lawyers are properly supervised.

[2]   Whether particular measures or efforts satisfy the requirements of paragraph (a) might depend upon the law firm's structure and the nature of

---

*   An asterisk (*) identifies a word or phrase defined in the terminology rule, rule 1.0.1.

its practice, including the size of the law firm,* whether it has more than one office location or practices in more than one jurisdiction, or whether the firm* or its partners* engage in any ancillary business.

[3] A partner,* shareholder or other lawyer in a law firm* who has intermediate managerial responsibilities satisfies paragraph (a) if the law firm* has a designated managing lawyer charged with that responsibility, or a management committee or other body that has appropriate managerial authority and is charged with that responsibility. For example, the managing lawyer of an office of a multi-office law firm* would not necessarily be required to promulgate firm-wide policies intended to reasonably* assure that the law firm's lawyers comply with the rules or State Bar Act. However, a lawyer remains responsible to take corrective steps if the lawyer knows* or reasonably should know* that the delegated body or person* is not providing or implementing measures as required by this rule.

[4] Paragraph (a) also requires managerial lawyers to make reasonable* efforts to assure that other lawyers in an agency or department comply with these rules and the State Bar Act. This rule contemplates, for example, the creation and implementation of reasonable* guidelines relating to the assignment of cases and the distribution of workload among lawyers in a public sector legal agency or other legal department. (See, e.g., State Bar of California, Guidelines on Indigent Defense Services Delivery Systems (2006).)

Paragraph (b)—Duties of Supervisory Lawyers

[5] Whether a lawyer has direct supervisory authority over another lawyer in particular circumstances is a question of fact.

Paragraph (c)—Responsibility for Another's Lawyer's Violation

[6] The appropriateness of remedial action under paragraph (c)(2) would depend on the nature and seriousness of the misconduct and the nature and immediacy of its harm. A managerial or supervisory lawyer must intervene to prevent avoidable consequences of misconduct if the lawyer knows* that the misconduct occurred.

[7] A supervisory lawyer violates paragraph (b) by failing to make the efforts required under that paragraph, even if the lawyer does not violate paragraph (c) by knowingly* directing or ratifying the conduct, or where feasible, failing to take reasonable* remedial action.

[8] Paragraphs (a), (b), and (c) create independent bases for discipline. This rule does not impose vicarious responsibility on a lawyer for the acts of another lawyer who is in or outside the law firm.* Apart from paragraph (c) of this rule and rule 8.4(a), a lawyer does not have disciplinary liability for the conduct of a partner,* associate, or subordinate lawyer. The question of whether a lawyer can be liable civilly or criminally for another lawyer's conduct is beyond the scope of these rules.

Rule 5.2   Responsibilities of a Subordinate Lawyer

(a) A lawyer shall comply with these rules and the State Bar Act notwithstanding that the lawyer acts at the direction of another lawyer or other person.*

---

* An asterisk (*) identifies a word or phrase defined in the terminology rule, rule 1.0.1.

(b)   A subordinate lawyer does not violate these rules or the State Bar Act if that lawyer acts in accordance with a supervisory lawyer's reasonable* resolution of an arguable question of professional duty.

Comment

When lawyers in a supervisor-subordinate relationship encounter a matter involving professional judgment as to the lawyers' responsibilities under these rules or the State Bar Act and the question can reasonably* be answered only one way, the duty of both lawyers is clear and they are equally responsible for fulfilling it. Accordingly, the subordinate lawyer must comply with his or her obligations under paragraph (a). If the question reasonably* can be answered more than one way, the supervisory lawyer may assume responsibility for determining which of the reasonable* alternatives to select, and the subordinate may be guided accordingly. If the subordinate lawyer believes* that the supervisor's proposed resolution of the question of professional duty would result in a violation of these rules or the State Bar Act, the subordinate is obligated to communicate his or her professional judgment regarding the matter to the supervisory lawyer.

Rule 5.3   Responsibilities Regarding Nonlawyer Assistants

With respect to a nonlawyer employed or retained by or associated with a lawyer:

(a)   a lawyer who individually or together with other lawyers possesses managerial authority in a law firm,* shall make reasonable* efforts to ensure that the firm* has in effect measures giving reasonable* assurance that the nonlawyer's conduct is compatible with the professional obligations of the lawyer;

(b)   a lawyer having direct supervisory authority over the nonlawyer, whether or not an employee of the same law firm,* shall make reasonable* efforts to ensure that the person's* conduct is compatible with the professional obligations of the lawyer; and

(c)   a lawyer shall be responsible for conduct of such a person* that would be a violation of these rules or the State Bar Act if engaged in by a lawyer if:

    (1)   the lawyer orders or, with knowledge of the relevant facts and of the specific conduct, ratifies the conduct involved; or

    (2)   the lawyer, individually or together with other lawyers, possesses managerial authority in the law firm* in which the person* is employed, or has direct supervisory authority over the person,* whether or not an employee of the same law firm,* and knows* of the conduct at a time when its consequences can be avoided or mitigated but fails to take reasonable* remedial action.

Comment

Lawyers often utilize nonlawyer personnel, including secretaries, investigators, law student interns, and paraprofessionals. Such assistants, whether employees or independent contractors, act for the lawyer in rendition of the lawyer's professional services. A lawyer must give such assistants appropriate instruction and supervision concerning all ethical aspects of their employment. The measures employed in instructing and supervising nonlawyers should take account of the fact that they might not have legal training.

---

   *   An asterisk (*) identifies a word or phrase defined in the terminology rule, rule 1.0.1.

Rule 5.3.1   Employment of Disbarred, Suspended, Resigned, or Involuntarily Inactive Lawyer

(a)   For purposes of this rule:

(1)   "Employ" means to engage the services of another, including employees, agents, independent contractors and consultants, regardless of whether any compensation is paid;

(2)   "Member" means a member of the State Bar of California;

(3)   "Involuntarily inactive member" means a member who is ineligible to practice law as a result of action taken pursuant to Business and Professions Code sections 6007, 6203, subdivision (d)(1), or California Rules of Court, rule 9.31(d);

(4)   "Resigned member" means a member who has resigned from the State Bar while disciplinary charges are pending; and

(5)   "Ineligible person" means a member whose current status with the State Bar of California is disbarred, suspended, resigned, or involuntarily inactive.

(b)   A lawyer shall not employ, associate in practice with, or assist a person* the lawyer knows* or reasonably should know* is an ineligible person to perform the following on behalf of the lawyer's client:

(1)   Render legal consultation or advice to the client;

(2)   Appear on behalf of a client in any hearing or proceeding or before any judicial officer, arbitrator, mediator, court, public agency, referee, magistrate, commissioner, or hearing officer;

(3)   Appear as a representative of the client at a deposition or other discovery matter;

(4)   Negotiate or transact any matter for or on behalf of the client with third parties;

(5)   Receive, disburse or otherwise handle the client's funds; or

(6)   Engage in activities that constitute the practice of law.

(c)   A lawyer may employ, associate in practice with, or assist an ineligible person to perform research, drafting or clerical activities, including but not limited to:

(1)   Legal work of a preparatory nature, such as legal research, the assemblage of data and other necessary information, drafting of pleadings, briefs, and other similar documents;

(2)   Direct communication with the client or third parties regarding matters such as scheduling, billing, updates, confirmation of receipt or sending of correspondence and messages; or

(3)   Accompanying an active lawyer in attending a deposition or other discovery matter for the limited purpose of providing clerical assistance to the active lawyer who will appear as the representative of the client.

(d)   Prior to or at the time of employing, associating in practice with, or assisting a person* the lawyer knows* or reasonably should know* is an ineligible person, the lawyer shall serve upon the State Bar written* notice of the employment, including a full description of such person's current bar

---

*   An asterisk (*) identifies a word or phrase defined in the terminology rule, rule 1.0.1.

status. The written* notice shall also list the activities prohibited in paragraph (b) and state that the ineligible person will not perform such activities. The lawyer shall serve similar written* notice upon each client on whose specific matter such person* will work, prior to or at the time of employing, associating with, or assisting such person* to work on the client's specific matter. The lawyer shall obtain proof of service of the client's written* notice and shall retain such proof and a true and correct copy of the client's written* notice for two years following termination of the lawyer's employment by the client.

(e)   A lawyer may, without client or State Bar notification, employ, associate in practice with, or assist an ineligible person whose sole function is to perform office physical plant or equipment maintenance, courier or delivery services, catering, reception, typing or transcription, or other similar support activities.

(f)   When the lawyer no longer employs, associates in practice with, or assists the ineligible person, the lawyer shall promptly serve upon the State Bar written* notice of the termination.

Comment

If the client is an organization, the lawyer shall serve the notice required by paragraph (d) on its highest authorized officer, employee, or constituent overseeing the particular engagement. (See rule 1.13.)

Rule 5.4   Financial and Similar Arrangements with Nonlawyers

(a)   A lawyer or law firm* shall not share legal fees directly or indirectly with a nonlawyer or with an organization that is not authorized to practice law, except that:

> (1)   an agreement by a lawyer with the lawyer's firm,* partner,* or associate may provide for the payment of money or other consideration over a reasonable* period of time after the lawyer's death, to the lawyer's estate or to one or more specified persons;*

> (2)   a lawyer purchasing the practice of a deceased, disabled or disappeared lawyer may pay the agreed-upon purchase price, pursuant to rule 1.17, to the lawyer's estate or other representative;

> (3)   a lawyer or law firm* may include nonlawyer employees in a compensation or retirement plan, even though the plan is based in whole or in part on a profit-sharing arrangement, provided the plan does not otherwise violate these rules or the State Bar Act;

> (4)   a lawyer or law firm* may pay a prescribed registration, referral, or other fee to a lawyer referral service established, sponsored and operated in accordance with the State Bar of California's Minimum Standards for Lawyer Referral Services; or

> (5)   a lawyer or law firm* may share with or pay a court-awarded legal fee to a nonprofit organization that employed, retained or recommended employment of the lawyer or law firm* in the matter.

(b)   A lawyer shall not form a partnership or other organization with a nonlawyer if any of the activities of the partnership or other organization consist of the practice of law.

---

*   An asterisk (*) identifies a word or phrase defined in the terminology rule, rule 1.0.1.

(c)   A lawyer shall not permit a person* who recommends, employs, or pays the lawyer to render legal services for another to direct or regulate the lawyer's independent professional judgment or interfere with the lawyer-client relationship in rendering legal services.

(d)   A lawyer shall not practice with or in the form of a professional corporation or other organization authorized to practice law for a profit if:

> (1)   a nonlawyer owns any interest in it, except that a fiduciary representative of a lawyer's estate may hold the lawyer's stock or other interest for a reasonable* time during administration;

> (2)   a nonlawyer is a director or officer of the corporation or occupies a position of similar responsibility in any other form of organization; or

> (3)   a nonlawyer has the right or authority to direct or control the lawyer's independent professional judgment.

(e)   The Board of Trustees of the State Bar shall formulate and adopt Minimum Standards for Lawyer Referral Services, which, as from time to time amended, shall be binding on lawyers. A lawyer shall not accept a referral from, or otherwise participate in, a lawyer referral service unless it complies with such Minimum Standards for Lawyer Referral Services.

(f)   A lawyer shall not practice with or in the form of a nonprofit legal aid, mutual benefit or advocacy group if the nonprofit organization allows any third person* to interfere with the lawyer's independent professional judgment, or with the lawyer-client relationship, or allows or aids any person* to practice law in violation of these rules or the State Bar Act.

Comment

[1]   Paragraph (a) does not prohibit a lawyer or law firm* from paying a bonus to or otherwise compensating a nonlawyer employee from general revenues received for legal services, provided the arrangement does not interfere with the independent professional judgment of the lawyer or lawyers in the firm* and does not violate these rules or the State Bar Act. However, a nonlawyer employee's bonus or other form of compensation may not be based on a percentage or share of fees in specific cases or legal matters.

[2]   Paragraph (a) also does not prohibit payment to a nonlawyer third-party for goods and services provided to a lawyer or law firm;* however, the compensation to a nonlawyer third-party may not be determined as a percentage or share of the lawyer's or law firm's overall revenues or tied to fees in particular cases or legal matters. A lawyer may pay to a nonlawyer third-party, such as a collection agency, a percentage of past due or delinquent fees in concluded matters that the third-party collects on the lawyer's behalf.

[3]   Paragraph (a)(5) permits a lawyer to share with or pay court-awarded legal fees to nonprofit legal aid, mutual benefit, and advocacy groups that are not engaged in the unauthorized practice of law. (See *Frye v. Tenderloin Housing Clinic, Inc.* (2006) 38 Cal.4th 23 [40 Cal.Rptr.3d 221]; see also rule 6.3.) Regarding a lawyer's contribution of legal fees to a legal services organization, see rule 1.0, Comment [5] on financial support for programs providing pro bono legal services.

[4]   This rule is not intended to affect case law regarding the relationship between insurers and lawyers providing legal services to insureds. (See, e.g.,

---

*   An asterisk (*) identifies a word or phrase defined in the terminology rule, rule 1.0.1.

Gafcon, Inc. v. Ponsor Associates (2002) 98 Cal.App.4th 1388 [120 Cal.Rptr.2d 392].)

[5]   Paragraph (c) is not intended to alter or diminish a lawyer's obligations under rule 1.8.6 (Compensation from One Other Than Client).

Rule 5.5   Unauthorized Practice of Law; Multijurisdictional Practice of Law

(a)   A lawyer admitted to practice law in California shall not:

(1)   practice law in a jurisdiction where to do so would be in violation of regulations of the profession in that jurisdiction; or

(2)   knowingly* assist a person* in the unauthorized practice of law in that jurisdiction.

(b)   A lawyer who is not admitted to practice law in California shall not:

(1)   except as authorized by these rules or other law, establish or maintain a resident office or other systematic or continuous presence in California for the practice of law; or

(2)   hold out to the public or otherwise represent that the lawyer is admitted to practice law in California.

Comment

Paragraph (b)(1) prohibits lawyers from practicing law in California unless otherwise entitled to practice law in this state by court rule or other law. (See, e.g., Bus. & Prof. Code, § 6125 et seq.; see also Cal. Rules of Court, rules 9.40 [counsel pro hac vice], 9.41 [appearances by military counsel], 9.42 [certified law students], 9.43 [out-of-state attorney arbitration counsel program], 9.44 [registered foreign legal consultant], 9.45 [registered legal services attorneys], 9.46 [registered in-house counsel], 9.47 [attorneys practicing temporarily in California as part of litigation], 9.48 [non-litigating attorneys temporarily in California to provide legal services].)

Rule 5.6   Restrictions on a Lawyer's Right to Practice

(a)   Unless authorized by law, a lawyer shall not participate in offering or making:

(1)   a partnership, shareholders, operating, employment, or other similar type of agreement that restricts the right of a lawyer to practice after termination of the relationship, except an agreement that concerns benefits upon retirement; or

(2)   an agreement that imposes a restriction on a lawyer's right to practice in connection with a settlement of a client controversy, or otherwise.

(b)   A lawyer shall not participate in offering or making an agreement which precludes the reporting of a violation of these rules.

(c)   This rule does not prohibit an agreement that is authorized by Business and Professions Code sections 6092.5, subdivision (i) or 6093.

Comment

[1]   Concerning the application of paragraph (a)(1), see Business and Professions Code section 16602; *Howard v. Babcock* (1993) 6 Cal.4th 409, 425 [25 Cal.Rptr.2d 80].

---

*   An asterisk (*) identifies a word or phrase defined in the terminology rule, rule 1.0.1.

[2]   Paragraph (a)(2) prohibits a lawyer from offering or agreeing not to represent other persons* in connection with settling a claim on behalf of a client.

[3]   This rule does not prohibit restrictions that may be included in the terms of the sale of a law practice pursuant to rule 1.17.

PUBLIC SERVICE

Rule 6.1   **[Reserved]**

Rule 6.2   **[Reserved]**

Rule 6.3   **Membership In Legal Services Organization**

A lawyer may serve as a director, officer or member of a legal services organization, apart from the law firm* in which the lawyer practices, notwithstanding that the organization serves persons* having interests adverse to a client of the lawyer. The lawyer shall not knowingly* participate in a decision or action of the organization:

(a)   if participating in the decision or action would be incompatible with the lawyer's obligations to a client under Business and Professions Code section 6068, subdivision (e)(1) or rules 1.6(a), 1.7, 1.9, or 1.18; or

(b)   where the decision or action could have a material adverse effect on the representation of a client of the organization whose interests are adverse to a client of the lawyer.

Comment

Lawyers should support and participate in legal service organizations. A lawyer who is an officer or a member of such an organization does not thereby have a client-lawyer relationship with persons* served by the organization. However, there is potential conflict between the interests of such persons* and the interests of the lawyer's clients. If the possibility of such conflict disqualified a lawyer from serving on the board of a legal services organization, the profession's involvement in such organizations would be severely curtailed.

Rule 6.4   **[Reserved]**

Rule 6.5   **Limited Legal Services Programs**

(a)   A lawyer who, under the auspices of a program sponsored by a court, government agency, bar association, law school, or nonprofit organization, provides short-term limited legal services to a client without expectation by either the lawyer or the client that the lawyer will provide continuing representation in the matter:

   (1)   is subject to rules 1.7 and 1.9(a) only if the lawyer knows* that the representation of the client involves a conflict of interest; and

   (2)   is subject to rule 1.10 only if the lawyer knows* that another lawyer associated with the lawyer in a law firm* is prohibited from representation by rule 1.7 or 1.9(a) with respect to the matter.

(b)   Except as provided in paragraph (a)(2), rule 1.10 is inapplicable to a representation governed by this rule.

(c)   The personal disqualification of a lawyer participating in the program will not be imputed to other lawyers participating in the program.

---

*   An asterisk (*) identifies a word or phrase defined in the terminology rule, rule 1.0.1.

Comment

[1]   Courts, government agencies, bar associations, law schools and various nonprofit organizations have established programs through which lawyers provide short-term limited legal services—such as advice or the completion of legal forms that will assist persons* in addressing their legal problems without further representation by a lawyer. In these programs, such as legal-advice hotlines, advice-only clinics or pro se counseling programs, whenever a lawyer-client relationship is established, there is no expectation that the lawyer's representation of the client will continue beyond that limited consultation. Such programs are normally operated under circumstances in which it is not feasible for a lawyer to systematically screen* for conflicts of interest as is generally required before undertaking a representation.

[2]   A lawyer who provides short-term limited legal services pursuant to this rule must secure the client's informed consent* to the limited scope of the representation. (See rule 1.2(b).) If a short-term limited representation would not be reasonable* under the circumstances, the lawyer may offer advice to the client but must also advise the client of the need for further assistance of counsel. Except as provided in this rule, these rules and the State Bar Act, including the lawyer's duty of confidentiality under Business and Professions Code section 6068, subdivision (e)(1) and rules 1.6 and 1.9, are applicable to the limited representation.

[3]   A lawyer who is representing a client in the circumstances addressed by this rule ordinarily is not able to check systematically for conflicts of interest. Therefore, paragraph (a)(1) requires compliance with rules 1.7 and 1.9(a) only if the lawyer knows* that the representation presents a conflict of interest for the lawyer. In addition, paragraph (a)(2) imputes conflicts of interest to the lawyer only if the lawyer knows* that another lawyer in the lawyer's law firm* would be disqualified under rules 1.7 or 1.9(a).

[4]   Because the limited nature of the services significantly reduces the risk of conflicts of interest with other matters being handled by the lawyer's law firm,* paragraph (b) provides that imputed conflicts of interest are inapplicable to a representation governed by this rule except as provided by paragraph (a)(2). Paragraph (a)(2) imputes conflicts of interest to the participating lawyer when the lawyer knows* that any lawyer in the lawyer's firm* would be disqualified under rules 1.7 or 1.9(a). By virtue of paragraph (b), moreover, a lawyer's participation in a short-term limited legal services program will not be imputed to the lawyer's law firm* or preclude the lawyer's law firm* from undertaking or continuing the representation of a client with interests adverse to a client being represented under the program's auspices. Nor will the personal disqualification of a lawyer participating in the program be imputed to other lawyers participating in the program.

[5]   If, after commencing a short-term limited representation in accordance with this rule, a lawyer undertakes to represent the client in the matter on an ongoing basis, rules 1.7, 1.9(a), and 1.10 become applicable.

INFORMATION ABOUT LEGAL SERVICES

Rule 7.1   Communications Concerning a Lawyer's Services

(a)   A lawyer shall not make a false or misleading communication about the lawyer or the lawyer's services. A communication is false or misleading if it

---

*   An asterisk (*) identifies a word or phrase defined in the terminology rule, rule 1.0.1.

contains a material misrepresentation of fact or law, or omits a fact necessary to make the communication considered as a whole not materially misleading.

(b)   The Board of Trustees of the State Bar may formulate and adopt standards as to communications that will be presumed to violate rule 7.1, 7.2, 7.3, 7.4 or 7.5. The standards shall only be used as presumptions affecting the burden of proof in disciplinary proceedings involving alleged violations of these rules. "Presumption affecting the burden of proof" means that presumption defined in Evidence Code sections 605 and 606. Such standards formulated and adopted by the Board, as from time to time amended, shall be effective and binding on all lawyers.

Comment

[1]   This rule governs all communications of any type whatsoever about the lawyer or the lawyer's services, including advertising permitted by rule 7.2. A communication includes any message or offer made by or on behalf of a lawyer concerning the availability for professional employment of a lawyer or a lawyer's law firm* directed to any person.*

[2]   A communication that contains an express guarantee or warranty of the result of a particular representation is a false or misleading communication under this rule. (See also Bus. & Prof. Code, § 6157.2, subd. (a).)

[3]   This rule prohibits truthful statements that are misleading. A truthful statement is misleading if it omits a fact necessary to make the lawyer's communication considered as a whole not materially misleading. A truthful statement is also misleading if it is presented in a manner that creates a substantial* likelihood that it will lead a reasonable* person* to formulate a specific conclusion about the lawyer or the lawyer's services for which there is no reasonable* factual foundation. Any communication that states or implies "no fee without recovery" is also misleading unless the communication also expressly discloses whether or not the client will be liable for costs.

[4]   A communication that truthfully reports a lawyer's achievements on behalf of clients or former clients, or a testimonial about or endorsement of the lawyer, may be misleading if presented so as to lead a reasonable* person* to form an unjustified expectation that the same results could be obtained for other clients in similar matters without reference to the specific factual and legal circumstances of each client's case. Similarly, an unsubstantiated comparison of the lawyer's services or fees with the services or fees of other lawyers may be misleading if presented with such specificity as would lead a reasonable* person* to conclude that the comparison can be substantiated. An appropriate disclaimer or qualifying language often avoids creating unjustified expectations.

[5]   This rule prohibits a lawyer from making a communication that states or implies that the lawyer is able to provide legal services in a language other than English unless the lawyer can actually provide legal services in that language or the communication also states in the language of the communication the employment title of the person* who speaks such language.

[6]   Rules 7.1 through 7.5 are not the sole basis for regulating communications concerning a lawyer's services. (See, e.g., Bus. & Prof. Code, §§ 6150–6159.2, 17000 et. seq.) Other state or federal laws may also apply.

---

*   An asterisk (*) identifies a word or phrase defined in the terminology rule, rule 1.0.1.

Rule 7.2   Advertising

(a)   Subject to the requirements of rules 7.1 and 7.3, a lawyer may advertise services through any written,* recorded or electronic means of communication, including public media.

(b)   A lawyer shall not compensate, promise or give anything of value to a person* for the purpose of recommending or securing the services of the lawyer or the lawyer's law firm,* except that a lawyer may:

(1)   pay the reasonable* costs of advertisements or communications permitted by this rule;

(2)   pay the usual charges of a legal services plan or a qualified lawyer referral service. A qualified lawyer referral service is a lawyer referral service established, sponsored and operated in accordance with the State Bar of California's Minimum Standards for a Lawyer Referral Service in California;

(3)   pay for a law practice in accordance with rule 1.17;

(4)   refer clients to another lawyer or a nonlawyer professional pursuant to an arrangement not otherwise prohibited under these Rules or the State Bar Act that provides for the other person* to refer clients or customers to the lawyer, if:

(i)   the reciprocal referral arrangement is not exclusive; and

(ii)   the client is informed of the existence and nature of the arrangement;

(5)   offer or give a gift or gratuity to a person* having made a recommendation resulting in the employment of the lawyer or the lawyer's law firm,* provided that the gift or gratuity was not offered or given in consideration of any promise, agreement, or understanding that such a gift or gratuity would be forthcoming or that referrals would be made or encouraged in the future.

(c)   Any communication made pursuant to this rule shall include the name and address of at least one lawyer or law firm* responsible for its content.

Comment

[1]   This rule permits public dissemination of accurate information concerning a lawyer and the lawyer's services, including for example, the lawyer's name or firm* name, the lawyer's contact information; the kinds of services the lawyer will undertake; the basis on which the lawyer's fees are determined, including prices for specific services and payment and credit arrangements; a lawyer's foreign language ability; names of references and, with their consent, names of clients regularly represented; and other information that might invite the attention of those seeking legal assistance. This rule, however, prohibits the dissemination of false or misleading information, for example, an advertisement that sets forth a specific fee or range of fees for a particular service where, in fact, the lawyer charges or intends to charge a greater fee than that stated in the advertisement.

[2]   Neither this rule nor rule 7.3 prohibits communications authorized by law, such as court-approved class action notices.

---

*   An asterisk (*) identifies a word or phrase defined in the terminology rule, rule 1.0.1.

Paying Others to Recommend a Lawyer

[3]   Paragraph (b)(1) permits a lawyer to compensate employees, agents, and vendors who are engaged to provide marketing or client-development services, such as publicists, public-relations personnel, business-development staff, and website designers. See rule 5.3 for the duties of lawyers and law firms* with respect to supervising the conduct of nonlawyers who prepare marketing materials and provide client development services.

[4]   Paragraph (b)(4) permits a lawyer to make referrals to another lawyer or nonlawyer professional, in return for the undertaking of that person* to refer clients or customers to the lawyer. Such reciprocal referral arrangements must not interfere with the lawyer's professional judgment as to making referrals or as to providing substantive legal services. (See rules 2.1 and 5.4(c).) Conflicts of interest created by arrangements made pursuant to paragraph (b)(4) are governed by rule 1.7. A division of fees between or among lawyers not in the same law firm* is governed by rule 1.5.1.

Rule 7.3   Solicitation of Clients

(a)   A lawyer shall not by in-person, live telephone or real-time electronic contact solicit professional employment when a significant motive for doing so is the lawyer's pecuniary gain, unless the person* contacted:

> (1)   is a lawyer; or

> (2)   has a family, close personal, or prior professional relationship with the lawyer.

(b)   A lawyer shall not solicit professional employment by written,* recorded or electronic communication or by in-person, telephone or real-time electronic contact even when not otherwise prohibited by paragraph (a), if:

> (1)   the person* being solicited has made known* to the lawyer a desire not to be solicited by the lawyer; or

> (2)   the solicitation is transmitted in any manner which involves intrusion, coercion, duress or harassment.

(c)   Every written,* recorded or electronic communication from a lawyer soliciting professional employment from any person* known* to be in need of legal services in a particular matter shall include the word "Advertisement" or words of similar import on the outside envelope, if any, and at the beginning and ending of any recorded or electronic communication, unless the recipient of the communication is a person* specified in paragraphs (a)(1) or (a)(2), or unless it is apparent from the context that the communication is an advertisement.

(d)   Notwithstanding the prohibitions in paragraph (a), a lawyer may participate with a prepaid or group legal service plan operated by an organization not owned or directed by the lawyer that uses in-person, live telephone or real-time electronic contact to solicit memberships or subscriptions for the plan from persons* who are not known* to need legal services in a particular matter covered by the plan.

(e)   As used in this rule, the terms "solicitation" and "solicit" refer to an oral or written* targeted communication initiated by or on behalf of the lawyer that is directed to a specific person* and that offers to provide, or can reasonably* be understood as offering to provide, legal services.

---

*   An asterisk (*) identifies a word or phrase defined in the terminology rule, rule 1.0.1.

Comment

[1]   A lawyer's communication does not constitute a solicitation if it is directed to the general public, such as through a billboard, an Internet banner advertisement, a website or a television commercial, or if it is in response to a request for information or is automatically generated in response to Internet searches.

[2]   Paragraph (a) does not apply to situations in which the lawyer is motivated by considerations other than the lawyer's pecuniary gain. Therefore, paragraph (a) does not prohibit a lawyer from participating in constitutionally protected activities of bona fide public or charitable legal-service organizations, or bona fide political, social, civic, fraternal, employee or trade organizations whose purposes include providing or recommending legal services to its members or beneficiaries. (See, e.g., *In re Primus* (1978) 436 U.S. 412 [98 S.Ct. 1893].)

[3]   This rule does not prohibit a lawyer from contacting representatives of organizations or groups that may be interested in establishing a bona fide group or prepaid legal plan for their members, insureds, beneficiaries or other third parties for the purpose of informing such entities of the availability of and details concerning the plan or arrangement which the lawyer or lawyer's firm* is willing to offer.

[4]   Lawyers who participate in a legal service plan as permitted under paragraph (d) must comply with rules 7.1, 7.2, and 7.3(b). (See also rules 5.4 and 8.4(a).)

Rule 7.4   Communication   of   Fields   of   Practice   and   Specialization

(a)   A lawyer shall not state that the lawyer is a certified specialist in a particular field of law, unless:

>   (1)   the lawyer is currently certified as a specialist by the Board of Legal Specialization, or any other entity accredited by the State Bar to designate specialists pursuant to standards adopted by the Board of Trustees; and

>   (2)   the name of the certifying organization is clearly identified in the communication.

(b)   Notwithstanding paragraph (a), a lawyer may communicate the fact that the lawyer does or does not practice in particular fields of law. A lawyer may also communicate that his or her practice specializes in, is limited to, or is concentrated in a particular field of law, subject to the requirements of rule 7.1.

Rule 7.5   Firm* Names and Trade Names

(a)   A lawyer shall not use a firm* name, trade name or other professional designation that violates rule 7.1.

(b)   A lawyer in private practice shall not use a firm* name, trade name or other professional designation that states or implies a relationship with a government agency or with a public or charitable legal services organization, or otherwise violates rule 7.1.

---

*   An asterisk (*) identifies a word or phrase defined in the terminology rule, rule 1.0.1.

(c)   A lawyer shall not state or imply that the lawyer practices in or has a professional relationship with a law firm* or other organization unless that is the fact.

Comment

The term "other professional designation" includes, but is not limited to, logos, letterheads, URLs, and signature blocks.

MAINTAINING THE INTEGRITY OF THE PROFESSION

Rule 8.1   False Statement Regarding Application for Admission to Practice Law

(a)   An applicant for admission to practice law shall not, in connection with that person's* own application for admission, make a statement of material fact that the lawyer knows* to be false, or make such a statement with reckless disregard as to its truth or falsity.

(b)   A lawyer shall not, in connection with another person's* application for admission to practice law, make a statement of material fact that the lawyer knows* to be false.

(c)   An applicant for admission to practice law, or a lawyer in connection with an application for admission, shall not fail to disclose a fact necessary to correct a statement known* by the applicant or the lawyer to have created a material misapprehension in the matter, except that this rule does not authorize disclosure of information protected by Business and Professions Code section 6068, subdivision (e) and rule 1.6.

(d)   As used in this rule, "admission to practice law" includes admission or readmission to membership in the State Bar; reinstatement to active membership in the State Bar; and any similar process relating to admission or certification to practice law in California or elsewhere.

Comment

[1]   A person* who makes a false statement in connection with that person's* own application for admission to practice law may be subject to discipline under this rule after that person* has been admitted. (See, e.g., *In re Gossage* (2000) 23 Cal.4th 1080 [99 Cal.Rptr.2d 130].)

[2]   A lawyer's duties with respect to a *pro hac vice* application or other application to a court for admission to practice law are governed by rule 3.3.

[3]   A lawyer representing an applicant for admission to practice law is governed by the rules applicable to the lawyer-client relationship, including Business and Professions Code section 6068, subdivision (e)(1) and rule 1.6. A lawyer representing a lawyer who is the subject of a disciplinary proceeding is not governed by this rule but is subject to the requirements of rule 3.3.

Rule 8.1.1   Compliance with Conditions of Discipline and Agreements in Lieu of Discipline

A lawyer shall comply with the terms and conditions attached to any agreement in lieu of discipline, any public or private reproval, or to other discipline administered by the State Bar pursuant to Business and Professions Code sections 6077 and 6078 and California Rules of Court, rule 9.19.

---

*   An asterisk (*) identifies a word or phrase defined in the terminology rule, rule 1.0.1.

Comment

Other provisions also require a lawyer to comply with agreements in lieu of discipline and conditions of discipline. (See, e.g., Bus. & Prof. Code, § 6068, subds. (k), (l).)

Rule 8.2   Judicial Officials

(a)   A lawyer shall not make a statement of fact that the lawyer knows* to be false or with reckless disregard as to its truth or falsity concerning the qualifications or integrity of a judge or judicial officer, or of a candidate for election or appointment to judicial office.

(b)   A lawyer who is a candidate for judicial office in California shall comply with canon 5 of the California Code of Judicial Ethics. For purposes of this rule, "candidate for judicial office" means a lawyer seeking judicial office by election. The determination of when a lawyer is a candidate for judicial office by election is defined in the terminology section of the California Code of Judicial Ethics. A lawyer's duty to comply with this rule shall end when the lawyer announces withdrawal of the lawyer's candidacy or when the results of the election are final, whichever occurs first.

(c)   A lawyer who seeks appointment to judicial office shall comply with canon 5B(1) of the California Code of Judicial Ethics. A lawyer becomes an applicant seeking judicial office by appointment at the time of first submission of an application or personal data questionnaire to the appointing authority. A lawyer's duty to comply with this rule shall end when the lawyer advises the appointing authority of the withdrawal of the lawyer's application.

Comment

To maintain the fair and independent administration of justice, lawyers should defend judges and courts unjustly criticized. Lawyers also are obligated to maintain the respect due to the courts of justice and judicial officers. (See Bus. & Prof. Code, § 6068, subd. (b).)

Rule 8.3   [Reserved]

Rule 8.4   Misconduct

It is professional misconduct for a lawyer to:

(a)   violate these rules or the State Bar Act, knowingly* assist, solicit, or induce another to do so, or do so through the acts of another;

(b)   commit a criminal act that reflects adversely on the lawyer's honesty, trustworthiness, or fitness as a lawyer in other respects;

(c)   engage in conduct involving dishonesty, fraud,* deceit, or reckless or intentional misrepresentation;

(d)   engage in conduct that is prejudicial to the administration of justice;

(e)   state or imply an ability to influence improperly a government agency or official, or to achieve results by means that violate these rules, the State Bar Act, or other law; or

(f)   knowingly* assist, solicit, or induce a judge or judicial officer in conduct that is a violation of an applicable code of judicial ethics or code of judicial

---

*   An asterisk (*) identifies a word or phrase defined in the terminology rule, rule 1.0.1.

conduct, or other law. For purposes of this rule, "judge" and "judicial officer" have the same meaning as in rule 3.5(c).

Comment

[1]   A violation of this rule can occur when a lawyer is acting in propria persona or when a lawyer is not practicing law or acting in a professional capacity.

[2]   Paragraph (a) does not prohibit a lawyer from advising a client concerning action the client is legally entitled to take.

[3]   A lawyer may be disciplined for criminal acts as set forth in Business and Professions Code sections 6101 et seq., or if the criminal act constitutes "other misconduct warranting discipline" as defined by California Supreme Court case law. (See *In re Kelley* (1990) 52 Cal.3d 487 [276 Cal.Rptr. 375].)

[4]   A lawyer may be disciplined under Business and Professions Code section 6106 for acts involving moral turpitude, dishonesty, or corruption, whether intentional, reckless, or grossly negligent.

[5]   Paragraph (c) does not apply where a lawyer advises clients or others about, or supervises, lawful covert activity in the investigation of violations of civil or criminal law or constitutional rights, provided the lawyer's conduct is otherwise in compliance with these rules and the State Bar Act.

[6]   This rule does not prohibit those activities of a particular lawyer that are protected by the First Amendment to the United States Constitution or by Article I, section 2 of the California Constitution.

Rule 8.4.1   Prohibited   Discrimination,   Harassment   and Retaliation

(a)   In representing a client, or in terminating or refusing to accept the representation of any client, a lawyer shall not:

> (1)   unlawfully harass or unlawfully discriminate against persons* on the basis of any protected characteristic; or

> (2)   unlawfully retaliate against persons.*

(b)   In relation to a law firm's operations, a lawyer shall not:

> (1)   on the basis of any protected characteristic,

>> (i)   unlawfully discriminate or knowingly* permit unlawful discrimination;

>> (ii)   unlawfully harass or knowingly* permit the unlawful harassment of an employee, an applicant, an unpaid intern or volunteer, or a person* providing services pursuant to a contract; or

>> (iii)   unlawfully refuse to hire or employ a person*, or refuse to select a person* for a training program leading to employment, or bar or discharge a person* from employment or from a training program leading to employment, or discriminate against a person* in compensation or in terms, conditions, or privileges of employment; or

> (2)   unlawfully retaliate against persons.*

---

*   An asterisk (*) identifies a word or phrase defined in the terminology rule, rule 1.0.1.

(c)   For purposes of this rule:

(1)   "protected characteristic" means race, religious creed, color, national origin, ancestry, physical disability, mental disability, medical condition, genetic information, marital status, sex, gender, gender identity, gender expression, sexual orientation, age, military and veteran status, or other category of discrimination prohibited by applicable law, whether the category is actual or perceived;

(2)   "knowingly permit" means to fail to advocate corrective action where the lawyer knows* of a discriminatory policy or practice that results in the unlawful discrimination or harassment prohibited by paragraph (b);

(3)   "unlawfully" and "unlawful" shall be determined by reference to applicable state and federal statutes and decisions making unlawful discrimination or harassment in employment and in offering goods and services to the public; and

(4)   "retaliate" means to take adverse action against a person* because that person* has (i) opposed, or (ii) pursued, participated in, or assisted any action alleging, any conduct prohibited by paragraphs (a)(1) or (b)(1) of this rule.

(d)   A lawyer who is the subject of a State Bar investigation or State Bar Court proceeding alleging a violation of this rule shall promptly notify the State Bar of any criminal, civil, or administrative action premised, whether in whole or part, on the same conduct that is the subject of the State Bar investigation or State Bar Court proceeding.

(e)   Upon being issued a notice of a disciplinary charge under this rule, a lawyer shall:

(1)   if the notice is of a disciplinary charge under paragraph (a) of this rule, provide a copy of the notice to the California Department of Fair Employment and Housing and the United States Department of Justice, Coordination and Review Section; or

(2)   if the notice is of a disciplinary charge under paragraph (b) of this rule, provide a copy of the notice to the California Department of Fair Employment and Housing and the United States Equal Employment Opportunity Commission.

(f)   This rule shall not preclude a lawyer from:

(1)   representing a client alleged to have engaged in unlawful discrimination, harassment, or retaliation;

(2)   declining or withdrawing from a representation as required or permitted by rule 1.16; or

(3)   providing advice and engaging in advocacy as otherwise required or permitted by these rules and the State Bar Act.

Comment

[1]   Conduct that violates this rule undermines confidence in the legal profession and our legal system and is contrary to the fundamental principle that all people are created equal. A lawyer may not engage in such conduct through the acts of another. (See rule 8.4(a).) In relation to a law firm's operations, this rule imposes on all law firm* lawyers the responsibility to

---

*   An asterisk (*) identifies a word or phrase defined in the terminology rule, rule 1.0.1.

advocate corrective action to address known* harassing or discriminatory conduct by the firm* or any of its other lawyers or nonlawyer personnel. Law firm* management and supervisorial lawyers retain their separate responsibility under rules 5.1 and 5.3. Neither this rule nor rule 5.1 or 5.3 imposes on the alleged victim of any conduct prohibited by this rule any responsibility to advocate corrective action.

[2]   The conduct prohibited by paragraph (a) includes the conduct of a lawyer in a proceeding before a judicial officer. (See Cal. Code Jud. Ethics, canon 3B(6) ["A judge shall require lawyers in proceedings before the judge to refrain from manifesting, by words or conduct, bias or prejudice based upon race, sex, gender, religion, national origin, ethnicity, disability, age, sexual orientation, marital status, socioeconomic status, or political affiliation against parties, witnesses, counsel, or others."].) A lawyer does not violate paragraph (a) by referring to any particular status or group when the reference is relevant to factual or legal issues or arguments in the representation. While both the parties and the court retain discretion to refer such conduct to the State Bar, a court's finding that peremptory challenges were exercised on a discriminatory basis does not alone establish a violation of paragraph (a).

[3]   A lawyer does not violate this rule by limiting the scope or subject matter of the lawyer's practice or by limiting the lawyer's practice to members of underserved populations. A lawyer also does not violate this rule by otherwise restricting who will be accepted as clients for advocacy-based reasons, as required or permitted by these rules or other law.

[4]   This rule does not apply to conduct protected by the First Amendment to the United States Constitution or by Article I, section 2 of the California Constitution.

[5]   What constitutes a failure to advocate corrective action under paragraph (c)(2) will depend on the nature and seriousness of the discriminatory policy or practice, the extent to which the lawyer knows* of unlawful discrimination or harassment resulting from that policy or practice, and the nature of the lawyer's relationship to the lawyer or law firm* implementing that policy or practice. For example, a law firm* non-management and nonsupervisorial lawyer who becomes aware that the law firm* is engaging in a discriminatory hiring practice may advocate corrective action by bringing that discriminatory practice to the attention of a law firm* management lawyer who would have responsibility under rule 5.1 or 5.3 to take reasonable* remedial action upon becoming aware of a violation of this rule.

[6]   Paragraph (d) ensures that the State Bar and the State Bar Court will be provided with information regarding related proceedings that may be relevant in determining whether a State Bar investigation or a State Bar Court proceeding relating to a violation of this rule should be abated.

[7]   Paragraph (e) recognizes the public policy served by enforcement of laws and regulations prohibiting unlawful discrimination, by ensuring that the state and federal agencies with primary responsibility for coordinating the enforcement of those laws and regulations is provided with notice of any allegation of unlawful discrimination, harassment, or retaliation by a lawyer that the State Bar finds has sufficient merit to warrant issuance of a notice of a disciplinary charge.

---

*   An asterisk (*) identifies a word or phrase defined in the terminology rule, rule 1.0.1.

[8]   This rule permits the imposition of discipline for conduct that would not necessarily result in the award of a remedy in a civil or administrative proceeding if such proceeding were filed.

[9]   A disciplinary investigation or proceeding for conduct coming within this rule may also be initiated and maintained if such conduct warrants discipline under California Business and Professions Code sections 6106 and 6068, the California Supreme Court's inherent authority to impose discipline, or other disciplinary standard.

Rule 8.5   Disciplinary Authority; Choice of Law

(a)   Disciplinary Authority.

A lawyer admitted to practice in California is subject to the disciplinary authority of California, regardless of where the lawyer's conduct occurs. A lawyer not admitted in California is also subject to the disciplinary authority of California if the lawyer provides or offers to provide any legal services in California. A lawyer may be subject to the disciplinary authority of both California and another jurisdiction for the same conduct.

(b)   Choice of Law.

In any exercise of the disciplinary authority of California, the rules of professional conduct to be applied shall be as follows:

(1)   for conduct in connection with a matter pending before a tribunal,* the rules of the jurisdiction in which the tribunal* sits, unless the rules of the tribunal* provide otherwise; and

(2)   for any other conduct, the rules of the jurisdiction in which the lawyer's conduct occurred, or, if the predominant effect of the conduct is in a different jurisdiction, the rules of that jurisdiction shall be applied to the conduct. A lawyer shall not be subject to discipline if the lawyer's conduct conforms to the rules of a jurisdiction in which the lawyer reasonably believes* the predominant effect of the lawyer's conduct will occur.

Comment

Disciplinary Authority

The conduct of a lawyer admitted to practice in California is subject to the disciplinary authority of California. (See Bus. & Prof. Code, §§ 6077, 6100.) Extension of the disciplinary authority of California to other lawyers who provide or offer to provide legal services in California is for the protection of the residents of California. A lawyer disciplined by a disciplinary authority in another jurisdiction may be subject to discipline in California for the same conduct. (See, e.g., § 6049.1.)

---

*   An asterisk (*) identifies a word or phrase defined in the terminology rule, rule 1.0.1.

SELECTED PROVISIONS FROM THE CALIFORNIA BUSINESS AND PROFESSIONS CODE

California is unusual in the number of statutory provisions it has that regulate the practice of law. Most are part of the state's Business and Professions Code. The following sections provide a sense of the range of topics covered. They are current through September 2018.

CHAPTER 4.   ATTORNEYS

ARTICLE 4.   ADMISSION TO THE PRACTICE OF LAW

ARTICLE 4.   ADMISSION TO THE PRACTICE OF LAW

§ 6067.   Oath

Every person on his admission shall take an oath to support the Constitution of the United States and the Constitution of the State of California, and faithfully to discharge the duties of any attorney at law to the best of his knowledge and ability. A certificate of the oath shall be indorsed upon his license.

§ 6068.   Duties of Attorney

It is the duty of an attorney to do all of the following:

(a)   To support the Constitution and laws of the United States and of this state.

(b)   To maintain the respect due to the courts of justice and judicial officers.

(c)   To counsel or maintain those actions, proceedings, or defenses only as appear to him or her legal or just, except the defense of a person charged with a public offense.

(d)   To employ, for the purpose of maintaining the causes confided to him or her those means only as are consistent with truth, and never to seek to mislead the judge or any judicial officer by an artifice or false statement of fact or law.

(e)   (1)   To maintain inviolate the confidence, and at every peril to himself or herself to preserve the secrets, of his or her client.

(2)   Notwithstanding paragraph (1), an attorney may, but is not required to, reveal confidential information relating to the representation of a client to the extent that the attorney reasonably believes the disclosure is necessary to prevent a criminal act that the

374

attorney reasonably believes is likely to result in death of, or substantial bodily harm to, an individual.

(f)   To advance no fact prejudicial to the honor or reputation of a party or witness, unless required by the justice of the cause with which he or she is charged.

(g)   Not to encourage either the commencement or the continuance of an action or proceeding from any corrupt motive of passion or interest.

(h)   Never to reject, for any consideration personal to himself or herself, the cause of the defenseless or the oppressed.

(i)   To cooperate and participate in any disciplinary investigation or other regulatory or disciplinary proceeding pending against himself or herself. However, this subdivision shall not be construed to deprive an attorney of any privilege guaranteed by the Fifth Amendment to the Constitution of the United States, or any other constitutional or statutory privileges. This subdivision shall not be construed to require an attorney to cooperate with a request that requires him or her to waive any constitutional or statutory privilege or to comply with a request for information or other matters within an unreasonable period of time in light of the time constraints of the attorney's practice. Any exercise by an attorney of any constitutional or statutory privilege shall not be used against the attorney in a regulatory or disciplinary proceeding against him or her.

(j)   To comply with the requirements of Section 6002.1.

(k)   To comply with all conditions attached to any disciplinary probation, including a probation imposed with the concurrence of the attorney.

(l)   To keep all agreements made in lieu of disciplinary prosecution with the agency charged with attorney discipline.

(m)   To respond promptly to reasonable status inquiries of clients and to keep clients reasonably informed of significant developments in matters with regard to which the attorney has agreed to provide legal services.

(n)   To provide copies to the client of certain documents under time limits and as prescribed in a rule of professional conduct which the board shall adopt.

(o)   To report to the agency charged with attorney discipline, in writing, within 30 days of the time the attorney has knowledge of any of the following:

(1)   The filing of three or more lawsuits in a 12-month period against the attorney for malpractice or other wrongful conduct committed in a professional capacity.

(2)   The entry of judgment against the attorney in a civil action for fraud, misrepresentation, breach of fiduciary duty, or gross negligence committed in a professional capacity.

(3)   The imposition of judicial sanctions against the attorney, except for sanctions for failure to make discovery or monetary sanctions of less than one thousand dollars ($1,000).

(4)   The bringing of an indictment or information charging a felony against the attorney.

(5)   The conviction of the attorney, including any verdict of guilty, or plea of guilty or no contest, of a felony, or a misdemeanor committed

in the course of the practice of law, or in a manner in which a client of the attorney was the victim, or a necessary element of which, as determined by the statutory or common law definition of the misdemeanor, involves improper conduct of an attorney, including dishonesty or other moral turpitude, or an attempt or a conspiracy or solicitation of another to commit a felony or a misdemeanor of that type.

(6) The imposition of discipline against the attorney by a professional or occupational disciplinary agency or licensing board, whether in California or elsewhere.

(7) Reversal of judgment in a proceeding based in whole or in part upon misconduct, grossly incompetent representation, or willful misrepresentation by an attorney.

(8) As used in this subdivision, "against the attorney" includes claims and proceedings against any firm of attorneys for the practice of law in which the attorney was a partner at the time of the conduct complained of and any law corporation in which the attorney was a shareholder at the time of the conduct complained of unless the matter has to the attorney's knowledge already been reported by the law firm or corporation.

(9) The State Bar may develop a prescribed form for the making of reports required by this section, usage of which it may require by rule or regulation.

(10) This subdivision is only intended to provide that the failure to report as required herein may serve as a basis of discipline.

ARTICLE 4.8.   PRO BONO SERVICES

§ 6073.   Pro Bono Legal Services; Financial Support in Lieu of Directly Providing Services

It has been the tradition of those learned in the law and licensed to practice law in this state to provide voluntary pro bono legal services to those who cannot afford the help of a lawyer. Every lawyer authorized and privileged to practice law in California is expected to make a contribution. In some circumstances, it may not be feasible for a lawyer to directly provide pro bono services. In those circumstances, a lawyer may instead fulfill his or her individual pro bono ethical commitment, in part, by providing financial support to organizations providing free legal services to persons of limited means. In deciding to provide that financial support, the lawyer should, at minimum, approximate the value of the hours of pro bono legal service that he or she would otherwise have provided. In some circumstances, pro bono contributions may be measured collectively, as by a firm's aggregate pro bono activities or financial contributions. Lawyers also make invaluable contributions through their other voluntary public service activities that increase access to justice or improve the law and the legal system. In view of their expertise in areas that critically affect the lives and well-being of members of the public, lawyers are uniquely situated to provide invaluable assistance in order to benefit those who might otherwise be unable to assert or protect their interests, and to support those legal organizations that advance these goals.

§ 6074. **Pro Bono Civil Legal Assistance to Veterans and their Families; Administration of Program by State Bar; Resources and Educational Materials**

(a) The State Bar shall administer a program to coordinate pro bono civil legal assistance to veterans and their families who otherwise cannot afford legal services.

(b) The State Bar shall engage with local bar associations, legal aid organizations, veterans service providers, and volunteer attorneys and encourage those groups to provide legal services throughout the state.

(c) The State Bar shall provide resources and educational materials to attorneys and the public in order to support the purposes of this section by, among other things, doing the following:

(1) Compiling a list of local bar associations, legal aid organizations, veterans service providers, and volunteer attorneys willing to provide pro bono legal services to veterans, organized by city and county, and posting the list on its Internet Web site.

(2) Conducting a statewide survey of programs that provide civil legal assistance to veterans in order to identify whether and where there is a need for legal advice clinics, publishing a report and recommendations based upon its findings no later than December 31, 2018, and posting the report on its Internet Web site.

ARTICLE 6. DISCIPLINARY AUTHORITY OF THE COURTS

§ 6100. **Disbarment or Suspension**

For any of the causes provided in this article, arising after an attorney's admission to practice, he or she may be disbarred or suspended by the Supreme Court. Nothing in this article limits the inherent power of the Supreme Court to discipline, including to summarily disbar, any attorney.

§ 6101. **Conviction of Crime; Notice of Pendency of Action; Record of Conviction; Proceedings**

(a) Conviction of a felony or misdemeanor, involving moral turpitude, constitutes a cause for disbarment or suspension.

In any proceeding, whether under this article or otherwise, to disbar or suspend an attorney on account of that conviction, the record of conviction shall be conclusive evidence of guilt of the crime of which he or she has been convicted.

. . .

(e) A plea or verdict of guilty, an acceptance of a nolo contendere plea, or a conviction after a plea of nolo contendere is deemed to be a conviction within the meaning of those sections.

§ 6102. **Immediate Suspension and Subsequent Disbarment Upon Conviction of Crime; Crimes Involving Moral Turpitude or Felonies; Procedure**

(a) Upon the receipt of the certified copy of the record of conviction, if it appears therefrom that the crime of which the attorney was convicted involved, or that there is probable cause to believe that it involved, moral turpitude or is a felony under the laws of California, the United States, or any state or territory thereof, the Supreme Court shall suspend the attorney until the time for appeal has elapsed, if no appeal has been taken, or until the judgment of conviction has been affirmed on appeal, or has otherwise become final, and until the further order of the court. Upon its own motion or upon good cause shown, the court may decline to impose, or may set aside, the suspension when it appears to be in the interest of justice to do so, with due regard being given to maintaining the integrity of, and confidence in, the profession.

. . .

§ 6103. Disobedience of Court Order; Violation of Oath or Attorney's Duties

A wilful disobedience or violation of an order of the court requiring him to do or forbear an act connected with or in the course of his profession, which he ought in good faith to do or forbear, and any violation of the oath taken by him, or of his duties as such attorney, constitute causes for disbarment or suspension.

§ 6103.5 Written Offers of Settlement; Required Communication to Client; Discovery

(a) A member of the State Bar shall promptly communicate to the member's client all amounts, terms, and conditions of any written offer of settlement made by or on behalf of an opposing party. As used in this section, "client" includes any person employing the member of the State Bar who possesses the authority to accept an offer of settlement, or in a class action, who is a representative of the class.

(b) Any written offer of settlement or any required communication of a settlement offer, as described in subdivision (a), shall be discoverable by either party in any action in which the existence or communication of the offer of settlement is an issue before the trier of fact.

§ 6103.6 Compensation for Trustee Services; Donative Transfers; Violations Constituting Grounds for Discipline

Violation of Section 15687 of the Probate Code, or of Part 3.5 (commencing with Section 21350) or Part 3.7 (commencing with Section 21360) of Division 11 of the Probate Code, shall be grounds for discipline, if the attorney knew or should have known of the facts leading to the violation. This section shall only apply to violations that occur on or after January 1, 1994.

§ 6103.7 Reporting or Threatening to Report Suspected Immigration Status

It is cause for suspension, disbarment, or other discipline for any member of the State Bar to report suspected immigration status or threaten to report suspected immigration status of a witness or party to a civil or administrative action or his or her family member to a federal, state, or local agency because the witness or party exercises or has exercised a right related to his or her employment or hiring of residential real property, broadly interpreted. As used in this section, "family member" means a spouse, parent, sibling, child, uncle, aunt, niece, nephew, cousin, grandparent, or grandchild related by blood, adoption, marriage, or domestic partnership.

§ 6104. Unauthorized Appearance

Corruptly or wilfully and without authority appearing as attorney for a party to an action or proceeding constitutes a cause for disbarment or suspension.

§ 6105. Permitting Misuse of Name

Lending his name to be used as attorney by another person who is not an attorney constitutes a cause for disbarment or suspension.

§ 6106. Moral Turpitude, Dishonesty or Corruption Irrespective of Criminal Conviction

The commission of any act involving moral turpitude, dishonesty or corruption, whether the act is committed in the course of his relations as an attorney or otherwise, and whether the act is a felony or misdemeanor or not, constitutes a cause for disbarment or suspension.

If the act constitutes a felony or misdemeanor, conviction thereof in a criminal proceeding is not a condition precedent to disbarment or suspension from practice therefor.

§ 6106.1 Advocacy of Overthrow of Government

Advocating the overthrow of the Government of the United States or of this State by force, violence, or other unconstitutional means, constitutes a cause for disbarment or suspension.

. . .

§ 6106.5 Insurance Claims; Fraud

It shall constitute cause for disbarment or suspension for an attorney to engage in any conduct prohibited under Section 1871.4 of the Insurance Code or Section 550 of the Penal Code.

. . .

§ 6106.7 Miller-Ayala Athlete Agents Act; Violation of Requirements

It shall constitute cause for the imposition of discipline of an attorney within the meaning of this chapter for an attorney to violate any provision of the Miller-Ayala Athlete Agents Act (Chapter 2.5 (commencing with Section 18895) of Division 8), or to violate any provision of Chapter 1 (commencing with Section 1500) of Part 6 of Division 2 of the Labor Code, prior to January 1, 1997, or to violate any provision of the law of any other state regulating athlete agents.

§ 6106.8 Sexual Involvement Between Lawyers and Clients; Rule of Professional Conduct

(a) The Legislature hereby finds and declares that there is no rule that governs propriety of sexual relationships between lawyers and clients. The Legislature further finds and declares that it is difficult to separate sound judgment from emotion or bias which may result from sexual involvement between a lawyer and his or her client during the period that an attorney-client relationship exists, and that emotional detachment is essential to the lawyer's ability to render competent legal services. Therefore, in order to ensure that a lawyer acts in the best interest of his or her client, a rule of professional conduct governing sexual relations between attorneys and their clients shall be adopted.

(b) With the approval of the Supreme Court, the State Bar shall adopt a rule of professional conduct governing sexual relations between attorneys and their clients in cases involving, but not limited to, probate matters and domestic relations, including dissolution proceedings, child custody cases, and settlement proceedings.

(c)   The State Bar shall submit the proposed rule to the Supreme Court for approval no later than January 1, 1991.

(d)   Intentional violation of this rule shall constitute a cause for suspension or disbarment.

§ 6106.9 Sexual Relations Between Attorney and Client; Cause for Discipline; Complaints to State Bar

(a)   It shall constitute cause for the imposition of discipline of an attorney within the meaning of this chapter for an attorney to do any of the following:

(1)   Expressly or impliedly condition the performance of legal services for a current or prospective client upon the client's willingness to engage in sexual relations with the attorney.

(2)   Employ coercion, intimidation, or undue influence in entering into sexual relations with a client.

(3)   Continue representation of a client with whom the attorney has sexual relations if the sexual relations cause the attorney to perform legal services incompetently in violation of Rule 3–110 of the Rules of Professional Conduct of the State Bar of California, or if the sexual relations would, or would be likely to, damage or prejudice the client's case.

(b)   Subdivision (a) shall not apply to sexual relations between attorneys and their spouses or persons in an equivalent domestic relationship or to ongoing consensual sexual relationships that predate the initiation of the attorney-client relationship.

(c)   Where an attorney in a firm has sexual relations with a client but does not participate in the representation of that client, the attorneys in the firm shall not be subject to discipline under this section solely because of the occurrence of those sexual relations.

(d)   For the purposes of this section, "sexual relations" means sexual intercourse or the touching of an intimate part of another person for the purpose of sexual arousal, gratification, or abuse.

(e)   Any complaint made to the State Bar alleging a violation of subdivision (a) shall be verified under oath by the person making the complaint.

ARTICLE 7. UNLAWFUL PRACTICE OF LAW

§ 6125.   Necessity of Active Membership in State Bar

No person shall practice law in California unless the person is an active member of the State Bar.

§ 6126.   Unauthorized Practice or Attempted Practice; Advertising or Holding Out; Penalties

(a)   Any person advertising or holding himself or herself out as practicing or entitled to practice law or otherwise practicing law who is not an active member of the State Bar, or otherwise authorized pursuant to statute or court rule to practice law in this state at the time of doing so, is guilty of a misdemeanor punishable by up to one year in a county jail or by a fine of up to one thousand dollars ($1,000), or by both that fine and imprisonment. Upon a second or subsequent conviction, the person shall be confined in a county jail for not less than 90 days, except in an unusual case where the interests of justice would be served by imposition of a lesser sentence or a fine. If the court imposes only a fine or a sentence of less than 90 days for a second or subsequent conviction under this subdivision, the court shall state the reasons for its sentencing choice on the record.

(b)   Any person who has been involuntarily enrolled as an inactive member of the State Bar, or has been suspended from membership from the State Bar, or has been disbarred, or has resigned from the State Bar with charges pending, and thereafter practices or attempts to practice law, advertises or holds himself or herself out as practicing or otherwise entitled to practice law, is guilty of a crime punishable by imprisonment pursuant to subdivision (h) of Section 1170 of the Penal Code or in a county jail for a period not to exceed six months. However, any person who has been involuntarily enrolled as an inactive member of the State Bar pursuant to paragraph (1) of subdivision (e) of Section 6007 and who knowingly thereafter practices or attempts to practice law, or advertises or holds himself or herself out as practicing or otherwise entitled to practice law, is guilty of a crime punishable by imprisonment pursuant to subdivision (h) of Section 1170 of the Penal Code or in a county jail for a period not to exceed six months.

(c)   The willful failure of a member of the State Bar, or one who has resigned or been disbarred, to comply with an order of the Supreme Court to comply with Rule 9.20 of California Rules of Court, constitutes a crime punishable by imprisonment pursuant to subdivision (h) of Section 1170 of the Penal Code or in a county jail for a period not to exceed six months.

(d)   The penalties provided in this section are cumulative to each other and to any other remedies or penalties provided by law.

. . .

§ 6127.   Contempt of Court

The following acts or omissions in respect to the practice of law are contempts of the authority of the courts:

(a)   Assuming to be an officer or attorney of a court and acting as such, without authority.

(b)   Advertising or holding oneself out as practicing or as entitled to practice law or otherwise practicing law in any court, without being an active member of the State Bar.

Proceedings to adjudge a person in contempt of court under this section are to be taken in accordance with the provisions of Title V of Part III of the Code of Civil Procedure.

§ 6128.   Deceit, Collusion, Delay of Suit and Improper Receipt of Money as Misdemeanor

Every attorney is guilty of a misdemeanor who either:

(a)   Is guilty of any deceit or collusion, or consents to any deceit or collusion, with intent to deceive the court or any party.

(b)   Willfully delays his client's suit with a view to his own gain.

(c)   Willfully receives any money or allowance for or on account of any money which he has not laid out or become answerable for.

Any violation of the provisions of this section is punishable by imprisonment in the county jail not exceeding six months, or by a fine not exceeding two thousand five hundred dollars ($2,500), or by both.

§ 6129.   Buying Claim as Misdemeanor

Every attorney who, either directly or indirectly, buys or is interested in buying any evidence of debt or thing in action, with intent to bring suit thereon, is guilty of a misdemeanor.

Any violation of the provisions of this section is punishable by imprisonment in the county jail not exceeding six months, or by a fine not exceeding two thousand five hundred dollars ($2,500), or by both.

§ 6130.   Disbarred or Suspended Attorney Suing as Assignee

No person, who has been an attorney, shall while a judgment of disbarment or suspension is in force appear on his own behalf as plaintiff in the prosecution of any action where the subject of the action has been assigned to him subsequent to the entry of the judgment of disbarment or suspension and solely for purpose of collection.

§ 6131.   Aiding Defense Where Partner or Self Has Acted as Public Prosecutor; Misdemeanor and Disbarment

Every attorney is guilty of a misdemeanor and, in addition to the punishment prescribed therefor, shall be disbarred:

(a)   Who directly or indirectly advises in relation to, or aids, or promotes the defense of any action or proceeding in any court the prosecution of which is carried on, aided or promoted by any person as district attorney or other public prosecutor with whom such person is directly or indirectly connected as a partner.

(b)   Who, having himself prosecuted or in any manner aided or promoted any action or proceeding in any court as district attorney or other public prosecutor, afterwards, directly or indirectly, advises in relation to or takes any part in the defense thereof, as attorney or otherwise, or who takes or receives any valuable consideration from or on behalf of any defendant in any such action upon any understanding or agreement whatever having relation to the defense thereof.

This section does not prohibit an attorney from defending himself in person, as attorney or counsel, when prosecuted, either civilly or criminally.

§ 6132.   Firm Names; Removal of Names of Attorneys Under Discipline

Any law firm, partnership, corporation, or association which contains the name of an attorney who is disbarred, or who resigned with charges pending, in its business name shall remove the name of that attorney from its business name, and from all signs, advertisements, letterhead, and other materials containing that name, within 60 days of the disbarment or resignation.

. . .

ARTICLE 8.5.   FEE AGREEMENTS

§ 6146.   Limitations; Periodic Payments

(a)   An attorney shall not contract for or collect a contingency fee for representing any person seeking damages in connection with an action for injury or damage against a health care provider based upon such person's alleged professional negligence in excess of the following limits:

(1)   Forty percent of the first fifty thousand dollars ($50,000) recovered.

(2)   Thirty-three and one-third percent of the next fifty thousand dollars ($50,000) recovered.

(3)   Twenty-five percent of the next five hundred thousand dollars ($500,000) recovered.

(4)   Fifteen percent of any amount on which the recovery exceeds six hundred thousand dollars ($600,000).

The limitations shall apply regardless of whether the recovery is by settlement, arbitration, or judgment, or whether the person for whom the recovery is made is a responsible adult, an infant, or a person of unsound mind.

(b)   If periodic payments are awarded to the plaintiff pursuant to Section 667.7 of the Code of Civil Procedure, the court shall place a total value on these payments based upon the projected life expectancy of the plaintiff and include this amount in computing the total award from which attorney's fees are calculated under this section.

(c)   For purposes of this section:

(1)   "Recovered" means the net sum recovered after deducting any disbursements or costs incurred in connection with prosecution or settlement of the claim. Costs of medical care incurred by the plaintiff and the attorney's office-overhead costs or charges are not deductible disbursements or costs for such purpose.

(2)   "Health care provider" means any person licensed or certified pursuant to Division 2 (commencing with Section 500), or licensed pursuant to the Osteopathic Initiative Act, or the Chiropractic Initiative Act, or licensed pursuant to Chapter 2.5 (commencing with Section 1440) of Division 2 of the Health and Safety Code; and any clinic, health dispensary, or health facility, licensed pursuant to Division 2 (commencing with Section 1200) of the Health and Safety Code. "Health care provider" includes the legal representatives of a health care provider.

(3)   "Professional negligence" is a negligent act or omission to act by a health care provider in the rendering of professional services, which act or omission is the proximate cause of a personal injury or wrongful death, provided that the services are within the scope of services for which the provider is licensed and which are not within any restriction imposed by the licensing agency or licensed hospital.

§ 6147. Contingency Fee Contracts; Duplicate Copy; Contents; Effect of Noncompliance; Recovery of Workers' Compensation Benefits

(a)   An attorney who contracts to represent a client on a contingency fee basis shall, at the time the contract is entered into, provide a duplicate copy of the contract, signed by both the attorney and the client, or the client's guardian or representative, to the plaintiff, or to the client's guardian or representative. The contract shall be in writing and shall include, but is not limited to, all of the following:

(1)   A statement of the contingency fee rate which the client and attorney have agreed upon.

(2)   A statement as to how disbursements and costs incurred in connection with the prosecution or settlement of the claim will affect the contingency fee and the client's recovery.

(3)   A statement as to what extent, if any, the client could be required to pay any compensation to the attorney for related matters that arise out of their relationship not covered by their contingency fee contract. This may include any amounts collected for the plaintiff by the attorney.

(4)   Unless the claim is subject to the provisions of Section 6146, a statement that the fee is not set by law but is negotiable between attorney and client.

(5)   If the claim is subject to the provisions of Section 6146, a statement that the rates set forth in that section are the maximum limits for the contingency fee agreement, and that the attorney and client may negotiate a lower rate.

(b)   Failure to comply with any provision of this section renders the agreement voidable at the option of the plaintiff, and the attorney shall thereupon be entitled to collect a reasonable fee.

(c)   This section shall not apply to contingency fee contracts for the recovery of workers' compensation benefits.

(d)   This section shall become operative on January 1, 2000.

§ 6147.5 Contingency Fee Contracts; Recovery of Claims Between Merchants

(a)   Sections 6147 and 6148 shall not apply to contingency fee contracts for the recovery of claims between merchants as defined in Section 2104 of the Commercial Code, arising from the sale or lease of goods or services rendered, or money loaned for use, in the conduct of a business or profession if the merchant contracting for legal services employs 10 or more individuals.

(b)(1)   In the instances in which no written contract for legal services exists as permitted by subdivision (a), an attorney shall not contract for or collect a contingency fee in excess of the following limits:

(A)   Twenty percent of the first three hundred dollars ($300) collected.

(B)   Eighteen percent of the next one thousand seven hundred dollars ($1,700) collected.

(C)   Thirteen percent of sums collected in excess of two thousand dollars ($2,000).

(2)   However, the following minimum charges may be charged and collected:

(A)   Twenty-five dollars ($25) in collections of seventy-five dollars ($75) to one hundred twenty-five dollars ($125).

(B)   Thirty-three and one-third percent of collections less than seventy-five dollars ($75).

§ 6148. Contracts for Services in Cases Not Coming Within § 6147; Bills Rendered by Attorney; Contents; Failure to Comply

(a)   In any case not coming within Section 6147 in which it is reasonably foreseeable that total expense to a client, including attorney fees, will exceed one thousand dollars ($1,000), the contract for services in the case shall be in writing. At the time the contract is entered into, the attorney shall provide a duplicate copy of the contract signed by both the attorney and the client, or the client's guardian or representative, to the client or to the client's guardian or representative. The written contract shall contain all of the following:

(1)   Any basis of compensation including, but not limited to, hourly rates, statutory fees or flat fees, and other standard rates, fees, and charges applicable to the case.

(2)   The general nature of the legal services to be provided to the client.

(3)   The respective responsibilities of the attorney and the client as to the performance of the contract.

(b)   All bills rendered by an attorney to a client shall clearly state the basis thereof. Bills for the fee portion of the bill shall include the amount, rate, basis for calculation, or other method of determination of the attorney's fees and costs. Bills for the cost and expense portion of the bill shall clearly identify the costs and expenses incurred and the amount of the costs and expenses. Upon request by the client, the attorney shall provide a bill to the client no later than 10 days following the request unless the attorney has provided a bill to the client within 31 days prior to the request, in which case the attorney may provide a bill to the client no later than 31 days following the date the most recent bill was provided. The client is entitled to make similar requests at intervals of no less than 30 days following the initial request. In providing responses to client requests for billing information, the attorney may use billing data that is currently effective on the date of the request, or, if any fees or costs to that date cannot be accurately determined, they shall be described and estimated.

(c)   Failure to comply with any provision of this section renders the agreement voidable at the option of the client, and the attorney shall, upon the agreement being voided, be entitled to collect a reasonable fee.

(d)   This section shall not apply to any of the following:

(1)   Services rendered in an emergency to avoid foreseeable prejudice to the rights or interests of the client or where a writing is otherwise impractical.

(2)   An arrangement as to the fee implied by the fact that the attorney's services are of the same general kind as previously rendered to and paid for by the client.

(3)   If the client knowingly states in writing, after full disclosure of this section, that a writing concerning fees is not required.

(4)   If the client is a corporation.

(e)   This section applies prospectively only to fee agreements following its operative date.

(f)   This section shall become operative on January 1, 2000.

§ 6149.   Written Fee Contract: Confidential Communication

A written fee contract shall be deemed to be a confidential communication within the meaning of subdivision (e) of Section 6068 and of Section 952 of the Evidence Code.

§ 6149.5 Third-Party Liability Claim; Settlement by Insurer; Notice to Claimant; Effect on Action or Defense

(a) Upon the payment of one hundred dollars ($100) or more in settlement of any third-party liability claim the insurer shall provide written notice to the claimant if both of the following apply:

(1) The claimant is a natural person.

(2) The payment is delivered to the claimant's lawyer or other representative by draft, check, or otherwise.

(b) For purposes of this section, "written notice" includes providing to the claimant a copy of the cover letter sent to the claimant's attorney or other representative that accompanied the settlement payment.

(c) This section shall not create any cause of action for any person against the insurer based upon the insurer's failure to provide the notice to a claimant required by this section. This section shall not create a defense for any party to any cause of action based upon the insurer's failure to provide this notice.

ARTICLE 9. UNLAWFUL SOLICITATION

§ 6151. Definitions

As used in this article:

(a) A runner or capper is any person, firm, association or corporation acting for consideration in any manner or in any capacity as an agent for an attorney at law or law firm, whether the attorney or any member of the law firm is admitted in California or any other jurisdiction, in the solicitation or procurement of business for the attorney at law or law firm as provided in this article.

(b) An agent is one who represents another in dealings with one or more third persons.

§ 6152. Prohibition of Solicitation

(a) It is unlawful for:

(1) Any person, in an individual capacity or in a capacity as a public or private employee, or for any firm, corporation, partnership or association to act as a runner or capper for any attorneys or to solicit any business for any attorneys in and about the state prisons, county jails, city jails, city prisons, or other places of detention of persons, city receiving hospitals, city and county receiving hospitals, county hospitals, superior courts, or in any public institution or in any public place or upon any public street or highway or in and about private hospitals, sanitariums or in and about any private institution or upon private property of any character whatsoever.

(2) Any person to solicit another person to commit or join in the commission of a violation of subdivision (a).

(b) A general release from a liability claim obtained from any person during the period of the first physical confinement, whether as an inpatient or outpatient, in a clinic or health facility as defined in Sections 1203 and 1250 of the Health and Safety Code, as a result of the injury alleged to have given rise to the claim and primarily for treatment of the injury, is presumed fraudulent if the release is executed within 15 days after the commencement of confinement or prior to release from confinement, whichever occurs first.

(c)   Nothing in this section shall be construed to prevent the recommendation of professional employment where that recommendation is not prohibited by the Rules of Professional Conduct of the State Bar of California.

(d)   Nothing in this section shall be construed to mean that a public defender or assigned counsel may not make known his or her services as a criminal defense attorney to persons unable to afford legal counsel whether such persons are in custody or otherwise.

§ 6153.   Violations; Penalty

Any person, firm, partnership, association, or corporation violating subdivision (a) of Section 6152 is punishable, upon a first conviction, by imprisonment in a county jail for not more than one year or by a fine not exceeding fifteen thousand dollars ($15,000), or by both that imprisonment and fine. Upon a second or subsequent conviction, a person, firm, partnership, association, or corporation is punishable by imprisonment in a county jail for not more than one year, or by imprisonment pursuant to subdivision (h) of Section 1170 of the Penal Code for two, three, or four years, or by a fine not exceeding fifteen thousand dollars ($15,000), or by both that imprisonment and fine.

Any person employed either as an officer, director, trustee, clerk, servant or agent of this state or of any county or other municipal corporation or subdivision thereof, who is found guilty of violating any of the provisions of this article, shall forfeit the right to his office and employment in addition to any other penalty provided in this article.

§ 6154.   Runner or Capper Used to Procure Business; Void Contract; Divesting of Fees and Other Compensation; Fees Recovered From Workers' Compensation Actions

(a)   Any contract for professional services secured by any attorney at law or law firm in this state through the services of a runner or capper is void. In any action against any attorney or law firm under the Unfair Practices Act, Chapter 4 (commencing with Section 17000) of Division 7, or Chapter 5 (commencing with Section 17200) of Division 7, any judgment shall include an order divesting the attorney or law firm of any fees and other compensation received pursuant to any such void contract. Those fees and compensation shall be recoverable as additional civil penalties under Chapter 4 (commencing with Section 17000) or Chapter 5 (commencing with Section 17200) of Division 7.

(b)   Notwithstanding section 17206 or any other provision of law, any fees recovered pursuant to subdivision (a) in an action involving professional services related to the provision of workers' compensation shall be allocated as follows: if the action is brought by the Attorney General, one-half of the penalty collected shall be paid to the State General Fund, and one-half of the penalty collected shall be paid to the Workers' Compensation Fraud Account in the Insurance Fund; if the action is brought by a district attorney, one-half of the penalty collected shall be paid to the treasurer of the county in which the judgment was entered, and one-half of the penalty collected shall be paid to the Workers' Compensation Fraud Account in the Insurance Fund; if the action is brought by a city attorney or city prosecutor, one-half of the penalty collected shall be paid to the treasurer of the city in which the judgment was entered, and one-half of the penalty collected shall be paid to the Workers' Compensation Fraud Account in the Insurance Fund. Moneys deposited into the Workers' Compensation Fraud Account pursuant to this subdivision shall be used in the investigation and prosecution of workers' compensation fraud, as appropriated by the Legislature.

§ 6155. Referral Services; Requirements; Conflicts of Interest; Enforcement; Rules and Regulations

(a)   An individual, partnership, corporation, association, or any other entity shall not operate for the direct or indirect purpose, in whole or in part, of referring potential clients to attorneys, and no attorney shall accept a referral of such potential clients, unless all of the following requirements are met:

(1)   The service is registered with the State Bar of California and (a) on July 1, 1988, is operated in conformity with minimum standards for a lawyer referral service established by the State Bar, or (b) upon approval by the Supreme Court of minimum standards for a lawyer referral service, is operated in conformity with those standards.

(2)   The combined charges to the potential client by the referral service and the attorney to whom the potential client is referred do not exceed the total cost that the client would normally pay if no referral service were involved.

(b)   A referral service shall not be owned or operated, in whole or in part, directly or indirectly, by those lawyers to whom, individually or collectively, more than 20 percent of referrals are made. For purposes of this subdivision, a referral service that is owned or operated by a bar association, as defined in the minimum standards, shall be deemed to be owned or operated by its governing committee so long as the governing committee is constituted and functions in the manner prescribed by the minimum standards.

(c)   None of the following is a lawyer referral service:

(1)   A plan of legal insurance as defined in Section 119.6 of the Insurance Code.

(2)   A group or prepaid legal plan, whether operated by a union, trust, mutual benefit or aid association, public or private corporation, or other entity or person, which meets both of the following conditions:

(A)   It recommends, furnishes, or pays for legal services to its members or beneficiaries.

(B)   It provides telephone advice or personal consultation.

(3)   A program having as its purpose the referral of clients to attorneys for representation on a pro bono basis.

(d)   The following are in the public interest and do not constitute an unlawful restraint of trade or commerce:

(1)   An agreement between a referral service and a participating attorney to eliminate or restrict the attorney's fee for an initial office consultation for each potential client or to provide free or reduced fee services.

(2)   Requirements by a referral service that attorneys meet reasonable participation requirements, including experience, education, and training requirements.

(3)   Provisions of the minimum standards as approved by the Supreme Court.

(4) Requirements that the application and renewal fees for certification as a lawyer referral service be determined, in whole or in part, by a consideration of any combination of the following factors: a referral service's gross annual revenues, number of panels, number of panel members, amount of fees charged to panel members, or for-profit or nonprofit status; provided that the application and renewal fees do not exceed ten thousand dollars ($10,000) or 1 percent of the gross annual revenues, whichever is less.

(5) Requirements that, to increase access to the justice system for all Californians, lawyer referral services establish separate ongoing activities or arrangements that serve persons of limited means.

(e) A violation or threatened violation of this section may be enjoined by any person.

(f) With the approval of the Supreme Court, the State Bar shall formulate and enforce rules and regulations for carrying out this section, including rules and regulations which do the following:

(1) Establish minimum standards for lawyer referral services. The minimum standards shall include provisions ensuring that panel membership shall be open to all attorneys practicing in the geographical area served who are qualified by virtue of suitable experience, and limiting attorney registration and membership fees to reasonable sums which do not discourage widespread attorney membership.

(2) Require that an entity seeking to qualify as a lawyer referral service register with the State Bar and obtain from the State Bar a certificate of compliance with the minimum standards for lawyer referral services.

(3) Require that the certificate may be obtained, maintained, suspended, or revoked pursuant to procedures set forth in the rules and regulations.

(4) Require the lawyer referral service to pay an application and renewal fee for the certificate in such reasonable amounts as may be determined by the State Bar. The State Bar shall adopt rules authorizing the waiver or reduction of the fees upon a demonstration of financial necessity. The State Bar may require that the application and renewal fees for certification as a lawyer referral service be determined, in whole or in part, by a consideration of any combination of the following factors: a referral service's gross annual revenues, number of panels, number of panel members, amount of fees charged to panel members, or for-profit or nonprofit status; provided that the application and renewal fees do not exceed ten thousand dollars ($10,000) or 1 percent of the gross annual revenues, whichever is less.

(5) Require that, to increase access to the justice system for all Californians, lawyer referral services establish separate ongoinq activities or arrangements that serve persons of limited means.

(6) Require each lawyer who is a member of a certified lawyer referral service to comply with all applicable professional standards, rules, and regulations, and to possess a policy of errors and omissions insurance in an amount not less than one hundred thousand dollars ($100,000) for each occurrence and three hundred thousand dollars ($300,000) aggregate, per year. By rule, the State Bar may provide for alternative proof of financial responsibility to meet this requirement.

(g)   Provide that cause for denial of certification or recertification or revocation of certification of a lawyer referral service shall include, but not be limited to:

(1)   Noncompliance with the statutes or minimum standards governing lawyer referral services as adopted and from time to time amended.

(2)   Sharing common or cross ownership, interests, or operations with any entity which engages in referrals to licensed or unlicensed health care providers.

(3)   Direct or indirect consideration regarding referrals between an owner, operator, or member of a lawyer referral service and any licensed or unlicensed health care provider.

(4)   Advertising on behalf of attorneys in violation of the Rules of Professional Conduct or the Business and Professions Code.

(h)   This section shall not be construed to prohibit attorneys from jointly advertising their services.

(1)   Permissible joint advertising, among other things, identifies by name the advertising attorneys or law firms whom the consumer of legal services may select and initiate contact with.

(2)   Certifiable referral activity involves, among other things, some person or entity other than the consumer and advertising attorney or law firms which, in person, electronically, or otherwise, refers the consumer to an attorney or law firm not identified in the advertising.

(i)   A lawyer referral service certified under this section and operating in full compliance with this section, and in full compliance with the minimum standards and the rules and regulations of the State Bar governing lawyer referral services, shall not be deemed to be in violation of Section 3215 of the Labor Code or Section 750 of the Insurance Code.

(j)   The payment by an attorney or law firm member of a certified referral service of the normal fees of that service shall not be deemed to be in violation of Section 3215 of the Labor Code or Section 750 of the Insurance Code, provided that the attorney or law firm member is in full compliance with the minimum standards and the rules and regulations of the State Bar governing lawyer referral services.

(k)   Certifications of lawyer referral services issued by the State Bar shall not be transferable.

ARTICLE 9.5.   LEGAL ADVERTISING

§ 6157.   Definitions

As used in this article, the following definitions apply:

(a)   "Member" means a member in good standing of the State Bar and includes any agent of the member and any law firm or law corporation doing business in the State of California.

(b)   "Lawyer" means a member of the State Bar or a person who is admitted in good standing and eligible to practice before the bar of any United States court or the highest court of the District of Columbia or any state, territory, or insular possession of the United States, or is licensed to practice law in, or is admitted in good standing and eligible to practice before the bar of the highest court of, a foreign country or any political subdivision thereof, and includes any agent of the lawyer, law firm, or law corporation doing business in the state.

(c) "Advertise" or "advertisement" means any communication, disseminated by television or radio, by any print medium, including, but not limited to, newspapers and billboards, or by means of a mailing directed generally to members of the public and not to a specific person, that solicits employment of legal services provided by a member, and is directed to the general public and is paid for by, or on the behalf of, an attorney.

(d) "Electronic medium" means television, radio, or computer networks.

§ 6157.1 False, Misleading or Deceptive Statements; Prohibition

No advertisement shall contain any false, misleading, or deceptive statement or omit to state any fact necessary to make the statements made, in light of circumstances under which they are made, not false, misleading, or deceptive.

§ 6157.2 Prohibited Statements Regarding Outcome; Dramatizations; Contingent Fee Basis Representations

No advertisement shall contain or refer to any of the following:

(a) Any guarantee or warranty regarding the outcome of a legal matter as a result of representation by the member.

(b) Statements or symbols stating that the member featured in the advertisement can generally obtain immediate cash or quick settlements.

(c) (1) An impersonation of the name, voice, photograph, or electronic image of any person other than the lawyer, directly or implicitly purporting to be that of a lawyer.

(2) An impersonation of the name, voice, photograph, or electronic image of any person, directly or implicitly purporting to be a client of the member featured in the advertisement, or a dramatization of events, unless disclosure of the impersonation or dramatization is made in the advertisement.

(3) A spokesperson, including a celebrity spokesperson, unless there is disclosure of the spokesperson's title.

(d) A statement that a member offers representation on a contingent basis unless the statement also advises whether a client will be held responsible for any costs advanced by the member when no recovery is obtained on behalf of the client. If the client will not be held responsible for costs, no disclosure is required.

. . .

§ 6158. Electronic Media Advertising; False, Misleading or Deceptive Message; Factual Substantiation

In advertising by electronic media, to comply with Sections 61571.1 and 6157.2, the message as a whole may not be false, misleading, or deceptive, and the message as a whole must be factually substantiated. The message means the effect in combination of the spoken word, sound, background, action, symbols, visual image, or any other technique employed to create the message. Factually substantiated means capable of verification by a credible source

§ 6158.1 False, Misleading or Deceptive Messages; Rebuttable Presumption

There shall be a rebuttable presumption affecting the burden of producing evidence that the following messages are false, misleading, or deceptive within the meaning of Section 6158:

(a) A message as to the ultimate result of a specific case or cases presented out of context without adequately providing information as to the facts or law giving rise to the result.

(b) The depiction of an event through methods such as the use of displays of injuries, accident scenes, or portrayals of other injurious events which may or may not be accompanied by sound effects and which may give rise to a claim for compensation.

(c) A message referring to or implying money received by or for a client in a particular case or cases, or to potential monetary recovery for a prospective client. A reference to money or monetary recovery includes, but is not limited to, a specific dollar amount, characterization of a sum of money, monetary symbols, or the implication of wealth.

§ 6158.2 Information Presumed to be in Compliance with Article

The following information shall be presumed to be in compliance with this article for purposes of advertising by electronic media, provided the message as a whole is not false, misleading, or deceptive:

(a) Name, including name of law firm, names of professional associates, addresses, telephone numbers, and the designation "lawyer," "attorney," "law firm," or the like.

(b) Fields of practice, limitation of practice, or specialization.

(c) Fees for routine legal services, subject to the requirements of subdivision (d) of Section 6157.2 and the Rules of Professional Conduct.

(d) Date and place of birth.

(e) Date and place of admission to the bar of state and federal courts.

(f) Schools attended, with dates of graduation, degrees, and other scholastic distinctions.

(g) Public or quasi-public offices.

(h) Military service.

(i) Legal authorship.

(j) Legal teaching positions.

(k) Memberships, offices, and committee assignments in bar associations.

(l) Memberships and offices in legal fraternities and legal societies.

(m) Technical and professional licenses.

(n) Memberships in scientific, technical, and professional associations and societies.

(o) Foreign language ability of the advertising lawyer or a member of lawyer's firm.

§ 6158.3 Electronic Media Advertising; Required Disclosures

In addition to any disclosure required by Section 6157.2, Section 6157.3, and the Rules of Professional Conduct, the following disclosure shall appear in advertising by electronic media. Use of the following disclosure alone may not rebut any presumption created in Section 6158.1. If an advertisement in the electronic media conveys a message portraying a result in a particular case or cases, the advertisement must state, in either an oral or printed communication, either of the following disclosures: The advertisement must adequately disclose the factual and legal circumstances that justify the result portrayed in the message, including the basis for liability and the nature of injury or damage sustained, or the advertisement must state that the result portrayed in the advertisement was dependent on the facts of that case, and that the results will differ if based on different facts.

. . .

ARTICLE 12. INCAPACITY TO ATTEND TO LAW PRACTICE— JURISDICTION OF COURTS

§ 6190. Authority of Courts; Attorney Incapable of Practice; Protection of Clients

The courts of the state shall have the jurisdiction as provided in this article when an attorney engaged in the practice of law in this state has, for any reason, including but not limited to excessive use of alcohol or drugs, physical or mental illness, or other infirmity or other cause, become incapable of devoting the time and attention to, and providing the quality of service for, his or her law practice which is necessary to protect the interest of a client if there is an unfinished client matter for which no other active member of the State Bar, with the consent of the client, has agreed to assume responsibility.

§ 6190.1 Application for Assumption by Court of Jurisdiction; Consent by Attorney; Appointment of Examiner or Coexaminer

(a) An application for assumption by the court of jurisdiction under this article shall be made to the superior court for the county where the attorney maintains or most recently has maintained his or her principal office for the practice of law or where such attorney resides. The court may assume jurisdiction over the law practice of an attorney to the extent provided in Article 11 (commencing with Section 6180) of Chapter 4 of Division 3.

(b) Where an attorney consents to the assumption by the court of jurisdiction under the article, the State Bar, a client, or an interested person or entity may apply to the court for assumption of jurisdiction over the law practice of the attorney. In any proceeding under this subdivision, the State Bar shall be permitted to intervene and to assume primary responsibility for conducting the action.

(c) Where an attorney does not consent to the assumption by the court of jurisdiction under this article, only the State Bar may apply to the court for assumption of jurisdiction over the law practice of the attorney.

(d) The chief trial counsel may appoint, pursuant to rules adopted by the board of trustees, an examiner or coexaminer from among the members of the State Bar in an investigation or formal proceeding under this article.

. . .

§ 6190.34 Findings; Orders

If the court finds that (a) the facts set forth in Section 6190 have occurred and, (b) that the interests of the client, or of an interested person or entity will be prejudiced if the proceeding provided herein is not maintained, the court shall order the applicant to mail a notice of cessation of law practice pursuant to Section 6180.1 and may make all orders provided for by the provisions of Article 11 (commencing with Section 6180) of Chapter 4 of Division 3. The court shall provide a copy of any order issued pursuant to this article to the Office of the Chief Trial Counsel of the State Bar.

. . .

ARTICLE 13. ARBITRATION OF ATTORNEYS' FEES

§ 6200. Establishment of System and Procedure; Arbitration and Mediation; Application of Article; Voluntary or Mandatory Nature; Rules; Immunity of Arbitrator and Mediator; Powers of Arbitrator; Confidentiality of Mediation

(a)   The board of trustees shall, by rule, establish, maintain, and administer a system and procedure for the arbitration, and may establish, maintain, and administer a system and procedure for mediation of disputes concerning fees, costs, or both, charged for professional services by members of the State Bar or by members of the bar of other jurisdictions. The rules may include provision for a filing fee in the amount as the board may, from time to time, determine.

(b)   This article shall not apply to any of the following:

(1)   Disputes where a member of the State Bar of California is also admitted to practice in another jurisdiction or where an attorney is only admitted to practice in another jurisdiction, and he or she maintains no office in the State of California, and no material portion of the services were rendered in the State of California.

(2)   Claims for affirmative relief against the attorney for damages or otherwise based upon alleged malpractice or professional misconduct, except as provided in subdivision (a) of Section 6203.

(3)   Disputes where the fee or cost to be paid by the client or on his or her behalf has been determined pursuant to statute or court order.

(c)   Unless the client has agreed in writing to arbitration under this article of all disputes concerning fees, costs, or both, arbitration under this article shall be voluntary for a client and shall be mandatory for an attorney if commenced by a client. Mediation under this article shall be voluntary for an attorney and a client.

(d)   The board of trustees shall adopt rules to allow arbitration and mediation of attorney fee and cost disputes under this article to proceed under arbitration and mediation systems sponsored by local bar associations in this state. Rules of procedure promulgated by local bar associations are subject to review by the board or a committee designated by the board to ensure that they provide for a fair, impartial, and speedy hearing and award.

(e)   In adopting or reviewing rules of arbitration under this section, the board shall provide that the panel shall include one attorney member whose area of practice is either, at the option of the client, civil law, if the attorney's representation involved civil law, or criminal law, if the attorney's representation involved criminal law, as follows:

(1) If the panel is composed of three members the panel shall include one attorney member whose area of practice is either, at the option of the client, civil or criminal law, and shall include one lay member.

(2) If the panel is composed of one member, that member shall be an attorney whose area of practice is either, at the option of the client, civil or criminal law.

(f) In any arbitration or mediation conducted pursuant to this article by the State Bar or by a local bar association, pursuant to rules of procedure approved by the board of trustees, an arbitrator or mediator, as well as the arbitrating association and its directors, officers, and employees, shall have the same immunity which attaches in judicial proceedings.

(g) In the conduct of arbitrations under this article the arbitrator or arbitrators may do all of the following:

(1) Take and hear evidence pertaining to the proceeding.

(2) Administer oaths and affirmations.

(3) Issue subpoenas for the attendance of witnesses and the production of books, papers, and documents pertaining to the proceeding.

(h) Participation in mediation is a voluntary consensual process, based on direct negotiations between the attorney and his or her client, and is an extension of the negotiated settlement process. All discussions and offers of settlement are confidential and shall not be disclosed pursuant to any state law, including, but not limited to, the California Public Records Act (Chapter 3.5 (commencing with Section 6250) of Division 7 of Title 1 of the Government Code), and may not be disclosed in any subsequent arbitration or other proceedings.

ARTICLE 14. FUNDS FOR THE PROVISION OF LEGAL SERVICES TO INDIGENT PERSONS

§ 6210. Legislative Findings; Purpose

The Legislature finds that, due to insufficient funding, existing programs providing free legal services in civil matters to indigent persons, especially underserved client groups, such as the elderly, the disabled, juveniles, and non-English-speaking persons, do not adequately meet the needs of these persons. It is the purpose of this article to expand the availability and improve the quality of existing free legal services in civil matters to indigent persons, and to initiate new programs that will provide services to them. The Legislature finds that the use of funds collected by the State Bar pursuant to this article for these purposes is in the public interest, is a proper use of the funds, and is consistent with essential public and governmental purposes in the judicial branch of government. The Legislature further finds that the expansion, improvement, and initiation of legal services to indigent persons will aid in the advancement of the science of jurisprudence and the improvement of the administration of justice.

§ 6211. Establishment by Attorney of IOLTA Account; Interest and Dividends Earned to Be Paid to State Bar; Other Accounts Not Prohibited; Rules of Professional Conduct, Authority of Supreme Court or State Bar Not Affected

(a) An attorney or law firm that, in the course of the practice of law, receives or disburses trust funds shall establish and maintain an IOLTA account in which the attorney or law firm shall deposit or invest all client deposits or funds that are nominal in amount or are on deposit or invested for a short period of time. All such client funds may be deposited or invested in a single unsegregated account. The interest and dividends earned on all those accounts shall be paid to the State Bar of California to be used for the purposes set forth in this article.

(b) Nothing in this article shall be construed to prohibit an attorney or law firm from establishing one or more interest bearing bank trust deposit accounts or dividend-paying trust investment accounts as may be permitted by the Supreme Court, with the interest or dividends earned on the accounts payable to clients for trust funds not deposited or invested in accordance with subdivision (a).

(c) With the approval of the Supreme Court, the State Bar may formulate and enforce rules of professional conduct pertaining to the use by attorneys or law firms of an IOLTA account for unsegregated client funds pursuant to this article.

(d) Nothing in this article shall be construed as affecting or impairing the disciplinary powers and authority of the Supreme Court or of the State Bar or as modifying the statutes and rules governing the conduct of members of the State Bar.

§ 6212. Establishment by Attorney of IOLTA Account; Amount of Interest; Remittance to State Bar; Reporting of IOLTA Account Compliance and Other Information; Statements and Reports

An attorney who, or a law firm that, establishes an IOLTA account pursuant to subdivision (a) of Section 6211 shall comply with all of the following provisions:

(a) The IOLTA account shall be established and maintained with an eligible institution offering or making available an IOLTA account that meets the requirements of this article. The IOLTA account shall be established and maintained consistent with the attorney's or law firm's duties of professional responsibility. An eligible financial institution shall have no responsibility for selecting the deposit or investment product chosen for the IOLTA account.

(b) Except as provided in subdivision (f), the rate of interest or dividends payable on any IOLTA account shall not be less than the interest rate or dividends generally paid by the eligible institution to nonattorney customers on accounts of the same type meeting the same minimum balance and other eligibility requirements as the IOLTA account. In determining the interest rate or dividend payable on any IOLTA account, an eligible institution may consider, in addition to the balance in the IOLTA account, risk or other factors customarily considered by the eligible institution when setting the interest rate or dividends for its non-IOLTA accounts, provided that the factors do not discriminate between IOLTA customers and non-IOLTA customers and that these factors do not include the fact that the account is an IOLTA account. The eligible institution shall calculate interest and dividends in accordance with its standard practice for non-IOLTA customers. Nothing in this article shall preclude an eligible institution from paying a higher interest rate or dividend on an IOLTA account or from electing to waive any fees and service charges on an IOLTA account.

(c)   Reasonable fees may be deducted from the interest or dividends remitted on an IOLTA account only at the rates and in accordance with the customary practices of the eligible institution for non-IOLTA customers. No other fees or service charges may be deducted from the interest or dividends earned on an IOLTA account. Unless and until the State Bar enacts regulations exempting from compliance with subdivision (a) of Section 6211 those accounts for which maintenance fees exceed the interest or dividends paid, an eligible institution may deduct the fees and service charges in excess of the interest or dividends paid on an IOLTA account from the aggregate interest and dividends remitted to the State Bar. Fees and service charges other than reasonable fees shall be the sole responsibility of, and may only be charged to, the attorney or law firm maintaining the IOLTA account. Fees and charges shall not be assessed against or deducted from the principal of any IOLTA account. It is the intent of the Legislature that the State Bar develop policies so that eligible institutions do not incur uncompensated administrative costs in adapting their systems to comply with the provisions of Chapter 422 of the Statutes of 2007 or in making investment products available to IOLTA members.

(d)   The attorney or law firm shall report IOLTA account compliance and all other IOLTA account information required by the State Bar in the manner specified by the State Bar.

(e)   The eligible institution shall be directed to do all of the following:

(1)   To remit interest or dividends on the IOLTA account, less reasonable fees, to the State Bar, at least quarterly.

(2)   To transmit to the State Bar with each remittance a statement showing the name of the attorney or law firm for which the remittance is sent, for each account the rate of interest applied or dividend paid, the amount and type of fees deducted, if any, and the average balance for each account for each month of the period for which the report is made.

(3)   To transmit to the attorney or law firm customer at the same time a report showing the amount paid to the State Bar for that period, the rate of interest or dividend applied, the amount of fees and service charges deducted, if any, and the average daily account balance for each month of the period for which the report is made.

(f)   An eligible institution has no affirmative duty to offer or make investment products available to IOLTA customers. However, if an eligible institution offers or makes investment products available to non-IOLTA customers, in order to remain an IOLTA-eligible institution, it shall make those products available to IOLTA customers or pay an interest rate on the IOLTA deposit account that is comparable to the rate of return or the dividends generally paid on that investment product for similar customers meeting the same minimum balance and other requirements applicable to the investment product. If the eligible institution elects to pay that higher interest rate, the eligible institution may subject the IOLTA deposit account to equivalent fees and charges assessable against the investment product.

§ 6213.   Definitions

As used in this article:

(a)   "Qualified legal services project" means either of the following:

(1)   A nonprofit project incorporated and operated exclusively in California that provides as its primary purpose and function legal services without charge to indigent persons and that has quality control procedures approved by the State Bar of California.

(2)   A program operated exclusively in California by a nonprofit law school accredited by the State Bar of California that meets the requirements of subparagraphs (A) and (B).

(A)   The program shall have operated for at least two years at a cost of at least twenty thousand dollars ($20,000) per year as an identifiable law school unit with a primary purpose and function of providing legal services without charge to indigent persons.

(B)   The program shall have quality control procedures approved by the State Bar of California.

(b)   "Qualified support center" means an incorporated nonprofit legal services center that has as its primary purpose and function the provision of legal training, legal technical assistance, or advocacy support without charge and which actually provides through an office in California a significant level of legal training, legal technical assistance, or advocacy support without charge to qualified legal services projects on a statewide basis in California.

(c)   "Recipient" means a qualified legal services project or support center receiving financial assistance under this article.

(d)   "Indigent person" means a person whose income is (1) 125 percent or less of the current poverty threshold established by the United States Office of Management and Budget, or (2) who is eligible for Supplemental Security Income or free services under the Older Americans Act or Developmentally Disabled Assistance Act. With regard to a project that provides free services of attorneys in private practice without compensation, "indigent person" also means a person whose income is 75 percent or less of the maximum levels of income for lower income households as defined in Section 50079.5 of the Health and Safety Code. For the purpose of this subdivision, the income of a person who is disabled shall be determined after deducting the costs of medical and other disability-related special expenses.

(e)   "Fee generating case" means a case or matter that, if undertaken on behalf of an indigent person by an attorney in private practice, reasonably may be expected to result in payment of a fee for legal services from an award to a client, from public funds, or from the opposing party. A case shall not be considered fee generating if adequate representation is unavailable and any of the following circumstances exist:

(1)   The recipient has determined that free referral is not possible because of any of the following reasons:

(A)   The case has been rejected by the local lawyer referral service, or if there is no such service, by two attorneys in private practice who have experience in the subject matter of the case.

(B)   Neither the referral service nor any attorney will consider the case without payment of a consultation fee.

(C)   The case is of the type that attorneys in private practice in the area ordinarily do not accept, or do not accept without prepayment of a fee.

(D)   Emergency circumstances compel immediate action before referral can be made, but the client is advised that, if appropriate and consistent with professional responsibility, referral will be attempted at a later time.

(2) Recovery of damages is not the principal object of the case and a request for damages is merely ancillary to an action for equitable or other nonpecuniary relief, or inclusion of a counterclaim requesting damages is necessary for effective defense or because of applicable rules governing joinder of counterclaims.

(3) A court has appointed a recipient or an employee of a recipient pursuant to a statute or a court rule or practice of equal applicability to all attorneys in the jurisdiction.

(4) The case involves the rights of a claimant under a publicly supported benefit program for which entitlement to benefit is based on need.

(f) "Legal Services Corporation" means the Legal Services Corporation established under the Legal Services Corporation Act of 1974 (P.L. 93–355; 42 U.S.C. Sec. 2996 et seq.).

(g) "Older Americans Act" means the Older Americans Act of 1965, as amended (P.L. 89–73; 42 U.S.C. Sec. 3001 et seq.).

(h) "Developmentally Disabled Assistance Act" means the Developmentally Disabled Assistance and Bill of Rights Act, as amended (P.L. 94–103; 42 U.S.C. Sec. 6001 et seq.).

(i) "Supplemental security income recipient" means an individual receiving or eligible to receive payments under Title XVI of the federal Social Security Act, or payments under Chapter 3 (commencing with Section 12000) of Part 3 of Division 9 of the Welfare and Institutions Code.

(j) "IOLTA account" means an account or investment product established and maintained pursuant to subdivision (a) of Section 6211 that is any of the following:

(1) An interest-bearing checking account.

(2) An investment sweep product that is a daily (overnight) financial institution repurchase agreement or an open-end money market fund.

(3) An investment product authorized by California Supreme Court rule or order.

A daily financial institution repurchase agreement shall be fully collateralized by United States Government Securities or other comparably conservative debt securities, and may be established only with any eligible institution that is "well-capitalized" or "adequately capitalized" as those terms are defined by applicable federal statutes and regulations. An open-end money market fund shall be invested solely in United States Government Securities or repurchase agreements fully collateralized by United States Government Securities or other comparably conservative debt securities, shall hold itself out as a "money market fund" as that term is defined by federal statutes and regulations under the Investment Company Act of 1940 (15 U.S.C. Sec. 80a–1 et seq.), and, at the time of the investment, shall have total assets of at least two hundred fifty million dollars ($250,000,000).

(k) "Eligible institution" means either of the following:

(1) A bank, savings and loan, or other financial institution regulated by a federal or state agency that pays interest or dividends in

the IOLTA account and carries deposit insurance from an agency of the federal government.

(2) Any other type of financial institution authorized by the California Supreme Court.

§ 6214. Qualified Legal Service Projects

(a) Projects meeting the requirements of subdivision (a) of Section 6213 which are funded either in whole or part by the Legal Services Corporation or with Older American Act funds shall be presumed qualified legal services projects for the purpose of this article.

(b) Projects meeting the requirements of subdivision (a) of Section 6213 but not qualifying under the presumption specified in subdivision (a) shall qualify for funds under this article if they meet all of the following additional criteria:

(1) They receive cash funds from other sources in the amount of at least twenty thousand dollars ($20,000) per year to support free legal representation to indigent persons.

(2) They have demonstrated community support for the operation of a viable ongoing program.

(3) They provide one or both of the following special services:

(A) The coordination of the recruitment of substantial numbers of attorneys in private practice to provide free legal representation to indigent persons or to qualified legal services projects in California.

(B) The provision of legal representation, training, or technical assistance on matters concerning special client groups, including the elderly, the disabled, juveniles, and non-English-speaking groups, or on matters of specialized substantive law important to the special client groups.

§ 6214.5 Qualified Legal Services Projects; Eligibility for Distributions of Funds

A law school program that meets the definition of a "qualified legal services project" as defined in paragraph (2) of subdivision (a) of Section 6213, and that applied to the State Bar for funding under this article not later than February 17, 1984, shall be deemed eligible for all distributions of funds made under Section 6216.

§ 6215. Qualified Support Centers

(a) Support centers satisfying the qualifications specified in subdivision (b) of Section 6213 which were operating an office and providing services in California on December 31, 1980, shall be presumed to be qualified support centers for the purposes of this article.

(b) Support centers not qualifying under the presumption specified in subdivision (a) may qualify as a support center by meeting both of the following additional criteria:

(1) Meeting quality control standards established by the State Bar.

(2) Being deemed to be of special need by a majority of the qualified legal services projects.

§ 6216. Distribution of Funds

The State Bar shall distribute all moneys received under the program established by this article for the provision of civil legal services to indigent persons. The funds first shall be distributed 18 months from the effective date of this article, or upon such a date, as shall be determined by the State Bar, that adequate funds are available to initiate the program. Thereafter, the funds shall be distributed on an annual basis. All distributions of funds shall be made in the following order and in the following manner:

(a) To pay the actual administrative costs of the program, including any costs incurred after the adoption of this article and a reasonable reserve therefor.

(b) Eighty-five percent of the funds remaining after payment of administrative costs allocated pursuant to this article shall be distributed to qualified legal services projects. Distribution shall be by a pro rata county-by-county formula based upon the number of persons whose income is 125 percent or less of the current poverty threshold per county. For the purposes of this section, the source of data identifying the number of persons per county shall be the latest available figures from the United States Department of Commerce, Bureau of the Census. Projects from more than one county may pool their funds to operate a joint, multicounty legal services project serving each of their respective counties.

(1) (A) In any county which is served by more than one qualified legal services project, the State Bar shall distribute funds for the county to those projects which apply on a pro rata basis, based upon the amount of their total budget expended in the prior year for legal services in that county as compared to the total expended in the prior year for legal services by all qualified legal services projects applying therefor in the county. In determining the amount of funds to be allocated to a qualified legal services project specified in paragraph (2) of subdivision (a) of Section 6213, the State Bar shall recognize only expenditures attributable to the representation of indigent persons as constituting the budget of the program.

(B) The State Bar shall reserve 10 percent of the funds allocated to the county for distribution to programs meeting the standards of subparagraph (A) of paragraph (3) and paragraphs (1) and (2) of subdivision (b) of Section 6214 and which perform the services described in subparagraph (A) of paragraph (3) of Section 6214 as their principal means of delivering legal services. The State Bar shall distribute the funds for that county to those programs which apply on a pro rata basis, based upon the amount of their total budget expended for free legal services in that county as compared to the total expended for free legal services by all programs meeting the standards of subparagraph (A) of paragraph (3) and paragraphs (1) and (2) of subdivision (b) of Section 6214 in that county. The State Bar shall distribute any funds for which no program has qualified pursuant hereto, in accordance with the provisions of subparagraph (A) of paragraph (1) of this subdivision.

(2) In any county in which there is no qualified legal services project providing services, the State Bar shall reserve for the remainder of the fiscal year for distribution the pro rata share of funds as provided for by this article. Upon application of a qualified legal services project proposing to provide legal services to the indigent of the county, the State Bar shall distribute the funds to the project. Any funds not so

distributed shall be added to the funds to be distributed the following year.

(c)   Fifteen percent of the funds remaining after payment of administrative costs allocated for the purposes of this article shall be distributed equally by the State Bar to qualified support centers which apply for the funds. The funds provided to support centers shall be used only for the provision of legal services within California. Qualified support centers that receive funds to provide services to qualified legal services projects from sources other than this article, shall submit and shall have approved by the State Bar a plan assuring that the services funded under this article are in addition to those already funded for qualified legal services projects by other sources.

§ 6217.   Maintenance of Quality Services, Professional Standards, Attorney-Client Privilege; Funds to Be Expended in Accordance With Article; Interference With Attorney Prohibited

With respect to the provision of legal assistance under this article, each recipient shall ensure all of the following:

(a)   The maintenance of quality service and professional standards.

(b)   The expenditure of funds received in accordance with the provisions of this article.

(c)   The preservation of the attorney-client privilege in any case, and the protection of the integrity of the adversary process from any impairment in furnishing legal assistance to indigent persons.

(d)   That no one shall interfere with any attorney funded in whole or in part by this article in carrying out his or her professional responsibility to his or her client as established by the rules of professional responsibility and this chapter.

§ 6218.   Eligibility for Services; Establishment of Guidelines; Funds to Be Expended in Accordance With Article

All legal services projects and support centers receiving funds pursuant to this article shall adopt financial eligibility guidelines for indigent persons.

(a)   Qualified legal services programs shall ensure that funds appropriated pursuant to this article shall be used solely to defray the costs of providing legal services to indigent persons or for such other purposes as set forth in this article.

(b)   Funds received pursuant to this article by support centers shall only be used to provide services to qualified legal services projects as defined in subdivision (a) of Section 6213 which are used pursuant to a plan as required by subdivision (c) of Section 6216, or as permitted by Section 6219.

§ 6219.   Provision of Work Opportunities and Scholarships for Disadvantaged Law Students

Qualified legal services projects and support centers may use funds provided under this article to provide work opportunities with pay, and where feasible, scholarships for disadvantaged law students to help defray their law school expenses.

§ 6220. Private Attorneys Providing Legal Services Without Charge; Support Center Services

Attorneys in private practice who are providing legal services without charge to indigent persons shall not be disqualified from receiving the services of the qualified support centers.

§ 6221. Services for Indigent Members of Disadvantaged and Underserved Groups

Qualified legal services projects shall make significant efforts to utilize 20 percent of the funds allocated under this article for increasing the availability of services to the elderly, the disabled, juveniles, or other indigent persons who are members of disadvantaged and underserved groups within their service area.

§ 6222. Financial Statements; Submission to State Bar; State Bar Report

A recipient of funds allocated pursuant to this article annually shall submit a financial statement to the State Bar, including an audit of the funds by a certified public accountant or a fiscal review approved by the State Bar, a report demonstrating the programs on which they were expended, a report on the recipient's compliance with the requirements of Section 6217, and progress in meeting the service expansion requirements of Section 6221.

The Board of Trustees of the State Bar shall include a report of receipts of funds under this article, expenditures for administrative costs, and disbursements of the funds, on a county-by-county basis, in the annual report of State Bar receipts and expenditures required pursuant to Section 6145.

§ 6223. Expenditure of Funds; Prohibitions

No funds allocated by the State Bar pursuant to this article shall be used for any of the following purposes:

(a) The provision of legal assistance with respect to any fee generating case, except in accordance with guidelines which shall be promulgated by the State Bar.

(b) The provision of legal assistance with respect to any criminal proceeding.

(c) The provision of legal assistance, except to indigent persons or except to provide support services to qualified legal services projects as defined by this article.

§ 6224. State Bar; Powers; Determination of Qualifications to Receive Funds; Denial of Funds; Termination; Procedures

The State Bar shall have the power to determine that an applicant for funding is not qualified to receive funding, to deny future funding, or to terminate existing funding because the recipient is not operating in compliance with the requirements or restrictions of this article.

A denial of an application for funding or for future funding or an action by the State Bar to terminate an existing grant of funds under this article shall not become final until the applicant or recipient has been afforded reasonable notice and an opportunity for a timely and fair hearing. Pending final determination of any hearing held with reference to termination of funding, financial assistance shall be continued at its existing level on a month-to-month basis. Hearings for denial shall be conducted by an impartial hearing officer whose decision shall be final. The hearing officer shall render a decision no later than 30 days after the conclusion of the hearing. Specific procedures governing the conduct of the hearings of this section shall be determined by the State Bar pursuant to Section 6225.

§ 6225. Implementation of Article; Adoption of Rules and Regulations; Procedures

The Board of Trustees of the State Bar shall adopt the regulations and procedures necessary to implement this article and to ensure that the funds allocated herein are utilized to provide civil legal services to indigent persons, especially underserved client groups such as but not limited to the elderly, the disabled, juveniles, and non-English-speaking persons.

In adopting the regulations the Board of Trustees shall comply with the following procedures:

(a) The board shall publish a preliminary draft of the regulations and procedures, which shall be distributed, together with notice of the hearings required by subdivision (b), to commercial banking institutions, to members of the State Bar, and to potential recipients of funds.

(b) The board shall hold at least two public hearings, one in southern California and one in northern California where affected and interested parties shall be afforded an opportunity to present oral and written testimony regarding the proposed regulations and procedures.

§ 6226. Implementation of Article; Resolution

The program authorized by this article shall become operative only upon the adoption of a resolution by the Board of Trustees of the State Bar stating that regulations have been adopted pursuant to Section 6225 which conform the program to all applicable tax and banking statutes, regulations, and rulings.

§ 6227. Credit of State Not Pledged

Nothing in this article shall create an obligation or pledge of the credit of the State of California or of the State Bar of California. Claims arising by reason of acts done pursuant to this article shall be limited to the moneys generated hereunder.

§ 6228. Severability

If any provision of this article or the application thereof to any group or circumstances is held invalid, such invalidity shall not affect the other provisions or applications of this article which can be given effect without the invalid provision or application, and to this end the provisions of this article are severable.

ARTICLE 15. ATTORNEY DIVERSION AND ASSISTANCE ACT

§ 6230. Legislative Intent and Findings

It is the intent of the Legislature that the State Bar of California seek ways and means to identify and rehabilitate attorneys with impairment due to abuse of drugs or alcohol, or due to mental illness, affecting competency so that attorneys so afflicted may be treated and returned to the practice of law in a manner that will not endanger the public health and safety.

§ 6231. Attorney Diversion and Assistance Program; Committee; Members; Terms; Rules and Regulations

(a)   The board shall establish and administer an Attorney Diversion and Assistance Program, and shall establish a committee to oversee the operation of the program. . . .

§ 6232. Practices and Procedures for Program; Entrance Into the Program

(a)   The committee shall establish practices and procedures for the acceptance, denial, completion, or termination of attorneys in the Attorney Diversion and Assistance Program, and may recommend rehabilitative criteria for adoption by the board for acceptance, denial, completion of, or termination from, the program.

(b)   An attorney currently under investigation by the State Bar may enter the program in the following ways:

(1)   By referral of the Office of the Chief Trial Counsel.

(2)   By referral of the State Bar Court following the initiation of a disciplinary proceeding.

(3)   Voluntarily, and in accordance with terms and conditions agreed upon by the attorney participant with the Office of the Chief Trial Counsel or upon approval by the State Bar Court, as long as the investigation is based primarily on the self-administration of drugs or alcohol or the illegal possession, prescription, or nonviolent procurement of drugs for self-administration, or on mental illness, and does not involve actual harm to the public or his or her clients. An attorney seeking entry under this paragraph may be required to execute an agreement that violations of this chapter, or other statutes that would otherwise be the basis for discipline, may nevertheless be prosecuted if the attorney is terminated from the program for failure to comply with program requirements.

(c)   Neither acceptance into nor participation in the Attorney Diversion and Assistance Program shall relieve the attorney of any lawful duties and obligations otherwise required by any agreements or stipulations with the Office of the Chief Trial Counsel, court orders, or applicable statutes relating to attorney discipline.

(d)   An attorney who is not the subject of a current investigation may voluntarily enter, whether by self-referral or referral by a third party, the diversion and assistance program on a confidential basis and such information shall not be disclosed pursuant to any state law, including, but not limited to, the California Public Records Act (Chapter 3.5 (commencing with Section 6250) of Division 7 of Title 1 of the Government Code). Confidentiality pursuant to this subdivision shall be absolute unless waived by the attorney.

(e)   By rules subject to the approval of the board and consistent with the requirements of this article, applicants who are in law school or have applied for admission to the State Bar may enter the program.

§ 6233.   Practice Restrictions; Inactive Membership of the State Bar

An attorney entering the diversion and assistance program pursuant to subdivision (b) of Section 6232 may be enrolled as an inactive member of the State Bar and not be entitled to practice law, or may be required to agree to various practice restrictions, including, where appropriate, restrictions on scope of practice and monetary accounting procedures. Upon the successful completion of the program, attorney participants who were placed on inactive status by the State Bar Court as a condition of program participation and who have complied with any and all conditions of probation may receive credit for the period of inactive enrollment towards any period of actual suspension imposed by the Supreme Court, and shall be eligible for reinstatement to active status and a dismissal of the underlying allegations or a reduction in the recommended discipline. Those attorneys who participated in the program with practice restrictions shall be eligible to have those restrictions removed and to a dismissal of the underlying allegations or a reduction in the recommended discipline.

§ 6234. Confidentiality

Any information provided to or obtained by the Attorney Diversion and Assistance Program, or any subcommittee or agent thereof, shall be as follows:

(a)   Confidential and shall not be disclosed pursuant to any state law, including, but not limited to, the California Public Records Act (Chapter 3.5 (commencing with Section 6250) of Division 7 of Title 1 of the Government Code). This confidentiality shall be absolute unless waived by the attorney.

(b)   Exempt from the provisions of Section 6086.1.

(c)   Not discoverable or admissible in any civil proceeding without the written consent of the attorney to whom the information pertains.

(d)   Not discoverable or admissible in any disciplinary proceeding without the written consent of the attorney to whom the information pertains.

(e)   Except with respect to the provisions of subdivision (d) of Section 6232, the limitations on the disclosure and admissibility of information in this section shall not apply to information relating to an attorney's noncooperation with, or unsuccessful completion of, the Attorney Diversion and Assistance Program, or any subcommittee or agent thereof, or to information otherwise obtained by the Office of the Chief Trial Counsel, by independent means, or from any other lawful source.

§ 6235. Program Expenses

(a)   Participants in the Attorney Diversion and Assistance Program shall be responsible for all expenses relating to treatment and recovery. In addition, the State Bar may charge a reasonable administrative fee to participants for the purpose of offsetting the costs of maintaining the program.

(b)   Notwithstanding subdivision (a), the State Bar shall establish a financial assistance program to ensure that no member is denied acceptance into the program solely due to the lack of ability to pay.

§ 6236. Outreach Activities by State Bar

The state bar shall actively engage in outreach activities to make members, the legal community, and the general public aware of the existence and availability of the attorney diversion and assistance program. Outreach shall include, but not be limited to, the development and certification of minimum continuing legal education courses relating to the prevention, detection, and treatment of substance abuse, including no-cost and low-cost programs and materials pursuant to subdivision (d) of section 6070, informing all members of the state bar of the program's existence and benefits through both direct communication and targeted advertising, working in coordination with the judicial branch to inform the state's judges of the program's existence and availability as a disciplinary option, and working in cooperation with organizations that provide services and support to attorneys with issues related to substance abuse

---

NOTE: SOME IMPORTANT STATUTES FOR LAWYERS IN CALIFORNIA GOVERNMENT

The State has a large number of statutes dealing with professional responsibilities of governmental officials, particularly if they are lawyers. West's California Government Code provides in part:

§ 8920.   Prohibited Acts

(a)   No Member of the Legislature, state elective or appointive officer, or judge or justice shall, while serving as such, have any interest, financial or otherwise, direct or indirect, or engage in any business or transaction or professional activity, or incur any obligation of any nature, which is in substantial conflict with the proper discharge of his duties in the public interest and of his responsibilities as prescribed in the laws of this state.

(b)   No Member of the Legislature shall do any of the following:

(1)   Accept other employment which he has reason to believe will either impair his independence of judgment as to his official duties or require him, or induce him, to disclose confidential information acquired by him in the course of and by reason of his official duties.

(2)   Willfully and knowingly disclose, for pecuniary gain, to any other person, confidential information acquired by him in the course of and by reason of his official duties or use any such information for the purpose of pecuniary gain.

(3)   Accept or agree to accept, or be in partnership with any person who accepts or agrees to accept, any employment, fee, or other thing of monetary value, or portion thereof, in consideration of his appearing, agreeing to appear, or taking any other action on behalf of another person before any state board or agency.

This subdivision shall not be construed to prohibit a member who is an attorney at law from practicing in that capacity before any court or before the Workers' Compensation Appeals Board and receiving compensation therefor. This subdivision shall not act to prohibit a member from acting as an advocate without compensation or making inquiry for information on behalf of a constituent before a state board or agency, or from engaging in activities on behalf of another which require purely ministerial acts by the board or agency and which in no way require the board or agency to exercise any discretion, or from engaging in activities involving a board or agency which are strictly on his or her own behalf. The prohibition contained in this subdivision shall not apply to a partnership or firm of which the Member of the Legislature is a member if the Member of the Legislature does not share directly or indirectly in the fee, less any expenses attributable to that fee, resulting from the transaction. The prohibition contained in this subdivision as it read immediately prior to January 1, 1983, shall not apply in connection with any matter pending before any state board or agency on or before January 2, 1967, if the affected Member of the Legislature was an attorney of record or representative in the matter prior to January 2, 1967. The prohibition contained in this subdivision, as amended and operative on January 1, 1983, shall not apply to any activity of any Member in connection with a matter pending before any state board or agency on January 1, 1983, which was not prohibited by this section prior to that date, if the affected Member of the Legislature was an attorney of record or representative in the matter prior to January 1, 1983.

(4)   Receive or agree to receive, directly or indirectly, any compensation, reward, or gift from any source except the State of California for any service, advice, assistance or other matter related to the legislative process, except fees for speeches or published works on legislative subjects and except, in connection therewith, reimbursement of expenses for actual expenditures for travel and reasonable subsistence for which no payment or reimbursement is made by the State of California;

(5)   Participate, by voting or any other action, on the floor of either house, in committee, or elsewhere, in the passage or defeat of legislation in which he has a personal interest, except as follows:

(i)   If, on the vote for final passage by the house of which he is a member, of the legislation in which he has a personal interest, he first files a statement (which shall be entered verbatim on the journal) stating in substance that he has a personal interest in the legislation to be voted on and, notwithstanding that interest, he is able to cast a fair and objective vote on that legislation, he may cast his vote without violating any provision of this article.

(ii)   If the member believes that, because of his personal interest, he should abstain from participating in the vote on the legislation, he shall so advise the presiding officer prior to the commencement of the vote and shall be excused from voting on the legislation without any entry on the journal of the fact of his personal interest. In the event a rule of the house requiring that each member who is present vote aye or nay is invoked, the presiding officer shall order the member excused from compliance and shall order entered on the journal a simple statement that the member was excused from voting on the legislation pursuant to law.

The provisions of this section do not apply to persons who are members of the state civil service as defined in Article VII of the California Constitution.

§ 8921.   Interest in Substantial Conflict With Proper Discharge of Duties

A person subject to this article has an interest which is in substantial conflict with the proper discharge of his duties in the public interest and of his responsibilities as prescribed in the laws of this state or a personal interest, arising from any situation, within the scope of this article, if he has reason to believe or expect that he will derive a direct monetary gain or suffer a direct monetary loss, as the case may be, by reason of his official activity. He does not have an interest which is in substantial conflict with the proper discharge of his duties in the public interest and of his responsibilities as prescribed in the laws of this state or a personal interest, arising from any situation, within the scope of this article, if any benefit or detriment accrues to him as a member of a business, profession, occupation, or group to no greater extent than any other member of that business, profession, occupation, or group.

NEW YORK RULES OF PROFESSIONAL CONDUCT

Effective April 1, 2009
As amended through January 1, 2017*

RULE 1.0: TERMINOLOGY

(a) "Advertisement" means any public or private communication made by or on behalf of a lawyer or law firm about that lawyer or law firm's services, the primary purpose of which is for the retention of the lawyer or law firm. It does not include communications to existing clients or other lawyers.

(b) "Belief" or "believes" denotes that the person involved actually believes the fact in question to be true. A person's belief may be inferred from circumstances.

(c) "Computer-accessed communication" means any communication made by or on behalf of a lawyer or law firm that is disseminated through the use of a computer or related electronic device, including, but not limited to, web sites, weblogs, search engines, electronic mail, banner advertisements, pop-up and pop-under advertisements, chat rooms, list servers, instant messaging, or other internet presences, and any attachments or links related thereto.

(d) "Confidential information" is defined in Rule 1.6.

(e) "Confirmed in writing" denotes (i) a writing from the person to the lawyer confirming that the person has given consent (ii) a writing that the lawyer promptly transmits to the person confirming the person's oral consent, or (iii) a statement by the person made on the record of any proceeding before a tribunal. If it is not feasible to obtain or transmit the writing at the time the person gives oral consent, then the lawyer must obtain or transmit it within a reasonable time thereafter.

(f) "Domestic relations matter" denotes representation of a client in a claim, action or proceeding, or preliminary to the filing of a claim, action or proceeding, in either Supreme Court or Family Court, or in any court of appellate jurisdiction, for divorce, separation, annulment, custody, visitation, maintenance, child support or alimony, or to enforce or modify a judgment or order in connection with any such claim, action or proceeding.

(g) "Domestic relations matter" denotes representation of a client in a claim, action or proceeding, or preliminary to the filing of a claim, action or proceeding, in either Supreme Court or Family

---

* Editors' note. The New York Rules of Professional Conduct have been adopted by the Appellate Division of the New York State Supreme Court and are published as Part 1200 of the Joint Rules of the Appellate Division (22 NYCRR Part 1200). The Appellate Division has not enacted the Preamble, Scope and Comments, which are published solely by the New York State Bar Association to provide guidance for attorneys in complying with the Rules. Where a conflict exists between a Rule and the Preamble, Scope or a Comment, the Rule controls. Hence, we have omitted the Preamble, Scope and Comments. They may be found at https://www.nysba.org/DownloadAsset.aspx?id=50671.

Court, or in any court of appellate jurisdiction, for divorce, separation, annulment, custody, visitation, maintenance, child support or alimony, or to enforce or modify a judgment or order in connection with any such claim, action or proceeding.

(h) "Firm" or "law firm" includes, but is not limited to, a lawyer or lawyers in a law partnership, professional corporation, sole proprietorship or other association authorized to practice law; or lawyers employed in a qualified legal assistance organization, a government law office, or the legal department of a corporation or other organization.

(i) "Fraud" or "fraudulent" denotes conduct that is fraudulent under the substantive or procedural law of the applicable jurisdiction or has a purpose to deceive, provided that it does not include conduct that, although characterized as fraudulent by statute or administrative rule, lacks an element of scienter, deceit, intent to mislead, or knowing failure to correct misrepresentations that can be reasonably expected to induce detrimental reliance by another.

(j) "Informed consent" denotes the agreement by a person to a proposed course of conduct after the lawyer has communicated information adequate for the person to make an informed decision, and after the lawyer has adequately explained to the person the material risks of the proposed course of conduct and reasonably available alternatives.

(k) "Knowingly," "known," "know," or "knows" denotes actual knowledge of the fact in question. A person's knowledge may be inferred from circumstances.

(*l*) "Matter" includes any litigation, judicial or administrative proceeding, case, claim, application, request for a ruling or other determination, contract, controversy, investigation, charge, accusation, arrest, negotiation, arbitration, mediation or any other representation involving a specific party or parties.

(m) "Partner" denotes a member of a partnership, a shareholder in a law firm organized as a professional legal corporation or a member of an association authorized to practice law.

(n) "Person" includes an individual, a corporation, an association, a trust, a partnership, and any other organization or entity.

(*o*) "Professional legal corporation" means a corporation, or an association treated as a corporation, authorized by law to practice law for profit.

(p) "Qualified legal assistance organization" means an office or organization of one of the four types listed in Rule 7.2(b)(1)–(4) that meets all of the requirements thereof.

(q) "Reasonable" or "reasonably," when used in relation to conduct by a lawyer, denotes the conduct of a reasonably prudent and competent lawyer. When used in the context of conflict of interest determinations, "reasonable lawyer" denotes a lawyer acting from the perspective of a reasonably prudent and competent lawyer who is personally disinterested in commencing or continuing the representation.

(r) "Reasonable belief" or "reasonably believes," when used in reference to a lawyer, denotes that the lawyer believes the matter in question and that the circumstances are such that the belief is reasonable.

(s) "Reasonably should know," when used in reference to a lawyer, denotes that a lawyer of reasonable prudence and competence would ascertain the matter in question.

(t) "Screened" or "screening" denotes the isolation of a lawyer from any participation in a matter through the timely imposition of procedures within a firm that are reasonably adequate under the circumstances to protect information that the isolated lawyer or the firm is obligated to protect under these Rules or other law.

(u) "Sexual relations" denotes sexual intercourse or the touching of an intimate part of the lawyer or another person for the purpose of sexual arousal, sexual gratification or sexual abuse.

(v) "State" includes the District of Columbia, Puerto Rico, and other federal territories and possessions.

(w) "Tribunal" denotes a court, an arbitrator in an arbitration proceeding or a legislative body, administrative agency or other body acting in an adjudicative capacity. A legislative body, administrative agency or other body acts in an adjudicative capacity when a neutral official, after the presentation of evidence or legal argument by a party or parties, will render a legal judgment directly affecting a party's interests in a particular matter.

(x) "Writing" or "written" denotes a tangible or electronic record of a communication or representation, including handwriting, typewriting, printing, photocopying, photography, audio or video recording, email or other electronic communication or any other form of recorded communication or recorded presentation. A "signed" writing includes an electronic sound, symbol or process attached to or logically associated with a writing and executed or adopted by a person with the intent to sign the writing.

RULE 1.1: COMPETENCE

(a) A lawyer should provide competent representation to a client. Competent representation requires the legal knowledge, skill, thoroughness and preparation reasonably necessary for the representation.

(b) A lawyer shall not handle a legal matter that the lawyer knows or should know that the lawyer is not competent to handle, without associating with a lawyer who is competent to handle it.

(c) A lawyer shall not intentionally:

(1) fail to seek the objectives of the client through reasonably available means permitted by law and these Rules; or

(2) prejudice or damage the client during the course of the representation except as permitted or required by these Rules.

RULE 1.2: SCOPE OF REPRESENTATION AND ALLOCATION OF AUTHORITY BETWEEN CLIENT AND LAWYER

(a) Subject to the provisions herein, a lawyer shall abide by a client's decisions concerning the objectives of representation and, as required by Rule 1.4, shall consult with the client as to the means by which they are to be pursued. A lawyer shall abide by a client's decision whether to settle a matter. In a criminal case, the lawyer shall abide by the client's decision, after consultation with the lawyer, as to a plea to be entered, whether to waive jury trial and whether the client will testify.

(b) A lawyer's representation of a client, including representation by appointment, does not constitute an endorsement of the client's political, economic, social or moral views or activities.

(c) A lawyer may limit the scope of the representation if the limitation is reasonable under the circumstances, the client gives informed consent and where necessary notice is provided to the tribunal and/or opposing counsel.

(d) A lawyer shall not counsel a client to engage, or assist a client, in conduct that the lawyer knows is illegal or fraudulent, except that the lawyer may discuss the legal consequences of any proposed course of conduct with a client.

(e) A lawyer may exercise professional judgment to waive or fail to assert a right or position of the client, or accede to reasonable requests of opposing counsel, when doing so does not prejudice the rights of the client.

(f) A lawyer may refuse to aid or participate in conduct that the lawyer believes to be unlawful, even though there is some support for an argument that the conduct is legal.

(g) A lawyer does not violate these Rules by being punctual in fulfilling all professional commitments, by avoiding offensive tactics, and by treating with courtesy and consideration all persons involved in the legal process.

RULE 1.3: DILIGENCE

(a) A lawyer shall act with reasonable diligence and promptness in representing a client.

(b) A lawyer shall not neglect a legal matter entrusted to the lawyer.

(c) A lawyer shall not intentionally fail to carry out a contract of employment entered into with a client for professional services, but the lawyer may withdraw as permitted under these Rules.

RULE 1.4: COMMUNICATION

(a) A lawyer shall:

   (1) promptly inform the client of:

      (i) any decision or circumstance with respect to which the client's informed consent, as defined in Rule 1.0(j), is required by these Rules;

      (ii) any information required by court rule or other law to be communicated to a client; and

(iii) material developments in the matter including settlement or plea offers.

(2) reasonably consult with the client about the means by which the client's objectives are to be accomplished;

(3) keep the client reasonably informed about the status of the matter;

(4) promptly comply with a client's reasonable requests for information; and

(5) consult with the client about any relevant limitation on the lawyer's conduct when the lawyer knows that the client expects assistance not permitted by these Rules or other law.

(b) A lawyer shall explain a matter to the extent reasonably necessary to permit the client to make informed decisions regarding the representation.

RULE 1.5: FEES AND DIVISION OF FEES

(a) A lawyer shall not make an agreement for, charge, or collect an excessive or illegal fee or expense. A fee is excessive when, after a review of the facts, a reasonable lawyer would be left with a definite and firm conviction that the fee is excessive. The factors to be considered in determining whether a fee is excessive may include the following:

(1) the time and labor required, the novelty and difficulty of the questions involved, and the skill requisite to perform the legal service properly;

(2) the likelihood, if apparent or made known to the client, that the acceptance of the particular employment will preclude other employment by the lawyer;

(3) the fee customarily charged in the locality for similar legal services;

(4) the amount involved and the results obtained;

(5) the time limitations imposed by the client or by circumstances;

(6) the nature and length of the professional relationship with the client;

(7) the experience, reputation and ability of the lawyer or lawyers performing the services; and

(8) whether the fee is fixed or contingent.

(b) A lawyer shall communicate to a client the scope of the representation and the basis or rate of the fee and expenses for which the client will be responsible. This information shall be communicated to the client before or within a reasonable time after commencement of the representation and shall be in writing where required by statute or court rule. This provision shall not apply when the lawyer will charge a regularly represented client on the same basis or rate and perform services that are of the same general kind as previously rendered to and paid for by the client. Any changes in the scope of the representation or the basis or rate of the fee or expenses shall also be communicated to the client.

(c)   A fee may be contingent on the outcome of the matter for which the service is rendered, except in a matter in which a contingent fee is prohibited by paragraph (d) or other law. Promptly after a lawyer has been employed in a contingent fee matter, the lawyer shall provide the client with a writing stating the method by which the fee is to be determined, including the percentage or percentages that shall accrue to the lawyer in the event of settlement, trial or appeal; litigation and other expenses to be deducted from the recovery; and whether such expenses are to be deducted before or, if not prohibited by statute or court rule, after the contingent fee is calculated. The writing must clearly notify the client of any expenses for which the client will be liable regardless of whether the client is the prevailing party. Upon conclusion of a contingent fee matter, the lawyer shall provide the client with a writing stating the outcome of the matter and, if there is a recovery, showing the remittance to the client and the method of its determination.

(d)   A lawyer shall not enter into an arrangement for, charge or collect:

(1)   a contingent fee for representing a defendant in a criminal matter;

(2)   a fee prohibited by law or rule of court;

(3)   a fee based on fraudulent billing;

(4)   a nonrefundable retainer fee; provided that a lawyer may enter into a retainer agreement with a client containing a reasonable minimum fee clause if it defines in plain language and sets forth the circumstances under which such fee may be incurred and how it will be calculated; or

(5)   any fee in a domestic relations matter if:

(i)   the payment or amount of the fee is contingent upon the securing of a divorce or of obtaining child custody or visitation or is in any way determined by reference to the amount of maintenance, support, equitable distribution, or property settlement;

(ii)   a written retainer agreement has not been signed by the lawyer and client setting forth in plain language the nature of the relationship and the details of the fee arrangement; or

(iii) the written retainer agreement includes a security interest, confession of judgment or other lien without prior notice being provided to the client in a signed retainer agreement and approval from a tribunal after notice to the adversary. A lawyer shall not foreclose on a mortgage placed on the marital residence while the spouse who consents to the mortgage remains the titleholder and the residence remains the spouse's primary residence.

(e)   In domestic relations matters, a lawyer shall provide a prospective client with a Statement of Client's Rights and Responsibilities at the initial conference and prior to the signing of a written retainer agreement.

(f) Where applicable, a lawyer shall resolve fee disputes by arbitration at the election of the client pursuant to a fee arbitration program established by the Chief Administrator of the Courts and approved by the Administrative Board of the Courts.

(g) A lawyer shall not divide a fee for legal services with another lawyer who is not associated in the same law firm unless:

(1) the division is in proportion to the services performed by each lawyer or, by a writing given to the client, each lawyer assumes joint responsibility for the representation;

(2) the client agrees to employment of the other lawyer after a full disclosure that a division of fees will be made, including the share each lawyer will receive, and the client's agreement is confirmed in writing; and

(3) the total fee is not excessive.

(h) Rule 1.5(g) does not prohibit payment to a lawyer formerly associated in a law firm pursuant to a separation or retirement agreement.

RULE 1.6: CONFIDENTIALITY OF INFORMATION

(a) A lawyer shall not knowingly reveal confidential information, as defined in this Rule, or use such information to the disadvantage of a client or for the advantage of the lawyer or a third person, unless:

(1) the client gives informed consent, as defined in Rule 1.0(j);

(2) the disclosure is impliedly authorized to advance the best interests of the client and is either reasonable under the circumstances or customary in the professional community; or

(3) the disclosure is permitted by paragraph (b).

"Confidential information" consists of information gained during or relating to the representation of a client, whatever its source, that is (a) protected by the attorney-client privilege (b) likely to be embarrassing or detrimental to the client if disclosed, or (c) information that the client has requested be kept confidential. "Confidential information" does not ordinarily include (i) a lawyer's legal knowledge or legal research or (ii) information that is generally known in the local community or in the trade, field or profession to which the information relates.

(b) A lawyer may reveal or use confidential information to the extent that the lawyer reasonably believes necessary:

(1) to prevent reasonably certain death or substantial bodily harm;

(2) to prevent the client from committing a crime;

(3) to withdraw a written or oral opinion or representation previously given by the lawyer and reasonably believed by the lawyer still to be relied upon by a third person, where the lawyer has discovered that the opinion or representation was based on materially inaccurate information or is being used to further a crime or fraud;

(4) to secure legal advice about compliance with these Rules or other law by the lawyer, another lawyer associated with the lawyer's firm or the law firm;

(5) (i) to defend the lawyer or the lawyer's employees and associates against an accusation of wrongful conduct; or

(ii) to establish or collect a fee; or

(6) when permitted or required under these Rules or to comply with other law or court order.

(c) A lawyer shall make reasonable efforts to prevent the inadvertent or unauthorized disclosure or use of, or unauthorized access to, information protected by Rules 1.6, 1.9(c), or 1.18(b).

RULE 1.7: CONFLICT OF INTEREST: CURRENT CLIENTS

(a) Except as provided in paragraph (b), a lawyer shall not represent a client if a reasonable lawyer would conclude that either:

(1) the representation will involve the lawyer in representing differing interests; or

(2) there is a significant risk that the lawyer's professional judgment on behalf of a client will be adversely affected by the lawyer's own financial, business, property or other personal interests.

(b) Notwithstanding the existence of a concurrent conflict of interest under paragraph (a), a lawyer may represent a client if:

(1) the lawyer reasonably believes that the lawyer will be able to provide competent and diligent representation to each affected client;

(2) the representation is not prohibited by law;

(3) the representation does not involve the assertion of a claim by one client against another client represented by the lawyer in the same litigation or other proceeding before a tribunal; and

(4) each affected client gives informed consent, confirmed in writing.

RULE 1.8: CURRENT CLIENTS: SPECIFIC CONFLICT OF INTEREST RULES

(a) A lawyer shall not enter into a business transaction with a client if they have differing interests therein and if the client expects the lawyer to exercise professional judgment therein for the protection of the client, unless:

(1) the transaction is fair and reasonable to the client and the terms of the transaction are fully disclosed and transmitted in writing in a manner that can be reasonably understood by the client;

(2) the client is advised in writing of the desirability of seeking, and is given a reasonable opportunity to seek, the advice of independent legal counsel on the transaction; and

(3) the client gives informed consent, in a writing signed by the client, to the essential terms of the transaction and the

lawyer's role in the transaction, including whether the lawyer is representing the client in the transaction.

(b) A lawyer shall not use information relating to representation of a client to the disadvantage of the client unless the client gives informed consent, except as permitted or required by these Rules.

(c) A lawyer shall not:

(1) solicit any gift from a client, including a testamentary gift, for the benefit of the lawyer or a person related to the lawyer; or

(2) prepare on behalf of a client an instrument giving the lawyer or a person related to the lawyer any gift, unless the lawyer or other recipient of the gift is related to the client and a reasonable lawyer would conclude that the transaction is fair and reasonable.

For purposes of this paragraph, related persons include a spouse, child, grandchild, parent, grandparent or other relative, or an individual with whom the lawyer or the client maintains a close, familial relationship.

(d) Prior to conclusion of all aspects of the matter giving rise to the representation or proposed representation of the client or prospective client, a lawyer shall not negotiate or enter into any arrangement or understanding with:

(1) a client or a prospective client by which the lawyer acquires an interest in literary or media rights with respect to the subject matter of the representation or proposed representation; or

(2) any person by which the lawyer transfers or assigns any interest in literary or media rights with respect to the subject matter of the representation of a client or prospective client.

(e) While representing a client in connection with contemplated or pending litigation, a lawyer shall not advance or guarantee financial assistance to the client, except that:

(1) a lawyer may advance court costs and expenses of litigation, the repayment of which may be contingent on the outcome of the matter;

(2) a lawyer representing an indigent or pro bono client may pay court costs and expenses of litigation on behalf of the client; and

(3) a lawyer, in an action in which an attorney's fee is payable in whole or in part as a percentage of the recovery in the action, may pay on the lawyer's own account court costs and expenses of litigation. In such case, the fee paid to the lawyer from the proceeds of the action may include an amount equal to such costs and expenses incurred.

(f) A lawyer shall not accept compensation for representing a client, or anything of value related to the lawyer's representation of the client, from one other than the client unless:

(1)   the client gives informed consent;

(2)   there is no interference with the lawyer's independent professional judgment or with the client-lawyer relationship; and

(3)   the client's confidential information is protected as required by Rule 1.6.

(g)   A lawyer who represents two or more clients shall not participate in making an aggregate settlement of the claims of or against the clients, absent court approval, unless each client gives informed consent in a writing signed by the client. The lawyer's disclosure shall include the existence and nature of all the claims involved and of the participation of each person in the settlement.

(h)   A lawyer shall not:

(1)   make an agreement prospectively limiting the lawyer's liability to a client for malpractice; or

(2)   settle a claim or potential claim for such liability with an unrepresented client or former client unless that person is advised in writing of the desirability of seeking, and is given a reasonable opportunity to seek, the advice of independent legal counsel in connection therewith.

(i)   A lawyer shall not acquire a proprietary interest in the cause of action or subject matter of litigation the lawyer is conducting for a client, except that the lawyer may:

(1)   acquire a lien authorized by law to secure the lawyer's fee or expenses; and

(2)   contract with a client for a reasonable contingent fee in a civil matter subject to Rule 1.5(d) or other law or court rule.

(j)   (1)   A lawyer shall not:

(i)   as a condition of entering into or continuing any professional representation by the lawyer or the lawyer's firm, require or demand sexual relations with any person;

(ii)   employ coercion, intimidation or undue influence in entering into sexual relations incident to any professional representation by the lawyer or the lawyer's firm; or

(iii)   in domestic relations matters, enter into sexual relations with a client during the course of the lawyer's representation of the client.

(2)   Rule 1.8(j)(1) shall not apply to sexual relations between lawyers and their spouses or to ongoing consensual sexual relationships that predate the initiation of the client-lawyer relationship.

(k)   Where a lawyer in a firm has sexual relations with a client but does not participate in the representation of that client, the lawyers in the firm shall not be subject to discipline under this Rule solely because of the occurrence of such sexual relations.

RULE 1.9: DUTIES TO FORMER CLIENTS

(a) A lawyer who has formerly represented a client in a matter shall not thereafter represent another person in the same or a substantially related matter in which that person's interests are materially adverse to the interests of the former client unless the former client gives informed consent, confirmed in writing.

(b) Unless the former client gives informed consent, confirmed in writing, a lawyer shall not knowingly represent a person in the same or a substantially related matter in which a firm with which the lawyer formerly was associated had previously represented a client:

   (1) whose interests are materially adverse to that person; and

   (2) about whom the lawyer had acquired information protected by Rules 1.6 or paragraph (c) of this Rule that is material to the matter.

(c) A lawyer who has formerly represented a client in a matter or whose present or former firm has formerly represented a client in a matter shall not thereafter:

   (1) use confidential information of the former client protected by Rule 1.6 to the disadvantage of the former client, except as these Rules would permit or require with respect to a current client or when the information has become generally known; or

   (2) reveal confidential information of the former client protected by Rule 1.6 except as these Rules would permit or require with respect to a current client.

RULE 1.10: IMPUTATION OF CONFLICTS OF INTEREST

(a) While lawyers are associated in a firm, none of them shall knowingly represent a client when any one of them practicing alone would be prohibited from doing so by Rule 1.7, 1.8 or 1.9, except as otherwise provided therein.

(b) When a lawyer has terminated an association with a firm, the firm is prohibited from thereafter representing a person with interests that the firm knows or reasonably should know are materially adverse to those of a client represented by the formerly associated lawyer and not currently represented by the firm if the firm or any lawyer remaining in the firm has information protected by Rule 1.6 or Rule 1.9(c) that is material to the matter.

(c) When a lawyer becomes associated with a firm, the firm may not knowingly represent a client in a matter that is the same as or substantially related to a matter in which the newly associated lawyer, or a firm with which that lawyer was associated, formerly represented a client whose interests are materially adverse to the prospective or current client unless the newly associated lawyer did not acquire any information protected by Rule 1.6 or Rule 1.9(c) that is material to the current matter.

(d) A disqualification prescribed by this Rule may be waived by the affected client or former client under the conditions stated in Rule 1.7.

(e)   A law firm shall make a written record of its engagements, at or near the time of each new engagement, and shall implement and maintain a system by which proposed engagements are checked against current and previous engagements when:

(1)   the firm agrees to represent a new client;

(2)   the firm agrees to represent an existing client in a new matter;

(3)   the firm hires or associates with another lawyer; or

(4)   an additional party is named or appears in a pending matter.

(f)   Substantial failure to keep records or to implement or maintain a conflict-checking system that complies with paragraph (e) shall be a violation thereof regardless of whether there is another violation of these Rules.

(g)   Where a violation of paragraph (e) by a law firm is a substantial factor in causing a violation of paragraph (a) by a lawyer, the law firm, as well as the individual lawyer, shall be responsible for the violation of paragraph (a).

(h)   A lawyer related to another lawyer as parent, child, sibling or spouse shall not represent in any matter a client whose interests differ from those of another party to the matter who the lawyer knows is represented by the other lawyer unless the client consents to the representation after full disclosure and the lawyer concludes that the lawyer can adequately represent the interests of the client.

RULE 1.11: SPECIFIC CONFLICTS OF INTEREST FOR FORMER AND CURRENT GOVERNMENT OFFICERS AND EMPLOYEES

(a)   Except as law may otherwise expressly provide, a lawyer who has formerly served as a public officer or employee of the government:

(1)   shall comply with Rule 1.9(c); and

(2)   shall not represent a client in connection with a matter in which the lawyer participated personally and substantially as a public officer or employee, unless the appropriate government agency gives its informed consent, confirmed in writing, to the representation. This provision shall not apply to matters governed by Rule 1.12(a).

(b)   When a lawyer is disqualified from representation under paragraph (a), no lawyer in a firm with which that lawyer is associated may knowingly undertake or continue representation in such a matter unless:

(1)   the firm acts promptly and reasonably to:

(i)   notify, as appropriate, lawyers and nonlawyer personnel within the firm that the personally disqualified lawyer is prohibited from participating in the representation of the current client;

(ii)   implement effective screening procedures to prevent the flow of information about the matter between the personally disqualified lawyer and the others in the firm;

(iii) ensure that the disqualified lawyer is apportioned no part of the fee therefrom; and

(iv) give written notice to the appropriate government agency to enable it to ascertain compliance with the provisions of this Rule; and

(2) there are no other circumstances in the particular representation that create an appearance of impropriety.

(c) Except as law may otherwise expressly provide, a lawyer having information that the lawyer knows is confidential government information about a person, acquired when the lawyer was a public officer or employee, may not represent a private client whose interests are adverse to that person in a matter in which the information could be used to the material disadvantage of that person. As used in this Rule, the term "confidential government information" means information that has been obtained under governmental authority and that, at the time this Rule is applied, the government is prohibited by law from disclosing to the public or has a legal privilege not to disclose, and that is not otherwise available to the public. A firm with which that lawyer is associated may undertake or continue representation in the matter only if the disqualified lawyer is timely and effectively screened from any participation in the matter in accordance with the provisions of paragraph (b).

(d) Except as law may otherwise expressly provide, a lawyer currently serving as a public officer or employee shall not:

(1) participate in a matter in which the lawyer participated personally and substantially while in private practice or nongovernmental employment, unless under applicable law no one is, or by lawful delegation may be, authorized to act in the lawyer's stead in the matter; or

(2) negotiate for private employment with any person who is involved as a party or as lawyer for a party in a matter in which the lawyer is participating personally and substantially.

(e) As used in this Rule, the term "matter" as defined in Rule 1.0(*l*) does not include or apply to agency rulemaking functions.

(f) A lawyer who holds public office shall not:

(1) use the public position to obtain, or attempt to obtain, a special advantage in legislative matters for the lawyer or for a client under circumstances where the lawyer knows or it is obvious that such action is not in the public interest;

(2) use the public position to influence, or attempt to influence, a tribunal to act in favor of the lawyer or of a client; or

(3) accept anything of value from any person when the lawyer knows or it is obvious that the offer is for the purpose of influencing the lawyer's action as a public official.

RULE 1.12: SPECIFIC CONFLICTS OF INTEREST FOR FORMER JUDGES, ARBITRATORS, MEDIATORS OR OTHER THIRD-PARTY NEUTRALS

(a) A lawyer shall not accept private employment in a matter upon the merits of which the lawyer has acted in a judicial capacity.

(b) Except as stated in paragraph (e), and unless all parties to the proceeding give informed consent, confirmed in writing, a lawyer shall not represent anyone in connection with a matter in which the lawyer participated personally and substantially as:

(1) an arbitrator, mediator or other third-party neutral; or

(2) a law clerk to a judge or other adjudicative officer or an arbitrator, mediator or other third-party neutral.

(c) A lawyer shall not negotiate for employment with any person who is involved as a party or as lawyer for a party in a matter in which the lawyer is participating personally and substantially as a judge or other adjudicative officer or as an arbitrator, mediator or other third-party neutral.

(d) When a lawyer is disqualified from representation under this Rule, no lawyer in a firm with which that lawyer is associated may knowingly undertake or continue representation in such a matter unless:

(1) the firm acts promptly and reasonably to:

(i) notify, as appropriate, lawyers and nonlawyer personnel within the firm that the personally disqualified lawyer is prohibited from participating in the representation of the current client;

(ii) implement effective screening procedures to prevent the flow of information about the matter between the personally disqualified lawyer and the others in the firm;

(iii) ensure that the disqualified lawyer is apportioned no part of the fee therefrom; and

(iv) give written notice to the parties and any appropriate tribunal to enable it to ascertain compliance with the provisions of this Rule; and

(2) there are no other circumstances in the particular representation that create an appearance of impropriety.

(e) An arbitrator selected as a partisan of a party in a multimember arbitration panel is not prohibited from subsequently representing that party.

RULE 1.13: ORGANIZATION AS CLIENT

(a) When a lawyer employed or retained by an organization is dealing with the organization's directors, officers, employees, members, shareholders or other constituents, and it appears that the organization's interests may differ from those of the constituents with whom the lawyer is dealing, the lawyer shall explain that the lawyer is the lawyer for the organization and not for any of the constituents.

(b) If a lawyer for an organization knows that an officer, employee or other person associated with the organization is engaged in action or intends to act or refuses to act in a matter related to the representation that (i) is a violation of a legal obligation to the organization or a violation of law that reasonably might be imputed to the organization, and (ii) is likely to result in substantial injury to the organization, then the lawyer shall proceed as is reasonably necessary in the best interest of the organization. In determining how to proceed, the lawyer shall give due consideration to the seriousness of the violation and its consequences, the scope and nature of the lawyer's representation, the responsibility in the organization and the apparent motivation of the person involved, the policies of the organization concerning such matters and any other relevant considerations. Any measures taken shall be designed to minimize disruption of the organization and the risk of revealing information relating to the representation to persons outside the organization. Such measures may include, among others:

(1) asking reconsideration of the matter;

(2) advising that a separate legal opinion on the matter be sought for presentation to an appropriate authority in the organization; and

(3) referring the matter to higher authority in the organization, including, if warranted by the seriousness of the matter, referral to the highest authority that can act in behalf of the organization as determined by applicable law.

(c) If, despite the lawyer's efforts in accordance with paragraph (b), the highest authority that can act on behalf of the organization insists upon action, or a refusal to act, that is clearly in violation of law and is likely to result in a substantial injury to the organization, the lawyer may reveal confidential information only if permitted by Rule 1.6, and may resign in accordance with Rule 1.16.

(d) A lawyer representing an organization may also represent any of its directors, officers, employees, members, shareholders or other constituents, subject to the provisions of Rule 1.7. If the organization's consent to the concurrent representation is required by Rule 1.7, the consent shall be given by an appropriate official of the organization other than the individual who is to be represented, or by the shareholders.

RULE 1.14: CLIENT WITH DIMINISHED CAPACITY

(a) When a client's capacity to make adequately considered decisions in connection with a representation is diminished, whether because of minority, mental impairment or for some other reason, the lawyer shall, as far as reasonably possible, maintain a conventional relationship with the client.

(b) When the lawyer reasonably believes that the client has diminished capacity, is at risk of substantial physical, financial or other harm unless action is taken and cannot adequately act in the client's own interest, the lawyer may take reasonably necessary protective action, including consulting with individuals or entities that have the ability to take action to protect the client and, in appropriate cases, seeking the appointment of a guardian ad litem, conservator or guardian.

(c) Information relating to the representation of a client with diminished capacity is protected by Rule 1.6. When taking protective action pursuant to paragraph (b), the lawyer is impliedly authorized under Rule 1.6(a) to reveal information about the client, but only to the extent reasonably necessary to protect the client's interests.

RULE 1.15: PRESERVING IDENTITY OF FUNDS AND PROPERTY OF OTHERS; FIDUCIARY RESPONSIBILITY; COMMINGLING AND MISAPPROPRIATION OF CLIENT FUNDS OR PROPERTY; MAINTENANCE OF BANK ACCOUNTS; RECORD KEEPING; EXAMINATION OF RECORDS

(a) Prohibition Against Commingling and Misappropriation of Client Funds or Property.

A lawyer in possession of any funds or other property belonging to another person, where such possession is incident to his or her practice of law, is a fiduciary, and must not misappropriate such funds or property or commingle such funds or property with his or her own.

(b) Separate Accounts.

(1) A lawyer who is in possession of funds belonging to another person incident to the lawyer's practice of law shall maintain such funds in a banking institution within New York State that agrees to provide dishonored check reports in accordance with the provisions of 22 N.Y.C.R.R. Part 1300. "Banking institution" means a state or national bank, trust company, savings bank, savings and loan association or credit union. Such funds shall be maintained, in the lawyer's own name, or in the name of a firm of lawyers of which the lawyer is a member, or in the name of the lawyer or firm of lawyers by whom the lawyer is employed, in a special account or accounts, separate from any business or personal accounts of the lawyer or lawyer's firm, and separate from any accounts that the lawyer may maintain as executor, guardian, trustee or receiver, or in any other fiduciary capacity; into such special account or accounts all funds held in escrow or otherwise entrusted to the lawyer or firm shall be deposited; provided, however, that such funds may be maintained in a banking institution located outside New York State if such banking institution complies with 22 N.Y.C.R.R. Part 1300 and the lawyer has obtained the prior written approval of the person to whom such funds belong specifying the name and address of the office or branch of the banking institution where such funds are to be maintained.

(2) A lawyer or the lawyer's firm shall identify the special bank account or accounts required by Rule 1.15(b)(1) as an "Attorney Special Account," "Attorney Trust Account," or "Attorney Escrow Account," and shall obtain checks and deposit slips that bear such title. Such title may be accompanied by such other descriptive language as the lawyer may deem appropriate, provided that such additional language distinguishes such special account or accounts from other bank accounts that are maintained by the lawyer or the lawyer's firm.

(3) Funds reasonably sufficient to maintain the account or to pay account charges may be deposited therein.

(4)   Funds belonging in part to a client or third person and in part currently or potentially to the lawyer or law firm shall be kept in such special account or accounts, but the portion belonging to the lawyer or law firm may be withdrawn when due unless the right of the lawyer or law firm to receive it is disputed by the client or third person, in which event the disputed portion shall not be withdrawn until the dispute is finally resolved.

(c)   Notification of Receipt of Property; Safekeeping; Rendering Accounts; Payment or Delivery of Property.

A lawyer shall:

(1)   promptly notify a client or third person of the receipt of funds, securities, or other properties in which the client or third person has an interest;

(2)   identify and label securities and properties of a client or third person promptly upon receipt and place them in a safe deposit box or other place of safekeeping as soon as practicable;

(3)   maintain complete records of all funds, securities, and other properties of a client or third person coming into the possession of the lawyer and render appropriate accounts to the client or third person regarding them; and

(4)   promptly pay or deliver to the client or third person as requested by the client or third person the funds, securities, or other properties in the possession of the lawyer that the client or third person is entitled to receive.

(d)   Required Bookkeeping Records.

(1)   A lawyer shall maintain for seven years after the events that they record:

(i)   the records of all deposits in and withdrawals from the accounts specified in Rule 1.15(b) and of any other bank account that concerns or affects the lawyer's practice of law; these records shall specifically identify the date, source and description of each item deposited, as well as the date, payee and purpose of each withdrawal or disbursement;

(ii)   a record for special accounts, showing the source of all funds deposited in such accounts, the names of all persons for whom the funds are or were held, the amount of such funds, the description and amounts, and the names of all persons to whom such funds were disbursed;

(iii) copies of all retainer and compensation agreements with clients;

(iv)   copies of all statements to clients or other persons showing the disbursement of funds to them or on their behalf;

(v)   copies of all bills rendered to clients;

(vi)   copies of all records showing payments to lawyers, investigators or other persons, not in the lawyer's regular employ, for services rendered or performed;

(vii) copies of all retainer and closing statements filed with the Office of Court Administration; and

(viii) all checkbooks and check stubs, bank statements, prenumbered canceled checks and duplicate deposit slips.

(2) Lawyers shall make accurate entries of all financial transactions in their records of receipts and disbursements, in their special accounts, in their ledger books or similar records, and in any other books of account kept by them in the regular course of their practice, which entries shall be made at or near the time of the act, condition or event recorded.

(3) For purposes of Rule 1.15(d), a lawyer may satisfy the requirements of maintaining "copies" by maintaining any of the following items: original records, photocopies, microfilm, optical imaging, and any other medium that preserves an image of the document that cannot be altered without detection.

(e) Authorized Signatories.

All special account withdrawals shall be made only to a named payee and not to cash. Such withdrawals shall be made by check or, with the prior written approval of the party entitled to the proceeds, by bank transfer. Only a lawyer admitted to practice law in New York State shall be an authorized signatory of a special account.

(f) Missing Clients.

Whenever any sum of money is payable to a client and the lawyer is unable to locate the client, the lawyer shall apply to the court in which the action was brought if in the unified court system, or, if no action was commenced in the unified court system, to the Supreme Court in the county in which the lawyer maintains an office for the practice of law, for an order directing payment to the lawyer of any fees and disbursements that are owed by the client and the balance, if any, to the Lawyers' Fund for Client Protection for safeguarding and disbursement to persons who are entitled thereto.

(g) Designation of Successor Signatories.

(1) Upon the death of a lawyer who was the sole signatory on an attorney trust, escrow or special account, an application may be made to the Supreme Court for an order designating a successor signatory for such trust, escrow or special account, who shall be a member of the bar in good standing and admitted to the practice of law in New York State.

(2) An application to designate a successor signatory shall be made to the Supreme Court in the judicial district in which the deceased lawyer maintained an office for the practice of law. The application may be made by the legal representative of the deceased lawyer's estate; a lawyer who was affiliated with the deceased lawyer in the practice of law; any person who has a beneficial interest in such trust, escrow or special account; an officer of a city or county bar association; or counsel for an attorney disciplinary committee. No lawyer may charge a legal fee for assisting with an application to designate a successor signatory pursuant to this Rule.

(3) The Supreme Court may designate a successor signatory and may direct the safeguarding of funds from such trust, escrow or special account, and the disbursement of such funds to persons who are entitled thereto, and may order that funds in such account be deposited with the Lawyers' Fund for Client Protection for safeguarding and disbursement to persons who are entitled thereto.

(h) Dissolution of a Firm.

Upon the dissolution of any firm of lawyers, the former partners or members shall make appropriate arrangements for the maintenance, by one of them or by a successor firm, of the records specified in Rule 1.15(d).

(i) Availability of Bookkeeping Records: Records Subject to Production in Disciplinary Investigations and Proceedings.

The financial records required by this Rule shall be located, or made available, at the principal New York State office of the lawyers subject hereto, and any such records shall be produced in response to a notice or subpoena duces tecum issued in connection with a complaint before or any investigation by the appropriate grievance or departmental disciplinary committee, or shall be produced at the direction of the appropriate Appellate Division before any person designated by it. All books and records produced pursuant to this Rule shall be kept confidential, except for the purpose of the particular proceeding, and their contents shall not be disclosed by anyone in violation of the attorney-client privilege.

(j) Disciplinary Action.

A lawyer who does not maintain and keep the accounts and records as specified and required by this Rule, or who does not produce any such records pursuant to this Rule, shall be deemed in violation of these Rules and shall be subject to disciplinary proceedings.

RULE 1.16: DECLINING OR
TERMINATING REPRESENTATION

(a) A lawyer shall not accept employment on behalf of a person if the lawyer knows or reasonably should know that such person wishes to:

(1) bring a legal action, conduct a defense, or assert a position in a matter, or otherwise have steps taken for such person, merely for the purpose of harassing or maliciously injuring any person; or

(2) present a claim or defense in a matter that is not warranted under existing law, unless it can be supported by a good faith argument for an extension, modification, or reversal of existing law.

(b) Except as stated in paragraph (d), a lawyer shall withdraw from the representation of a client when:

(1) the lawyer knows or reasonably should know that the representation will result in a violation of these Rules or of law;

(2) the lawyer's physical or mental condition materially impairs the lawyer's ability to represent the client;

(3) the lawyer is discharged; or

(4) the lawyer knows or reasonably should know that the client is bringing the legal action, conducting the defense, or asserting a position in the matter, or is otherwise having steps taken, merely for the purpose of harassing or maliciously injuring any person.

(c) Except as stated in paragraph (d), a lawyer may withdraw from representing a client when:

(1) withdrawal can be accomplished without material adverse effect on the interests of the client;

(2) the client persists in a course of action involving the lawyer's services that the lawyer reasonably believes is criminal or fraudulent;

(3) the client has used the lawyer's services to perpetrate a crime or fraud;

(4) the client insists upon taking action with which the lawyer has a fundamental disagreement;

(5) the client deliberately disregards an agreement or obligation to the lawyer as to expenses or fees;

(6) the client insists upon presenting a claim or defense that is not warranted under existing law and cannot be supported by good faith argument for an extension, modification, or reversal of existing law;

(7) the client fails to cooperate in the representation or otherwise renders the representation unreasonably difficult for the lawyer to carry out employment effectively;

(8) the lawyer's inability to work with co-counsel indicates that the best interest of the client likely will be served by withdrawal;

(9) the lawyer's mental or physical condition renders it difficult for the lawyer to carry out the representation effectively;

(10) the client knowingly and freely assents to termination of the employment;

(11) withdrawal is permitted under Rule 1.13(c) or other law;

(12) the lawyer believes in good faith, in a matter pending before a tribunal, that the tribunal will find the existence of other good cause for withdrawal; or

(13) the client insists that the lawyer pursue a course of conduct which is illegal or prohibited under these Rules.

(d) If permission for withdrawal from employment is required by the rules of a tribunal, a lawyer shall not withdraw from employment in a matter before that tribunal without its permission. When ordered to do so by a tribunal, a lawyer shall continue representation notwithstanding good cause for terminating the representation.

(e) Even when withdrawal is otherwise permitted or required, upon termination of representation, a lawyer shall take steps, to the extent reasonably practicable, to avoid foreseeable prejudice to the rights of the client, including giving reasonable notice to the client, allowing time for employment of other counsel, delivering to the client all papers and property to which the client is entitled, promptly refunding any part of a fee paid in advance that has not been earned and complying with applicable laws and rules.

RULE 1.17: SALE OF LAW PRACTICE

(a) A lawyer retiring from a private practice of law; a law firm, one or more members of which are retiring from the private practice of law with the firm; or the personal representative of a deceased, disabled or missing lawyer, may sell a law practice, including goodwill, to one or more lawyers or law firms, who may purchase the practice. The seller and the buyer may agree on reasonable restrictions on the seller's private practice of law, notwithstanding any other provision of these Rules. Retirement shall include the cessation of the private practice of law in the geographic area, that is, the county and city and any county or city contiguous thereto, in which the practice to be sold has been conducted.

(b) Confidential information.

(1) With respect to each matter subject to the contemplated sale, the seller may provide prospective buyers with any information not protected as confidential information under Rule 1.6.

(2) Notwithstanding Rule 1.6, the seller may provide the prospective buyer with information as to individual clients:

(i) concerning the identity of the client, except as provided in paragraph (b)(6);

(ii) concerning the status and general nature of the matter;

(iii) available in public court files; and

(iv) concerning the financial terms of the client-lawyer relationship and the payment status of the client's account.

(3) Prior to making any disclosure of confidential information that may be permitted under paragraph (b)(2), the seller shall provide the prospective buyer with information regarding the matters involved in the proposed sale sufficient to enable the prospective buyer to determine whether any conflicts of interest exist. Where sufficient information cannot be disclosed without revealing client confidential information, the seller may make the disclosures necessary for the prospective buyer to determine whether any conflict of interest exists, subject to paragraph (b)(6). If the prospective buyer determines that conflicts of interest exist prior to reviewing the information, or determines during the course of review that a conflict of interest exists, the prospective buyer shall not review or continue to review the information unless the seller shall

431

have obtained the consent of the client in accordance with Rule 1.6(a)(1).

(4)   Prospective buyers shall maintain the confidentiality of and shall not use any client information received in connection with the proposed sale in the same manner and to the same extent as if the prospective buyers represented the client.

(5)   Absent the consent of the client after full disclosure, a seller shall not provide a prospective buyer with information if doing so would cause a violation of the attorney-client privilege.

(6)   If the seller has reason to believe that the identity of the client or the fact of the representation itself constitutes confidential information in the circumstances, the seller may not provide such information to a prospective buyer without first advising the client of the identity of the prospective buyer and obtaining the client's consent to the proposed disclosure.

(c)   Written notice of the sale shall be given jointly by the seller and the buyer to each of the seller's clients and shall include information regarding:

(1)   the client's right to retain other counsel or to take possession of the file;

(2)   the fact that the client's consent to the transfer of the client's file or matter to the buyer will be presumed if the client does not take any action or otherwise object within 90 days of the sending of the notice, subject to any court rule or statute requiring express approval by the client or a court;

(3)   the fact that agreements between the seller and the seller's clients as to fees will be honored by the buyer;

(4)   proposed fee increases, if any, permitted under paragraph (e); and

(5)   the identity and background of the buyer or buyers, including principal office address, bar admissions, number of years in practice in New York State, whether the buyer has ever been disciplined for professional misconduct or convicted of a crime, and whether the buyer currently intends to resell the practice.

(d)   When the buyer's representation of a client of the seller would give rise to a waivable conflict of interest, the buyer shall not undertake such representation unless the necessary waiver or waivers have been obtained in writing.

(e)   The fee charged a client by the buyer shall not be increased by reason of the sale, unless permitted by a retainer agreement with the client or otherwise specifically agreed to by the client.

RULE 1.18: DUTIES TO PROSPECTIVE CLIENTS

(a)   Except as provided in Rule 1.18(e), a person who consults with a lawyer about the possibility of forming a client-lawyer relationship with respect to a matter is a "prospective client."

(b)   Even when no client-lawyer relationship ensues, a lawyer who has learned information from a prospective client shall not use or reveal that information, except as Rule 1.9 would permit with respect to information of a former client.

(c) A lawyer subject to paragraph (b) shall not represent a client with interests materially adverse to those of a prospective client in the same or a substantially related matter if the lawyer received information from the prospective client that could be significantly harmful to that person in the matter, except as provided in paragraph (d). If a lawyer is disqualified from representation under this paragraph, no lawyer in a firm with which that lawyer is associated may knowingly undertake or continue representation in such a matter, except as provided in paragraph (d).

(d) When the lawyer has received disqualifying information as defined in paragraph (c), representation is permissible if:

(1) both the affected client and the prospective client have given informed consent, confirmed in writing; or

(2) the lawyer who received the information took reasonable measures to avoid exposure to more disqualifying information than was reasonably necessary to determine whether to represent the prospective client; and

(i) the firm acts promptly and reasonably to notify, as appropriate, lawyers and nonlawyer personnel within the firm that the personally disqualified lawyer is prohibited from participating in the representation of the current client;

(ii) the firm implements effective screening procedures to prevent the flow of information about the matter between the disqualified lawyer and the others in the firm;

(iii) the disqualified lawyer is apportioned no part of the fee therefrom; and

(iv) written notice is promptly given to the prospective client; and

(3) a reasonable lawyer would conclude that the law firm will be able to provide competent and diligent representation in the matter.

(e) A person is not a prospective client within the meaning of paragraph (a) if the person:

(1) communicates information unilaterally to a lawyer, without any reasonable expectation that the lawyer is willing to discuss the possibility of forming a client-lawyer relationship; or

(2) communicates with a lawyer for the purpose of disqualifying the lawyer from handling a materially adverse representation on the same or a substantially related matter.

RULE 2.1: ADVISOR

In representing a client, a lawyer shall exercise professional judgment and render candid advice. In rendering advice, a lawyer may refer not only to law but to other considerations such as moral, economic, social, psychological, and political factors that may be relevant to the client's situation.

RULE 2.2: [RESERVED]

RULE 2.3: EVALUATION FOR USE BY THIRD PERSONS

(a) A lawyer may provide an evaluation of a matter affecting a client for the use of someone other than the client if the lawyer reasonably believes that making the evaluation is compatible with other aspects of the lawyer's relationship with the client.

(b) When the lawyer knows or reasonably should know that the evaluation is likely to affect the client's interests materially and adversely, the lawyer shall not provide the evaluation unless the client gives informed consent.

(c) Unless disclosure is authorized in connection with a report of an evaluation, information relating to the evaluation is protected by Rule 1.6.

RULE 2.4: LAWYER SERVING AS THIRD-PARTY NEUTRAL

(a) A lawyer serves as a "third-party neutral" when the lawyer assists two or more persons who are not clients of the lawyer to reach a resolution of a dispute or other matter that has arisen between them. Service as a third-party neutral may include service as an arbitrator, a mediator or in such other capacity as will enable the lawyer to assist the parties to resolve the matter.

(b) A lawyer serving as a third-party neutral shall inform unrepresented parties that the lawyer is not representing them. When the lawyer knows or reasonably should know that a party does not understand the lawyer's role in the matter, the lawyer shall explain the difference between the lawyer's role as a third-party neutral and a lawyer's role as one who represents a client.

RULE 3.1: NON-MERITORIOUS CLAIMS AND CONTENTIONS

(a) A lawyer shall not bring or defend a proceeding, or assert or controvert an issue therein, unless there is a basis in law and fact for doing so that is not frivolous. A lawyer for the defendant in a criminal proceeding or for the respondent in a proceeding that could result in incarceration may nevertheless so defend the proceeding as to require that every element of the case be established.

(b) A lawyer's conduct is "frivolous" for purposes of this Rule if:

(1) the lawyer knowingly advances a claim or defense that is unwarranted under existing law, except that the lawyer may advance such claim or defense if it can be supported by good faith argument for an extension, modification, or reversal of existing law;

(2) the conduct has no reasonable purpose other than to delay or prolong the resolution of litigation, in violation of Rule 3.2, or serves merely to harass or maliciously injure another; or

(3) the lawyer knowingly asserts material factual statements that are false.

RULE 3.2: DELAY OF LITIGATION

In representing a client, a lawyer shall not use means that have no substantial purpose other than to delay or prolong the proceeding or to cause needless expense.

RULE 3.3: CONDUCT BEFORE A TRIBUNAL

(a)   A lawyer shall not knowingly:

(1)   make a false statement of fact or law to a tribunal or fail to correct a false statement of material fact or law previously made to the tribunal by the lawyer;

(2)   fail to disclose to the tribunal controlling legal authority known to the lawyer to be directly adverse to the position of the client and not disclosed by opposing counsel; or

(3)   offer or use evidence that the lawyer knows to be false. If a lawyer, the lawyer's client, or a witness called by the lawyer has offered material evidence and the lawyer comes to know of its falsity, the lawyer shall take reasonable remedial measures, including, if necessary, disclosure to the tribunal. A lawyer may refuse to offer evidence, other than the testimony of a defendant in a criminal matter, that the lawyer reasonably believes is false.

(b)   A lawyer who represents a client before a tribunal and who knows that a person intends to engage, is engaging or has engaged in criminal or fraudulent conduct related to the proceeding shall take reasonable remedial measures, including, if necessary, disclosure to the tribunal.

(c)   The duties stated in paragraphs (a) and (b) apply even if compliance requires disclosure of information otherwise protected by Rule 1.6.

(d)   In an ex parte proceeding, a lawyer shall inform the tribunal of all material facts known to the lawyer that will enable the tribunal to make an informed decision, whether or not the facts are adverse.

(e)   In presenting a matter to a tribunal, a lawyer shall disclose, unless privileged or irrelevant, the identities of the clients the lawyer represents and of the persons who employed the lawyer.

(f)   In appearing as a lawyer before a tribunal, a lawyer shall not:

(1)   fail to comply with known local customs of courtesy or practice of the bar or a particular tribunal without giving to opposing counsel timely notice of the intent not to comply;

(2)   engage in undignified or discourteous conduct;

(3)   intentionally or habitually violate any established rule of procedure or of evidence; or

(4)   engage in conduct intended to disrupt the tribunal.

RULE 3.4: FAIRNESS TO OPPOSING PARTY AND COUNSEL

A lawyer shall not:

(a)   (1)   suppress any evidence that the lawyer or the client has a legal obligation to reveal or produce;

(2) advise or cause a person to hide or leave the jurisdiction of a tribunal for the purpose of making the person unavailable as a witness therein;

(3) conceal or knowingly fail to disclose that which the lawyer is required by law to reveal;

(4) knowingly use perjured testimony or false evidence;

(5) participate in the creation or preservation of evidence when the lawyer knows or it is obvious that the evidence is false; or

(6) knowingly engage in other illegal conduct or conduct contrary to these Rules;

(b) offer an inducement to a witness that is prohibited by law or pay, offer to pay or acquiesce in the payment of compensation to a witness contingent upon the content of the witness's testimony or the outcome of the matter. A lawyer may advance, guarantee or acquiesce in the payment of:

(1) reasonable compensation to a witness for the loss of time in attending, testifying, preparing to testify or otherwise assisting counsel, and reasonable related expenses; or

(2) a reasonable fee for the professional services of an expert witness and reasonable related expenses;

(c) disregard or advise the client to disregard a standing rule of a tribunal or a ruling of a tribunal made in the course of a proceeding, but the lawyer may take appropriate steps in good faith to test the validity of such rule or ruling;

(d) in appearing before a tribunal on behalf of a client:

(1) state or allude to any matter that the lawyer does not reasonably believe is relevant or that will not be supported by admissible evidence;

(2) assert personal knowledge of facts in issue except when testifying as a witness;

(3) assert a personal opinion as to the justness of a cause, the credibility of a witness, the culpability of a civil litigant or the guilt or innocence of an accused but the lawyer may argue, upon analysis of the evidence, for any position or conclusion with respect to the matters stated herein; or

(4) ask any question that the lawyer has no reasonable basis to believe is relevant to the case and that is intended to degrade a witness or other person; or

(e) present, participate in presenting, or threaten to present criminal charges solely to obtain an advantage in a civil matter.

RULE 3.5: MAINTAINING AND PRESERVING THE IMPARTIALITY OF TRIBUNALS AND JURORS

(a) A lawyer shall not:

(1) seek to or cause another person to influence a judge, official or employee of a tribunal by means prohibited by law or give or lend anything of value to such judge, official, or

employee of a tribunal when the recipient is prohibited from accepting the gift or loan but a lawyer may make a contribution to the campaign fund of a candidate for judicial office in conformity with Part 100 of the Rules of the Chief Administrator of the Courts;

(2) in an adversarial proceeding communicate or cause another person to do so on the lawyer's behalf, as to the merits of the matter with a judge or official of a tribunal or an employee thereof before whom the matter is pending, except:

    (i) in the course of official proceedings in the matter;

    (ii) in writing, if the lawyer promptly delivers a copy of the writing to counsel for other parties and to a party who is not represented by a lawyer;

    (iii) orally, upon adequate notice to counsel for the other parties and to any party who is not represented by a lawyer; or

    (iv) as otherwise authorized by law, or by Part 100 of the Rules of the Chief Administrator of the Courts;

(3) seek to or cause another person to influence a juror or prospective juror by means prohibited by law;

(4) communicate or cause another to communicate with a member of the jury venire from which the jury will be selected for the trial of a case or, during the trial of a case, with any member of the jury unless authorized to do so by law or court order;

(5) communicate with a juror or prospective juror after discharge of the jury if:

    (i) the communication is prohibited by law or court order;

    (ii) the juror has made known to the lawyer a desire not to communicate;

    (iii) the communication involves misrepresentation, coercion, duress or harassment; or

    (iv) the communication is an attempt to influence the juror's actions in future jury service; or

(6) conduct a vexatious or harassing investigation of either a member of the venire or a juror or, by financial support or otherwise, cause another to do so.

(b) During the trial of a case a lawyer who is not connected therewith shall not communicate with or cause another to communicate with a juror concerning the case.

(c) All restrictions imposed by this Rule also apply to communications with or investigations of members of a family of a member of the venire or a juror.

(d) A lawyer shall reveal promptly to the court improper conduct by a member of the venire or a juror, or by another toward a member of the venire or a juror or a member of his or her family of which the lawyer has knowledge.

RULE 3.6: TRIAL PUBLICITY

(a) A lawyer who is participating in or has participated in a criminal or civil matter shall not make an extrajudicial statement that the lawyer knows or reasonably should know will be disseminated by means of public communication and will have a substantial likelihood of materially prejudicing an adjudicative proceeding in the matter.

(b) A statement ordinarily is likely to prejudice materially an adjudicative proceeding when it refers to a civil matter triable to a jury, a criminal matter or any other proceeding that could result in incarceration, and the statement relates to:

(1) the character, credibility, reputation or criminal record of a party, suspect in a criminal investigation or witness, or the identity of a witness or the expected testimony of a party or witness;

(2) in a criminal matter that could result in incarceration, the possibility of a plea of guilty to the offense or the existence or contents of any confession, admission or statement given by a defendant or suspect, or that person's refusal or failure to make a statement;

(3) the performance or results of any examination or test, or the refusal or failure of a person to submit to an examination or test, or the identity or nature of physical evidence expected to be presented;

(4) any opinion as to the guilt or innocence of a defendant or suspect in a criminal matter that could result in incarceration;

(5) information the lawyer knows or reasonably should know is likely to be inadmissible as evidence in a trial and would, if disclosed, create a substantial risk of prejudicing an impartial trial; or

(6) the fact that a defendant has been charged with a crime, unless there is included therein a statement explaining that the charge is merely an accusation and that the defendant is presumed innocent until and unless proven guilty.

(c) Provided that the statement complies with paragraph (a), a lawyer may state the following without elaboration:

(1) the claim, offense or defense and, except when prohibited by law, the identity of the persons involved;

(2) information contained in a public record;

(3) that an investigation of a matter is in progress;

(4) the scheduling or result of any step in litigation;

(5) a request for assistance in obtaining evidence and information necessary thereto;

(6) a warning of danger concerning the behavior of a person involved, when there is reason to believe that there exists the likelihood of substantial harm to an individual or to the public interest; and

(7)   in a criminal matter:

(i)   the identity, age, residence, occupation and family status of the accused;

(ii) if the accused has not been apprehended, information necessary to aid in apprehension of that person;

(iii) the identity of investigating and arresting officers or agencies and the length of the investigation; and

(iv) the fact, time and place of arrest, resistance, pursuit and use of weapons, and a description of physical evidence seized, other than as contained only in a confession, admission or statement.

(d)   Notwithstanding paragraph (a), a lawyer may make a statement that a reasonable lawyer would believe is required to protect a client from the substantial prejudicial effect of recent publicity not initiated by the lawyer or the lawyer's client. A statement made pursuant to this paragraph shall be limited to such information as is necessary to mitigate the recent adverse publicity.

(e)   No lawyer associated in a firm or government agency with a lawyer subject to paragraph (a) shall make a statement prohibited by paragraph (a).

RULE 3.7: LAWYER AS WITNESS

(a)   A lawyer shall not act as advocate before a tribunal in a matter in which the lawyer is likely to be a witness on a significant issue of fact unless:

(1)   the testimony relates solely to an uncontested issue;

(2)   the testimony relates solely to the nature and value of legal services rendered in the matter;

(3)   disqualification of the lawyer would work substantial hardship on the client;

(4)   the testimony will relate solely to a matter of formality, and there is no reason to believe that substantial evidence will be offered in opposition to the testimony; or

(5)   the testimony is authorized by the tribunal.

(b)   A lawyer may not act as advocate before a tribunal in a matter if:

(1)   another lawyer in the lawyer's firm is likely to be called as a witness on a significant issue other than on behalf of the client, and it is apparent that the testimony may be prejudicial to the client; or

(2)   the lawyer is precluded from doing so by Rule 1.7 or Rule 1.9.

RULE 3.8: SPECIAL RESPONSIBILITIES OF PROSECUTORS AND OTHER GOVERNMENT LAWYERS

(a)   A prosecutor or other government lawyer shall not institute, cause to be instituted or maintain a criminal charge when the prosecutor or other government lawyer knows or it is obvious that the charge is not supported by probable cause.

(b) A prosecutor or other government lawyer in criminal litigation shall make timely disclosure to counsel for the defendant or to a defendant who has no counsel of the existence of evidence or information known to the prosecutor or other government lawyer that tends to negate the guilt of the accused, mitigate the degree of the offense, or reduce the sentence, except when relieved of this responsibility by a protective order of a tribunal.

(c) When a prosecutor knows of new, credible and material evidence creating a reasonable likelihood that a convicted defendant did not commit an offense of which the defendant was convicted, the prosecutor shall within a reasonable time:

(1) disclose that evidence to an appropriate court or prosecutor's office; or

(2) if the conviction was obtained by that prosecutor's office,

(A) notify the appropriate court and the defendant that the prosecutor's office possesses such evidence unless a court authorizes delay for good cause shown;

(B) disclose that evidence to the defendant unless the disclosure would interfere with an ongoing investigation or endanger the safety of a witness or other person, and a court authorizes delay for good cause shown; and

(C) undertake or make reasonable efforts to cause to be undertaken such further inquiry or investigation as may be necessary to provide a reasonable belief that the conviction should or should not be set aside.

(d) When a prosecutor knows of clear and convincing evidence establishing that a defendant was convicted, in a prosecution by the prosecutor's office, of an offense that the defendant did not commit, the prosecutor shall seek a remedy consistent with justice, applicable law, and the circumstances of the case.

(e) A prosecutor's independent judgment, made in good faith, that the new evidence is not of such nature as to trigger the obligations of sections (c) and (d), though subsequently determined to have been erroneous, does not constitute a violation of this rule.

RULE 3.9: ADVOCATE IN NON-ADJUDICATIVE MATTERS

A lawyer communicating in a representative capacity with a legislative body or administrative agency in connection with a pending non-adjudicative matter or proceeding shall disclose that the appearance is in a representative capacity, except when the lawyer seeks information from an agency that is available to the public.

RULE 4.1: TRUTHFULNESS IN STATEMENTS TO OTHERS

In the course of representing a client, a lawyer shall not knowingly make a false statement of fact or law to a third person.

RULE 4.2: COMMUNICATION WITH PERSON REPRESENTED BY COUNSEL

(a) In representing a client, a lawyer shall not communicate or cause another to communicate about the subject of the representation with a party the lawyer knows to be represented by another lawyer in the matter, unless the lawyer has the prior consent of the other lawyer or is authorized to do so by law.

(b) Notwithstanding the prohibitions of paragraph (a), and unless otherwise prohibited by law, a lawyer may cause a client to communicate with a represented person unless the represented person is not legally competent, and may counsel the client with respect to those communications, provided the lawyer gives reasonable advance notice to the represented person's counsel that such communications will be taking place.

(c) A lawyer who is acting *pro se* or is represented by counsel in a matter is subject to paragraph (a), but may communicate with a represented person, unless otherwise prohibited by law and unless the represented person is not legally competent, provided the lawyer or the lawyer's counsel gives reasonable advance notice to the represented person's counsel that such communications will be taking place.

RULE 4.3: COMMUNICATING WITH UNREPRESENTED PERSONS

In communicating on behalf of a client with a person who is not represented by counsel, a lawyer shall not state or imply that the lawyer is disinterested. When the lawyer knows or reasonably should know that the unrepresented person misunderstands the lawyer's role in the matter, the lawyer shall make reasonable efforts to correct the misunderstanding. The lawyer shall not give legal advice to an unrepresented person other than the advice to secure counsel if the lawyer knows or reasonably should know that the interests of such a person are or have a reasonable possibility of being in conflict with the interests of the client.

RULE 4.4: RESPECT FOR RIGHTS OF THIRD PERSONS

(a) In representing a client, a lawyer shall not use means that have no substantial purpose other than to embarrass or harm a third person or use methods of obtaining evidence that violate the legal rights of such a person.

(b) A lawyer who receives a document, electronically stored information, or other writing relating to the representation of the lawyer's client and knows or reasonably should know that it was inadvertently sent shall promptly notify the sender.

RULE 4.5: COMMUNICATION AFTER INCIDENTS INVOLVING PERSONAL INJURY OR WRONGFUL DEATH

(a) In the event of a specific incident involving potential claims for personal injury or wrongful death, no unsolicited communication shall be made to an individual injured in the incident or to a family member or legal representative of such an individual, by a lawyer or law firm, or by any associate, agent, employee or other representative of a lawyer or law firm representing actual or potential defendants or entities that may defend and/or indemnify said defendants, before the 30th day after the date of the incident, unless a filing must be made within 30 days of the incident as a legal prerequisite to the particular claim, in which case no unsolicited communication shall be made before the 15th day after the date of the incident.

(b)   An unsolicited communication by a lawyer or law firm, seeking to represent an injured individual or the legal representative thereof under the circumstance described in paragraph (a) shall comply with Rule 7.3(e).

RULE 5.1: RESPONSIBILITIES OF LAW FIRMS, PARTNERS, MANAGERS AND SUPERVISORY LAWYERS

(a)   A law firm shall make reasonable efforts to ensure that all lawyers in the firm conform to these Rules.

(b)   (1)   A lawyer with management responsibility in a law firm shall make reasonable efforts to ensure that other lawyers in the law firm conform to these Rules.

(2)   A lawyer with direct supervisory authority over another lawyer shall make reasonable efforts to ensure that the supervised lawyer conforms to these Rules.

(c)   A law firm shall ensure that the work of partners and associates is adequately supervised, as appropriate. A lawyer with direct supervisory authority over another lawyer shall adequately supervise the work of the other lawyer, as appropriate. In either case, the degree of supervision required is that which is reasonable under the circumstances, taking into account factors such as the experience of the person whose work is being supervised, the amount of work involved in a particular matter, and the likelihood that ethical problems might arise in the course of working on the matter.

(d)   A lawyer shall be responsible for a violation of these Rules by another lawyer if:

(1)   the lawyer orders or directs the specific conduct or, with knowledge of the specific conduct, ratifies it; or

(2)   the lawyer is a partner in a law firm or is a lawyer who individually or together with other lawyers possesses comparable managerial responsibility in a law firm in which the other lawyer practices or is a lawyer who has supervisory authority over the other lawyer; and

(i)   knows of such conduct at a time when it could be prevented or its consequences avoided or mitigated but fails to take reasonable remedial action; or

(ii)   in the exercise of reasonable management or supervisory authority should have known of the conduct so that reasonable remedial action could have been taken at a time when the consequences of the conduct could have been avoided or mitigated.

RULE 5.2: RESPONSIBILITIES OF A SUBORDINATE LAWYER

(a)   A lawyer is bound by these Rules notwithstanding that the lawyer acted at the direction of another person.

(b) A subordinate lawyer does not violate these Rules if that lawyer acts in accordance with a supervisory lawyer's reasonable resolution of an arguable question of professional duty.

RULE 5.3: LAWYER'S RESPONSIBILITY FOR CONDUCT OF NONLAWYERS

(a) A law firm shall ensure that the work of nonlawyers who work for the firm is adequately supervised, as appropriate. A lawyer with direct supervisory authority over a nonlawyer shall adequately supervise the work of the nonlawyer, as appropriate. In either case, the degree of supervision required is that which is reasonable under the circumstances, taking into account factors such as the experience of the person whose work is being supervised, the amount of work involved in a particular matter and the likelihood that ethical problems might arise in the course of working on the matter.

(b) A lawyer shall be responsible for conduct of a nonlawyer employed or retained by or associated with the lawyer that would be a violation of these Rules if engaged in by a lawyer, if:

(1) the lawyer orders or directs the specific conduct or, with knowledge of the specific conduct, ratifies it; or

(2) the lawyer is a partner in a law firm or is a lawyer who individually or together with other lawyers possesses comparable managerial responsibility in a law firm in which the nonlawyer is employed or is a lawyer who has supervisory authority over the nonlawyer; and

(i) knows of such conduct at a time when it could be prevented or its consequences avoided or mitigated but fails to take reasonable remedial action; or

(ii) in the exercise of reasonable management or supervisory authority should have known of the conduct so that reasonable remedial action could have been taken at a time when the consequences of the conduct could have been avoided or mitigated.

RULE 5.4: PROFESSIONAL INDEPENDENCE OF A LAWYER

(a) A lawyer or law firm shall not share legal fees with a nonlawyer, except that:

(1) an agreement by a lawyer with the lawyer's firm or another lawyer associated in the firm may provide for the payment of money, over a reasonable period of time after the lawyer's death, to the lawyer's estate or to one or more specified persons;

(2) a lawyer who undertakes to complete unfinished legal business of a deceased lawyer may pay to the estate of the deceased lawyer that portion of the total compensation that fairly represents the services rendered by the deceased lawyer; and

(3) a lawyer or law firm may compensate a nonlawyer employee or include a nonlawyer employee in a retirement plan based in whole or in part on a profit-sharing arrangement.

(b) A lawyer shall not form a partnership with a nonlawyer if any of the activities of the partnership consist of the practice of law.

(c) Unless authorized by law, a lawyer shall not permit a person who recommends, employs or pays the lawyer to render legal service for another to direct or regulate the lawyer's professional judgment in rendering such legal services or to cause the lawyer to compromise the lawyer's duty to maintain the confidential information of the client under Rule 1.6.

(d) A lawyer shall not practice with or in the form of an entity authorized to practice law for profit, if:

> (1) a nonlawyer owns any interest therein, except that a fiduciary representative of the estate of a lawyer may hold the stock or interest of the lawyer for a reasonable time during administration;

> (2) a nonlawyer is a member, corporate director or officer thereof or occupies a position of similar responsibility in any form of association other than a corporation; or

> (3) a nonlawyer has the right to direct or control the professional judgment of a lawyer.

RULE 5.5: UNAUTHORIZED PRACTICE OF LAW

(a) A lawyer shall not practice law in a jurisdiction in violation of the regulation of the legal profession in that jurisdiction.

(b) A lawyer shall not aid a nonlawyer in the unauthorized practice of law.

RULE 5.6: RESTRICTIONS ON RIGHT TO PRACTICE

(a) A lawyer shall not participate in offering or making:

> (1) a partnership, shareholder, operating, employment, or other similar type of agreement that restricts the right of a lawyer to practice after termination of the relationship, except an agreement concerning benefits upon retirement; or

> (2) an agreement in which a restriction on a lawyer's right to practice is part of the settlement of a client controversy.

(b) This Rule does not prohibit restrictions that may be included in the terms of the sale of a law practice pursuant to Rule 1.17.

RULE 5.7: RESPONSIBILITIES REGARDING NONLEGAL SERVICES

(a) With respect to lawyers or law firms providing nonlegal services to clients or other persons:

> (1) A lawyer or law firm that provides nonlegal services to a person that are not distinct from legal services being provided to that person by the lawyer or law firm is subject to these Rules with respect to the provision of both legal and nonlegal services.

> (2) A lawyer or law firm that provides nonlegal services to a person that are distinct from legal services being provided to that person by the lawyer or law firm is subject to these Rules with respect to the nonlegal services if the person receiving the

services could reasonably believe that the nonlegal services are the subject of a client-lawyer relationship.

(3) A lawyer or law firm that is an owner, controlling party or agent of, or that is otherwise affiliated with, an entity that the lawyer or law firm knows to be providing nonlegal services to a person is subject to these Rules with respect to the nonlegal services if the person receiving the services could reasonably believe that the nonlegal services are the subject of a client-lawyer relationship.

(4) For purposes of paragraphs (a)(2) and (a)(3), it will be presumed that the person receiving nonlegal services believes the services to be the subject of a client-lawyer relationship unless the lawyer or law firm has advised the person receiving the services in writing that the services are not legal services and that the protection of a client-lawyer relationship does not exist with respect to the nonlegal services, or if the interest of the lawyer or law firm in the entity providing nonlegal services is *de minimis*.

(b) Notwithstanding the provisions of paragraph (a), a lawyer or law firm that is an owner, controlling party, agent, or is otherwise affiliated with an entity that the lawyer or law firm knows is providing nonlegal services to a person shall not permit any nonlawyer providing such services or affiliated with that entity to direct or regulate the professional judgment of the lawyer or law firm in rendering legal services to any person, or to cause the lawyer or law firm to compromise its duty under Rule 1.6(a) and Rule 1.6(c) with respect to the confidential information of a client receiving legal services.

(c) For purposes of this Rule, "nonlegal services" shall mean those services that lawyers may lawfully provide and that are not prohibited as an unauthorized practice of law when provided by a nonlawyer.

RULE 5.8: CONTRACTUAL RELATIONSHIPS BETWEEN LAWYERS AND NONLEGAL PROFESSIONALS

(a) The practice of law has an essential tradition of complete independence and uncompromised loyalty to those it serves. Recognizing this tradition, clients of lawyers practicing in New York State are guaranteed "independent professional judgment and undivided loyalty uncompromised by conflicts of interest." Indeed, these guarantees represent the very foundation of the profession and allow and foster its continued role as a protector of the system of law. Therefore, a lawyer must remain completely responsible for his or her own independent professional judgment, maintain the confidences and secrets of clients, preserve funds of clients and third parties in his or her control, and otherwise comply with the legal and ethical principles governing lawyers in New York State.

Multi-disciplinary practice between lawyers and nonlawyers is incompatible with the core values of the legal profession and therefore, a strict division between services provided by lawyers and those provided by nonlawyers is essential to protect those values. However, a lawyer or law firm may enter into and maintain a contractual relationship with a nonlegal professional or nonlegal professional service firm for the purpose of offering to the public, on a systematic and continuing basis, legal services performed by the lawyer or law firm as well as other nonlegal professional services, notwithstanding the provisions of Rule 1.7(a), provided that:

(1)   the profession of the nonlegal professional or nonlegal professional service firm is included in a list jointly established and maintained by the Appellate Divisions pursuant to Section 1205.3 of the Joint Appellate Division Rules;

(2)   the lawyer or law firm neither grants to the nonlegal professional or nonlegal professional service firm, nor permits such person or firm to obtain, hold or exercise, directly or indirectly, any ownership or investment interest in, or managerial or supervisory right, power or position in connection with the practice of law by the lawyer or law firm, nor, as provided in Rule 7.2(a)(1), shares legal fees with a nonlawyer or receives or gives any monetary or other tangible benefit for giving or receiving a referral; and

(3)   the fact that the contractual relationship exists is disclosed by the lawyer or law firm to any client of the lawyer or law firm before the client is referred to the nonlegal professional service firm, or to any client of the nonlegal professional service firm before that client receives legal services from the lawyer or law firm; and the client has given informed written consent and has been provided with a copy of the "Statement of Client's Rights In Cooperative Business Arrangements" pursuant to section 1205.4 of the Joint Appellate Divisions Rules.

(b)   For purposes of paragraph (a):

(1)   each profession on the list maintained pursuant to a Joint Rule of the Appellate Divisions shall have been designated sua sponte, or approved by the Appellate Divisions upon application of a member of a nonlegal profession or nonlegal professional service firm, upon a determination that the profession is composed of individuals who, with respect to their profession:

(i)   have been awarded a bachelor's degree or its equivalent from an accredited college or university, or have attained an equivalent combination of educational credit from such a college or university and work experience;

(ii)   are licensed to practice the profession by an agency of the State of New York or the United States Government; and

(iii) are required under penalty of suspension or revocation of license to adhere to a code of ethical conduct that is reasonably comparable to that of the legal profession;

(2)   the term "ownership or investment interest" shall mean any such interest in any form of debt or equity, and shall include any interest commonly considered to be an interest accruing to or enjoyed by an owner or investor.

(c)   This Rule shall not apply to relationships consisting solely of non-exclusive reciprocal referral agreements or understandings between a lawyer or law firm and a nonlegal professional or nonlegal professional service firm.

RULE 6.1: VOLUNTARY PRO BONO SERVICE

Lawyers are strongly encouraged to provide pro bono legal services to benefit poor persons.

(a)   Every lawyer should aspire to:

(1)   provide at least 50 hours of pro bono legal services each year to poor persons; and

(2)   contribute financially to organizations that provide legal services to poor persons. Lawyers in private practice or employed by a for-profit entity should aspire to contribute annually in an amount at least equivalent to (i) the amount typically billed by the lawyer (or the firm with which the lawyer is associated) for one hour of time; or (ii) if the lawyer's work is performed on a contingency basis, the amount typically billed by lawyers in the community for one hour of time; or (iii) the amount typically paid by the organization employing the lawyer for one hour of the lawyer's time; or (iv) if the lawyer is underemployed, an amount not to exceed one-tenth of one percent of the lawyer's income.

(b)   Pro bono legal services that meet this goal are:

(1)   professional services rendered in civil matters, and in those criminal matters for which the government is not obliged to provide funds for legal representation, to persons who are financially unable to compensate counsel;

(2)   activities related to improving the administration of justice by simplifying the legal process for, or increasing the availability and quality of legal services to, poor persons; and

(3)   professional services to charitable, religious, civic and educational organizations in matters designed predominantly to address the needs of poor persons.

(c)   Appropriate organizations for financial contributions are:

(1)   organizations primarily engaged in the provision of legal services to the poor; and

(2)   organizations substantially engaged in the provision of legal services to the poor, provided that the donated funds are to be used for the provision of such legal services.

(d)   This Rule is not intended to be enforced through the disciplinary process, and the failure to fulfill the aspirational goals contained herein should be without legal consequence.

RULE 6.2: [RESERVED]

RULE 6.3: MEMBERSHIP IN A LEGAL SERVICES ORGANIZATION

A lawyer may serve as a director, officer or member of a not-for-profit legal services organization, apart from the law firm in which the lawyer practices, notwithstanding that the organization serves persons having interests that differ from those of a client of the lawyer or the lawyer's firm. The lawyer shall not knowingly participate in a decision or action of the organization:

(a) if participating in the decision or action would be incompatible with the lawyer's obligations to a client under Rules 1.7 through 1.13; or

(b) where the decision or action could have a material adverse effect on the representation of a client of the organization whose interests differ from those of a client of the lawyer or the lawyer's firm.

RULE 6.4: LAW REFORM ACTIVITIES AFFECTING CLIENT INTERESTS

A lawyer may serve as a director, officer or member of an organization involved in reform of the law or its administration, notwithstanding that the reform may affect the interests of a client of the lawyer. When the lawyer knows that the interests of a client may be materially benefitted by a decision in which the lawyer actively participates, the lawyer shall disclose that fact to the organization, but need not identify the client. In determining the nature and scope of participation in such activities, a lawyer should be mindful of obligations to clients under other Rules, particularly Rule 1.7.

RULE 6.5: PARTICIPATION IN LIMITED PRO BONO LEGAL SERVICES PROGRAMS

(a) A lawyer who, under the auspices of a program sponsored by a court, government agency, bar association or not-for-profit legal services organization, provides short-term limited legal services to a client without expectation by either the lawyer or the client that the lawyer will provide continuing representation in the matter:

(1) shall comply with Rules 1.7, 1.8 and 1.9, concerning restrictions on representations where there are or may be conflicts of interest as that term is defined in these Rules, only if the lawyer has actual knowledge at the time of commencement of representation that the representation of the client involves a conflict of interest; and

(2) shall comply with Rule 1.10 only if the lawyer has actual knowledge at the time of commencement of representation that another lawyer associated with the lawyer in a law firm is affected by Rules 1.7, 1.8 and 1.9.

(b) Except as provided in paragraph (a)(2), Rule 1.7 and Rule 1.9 are inapplicable to a representation governed by this Rule.

(c) Short-term limited legal services are services providing legal advice or representation free of charge as part of a program described in paragraph (a) with no expectation that the assistance will continue beyond what is necessary to complete an initial consultation, representation or court appearance.

(d) The lawyer providing short-term limited legal services must secure the client's informed consent to the limited scope of the representation, and such representation shall be subject to the provisions of Rule 1.6.

(e)   This Rule shall not apply where the court before which the matter is pending determines that a conflict of interest exists or, if during the course of the representation, the lawyer providing the services becomes aware of the existence of a conflict of interest precluding continued representation.

RULE 7.1: ADVERTISING

(a) A lawyer or law firm shall not use or disseminate or participate in the use or dissemination of any advertisement that:

(1)   contains statements or claims that are false, deceptive or misleading; or

(2)   violates a Rule.

(b)   Subject to the provisions of paragraph (a), an advertisement may include information as to:

(1)   legal and nonlegal education; degrees and other scholastic distinctions; dates of admission to any bar; areas of the law in which the lawyer or law firm practices, as authorized by these Rules; public offices and teaching positions held; publications of law-related matters authored by the lawyer; memberships in bar associations or other professional societies or organizations, including offices and committee assignments therein; foreign language fluency; and bona fide professional ratings;

(2)   names of clients regularly represented, provided that the client has given prior written consent;

(3)   bank references; credit arrangements accepted; prepaid or group legal services programs in which the lawyer or law firm participates; nonlegal services provided by the lawyer or law firm or by an entity owned and controlled by the lawyer or law firm; the existence of contractual relationships between the lawyer or law firm and a nonlegal professional or nonlegal professional service firm, to the extent permitted by Rule 5.8, and the nature and extent of services available through those contractual relationships; and

(4)   legal fees for initial consultation; contingent fee rates in civil matters, when accompanied by a statement disclosing the information required by paragraph (p); range of fees for legal and nonlegal services, provided that there be available to the public free of charge a written statement clearly describing the scope of each advertised service, hourly rates, and fixed fees for specified legal and nonlegal services.

(c)   An advertisement shall not:

(1)   include a paid endorsement of, or testimonial about, a lawyer or law firm without disclosing that the person is being compensated therefor;

(2)   include the portrayal of a fictitious law firm, the use of a fictitious name to refer to lawyers not associated together in a law firm, or otherwise imply that lawyers are associated in a law firm if that is not the case;

(3)　use actors to portray a judge, the lawyer, members of the law firm, or clients, or utilize depictions of fictionalized events or scenes, without disclosure of same;

(4)　be made to resemble legal documents.

(d)　An advertisement that complies with paragraph (e) may contain the following:

(1)　statements that are reasonably likely to create an expectation about results the lawyer can achieve;

(2)　statements that compare the lawyer's services with the services of other lawyers;

(3)　testimonials or endorsements of clients, where not prohibited by paragraph (c)(1), and of former clients; or

(4)　statements describing or characterizing the quality of the lawyer's or law firm's services.

(e)　It is permissible to provide the information set forth in paragraph (d) provided:

(1)　its dissemination does not violate paragraph (a);

(2)　it can be factually supported by the lawyer or law firm as of the date on which the advertisement is published or disseminated;

(3)　it is accompanied by the following disclaimer: "Prior results do not guarantee a similar outcome"; and

(4)　in the case of a testimonial or endorsement from a client with respect to a matter still pending, the client gives informed consent confirmed in writing.

(f)　Every advertisement other than those appearing in a radio, television or billboard advertisement, in a directory, newspaper, magazine or other periodical (and any web sites related thereto), or made in person pursuant to Rule 7.3(a)(1), shall be labeled "Attorney Advertising" on the first page, or on the home page in the case of a web site. If the communication is in the form of a self-mailing brochure or postcard, the words "Attorney Advertising" shall appear therein. In the case of electronic mail, the subject line shall contain the notation "ATTORNEY ADVERTISING."

(g)　A lawyer or law firm shall not utilize meta-tags or other hidden computer codes that, if displayed, would violate these Rules.

(h)　All advertisements shall include the name, principal law office address and telephone number of the lawyer or law firm whose services are being offered.

(i)　Any words or statements required by this Rule to appear in an advertisement must be clearly legible and capable of being read by the average person, if written, and intelligible if spoken aloud. In the case of a web site, the required words or statements shall appear on the home page.

(j)　A lawyer or law firm advertising any fixed fee for specified legal services shall, at the time of fee publication, have available to the public a written statement clearly describing the scope of each advertised service, which statement shall be available to the client at the time of retainer for any such service. Such legal services shall include all those services that are recognized as reasonable and necessary under local custom in the area of practice in the community where the services are performed.

(k) All advertisements shall be pre-approved by the lawyer or law firm, and a copy shall be retained for a period of not less than three years following its initial dissemination. Any advertisement contained in a computer-accessed communication shall be retained by the lawyer for a period of not less than one year. A copy of the contents of any web site covered by this Rule shall be preserved upon the initial publication of the web site, any major web site redesign, or a meaningful and extensive content change, but in no event less frequently than once every 90 days.

(*l*) If a lawyer or law firm advertises a range of fees or an hourly rate for services, the lawyer or law firm shall not charge more than the fee advertised for such services. If a lawyer or law firm advertises a fixed fee for specified legal services, or performs services described in a fee schedule, the lawyer or law firm shall not charge more than the fixed fee for such stated legal service as set forth in the advertisement or fee schedule, unless the client agrees in writing that the services performed or to be performed were not legal services referred to or implied in the advertisement or in the fee schedule and, further, that a different fee arrangement shall apply to the transaction.

(m) Unless otherwise specified in the advertisement, if a lawyer publishes any fee information authorized under this Rule in a publication that is published more frequently than once per month, the lawyer shall be bound by any representation made therein for a period of not less than 30 days after such publication. If a lawyer publishes any fee information authorized under this Rule in a publication that is published once per month or less frequently, the lawyer shall be bound by any representation made therein until the publication of the succeeding issue. If a lawyer publishes any fee information authorized under this Rule in a publication that has no fixed date for publication of a succeeding issue, the lawyer shall be bound by any representation made therein for a reasonable period of time after publication, but in no event less than 90 days.

(n) Unless otherwise specified, if a lawyer broadcasts any fee information authorized under this Rule, the lawyer shall be bound by any representation made therein for a period of not less than 30 days after such broadcast.

(*o*) A lawyer shall not compensate or give anything of value to representatives of the press, radio, television or other communication medium in anticipation of or in return for professional publicity in a news item.

(p) All advertisements that contain information about the fees charged by the lawyer or law firm, including those indicating that in the absence of a recovery no fee will be charged, shall comply with the provisions of Judiciary Law § 488(3).

(q) A lawyer may accept employment that results from participation in activities designed to educate the public to recognize legal problems, to make intelligent selection of counsel or to utilize available legal services.

(r)   Without affecting the right to accept employment, a lawyer may speak publicly or write for publication on legal topics so long as the lawyer does not undertake to give individual advice.

RULE 7.2: PAYMENT FOR REFERRALS

(a)   A lawyer shall not compensate or give anything of value to a person or organization to recommend or obtain employment by a client, or as a reward for having made a recommendation resulting in employment by a client, except that:

(1)   a lawyer or law firm may refer clients to a nonlegal professional or nonlegal professional service firm pursuant to a contractual relationship with such nonlegal professional or nonlegal professional service firm to provide legal and other professional services on a systematic and continuing basis as permitted by Rule 5.8, provided however that such referral shall not otherwise include any monetary or other tangible consideration or reward for such, or the sharing of legal fees; and

(2)   a lawyer may pay the usual and reasonable fees or dues charged by a qualified legal assistance organization or referral fees to another lawyer as permitted by Rule 1.5(g).

(b)   A lawyer or the lawyer's partner or associate or any other affiliated lawyer may be recommended, employed or paid by, or may cooperate with one of the following offices or organizations that promote the use of the lawyer's services or those of a partner or associate or any other affiliated lawyer, or request one of the following offices or organizations to recommend or promote the use of the lawyer's services or those of the lawyer's partner or associate, or any other affiliated lawyer as a private practitioner, if there is no interference with the exercise of independent professional judgment on behalf of the client:

(1)   a legal aid office or public defender office:

(i)   operated or sponsored by a duly accredited law school;

(ii)   operated or sponsored by a bona fide, non-profit community organization;

(iii)   operated or sponsored by a governmental agency; or

(iv)   operated, sponsored, or approved by a bar association;

(2)   a military legal assistance office;

(3)   a lawyer referral service operated, sponsored or approved by a bar association or authorized by law or court rule; or

(4)   any bona fide organization that recommends, furnishes or pays for legal services to its members or beneficiaries provided the following conditions are satisfied:

(i)   Neither the lawyer, nor the lawyer's partner, nor associate, nor any other affiliated lawyer nor any nonlawyer, shall have initiated or promoted such organization for the primary purpose of providing financial or other benefit to such lawyer, partner, associate or affiliated lawyer;

(ii) Such organization is not operated for the purpose of procuring legal work or financial benefit for any lawyer as a private practitioner outside of the legal services program of the organization;

(iii) The member or beneficiary to whom the legal services are furnished, and not such organization, is recognized as the client of the lawyer in the matter;

(iv) The legal service plan of such organization provides appropriate relief for any member or beneficiary who asserts a claim that representation by counsel furnished, selected or approved by the organization for the particular matter involved would be unethical, improper or inadequate under the circumstances of the matter involved; and the plan provides an appropriate procedure for seeking such relief;

(v) The lawyer does not know or have cause to know that such organization is in violation of applicable laws, rules of court or other legal requirements that govern its legal service operations; and

(vi) Such organization has filed with the appropriate disciplinary authority, to the extent required by such authority, at least annually a report with respect to its legal service plan, if any, showing its terms, its schedule of benefits, its subscription charges, agreements with counsel and financial results of its legal service activities or, if it has failed to do so, the lawyer does not know or have cause to know of such failure.

RULE 7.3: SOLICITATION AND RECOMMENDATION
OF PROFESSIONAL EMPLOYMENT

(a)   A lawyer shall not engage in solicitation:

(1) by in-person or telephone contact, or by real-time or interactive computer-accessed communication unless the recipient is a close friend, relative, former client or existing client; or

(2) by any form of communication if:

(i)   the communication or contact violates Rule 4.5, Rule 7.1(a), or paragraph (e) of this Rule;

(ii) the recipient has made known to the lawyer a desire not to be solicited by the lawyer;

(iii) the solicitation involves coercion, duress or harassment;

(iv) the lawyer knows or reasonably should know that the age or the physical, emotional or mental state of the recipient makes it unlikely that the recipient will be able to exercise reasonable judgment in retaining a lawyer; or

(v) the lawyer intends or expects, but does not disclose, that the legal services necessary to handle the matter competently will be performed primarily by another lawyer who is not affiliated with the soliciting lawyer as a partner, associate or of counsel.

(b) For purposes of this Rule, "solicitation" means any advertisement initiated by or on behalf of a lawyer or law firm that is directed to, or targeted at, a specific recipient or group of recipients, or their family members or legal representatives, the primary purpose of which is the retention of the lawyer or law firm, and a significant motive for which is pecuniary gain. It does not include a proposal or other writing prepared and delivered in response to a specific request.

(c) A solicitation directed to a recipient in this State shall be subject to the following provisions:

(1) A copy of the solicitation shall at the time of its dissemination be filed with the attorney disciplinary committee of the judicial district or judicial department wherein the lawyer or law firm maintains its principal office. Where no such office is maintained, the filing shall be made in the judicial department where the solicitation is targeted. A filing shall consist of:

(i)   a copy of the solicitation;

(ii) a transcript of the audio portion of any radio or television solicitation; and

(iii) if the solicitation is in a language other than English, an accurate English-language translation.

(2) Such solicitation shall contain no reference to the fact of filing.

(3) If a solicitation is directed to a predetermined recipient, a list containing the names and addresses of all recipients shall be retained by the lawyer or law firm for a period of not less than three years following the last date of its dissemination.

(4) Solicitations filed pursuant to this subdivision shall be open to public inspection.

(5) The provisions of this paragraph shall not apply to:

(i)   a solicitation directed or disseminated to a close friend, relative, or former or existing client;

(ii) a web site maintained by the lawyer or law firm, unless the web site is designed for and directed to or targeted at persons affected by an identifiable actual event or occurrence or by an identifiable prospective defendant; or

(iii) professional cards or other announcements the distribution of which is authorized by Rule 7.5(a).

(d) A written solicitation shall not be sent by a method that requires the recipient to travel to a location other than that at which the recipient ordinarily receives business or personal mail or that requires a signature on the part of the recipient.

(e) No solicitation relating to a specific incident involving potential claims for personal injury or wrongful death shall be disseminated before the 30th day after the date of the incident, unless a filing must be made within 30 days of the incident as a legal prerequisite to the particular claim, in which case no unsolicited communication shall be made before the 15th day after the date of the incident.

(f) Any solicitation made in writing or by computer-accessed communication and directed to a pre-determined recipient, if prompted by a specific occurrence involving or affecting a recipient, shall disclose how the lawyer obtained the identity of the recipient and learned of the recipient's potential legal need.

(g) If a retainer agreement is provided with any solicitation, the top of each page shall be marked "SAMPLE" in red ink in a type size equal to the largest type size used in the agreement and the words "DO NOT SIGN" shall appear on the client signature line.

(h) Any solicitation covered by this section shall include the name, principal law office address and telephone number of the lawyer or law firm whose services are being offered.

(i) The provisions of this Rule shall apply to a lawyer or members of a law firm not admitted to practice in this State who shall solicit retention by residents of this State.

RULE 7.4: IDENTIFICATION OF PRACTICE AND SPECIALTY

(a) A lawyer or law firm may publicly identify one or more areas of law in which the lawyer or the law firm practices, or may state that the practice of the lawyer or law firm is limited to one or more areas of law, provided that the lawyer or law firm shall not state that the lawyer or law firm is a specialist or specializes in a particular field of law, except as provided in Rule 7.4(c).

(b) A lawyer admitted to engage in patent practice before the United States Patent and Trademark Office may use the designation "Patent Attorney" or a substantially similar designation.

(c) A lawyer may state that the lawyer has been recognized or certified as a specialist only as follows:

(1) A lawyer who is certified as a specialist in a particular area of law or law practice by a private organization approved for that purpose by the American Bar Association may state the fact of certification if, in conjunction therewith, the certifying organization is identified and the following statement is prominently made: "This certification is not granted by any governmental authority."

(2) A lawyer who is certified as a specialist in a particular area of law or law practice by the authority having jurisdiction over specialization under the laws of another state or territory may state the fact of certification if, in conjunction therewith, the certifying state or territory is identified and the following

statement is prominently made: "This certification granted is not granted by any governmental authority within the State of New York."

(3) A statement is prominently made if:

(i) when written, it is clearly legible and capable of being read by the average person, and is at least two font sizes larger than the largest text used to state the fact of certification; and

(ii) when spoken, it is intelligible to the average person, and is at a cadence no faster, and a level of audibility no lower, than the cadence and level of audibility used to state the fact of certification.

RULE 7.5: PROFESSIONAL NOTICES, LETTERHEADS AND SIGNS

(a) A lawyer or law firm may use internet web sites, professional cards, professional announcement cards, office signs, letterheads or similar professional notices or devices, provided the same do not violate any statute or court rule and are in accordance with Rule 7.1, including the following:

(1) a professional card of a lawyer identifying the lawyer by name and as a lawyer, and giving addresses, telephone numbers, the name of the law firm, and any information permitted under Rule 7.1(b) or Rule 7.4. A professional card of a law firm may also give the names of members and associates;

(2) a professional announcement card stating new or changed associations or addresses, change of firm name, or similar matters pertaining to the professional offices of a lawyer or law firm or any nonlegal business conducted by the lawyer or law firm pursuant to Rule 5.7. It may state biographical data, the names of members of the firm and associates, and the names and dates of predecessor firms in a continuing line of succession. It may state the nature of the legal practice if permitted under Rule 7.4;

(3) a sign in or near the office and in the building directory identifying the law office and any nonlegal business conducted by the lawyer or law firm pursuant to Rule 5.7. The sign may state the nature of the legal practice if permitted under Rule 7.4; or

(4) a letterhead identifying the lawyer by name and as a lawyer, and giving addresses, telephone numbers, the name of the law firm, associates and any information permitted under Rule 7.1(b) or Rule 7.4. A letterhead of a law firm may also give the names of members and associates, and names and dates relating to deceased and retired members. A lawyer or law firm may be designated "Of Counsel" on a letterhead if there is a continuing relationship with a lawyer or law firm, other than as a partner or associate. A lawyer or law firm may be designated as "General Counsel" or by similar professional reference on stationery of a client if the lawyer or the firm devotes a substantial amount of professional time in the representation of

that client. The letterhead of a law firm may give the names and dates of predecessor firms in a continuing line of succession.

(b)   A lawyer in private practice shall not practice under a trade name, a name that is misleading as to the identity of the lawyer or lawyers practicing under such name, or a firm name containing names other than those of one or more of the lawyers in the firm, except that the name of a professional corporation shall contain "PC" or such symbols permitted by law, the name of a limited liability company or partnership shall contain "LLC," "LLP" or such symbols permitted by law and, if otherwise lawful, a firm may use as, or continue to include in its name the name or names of one or more deceased or retired members of the firm or of a predecessor firm in a continuing line of succession. Such terms as "legal clinic," "legal aid," "legal service office," "legal assistance office," "defender office" and the like may be used only by qualified legal assistance organizations, except that the term "legal clinic" may be used by any lawyer or law firm provided the name of a participating lawyer or firm is incorporated therein. A lawyer or law firm may not include the name of a nonlawyer in its firm name, nor may a lawyer or law firm that has a contractual relationship with a nonlegal professional or nonlegal professional service firm pursuant to Rule 5.8 to provide legal and other professional services on a systematic and continuing basis include in its firm name the name of the nonlegal professional service firm or any individual nonlegal professional affiliated therewith. A lawyer who assumes a judicial, legislative or public executive or administrative post or office shall not permit the lawyer's name to remain in the name of a law firm or to be used in professional notices of the firm during any significant period in which the lawyer is not actively and regularly practicing law as a member of the firm and, during such period, other members of the firm shall not use the lawyer's name in the firm name or in professional notices of the firm.

(c)   Lawyers shall not hold themselves out as having a partnership with one or more other lawyers unless they are in fact partners.

(d)   A partnership shall not be formed or continued between or among lawyers licensed in different jurisdictions unless all enumerations of the members and associates of the firm on its letterhead and in other permissible listings make clear the jurisdictional limitations on those members and associates of the firm not licensed to practice in all listed jurisdictions; however, the same firm name may be used in each jurisdiction.

(e)   A lawyer or law firm may utilize a domain name for an internet web site that does not include the name of the lawyer or law firm provided:

(1)   all pages of the web site clearly and conspicuously include the actual name of the lawyer or law firm;

(2)   the lawyer or law firm in no way attempts to engage in the practice of law using the domain name;

(3)   the domain name does not imply an ability to obtain results in a matter; and

(4) the domain name does not otherwise violate these Rules.

(f)   A lawyer or law firm may utilize a telephone number which contains a domain name, nickname, moniker or motto that does not otherwise violate these Rules.

RULE 8.1: CANDOR IN THE BAR ADMISSION PROCESS

(a)   A lawyer shall be subject to discipline if, in connection with the lawyer's own application for admission to the bar previously filed in this state or in any other jurisdiction, or in connection with the application of another person for admission to the bar, the lawyer knowingly:

(1) has made or failed to correct a false statement of material fact; or

(2) has failed to disclose a material fact requested in connection with a lawful demand for information from an admissions authority.

RULE 8.2: JUDICIAL OFFICERS AND CANDIDATES

(a)   A lawyer shall not knowingly make a false statement of fact concerning the qualifications, conduct or integrity of a judge or other adjudicatory officer or of a candidate for election or appointment to judicial office.

(b)   A lawyer who is a candidate for judicial office shall comply with the applicable provisions of Part 100 of the Rules of the Chief Administrator of the Courts.

RULE 8.3: REPORTING PROFESSIONAL MISCONDUCT

(a)   A lawyer who knows that another lawyer has committed a violation of the Rules of Professional Conduct that raises a substantial question as to that lawyer's honesty, trustworthiness or fitness as a lawyer shall report such knowledge to a tribunal or other authority empowered to investigate or act upon such violation.

(b)   A lawyer who possesses knowledge or evidence concerning another lawyer or a judge shall not fail to respond to a lawful demand for information from a tribunal or other authority empowered to investigate or act upon such conduct.

(c)   This Rule does not require disclosure of:

(1)   information otherwise protected by Rule 1.6; or

(2)   information gained by a lawyer or judge while participating in a bona fide lawyer assistance program.

RULE 8.4: MISCONDUCT

A lawyer or law firm shall not:

(a)   violate or attempt to violate the Rules of Professional Conduct, knowingly assist or induce another to do so, or do so through the acts of another;

(b)   engage in illegal conduct that adversely reflects on the lawyer's honesty, trustworthiness or fitness as a lawyer;

(c)   engage in conduct involving dishonesty, fraud, deceit or misrepresentation;

(d)   engage in conduct that is prejudicial to the administration of justice;

(e)   state or imply an ability:

(1)   to influence improperly or upon irrelevant grounds any tribunal, legislative body or public official; or

(2)   to achieve results using means that violate these Rules or other law;

(f)   knowingly assist a judge or judicial officer in conduct that is a violation of applicable rules of judicial conduct or other law;

(g)   unlawfully discriminate in the practice of law, including in hiring, promoting or otherwise determining conditions of employment on the basis of age, race, creed, color, national origin, sex, disability, marital status or sexual orientation. Where there is a tribunal with jurisdiction to hear a complaint, if timely brought, other than a Departmental Disciplinary Committee, a complaint based on unlawful discrimination shall be brought before such tribunal in the first instance. A certified copy of a determination by such a tribunal, which has become final and enforceable and as to which the right to judicial or appellate review has been exhausted, finding that the lawyer has engaged in an unlawful discriminatory practice shall constitute prima facie evidence of professional misconduct in a disciplinary proceeding; or

(h)   engage in any other conduct that adversely reflects on the lawyer's fitness as a lawyer.

RULE 8.5: DISCIPLINARY AUTHORITY AND CHOICE OF LAW

(a)   A lawyer admitted to practice in this state is subject to the disciplinary authority of this state, regardless of where the lawyer's conduct occurs. A lawyer may be subject to the disciplinary authority of both this state and another jurisdiction where the lawyer is admitted for the same conduct.

(b)   In any exercise of the disciplinary authority of this state, the Rules of Professional Conduct to be applied shall be as follows:

(1)   For conduct in connection with a proceeding in a court before which a lawyer has been admitted to practice (either generally or for purposes of that proceeding), the rules to be applied shall be the rules of the jurisdiction in which the court sits, unless the rules of the court provide otherwise; and

(2)   For any other conduct:

(i)   If the lawyer is licensed to practice only in this state, the rules to be applied shall be the rules of this state, and

(ii)   If the lawyer is licensed to practice in this state and another jurisdiction, the rules to be applied shall be the rules of the admitting jurisdiction in which the lawyer principally practices; provided, however, that if particular conduct clearly has its predominant effect in another jurisdiction in which the lawyer is licensed to practice, the rules of that jurisdiction shall be applied to that conduct.

SELECTED FEDERAL STATUTES AND RULES APPLICABLE TO LAWYERS

Obviously, many federal laws apply to lawyers. The ones in this part of this Supplement most closely mirror issues in the state Rules of Professional Conduct, illustrate how a lawyer is admitted to practice in federal courts, and provide the text of federal rules of civil procedure relevant to ethical decisions faced in litigation.

1. 15 U.S.C.A. § 7245 (Sarbanes-Oxley Act of 2002, § 307)

§ 7245. Rules of professional responsibility for attorneys

Not later than 180 days after July 30, 2002, the [Securities and Exchange] Commission shall issue rules, in the public interest and for the protection of investors, setting forth minimum standards of professional conduct for attorneys appearing and practicing before the Commission in any way in the representation of issuers, including a rule—

    (1) requiring an attorney to report evidence of a material violation of securities law or breach of fiduciary duty or similar violation by the company or any agent thereof, to the chief legal counsel or the chief executive officer of the company (or the equivalent thereof); and

    (2) if the counsel or officer does not appropriately respond to the evidence (adopting, as necessary, appropriate remedial measures or sanctions with respect to the violation), requiring the attorney to report the evidence to the audit committee of the board of directors of the issuer or to another committee of the board of directors comprised solely of directors not employed directly or indirectly by the issuer, or to the board of directors.

Sarbanes-Oxley Act of 2002, Pub.L. 107–204, Title III, § 307, July 30, 2002, 116 Stat. 784.

2. Regulations Implementing the Sarbanes-Oxley Act, § 307

17 Code of Federal Regulations, Part 205

STANDARDS OF PROFESSIONAL CONDUCT FOR ATTORNEYS APPEARING AND PRACTICING BEFORE THE COMMISSION IN THE REPRESENTATION OF AN ISSUER

75 Federal Register 52479

§ 205.1   Purpose and scope.

§ 205.2   Definitions.

§ 205.3   Issuer as client.

§ 205.4   Responsibilities of supervisory attorneys.

§ 205.5   Responsibilities of a subordinate attorney.

§ 205.6   Sanctions and discipline.

§ 205.7   No private right of action.

Authority: 15 U.S.C. 77s, 78d–3, 78w, 80a–37, 80a–38, 80b–11, 7202, 7245, and 7262.

§ 205.1 Purpose and scope.

This part sets forth minimum standards of professional conduct for attorneys appearing and practicing before the Commission in the representation of an issuer. These standards supplement applicable standards of any jurisdiction where an attorney is admitted or practices and are not intended to limit the ability of any jurisdiction to impose additional obligations on an attorney not inconsistent with the application of this part. Where the standards of a state or other United States jurisdiction where an attorney is admitted or practices conflict with this part, this part shall govern.

§ 205.2 Definitions.

For purposes of this part, the following definitions apply:

(a) Appearing and practicing before the Commission:

(1) Means:

(i) Transacting any business with the Commission, including communications in any form;

(ii) Representing an issuer in a Commission administrative proceeding or in connection with any Commission investigation, inquiry, information request, or subpoena;

(iii) Providing advice in respect of the United States securities laws or the Commission's rules or regulations thereunder regarding any document that the attorney has notice will be filed with or submitted to, or incorporated into any document that will be filed with or submitted to, the Commission, including the provision of such advice in the context of preparing, or participating in the preparation of, any such document; or

(iv) Advising an issuer as to whether information or a statement, opinion, or other writing is required under the United States securities laws or the Commission's rules or regulations thereunder to be filed with or submitted to, or incorporated into any document that will be filed with or submitted to, the Commission; but

(2) Does not include an attorney who:

(i) Conducts the activities in paragraphs (a)(1)(i) through (a)(1)(iv) of this section other than in the context of providing legal services to an issuer with whom the attorney has an attorney-client relationship; or

(ii) Is a non-appearing foreign attorney.

(b) Appropriate response means a response to an attorney regarding reported evidence of a material violation as a result of which the attorney reasonably believes:

(1) That no material violation, as defined in paragraph (i) of this section, has occurred, is ongoing, or is about to occur;

(2) That the issuer has, as necessary, adopted appropriate remedial measures, including appropriate steps or sanctions to stop any material violations that are ongoing, to prevent any material violation that has yet to occur, and to remedy or otherwise appropriately address

any material violation that has already occurred and to minimize the likelihood of its recurrence; or

(3) That the issuer, with the consent of the issuer's board of directors, a committee thereof to whom a report could be made pursuant to § 205.3(b)(3), or a qualified legal compliance committee, has retained or directed an attorney to review the reported evidence of a material violation and either:

(i) Has substantially implemented any remedial recommendations made by such attorney after a reasonable investigation and evaluation of the reported evidence; or

(ii) Has been advised that such attorney may, consistent with his or her professional obligations, assert a colorable defense on behalf of the issuer (or the issuer's officer, director, employee, or agent, as the case may be) in any investigation or judicial or administrative proceeding relating to the reported evidence of a material violation.

(c) Attorney means any person who is admitted, licensed, or otherwise qualified to practice law in any jurisdiction, domestic or foreign, or who holds himself or herself out as admitted, licensed, or otherwise qualified to practice law.

(d) Breach of fiduciary duty refers to any breach of fiduciary or similar duty to the issuer recognized under an applicable Federal or State statute or at common law, including but not limited to misfeasance, nonfeasance, abdication of duty, abuse of trust, and approval of unlawful transactions.

(e) Evidence of a material violation means credible evidence, based upon which it would be unreasonable, under the circumstances, for a prudent and competent attorney not to conclude that it is reasonably likely that a material violation has occurred, is ongoing, or is about to occur.

(f) Foreign government issuer means a foreign issuer as defined in 17 CFR 230.405 eligible to register securities on Schedule B of the Securities Act of 1933 (15 U.S.C. 77a et seq., Schedule B).

(g) In the representation of an issuer means providing legal services as an attorney for an issuer, regardless of whether the attorney is employed or retained by the issuer.

(h) Issuer means an issuer (as defined in section 3 of the Securities Exchange Act of 1934 (15 U.S.C. 78c)), the securities of which are registered under section 12 of that Act (15 U.S.C. 78l), or that is required to file reports under section 15(d) of that Act (15 U.S.C. 78o(d)), or that files or has filed a registration statement that has not yet become effective under the Securities Act of 1933 (15 U.S.C. 77a et seq.), and that it has not withdrawn, but does not include a foreign government issuer. For purposes of paragraphs (a) and (g) of this section, the term "issuer" includes any person controlled by an issuer, where an attorney provides legal services to such person on behalf of, or at the behest, or for the benefit of the issuer, regardless of whether the attorney is employed or retained by the issuer.

(i) Material violation means a material violation of an applicable United States federal or state securities law, a material breach of fiduciary duty arising under United States federal or state law, or a similar material violation of any United States federal or state law.

(j) Non-appearing foreign attorney means an attorney:

(1)   Who is admitted to practice law in a jurisdiction outside the United States;

(2)   Who does not hold himself or herself out as practicing, and does not give legal advice regarding, United States federal or state securities or other laws (except as provided in paragraph (j)(3)(ii) of this section); and

(3)   Who:

(i)   Conducts activities that would constitute appearing and practicing before the Commission only incidentally to, and in the ordinary course of, the practice of law in a jurisdiction outside the United States; or

(ii)   Is appearing and practicing before the Commission only in consultation with counsel, other than a non-appearing foreign attorney, admitted or licensed to practice in a state or other United States jurisdiction.

(k)   Qualified legal compliance committee means a committee of an issuer (which also may be an audit or other committee of the issuer) that:

(1)   Consists of at least one member of the issuer's audit committee (or, if the issuer has no audit committee, one member from an equivalent committee of independent directors) and two or more members of the issuer's board of directors who are not employed, directly or indirectly, by the issuer and who are not, in the case of a registered investment company, "interested persons" as defined in section 2(a)(19) of the Investment Company Act of 1940 (15 U.S.C. 80a–2(a)(19));

(2)   Has adopted written procedures for the confidential receipt, retention, and consideration of any report of evidence of a material violation under § 205.3;

(3)   Has been duly established by the issuer's board of directors, with the authority and responsibility:

(i)   To inform the issuer's chief legal officer and chief executive officer (or the equivalents thereof) of any report of evidence of a material violation (except in the circumstances described in § 205.3(b)(4));

(ii)   To determine whether an investigation is necessary regarding any report of evidence of a material violation by the issuer, its officers, directors, employees or agents and, if it determines an investigation is necessary or appropriate, to:

(A)   Notify the audit committee or the full board of directors;

(B)   Initiate an investigation, which may be conducted either by the chief legal officer (or the equivalent thereof) or by outside attorneys; and

(C)   Retain such additional expert personnel as the committee deems necessary; and

(iii)   At the conclusion of any such investigation, to:

(A)   Recommend, by majority vote, that the issuer implement an appropriate response to evidence of a material violation; and

(B) Inform the chief legal officer and the chief executive officer (or the equivalents thereof) and the board of directors of the results of any such investigation under this section and the appropriate remedial measures to be adopted; and

(4) Has the authority and responsibility, acting by majority vote, to take all other appropriate action, including the authority to notify the Commission in the event that the issuer fails in any material respect to implement an appropriate response that the qualified legal compliance committee has recommended the issuer to take.

(l) Reasonable or reasonably denotes, with respect to the actions of an attorney, conduct that would not be unreasonable for a prudent and competent attorney.

(m) Reasonably believes means that an attorney believes the matter in question and that the circumstances are such that the belief is not unreasonable.

(n) Report means to make known to directly, either in person, by telephone, by e-mail, electronically, or in writing.

§ 205.3   Issuer as client.

(a) Representing an issuer. An attorney appearing and practicing before the Commission in the representation of an issuer owes his or her professional and ethical duties to the issuer as an organization. That the attorney may work with and advise the issuer's officers, directors, or employees in the course of representing the issuer does not make such individuals the attorney's clients.

(b) Duty to report evidence of a material violation.

(1) If an attorney, appearing and practicing before the Commission in the representation of an issuer, becomes aware of evidence of a material violation by the issuer or by any officer, director, employee, or agent of the issuer, the attorney shall report such evidence to the issuer's chief legal officer (or the equivalent thereof) or to both the issuer's chief legal officer and its chief executive officer (or the equivalents thereof) forthwith. By communicating such information to the issuer's officers or directors, an attorney does not reveal client confidences or secrets or privileged or otherwise protected information related to the attorney's representation of an issuer.

(2) The chief legal officer (or the equivalent thereof) shall cause such inquiry into the evidence of a material violation as he or she reasonably believes is appropriate to determine whether the material violation described in the report has occurred, is ongoing, or is about to occur. If the chief legal officer (or the equivalent thereof) determines no material violation has occurred, is ongoing, or is about to occur, he or she shall notify the reporting attorney and advise the reporting attorney of the basis for such determination. Unless the chief legal officer (or the equivalent thereof) reasonably believes that no material violation has occurred, is ongoing, or is about to occur, he or she shall take all reasonable steps to cause the issuer to adopt an appropriate response, and shall advise the reporting attorney thereof. In lieu of causing an inquiry under this paragraph (b), a chief legal officer (or the equivalent thereof) may refer a report of evidence of a material violation to a qualified legal compliance committee under paragraph (c)(2) of this

section if the issuer has duly established a qualified legal compliance committee prior to the report of evidence of a material violation.

(3)   Unless an attorney who has made a report under paragraph (b)(1) of this section reasonably believes that the chief legal officer or the chief executive officer of the issuer (or the equivalent thereof) has provided an appropriate response within a reasonable time, the attorney shall report the evidence of a material violation to:

    (i)   The audit committee of the issuer's board of directors;

    (ii)   Another committee of the issuer's board of directors consisting solely of directors who are not employed, directly or indirectly, by the issuer and are not, in the case of a registered investment company, "interested persons" as defined in section 2(a)(19) of the Investment Company Act of 1940 (15 U.S.C. 80a–2(a)(19)) (if the issuer's board of directors has no audit committee); or

    (iii)   The issuer's board of directors (if the issuer's board of directors has no committee consisting solely of directors who are not employed, directly or indirectly, by the issuer and are not, in the case of a registered investment company, "interested persons" as defined in section 2(a)(19) of the Investment Company Act of 1940 (15 U.S.C. 80a–2(a)(19))).

(4)   If an attorney reasonably believes that it would be futile to report evidence of a material violation to the issuer's chief legal officer and chief executive officer (or the equivalents thereof) under paragraph (b)(1) of this section, the attorney may report such evidence as provided under paragraph (b)(3) of this section.

(5)   An attorney retained or directed by an issuer to investigate evidence of a material violation reported under paragraph (b)(1) (b)(3), or (b)(4) of this section shall be deemed to be appearing and practicing before the Commission. Directing or retaining an attorney to investigate reported evidence of a material violation does not relieve an officer or director of the issuer to whom such evidence has been reported under paragraph (b)(1) (b)(3), or (b)(4) of this section from a duty to respond to the reporting attorney.

(6)   An attorney shall not have any obligation to report evidence of a material violation under this paragraph (b) if:

    (i)   The attorney was retained or directed by the issuer's chief legal officer (or the equivalent thereof) to investigate such evidence of a material violation and:

        (A) The attorney reports the results of such investigation to the chief legal officer (or the equivalent thereof); and

        (B) Except where the attorney and the chief legal officer (or the equivalent thereof) each reasonably believes that no material violation has occurred, is ongoing, or is about to occur, the chief legal officer (or the equivalent thereof) reports the results of the investigation to the issuer's board of directors, a committee thereof to whom a report could be made pursuant to paragraph (b)(3) of this section, or a qualified legal compliance committee; or

(ii)   The attorney was retained or directed by the chief legal officer (or the equivalent thereof) to assert, consistent with his or her professional obligations, a colorable defense on behalf of the issuer (or the issuer's officer, director, employee, or agent, as the case may be) in any investigation or judicial or administrative proceeding relating to such evidence of a material violation, and the chief legal officer (or the equivalent thereof) provides reasonable and timely reports on the progress and outcome of such proceeding to the issuer's board of directors, a committee thereof to whom a report could be made pursuant to paragraph (b)(3) of this section, or a qualified legal compliance committee.

(7)   An attorney shall not have any obligation to report evidence of a material violation under this paragraph (b) if such attorney was retained or directed by a qualified legal compliance committee:

(i)   To investigate such evidence of a material violation; or

(ii)   To assert, consistent with his or her professional obligations, a colorable defense on behalf of the issuer (or the issuer's officer, director, employee, or agent, as the case may be) in any investigation or judicial or administrative proceeding relating to such evidence of a material violation.

(8)   An attorney who receives what he or she reasonably believes is an appropriate and timely response to a report he or she has made pursuant to paragraph (b)(1) (b)(3), or (b)(4) of this section need do nothing more under this section with respect to his or her report.

(9)   An attorney who does not reasonably believe that the issuer has made an appropriate response within a reasonable time to the report or reports made pursuant to paragraph (b)(1) (b)(3), or (b)(4) of this section shall explain his or her reasons therefor to the chief legal officer (or the equivalent thereof), the chief executive officer (or the equivalent thereof), and directors to whom the attorney reported the evidence of a material violation pursuant to paragraph (b)(1) (b)(3), or (b)(4) of this section.

(10) An attorney formerly employed or retained by an issuer who has reported evidence of a material violation under this part and reasonably believes that he or she has been discharged for so doing may notify the issuer's board of directors or any committee thereof that he or she believes that he or she has been discharged for reporting evidence of a material violation under this section.

(c)   Alternative reporting procedures for attorneys retained or employed by an issuer that has established a qualified legal compliance committee.

(1)   If an attorney, appearing and practicing before the Commission in the representation of an issuer, becomes aware of evidence of a material violation by the issuer or by any officer, director, employee, or agent of the issuer, the attorney may, as an alternative to the reporting requirements of paragraph (b) of this section, report such evidence to a qualified legal compliance committee, if the issuer has previously formed such a committee. An attorney who reports evidence of a material violation to such a qualified legal compliance committee has satisfied his or her obligation to report such evidence and is not required to assess the issuer's response to the reported evidence of a material violation.

(2)   A chief legal officer (or the equivalent thereof) may refer a report of evidence of a material violation to a previously established qualified legal compliance committee in lieu of causing an inquiry to be conducted under paragraph (b)(2) of this section. The chief legal officer (or the equivalent thereof) shall inform the reporting attorney that the report has been referred to a qualified legal compliance committee. Thereafter, pursuant to the requirements under § 205.2(k), the qualified legal compliance committee shall be responsible for responding to the evidence of a material violation reported to it under this paragraph (c).

(d)   Issuer confidences.

(1)   Any report under this section (or the contemporaneous record thereof) or any response thereto (or the contemporaneous record thereof) may be used by an attorney in connection with any investigation, proceeding, or litigation in which the attorney's compliance with this part is in issue.

(2)   An attorney appearing and practicing before the Commission in the representation of an issuer may reveal to the Commission, without the issuer's consent, confidential information related to the representation to the extent the attorney reasonably believes necessary:

(i)   To prevent the issuer from committing a material violation that is likely to cause substantial injury to the financial interest or property of the issuer or investors;

(ii)   To prevent the issuer, in a Commission investigation or administrative proceeding from committing perjury, proscribed in 18 U.S.C. 1621; suborning perjury, proscribed in 18 U.S.C. 1622; or committing any act proscribed in 18 U.S.C. 1001 that is likely to perpetrate a fraud upon the Commission; or

(iii)   To rectify the consequences of a material violation by the issuer that caused, or may cause, substantial injury to the financial interest or property of the issuer or investors in the furtherance of which the attorney's services were used.

§ 205.4   Responsibilities of supervisory attorneys.

(a)   An attorney supervising or directing another attorney who is appearing and practicing before the Commission in the representation of an issuer is a supervisory attorney. An issuer's chief legal officer (or the equivalent thereof) is a supervisory attorney under this section.

(b)   A supervisory attorney shall make reasonable efforts to ensure that a subordinate attorney, as defined in § 205.5(a), that he or she supervises or directs conforms to this part. To the extent a subordinate attorney appears and practices before the Commission in the representation of an issuer, that subordinate attorney's supervisory attorneys also appear and practice before the Commission.

(c)   A supervisory attorney is responsible for complying with the reporting requirements in § 205.3 when a subordinate attorney has reported to the supervisory attorney evidence of a material violation.

(d)   A supervisory attorney who has received a report of evidence of a material violation from a subordinate attorney under § 205.3 may report such evidence to the issuer's qualified legal compliance committee if the issuer has duly formed such a committee.

§ 205.5   Responsibilities of a subordinate attorney.

(a) An attorney who appears and practices before the Commission in the representation of an issuer on a matter under the supervision or direction of another attorney (other than under the direct supervision or direction of the issuer's chief legal officer (or the equivalent thereof)) is a subordinate attorney.

(b) A subordinate attorney shall comply with this part notwithstanding that the subordinate attorney acted at the direction of or under the supervision of another person.

(c) A subordinate attorney complies with § 205.3 if the subordinate attorney reports to his or her supervising attorney under § 205.3(b) evidence of a material violation of which the subordinate attorney has become aware in appearing and practicing before the Commission.

(d) A subordinate attorney may take the steps permitted or required by § 205.3(b) or (c) if the subordinate attorney reasonably believes that a supervisory attorney to whom he or she has reported evidence of a material violation under § 205.3(b) has failed to comply with § 205.3.

§ 205.6   Sanctions and discipline.

(a) A violation of this part by any attorney appearing and practicing before the Commission in the representation of an issuer shall subject such attorney to the civil penalties and remedies for a violation of the federal securities laws available to the Commission in an action brought by the Commission thereunder.

(b) An attorney appearing and practicing before the Commission who violates any provision of this part is subject to the disciplinary authority of the Commission, regardless of whether the attorney may also be subject to discipline for the same conduct in a jurisdiction where the attorney is admitted or practices. An administrative disciplinary proceeding initiated by the Commission for violation of this part may result in an attorney being censured, or being temporarily or permanently denied the privilege of appearing or practicing before the Commission.

(c) An attorney who complies in good faith with the provisions of this part shall not be subject to discipline or otherwise liable under inconsistent standards imposed by any state or other United States jurisdiction where the attorney is admitted or practices.

(d) An attorney practicing outside the United States shall not be required to comply with the requirements of this part to the extent that such compliance is prohibited by applicable foreign law.

§ 205.7   No private right of action.

(a) Nothing in this part is intended to, or does, create a private right of action against any attorney, law firm, or issuer based upon compliance or noncompliance with its provisions.

(b) Authority to enforce compliance with this part is vested exclusively in the Commission.

3.   Bribery, Graft, and Conflicts of Interest, 18 U.S.C.A. §§ 201–216—Excerpts

§ 201.   Bribery of public officials and witnesses

(a)   For the purpose of this section—

(1)   the term "public official" means Member of Congress, Delegate, or Resident Commissioner, either before or after such official has qualified, or an officer or employee or person acting for or on behalf of the United States, or any department, agency or branch of Government thereof, including the District of Columbia, in any official function, under or by authority of any such department, agency, or branch of Government, or a juror;

(2)   the term "person who has been selected to be a public official" means any person who has been nominated or appointed to be a public official, or has been officially informed that such person will be so nominated or appointed; and

(3)   the term "official act" means any decision or action on any question, matter, cause, suit, proceeding or controversy, which may at any time be pending, or which may by law be brought before any public official, in such official's official capacity, or in such official's place of trust or profit.

(b)   Whoever—

(1)   directly or indirectly, corruptly gives, offers or promises anything of value to any public official or person who has been selected to be a public official, or offers or promises any public official or any person who has been selected to be a public official to give anything of value to any other person or entity, with intent—

>   (A)   to influence any official act; or

>   (B)   to influence such public official or person who has been selected to be a public official to commit or aid in committing, or collude in, or allow, any fraud, or make opportunity for the commission of any fraud, on the United States; or

>   (C)   to induce such public official or such person who has been selected to be a public official to do or omit to do any act in violation of the lawful duty of such official or person;

(2)   being a public official or person selected to be a public official, directly or indirectly, corruptly demands, seeks, receives, accepts, or agrees to receive or accept anything of value personally or for any other person or entity, in return for:

>   (A)   being influenced in the performance of any official act;

>   (B)   being influenced to commit or aid in committing, or to collude in, or allow, any fraud, or make opportunity for the commission of any fraud, on the United States; or

>   (C)   being induced to do or omit to do any act in violation of the official duty of such official or person;

(3)   directly or indirectly, corruptly gives, offers, or promises anything of value to any person, or offers or promises such person to give anything of value to any other person or entity, with intent to influence the testimony under oath or affirmation of such first-mentioned person

470

as a witness upon a trial, hearing, or other proceeding, before any court, any committee of either House or both Houses of Congress, or any agency, commission, or officer authorized by the laws of the United States to hear evidence or take testimony, or with intent to influence such person to absent himself therefrom;

(4) directly or indirectly, corruptly demands, seeks, receives, accepts, or agrees to receive or accept anything of value personally or for any other person or entity in return for being influenced in testimony under oath or affirmation as a witness upon any such trial, hearing, or other proceeding, or in return for absenting himself therefrom;

shall be fined under this title or not more than three times the monetary equivalent of the thing of value, whichever is greater, or imprisoned for not more than fifteen years, or both, and may be disqualified from holding any office of honor, trust, or profit under the United States.

(c) Whoever—

(1) otherwise than as provided by law for the proper discharge of official duty—

(A) directly or indirectly gives, offers, or promises anything of value to any public official, former public official, or person selected to be a public official, for or because of any official act performed or to be performed by such public official, former public official, or person selected to be a public official; or

(B) being a public official, former public official, or person selected to be a public official, otherwise than as provided by law for the proper discharge of official duty, directly or indirectly demands, seeks, receives, accepts, or agrees to receive or accept anything of value personally for or because of any official act performed or to be performed by such official or person;

(2) directly or indirectly, gives, offers, or promises anything of value to any person, for or because of the testimony under oath or affirmation given or to be given by such person as a witness upon a trial, hearing, or other proceeding, before any court, any committee of either House or both Houses of Congress, or any agency, commission, or officer authorized by the laws of the United States to hear evidence or take testimony, or for or because of such person's absence therefrom;

(3) directly or indirectly, demands, seeks, receives, accepts, or agrees to receive or accept anything of value personally for or because of the testimony under oath or affirmation given or to be given by such person as a witness upon any such trial, hearing, or other proceeding, or for or because of such person's absence therefrom;

shall be fined under this title or imprisoned for not more than two years, or both.

(d) Paragraphs (3) and (4) of subsection (b) and paragraphs (2) and (3) of subsection (c) shall not be construed to prohibit the payment or receipt of witness fees provided by law, or the payment, by the party upon whose behalf a witness is called and receipt by a witness, of the reasonable cost of travel and subsistence incurred and the reasonable value of time lost in attendance at any such trial, hearing, or proceeding, or in the case of expert witnesses, a reasonable fee for time spent in the preparation of such opinion, and in appearing and testifying.

(e) The offenses and penalties prescribed in this section are separate from and in addition to those prescribed in sections 1503, 1504, and 1505 of this title.

§ 202.   Definitions

(a) For the purpose of sections 203, 205, 207, 208, and 209 of this title the term "special Government employee" shall mean an officer or employee of the executive or legislative branch of the United States Government, of any independent agency of the United States or of the District of Columbia, who is retained, designated, appointed, or employed to perform, with or without compensation, for not to exceed one hundred and thirty days during any period of three hundred and sixty-five consecutive days, temporary duties either on a full-time or intermittent basis, a part-time United States commissioner, or a part-time United States magistrate judge, or, regardless of the number of days of appointment, an independent counsel appointed under chapter 40 of title 28 and any person appointed by that independent counsel under section 594(c) of title 28. Notwithstanding the next preceding sentence, every person serving as a part-time local representative of a Member of Congress in the Member's home district or State shall be classified as a special Government employee. Notwithstanding section 29(c) and (d) of the Act of August 10, 1956 (70A Stat. 632; 5 U.S.C. 30r(c) and (d)), a Reserve officer of the Armed Forces, or an officer of the National Guard of the United States, unless otherwise an officer or employee of the United States, shall be classified as a special Government employee while on active duty solely for training. A Reserve officer of the Armed Forces or an officer of the National Guard of the United States who is voluntarily serving a period of extended active duty in excess of one hundred and thirty days shall be classified as an officer of the United States within the meaning of section 203 and sections 205 through 209 and 218. A Reserve officer of the Armed Forces or an officer of the National Guard of the United States who is serving involuntarily shall be classified as a special Government employee. The terms "officer or employee" and "special Government employee" as used in sections 203, 205, 207 through 209, and 218, shall not include enlisted members of the Armed Forces.

(b) For the purposes of sections 205 and 207 of this title, the term "official responsibility" means the direct administrative or operating authority, whether intermediate or final, and either exercisable alone or with others, and either personally or through subordinates, to approve, disapprove, or otherwise direct Government action.

(c) Except as otherwise provided in such sections, the terms "officer" and "employee" in sections 203, 205, 207 through 209, and 218 of this title shall not include the President, the Vice President, a Member of Congress, or a Federal judge.

(d) The term "Member of Congress" in sections 204 and 207 means—

(1)   a United States Senator; and

(2)   a Representative in, or a Delegate or Resident Commissioner to, the House of Representatives.

(e) As used in this chapter [18 U.S.C.A. §§ 201 et seq.], the term—

(1)   "executive branch" includes each executive agency as defined in title 5, and any other entity or administrative unit in the executive branch;

(2) "judicial branch" means the Supreme Court of the United States; the United States courts of appeals; the United States district courts; the Court of International Trade; the United States bankruptcy courts; any court created pursuant to article I of the United States Constitution, including the Court of Appeals for the Armed Forces, the United States Court of Federal Claims, and the United States Tax Court, but not including a court of a territory or possession of the United States; the Federal Judicial Center; and any other agency, office, or entity in the judicial branch; and

(3) "legislative branch" means—

(A) the Congress; and

(B) the Office of the Architect of the Capitol, the United States Botanic Garden, the Government Accountability Office, the Government Printing Office, the Library of Congress, the Office of Technology Assessment, the Congressional Budget Office, the United States Capitol Police, and any other agency, entity, office, or commission established in the legislative branch.

§ 203. **Compensation to Members of Congress, officers, and others in matters affecting the Government**

(a) Whoever, otherwise than as provided by law for the proper discharge of official duties, directly or indirectly—

(1) demands, seeks, receives, accepts, or agrees to receive or accept any compensation for any representational services, as agent or attorney or otherwise, rendered or to be rendered either personally or by another—

(A) at a time when such person is a Member of Congress, Member of Congress Elect, Delegate, Delegate Elect, Resident Commissioner, or Resident Commissioner Elect; or

(B) at a time when such person is an officer or employee or Federal judge of the United States in the executive, legislative, or judicial branch of the Government, or in any agency of the United States,

in relation to any proceeding, application, request for a ruling or other determination, contract, claim, controversy, charge, accusation, arrest, or other particular matter in which the United States is a party or has a direct and substantial interest, before any department, agency, court, court-martial, officer, or any civil, military, or naval commission; or

(2) knowingly gives, promises, or offers any compensation for any such representational services rendered or to be rendered at a time when the person to whom the compensation is given, promised, or offered, is or was such a Member, Member Elect, Delegate, Delegate Elect, Commissioner, Commissioner Elect, Federal judge, officer, or employee;

shall be subject to the penalties set forth in section 216 of this title.

(b) Whoever, otherwise than as provided by law for the proper discharge of official duties, directly or indirectly—

(1) demands, seeks, receives, accepts, or agrees to receive or accept any compensation for any representational services, as agent or attorney or otherwise, rendered or to be rendered either personally or by another, at a time when such person is an officer or employee of the

District of Columbia, in relation to any proceeding, application, request for a ruling or other determination, contract, claim, controversy, charge, accusation, arrest, or other particular matter in which the District of Columbia is a party or has a direct and substantial interest, before any department, agency, court, officer, or commission; or

(2)   knowingly gives, promises, or offers any compensation for any such representational services rendered or to be rendered at a time when the person to whom the compensation is given, promised, or offered, is or was an officer or employee of the District of Columbia;

shall be subject to the penalties set forth in section 216 of this title.

(c)   A special Government employee shall be subject to subsections (a) and (b) only in relation to a particular matter involving a specific party or parties—

(1)   in which such employee has at any time participated personally and substantially as a Government employee or as a special Government employee through decision, approval, disapproval, recommendation, the rendering of advice, investigation or otherwise; or

(2)   which is pending in the department or agency of the Government in which such employee is serving except that paragraph (2) of this subsection shall not apply in the case of a special Government employee who has served in such department or agency no more than sixty days during the immediately preceding period of three hundred and sixty-five consecutive days.

(d)   Nothing in this section prevents an officer or employee, including a special Government employee, from acting, with or without compensation, as agent or attorney for or otherwise representing his parents, spouse, child, or any person for whom, or for any estate for which, he is serving as guardian, executor, administrator, trustee, or other personal fiduciary except—

(1)   in those matters in which he has participated personally and substantially as a Government employee or as a special Government employee through decision, approval, disapproval, recommendation, the rendering of advice, investigation, or otherwise; or

(2)   in those matters that are the subject of his official responsibility,

subject to approval by the Government official responsible for appointment to his position.

(e)   Nothing in this section prevents a special Government employee from acting as agent or attorney for another person in the performance of work under a grant by, or a contract with or for the benefit of, the United States if the head of the department or agency concerned with the grant or contract certifies in writing that the national interest so requires and publishes such certification in the Federal Register.

(f)   Nothing in this section prevents an individual from giving testimony under oath or from making statements required to be made under penalty of perjury.

§ 204. Practice in United States Court of Federal Claims or the United States Court of Appeals for the Federal Circuit by Members of Congress

Whoever, being a Member of Congress or Member of Congress Elect, practices in the United States Court of Federal Claims or the United States Court of Appeals for the Federal Circuit shall be subject to the penalties set forth in section 216 of this title.

§ 205. Activities of officers and employees in claims against and other matters affecting the Government

(a) Whoever, being an officer or employee of the United States in the executive, legislative, or judicial branch of the Government or in any agency of the United States, other than in the proper discharge of his official duties—

(1) acts as agent or attorney for prosecuting any claim against the United States, or receives any gratuity, or any share of or interest in any such claim, in consideration of assistance in the prosecution of such claim; or

(2) acts as agent or attorney for anyone before any department, agency, court, court-martial, officer, or civil, military, or naval commission in connection with any covered matter in which the United States is a party or has a direct and substantial interest;

shall be subject to the penalties set forth in section 216 of this title.

(b) Whoever, being an officer or employee of the District of Columbia or an officer or employee of the Office of the United States Attorney for the District of Columbia, otherwise than in the proper discharge of official duties—

(1) acts as agent or attorney for prosecuting any claim against the District of Columbia, or receives any gratuity, or any share of or interest in any such claim in consideration of assistance in the prosecution of such claim; or

(2) acts as agent or attorney for anyone before any department, agency, court, officer, or commission in connection with any covered matter in which the District of Columbia is a party or has a direct and substantial interest;

shall be subject to the penalties set forth in section 216 of this title.

(c) A special Government employee shall be subject to subsections (a) and (b) only in relation to a covered matter involving a specific party or parties—

(1) in which he has at any time participated personally and substantially as a Government employee or special Government employee through decision, approval, disapproval, recommendation, the rendering of advice, investigation, or otherwise; or

(2) which is pending in the department or agency of the Government in which he is serving.

Paragraph (2) shall not apply in the case of a special Government employee who has served in such department or agency no more than sixty days during the immediately preceding period of three hundred and sixty-five consecutive days.

(d)(1)   Nothing in subsection (a) or (b) prevents an officer or employee, if not inconsistent with the faithful performance of that officer's or employee's duties, from acting without compensation as agent or attorney for, or otherwise representing—

(A)   any person who is the subject of disciplinary, loyalty, or other personnel administration proceedings in connection with those proceedings; or

(B) except as provided in paragraph (2), any cooperative, voluntary, professional, recreational, or similar organization or group not established or operated for profit, if a majority of the organization's or group's members are current officers or employees of the United States or of the District of Columbia, or their spouses or dependent children.

(2)   Paragraph (1)(B) does not apply with respect to a covered matter that—

(A)   is a claim under subsection (a)(1) or (b)(1);

(B) is a judicial or administrative proceeding where the organization or group is a party; or

(C) involves a grant, contract, or other agreement (including a request for any such grant, contract, or agreement) providing for the disbursement of Federal funds to the organization or group.

(e)   Nothing in subsection (a) or (b) prevents an officer or employee, including a special Government employee, from acting, with or without compensation, as agent or attorney for, or otherwise representing, his parents, spouse, child, or any person for whom, or for any estate for which, he is serving as guardian, executor, administrator, trustee, or other personal fiduciary except—

(1)   in those matters in which he has participated personally and substantially as a Government employee or special Government employee through decision, approval, disapproval, recommendation, the rendering of advice, investigation, or otherwise, or

(2)   in those matters which are the subject of his official responsibility,

subject to approval by the Government official responsible for appointment to his position.

(f)   Nothing in subsection (a) or (b) prevents a special Government employee from acting as agent or attorney for another person in the performance of work under a grant by, or a contract with or for the benefit of, the United States if the head of the department or agency concerned with the grant or contract certifies in writing that the national interest so requires and publishes such certification in the Federal Register.

(g)   Nothing in this section prevents an officer or employee from giving testimony under oath or from making statements required to be made under penalty for perjury or contempt.

(h)   For the purpose of this section, the term "covered matter" means any judicial or other proceeding, application, request for a ruling or other determination, contract, claim, controversy, investigation, charge, accusation, arrest, or other particular matter.

(i) Nothing in this section prevents an employee from acting pursuant to—

(1) chapter 71 of title 5;

(2) section 1004 or chapter 12 of title 39;

(3) section 3 of the Tennessee Valley Authority Act of 1933 (16 U.S.C. 831b);

(4) chapter 10 of title I of the Foreign Service Act of 1980 (22 U.S.C. 4104 et seq.); or

(5) any provision of any other Federal or District of Columbia law that authorizes labor-management relations between an agency or instrumentality of the United States or the District of Columbia and any labor organization that represents its employees.

§ 207. Restrictions on former officers, employees, and elected officials of the executive and legislative branches

(a) Restrictions on all officers and employees of the executive branch and certain other agencies.—

(1) Permanent restrictions on representation on particular matters.—Any person who is an officer or employee (including any special Government employee) of the executive branch of the United States (including any independent agency of the United States), or of the District of Columbia, and who, after the termination of his or her service or employment with the United States or the District of Columbia, knowingly makes, with the intent to influence, any communication to or appearance before any officer or employee of any department, agency, court, or court-martial of the United States or the District of Columbia, on behalf of any other person (except the United States or the District of Columbia) in connection with a particular matter—

(A) in which the United States or the District of Columbia is a party or has a direct and substantial interest,

(B) in which the person participated personally and substantially as such officer or employee, and

(C) which involved a specific party or specific parties at the time of such participation,

shall be punished as provided in section 216 of this title.

(2) Two-year restrictions concerning particular matters under official responsibility.—Any person subject to the restrictions contained in paragraph (1) who, within 2 years after the termination of his or her service or employment with the United States or the District of Columbia, knowingly makes, with the intent to influence, any communication to or appearance before any officer or employee of any department, agency, court, or court-martial of the United States or the District of Columbia, on behalf of any other person (except the United States or the District of Columbia), in connection with a particular matter—

(A) in which the United States or the District of Columbia is a party or has a direct and substantial interest,

(B) which such person knows or reasonably should know was actually pending under his or her official responsibility as such officer or employee within a period of 1 year before the termination of his or her service or employment with the United States or the District of Columbia, and

(C) which involved a specific party or specific parties at the time it was so pending,

shall be punished as provided in section 216 of this title.

(3) Clarification of restrictions.—The restrictions contained in paragraphs (1) and (2) shall apply—

(A) in the case of an officer or employee of the executive branch of the United States (including any independent agency), only with respect to communications to or appearances before any officer or employee of any department, agency, court, or court-martial of the United States on behalf of any other person (except the United States), and only with respect to a matter in which the United States is a party or has a direct and substantial interest; and

(B) in the case of an officer or employee of the District of Columbia, only with respect to communications to or appearances before any officer or employee of any department, agency, or court of the District of Columbia on behalf of any other person (except the District of Columbia), and only with respect to a matter in which the District of Columbia is a party or has a direct and substantial interest.

(b) One-year restrictions on aiding or advising.—

(1) In general.—Any person who is a former officer or employee of the executive branch of the United States (including any independent agency) and is subject to the restrictions contained in subsection (a)(1), or any person who is a former officer or employee of the legislative branch or a former Member of Congress, who personally and substantially participated in any ongoing trade or treaty negotiation on behalf of the United States within the 1-year period preceding the date on which his or her service or employment with the United States terminated, and who had access to information concerning such trade or treaty negotiation which is exempt from disclosure under section 552 of title 5, which is so designated by the appropriate department or agency, and which the person knew or should have known was so designated, shall not, on the basis of that information, knowingly represent, aid, or advise any other person (except the United States) concerning such ongoing trade or treaty negotiation for a period of 1 year after his or her service or employment with the United States terminates. Any person who violates this subsection shall be punished as provided in section 216 of this title.

(2) Definition.—For purposes of this paragraph—

(A) the term "trade negotiation" means negotiations which the President determines to undertake to enter into a trade agreement pursuant to section 1102 of the Omnibus Trade and Competitiveness Act of 1988, and does not include any action taken before that determination is made; and

(B) the term "treaty" means an international agreement made by the President that requires the advice and consent of the Senate.

(c) One-year restrictions on certain senior personnel of the executive branch and independent agencies.—

(1) Restrictions.—In addition to the restrictions set forth in subsections (a) and (b), any person who is an officer or employee (including any special Government employee) of the executive branch of the United States (including an independent agency), who is referred to in paragraph (2), and who, within 1 year after the termination of his or her service or employment as such officer or employee, knowingly makes, with the intent to influence, any communication to or appearance before any officer or employee of the department or agency in which such person served within 1 year before such termination, on behalf of any other person (except the United States), in connection with any matter on which such person seeks official action by any officer or employee of such department or agency, shall be punished as provided in section 216 of this title.

(2) Persons to whom restrictions apply.—(A) Paragraph (1) shall apply to a person (other than a person subject to the restrictions of subsection (d))—

(i) employed at a rate of pay specified in or fixed according to subchapter II of chapter 53 of title 5,

(ii) employed in a position which is not referred to in clause (i) and for which that person is paid at a rate of basic pay which is equal to or greater than 86.5 percent of the rate of basic pay for level II of the Executive Schedule, or, for a period of 2 years following the enactment of the National Defense Authorization Act for Fiscal Year 2004, a person who, on the day prior to the enactment of that Act, was employed in a position which is not referred to in clause (i) and for which the rate of basic pay, exclusive of any locality-based pay adjustment under section 5304 or section 5304a of title 5, was equal to or greater than the rate of basic pay payable for level 5 of the Senior Executive Service on the day prior to the enactment of that Act,

(iii) appointed by the President to a position under section 105(a)(2)(B) of title 3 or by the Vice President to a position under section 106(a)(1)(B) of title 3,

(iv) employed in a position which is held by an active duty commissioned officer of the uniformed services who is serving in a grade or rank for which the pay grade (as specified in section 201 of title 37) is pay grade O–7 or above; or

(v) assigned from a private sector organization to an agency under chapter 37 of title 5.

(B) Paragraph (1) shall not apply to a special Government employee who serves less than 60 days in the 1-year period before his or her service or employment as such employee terminates.

(C) At the request of a department or agency, the Director of the Office of Government Ethics may waive the restrictions contained in paragraph (1) with respect to any position, or category of positions, referred to in clause (ii) or (iv) of subparagraph (A), in such department or agency if the Director determines that—

    (i) the imposition of the restrictions with respect to such position or positions would create an undue hardship on the department or agency in obtaining qualified personnel to fill such position or positions, and

    (ii) granting the waiver would not create the potential for use of undue influence or unfair advantage.

(d) Restrictions on very senior personnel of the executive branch and independent agencies.—

    (1) Restrictions.—In addition to the restrictions set forth in subsections (a) and (b), any person who—

        (A) serves in the position of Vice President of the United States,

        (B) is employed in a position in the executive branch of the United States (including any independent agency) at a rate of pay payable for level I of the Executive Schedule or employed in a position in the Executive Office of the President at a rate of pay payable for level II of the Executive Schedule, or

        (C) is appointed by the President to a position under section 105(a)(2)(A) of title 3 or by the Vice President to a position under section 106(a)(1)(A) of title 3,

and who, within 2 years after the termination of that person's service in that position, knowingly makes, with the intent to influence, any communication to or appearance before any person described in paragraph (2), on behalf of any other person (except the United States), in connection with any matter on which such person seeks official action by any officer or employee of the executive branch of the United States, shall be punished as provided in section 216 of this title.

    (2) Persons who may not be contacted.—The persons referred to in paragraph (1) with respect to appearances or communications by a person in a position described in subparagraph (A) (B), or (C) of paragraph (1) are—

        (A) any officer or employee of any department or agency in which such person served in such position within a period of 1 year before such person's service or employment with the United States Government terminated, and

        (B) any person appointed to a position in the executive branch which is listed in sections 5312, 5313, 5314, 5315, or 5316 of title 5.

* * *

(i) Definitions.—For purposes of this section—

    (1) the term "officer or employee", when used to describe the person to whom a communication is made or before whom an appearance is made, with the intent to influence, shall include—

        (A) in subsections (a) (c), and (d), the President and the Vice President; and

(B) in subsection (f), the President, the Vice President, and Members of Congress;

(2) the term "participated" means an action taken as an officer or employee through decision, approval, disapproval, recommendation, the rendering of advice, investigation, or other such action; and

(3) the term "particular matter" includes any investigation, application, request for a ruling or determination, rulemaking, contract, controversy, claim, charge, accusation, arrest, or judicial or other proceeding.

(j) **Exceptions.—**

(1) **Official government duties.—**

(A) In general.—The restrictions contained in this section shall not apply to acts done in carrying out official duties on behalf of the United States or the District of Columbia or as an elected official of a State or local government.

(B) Tribal organizations and inter-tribal consortiums.—The restrictions contained in this section shall not apply to acts authorized by section 104(j) of the Indian Self-Determination and Education Assistance Act (25 U.S.C. 450i(j)).

(2) **State and local governments and institutions, hospitals, and organizations.—**The restrictions contained in subsections (c) (d), and (e) shall not apply to acts done in carrying out official duties as an employee of—

(A) an agency or instrumentality of a State or local government if the appearance, communication, or representation is on behalf of such government, or

(B) an accredited, degree-granting institution of higher education, as defined in section 101 of the Higher Education Act of 1965, or a hospital or medical research organization, exempted and defined under section 501(c)(3) of the Internal Revenue Code of 1986, if the appearance, communication, or representation is on behalf of such institution, hospital, or organization.

(3) **International organizations.—**The restrictions contained in this section shall not apply to an appearance or communication on behalf of, or advice or aid to, an international organization in which the United States participates, if the Secretary of State certifies in advance that such activity is in the interests of the United States.

(4) **Special knowledge.—**The restrictions contained in subsections (c) (d), and (e) shall not prevent an individual from making or providing a statement, which is based on the individual's own special knowledge in the particular area that is the subject of the statement, if no compensation is thereby received.

(5) **Exception for scientific or technological information.—**The restrictions contained in subsections (a) (c), and (d) shall not apply with respect to the making of communications solely for the purpose of furnishing scientific or technological information, if such communications are made under procedures acceptable to the department or agency concerned or if the head of the department or agency concerned with the particular matter, in consultation with the Director of the Office of Government Ethics, makes a certification, published in the Federal Register, that the former officer or employee has outstanding qualifications in a scientific, technological, or other technical discipline, and is acting with respect to a particular matter which requires such qualifications, and that the national interest would be served by the participation of the former officer or employee. For purposes of this paragraph, the term "officer or employee" includes the Vice President.

(6) **Exception for testimony.**—Nothing in this section shall prevent an individual from giving testimony under oath, or from making statements required to be made under penalty of perjury. Notwithstanding the preceding sentence—

(A) a former officer or employee of the executive branch of the United States (including any independent agency) who is subject to the restrictions contained in subsection (a)(1) with respect to a particular matter may not, except pursuant to court order, serve as an expert witness for any other person (except the United States) in that matter; and

(B) a former officer or employee of the District of Columbia who is subject to the restrictions contained in subsection (a)(1) with respect to a particular matter may not, except pursuant to court order, serve as an expert witness for any other person (except the District of Columbia) in that matter.

(7) **Political parties and campaign committees.**—(A) Except as provided in subparagraph **(B)** [omitted here], the restrictions contained in subsections (c) (d), and (e) shall not apply to a communication or appearance made solely on behalf of a candidate in his or her capacity as a candidate, an authorized committee, a national committee, a national Federal campaign committee, a State committee, or a political party.

* * *

§ 208.   **Acts affecting a personal financial interest**

(a) Except as permitted by subsection (b) hereof, whoever, being an officer or employee of the executive branch of the United States Government, or of any independent agency of the United States, a Federal Reserve bank director, officer, or employee, or an officer or employee of the District of Columbia, including a special Government employee, participates personally and substantially as a Government officer or employee, through decision, approval, disapproval, recommendation, the rendering of advice, investigation, or otherwise, in a judicial or other proceeding, application, request for a ruling or other determination, contract, claim, controversy, charge, accusation, arrest, or other particular matter in which, to his knowledge, he, his spouse, minor child, general partner, organization in which he is serving as officer, director, trustee, general partner or employee, or any person or organization with whom he is negotiating or has any arrangement concerning prospective employment, has a financial interest—

Shall be subject to the penalties set forth in section 216 of this title.

(b) Subsection (a) shall not apply—

(1) if the officer or employee first advises the Government official responsible for appointment to his or her position of the nature and circumstances of the judicial or other proceeding, application, request for a ruling or other determination, contract, claim, controversy, charge,

accusation, arrest, or other particular matter and makes full disclosure of the financial interest and receives in advance a written determination made by such official that the interest is not so substantial as to be deemed likely to affect the integrity of the services which the Government may expect from such officer or employee;

(2) if, by regulation issued by the Director of the Office of Government Ethics, applicable to all or a portion of all officers and employees covered by this section, and published in the Federal Register, the financial interest has been exempted from the requirements of subsection (a) as being too remote or too inconsequential to affect the integrity of the services of the Government officers or employees to which such regulation applies;

(3) in the case of a special Government employee serving on an advisory committee within the meaning of the Federal Advisory Committee Act (including an individual being considered for an appointment to such a position), the official responsible for the employee's appointment, after review of the financial disclosure report filed by the individual pursuant to the Ethics in Government Act of 1978, certifies in writing that the need for the individual's services outweighs the potential for a conflict of interest created by the financial interest involved; or

(4) if the financial interest that would be affected by the particular matter involved is that resulting solely from the interest of the officer or employee, or his or her spouse or minor child, in birthrights—

(A) in an Indian tribe, band, nation, or other organized group or community, including any Alaska Native village corporation as defined in or established pursuant to the Alaska Native Claims Settlement Act, which is recognized as eligible for the special programs and services provided by the United States to Indians because of their status as Indians,

(B) in an Indian allotment the title to which is held in trust by the United States or which is inalienable by the allottee without the consent of the United States, or

(C) in an Indian claims fund held in trust or administered by the United States,

if the particular matter does not involve the Indian allotment or claims fund or the Indian tribe, band, nation, organized group or community, or Alaska Native village corporation as a specific party or parties.

(c)(1) For the purpose of paragraph (1) of subsection (b), in the case of class A and B directors of Federal Reserve banks, the Board of Governors of the Federal Reserve System shall be deemed to be the Government official responsible for appointment.

(2) The potential availability of an exemption under any particular paragraph of subsection (b) does not preclude an exemption being granted pursuant to another paragraph of subsection (b).

(d)(1) Upon request, a copy of any determination granting an exemption under subsection (b)(1) or (b)(3) shall be made available to the public by the agency granting the exemption pursuant to the procedures set forth in section 105 of the Ethics in Government Act of 1978. In making such determination available, the agency may withhold from disclosure any information contained in the determination that would be exempt from disclosure under section 552 of title 5. For purposes of determinations under subsection (b)(3), the information describing each financial interest shall be no more extensive than that required of the individual in his or her financial disclosure report under the Ethics in Government Act of 1978.

(2) The Office of Government Ethics, after consultation with the Attorney General, shall issue uniform regulations for the issuance of waivers and exemptions under subsection (b) which shall—

    (A) list and describe exemptions; and

    (B) provide guidance with respect to the types of interests that are not so substantial as to be deemed likely to affect the integrity of the services the Government may expect from the employee.

§ 209.   Salary of Government officials and employees payable only by United States

(a) Whoever receives any salary, or any contribution to or supplementation of salary, as compensation for his services as an officer or employee of the executive branch of the United States Government, of any independent agency of the United States, or of the District of Columbia, from any source other than the Government of the United States, except as may be contributed out of the treasury of any State, county, or municipality; or

Whoever, whether an individual, partnership, association, corporation, or other organization pays, makes any contribution to, or in any way supplements, the salary of any such officer or employee under circumstances which would make its receipt a violation of this subsection—

Shall be subject to the penalties set forth in section 216 of this title.

(b) Nothing herein prevents an officer or employee of the executive branch of the United States Government, or of any independent agency of the United States, or of the District of Columbia, from continuing to participate in a bona fide pension, retirement, group life, health or accident insurance, profit-sharing, stock bonus, or other employee welfare or benefit plan maintained by a former employer.

(c) This section does not apply to a special Government employee or to an officer or employee of the Government serving without compensation, whether or not he is a special Government employee, or to any person paying, contributing to, or supplementing his salary as such.

(d) This section does not prohibit payment or acceptance of contributions, awards, or other expenses under the terms of Chapter 41 of title 5.

(e) This section does not prohibit the payment of actual relocation expenses incident to participation, or the acceptance of same by a participant in an executive exchange or fellowship program in an executive agency: *Provided*, That such program has been established by statute or Executive order of the President, offers appointments not to exceed three hundred and sixty-five days, and permits no extensions in excess of ninety additional days or, in the case of participants in overseas assignments, in excess of three hundred and sixty-five days.

(f) This section does not prohibit acceptance or receipt, by any officer or employee injured during the commission of an offense described in section 351 or 1751 of this title, of contributions or payments from an organization which is described in section 501(c)(3) of the Internal Revenue Code of 1986 and which is exempt from taxation under section 501(a) of such Code.

(g)(1) This section does not prohibit an employee of a private sector organization, while assigned to an agency under chapter 37 of title 5, from continuing to receive pay and benefits from such organization in accordance with such chapter.

(2) For purposes of this subsection, the term "agency" means an agency (as defined by section 3701 of title 5) and the Office of the Chief Technology Officer of the District of Columbia.

(h) This section does not prohibit a member of the reserve components of the armed forces on active duty pursuant to a call or order to active duty under a provision of law referred to in section 101(a)(13) of title 10 from receiving from any person that employed such member before the call or order to active duty any payment of any part of the salary or wages that such person would have paid the member if the member's employment had not been interrupted by such call or order to active duty.

. . .

§ 216.   **Penalties and injunctions**

(a) The punishment for an offense under section 203, 204, 205, 207, 208, or 209 of this title is the following:

(1) Whoever engages in the conduct constituting the offense shall be imprisoned for not more than one year or fined in the amount set forth in this title, or both.

(2) Whoever willfully engages in the conduct constituting the offense shall be imprisoned for not more than five years or fined in the amount set forth in this title, or both.

(b) The Attorney General may bring a civil action in the appropriate United States district court against any person who engages in conduct constituting an offense under section 203, 204, 205, 207, 208, or 209 of this title and, upon proof of such conduct by a preponderance of the evidence, such person shall be subject to a civil penalty of not more than $50,000 for each violation or the amount of compensation which the person received or offered for the prohibited conduct, whichever amount is greater. The imposition of a civil penalty under this subsection does not preclude any other criminal or civil statutory, common law, or administrative remedy, which is available by law to the United States or any other person.

(c) If the Attorney General has reason to believe that a person is engaging in conduct constituting an offense under section 203, 204, 205, 207, 208, or 209 of this title, the Attorney General may petition an appropriate United States district court for an order prohibiting that person from engaging in such conduct. The court may issue an order prohibiting that person from engaging in such conduct if the court finds that the conduct constitutes such an offense. The filing of a petition under this section does not preclude any other remedy which is available by law to the United States or any other person.

4.   18 U.S.C.A. § 1519

§ 1519. Destruction, alteration, or falsification of records in Federal investigations and bankruptcy

Whoever knowingly alters, destroys, mutilates, conceals, covers up, falsifies, or makes a false entry in any record, document, or tangible object with the intent to impede, obstruct, or influence the investigation or proper administration of any matter within the jurisdiction of any department or agency of the United States or any case filed under title 11, or in relation to or contemplation of any such matter or case, shall be fined under this title, imprisoned not more than 20 years, or both.

5.   18 U.S.C.A. § 1905

§ 1905. Disclosure of confidential information generally

Whoever, being an officer or employee of the United States or of any department or agency thereof, any person acting on behalf of the Federal Housing Finance Agency, or agent of the Department of Justice as defined in the Antitrust Civil Process Act (15 U.S.C. 1311–1314), or being an employee of a private sector organization who is or was assigned to an agency under chapter 37 of title 5, publishes, divulges, discloses, or makes known in any manner or to any extent not authorized by law any information coming to him in the course of his employment or official duties or by reason of any examination or investigation made by, or return, report or record made to or filled with, such department or agency or officer or employee thereof, which information concerns or relates to the trade secrets, processes, operations, style of work, or apparatus, or to the identity, confidential statistical data, amount or source of any income, profits, losses, or expenditures of any person, firm, partnership, corporation, or association; or permits any income return or copy thereof or any book containing any abstract or particulars thereof to be seen or examined by any person except as provided by law; shall be fined under this title, or imprisoned not more than one year, or both; and shall be removed from office or employment.

6.   Citizens Protection Act of 1998, 28 U.S.C.A. § 530B

§ 530B. Ethical standards for attorneys for the Government

(a) An attorney for the Government shall be subject to State laws and rules, and local Federal court rules, governing attorneys in each State where such attorney engages in that attorney's duties, to the same extent and in the same manner as other attorneys in that State.

(b) The Attorney General shall make and amend rules of the Department of Justice to assure compliance with this section.

(c) As used in this section, the term "attorney for the Government" includes any attorney described in section 77.2(a) of part 77 of title 28 of the Code of Federal Regulations and also includes any independent counsel, or employee of such a counsel, appointed under chapter 40.

7.   Sample Federal District Court Rule

LOCAL RULE OF THE UNITED STATES DISTRICT COURTS FOR THE SOUTHERN AND EASTERN DISTRICTS OF NEW YORK

Local Civil Rule 1.3.   Admission to the Bar

(a) A member in good standing of the bar of the state of New York, or a member in good standing of the bar of the United States District Court in

Connecticut or Vermont and of the bar of the State in which such district court is located, provided such district court by its rule extends a corresponding privilege to members of the bar of this Court, may be admitted to practice in this Court on compliance with the following provisions:

In the first instance, each applicant for admission is required to file an application for admission in electronic form on the Court's Web site [www.nysd.uscourts.gov]. This one application will be utilized both to admit and then to provide the applicant to the bar of this Court with a password and login for use on the Court's Electronic Case Filing (ECF) system. The applicant shall adhere to all applicable rules of admission.

The applicant shall (a) complete the application on-line (b) submit the application electronically (c) print and sign a copy of the application, and (d) file the printed application and fee with the Clerk, together with a certificate(s) of good standing and supporting affidavit(s).

After submitting the application in electronic form, each applicant for admission shall file with the Clerk, at least ten (10) days prior to hearing (unless, for good cause shown, the Judge shall shorten the time), the signed paper copy of the verified written petition for admission stating: (1) applicant's residence and office address; (2) the time when, and courts where, admitted; (3) applicant's legal training and experience; (4) whether applicant has ever been held in contempt of court, and, if so, the nature of the contempt and the final disposition thereof; (5) whether applicant has ever been censured, suspended, disbarred or denied admission or readmission by any court, and, if so, the facts and circumstances connected therewith; (6) that applicant has read and is familiar with (a) the provisions of the Judicial Code (Title 28, U.S.C.) which pertain to the jurisdiction of, and practice in, the United States District Courts; (b) the Federal Rules of Civil Procedure; (c) the Federal Rules of Criminal Procedure; (d) the Federal Rules of Evidence; (e) the Local Rules of the United States District Court for the Southern and Eastern Districts of New York; and (f) the New York State Rules of Professional Conduct as adopted from time to time by the Appellate Divisions of the State of New York; and (7) that applicant will faithfully adhere to all rules applicable to applicant's conduct in connection with any activities in this court.

The petition shall be accompanied by a certificate of the clerk of the court for each of the states in which the applicant is a member of the bar, which has been issued within thirty (30) days of filing and states that the applicant is a member in good standing of the bar of that state court. The petition shall also be accompanied by an affidavit of an attorney of this Court who has known the applicant for at least one year, stating when the affiant was admitted to practice in this Court, how long and under what circumstances the attorney has known the applicant, and what the attorney knows of the applicant's character and experience at the bar. Such petition shall be placed at the head of the calendar and, on the call thereof, the attorney whose affidavit accompanied the petition shall personally move the admission of the applicant. If the petition is granted, the applicant shall take the oath of office and sign the roll of attorneys.

A member of the bar of the state of New York, Connecticut, or Vermont who has been admitted to the bar of this Court pursuant to this subsection and who thereafter voluntarily resigns from membership in the bar of the state pursuant to which he was admitted to the bar of this Court, and who does not within 30 days of that voluntary resignation file an affidavit with the Clerk of this Court indicating that such person remains eligible to be admitted to the bar of this Court pursuant to other provisions of this subsection (such as because he is still a member of the bar of another eligible state and, where applicable, a corresponding district court), shall be deemed to have voluntarily resigned from the bar of this Court as of the same date the member resigned from the bar of the underlying state, provided that such resignation shall not be deemed to deprive this Court of jurisdiction to impose discipline on this person, pursuant to Rule 1.5 infra, for conduct preceding the date of such resignation.

(b) A member in good standing of the bar of either the Southern or Eastern District of New York may be admitted to the bar of the other district without formal application (1) upon filing in that district a certificate of the Clerk of the United States District Court for the district in which the applicant is a member of the bar, which has been issued within thirty (30) days of filing and states that the applicant is a member in good standing of the bar of that Court; (2) an affidavit by the applicant stating (a) whether the applicant has ever been convicted of a felony, (b) whether the applicant has ever been censured, suspended, disbarred or denied admission or readmission by any court, (c) whether there are any disciplinary proceedings presently against the applicant and (d) the facts and circumstances surrounding any affirmative responses to (a) through (c); and (3) upon taking the oath of office, signing the roll of attorneys of that district, and paying the fee required in that district. Each district retains the right to deny admission based upon the content of the affidavit in response to item (2).

(c) A member in good standing of the bar of any state or of any United States District Court may be permitted to argue or try a particular case in whole or in part as counsel or advocate, upon motion (which may be made by the applicant) and (1) upon filing with the Clerk of the District Court a certificate of the court for each of the states in which the applicant is a member of the bar, which has been issued within thirty (30) days of filing and states that the applicant is a member in good standing of the bar of that state court, and an affidavit stating (a) whether the applicant has ever been convicted of a felony, (b) whether the applicant has ever been censured, suspended, disbarred or denied admission or readmission by any court, (c) whether there are any disciplinary proceedings presently against the applicant and (d) the facts and circumstances surrounding any affirmative responses to (a) through (c); and (2) upon paying the required fee. Attorneys appearing for the Department of Justice may appear before the Court without requesting pro hac vice admission. Attorney appearing for other federal agencies must move for pro hac vice admission but the fee requirement is waived and the certificate(s) of good standing may have been issued within one year of filing. Only an attorney who has been so admitted or who is a member of the bar of this Court may enter appearances for parties, sign stipulations or receive payments upon judgments, decrees or orders.

(d) If an attorney who is a member of the bar of this Court, or who has been authorized to appear in a case in this Court, changes his or her residence or office address, the attorney shall immediately notify the Clerk of the Court, in addition to serving and filing a notice of change of address in each pending case in which the attorney has appeared.

8.   Federal Rules of Appellate Procedure, 28 U.S.C.A

RULE 45.   Clerk's Duties

(a)   General Provisions.

(1)   Qualifications. * * * Neither the clerk nor any deputy clerk may practice as an attorney or counselor in any court while in office. * * *

RULE 46.   Attorneys

(a)   Admission to the Bar.

(1)   Eligibility. An attorney is eligible for admission to the bar of a court of appeals if that attorney is of good moral and professional character and is admitted to practice before the Supreme Court of the United States, the highest court of a state, another United States court of appeals, or a United States district court (including the district courts for Guam, the Northern Mariana Islands, and the Virgin Islands).

(2)   Application. An applicant must file an application for admission, on a form approved by the court that contains the applicant's personal statement showing eligibility for membership. The applicant must subscribe to the following oath or affirmation:

"I, _____, do solemnly swear [or affirm] that I will conduct myself as an attorney and counselor of this court, uprightly and according to law; and that I will support the Constitution of the United States."

(3)   Admission Procedures. On written or oral motion of a member of the court's bar, the court will act on the application. An applicant may be admitted by oral motion in open court. But, unless the court orders otherwise, an applicant need not appear before the court to be admitted. Upon admission, an applicant must pay the clerk the fee prescribed by local rule or court order.

(b)   Suspension or Disbarment.

(1)   Standard. A member of the court's bar is subject to suspension or disbarment by the court if the member:

     (A) has been suspended or disbarred from practice in any other court; or

     (B) is guilty of conduct unbecoming a member of the court's bar.

(2)   Procedure. The member must be given an opportunity to show good cause, within the time prescribed by the court, why the member should not be suspended or disbarred.

(3)   Order. The court must enter an appropriate order after the member responds and a hearing is held, if requested, or after the time prescribed for a response expires, if no response is made.

(c)   Discipline.
A court of appeals may discipline an attorney who practices before it for conduct unbecoming a member of the bar or for failure to comply with any court rule. First, however, the court must afford the attorney reasonable notice, an opportunity to show cause to the contrary, and, if requested, a hearing.

9. Rules of the Supreme Court of the United States

RULE 7. Prohibition Against Practice

No employee of this Court shall practice as an attorney or counselor in any court or before any agency of government while employed by the Court; nor shall any person after leaving such employment participate in any professional capacity in any case pending before this Court or in any case being considered for filing in this Court, until two years have elapsed after separation; nor shall a former employee ever participate in any professional capacity in any case that was pending in this Court during the employee's tenure.

RULE 8. Disbarment and Disciplinary Action

1. Whenever a member of the Bar of this Court has been disbarred or suspended from practice in any court of record, or has engaged in conduct unbecoming a member of the Bar of this Court, the Court will enter an order suspending that member from practice before this Court and affording the member an opportunity to show cause, within 40 days, why a disbarment order should not be entered. Upon response, or if no response is timely filed, the Court will enter an appropriate order.

2. After reasonable notice and an opportunity to show cause why disciplinary action should not be taken, and after a hearing if material facts are in dispute, the Court may take any appropriate disciplinary action against any attorney who is admitted to practice before it for conduct unbecoming a member of the Bar or for failure to comply with these Rules or any Rule or order of the Court.

10. Federal Rules of Civil Procedure, Rules 11, 23, 26, 34 & 37

RULE 11. Signing Pleadings, Motions, and Other Papers; Representations to the Court; Sanctions

(a) Signature. Every pleading, written motion, and other paper must be signed by at least one attorney of record in the attorney's name—or by a party personally if the party is unrepresented. The paper must state the signer's address, e-mail address, and telephone number. Unless a rule or statute specifically states otherwise, a pleading need not be verified or accompanied by an affidavit. The court must strike an unsigned paper unless the omission is promptly corrected after being called to the attorney's or party's attention.

(b) Representations to the Court. By presenting to the court a pleading, written motion, or other paper—whether by signing, filing, submitting, or later advocating it—an attorney or unrepresented party certifies that to the best of the person's knowledge, information, and belief, formed after an inquiry reasonable under the circumstances:

    (1) it is not being presented for any improper purpose, such as to harass, cause unnecessary delay, or needlessly increase the cost of litigation;

    (2) the claims, defenses, and other legal contentions are warranted by existing law or by a nonfrivolous argument for extending, modifying, or reversing existing law or for establishing new law;

(3) the factual contentions have evidentiary support or, if specifically so identified, will likely have evidentiary support after a reasonable opportunity for further investigation or discovery; and

(4) the denials of factual contentions are warranted on the evidence or, if specifically so identified, are reasonably based on belief or a lack of information.

(c) Sanctions.

(1) *In General.* If, after notice and a reasonable opportunity to respond, the court determines that Rule 11(b) has been violated, the court may impose an appropriate sanction on any attorney, law firm, or party that violated the rule or is responsible for the violation. Absent exceptional circumstances, a law firm must be held jointly responsible for a violation committed by its partner, associate, or employee.

(2) *Motion for Sanctions.* A motion for sanctions must be made separately from any other motion and must describe the specific conduct that allegedly violates Rule 11(b). The motion must be served under Rule 5, but it must not be filed or be presented to the court if the challenged paper, claim, defense, contention, or denial is withdrawn or appropriately corrected within 21 days after service or within another time the court sets. If warranted, the court may award to the prevailing party the reasonable expenses, including attorney's fees, incurred for the motion.

(3) *On the Court's Initiative.* On its own, the court may order an attorney, law firm, or party to show cause why conduct specifically described in the order has not violated Rule 11(b).

(4) *Nature of a Sanction.* A sanction imposed under this rule must be limited to what suffices to deter repetition of the conduct or comparable conduct by others similarly situated. The sanction may include nonmonetary directives; an order to pay a penalty into court; or, if imposed on motion and warranted for effective deterrence, an order directing payment to the movant of part or all of the reasonable attorney's fees and other expenses directly resulting from the violation.

(5) *Limitations on Monetary Sanctions.* The court must not impose a monetary sanction:

(A) against a represented party for violating Rule 11(b)(2); or

(B) on its own, unless it issued the show-cause order under Rule 11(c)(3) before voluntary dismissal or settlement of the claims made by or against the party that is, or whose attorneys are, to be sanctioned.

(6) *Requirements for an Order.* An order imposing a sanction must describe the sanctioned conduct and explain the basis for the sanction.

(d) Inapplicability to Discovery. This rule does not apply to disclosures and discovery requests, responses, objections, and motions under Rules 26 through 37.

RULE 23.   Class Actions

(a) Prerequisites. One or more members of a class may sue or be sued as representative parties on behalf of all members only if:

(1) the class is so numerous that joinder of all members is impracticable;

(2) there are questions of law or fact common to the class;

(3) the claims or defenses of the representative parties are typical of the claims or defenses of the class; and

(4) the representative parties will fairly and adequately protect the interests of the class.

(b) Types of Class Actions. A class action may be maintained if Rule 23(a) is satisfied and if:

(1) prosecuting separate actions by or against individual class members would create a risk of:

(A) inconsistent or varying adjudications with respect to individual class members that would establish incompatible standards of conduct for the party opposing the class; or

(B) adjudications with respect to individual class members that, as a practical matter, would be dispositive of the interests of the other members not parties to the individual adjudications or would substantially impair or impede their ability to protect their interests;

(2) the party opposing the class has acted or refused to act on grounds that apply generally to the class, so that final injunctive relief or corresponding declaratory relief is appropriate respecting the class as a whole; or

(3) the court finds that the questions of law or fact common to class members predominate over any questions affecting only individual members, and that a class action is superior to other available methods for fairly and efficiently adjudicating the controversy. The matters pertinent to these findings include:

(A) the class members' interests in individually controlling the prosecution or defense of separate actions;

(B) the extent and nature of any litigation concerning the controversy already begun by or against class members;

(C) the desirability or undesirability of concentrating the litigation of the claims in the particular forum; and

(D) the likely difficulties in managing a class action.

(c) Certification Order; Notice to Class Members; Judgment; Issues Classes; Subclasses.

(1) *Certification Order.*

(A) *Time to Issue.* At an early practicable time after a person sues or is sued as a class representative, the court must determine by order whether to certify the action as a class action.

(B) *Defining the Class; Appointing Class Counsel.* An order that certifies a class action must define the class and the class claims, issues, or defenses, and must appoint class counsel under Rule 23(g).

(C) *Altering or Amending the Order.* An order that grants or denies class certification may be altered or amended before final judgment.

(2) *Notice.*

(A) *For (b)(1) or (b)(2) Classes.* For any class certified under Rule 23(b)(1) or (b)(2), the court may direct appropriate notice to the class.

(B) *For (b)(3) Classes.* For any class certified under Rule 23(b)(3), the court must direct to class members the best notice that is practicable under the circumstances, including individual notice to all members who can be identified through reasonable effort. The notice must clearly and concisely state in plain, easily understood language:

> **(i)** the nature of the action;

> **(ii)** the definition of the class certified;

> **(iii)** the class claims, issues, or defenses;

> **(iv)** that a class member may enter an appearance through an attorney if the member so desires;

> **(v)** that the court will exclude from the class any member who requests exclusion;

> **(vi)** the time and manner for requesting exclusion; and

> **(vii)** the binding effect of a class judgment on members under Rule 23(c)(3).

(3) *Judgment.* Whether or not favorable to the class, the judgment in a class action must:

(A) for any class certified under Rule 23(b)(1) or (b)(2), include and describe those whom the court finds to be class members; and

(B) for any class certified under Rule 23(b)(3), include and specify or describe those to whom the Rule 23(c)(2) notice was directed, who have not requested exclusion, and whom the court finds to be class members.

(4) *Particular Issues.* When appropriate, an action may be brought or maintained as a class action with respect to particular issues.

(5) *Subclasses.* When appropriate, a class may be divided into subclasses that are each treated as a class under this rule.

(d) **Conducting the Action.**

(1) *In General.* In conducting an action under this rule, the court may issue orders that:

(A) determine the course of proceedings or prescribe measures to prevent undue repetition or complication in presenting evidence or argument;

(B) require—to protect class members and fairly conduct the action—giving appropriate notice to some or all class members of:

> **(i)** any step in the action;

(ii) the proposed extent of the judgment; or

(iii) the members' opportunity to signify whether they consider the representation fair and adequate, to intervene and present claims or defenses, or to otherwise come into the action;

(C) impose conditions on the representative parties or on intervenors;

(D) require that the pleadings be amended to eliminate allegations about representation of absent persons and that the action proceed accordingly; or

(E) deal with similar procedural matters.

(2) *Combining and Amending Orders.* An order under Rule 23(d)(1) may be altered or amended from time to time and may be combined with an order under Rule 16.

(e) **Settlement, Voluntary Dismissal, or Compromise.** The claims, issues, or defenses of a certified class may be settled, voluntarily dismissed, or compromised only with the court's approval. The following procedures apply to a proposed settlement, voluntary dismissal, or compromise:

(1) The court must direct notice in a reasonable manner to all class members who would be bound by the proposal.

(2) If the proposal would bind class members, the court may approve it only after a hearing and on finding that it is fair, reasonable, and adequate.

(3) The parties seeking approval must file a statement identifying any agreement made in connection with the proposal.

(4) If the class action was previously certified under Rule 23(b)(3), the court may refuse to approve a settlement unless it affords a new opportunity to request exclusion to individual class members who had an earlier opportunity to request exclusion but did not do so.

(5) Any class member may object to the proposal if it requires court approval under this subdivision (e); the objection may be withdrawn only with the court's approval.

(f) **Appeals.** A court of appeals may permit an appeal from an order granting or denying class-action certification under this rule if a petition for permission to appeal is filed with the circuit clerk within 14 days after the order is entered. An appeal does not stay proceedings in the district court unless the district judge or the court of appeals so orders.

(g) **Class Counsel.**

(1) *Appointing Class Counsel.* Unless a statute provides otherwise, a court that certifies a class must appoint class counsel. In appointing class counsel, the court:

(A) must consider:

(i) the work counsel has done in identifying or investigating potential claims in the action;

(ii) counsel's experience in handling class actions, other complex litigation, and the types of claims asserted in the action;

(iii) counsel's knowledge of the applicable law; and

(iv) the resources that counsel will commit to representing the class;

(B) may consider any other matter pertinent to counsel's ability to fairly and adequately represent the interests of the class;

(C) may order potential class counsel to provide information on any subject pertinent to the appointment and to propose terms for attorney's fees and nontaxable costs;

(D) may include in the appointing order provisions about the award of attorney's fees or nontaxable costs under Rule 23(h); and

(E) may make further orders in connection with the appointment.

(2) *Standard for Appointing Class Counsel.* When one applicant seeks appointment as class counsel, the court may appoint that applicant only if the applicant is adequate under Rule 23(g)(1) and (4). If more than one adequate applicant seeks appointment, the court must appoint the applicant best able to represent the interests of the class.

(3) *Interim Counsel.* The court may designate interim counsel to act on behalf of a putative class before determining whether to certify the action as a class action.

(4) *Duty of Class Counsel.* Class counsel must fairly and adequately represent the interests of the class.

(h) Attorney's Fees and Nontaxable Costs. In a certified class action, the court may award reasonable attorney's fees and nontaxable costs that are authorized by law or by the parties' agreement. The following procedures apply:

(1) A claim for an award must be made by motion under Rule 54(d)(2), subject to the provisions of this subdivision (h), at a time the court sets. Notice of the motion must be served on all parties and, for motions by class counsel, directed to class members in a reasonable manner.

(2) A class member, or a party from whom payment is sought, may object to the motion.

(3) The court may hold a hearing and must find the facts and state its legal conclusions under Rule 52(a).

(4) The court may refer issues related to the amount of the award to a special master or a magistrate judge, as provided in Rule 54(d)(2)(D).

RULE 26. Duty to Disclose; General Provisions Governing Discovery

(a) Required Disclosures.

(1) *Initial Disclosure.*

(A) *In General.* Except as exempted by Rule 26(a)(1)(B) or as otherwise stipulated or ordered by the court, a party must, without awaiting a discovery request, provide to the other parties:

(i) the name and, if known, the address and telephone number of each individual likely to have discoverable information—along with the subjects of that information—that the disclosing party may use to support its claims or defenses, unless the use would be solely for impeachment;

(ii) a copy—or a description by category and location—of all documents, electronically stored information, and tangible things that the disclosing party has in its possession, custody, or control and may use to support its claims or defenses, unless the use would be solely for impeachment;

(iii) a computation of each category of damages claimed by the disclosing party—who must also make available for inspection and copying as under Rule 34 the documents or other evidentiary material, unless privileged or protected from disclosure, on which each computation is based, including materials bearing on the nature and extent of injuries suffered; and

(iv) for inspection and copying as under Rule 34, any insurance agreement under which an insurance business may be liable to satisfy all or part of a possible judgment in the action or to indemnify or reimburse for payments made to satisfy the judgment.

(B) *Proceedings Exempt from Initial Disclosure.* The following proceedings are exempt from initial disclosure:

(i) an action for review on an administrative record;

(ii) a forfeiture action in rem arising from a federal statute;

(iii) a petition for habeas corpus or any other proceeding to challenge a criminal conviction or sentence;

(iv) an action brought without an attorney by a person in the custody of the United States, a state, or a state subdivision;

(v) an action to enforce or quash an administrative summons or subpoena;

(vi) an action by the United States to recover benefit payments;

(vii) an action by the United States to collect on a student loan guaranteed by the United States;

(viii) a proceeding ancillary to a proceeding in another court; and

(ix) an action to enforce an arbitration award.

(C) *Time for Initial Disclosures—In General.* A party must make the initial disclosures at or within 14 days after the parties' Rule 26(f) conference unless a different time is set by stipulation or court order, or unless a party objects during the conference that initial disclosures are not appropriate in this action and states the objection in the proposed discovery plan. In ruling on the objection, the court must determine what disclosures, if any, are to be made and must set the time for disclosure.

(D) *Time for Initial Disclosures—For Parties Served or Joined Later.* A party that is first served or otherwise joined after the Rule 26(f) conference must make the initial disclosures within 30 days after being served or joined, unless a different time is set by stipulation or court order.

(E) *Basis for Initial Disclosure; Unacceptable Excuses.* A party must make its initial disclosures based on the information then reasonably available to it. A party is not excused from making its disclosures because it has not fully investigated the case or because it challenges the sufficiency of another party's disclosures or because another party has not made its disclosures.

(2) *Disclosure of Expert Testimony.*

(A) *In General.* In addition to the disclosures required by Rule 26(a)(1), a party must disclose to the other parties the identity of any witness it may use at trial to present evidence under Federal Rule of Evidence 702, 703, or 705.

(B) *Witnesses Who Must Provide a Written Report.* Unless otherwise stipulated or ordered by the court, this disclosure must be accompanied by a written report—prepared and signed by the witness—if the witness is one retained or specially employed to provide expert testimony in the case or one whose duties as the party's employee regularly involve giving expert testimony. The report must contain:

   (i) a complete statement of all opinions the witness will express and the basis and reasons for them;

   (ii) the facts or data considered by the witness in forming them;

   (iii) any exhibits that will be used to summarize or support them;

   (iv) the witness's qualifications, including a list of all publications authored in the previous 10 years;

   (v) a list of all other cases in which, during the previous 4 years, the witness testified as an expert at trial or by deposition; and

   (vi) a statement of the compensation to be paid for the study and testimony in the case.

(C) *Witnesses Who Do Not Provide a Written Report.* Unless otherwise stipulated or ordered by the court, if the witness is not required to provide a written report, this disclosure must state:

   (i) the subject matter on which the witness is expected to present evidence under Federal Rule of Evidence 702, 703, or 705; and

   (ii) a summary of the facts and opinions to which the witness is expected to testify.

(D) *Time to Disclose Expert Testimony.* A party must make these disclosures at the times and in the sequence that the court orders. Absent a stipulation or a court order, the disclosures must be made:

(i) at least 90 days before the date set for trial or for the case to be ready for trial; or

(ii) if the evidence is intended solely to contradict or rebut evidence on the same subject matter identified by another party under Rule 26(a)(2)(B) or (C), within 30 days after the other party's disclosure.

(E) *Supplementing the Disclosure.* The parties must supplement these disclosures when required under Rule 26(e).

(3) *Pretrial Disclosures.*

(A) *In General.* In addition to the disclosures required by Rule 26(a)(1) and (2), a party must provide to the other parties and promptly file the following information about the evidence that it may present at trial other than solely for impeachment:

(i) the name and, if not previously provided, the address and telephone number of each witness—separately identifying those the party expects to present and those it may call if the need arises;

(ii) the designation of those witnesses whose testimony the party expects to present by deposition and, if not taken stenographically, a transcript of the pertinent parts of the deposition; and

(iii) an identification of each document or other exhibit, including summaries of other evidence—separately identifying those items the party expects to offer and those it may offer if the need arises.

(B) *Time for Pretrial Disclosures; Objections.* Unless the court orders otherwise, these disclosures must be made at least 30 days before trial. Within 14 days after they are made, unless the court sets a different time, a party may serve and promptly file a list of the following objections: any objections to the use under Rule 32(a) of a deposition designated by another party under Rule 26(a)(3)(A)(ii); and any objection, together with the grounds for it, that may be made to the admissibility of materials identified under Rule 26(a)(3)(A)(iii). An objection not so made—except for one under Federal Rule of Evidence 402 or 403—is waived unless excused by the court for good cause.

(4) *Form of Disclosures.* Unless the court orders otherwise, all disclosures under Rule 26(a) must be in writing, signed, and served.

(b) Discovery Scope and Limits.

(1) *Scope in General.* Unless otherwise limited by court order, the scope of discovery is as follows: Parties may obtain discovery regarding any nonprivileged matter that is relevant to any party's claim or defense and proportional to the needs of the case, considering the importance of the issues at stake in the action, the amount in controversy, the parties' relative access to relevant information, the parties' resources, the importance of the discovery in resolving the issues, and whether the burden or expense of the proposed discovery outweighs its likely benefit. Information within this scope of discovery need not be admissible in evidence to be discoverable.

(2) *Limitations on Frequency and Extent.*

(A) *When Permitted.* By order, the court may alter the limits in these rules on the number of depositions and interrogatories or on the length of depositions under Rule 30. By order or local rule, the court may also limit the number of requests under Rule 36.

(B) *Specific   Limitations   on   Electronically   Stored Information.* A party need not provide discovery of electronically stored information from sources that the party identifies as not reasonably accessible because of undue burden or cost. On motion to compel discovery or for a protective order, the party from whom discovery is sought must show that the information is not reasonably accessible because of undue burden or cost. If that showing is made, the court may nonetheless order discovery from such sources if the requesting party shows good cause, considering the limitations of Rule 26(b)(2)(C). The court may specify conditions for the discovery.

(C) *When Required.* On motion or on its own, the court must limit the frequency or extent of discovery otherwise allowed by these rules or by local rule if it determines that:

(i)   the discovery sought is unreasonably cumulative or duplicative, or can be obtained from some other source that is more convenient, less burdensome, or less expensive;

(ii) the party seeking discovery has had ample opportunity to obtain the information by discovery in the action; or

(iii) the proposed discovery is outside the scope permitted by Rule 26(b)(1).

(3) *Trial Preparation: Materials.*

(A) *Documents and Tangible Things.* Ordinarily, a party may not discover documents and tangible things that are prepared in anticipation of litigation or for trial by or for another party or its representative (including the other party's attorney, consultant, surety, indemnitor, insurer, or agent). But, subject to Rule 26(b)(4), those materials may be discovered if:

(i)   they are otherwise discoverable under Rule 26(b)(1); and

(ii) the party shows that it has substantial need for the materials to prepare its case and cannot, without undue hardship, obtain their substantial equivalent by other means.

(B) *Protection Against Disclosure.* If the court orders discovery of those materials, it must protect against disclosure of the mental impressions, conclusions, opinions, or legal theories of a party's attorney or other representative concerning the litigation.

(C) *Previous Statement.* Any party or other person may, on request and without the required showing, obtain the person's own previous statement about the action or its subject matter. If the request is refused, the person may move for a court order, and Rule 37(a)(5) applies to the award of expenses. A previous statement is either:

    (i) a written statement that the person has signed or otherwise adopted or approved; or

    (ii) a contemporaneous stenographic, mechanical, electrical, or other recording—or a transcription of it—that recites substantially verbatim the person's oral statement.

(4) *Trial Preparation: Experts.*

    (A) *Deposition of an Expert Who May Testify.* A party may depose any person who has been identified as an expert whose opinions may be presented at trial. If Rule 26(a)(2)(B) requires a report from the expert, the deposition may be conducted only after the report is provided.

    (B) *Trial-Preparation Protection for Draft Reports or Disclosures.* Rules 26(b)(3)(A) and (B) protect drafts of any report or disclosure required under Rule 26(a)(2), regardless of the form in which the draft is recorded.

    (C) *Trial-Preparation Protection for Communications Between a Party's Attorney and Expert Witnesses.* Rules 26(b)(3)(A) and (B) protect communications between the party's attorney and any witness required to provide a report under Rule 26(a)(2)(B), regardless of the form of the communications, except to the extent that the communications:

        (i) relate to compensation for the expert's study or testimony;

        (ii) identify facts or data that the party's attorney provided and that the expert considered in forming the opinions to be expressed; or

        (iii) identify assumptions that the party's attorney provided and that the expert relied on in forming the opinions to be expressed.

    (D) *Expert Employed Only for Trial Preparation.* Ordinarily, a party may not, by interrogatories or deposition, discover facts known or opinions held by an expert who has been retained or specially employed by another party in anticipation of litigation or to prepare for trial and who is not expected to be called as a witness at trial. But a party may do so only:

        (i) as provided in Rule 35(b); or

        (ii) on showing exceptional circumstances under which it is impracticable for the party to obtain facts or opinions on the same subject by other means.

    (E) *Payment.* Unless manifest injustice would result, the court must require that the party seeking discovery:

        (i) pay the expert a reasonable fee for time spent in responding to discovery under Rule 26(b)(4)(A) or (D); and

        (ii) for discovery under (D), also pay the other party a fair portion of the fees and expenses it reasonably incurred in obtaining the expert's facts and opinions.

    (5) *Claiming Privilege or Protecting Trial-Preparation Materials.*

(A) *Information Withheld.* When a party withholds information otherwise discoverable by claiming that the information is privileged or subject to protection as trial-preparation material, the party must:

(i) expressly make the claim; and

(ii) describe the nature of the documents, communications, or tangible things not produced or disclosed—and do so in a manner that, without revealing information itself privileged or protected, will enable other parties to assess the claim.

(B) *Information Produced.* If information produced in discovery is subject to a claim of privilege or of protection as trial-preparation material, the party making the claim may notify any party that received the information of the claim and the basis for it. After being notified, a party must promptly return, sequester, or destroy the specified information and any copies it has; must not use or disclose the information until the claim is resolved; must take reasonable steps to retrieve the information if the party disclosed it before being notified; and may promptly present the information to the court under seal for a determination of the claim. The producing party must preserve the information until the claim is resolved.

(c) Protective Orders.

(1) *In General.* A party or any person from whom discovery is sought may move for a protective order in the court where the action is pending—or as an alternative on matters relating to a deposition, in the court for the district where the deposition will be taken. The motion must include a certification that the movant has in good faith conferred or attempted to confer with other affected parties in an effort to resolve the dispute without court action. The court may, for good cause, issue an order to protect a party or person from annoyance, embarrassment, oppression, or undue burden or expense, including one or more of the following:

(A) *forbidding* the disclosure or discovery;

(B) *specifying* terms, including time and place or the allocation of expenses, for the disclosure or discovery;

(C) *prescribing* a discovery method other than the one selected by the party seeking discovery;

(D) *forbidding* inquiry into certain matters, or limiting the scope of disclosure or discovery to certain matters;

(E) *designating* the persons who may be present while the discovery is conducted;

(F) *requiring* that a deposition be sealed and opened only on court order;

(G) *requiring* that a trade secret or other confidential research, development, or commercial information not be revealed or be revealed only in a specified way; and

(H) *requiring* that the parties simultaneously file specified documents or information in sealed envelopes, to be opened as the court directs.

(2) *Ordering Discovery.* If a motion for a protective order is wholly or partly denied, the court may, on just terms, order that any party or person provide or permit discovery.

(3) *Awarding Expenses.* Rule 37(a)(5) applies to the award of expenses.

(d) Timing and Sequence of Discovery.

(1) *Timing.* A party may not seek discovery from any source before the parties have conferred as required by Rule 26(f), except in a proceeding exempted from initial disclosure under Rule 26(a)(1)(B), or when authorized by these rules, by stipulation, or by court order.

(2) *Early Rule 34 Requests.*

(A) *Time to Deliver.* More than 21 days after the summons and complaint are served on a party, a request under Rule 34 may be delivered:

(i) to that party by any other party, and

(ii) by that party to any plaintiff or to any other party that has been served.

(B) *When Considered Served.* The request is considered to have been served at the first Rule 26(f) conference.

(3) *Sequence.* Unless the parties stipulate or the court orders otherwise for the parties' and witnesses' convenience and in the interests of justice:

(A) *methods* of discovery may be used in any sequence; and

(B) *discovery* by one party does not require any other party to delay its discovery.

(e) Supplementing Disclosures and Responses.

(1) *In General.* A party who has made a disclosure under Rule 26(a)—or who has responded to an interrogatory, request for production, or request for admission—must supplement or correct its disclosure or response:

(A) in a timely manner if the party learns that in some material respect the disclosure or response is incomplete or incorrect, and if the additional or corrective information has not otherwise been made known to the other parties during the discovery process or in writing; or

(B) as ordered by the court.

(2) *Expert Witness.* For an expert whose report must be disclosed under Rule 26(a)(2)(B), the party's duty to supplement extends both to information included in the report and to information given during the expert's deposition. Any additions or changes to this information must be disclosed by the time the party's pretrial disclosures under Rule 26(a)(3) are due.

(f) Conference of the Parties; Planning for Discovery.

(1) *Conference Timing.* Except in a proceeding exempted from initial disclosure under Rule 26(a)(1)(B) or when the court orders otherwise, the parties must confer as soon as practicable—and in any event at least 21 days before a scheduling conference is to be held or a scheduling order is due under Rule 16(b).

(2) *Conference Content; Parties' Responsibilities.* In conferring, the parties must consider the nature and basis of their claims and defenses and the possibilities for promptly settling or resolving the case; make or arrange for the disclosures required by Rule 26(a)(1); discuss any issues about preserving discoverable information; and develop a proposed discovery plan. The attorneys of record and all unrepresented parties that have appeared in the case are jointly responsible for arranging the conference, for attempting in good faith to agree on the proposed discovery plan, and for submitting to the court within 14 days after the conference a written report outlining the plan. The court may order the parties or attorneys to attend the conference in person.

(3) *Discovery Plan.* A discovery plan must state the parties' views and proposals on:

(A) what changes should be made in the timing, form, or requirement for disclosures under Rule 26(a), including a statement of when initial disclosures were made or will be made;

(B) the subjects on which discovery may be needed, when discovery should be completed, and whether discovery should be conducted in phases or be limited to or focused on particular issues;

(C) any issues about disclosure, discovery, or preservation of electronically stored information, including the form or forms in which it should be produced;

(D) any issues about claims of privilege or of protection as trial-preparation materials, including—if the parties agree on a procedure to assert these claims after production—whether to ask the court to include their agreement in an order under Federal Rule of Evidence 502;

(E) what changes should be made in the limitations on discovery imposed under these rules or by local rule, and what other limitations should be imposed; and

(F) any other orders that the court should issue under Rule 26(c) or under Rule 16(b)and (c).

(4) *Expedited Schedule.* If necessary to comply with its expedited schedule for Rule 16(b) conferences, a court may by local rule:

(A) require the parties' conference to occur less than 21 days before the scheduling conference is held or a scheduling order is due under Rule 16(b); and

(B) require the written report outlining the discovery plan to be filed less than 14 days after the parties' conference, or excuse the parties from submitting a written report and permit them to report orally on their discovery plan at the Rule 16(b) conference.

(g) Signing Disclosures and Discovery Requests, Responses, and Objections.

(1) *Signature Required; Effect of Signature.* Every disclosure under Rule 26(a)(1) or (a)(3) and every discovery request, response, or objection must be signed by at least one attorney of record in the attorney's own name—or by the party personally, if unrepresented—and must state the signer's address, e-mail address, and telephone number. By signing, an attorney or party certifies that to the best of the person's knowledge, information, and belief formed after a reasonable inquiry:

(A) with respect to a disclosure, it is complete and correct as of the time it is made; and

(B) with respect to a discovery request, response, or objection, it is:

(i) consistent with these rules and warranted by existing law or by a nonfrivolous argument for extending, modifying, or reversing existing law, or for establishing new law;

(ii) not interposed for any improper purpose, such as to harass, cause unnecessary delay, or needlessly increase the cost of litigation; and

(iii) neither unreasonable nor unduly burdensome or expensive, considering the needs of the case, prior discovery in the case, the amount in controversy, and the importance of the issues at stake in the action.

(2) *Failure to Sign.* Other parties have no duty to act on an unsigned disclosure, request, response, or objection until it is signed, and the court must strike it unless a signature is promptly supplied after the omission is called to the attorney's or party's attention.

(3) *Sanction for Improper Certification.* If a certification violates this rule without substantial justification, the court, on motion or on its own, must impose an appropriate sanction on the signer, the party on whose behalf the signer was acting, or both. The sanction may include an order to pay the reasonable expenses, including attorney's fees, caused by the violation.

RULE 34. Producing Documents, Electronically Stored Information, and Tangible Things, or Entering Onto Land, for Inspection and Other Purposes

(a) In General. A party may serve on any other party a request within the scope of Rule 26(b):

(1) to produce and permit the requesting party or its representative to inspect, copy, test, or sample the following items in the responding party's possession, custody, or control:

(A) any designated documents or electronically stored information—including writings, drawings, graphs, charts, photographs, sound recordings, images, and other data or data compilations—stored in any medium from which information can be obtained either directly or, if necessary, after translation by the responding party into a reasonably usable form; or

(B) any designated tangible things; or

(2) to permit entry onto designated land or other property possessed or controlled by the responding party, so that the requesting party may inspect, measure, survey, photograph, test, or sample the property or any designated object or operation on it.

(b) Procedure.

(1) *Contents of the Request.* The request:

(A) must describe with reasonable particularity each item or category of items to be inspected;

(B) must specify a reasonable time, place, and manner for the inspection and for performing the related acts; and

(C) may specify the form or forms in which electronically stored information is to be produced.

(2) *Responses and Objections.*

(A) *Time to Respond.* The party to whom the request is directed must respond in writing within 30 days after being served or—if the request was delivered under Rule 26(d)(2)—within 30 days after the parties' first Rule 26(f) conference. A shorter or longer time may be stipulated to under Rule 29 or be ordered by the court.

(B) *Responding to Each Item.* For each item or category, the response must either state that inspection and related activities will be permitted as requested or state with specificity the grounds for objecting to the request, including the reasons. The responding party may state that it will produce copies of documents or of electronically stored information instead of permitting inspection. The production must then be completed no later than the time for inspection specified in the request or another reasonable time specified in the response.

(C) *Objections.* An objection must state whether any responsive materials are being withheld on the basis of that objection. An objection to part of a request must specify the part and permit inspection of the rest.

(D) *Responding to a Request for Production of Electronically Stored Information.* The response may state an objection to a requested form for producing electronically stored information. If the responding party objects to a requested form—or if no form was specified in the request—the party must state the form or forms it intends to use.

(E) *Producing the Documents or Electronically Stored Information.* Unless otherwise stipulated or ordered by the court, these procedures apply to producing documents or electronically stored information:

(i) A party must produce documents as they are kept in the usual course of business or must organize and label them to correspond to the categories in the request;

(ii) If a request does not specify a form for producing electronically stored information, a party must produce it in a form or forms in which it is ordinarily maintained or in a reasonably usable form or forms; and

> **(iii)** A party need not produce the same electronically stored information in more than one form.

(c) Nonparties. As provided in Rule 45, a nonparty may be compelled to produce documents and tangible things or to permit an inspection.

RULE 37.   Failure to Make Disclosures or to Cooperate in Discovery; Sanctions

* * *

(e) Failure to Preserve Electronically Stored Information. If electronically stored information that should have been preserved in the anticipation or conduct of litigation is lost because a party failed to take reasonable steps to preserve it, and it cannot be restored or replaced through additional discovery, the court:

> **(1)** upon finding prejudice to another party from loss of the information, may order measures no greater than necessary to cure the prejudice; or

> **(2)** only upon finding that the party acted with the intent to deprive another party of the information's use in the litigation may:

>> **(A)** presume that the lost information was unfavorable to the party;

>> **(B)** instruct the jury that it may or must presume the information was unfavorable to the party; or

>> **(C)** dismiss the action or enter a default judgment.

ABA MODEL CODE OF JUDICIAL CONDUCT (2007)

Editor's Note: The ABA Joint Commission to Evaluate the Model Code of Judicial Conduct began its work in 2003. On 12 February 2007, the ABA House of Delegates approved a new version of the Model Code of Judicial Conduct, later amended in August 2010. That current version is reprinted here.

Table of Contents

CANON 1

A JUDGE SHALL UPHOLD AND PROMOTE THE INDEPENDENCE, INTEGRITY, AND IMPARTIALITY OF THE JUDICIARY, AND SHALL AVOID IMPROPRIETY AND THE APPEARANCE OF IMPROPRIETY.

Rule

CANON 2

A JUDGE SHALL PERFORM THE DUTIES OF JUDICIAL OFFICE IMPARTIALLY, COMPETENTLY, AND DILIGENTLY.

Rule

CANON 3

A JUDGE SHALL CONDUCT THE JUDGE'S PERSONAL AND EXTRAJUDICIAL ACTIVITIES TO MINIMIZE THE RISK OF CONFLICT WITH THE OBLIGATIONS OF JUDICIAL OFFICE.

CANON 4

A JUDGE OR CANDIDATE FOR JUDICIAL OFFICE SHALL NOT ENGAGE IN POLITICAL OR CAMPAIGN ACTIVITY THAT IS INCONSISTENT WITH THE INDEPENDENCE, INTEGRITY, OR IMPARTIALITY OF THE JUDICIARY.

PREAMBLE

[1]   An independent, fair and impartial judiciary is indispensable to our system of justice. The United States legal system is based upon the principle that an independent, impartial, and competent judiciary, composed of men and women of integrity, will interpret and apply the law that governs our society. Thus, the judiciary plays a central role in preserving the principles of justice and the rule of law. Inherent in all the Rules contained in this Code are the precepts that judges, individually and collectively, must respect and honor the judicial office as a public trust and strive to maintain and enhance confidence in the legal system.

[2]   Judges should maintain the dignity of judicial office at all times, and avoid both impropriety and the appearance of impropriety in their professional and personal lives. They should aspire at all times to conduct that ensures the greatest possible public confidence in their independence, impartiality, integrity, and competence.

[3]   The Model Code of Judicial Conduct establishes standards for the ethical conduct of judges and judicial candidates. It is not intended as an exhaustive guide for the conduct of judges and judicial candidates, who are governed in their judicial and personal conduct by general ethical standards as well as by the Code. The Code is intended, however, to provide guidance and assist judges in maintaining the highest standards of judicial and personal conduct, and to provide a basis for regulating their conduct through disciplinary agencies.

SCOPE

[1]   The Model Code of Judicial Conduct consists of four Canons, numbered Rules under each Canon, and Comments that generally follow and explain each Rule. Scope and Terminology sections provide additional guidance in interpreting and applying the Code. An Application section establishes when the various Rules apply to a judge or judicial candidate.

[2]   The Canons state overarching principles of judicial ethics that all judges must observe. Although a judge may be disciplined only for violating a Rule, the Canons provide important guidance in interpreting the Rules. Where a Rule contains a permissive term, such as "may" or "should," the conduct being addressed is committed to the personal and professional discretion of the judge or candidate in question, and no disciplinary action should be taken for action or inaction within the bounds of such discretion.

[3]   The Comments that accompany the Rules serve two functions. First, they provide guidance regarding the purpose, meaning, and proper application of the Rules. They contain explanatory material and, in some instances, provide examples of permitted or prohibited conduct. Comments neither add to nor subtract from the binding obligations set forth in the Rules. Therefore, when a Comment contains the term "must," it does not mean that the Comment itself is binding or enforceable; it signifies that the Rule in question, properly understood, is obligatory as to the conduct at issue.

[4]   Second, the Comments identify aspirational goals for judges. To implement fully the principles of this Code as articulated in the Canons, judges should strive to exceed the standards of conduct established by the Rules, holding themselves to the highest ethical standards and seeking to achieve those aspirational goals, thereby enhancing the dignity of the judicial office.

[5]   The Rules of the Model Code of Judicial Conduct are rules of reason that should be applied consistent with constitutional requirements, statutes, other court rules, and decisional law, and with due regard for all relevant circumstances. The Rules should not be interpreted to impinge upon the essential independence of judges in making judicial decisions.

[6]   Although the black letter of the Rules is binding and enforceable, it is not contemplated that every transgression will result in the imposition of discipline. Whether discipline should be imposed should be determined through a reasonable and reasoned application of the Rules, and should depend upon factors such as the seriousness of the transgression, the facts and circumstances that existed at the time of the transgression, the extent of any pattern of improper activity, whether there have been previous violations, and the effect of the improper activity upon the judicial system or others.

[7]   The Code is not designed or intended as a basis for civil or criminal liability. Neither is it intended to be the basis for litigants to seek collateral remedies against each other or to obtain tactical advantages in proceedings before a court.

TERMINOLOGY

The first time any term listed below is used in a Rule in its defined sense, it is followed by an asterisk (*).

[1]   **"Aggregate,"** in relation to contributions for a candidate, means not only contributions in cash or in kind made directly to a candidate's campaign committee, but also all contributions made indirectly with the understanding that they will be used to support the election of a candidate or to oppose the election of the candidate's opponent. See Rules 2.11 and 4.4.

[2]   **"Appropriate authority"** means the authority having responsibility for initiation of disciplinary process in connection with the violation to be reported. See Rules 2.14 and 2.15.

[3]   **"Contribution"** means both financial and in-kind contributions, such as goods, professional or volunteer services, advertising, and other types of assistance, which, if obtained by the recipient otherwise, would require a financial expenditure. See Rules 2.11, 2.13, 3.7, 4.1, and 4.4.

[4]   **"De minimis,"** in the context of interests pertaining to disqualification of a judge, means an insignificant interest that could not raise a reasonable question regarding the judge's impartiality. See Rule 2.11.

[5]   **"Domestic partner"** means a person with whom another person maintains a household and an intimate relationship, other than a person to whom he or she is legally married. See Rules 2.11, 2.13, 3.13, and 3.14.

[6]   **"Economic interest"** means ownership of more than a de minimis legal or equitable interest. Except for situations in which the judge participates in the management of such a legal or equitable interest, or the interest could be substantially affected by the outcome of a proceeding before a judge, it does not include:

(1)   an interest in the individual holdings within a mutual or common investment fund;

(2)   an interest in securities held by an educational, religious, charitable, fraternal, or civic organization in which the judge or the judge's spouse, domestic partner, parent, or child serves as a director, an officer, an advisor, or other participant;

(3)   a deposit in a financial institution or deposits or proprietary interests the judge may maintain as a member of a mutual savings association or credit union, or similar proprietary interests; or

(4)   an interest in the issuer of government securities held by the judge.

See Rules 1.3 and 2.11.

[7] **"Fiduciary"** includes relationships such as executor, administrator, trustee, or guardian. See Rules 2.11, 3.2, and 3.8.

[8] **"Impartial," "impartiality,"** and **"impartially"** mean absence of bias or prejudice in favor of, or against, particular parties or classes of parties, as well as maintenance of an open mind in considering issues that may come before a judge. See Canons 1, 2, and 4, and Rules 1.2, 2.2, 2.10, 2.11, 2.13, 3.1, 3.12, 3.13, 4.1, and 4.2.

[9] **"Impending matter"** is a matter that is imminent or expected to occur in the near future. See Rules 2.9, 2.10, 3.13, and 4.1.

[10] **"Impropriety"** includes conduct that violates the law, court rules, or provisions of this Code, and conduct that undermines a judge's independence, integrity, or impartiality. See Canon 1 and Rule 1.2.

[11] **"Independence"** means a judge's freedom from influence or controls other than those established by law. See Canons 1 and 4, and Rules 1.2, 3.1, 3.12, 3.13, and 4.2.

[12] **"Integrity"** means probity, fairness, honesty, uprightness, and soundness of character. See Canon 1 and 4 and Rules 1.2, 3.1, 3.12, 3.13, and 4.2.

[13] **"Judicial candidate"** means any person, including a sitting judge, who is seeking selection for or retention in judicial office by election or appointment. A person becomes a candidate for judicial office as soon as he or she makes a public announcement of candidacy, declares or files as a candidate with the election or appointment authority, authorizes or, where permitted, engages in solicitation or acceptance of contributions or support, or is nominated for election or appointment to office. See Rules 2.11, 4.1, 4.2, and 4.4.

[14] **"Knowingly," "knowledge," "known,"** and **"knows"** mean actual knowledge of the fact in question. A person's knowledge may be inferred from circumstances. See Rules 2.11, 2.13, 2.15, 2.16, 3.6, and 4.1.

[15] **"Law"** encompasses court rules as well as statutes, constitutional provisions, and decisional law. See Rules 1.1, 2.1, 2.2, 2.6, 2.7, 2.9, 3.1, 3.4, 3.9, 3.12, 3.13, 3.14, 3.15, 4.1, 4.2, 4.4, and 4.5.

[16] **"Member of the candidate's family"** means a spouse, domestic partner, child, grandchild, parent, grandparent, or other relative or person with whom the candidate maintains a close familial relationship.

[17] **"Member of the judge's family"** means a spouse, domestic partner, child, grandchild, parent, grandparent, or other relative or person with whom the judge maintains a close familial relationship. See Rules 3.7, 3.8, 3.10, and 3.11.

[18] **"Member of a judge's family residing in the judge's household"** means any relative of a judge by blood or marriage, or a person treated by a judge as a member of the judge's family, who resides in the judge's household. See Rules 2.11 and 3.13.

[19] **"Nonpublic information"** means information that is not available to the public. Nonpublic information may include, but is not limited to, information that is sealed by statute or court order or impounded or communicated in camera, and information offered in grand jury proceedings, presentencing reports, dependency cases, or psychiatric reports. See Rule 3.5.

[20] **"Pending matter"** is a matter that has commenced. A matter continues to be pending through any appellate process until final disposition. See Rules 2.9, 2.10, 3.13, and 4.1.

[21] **"Personally solicit"** means a direct request made by a judge or a judicial candidate for financial support or in-kind services, whether made by letter, telephone, or any other means of communication. See Rule 4.1.

[22] **"Political organization"** means a political party or other group sponsored by or affiliated with a political party or candidate, the principal purpose of which is to further the election or appointment of candidates for political office. For purposes of this Code, the term does not include a judicial candidate's campaign committee created as authorized by Rule 4.4. See Rules 4.1 and 4.2.

[23] **"Public election"** includes primary and general elections, partisan elections, nonpartisan elections, and retention elections. See Rules 4.2 and 4.4.

[24] **"Third degree of relationship"** includes the following persons: great-grandparent, grandparent, parent, uncle, aunt, brother, sister, child, grandchild, great-grandchild, nephew, and niece. See Rule 2.11.

APPLICATION

The Application section establishes when the various Rules apply to a judge or judicial candidate.

I. APPLICABILITY OF THIS CODE

(A) The provisions of the Code apply to all full-time judges. Parts II through V of this section identify provisions that apply to the four categories of part-time judges only while they are serving as judges, and provisions that do not apply to part-time judges at any time. All other Rules are therefore applicable to part-time judges at all times. The four categories of judicial service in other than a full-time capacity are necessarily defined in general terms because of the widely varying forms of judicial service. Canon 4 applies to judicial candidates.

(B) A judge, within the meaning of this Code, is anyone who is authorized to perform judicial functions, including an officer such as a justice of the peace, magistrate, court commissioner, special master, referee, or member of the administrative law judiciary.[1]

---

[1] Each jurisdiction should consider the characteristics of particular positions within the administrative law judiciary in adopting, adapting, applying, and enforcing the Code for the administrative law judiciary. *See, e.g.,* Model Code of Judicial Conduct for Federal Administrative Law Judges (1989) and Model Code of Judicial Conduct for State Administrative Law Judges (1995). Both Model Codes are endorsed by the ABA National Conference of Administrative Law Judiciary.

Comment

[1]   The Rules in this Code have been formulated to address the ethical obligations of any person who serves a judicial function, and are premised upon the supposition that a uniform system of ethical principles should apply to all those authorized to perform judicial functions.

[2]   The determination of which category and, accordingly, which specific Rules apply to an individual judicial officer, depends upon the facts of the particular judicial service.

[3]   In recent years many jurisdictions have created what are often called "problem solving" courts, in which judges are authorized by court rules to act in nontraditional ways. For example, judges presiding in drug courts and monitoring the progress of participants in those courts' programs may be authorized, and even encouraged, to communicate directly with social workers, probation officers, and others outside the context of their usual judicial role as independent decision makers on issues of fact and law. When local rules specifically authorize conduct not otherwise permitted under these Rules, they take precedence over the provisions set forth in the Code. Nevertheless, judges serving on "problem solving" courts shall comply with this Code except to the extent local rules provide and permit otherwise.

II.   RETIRED JUDGE SUBJECT TO RECALL

A retired judge subject to recall for service, who by law is not permitted to practice law, is not required to comply:

(A) with Rule 3.9 (Service as Arbitrator or Mediator), except while serving as a judge.

(B) at any time with Rule 3.8 (A) (Appointments to Fiduciary Positions).

Comment

[1]   For the purposes of this section, as long as a retired judge is subject to being recalled for service, the judge is considered to "perform judicial functions."

III.   CONTINUING PART-TIME JUDGE

A judge who serves repeatedly on a part-time basis by election or under a continuing appointment, including a retired judge subject to recall who is permitted to practice law ("continuing part-time judge"),

(A) is not required to comply:

(1) with Rule 4.1 (Political and Campaign Activities of Judges and Judicial Candidates in General) (A)(1) through (7), except while serving as a judge; or

(2) at any time with Rules 3.4 (Appointments to Governmental Positions), 3.8 (A) (Appointments to Fiduciary Positions), 3.9 (Service as Arbitrator or Mediator), 3.10 (Practice of Law), and 3.11(B) (Financial, Business, or Remunerative Activities); and

(B) shall not practice law in the court on which the judge serves, or in any court subject to the appellate jurisdiction of the court on which the judge serves, and shall not act as a lawyer in a proceeding in which the judge has served as a judge or in any other proceeding related thereto.

Comment

[1] When a person who has been a continuing part-time judge is no longer a continuing part-time judge, including a retired judge no longer subject to recall, that person may act as a lawyer in a proceeding in which he or she has served as a judge, or in any other proceeding related thereto, only with the informed consent of all parties, and pursuant to any applicable Model Rules of Professional Conduct. An adopting jurisdiction should substitute a reference to its applicable rule.

IV. PERIODIC PART-TIME JUDGE

A periodic part-time judge who serves or expects to serve repeatedly on a part-time basis, but under a separate appointment for each limited period of service or for each matter,

(A) is not required to comply:

(1) with Rule 4.1 (Political and Campaign Activities of Judges and Judicial Candidates in General) (A)(1) through (7), except while serving as a judge; or

(2) at any time with Rules 3.4 (Appointments to Governmental Positions), 3.8 (A) (Appointments to Fiduciary Positions), 3.9 (Service as Arbitrator or Mediator), 3.10 (Practice of Law), and 3.11(B) (Financial, Business, or Remunerative Activities); and

(B) shall not practice law in the court on which the judge serves, or in any court subject to the appellate jurisdiction of the court on which the judge serves, and shall not act as a lawyer in a proceeding in which the judge has served as a judge or in any other proceeding related thereto.

V. PRO TEMPORE PART-TIME JUDGE

A pro tempore part-time judge who serves or expects to serve once or only sporadically on a part-time basis under a separate appointment for each period of service or for each case heard is not required to comply:

(A) except while serving as a judge, with Rules 2.4 (External Influences on Judicial Conduct), 3.2 (Appearances before Governmental Bodies and Consultation with Government Officials); and 4.1 (Political and Campaign Activities of Judges and Judicial Candidates in General) (A)(1) through (7); or

(B) at any time with Rules 3.4 (Appointments to Governmental Positions), 3.8 (A) (Appointments to Fiduciary Positions), 3.9 (Service as Arbitrator or Mediator), 3.10 (Practice of Law), and 3.11 (B) (Financial, Business, or Remunerative Activities).

VI. TIME FOR COMPLIANCE

A person to whom this Code becomes applicable shall comply immediately with its provisions, except that those judges to whom Rules 3.8 (Appointments to Fiduciary Positions) and 3.11 (Financial, Business, or Remunerative Activities) apply shall comply with those

Rules as soon as reasonably possible, but in no event later than one year after the Code becomes applicable to the judge.

Comment

[1]   If serving as a fiduciary when selected as judge, a new judge may, notwithstanding the prohibitions in Rule 3.8, continue to serve as fiduciary, but only for that period of time necessary to avoid serious adverse consequences to the beneficiaries of the fiduciary relationship, and in no event longer than one year. Similarly, if engaged at the time of judicial selection in a business activity, a new judge may, notwithstanding the prohibitions in Rule 3.11, continue in that activity for a reasonable period, but in no event longer than one year.

CANON 1

A judge shall uphold and promote the independence, integrity, and impartiality of the judiciary, and shall avoid impropriety and the appearance of impropriety.

RULE 1.1: Compliance with the Law

A judge shall comply with the law,* including the Code of Judicial Conduct.

RULE 1.2: Promoting Confidence in the Judiciary

A judge shall act at all times in a manner that promotes public confidence in the independence,* integrity,* and impartiality* of the judiciary, and shall avoid impropriety and the appearance of impropriety.

Comment

[1]   Public confidence in the judiciary is eroded by improper conduct and conduct that creates the appearance of impropriety. This principle applies to both the professional and personal conduct of a judge.

[2]   A judge should expect to be the subject of public scrutiny that might be viewed as burdensome if applied to other citizens, and must accept the restrictions imposed by the Code.

[3]   Conduct that compromises or appears to compromise the independence, integrity, and impartiality of a judge undermines public confidence in the judiciary. Because it is not practicable to list all such conduct, the Rule is necessarily cast in general terms.

[4]   Judges should participate in activities that promote ethical conduct among judges and lawyers, support professionalism within the judiciary and the legal profession, and promote access to justice for all.

[5]   Actual improprieties include violations of law, court rules or provisions of this Code. The test for appearance of impropriety is whether the conduct would create in reasonable minds a perception that the judge violated this Code or engaged in other conduct that reflects adversely on the judge's honesty, impartiality, temperament, or fitness to serve as a judge.

[6]   A judge should initiate and participate in community outreach activities for the purpose of promoting public understanding of and

---

*   See, Terminology.

confidence in the administration of justice. In conducting such activities, the judge must act in a manner consistent with this Code.

RULE 1.3: Avoiding Abuse of the Prestige of Judicial Office

A judge shall not abuse the prestige of judicial office to advance the personal or economic interests* of the judge or others, or allow others to do so.

Comment

[1] It is improper for a judge to use or attempt to use his or her position to gain personal advantage or deferential treatment of any kind. For example, it would be improper for a judge to allude to his or her judicial status to gain favorable treatment in encounters with traffic officials. Similarly, a judge must not use judicial letterhead to gain an advantage in conducting his or her personal business.

[2] A judge may provide a reference or recommendation for an individual based upon the judge's personal knowledge. The judge may use official letterhead if the judge indicates that the reference is personal and if there is no likelihood that the use of the letterhead would reasonably be perceived as an attempt to exert pressure by reason of the judicial office.

[3] Judges may participate in the process of judicial selection by cooperating with appointing authorities and screening committees, and by responding to inquiries from such entities concerning the professional qualifications of a person being considered for judicial office.

[4] Special considerations arise when judges write or contribute to publications of for-profit entities, whether related or unrelated to the law. A judge should not permit anyone associated with the publication of such materials to exploit the judge's office in a manner that violates this Rule or other applicable law. In contracts for publication of a judge's writing, the judge should retain sufficient control over the advertising to avoid such exploitation.

CANON 2

A judge shall perform the duties of judicial office impartially, competently, and diligently.

RULE 2.1: Giving Precedence to the Duties of Judicial Office

The duties of judicial office, as prescribed by law,* shall take precedence over all of a judge's personal and extrajudicial activities.

Comment

[1] To ensure that judges are available to fulfill their judicial duties, judges must conduct their personal and extrajudicial activities to minimize the risk of conflicts that would result in frequent disqualification. See Canon 3.

[2] Although it is not a duty of judicial office unless prescribed by law, judges are encouraged to participate in activities that promote public understanding of and confidence in the justice system.

---

*   See, Terminology.

RULE 2.2: Impartiality and Fairness

A judge shall uphold and apply the law,* and shall perform all duties of judicial office fairly and impartially.*

Comment

[1]   To ensure impartiality and fairness to all parties, a judge must be objective and open-minded.

[2]   Although each judge comes to the bench with a unique background and personal philosophy, a judge must interpret and apply the law without regard to whether the judge approves or disapproves of the law in question.

[3]   When applying and interpreting the law, a judge sometimes may make good-faith errors of fact or law. Errors of this kind do not violate this Rule.

[4]   It is not a violation of this Rule for a judge to make reasonable accommodations to ensure pro se litigants the opportunity to have their matters fairly heard.

RULE 2.3: Bias, Prejudice, and Harassment

(A) A judge shall perform the duties of judicial office, including administrative duties, without bias or prejudice.

(B) A judge shall not, in the performance of judicial duties, by words or conduct manifest bias or prejudice, or engage in harassment, including but not limited to bias, prejudice, or harassment based upon race, sex, gender, religion, national origin, ethnicity, disability, age, sexual orientation, marital status, socioeconomic status, or political affiliation, and shall not permit court staff, court officials, or others subject to the judge's direction and control to do so.

(C) A judge shall require lawyers in proceedings before the court to refrain from manifesting bias or prejudice, or engaging in harassment, based upon attributes including but not limited to race, sex, gender, religion, national origin, ethnicity, disability, age, sexual orientation, marital status, socioeconomic status, or political affiliation, against parties, witnesses, lawyers, or others.

(D) The restrictions of paragraphs (B) and (C) do not preclude judges or lawyers from making legitimate reference to the listed factors, or similar factors, when they are relevant to an issue in a proceeding.

Comment

[1]   A judge who manifests bias or prejudice in a proceeding impairs the fairness of the proceeding and brings the judiciary into disrepute.

[2]   Examples of manifestations of bias or prejudice include but are not limited to epithets; slurs; demeaning nicknames; negative stereotyping; attempted humor based upon stereotypes; threatening, intimidating, or hostile acts; suggestions of connections between race, ethnicity, or nationality and crime; and irrelevant references to personal characteristics. Even facial expressions and body language can convey to parties and lawyers in the proceeding, jurors, the media, and others an appearance of bias or prejudice.

---

*   See, Terminology.

A judge must avoid conduct that may reasonably be perceived as prejudiced or biased.

[3] Harassment, as referred to in paragraphs (B) and (C), is verbal or physical conduct that denigrates or shows hostility or aversion toward a person on bases such as race, sex, gender, religion, national origin, ethnicity, disability, age, sexual orientation, marital status, socioeconomic status, or political affiliation.

[4] Sexual harassment includes but is not limited to sexual advances, requests for sexual favors, and other verbal or physical conduct of a sexual nature that is unwelcome.

RULE 2.4: External Influences on Judicial Conduct

(A) A judge shall not be swayed by public clamor or fear of criticism.

(B) A judge shall not permit family, social, political, financial, or other interests or relationships to influence the judge's judicial conduct or judgment.

(C) A judge shall not convey or permit others to convey the impression that any person or organization is in a position to influence the judge.

Comment

[1] An independent judiciary requires that judges decide cases according to the law and facts, without regard to whether particular laws or litigants are popular or unpopular with the public, the media, government officials, or the judge's friends or family. Confidence in the judiciary is eroded if judicial decision making is perceived to be subject to inappropriate outside influences.

RULE 2.5: Competence, Diligence, and Cooperation

(A) A judge shall perform judicial and administrative duties, competently and diligently.

(B) A judge shall cooperate with other judges and court officials in the administration of court business.

Comment

[1] Competence in the performance of judicial duties requires the legal knowledge, skill, thoroughness, and preparation reasonably necessary to perform a judge's responsibilities of judicial office.

[2] A judge should seek the necessary docket time, court staff, expertise, and resources to discharge all adjudicative and administrative responsibilities.

[3] Prompt disposition of the court's business requires a judge to devote adequate time to judicial duties, to be punctual in attending court and expeditious in determining matters under submission, and to take reasonable measures to ensure that court officials, litigants, and their lawyers cooperate with the judge to that end.

[4] In disposing of matters promptly and efficiently, a judge must demonstrate due regard for the rights of parties to be heard and to have issues resolved without unnecessary cost or delay. A judge should monitor

and supervise cases in ways that reduce or eliminate dilatory practices, avoidable delays, and unnecessary costs.

RULE 2.6: Ensuring the Right to Be Heard

(A) A judge shall accord to every person who has a legal interest in a proceeding, or that person's lawyer, the right to be heard according to law.*

(B) A judge may encourage parties to a proceeding and their lawyers to settle matters in dispute but shall not act in a manner that coerces any party into settlement.

Comment

[1]   The right to be heard is an essential component of a fair and impartial system of justice. Substantive rights of litigants can be protected only if procedures protecting the right to be heard are observed.

[2]   The judge plays an important role in overseeing the settlement of disputes, but should be careful that efforts to further settlement do not undermine any party's right to be heard according to law. The judge should keep in mind the effect that the judge's participation in settlement discussions may have, not only on the judge's own views of the case, but also on the perceptions of the lawyers and the parties if the case remains with the judge after settlement efforts are unsuccessful. Among the factors that a judge should consider when deciding upon an appropriate settlement practice for a case are (1) whether the parties have requested or voluntarily consented to a certain level of participation by the judge in settlement discussions (2) whether the parties and their counsel are relatively sophisticated in legal matters (3) whether the case will be tried by the judge or a jury (4) whether the parties participate with their counsel in settlement discussions (5) whether any parties are unrepresented by counsel, and (6) whether the matter is civil or criminal.

[3]   Judges must be mindful of the effect settlement discussions can have, not only on their objectivity and impartiality, but also on the appearance of their objectivity and impartiality. Despite a judge's best efforts, there may be instances when information obtained during settlement discussions could influence a judge's decision making during trial, and, in such instances, the judge should consider whether disqualification may be appropriate. See Rule 2.11(A)(1).

RULE 2.7: Responsibility to Decide

A judge shall hear and decide matters assigned to the judge, except when disqualification is required by Rule 2.11 or other law.*

Comment

[1]   Judges must be available to decide the matters that come before the court. Although there are times when disqualification is necessary to protect the rights of litigants and preserve public confidence in the independence, integrity, and impartiality of the judiciary, judges must be available to decide matters that come before the courts. Unwarranted disqualification may bring public disfavor to the court and to the judge personally. The dignity of the court, the judge's respect for fulfillment of judicial duties, and a proper concern for the burdens that may be imposed

---

*   See, Terminology.

upon the judge's colleagues require that a judge not use disqualification to avoid cases that present difficult, controversial, or unpopular issues.

RULE 2.8: Decorum, Demeanor, and Communication with Jurors

(A) A judge shall require order and decorum in proceedings before the court.

(B) A judge shall be patient, dignified, and courteous to litigants, jurors, witnesses, lawyers, court staff, court officials, and others with whom the judge deals in an official capacity, and shall require similar conduct of lawyers, court staff, court officials, and others subject to the judge's direction and control.

(C) A judge shall not commend or criticize jurors for their verdict other than in a court order or opinion in a proceeding.

Comment

[1] The duty to hear all proceedings with patience and courtesy is not inconsistent with the duty imposed in Rule 2.5 to dispose promptly of the business of the court. Judges can be efficient and businesslike while being patient and deliberate.

[2] Commending or criticizing jurors for their verdict may imply a judicial expectation in future cases and may impair a juror's ability to be fair and impartial in a subsequent case.

[3] A judge who is not otherwise prohibited by law from doing so may meet with jurors who choose to remain after trial but should be careful not to discuss the merits of the case.

RULE 2.9: Ex Parte Communications

(A) A judge shall not initiate, permit, or consider ex parte communications, or consider other communications made to the judge outside the presence of the parties or their lawyers, concerning a pending* or impending matter,* except as follows:

(1) When circumstances require it, ex parte communication for scheduling, administrative, or emergency purposes, which does not address substantive matters, is permitted, provided:

(a) the judge reasonably believes that no party will gain a procedural, substantive, or tactical advantage as a result of the ex parte communication; and

(b) the judge makes provision promptly to notify all other parties of the substance of the ex parte communication, and gives the parties an opportunity to respond.

(2) A judge may obtain the written advice of a disinterested expert on the law applicable to a proceeding before the judge, if the judge gives advance notice to the parties of the person to be consulted and the subject matter of the advice to be solicited, and affords the parties a reasonable

---

*   See, Terminology.

opportunity to object and respond to the notice and to the advice received.

(3)   A judge may consult with court staff and court officials whose functions are to aid the judge in carrying out the judge's adjudicative responsibilities, or with other judges, provided the judge makes reasonable efforts to avoid receiving factual information that is not part of the record, and does not abrogate the responsibility personally to decide the matter.

(4)   A judge may, with the consent of the parties, confer separately with the parties and their lawyers in an effort to settle matters pending before the judge.

(5)   A judge may initiate, permit, or consider any ex parte communication when expressly authorized by law* to do so.

(B)   If a judge inadvertently receives an unauthorized ex parte communication bearing upon the substance of a matter, the judge shall make provision promptly to notify the parties of the substance of the communication and provide the parties with an opportunity to respond.

(C)   A judge shall not investigate facts in a matter independently, and shall consider only the evidence presented and any facts that may properly be judicially noticed.

(D)   A judge shall make reasonable efforts, including providing appropriate supervision, to ensure that this Rule is not violated by court staff, court officials, and others subject to the judge's direction and control.

Comment

[1]   To the extent reasonably possible, all parties or their lawyers shall be included in communications with a judge.

[2]   Whenever the presence of a party or notice to a party is required by this Rule, it is the party's lawyer, or if the party is unrepresented, the party, who is to be present or to whom notice is to be given.

[3]   The proscription against communications concerning a proceeding includes communications with lawyers, law teachers, and other persons who are not participants in the proceeding, except to the limited extent permitted by this Rule.

[4]   A judge may initiate, permit, or consider ex parte communications expressly authorized by law, such as when serving on therapeutic or problem-solving courts, mental health courts, or drug courts. In this capacity, judges may assume a more interactive role with parties, treatment providers, probation officers, social workers, and others.

[5]   A judge may consult with other judges on pending matters, but must avoid ex parte discussions of a case with judges who have previously been disqualified from hearing the matter, and with judges who have appellate jurisdiction over the matter.

[6]   The prohibition against a judge investigating the facts in a matter extends to information available in all mediums, including electronic.

---

*   See, Terminology.

[7]   A judge may consult ethics advisory committees, outside counsel, or legal experts concerning the judge's compliance with this Code. Such consultations are not subject to the restrictions of paragraph (A)(2).

RULE 2.10: Judicial Statements on Pending and Impending Cases

(A) A judge shall not make any public statement that might reasonably be expected to affect the outcome or impair the fairness of a matter pending* or impending* in any court, or make any nonpublic statement that might substantially interfere with a fair trial or hearing.

(B) A judge shall not, in connection with cases, controversies, or issues that are likely to come before the court, make pledges, promises, or commitments that are inconsistent with the impartial* performance of the adjudicative duties of judicial office.

(C) A judge shall require court staff, court officials, and others subject to the judge's direction and control to refrain from making statements that the judge would be prohibited from making by paragraphs (A) and (B).

(D) Notwithstanding the restrictions in paragraph (A), a judge may make public statements in the course of official duties, may explain court procedures, and may comment on any proceeding in which the judge is a litigant in a personal capacity.

(E) Subject to the requirements of paragraph (A), a judge may respond directly or through a third party to allegations in the media or elsewhere concerning the judge's conduct in a matter.

Comment

[1]   This Rule's restrictions on judicial speech are essential to the maintenance of the independence, integrity, and impartiality of the judiciary.

[2]   This Rule does not prohibit a judge from commenting on proceedings in which the judge is a litigant in a personal capacity, or represents a client as permitted by these Rules. In cases in which the judge is a litigant in an official capacity, such as writ of mandamus, the judge must not comment publicly.

[3]   Depending upon the circumstances, the judge should consider whether it may be preferable for a third party, rather than the judge, to respond or issue statements in connection with allegations concerning the judge's conduct in a matter.

RULE 2.11: Disqualification

(A) A judge shall disqualify himself or herself in any proceeding in which the judge's impartiality* might reasonably be questioned, including but not limited to the following circumstances:

(1)   The judge has a personal bias or prejudice concerning a party or a party's lawyer, or personal knowledge* of facts that are in dispute in the proceeding.

(2)   The judge knows* that the judge, the judge's spouse or domestic partner,* or a person within the third degree of

---

*   See, Terminology.

relationship* to either of them, or the spouse or domestic partner of such a person is:

> (a) a party to the proceeding, or an officer, director, general partner, managing member, or trustee of a party;

> (b) acting as a lawyer in the proceeding;

> (c) a person who has more than a de minimis* interest that could be substantially affected by the proceeding; or

> (d) likely to be a material witness in the proceeding.

(3) The judge knows that he or she, individually or as a fiduciary,* or the judge's spouse, domestic partner, parent, or child, or any other member of the judge's family residing in the judge's household,* has an economic interest* in the subject matter in controversy or is a party to the proceeding.

(4) The judge knows or learns by means of a timely motion that a party, a party's lawyer, or the law firm of a party's lawyer has within the previous [insert number] year[s] made aggregate* contributions* to the judge's campaign in an amount that [is greater than $[insert amount] for an individual or $[insert amount] for an entity] [is reasonable and appropriate for an individual or an entity].

(5) The judge, while a judge or a judicial candidate,* has made a public statement, other than in a court proceeding, judicial decision, or opinion, that commits or appears to commit the judge to reach a particular result or rule in a particular way in the proceeding or controversy.

(6) The judge:

> (a) served as a lawyer in the matter in controversy, or was associated with a lawyer who participated substantially as a lawyer in the matter during such association;

> (b) served in governmental employment, and in such capacity participated personally and substantially as a lawyer or public official concerning the proceeding, or has publicly expressed in such capacity an opinion concerning the merits of the particular matter in controversy;

> (c) was a material witness concerning the matter; or

> (d) previously presided as a judge over the matter in another court.

(B) A judge shall keep informed about the judge's personal and fiduciary economic interests, and make a reasonable effort to keep informed about the personal economic interests of the judge's spouse or domestic partner and minor children residing in the judge's household.

(C) A judge subject to disqualification under this Rule, other than for bias or prejudice under paragraph (A)(1), may disclose on the record the basis of the judge's disqualification and may ask the parties and their lawyers to consider, outside the presence of the

---

*   See, Terminology.

judge and court personnel, whether to waive disqualification. If, following the disclosure, the parties and lawyers agree, without participation by the judge or court personnel, that the judge should not be disqualified, the judge may participate in the proceeding. The agreement shall be incorporated into the record of the proceeding.

Comment

[1]   Under this Rule, a judge is disqualified whenever the judge's impartiality might reasonably be questioned, regardless of whether any of the specific provisions of paragraphs (A)(1) through (6) apply. In many jurisdictions, the term "recusal" is used interchangeably with the term "disqualification."

[2]   A judge's obligation not to hear or decide matters in which disqualification is required applies regardless of whether a motion to disqualify is filed.

[3]   The rule of necessity may override the rule of disqualification. For example, a judge might be required to participate in judicial review of a judicial salary statute, or might be the only judge available in a matter requiring immediate judicial action, such as a hearing on probable cause or a temporary restraining order. In matters that require immediate action, the judge must disclose on the record the basis for possible disqualification and make reasonable efforts to transfer the matter to another judge as soon as practicable.

[4]   The fact that a lawyer in a proceeding is affiliated with a law firm with which a relative of the judge is affiliated does not itself disqualify the judge. If, however, the judge's impartiality might reasonably be questioned under paragraph (A), or the relative is known by the judge to have an interest in the law firm that could be substantially affected by the proceeding under paragraph (A)(2)(c), the judge's disqualification is required.

[5]   A judge should disclose on the record information that the judge believes the parties or their lawyers might reasonably consider relevant to a possible motion for disqualification, even if the judge believes there is no basis for disqualification.

[6]   "Economic interest," as set forth in the Terminology section, means ownership of more than a de minimis legal or equitable interest. Except for situations in which a judge participates in the management of such a legal or equitable interest, or the interest could be substantially affected by the outcome of a proceeding before a judge, it does not include:

(1)   an interest in the individual holdings within a mutual or common investment fund;

(2)   an interest in securities held by an educational, religious, charitable, fraternal, or civic organization in which the judge or the judge's spouse, domestic partner, parent, or child serves as a director, officer, advisor, or other participant;

(3)   a deposit in a financial institution or deposits or proprietary interests the judge may maintain as a member of a mutual savings association or credit union, or similar proprietary interests; or

(4)   an interest in the issuer of government securities held by the judge.

RULE 2.12: Supervisory Duties

(A) A judge shall require court staff, court officials, and others subject to the judge's direction and control to act in a manner consistent with the judge's obligations under this Code.

(B) A judge with supervisory authority for the performance of other judges shall take reasonable measures to ensure that those judges properly discharge their judicial responsibilities, including the prompt disposition of matters before them.

Comment

[1]   A judge is responsible for his or her own conduct and for the conduct of others, such as staff, when those persons are acting at the judge's direction or control. A judge may not direct court personnel to engage in conduct on the judge's behalf or as the judge's representative when such conduct would violate the Code if undertaken by the judge.

[2]   Public confidence in the judicial system depends upon timely justice. To promote the efficient administration of justice, a judge with supervisory authority must take the steps needed to ensure that judges under his or her supervision administer their workloads promptly.

RULE 2.13: Administrative Appointments

(A) In making administrative appointments, a judge:

(1)   shall exercise the power of appointment impartially* and on the basis of merit; and

(2)   shall avoid nepotism, favoritism, and unnecessary appointments.

(B) A judge shall not appoint a lawyer to a position if the judge either knows* that the lawyer, or the lawyer's spouse or domestic partner,* has contributed more than \$[insert amount] within the prior [insert number] year[s] to the judge's election campaign, or learns of such a contribution* by means of a timely motion by a party or other person properly interested in the matter, unless:

(1)   the position is substantially uncompensated;

(2)   the lawyer has been selected in rotation from a list of qualified and available lawyers compiled without regard to their having made political contributions; or

(3)   the judge or another presiding or administrative judge affirmatively finds that no other lawyer is willing, competent, and able to accept the position.

(C) A judge shall not approve compensation of appointees beyond the fair value of services rendered.

Comment

[1]   Appointees of a judge include assigned counsel, officials such as referees, commissioners, special masters, receivers, and guardians, and personnel such as clerks, secretaries, and bailiffs. Consent by the parties to an appointment or an award of compensation does not relieve the judge of the obligation prescribed by paragraph (A).

---

*   See, Terminology.

[2]   Unless otherwise defined by law, nepotism is the appointment or hiring of any relative within the third degree of relationship of either the judge or the judge's spouse or domestic partner, or the spouse or domestic partner of such relative.

[3]   The rule against making administrative appointments of lawyers who have contributed in excess of a specified dollar amount to a judge's election campaign includes an exception for positions that are substantially uncompensated, such as those for which the lawyer's compensation is limited to reimbursement for out-of-pocket expenses.

RULE 2.14: Disability and Impairment

A judge having a reasonable belief that the performance of a lawyer or another judge is impaired by drugs or alcohol, or by a mental, emotional, or physical condition, shall take appropriate action, which may include a confidential referral to a lawyer or judicial assistance program.

Comment

[1]   "Appropriate action" means action intended and reasonably likely to help the judge or lawyer in question address the problem and prevent harm to the justice system. Depending upon the circumstances, appropriate action may include but is not limited to speaking directly to the impaired person, notifying an individual with supervisory responsibility over the impaired person, or making a referral to an assistance program.

[2]   Taking or initiating corrective action by way of referral to an assistance program may satisfy a judge's responsibility under this Rule. Assistance programs have many approaches for offering help to impaired judges and lawyers, such as intervention, counseling, or referral to appropriate health care professionals. Depending upon the gravity of the conduct that has come to the judge's attention, however, the judge may be required to take other action, such as reporting the impaired judge or lawyer to the appropriate authority, agency, or body. See Rule 2.15.

RULE 2.15: Responding to Judicial and Lawyer Misconduct

(A) A judge having knowledge* that another judge has committed a violation of this Code that raises a substantial question regarding the judge's honesty, trustworthiness, or fitness as a judge in other respects shall inform the appropriate authority.*

(B) A judge having knowledge that a lawyer has committed a violation of the Rules of Professional Conduct that raises a substantial question regarding the lawyer's honesty, trustworthiness, or fitness as a lawyer in other respects shall inform the appropriate authority.

(C) A judge who receives information indicating a substantial likelihood that another judge has committed a violation of this Code shall take appropriate action.

(D) A judge who receives information indicating a substantial likelihood that a lawyer has committed a violation of the Rules of Professional Conduct shall take appropriate action.

---

*   See, Terminology.

Comment

[1]   Taking action to address known misconduct is a judge's obligation. Paragraphs (A) and (B) impose an obligation on the judge to report to the appropriate disciplinary authority the known misconduct of another judge or a lawyer that raises a substantial question regarding the honesty, trustworthiness, or fitness of that judge or lawyer. Ignoring or denying known misconduct among one's judicial colleagues or members of the legal profession undermines a judge's responsibility to participate in efforts to ensure public respect for the justice system. This Rule limits the reporting obligation to those offenses that an independent judiciary must vigorously endeavor to prevent.

[2]   A judge who does not have actual knowledge that another judge or a lawyer may have committed misconduct, but receives information indicating a substantial likelihood of such misconduct, is required to take appropriate action under paragraphs (C) and (D). Appropriate action may include, but is not limited to, communicating directly with the judge who may have violated this Code, communicating with a supervising judge, or reporting the suspected violation to the appropriate authority or other agency or body. Similarly, actions to be taken in response to information indicating that a lawyer has committed a violation of the Rules of Professional Conduct may include but are not limited to communicating directly with the lawyer who may have committed the violation, or reporting the suspected violation to the appropriate authority or other agency or body.

RULE 2.16: Cooperation with Disciplinary Authorities

(A) A judge shall cooperate and be candid and honest with judicial and lawyer disciplinary agencies.

(B) A judge shall not retaliate, directly or indirectly, against a person known* or suspected to have assisted or cooperated with an investigation of a judge or a lawyer.

Comment

[1]   Cooperation with investigations and proceedings of judicial and lawyer discipline agencies, as required in paragraph (A), instills confidence in judges' commitment to the integrity of the judicial system and the protection of the public.

CANON 3

A judge shall conduct the judge's personal and extrajudicial activities to minimize the risk of conflict with the obligations of judicial office.

RULE 3.1: Extrajudicial Activities in General

A judge may engage in extrajudicial activities, except as prohibited by law* or this Code. However, when engaging in extrajudicial activities, a judge shall not:

(A) participate in activities that will interfere with the proper performance of the judge's judicial duties;

(B) participate in activities that will lead to frequent disqualification of the judge;

---

*   See, Terminology.

(C) participate in activities that would appear to a reasonable person to undermine the judge's independence,* integrity,* or impartiality;*

(D) engage in conduct that would appear to a reasonable person to be coercive; or

(E) make use of court premises, staff, stationery, equipment, or other resources, except for incidental use for activities that concern the law, the legal system, or the administration of justice, or unless such additional use is permitted by law.

Comment

[1] To the extent that time permits, and judicial independence and impartiality are not compromised, judges are encouraged to engage in appropriate extrajudicial activities. Judges are uniquely qualified to engage in extrajudicial activities that concern the law, the legal system, and the administration of justice, such as by speaking, writing, teaching, or participating in scholarly research projects. In addition, judges are permitted and encouraged to engage in educational, religious, charitable, fraternal or civic extrajudicial activities not conducted for profit, even when the activities do not involve the law. See Rule 3.7.

[2] Participation in both law-related and other extrajudicial activities helps integrate judges into their communities, and furthers public understanding of and respect for courts and the judicial system.

[3] Discriminatory actions and expressions of bias or prejudice by a judge, even outside the judge's official or judicial actions, are likely to appear to a reasonable person to call into question the judge's integrity and impartiality. Examples include jokes or other remarks that demean individuals based upon their race, sex, gender, religion, national origin, ethnicity, disability, age, sexual orientation, or socioeconomic status. For the same reason, a judge's extrajudicial activities must not be conducted in connection or affiliation with an organization that practices invidious discrimination. See Rule 3.6.

[4] While engaged in permitted extrajudicial activities, judges must not coerce others or take action that would reasonably be perceived as coercive. For example, depending upon the circumstances, a judge's solicitation of contributions or memberships for an organization, even as permitted by Rule 3.7(A), might create the risk that the person solicited would feel obligated to respond favorably, or would do so to curry favor with the judge.

RULE 3.2: Appearances before Governmental Bodies and Consultation with Government Officials

A judge shall not appear voluntarily at a public hearing before, or otherwise consult with, an executive or a legislative body or official, except:

(A) in connection with matters concerning the law, the legal system, or the administration of justice;

---

* See, Terminology.

(B) in connection with matters about which the judge acquired knowledge or expertise in the course of the judge's judicial duties; or

(C) when the judge is acting pro se in a matter involving the judge's legal or economic interests, or when the judge is acting in a fiduciary* capacity.

Comment

[1]   Judges possess special expertise in matters of law, the legal system, and the administration of justice, and may properly share that expertise with governmental bodies and executive or legislative branch officials.

[2]   In appearing before governmental bodies or consulting with government officials, judges must be mindful that they remain subject to other provisions of this Code, such as Rule 1.3, prohibiting judges from using the prestige of office to advance their own or others' interests, Rule 2.10, governing public comment on pending and impending matters, and Rule 3.1(C), prohibiting judges from engaging in extrajudicial activities that would appear to a reasonable person to undermine the judge's independence, integrity, or impartiality.

[3]   In general, it would be an unnecessary and unfair burden to prohibit judges from appearing before governmental bodies or consulting with government officials on matters that are likely to affect them as private citizens, such as zoning proposals affecting their real property. In engaging in such activities, however, judges must not refer to their judicial positions, and must otherwise exercise caution to avoid using the prestige of judicial office.

RULE 3.3: Testifying as a Character Witness

A judge shall not testify as a character witness in a judicial, administrative, or other adjudicatory proceeding or otherwise vouch for the character of a person in a legal proceeding, except when duly summoned.

Comment

[1]   A judge who, without being subpoenaed, testifies as a character witness abuses the prestige of judicial office to advance the interests of another. See Rule 1.3. Except in unusual circumstances where the demands of justice require, a judge should discourage a party from requiring the judge to testify as a character witness.

RULE 3.4: Appointments to Governmental Positions

A judge shall not accept appointment to a governmental committee, board, commission, or other governmental position, unless it is one that concerns the law, the legal system, or the administration of justice.

Comment

[1]   Rule 3.4 implicitly acknowledges the value of judges accepting appointments to entities that concern the law, the legal system, or the administration of justice. Even in such instances, however, a judge should assess the appropriateness of accepting an appointment, paying particular

---

*   See, Terminology.

attention to the subject matter of the appointment and the availability and allocation of judicial resources, including the judge's time commitments, and giving due regard to the requirements of the independence and impartiality of the judiciary.

[2]   A judge may represent his or her country, state, or locality on ceremonial occasions or in connection with historical, educational, or cultural activities. Such representation does not constitute acceptance of a government position.

RULE 3.5: Use of Nonpublic Information

A judge shall not intentionally disclose or use nonpublic information* acquired in a judicial capacity for any purpose unrelated to the judge's judicial duties.

Comment

[1]   In the course of performing judicial duties, a judge may acquire information of commercial or other value that is unavailable to the public. The judge must not reveal or use such information for personal gain or for any purpose unrelated to his or her judicial duties.

[2]   This rule is not intended, however, to affect a judge's ability to act on information as necessary to protect the health or safety of the judge or a member of a judge's family, court personnel, or other judicial officers if consistent with other provisions of this Code.

RULE 3.6: Affiliation with Discriminatory Organizations

(A) A judge shall not hold membership in any organization that practices invidious discrimination on the basis of race, sex, gender, religion, national origin, ethnicity, or sexual orientation.

(B) A judge shall not use the benefits or facilities of an organization if the judge knows* or should know that the organization practices invidious discrimination on one or more of the bases identified in paragraph (A). A judge's attendance at an event in a facility of an organization that the judge is not permitted to join is not a violation of this Rule when the judge's attendance is an isolated event that could not reasonably be perceived as an endorsement of the organization's practices.

Comment

[1]   A judge's public manifestation of approval of invidious discrimination on any basis gives rise to the appearance of impropriety and diminishes public confidence in the integrity and impartiality of the judiciary. A judge's membership in an organization that practices invidious discrimination creates the perception that the judge's impartiality is impaired.

[2]   An organization is generally said to discriminate invidiously if it arbitrarily excludes from membership on the basis of race, sex, gender, religion, national origin, ethnicity, or sexual orientation persons who would otherwise be eligible for admission. Whether an organization practices invidious discrimination is a complex question to which judges should be attentive. The answer cannot be determined from a mere examination of an organization's current membership rolls, but rather, depends upon how the

---

*   See, Terminology.

organization selects members, as well as other relevant factors, such as whether the organization is dedicated to the preservation of religious, ethnic, or cultural values of legitimate common interest to its members, or whether it is an intimate, purely private organization whose membership limitations could not constitutionally be prohibited.

[3]   When a judge learns that an organization to which the judge belongs engages in invidious discrimination, the judge must resign immediately from the organization.

[4]   A judge's membership in a religious organization as a lawful exercise of the freedom of religion is not a violation of this Rule.

[5]   This Rule does not apply to national or state military service.

RULE 3.7: Participation in Educational, Religious, Charitable, Fraternal, or Civic Organizations and Activities

(A) Subject to the requirements of Rule 3.1, a judge may participate in activities sponsored by organizations or governmental entities concerned with the law, the legal system, or the administration of justice, and those sponsored by or on behalf of educational, religious, charitable, fraternal, or civic organizations not conducted for profit, including but not limited to the following activities:

(1)   assisting such an organization or entity in planning related to fund-raising, and participating in the management and investment of the organization's or entity's funds;

(2)   soliciting* contributions* for such an organization or entity, but only from members of the judge's family,* or from judges over whom the judge does not exercise supervisory or appellate authority;

(3)   soliciting membership for such an organization or entity, even though the membership dues or fees generated may be used to support the objectives of the organization or entity, but only if the organization or entity is concerned with the law, the legal system, or the administration of justice;

(4)   appearing or speaking at, receiving an award or other recognition at, being featured on the program of, and permitting his or her title to be used in connection with an event of such an organization or entity, but if the event serves a fund-raising purpose, the judge may participate only if the event concerns the law, the legal system, or the administration of justice;

(5)   making recommendations to such a public or private fund-granting organization or entity in connection with its programs and activities, but only if the organization or entity is concerned with the law, the legal system, or the administration of justice; and

(6)   serving as an officer, director, trustee, or nonlegal advisor of such an organization or entity, unless it is likely that the organization or entity:

---

*   See, Terminology.

(a) will be engaged in proceedings that would ordinarily come before the judge; or

(b) will frequently be engaged in adversary proceedings in the court of which the judge is a member, or in any court subject to the appellate jurisdiction of the court of which the judge is a member.

(B) A judge may encourage lawyers to provide pro bono publico legal services.

Comment

[1]   The activities permitted by paragraph (A) generally include those sponsored by or undertaken on behalf of public or private not-for-profit educational institutions, and other not-for-profit organizations, including law-related, charitable, and other organizations.

[2]   Even for law-related organizations, a judge should consider whether the membership and purposes of the organization, or the nature of the judge's participation in or association with the organization, would conflict with the judge's obligation to refrain from activities that reflect adversely upon a judge's independence, integrity, and impartiality.

[3]   Mere attendance at an event, whether or not the event serves a fund-raising purpose, does not constitute a violation of paragraph 4(A). It is also generally permissible for a judge to serve as an usher or a food server or preparer, or to perform similar functions, at fund-raising events sponsored by educational, religious, charitable, fraternal, or civic organizations. Such activities are not solicitation and do not present an element of coercion or abuse the prestige of judicial office.

[4]   Identification of a judge's position in educational, religious, charitable, fraternal, or civic organizations on letterhead used for fund-raising or membership solicitation does not violate this Rule. The letterhead may list the judge's title or judicial office if comparable designations are used for other persons.

[5]   In addition to appointing lawyers to serve as counsel for indigent parties in individual cases, a judge may promote broader access to justice by encouraging lawyers to participate in pro bono publico legal services, if in doing so the judge does not employ coercion, or abuse the prestige of judicial office. Such encouragement may take many forms, including providing lists of available programs, training lawyers to do pro bono publico legal work, and participating in events recognizing lawyers who have done pro bono publico work.

RULE 3.8: Appointments to Fiduciary Positions

(A) A judge shall not accept appointment to serve in a fiduciary* position, such as executor, administrator, trustee, guardian, attorney in fact, or other personal representative, except for the estate, trust, or person of a member of the judge's family,* and then only if such service will not interfere with the proper performance of judicial duties.

(B) A judge shall not serve in a fiduciary position if the judge as fiduciary will likely be engaged in proceedings that would ordinarily come before the judge, or if the estate, trust, or ward becomes

---

*   See, Terminology.

involved in adversary proceedings in the court on which the judge serves, or one under its appellate jurisdiction.

(C) A judge acting in a fiduciary capacity shall be subject to the same restrictions on engaging in financial activities that apply to a judge personally.

(D) If a person who is serving in a fiduciary position becomes a judge, he or she must comply with this Rule as soon as reasonably practicable, but in no event later than [one year] after becoming a judge.

Comment

[1]   A judge should recognize that other restrictions imposed by this Code may conflict with a judge's obligations as a fiduciary; in such circumstances, a judge should resign as fiduciary. For example, serving as a fiduciary might require frequent disqualification of a judge under Rule 2.11 because a judge is deemed to have an economic interest in shares of stock held by a trust if the amount of stock held is more than de minimis.

RULE 3.9: Service as Arbitrator or Mediator

A judge shall not act as an arbitrator or a mediator or perform other judicial functions apart from the judge's official duties unless expressly authorized by law.*

Comment

[1]   This Rule does not prohibit a judge from participating in arbitration, mediation, or settlement conferences performed as part of assigned judicial duties. Rendering dispute resolution services apart from those duties, whether or not for economic gain, is prohibited unless it is expressly authorized by law.

RULE 3.10: Practice of Law

A judge shall not practice law. A judge may act pro se and may, without compensation, give legal advice to and draft or review documents for a member of the judge's family,* but is prohibited from serving as the family member's lawyer in any forum.

Comment

[1]   A judge may act pro se in all legal matters, including matters involving litigation and matters involving appearances before or other dealings with governmental bodies. A judge must not use the prestige of office to advance the judge's personal or family interests. See Rule 1.3.

RULE 3.11: Financial, Business, or Remunerative Activities

(A) A judge may hold and manage investments of the judge and members of the judge's family.*

(B) A judge shall not serve as an officer, director, manager, general partner, advisor, or employee of any business entity except that a judge may manage or participate in:

   (1)   a business closely held by the judge or members of the judge's family; or

---

*   See, Terminology.

(2) a business entity primarily engaged in investment of the financial resources of the judge or members of the judge's family.

(C) A judge shall not engage in financial activities permitted under paragraphs (A) and (B) if they will:

(1) interfere with the proper performance of judicial duties;

(2) lead to frequent disqualification of the judge;

(3) involve the judge in frequent transactions or continuing business relationships with lawyers or other persons likely to come before the court on which the judge serves; or

(4) result in violation of other provisions of this Code.

Comment

[1] Judges are generally permitted to engage in financial activities, including managing real estate and other investments for themselves or for members of their families. Participation in these activities, like participation in other extrajudicial activities, is subject to the requirements of this Code. For example, it would be improper for a judge to spend so much time on business activities that it interferes with the performance of judicial duties. See Rule 2.1. Similarly, it would be improper for a judge to use his or her official title or appear in judicial robes in business advertising, or to conduct his or her business or financial affairs in such a way that disqualification is frequently required. See Rules 1.3 and 2.11.

[2] As soon as practicable without serious financial detriment, the judge must divest himself or herself of investments and other financial interests that might require frequent disqualification or otherwise violate this Rule.

RULE 3.12: Compensation for Extrajudicial Activities

A judge may accept reasonable compensation for extrajudicial activities permitted by this Code or other law* unless such acceptance would appear to a reasonable person to undermine the judge's independence,* integrity,* or impartiality.*

Comment

[1] A judge is permitted to accept honoraria, stipends, fees, wages, salaries, royalties, or other compensation for speaking, teaching, writing, and other extrajudicial activities, provided the compensation is reasonable and commensurate with the task performed. The judge should be mindful, however, that judicial duties must take precedence over other activities. See Rule 2.1.

[2] Compensation derived from extrajudicial activities may be subject to public reporting. See Rule 3.15.

RULE 3.13: Acceptance and Reporting of Gifts, Loans, Bequests, Benefits, or Other Things of Value

(A) A judge shall not accept any gifts, loans, bequests, benefits, or other things of value, if acceptance is prohibited by law* or would

---

* See, Terminology.

appear to a reasonable person to undermine the judge's independence,* integrity,* or impartiality.*

(B) Unless otherwise prohibited by law, or by paragraph (A), a judge may accept the following without publicly reporting such acceptance:

(1) items with little intrinsic value, such as plaques, certificates, trophies, and greeting cards;

(2) gifts, loans, bequests, benefits, or other things of value from friends, relatives, or other persons, including lawyers, whose appearance or interest in a proceeding pending* or impending* before the judge would in any event require disqualification of the judge under Rule 2.11;

(3) ordinary social hospitality;

(4) commercial or financial opportunities and benefits, including special pricing and discounts, and loans from lending institutions in their regular course of business, if the same opportunities and benefits or loans are made available on the same terms to similarly situated persons who are not judges;

(5) rewards and prizes given to competitors or participants in random drawings, contests, or other events that are open to persons who are not judges;

(6) scholarships, fellowships, and similar benefits or awards, if they are available to similarly situated persons who are not judges, based upon the same terms and criteria;

(7) books, magazines, journals, audiovisual materials, and other resource materials supplied by publishers on a complimentary basis for official use; or

(8) gifts, awards, or benefits associated with the business, profession, or other separate activity of a spouse, a domestic partner,* or other family member of a judge residing in the judge's household,* but that incidentally benefit the judge.

(C) Unless otherwise prohibited by law or by paragraph (A), a judge may accept the following items, and must report such acceptance to the extent required by Rule 3.15:

(1) gifts incident to a public testimonial;

(2) invitations to the judge and the judge's spouse, domestic partner, or guest to attend without charge:

(a) an event associated with a bar-related function or other activity relating to the law, the legal system, or the administration of justice; or

(b) an event associated with any of the judge's educational, religious, charitable, fraternal or civic activities permitted by this Code, if the same invitation is offered to nonjudges who are engaged in similar ways in the activity as is the judge; and

---

*   See, Terminology.

(3) gifts, loans, bequests, benefits, or other things of value, if the source is a party or other person, including a lawyer, who has come or is likely to come before the judge, or whose interests have come or are likely to come before the judge.

Comment

[1] Whenever a judge accepts a gift or other thing of value without paying fair market value, there is a risk that the benefit might be viewed as intended to influence the judge's decision in a case. Rule 3.13 imposes restrictions upon the acceptance of such benefits, according to the magnitude of the risk. Paragraph (B) identifies circumstances in which the risk that the acceptance would appear to undermine the judge's independence, integrity, or impartiality is low, and explicitly provides that such items need not be publicly reported. As the value of the benefit or the likelihood that the source of the benefit will appear before the judge increases, the judge is either prohibited under paragraph (A) from accepting the gift, or required under paragraph (C) to publicly report it.

[2] Gift-giving between friends and relatives is a common occurrence, and ordinarily does not create an appearance of impropriety or cause reasonable persons to believe that the judge's independence, integrity, or impartiality has been compromised. In addition, when the appearance of friends or relatives in a case would require the judge's disqualification under Rule 2.11, there would be no opportunity for a gift to influence the judge's decision making. Paragraph (B)(2) places no restrictions upon the ability of a judge to accept gifts or other things of value from friends or relatives under these circumstances, and does not require public reporting.

[3] Businesses and financial institutions frequently make available special pricing, discounts, and other benefits, either in connection with a temporary promotion or for preferred customers, based upon longevity of the relationship, volume of business transacted, and other factors. A judge may freely accept such benefits if they are available to the general public, or if the judge qualifies for the special price or discount according to the same criteria as are applied to persons who are not judges. As an example, loans provided at generally prevailing interest rates are not gifts, but a judge could not accept a loan from a financial institution at below-market interest rates unless the same rate was being made available to the general public for a certain period of time or only to borrowers with specified qualifications that the judge also possesses.

[4] Rule 3.13 applies only to acceptance of gifts or other things of value by a judge. Nonetheless, if a gift or other benefit is given to the judge's spouse, domestic partner, or member of the judge's family residing in the judge's household, it may be viewed as an attempt to evade Rule 3.13 and influence the judge indirectly. Where the gift or benefit is being made primarily to such other persons, and the judge is merely an incidental beneficiary, this concern is reduced. A judge should, however, remind family and household members of the restrictions imposed upon judges, and urge them to take these restrictions into account when making decisions about accepting such gifts or benefits.

[5] Rule 3.13 does not apply to contributions to a judge's campaign for judicial office. Such contributions are governed by other Rules of this Code, including Rules 4.3 and 4.4.

RULE 3.14: Reimbursement of Expenses and Waivers of Fees or Charges

(A) Unless otherwise prohibited by Rules 3.1 and 3.13(A) or other law,* a judge may accept reimbursement of necessary and reasonable expenses for travel, food, lodging, or other incidental expenses, or a waiver or partial waiver of fees or charges for registration, tuition, and similar items, from sources other than the judge's employing entity, if the expenses or charges are associated with the judge's participation in extrajudicial activities permitted by this Code.

(B) Reimbursement of expenses for necessary travel, food, lodging, or other incidental expenses shall be limited to the actual costs reasonably incurred by the judge and, when appropriate to the occasion, by the judge's spouse, domestic partner,* or guest.

(C) A judge who accepts reimbursement of expenses or waivers or partial waivers of fees or charges on behalf of the judge or the judge's spouse, domestic partner, or guest shall publicly report such acceptance as required by Rule 3.15.

Comment

[1] Educational, civic, religious, fraternal, and charitable organizations often sponsor meetings, seminars, symposia, dinners, awards ceremonies, and similar events. Judges are encouraged to attend educational programs, as both teachers and participants, in law-related and academic disciplines, in furtherance of their duty to remain competent in the law. Participation in a variety of other extrajudicial activity is also permitted and encouraged by this Code.

[2] Not infrequently, sponsoring organizations invite certain judges to attend seminars or other events on a fee-waived or partial-fee-waived basis, and sometimes include reimbursement for necessary travel, food, lodging, or other incidental expenses. A judge's decision whether to accept reimbursement of expenses or a waiver or partial waiver of fees or charges in connection with these or other extrajudicial activities must be based upon an assessment of all the circumstances. The judge must undertake a reasonable inquiry to obtain the information necessary to make an informed judgment about whether acceptance would be consistent with the requirements of this Code.

[3] A judge must assure himself or herself that acceptance of reimbursement or fee waivers would not appear to a reasonable person to undermine the judge's independence, integrity, or impartiality. The factors that a judge should consider when deciding whether to accept reimbursement or a fee waiver for attendance at a particular activity include:

(a) whether the sponsor is an accredited educational institution or bar association rather than a trade association or a for-profit entity;

(b) whether the funding comes largely from numerous contributors rather than from a single entity and is earmarked for programs with specific content;

---

*　See, Terminology.

(c)   whether the content is related or unrelated to the subject matter of litigation pending or impending before the judge, or to matters that are likely to come before the judge;

(d)   whether the activity is primarily educational rather than recreational, and whether the costs of the event are reasonable and comparable to those associated with similar events sponsored by the judiciary, bar associations, or similar groups;

(e)   whether information concerning the activity and its funding sources is available upon inquiry;

(f)   whether the sponsor or source of funding is generally associated with particular parties or interests currently appearing or likely to appear in the judge's court, thus possibly requiring disqualification of the judge under Rule 2.11;

(g)   whether differing viewpoints are presented; and

(h)   whether a broad range of judicial and nonjudicial participants are invited, whether a large number of participants are invited, and whether the program is designed specifically for judges.

RULE 3.15: Reporting Requirements

(A) A judge shall publicly report the amount or value of:

(1)   compensation received for extrajudicial activities as permitted by Rule 3.12;

(2)   gifts and other things of value as permitted by Rule 3.13(C), unless the value of such items, alone or in the aggregate with other items received from the same source in the same calendar year, does not exceed $[insert amount]; and

(3)   reimbursement of expenses and waiver of fees or charges permitted by Rule 3.14(A), unless the amount of reimbursement or waiver, alone or in the aggregate with other reimbursements or waivers received from the same source in the same calendar year, does not exceed $[insert amount].

(B) When public reporting is required by paragraph (A), a judge shall report the date, place, and nature of the activity for which the judge received any compensation; the description of any gift, loan, bequest, benefit, or other thing of value accepted; and the source of reimbursement of expenses or waiver or partial waiver of fees or charges.

(C) The public report required by paragraph (A) shall be made at least annually, except that for reimbursement of expenses and waiver or partial waiver of fees or charges, the report shall be made within thirty days following the conclusion of the event or program.

(D) Reports made in compliance with this Rule shall be filed as public documents in the office of the clerk of the court on which the judge serves or other office designated by law,* and, when technically feasible, posted by the court or office personnel on the court's website.

---

*   See, Terminology.

CANON 4

A judge or candidate for judicial office shall not engage in political or campaign activity that is inconsistent with the independence, integrity, or impartiality of the judiciary.

RULE 4.1: Political and Campaign Activities of Judges and Judicial Candidates in General

(A) Except as permitted by law,* or by Rules 4.2, 4.3, and 4.4, a judge or a judicial candidate* shall not:

(1) act as a leader in, or hold an office in, a political organization;*

(2) make speeches on behalf of a political organization;

(3) publicly endorse or oppose a candidate for any public office;

(4) solicit funds for, pay an assessment to, or make a contribution* to a political organization or a candidate for public office;

(5) attend or purchase tickets for dinners or other events sponsored by a political organization or a candidate for public office;

(6) publicly identify himself or herself as a candidate of a political organization;

(7) seek, accept, or use endorsements from a political organization;

(8) personally solicit* or accept campaign contributions other than through a campaign committee authorized by Rule 4.4;

(9) use or permit the use of campaign contributions for the private benefit of the judge, the candidate, or others;

(10) use court staff, facilities, or other court resources in a campaign for judicial office;

(11) knowingly,* or with reckless disregard for the truth, make any false or misleading statement;

(12) make any statement that would reasonably be expected to affect the outcome or impair the fairness of a matter pending* or impending* in any court; or

(13) in connection with cases, controversies, or issues that are likely to come before the court, make pledges, promises, or commitments that are inconsistent with the impartial* performance of the adjudicative duties of judicial office.

(B) A judge or judicial candidate shall take reasonable measures to ensure that other persons do not undertake, on behalf of the judge or judicial candidate, any activities prohibited under paragraph (A).

---

*   See, Terminology.

Comment

GENERAL CONSIDERATIONS

[1]   Even when subject to public election, a judge plays a role different from that of a legislator or executive branch official. Rather than making decisions based upon the expressed views or preferences of the electorate, a judge makes decisions based upon the law and the facts of every case. Therefore, in furtherance of this interest, judges and judicial candidates must, to the greatest extent possible, be free and appear to be free from political influence and political pressure. This Canon imposes narrowly tailored restrictions upon the political and campaign activities of all judges and judicial candidates, taking into account the various methods of selecting judges.

[2]   When a person becomes a judicial candidate, this Canon becomes applicable to his or her conduct.

PARTICIPATION IN POLITICAL ACTIVITIES

[3]   Public confidence in the independence and impartiality of the judiciary is eroded if judges or judicial candidates are perceived to be subject to political influence. Although judges and judicial candidates may register to vote as members of a political party, they are prohibited by paragraph (A)(1) from assuming leadership roles in political organizations.

[4]   Paragraphs (A)(2) and (A)(3) prohibit judges and judicial candidates from making speeches on behalf of political organizations or publicly endorsing or opposing candidates for public office, respectively, to prevent them from abusing the prestige of judicial office to advance the interests of others. See Rule 1.3. These Rules do not prohibit candidates from campaigning on their own behalf, or from endorsing or opposing candidates for the same judicial office for which they are running. See Rules 4.2(B)(2) and 4.2(B)(3).

[5]   Although members of the families of judges and judicial candidates are free to engage in their own political activity, including running for public office, there is no "family exception" to the prohibition in paragraph (A)(3) against a judge or candidate publicly endorsing candidates for public office. A judge or judicial candidate must not become involved in, or publicly associated with, a family member's political activity or campaign for public office. To avoid public misunderstanding, judges and judicial candidates should take, and should urge members of their families to take, reasonable steps to avoid any implication that they endorse any family member's candidacy or other political activity.

[6]   Judges and judicial candidates retain the right to participate in the political process as voters in both primary and general elections. For purposes of this Canon, participation in a caucus-type election procedure does not constitute public support for or endorsement of a political organization or candidate, and is not prohibited by paragraphs (A)(2) or (A)(3).

STATEMENTS AND COMMENTS MADE DURING A CAMPAIGN FOR JUDICIAL OFFICE

[7]   Judicial candidates must be scrupulously fair and accurate in all statements made by them and by their campaign committees. Paragraph (A)(11) obligates candidates and their committees to refrain from making statements that are false or misleading, or that omit facts necessary to make the communication considered as a whole not materially misleading.

[8]   Judicial candidates are sometimes the subject of false, misleading, or unfair allegations made by opposing candidates, third parties, or the media. For example, false or misleading statements might be made regarding the identity, present position, experience, qualifications, or judicial rulings of a candidate. In other situations, false or misleading allegations may be made that bear upon a candidate's integrity or fitness for judicial office. As long as the candidate does not violate paragraphs (A)(11) (A)(12), or (A)(13), the candidate may make a factually accurate public response. In addition, when an independent third party has made unwarranted attacks on a candidate's opponent, the candidate may disavow the attacks, and request the third party to cease and desist.

[9]   Subject to paragraph (A)(12), a judicial candidate is permitted to respond directly to false, misleading, or unfair allegations made against him or her during a campaign, although it is preferable for someone else to respond if the allegations relate to a pending case.

[10] Paragraph (A)(12) prohibits judicial candidates from making comments that might impair the fairness of pending or impending judicial proceedings. This provision does not restrict arguments or statements to the court or jury by a lawyer who is a judicial candidate, or rulings, statements, or instructions by a judge that may appropriately affect the outcome of a matter.

PLEDGES, PROMISES, OR COMMITMENTS INCONSISTENT WITH IMPARTIAL PERFORMANCE OF THE ADJUDICATIVE DUTIES OF JUDICIAL OFFICE

[11] The role of a judge is different from that of a legislator or executive branch official, even when the judge is subject to public election. Campaigns for judicial office must be conducted differently from campaigns for other offices. The narrowly drafted restrictions upon political and campaign activities of judicial candidates provided in Canon 4 allow candidates to conduct campaigns that provide voters with sufficient information to permit them to distinguish between candidates and make informed electoral choices.

[12] Paragraph (A)(13) makes applicable to both judges and judicial candidates the prohibition that applies to judges in Rule 2.10(B), relating to pledges, promises, or commitments that are inconsistent with the impartial performance of the adjudicative duties of judicial office.

[13] The making of a pledge, promise, or commitment is not dependent upon, or limited to, the use of any specific words or phrases; instead, the totality of the statement must be examined to determine if a reasonable person would believe that the candidate for judicial office has specifically undertaken to reach a particular result. Pledges, promises, or commitments must be contrasted with statements or announcements of personal views on legal, political, or other issues, which are not prohibited. When making such statements, a judge should acknowledge the overarching judicial obligation to apply and uphold the law, without regard to his or her personal views.

[14] A judicial candidate may make campaign promises related to judicial organization, administration, and court management, such as a promise to dispose of a backlog of cases, start court sessions on time, or avoid favoritism in appointments and hiring. A candidate may also pledge to take action outside the courtroom, such as working toward an improved jury selection system, or advocating for more funds to improve the physical plant and amenities of the courthouse.

[15] Judicial candidates may receive questionnaires or requests for interviews from the media and from issue advocacy or other community

organizations that seek to learn their views on disputed or controversial legal or political issues. Paragraph (A)(13) does not specifically address judicial responses to such inquiries. Depending upon the wording and format of such questionnaires, candidates' responses might be viewed as pledges, promises, or commitments to perform the adjudicative duties of office other than in an impartial way. To avoid violating paragraph (A)(13), therefore, candidates who respond to media and other inquiries should also give assurances that they will keep an open mind and will carry out their adjudicative duties faithfully and impartially if elected. Candidates who do not respond may state their reasons for not responding, such as the danger that answering might be perceived by a reasonable person as undermining a successful candidate's independence or impartiality, or that it might lead to frequent disqualification. See Rule 2.11.

RULE 4.2: Political and Campaign Activities of Judicial Candidates in Public Elections

(A) A judicial candidate* in a partisan, nonpartisan, or retention public election* shall:

(1) act at all times in a manner consistent with the independence,* integrity,* and impartiality* of the judiciary;

(2) comply with all applicable election, election campaign, and election campaign fund-raising laws and regulations of this jurisdiction;

(3) review and approve the content of all campaign statements and materials produced by the candidate or his or her campaign committee, as authorized by Rule 4.4, before their dissemination; and

(4) take reasonable measures to ensure that other persons do not undertake on behalf of the candidate activities, other than those described in Rule 4.4, that the candidate is prohibited from doing by Rule 4.1.

(B) A candidate for elective judicial office may, unless prohibited by law,* and not earlier than [insert amount of time] before the first applicable primary election, caucus, or general or retention election:

(1) establish a campaign committee pursuant to the provisions of Rule 4.4;

(2) speak on behalf of his or her candidacy through any medium, including but not limited to advertisements, websites, or other campaign literature;

(3) publicly endorse or oppose candidates for the same judicial office for which he or she is running;

(4) attend or purchase tickets for dinners or other events sponsored by a political organization* or a candidate for public office;

(5) seek, accept, or use endorsements from any person or organization other than a partisan political organization; and

---

*   See, Terminology.

(6) contribute to a political organization or candidate for public office, but not more than $[insert amount] to any one organization or candidate.

(C) A judicial candidate in a partisan public election may, unless prohibited by law, and not earlier than [insert amount of time] before the first applicable primary election, caucus, or general election:

(1) identify himself or herself as a candidate of a political organization; and

(2) seek, accept, and use endorsements of a political organization.

Comment

[1] Paragraphs (B) and (C) permit judicial candidates in public elections to engage in some political and campaign activities otherwise prohibited by Rule 4.1. Candidates may not engage in these activities earlier than [insert amount of time] before the first applicable electoral event, such as a caucus or a primary election.

[2] Despite paragraphs (B) and (C), judicial candidates for public election remain subject to many of the provisions of Rule 4.1. For example, a candidate continues to be prohibited from soliciting funds for a political organization, knowingly making false or misleading statements during a campaign, or making certain promises, pledges, or commitments related to future adjudicative duties. See Rule 4.1(A), paragraphs (4), (11), and (13).

[3] In partisan public elections for judicial office, a candidate may be nominated by, affiliated with, or otherwise publicly identified or associated with a political organization, including a political party. This relationship may be maintained throughout the period of the public campaign, and may include use of political party or similar designations on campaign literature and on the ballot.

[4] In nonpartisan public elections or retention elections, paragraph (B)(5) prohibits a candidate from seeking, accepting, or using nominations or endorsements from a partisan political organization.

[5] Judicial candidates are permitted to attend or purchase tickets for dinners and other events sponsored by political organizations.

[6] For purposes of paragraph (B)(3), candidates are considered to be running for the same judicial office if they are competing for a single judgeship or if several judgeships on the same court are to be filled as a result of the election. In endorsing or opposing another candidate for a position on the same court, a judicial candidate must abide by the same rules governing campaign conduct and speech as apply to the candidate's own campaign.

[7] Although judicial candidates in nonpartisan public elections are prohibited from running on a ticket or slate associated with a political organization, they may group themselves into slates or other alliances to conduct their campaigns more effectively. Candidates who have grouped themselves together are considered to be running for the same judicial office if they satisfy the conditions described in Comment [6].

RULE 4.3: Activities of Candidates for Appointive Judicial Office

A candidate for appointment to judicial office may:

(A) communicate with the appointing or confirming authority, including any selection, screening, or nominating commission or similar agency; and

(B) seek endorsements for the appointment from any person or organization other than a partisan political organization.

Comment

[1] When seeking support or endorsement, or when communicating directly with an appointing or confirming authority, a candidate for appointive judicial office must not make any pledges, promises, or commitments that are inconsistent with the impartial performance of the adjudicative duties of the office. See Rule 4.1(A)(13).

RULE 4.4: Campaign Committees

(A) A judicial candidate* subject to public election* may establish a campaign committee to manage and conduct a campaign for the candidate, subject to the provisions of this Code. The candidate is responsible for ensuring that his or her campaign committee complies with applicable provisions of this Code and other applicable law.*

(B) A judicial candidate subject to public election shall direct his or her campaign committee:

(1) to solicit and accept only such campaign contributions* as are reasonable, in any event not to exceed, in the aggregate,* $[insert amount] from any individual or $[insert amount] from any entity or organization;

(2) not to solicit or accept contributions for a candidate's current campaign more than [insert amount of time] before the applicable primary election, caucus, or general or retention election, nor more than [insert number] days after the last election in which the candidate participated; and

(3) to comply with all applicable statutory requirements for disclosure and divestiture of campaign contributions, and to file with [name of appropriate regulatory authority] a report stating the name, address, occupation, and employer of each person who has made campaign contributions to the committee in an aggregate value exceeding $[insert amount]. The report must be filed within [insert number] days following an election, or within such other period as is provided by law.

Comment

[1] Judicial candidates are prohibited from personally soliciting campaign contributions or personally accepting campaign contributions. See Rule 4.1(A)(8). This Rule recognizes that in many jurisdictions, judicial candidates must raise campaign funds to support their candidacies, and permits candidates, other than candidates for appointive judicial office, to

---

* See, Terminology.

establish campaign committees to solicit and accept reasonable financial contributions or in-kind contributions.

[2] Campaign committees may solicit and accept campaign contributions, manage the expenditure of campaign funds, and generally conduct campaigns. Candidates are responsible for compliance with the requirements of election law and other applicable law, and for the activities of their campaign committees.

[3] At the start of a campaign, the candidate must instruct the campaign committee to solicit or accept only such contributions as are reasonable in amount, appropriate under the circumstances, and in conformity with applicable law. Although lawyers and others who might appear before a successful candidate for judicial office are permitted to make campaign contributions, the candidate should instruct his or her campaign committee to be especially cautious in connection with such contributions, so they do not create grounds for disqualification if the candidate is elected to judicial office. See Rule 2.11.

RULE 4.5: Activities of Judges Who Become Candidates for Nonjudicial Office

(A)   Upon becoming a candidate for a nonjudicial elective office, a judge shall resign from judicial office, unless permitted by law* to continue to hold judicial office.

(B)   Upon becoming a candidate for a nonjudicial appointive office, a judge is not required to resign from judicial office, provided that the judge complies with the other provisions of this Code.

Comment

[1]   In campaigns for nonjudicial elective public office, candidates may make pledges, promises, or commitments related to positions they would take and ways they would act if elected to office. Although appropriate in nonjudicial campaigns, this manner of campaigning is inconsistent with the role of a judge, who must remain fair and impartial to all who come before him or her. The potential for misuse of the judicial office, and the political promises that the judge would be compelled to make in the course of campaigning for nonjudicial elective office, together dictate that a judge who wishes to run for such an office must resign upon becoming a candidate.

[2]   The "resign to run" rule set forth in paragraph (A) ensures that a judge cannot use the judicial office to promote his or her candidacy, and prevents post-campaign retaliation from the judge in the event the judge is defeated in the election. When a judge is seeking appointive nonjudicial office, however, the dangers are not sufficient to warrant imposing the "resign to run" rule.

---

*   See, Terminology.

CALIFORNIA CODE OF JUDICIAL ETHICS

Effective December 1, 2016

Adopted by the Supreme Court of California effective January 15, 1996. Amended March 4, 1999, December 13, 2000, December 30, 2002, June 18, 2003, December 22, 2003, January 1, 2005, June 1, 2005, July 1, 2006, January 1, 2007, January 1, 2008, April 29, 2009, January 1, 2013, January 21, 2015, and August 19, 2016.

Preface

Preamble

Terminology

Canon 1. A Judge Shall Uphold the Integrity and Independence of the Judiciary.

Canon 2. A Judge Shall Avoid Impropriety and the Appearance of Impropriety in All of the Judge's Activities.

Canon 3. A Judge Shall Perform the Duties of Judicial Office Impartially, Competently, and Diligently.

Canon 4. A Judge Shall So Conduct the Judge's Quasi-Judicial and Extrajudicial Activities as to Minimize the Risk of Conflict With Judicial Obligations.

Canon 5. A Judge or Candidate for Judicial Office Shall Not Engage in Political or Campaign Activity That Is Inconsistent With the Independence, Integrity, or Impartiality of the Judiciary.

Canon 6. Compliance With the Code of Judicial Ethics.

PREFACE

Formal standards of judicial conduct have existed for more than 65 years. The original Canons of Judicial Ethics promulgated by the American Bar Association were modified and adopted in 1949 for application in California by the Conference of California Judges (now the California Judges Association).

In 1969, the American Bar Association determined that then current needs and problems warranted revision of the canons. In the revision process, a special American Bar Association committee, headed by former California Chief Justice Roger Traynor, sought and considered the views of the bench and bar and other interested persons. The American Bar Association Code of Judicial Conduct was adopted by the House of Delegates of the American Bar Association August 16, 1972.

Effective January 5, 1975, the California Judges Association adopted a new California Code of Judicial Conduct adapted from the American Bar Association 1972 Model Code. The California code was recast in gender-neutral form in 1986.

In 1990, the American Bar Association Model Code was further revised after a lengthy study. The California Judges Association again reviewed the model code and adopted a revised California Code of Judicial Conduct on October 5, 1992.

Proposition 190 (amending Cal. Const., art. VI, § 18, subd. (m), operative March 1, 1995) created a new constitutional provision that states, "The Supreme Court shall make rules for the conduct of judges, both on and off the bench, and for judicial candidates in the conduct of their campaigns. These rules shall be referred to as the Code of Judicial Ethics."

The Supreme Court formally adopted the 1992 Code of Judicial Conduct in March 1995, as a transitional measure pending further review.

The Supreme Court formally adopted the Code of Judicial Ethics effective January 15, 1996.

The Supreme Court has formally adopted amendments to the Code of Judicial Ethics on several occasions. The Advisory Committee Commentary is published by the Supreme Court Advisory Committee on the Code of Judicial Ethics.

PREAMBLE

Our legal system is based on the principle that an independent, fair, and competent judiciary will interpret and apply the laws that govern us. The role of the judiciary is central to American concepts of justice and the rule of law. Intrinsic to this code are the precepts that judges, individually and collectively, must respect and honor the judicial office as a public trust and must strive to enhance and maintain confidence in our legal system. The judge is an arbiter of facts and law for the resolution of disputes and is a highly visible member of government under the rule of law.

The Code of Judicial Ethics ("code") establishes standards for ethical conduct of judges on and off the bench and for candidates for judicial office.* The code consists of broad declarations called canons, with subparts, and a terminology section. Following many canons is a commentary section prepared by the Supreme Court Advisory Committee on the Code of Judicial Ethics. The commentary, by explanation and example, provides guidance as to the purpose and meaning of the canons. The commentary does not constitute additional rules and should not be so construed. All members of the judiciary must comply with the code. Compliance is required to preserve the integrity* of the bench and to ensure the confidence of the public.

The canons should be read together as a whole, and each provision should be construed in context and consistent with every other provision. They are to be applied in conformance with constitutional requirements, statutes, other court rules, and decisional law. Nothing in the code shall either impair the essential independence* of judges in making judicial decisions or provide a separate basis for civil liability or criminal prosecution.

The code governs the conduct of judges and candidates for judicial office* and is binding upon them. Whether disciplinary action is appropriate, and the degree of discipline to be imposed, requires a reasoned application of the text and consideration of such factors as the seriousness of the transgression, if there is a pattern of improper activity, and the effect of the improper activity on others or on the judicial system.

TERMINOLOGY

Terms explained below are noted with an asterisk (*) in the canons where they appear. In addition, the canons in which these terms appear are cited after the explanation of each term below.

"**Candidate for judicial office**" is a person seeking election to or retention of a judicial office. A person becomes a candidate for judicial office as soon as he or she makes a public announcement of candidacy, declares or files as a candidate with the election authority, or authorizes solicitation or acceptance of contributions or support. See Preamble and Canons 3E(2)(b)(i), 3E(3)(a), 5, 5A, 5A (Commentary), 5B(1), 5B(2), 5B(3), 5B (Commentary), 5C, 5D, and 6E.

"**Fiduciary**" includes such relationships as executor, administrator, trustee, and guardian. See Canons 3E(5)(d), 4E(1), 4E(2), 4E(3), 4E (Commentary), 6B, and 6F (Commentary).

"**Gift**" means anything of value to the extent that consideration of equal or greater value is not received and includes a rebate or discount in the price of anything of value unless the rebate or discount is made in the regular course of business to members of the public without regard to official status. See Canons 4D(5), 4D(5) (Commentary), 4D(6), 4D(6)(a), 4D(6)(b), 4D(6)(b) (Commentary), 4D(6)(d), 4D(6)(f), 4H (Commentary), 5A (Commentary), 6D(2)(c), and 6D(7).

"**Impartial**," "**impartiality**," and "**impartially**" mean the absence of bias or prejudice in favor of, or against, particular parties or classes of parties, as well as the maintenance of an open mind in considering issues that may come before a judge. See Canons 1, 1(Commentary), 2A, 2A (Commentary), 2B (Commentary), 2C (Commentary), 3, 3B(9) (Commentary), 3B(10) (Commentary), 3B(12), 3B(12) (Commentary), 3C(1), 3C(5), 3E(4)(b), 3E(4)(c), 4A(1), 4A (Commentary), 4C(3)(b) (Commentary), 4C(3)(c) (Commentary), 4D(1) (Commentary), 4D(6)(a) (Commentary), 4D(6)(b) (Commentary), 4D(6)(g) (Commentary), 4H (Commentary), 5, 5A, 5A (Commentary), 5B (Commentary), 6D(2)(a), and 6D(3)(a)(vii).

"**Impending proceeding**" is a proceeding or matter that is imminent or expected to occur in the near future. The words "proceeding" and "matter" are used interchangeably, and are intended to have the same meaning. See Canons 3B(7), 3B(7)(a), 3B(9), 3B(9) (Commentary), 4H (Commentary), and 6D(6). "Pending proceeding" is defined below.

"**Impropriety**" includes conduct that violates the law, court rules, or provisions of this code, as well as conduct that undermines a judge's independence, integrity, or impartiality. See Canons 2, 2A (Commentary), 2B (Commentary), 2C (Commentary), 3B(9) (Commentary), 4D(1)(b) (Commentary), 4D(6)(g) (Commentary), 4H, 5, and 5A (Commentary).

"**Independence**" means a judge's freedom from influence or controls other than as established by law. See Preamble, Canons 1, 1 (Commentary), 4C(2) (Commentary), 4D(6)(a) (Commentary), 4D(6)(g) (Commentary), 4H(3) (Commentary), 5, 5A (Commentary), 5B (Commentary), and 6D(1).

"**Integrity**" means probity, fairness, honesty, uprightness, and soundness of character. See Preamble, Canons 1, 1 (Commentary), 2A, 2A (Commentary), 2B (Commentary), 2C (Commentary), 3B(9) (Commentary), 3C(1), 3C(5), 4D(6)(a) (Commentary), 4D(6)(b) (Commentary), 4D(6)(g) (Commentary), 4H (Commentary), 5, 5A (Commentary), 5B (Commentary), and 6D(1).

"**Knowingly,**" "**knowledge,**" "**known,**" and "**knows**" mean actual knowledge of the fact in question. A person's knowledge may be inferred from circumstances. See Canons 2B(2)(b), 2B(2)(e), 2C (Commentary), 3B(2) (Commentary), 3B(7)(a), 3B(7)(a) (Commentary), 3D(2), 3D(5), 3E(5)(f), 5B(1)(b), 6D(3)(a)(i), 6D(3)(a) (Commentary), 6D(4) (Commentary), and 6D(5)(a).

"**Law**" means constitutional provisions, statutes, court rules, and decisional law. See Canons 1 (Commentary), 2A, 2C (Commentary), 3A, 3B(2), 3B(7), 3B(7)(c), 3B(8), 3B(8) (Commentary), 3B(12) (Commentary), 3E(1), 4C(3)(c) (Commentary), 4F, and 4H.

"**Law, the legal system, or the administration of justice.**" When a judge engages in an activity that relates to the law, the legal system, or the administration of justice, the judge should also consider factors such as whether the activity upholds the integrity, impartiality, and independence of the judiciary (Canons 1 and 2A), whether the activity impairs public confidence in the judiciary (Canon 2), whether the judge is allowing the activity to take precedence over judicial duties (Canon 3A), and whether engaging in the activity would cause the judge to be disqualified (Canon 4A(4)). See Canons 4B (Commentary), 4C(1), 4C(1) (Commentary), 4C(2), 4C(2) (Commentary), 4C(3)(a), 4C(3)(b) (Commentary), 4C(3)(d)(ii), 4C(3)(d) (Commentary), 4D(6)(d), 4D(6)(e), 5A (Commentary), 5D, and 5D (Commentary).

"**Member of the judge's family**" means a spouse, registered domestic partner, child, grandchild, parent, grandparent, or other relative or person with whom the judge maintains a close familial relationship. See Canons 2B(3)(c), 2B (Commentary), 4C(3)(d)(i), 4D(1) (Commentary), 4D(2), 4D(5) (Commentary), 4E(1), and 4G (Commentary).

"**Member of the judge's family residing in the judge's household**" means a spouse or registered domestic partner and those persons who reside in the judge's household and who are relatives of the judge, including relatives by marriage, or persons with whom the judge maintains a close familial relationship. See Canons 4D(5), 4D(5) (Commentary), 4D(6), 4D(6)(b) (Commentary), 4D(6)(f) and 6D(2)(c).

"**Nonpublic information**" means information that, by law, is not available to the public. Nonpublic information may include, but is not limited to, information that is sealed by statute or court order, impounded, or communicated in camera, and information offered in grand jury proceedings, presentencing reports, dependency cases, or psychiatric reports. Nonpublic information also includes information from affidavits, jury results, or court rulings before it becomes public knowledge. See Canons 3B(11) and 6D(8)(a).

"**Pending proceeding**" is a proceeding or matter that has commenced. A proceeding continues to be pending through any period during which an appeal may be filed and any appellate process until final disposition. The words "proceeding" and "matter" are used interchangeably, and are intended to have the same meaning. See Canons 2A (Commentary), 2B(3)(a), 3B(7), 3B(9), 3B(9) (Commentary), 3E(5)(a), 4H (Commentary), and 6D(6). "Impending proceeding" is defined above. 26

"**Political organization**" means a political party, political action committee, or other group, the principal purpose of which is to further the election or appointment of candidates to nonjudicial office. See Canon 5A.

"**Registered domestic partner**" means a person who has registered for domestic partnership pursuant to state law or who is recognized as a domestic partner pursuant to Family Code section 299.2. See Canons 3E(5)(d), 3E(5)(e), 3E(5)(i), 4D(6)(d), 4D(6)(f), 4D(6)(j), 4H(2), 5A (Commentary), 6D(3)(a)(v), and 6D(3)(a)(vi).

"**Require**." Any canon prescribing that a judge "require" certain conduct of others means that a judge is to exercise reasonable direction and control over the conduct of those persons subject to the judge's direction and control. See Canons 3B(3), 3B(4), 3B(6), 3B(8) (Commentary), 3B(9), 3C(3), 6D(1), 6D(2)(a), and 6D(6).

"**Service organization**" includes any organization commonly referred to as a "fraternal organization." See Canons 3E(5)(d), 4C(2) (Commentary), 4C(3)(b), 4C(3)(b) (Commentary), 4C(3)(d) (Commentary), 4D(6)(j), and 6D(2)(b).

"**Subordinate judicial officer**" A subordinate judicial officer is, for the purposes of this code, a person appointed pursuant to article VI, section 22 of the California Constitution, including, but not limited to, a commissioner, referee, and hearing officer. See Canons 3D(3), 4G (Commentary), and 6A.

"**Temporary Judge**" means an active or inactive member of the bar who, pursuant to article VI, section 21 of the California Constitution, serves or expects to serve as a judge once, sporadically, or regularly on a part-time basis under a separate court appointment for each period of service or for each case heard. See Canons 3E(5)(h), 4C(3)(d)(i), 4C(3)(d) (Commentary), 6A, and 6D.

"**Third degree of relationship**" includes the following persons: great-grandparent, grandparent, parent, uncle, aunt, brother, sister, child, grandchild, great-grandchild, nephew, and niece. See Canons 3E(5)(e), 3E(5)(i), and 6D(3)(a)(v).

CANON 1

A Judge Shall Uphold the Integrity* and Independence* of the Judiciary

An independent, impartial,* and honorable judiciary is indispensable to justice in our society. A judge should participate in establishing, maintaining, and enforcing high standards of conduct, and shall personally observe those standards so that the integrity* and independence* of the judiciary is preserved. The provisions of this code are to be construed and applied to further that objective. A judicial decision or administrative act later determined to be incorrect legally is not itself a violation of this code.

Advisory Committee Commentary: Canon 1

Deference to the judgments and rulings of courts depends upon public confidence in the integrity and independence* of judges. The integrity* and independence* of judges depend in turn upon their acting without fear or favor. Although judges should be independent, they must comply with the law* and the provisions of this code. Public confidence in the impartiality* of the judiciary is maintained by the adherence of each judge to this responsibility. Conversely, violations of this code diminish public confidence in the judiciary and thereby do injury to the system of government under law.*

---

* [Ed. Note: Terms noted with an asterisk (*) in the canons are defined in the Terminology section.]

The basic function of an independent, impartial,* and honorable judiciary is to maintain the utmost integrity* in decisionmaking, and this code should be read and interpreted with that function in mind.

CANON 2

A Judge Shall Avoid Impropriety* and the Appearance of Impropriety* in All of the Judge's Activities

A. Promoting Public Confidence

A judge shall respect and comply with the law* and shall act at all times in a manner that promotes public confidence in the integrity* and impartiality* of the judiciary. A judge shall not make statements, whether public or nonpublic, that commit the judge with respect to cases, controversies, or issues that are likely to come before the courts or that are inconsistent with the impartial performance of the adjudicative duties of judicial office.

Advisory Committee Commentary: Canons 2 and 2A

Public confidence in the judiciary is eroded by irresponsible or improper conduct by judges.

A judge must avoid all impropriety* and appearance of impropriety.* A judge must expect to be the subject of constant public scrutiny. A judge must therefore accept restrictions on the judge's conduct that might be viewed as burdensome by other members of the community and should do so freely and willingly.

The prohibition against behaving with impropriety* or the appearance of impropriety* applies to both the professional and personal conduct of a judge.

The test for the appearance of impropriety* is whether a person aware of the facts might reasonably entertain a doubt that the judge would be able to act with integrity,* impartiality,* and competence.

As to membership in organizations that practice invidious discrimination, see Commentary under Canon 2C.

As to judges making statements that commit the judge with respect to cases, controversies, or issues that are likely to come before the courts, see Canon 3B(9) and its commentary concerning comments about a pending proceeding,* Canon 3E(3)(a) concerning the disqualification of a judge who makes statements that commit the judge to a particular result, and Canon 5B(1)(a) concerning statements made during an election campaign that commit the candidate to a particular result. In addition, Code of Civil Procedure section 170.2, subdivision (b), provides that, with certain exceptions, a judge is not disqualified on the ground that the judge has, in any capacity, expressed a view on a legal or factual issue presented in the proceeding before the judge.

B. Use of the Prestige of Judicial Office

(1) A judge shall not allow family, social, political, or other relationships to influence the judge's judicial conduct or judgment, nor shall a judge convey or permit others to convey the impression that any individual is in a special position to influence the judge.

(2) A judge shall not lend the prestige of judicial office or use the judicial title in any manner, including any oral or written communication, to advance the pecuniary or personal interests of the judge or others. This canon does not prohibit the following:

(a)   A judge may testify as a character witness, provided the judge does so only when subpoenaed.

(b)   A judge may, without a subpoena, provide the Commission on Judicial Performance with a written communication containing (i) factual information regarding a matter pending before the commission or (ii) information related to the character of a judge who has a matter pending before the commission, provided that any such factual or character information is based on personal knowledge.* In commission proceedings, a judge shall provide information responsive to a subpoena or when officially requested to do so by the commission.

(c)   A judge may provide factual information in State Bar disciplinary proceedings and shall provide information responsive to a subpoena or when officially requested to do so by the State Bar.

(d)   A judge may respond to judicial selection inquiries, provide recommendations (including a general character reference relating to the evaluation of persons being considered for a judgeship), and otherwise participate in the process of judicial selection.

(e)   A judge may serve as a reference or provide a letter of recommendation only if based on the judge's personal knowledge* of the individual. These written communications may include the judge's title and may be written on stationery that uses the judicial title.

(3)   Except as permitted in subdivision (c) or otherwise authorized by law* or these canons:

(a)   A judge shall not advance the pecuniary or personal interests of the judge or others by initiating communications with a sentencing judge or a representative of a probation department about a proceeding pending* before the sentencing judge, but may provide information in response to an official request. "Sentencing judge" includes a judge who makes a disposition pursuant to Welfare and Institutions Code section 725.

(b)   A judge, other than the judge who presided over the trial of or sentenced the person seeking parole, pardon, or commutation of sentence, shall not initiate communications with the Board of Parole Hearings regarding parole or the Office of the Governor regarding parole, pardon, or commutation of sentence, but may provide these entities with information for the record in response to an official request.

(c)   A judge may initiate communications concerning a member of the judge's family* with a representative of a probation department regarding sentencing, the Board of Parole Hearings regarding parole, or the Office of the Governor regarding parole, pardon, or commutation of sentence, provided the judge is not identified as a judge in the communication.

Advisory Committee Commentary: Canon 2B

A strong judicial branch, based on the prestige that comes from effective and ethical performance, is essential to a system of government in which the judiciary functions independently of the executive and legislative branches. A judge should distinguish between proper and improper use of the prestige of office in all of his or her activities.

As to those communications that are permitted under this canon, a judge must keep in mind the general obligations to maintain high standards of conduct, as set forth in Canon 1, and to avoid any impropriety* or the *appearance of impropriety* as set forth in Canon 2. A judge must also be mindful of Canon 2A, which requires a judge to act at all times in a manner that promotes public confidence in the integrity* and impartiality* of the courts.*

A judge must avoid lending the prestige of judicial office for the advancement of the private interests of the judge or others. For example, a judge must not use the judicial position to gain advantage in a civil suit involving a member of the judge's family,* or use his or her position to gain deferential treatment when stopped by a police officer for a traffic offense.

As to the use of a judge's title to identify a judge's role in the presentation and creation of legal education programs and materials, see Commentary to Canon 4B. In contracts for publication of a judge's writings, a judge should retain control over the advertising, to the extent feasible, to avoid exploitation of the judge's office.

This canon does not afford a judge a privilege against testifying in response to any official summons.

See also Canons 3D(1) and 3D(2) concerning a judge's obligation to take appropriate corrective action regarding other judges who violate any provision of the Code of Judicial Ethics and attorneys who violate any provision of the Rules of Professional Conduct.

Except as set forth in Canon 2B(3)(a), this canon does not preclude consultations among judges. Additional limitations on such consultations among judges are set forth in Canon 3B(7)(a).

C. Membership in Organizations

A judge shall not hold membership in any organization that practices invidious discrimination on the basis of race, sex, gender, religion, national origin, ethnicity, or sexual orientation.

This canon does not apply to membership in a religious organization.

Advisory Committee Commentary: Canon 2C

Membership by a judge in an organization that practices invidious discrimination on the basis of race, sex, gender, religion, national origin, ethnicity, or sexual orientation gives rise to a perception that the judge's impartiality* is impaired. The code prohibits such membership by judges who preserve the fairness, impartiality,* independence,* and honor of the judiciary, to treat all parties equally under the law,* and to avoid impropriety* and the appearance of impropriety.*

Previously, Canon 2C contained exceptions to this prohibition for membership in religious organizations, membership in an official military organization of the United States and, so long as membership did not violate Canon 4A, membership in a nonprofit youth organization. The exceptions for membership in an official military organization of the United States and nonprofit youth organizations have been eliminated as exceptions to the canon. The exception for membership in religious organizations has been preserved.

Canon 2C refers to the current practices of the organization. Whether an organization practices invidious discrimination is often a complex question to which judges should be sensitive. The answer cannot be determined from a mere examination of an organization's current membership rolls but rather depends on how the organization selects members and other relevant factors, such as whether the organization is dedicated to the preservation of religious, ethnic, or cultural values of legitimate common interest to its members, or whether it is in fact and effect an intimate, purely private organization whose membership limitations could not be constitutionally prohibited. Absent such factors, an organization is generally said to discriminate invidiously if it arbitrarily excludes from membership on the basis of race, religion, sex, gender, national origin, ethnicity, or sexual orientation persons who would otherwise be admitted to membership.

Although Canon 2C relates only to membership in organizations that invidiously discriminate on the basis of race, sex, gender, religion, national origin, ethnicity, or sexual orientation, a judge's membership in an organization that engages in any discriminatory membership practices prohibited by law* also violates Canon 2 and Canon 2A and gives the appearance of impropriety.* In addition, it would be a violation of Canon 2 and Canon 2A for a judge to arrange a meeting at a club that the judge knows* practices such invidious discrimination or for the judge to use such a club regularly. Moreover, public manifestation by a judge of the judge's knowing* approval of invidious discrimination on any basis gives the appearance of impropriety* under Canon 2 and diminishes public confidence in the integrity* and impartiality* of the judiciary in violation of Canon 2A.

CANON 3

A Judge Shall Perform the Duties of Judicial Office Impartially,* Competently, and Diligently

A. Judicial Duties in General

All of the judicial duties prescribed by law* shall take precedence over all other activities of every judge. In the performance of these duties, the following standards apply.

B. Adjudicative Responsibilities

(1) A judge shall hear and decide all matters assigned to the judge except those in which he or she is disqualified.

Advisory Committee Commentary: Canon 3B(1)

Canon 3B(1) is based upon the affirmative obligation contained in Code of Civil Procedure section 170.

(2) A judge shall be faithful to the law* regardless of partisan interests, public clamor, or fear of criticism, and shall maintain professional competence in the law.*

Advisory Committee Commentary: Canon 3B(2)

Competence in the performance of judicial duties requires the legal knowledge,* skill, thoroughness, and preparation reasonably necessary to perform a judge's responsibilities of judicial office. Canon 1 provides that an incorrect legal ruling is not itself a violation of this code.

(3) A judge shall require* order and decorum in proceedings before the judge.

(4) A judge shall be patient, dignified, and courteous to litigants, jurors, witnesses, lawyers, and others with whom the judge deals in an official capacity, and shall require* similar conduct of lawyers and of all staff and court personnel under the judge's direction and control.

(5) A judge shall perform judicial duties without bias or prejudice. A judge shall not, in the performance of judicial duties, engage in speech, gestures, or other conduct that would reasonably be perceived as (a) bias or prejudice, including but not limited to bias or prejudice based upon race, sex, gender, religion, national origin, ethnicity, disability, age, sexual orientation,

marital status, socioeconomic status, or political affiliation, or (b) sexual harassment.

(6) A judge shall require* lawyers in proceedings before the judge to refrain from manifesting, by words or conduct, bias or prejudice based upon race, sex, gender, religion, national origin, ethnicity, disability, age, sexual orientation, marital status, socioeconomic status, or political affiliation against parties, witnesses, counsel, or others. This canon does not preclude legitimate advocacy when race, sex, gender, religion, national origin, ethnicity, disability, age, sexual orientation, marital status, socioeconomic status, political affiliation, or other similar factors are issues in the proceeding.

(7) A judge shall accord to every person who has a legal interest in a proceeding, or that person's lawyer, the full right to be heard according to law.* Unless otherwise authorized by law,* a judge shall not independently investigate facts in a proceeding and shall consider only the evidence presented or facts that may be properly judicially noticed. This prohibition extends to information available in all media, including electronic. A judge shall not initiate, permit, or consider ex parte communications, that is, any communications to or from the judge outside the presence of the parties concerning a pending* or impending* proceeding, and shall make reasonable efforts to avoid such communications, except as follows:

(a) Except as stated below, a judge may consult with other judges. A judge shall not engage in discussions about a case with a judge who has previously been disqualified from hearing that matter; likewise, a judge who knows* he or she is or would be disqualified from hearing a case shall not discuss that matter with the judge assigned to the case. A judge also shall not engage in discussions with a judge who may participate in appellate review of the matter, nor shall a judge who may participate in appellate review of a matter engage in discussions with the judge presiding over the case.

A judge may consult with court personnel or others authorized by law,* so as long as the communication relates to that person's duty to aid the judge in carrying out the judge's adjudicative responsibilities.

In any discussion with judges or court personnel, a judge shall make reasonable efforts to avoid receiving factual information that is not part of the record or an evaluation of that factual information. In such consultations, the judge shall not abrogate the responsibility personally to decide the matter.

For purposes of Canon 3B(7)(a), "court personnel" includes bailiffs, court reporters, court externs, research attorneys, courtroom clerks, and other employees of the court, but does not include the lawyers in a proceeding before a judge, persons who are appointed by the court to serve in some capacity in a proceeding, or employees of other governmental entities, such as lawyers, social workers, or 3 representatives of the probation department.

Advisory Committee Commentary: Canon 3B(7)(a)

Regarding communications between a judge presiding over a matter and a judge of a court with appellate jurisdiction over that matter, see *Government Code section 68070.5*

Though a judge may have ex parte discussions with appropriate court personnel, a judge may do so only on matters that are within the proper performance of that person's duties. For example, a bailiff may inform the judge of a threat to the judge or to the safety and security of the courtroom, but may not tell the judge ex parte that a defendant was overheard making an incriminating statement during a court recess. A clerk may point out to the judge a technical defect in a proposed sentence, but may not suggest to the judge that a defendant deserves a certain sentence.

A sentencing judge may not consult ex parte with a representative of the probation department about a matter pending before the sentencing judge.

This canon prohibits a judge from discussing a case with another judge who has already been disqualified. A judge also must be careful not to talk to a judge whom the judge knows* would be disqualified from hearing the matter.

(b) A judge may initiate, permit, or consider ex parte communications, where circumstances require, for scheduling, administrative purposes, or emergencies that do not deal with substantive matters provided:

(i) the judge reasonably believes that no party will gain a procedural or tactical advantage as a result of the ex parte communication, and

(ii) the judge makes provision promptly to notify all other parties of the substance of the ex parte communication and allows an opportunity to respond.

(c) A judge may initiate, permit, or consider any ex parte communication when expressly authorized by law* to do so or when authorized to do so by stipulation of the parties.

(d) If a judge receives an unauthorized ex parte communication, the judge shall make provision promptly to notify the parties of the substance of the communication and provide the parties with an opportunity to respond.

Advisory Committee Commentary: Canon 3B(7)

An exception allowing a judge, under certain circumstances, to obtain the advice of a disinterested expert on the law* has been eliminated from Canon 3B(7) because consulting with legal experts outside the presence of the parties is inconsistent with the core tenets of the adversarial system. Therefore, a judge shall not consult with legal experts outside the presence of the parties. Evidence Code section 730 provides for the appointment of an expert if a judge determines that expert testimony is necessary. A court may also invite the filing of amicus curiae briefs.

An exception allowing a judge to confer with the parties separately in an effort to settle the matter before the judge has been moved from this canon to Canon 3B(12).

This canon does not prohibit court personnel from communicating scheduling information or carrying out similar administrative functions.

A judge is statutorily authorized to investigate and consult witnesses informally in small claims cases. Code of Civil Procedure section 116.520, subdivision (c).

(8) A judge shall dispose of all judicial matters fairly, promptly, and efficiently. A judge shall manage the courtroom in a manner that provides all litigants the opportunity to have their matters fairly adjudicated in accordance with the law.*

Advisory Committee Commentary: Canon 3B(8)

The obligation of a judge to dispose of matters promptly and efficiently must not take precedence over the judge's obligation to dispose of the matters fairly and with patience. For example, when a litigant is self-represented, a judge has the discretion to take reasonable steps, appropriate under the circumstances and consistent with the law* and the canons, to enable the litigant to be heard. A judge should monitor and supervise cases so as to reduce or eliminate dilatory practices, avoidable delays, and unnecessary costs.

Prompt disposition of the court's business requires a judge to devote adequate time to judicial duties, to be punctual in attending court and expeditious in determining matters under submission, and to require* that court officials, litigants, and their lawyers cooperate with the judge to those ends.

(9) A judge shall not make any public comment about a pending* or impending* proceeding in any court, and shall not make any nonpublic comment that might substantially interfere with a fair trial or hearing. The judge shall require* similar abstention on the part of staff and court personnel subject to the judge's direction and control. This canon does not prohibit judges from making statements in the course of their official duties or from explaining the procedures of the court, and does not apply to proceedings in which the judge is a litigant in a personal capacity. Other than cases in which the judge has personally participated, this canon does not prohibit judges from discussing, in legal education programs and materials, cases and issues pending in appellate courts. This educational exemption does not apply to cases over which the judge has presided or to comments or discussions that might interfere with a fair hearing of the case.

Advisory Committee Commentary: Canon 3B(9)

The requirement that judges abstain from public comment regarding a pending* or impending* proceeding continues during any appellate process and until final disposition. A judge shall make reasonable efforts to ascertain whether a case is pending* or impending* before commenting on it. This canon does not prohibit a judge from commenting on proceedings in which the judge is a litigant in a personal capacity, but in cases such as a writ of mandamus where the judge is a litigant in an official capacity, the judge must not comment publicly.

"Making statements in the course of their official duties" and "explaining the procedures of the court" include providing an official transcript or partial official transcript of a court proceeding open to the public and explaining the rules of court and procedures related to a decision rendered by a judge.

Although this canon does not prohibit a judge from commenting on cases that are not pending* or impending* in any court, a judge must be cognizant of the general prohibition in Canon 2 against conduct involving impropriety* or the appearance of impropriety.* A judge should also be aware of the mandate in Canon 2A that a judge must act at all times in a manner that promotes public confidence in the integrity* and impartiality* of the judiciary. In addition, when commenting on a case pursuant to this canon, a judge must maintain the high standards of conduct, as set forth in Canon 1.

Although a judge is permitted to make nonpublic comments about pending* or impending* cases that will not substantially interfere with a fair trial or hearing, the judge should be cautious when making any such comments. There is always a risk that a comment can be misheard, misinterpreted, or repeated. A judge making such a comment must be *mindful of the judge's obligation under Canon 2A to act at all times in a manner that promotes public confidence in the integrity* and impartiality* of the judiciary. When a judge makes a nonpublic comment about a case pending* before that judge, the judge must keep an open mind and not form an opinion prematurely or create the appearance of having formed an opinion prematurely.*

(10) A judge shall not commend or criticize jurors for their verdict other than in a court order or opinion in a proceeding, but may express appreciation to jurors for their service to the judicial system and the community.

Advisory Committee Commentary: Canon 3B(10)

Commending or criticizing jurors for their verdict may imply a judicial expectation in future cases and may impair a juror's ability to be fair and impartial* in a subsequent case.

(11) A judge shall not disclose or use, for any purpose unrelated to judicial duties, nonpublic information* acquired in a judicial capacity.

(12) A judge may participate in settlement conferences or in other efforts to resolve matters in dispute, including matters pending before the judge. A judge may, with the express consent of the parties or their lawyers, confer separately with the parties and/or their lawyers during such resolution efforts. At all times during such resolution efforts, a judge shall remain impartial* and shall not engage in conduct that may reasonably be perceived as coercive.

Advisory Committee Commentary: Canon 3B(12)

While the judge plays an important role in overseeing efforts to resolve disputes, including conducting settlement discussions, a judge should be careful that efforts to resolve disputes do not undermine any party's right to be heard according to law.*

The judge should keep in mind the effect that the judge's participation in dispute resolution efforts may have on the judge's impartiality* or the appearance of impartiality* if the case remains with the judge for trial after resolution efforts are unsuccessful. Accordingly, a judge may wish to consider whether: (1) the parties or their counsel have requested or objected to the participation by the trial judge in such discussions; (2) the parties and their counsel are relatively sophisticated in legal matters or the particular legal issues involved in the case; (3) a party is unrepresented; (4) the case will be tried by the judge or a jury; (5) the parties will participate with their counsel in settlement discussions and, if so, the effect of personal contact between the judge and parties; and (6) it is appropriate during the settlement conference for the judge to express an opinion on the merits or worth of the case or express an opinion on the legal issues that the judge may later have to rule upon.

If a judge assigned to preside over a trial believes participation in resolution efforts could influence the judge's decisionmaking during trial, the judge may decline to engage in such efforts.

Where dispute resolution efforts of any type are unsuccessful, the judge should consider whether, due to events that occurred during the resolution efforts, the judge may be disqualified under the law* from presiding over the trial. See, e.g., Code of Civil Procedure section 170.1, subdivision (a)(6)(A).

C. Administrative Responsibilities

(1) A judge shall diligently discharge the judge's administrative responsibilities impartially,* on the basis of merit, without bias or prejudice, free of conflict of interest, and in a manner that promotes public confidence

in the integrity* of the judiciary. A judge shall not, in the performance of administrative duties, engage in speech, gestures, or other conduct that would reasonably be perceived as (a) bias or prejudice, including but not limited to bias or prejudice based upon race, sex, gender, religion, national origin, ethnicity, disability, age, sexual orientation, marital status, socioeconomic status, or political affiliation, or (b) sexual harassment.

Advisory Committee Commentary: Canon 3C(1)

In considering what constitutes a conflict of interest under this canon, a judge should be informed by Code of Civil Procedure section 170.1, subdivision (a)(6).

(2) A judge shall maintain professional competence in judicial administration, and shall cooperate with other judges and court officials in the administration of court business.

(3) A judge shall require* staff and court personnel under the judge's direction and control to observe appropriate standards of conduct and to refrain from manifesting bias or prejudice based upon race, sex, gender, religion, national origin, ethnicity, disability, age, sexual orientation, marital status, socioeconomic status, or political affiliation in the performance of their official duties.

(4) A judge with supervisory authority for the judicial performance of other judges shall take reasonable measures to ensure the prompt disposition of matters before them and the proper performance of their other judicial responsibilities.

(5) A judge shall not make unnecessary court appointments. A judge shall exercise the power of appointment impartially,* on the basis of merit, without bias or prejudice, free of conflict of interest, and in a manner that promotes public confidence in the integrity* of the judiciary. A judge shall avoid nepotism and favoritism. A judge shall not approve compensation of appointees above the reasonable value of services rendered.

Advisory Committee Commentary: Canon 3(C)(5)

Appointees of a judge include assigned counsel and officials such as referees, commissioners, special masters, receivers, and guardians. Consent by the parties to an appointment or an award of compensation does not relieve the judge of the obligation prescribed by Canon 3C(5).

D. Disciplinary Responsibilities

(1) Whenever a judge has reliable information that another judge has violated any provision of the Code of Judicial Ethics, that judge shall take appropriate corrective action, which may include reporting the violation to the appropriate authority. (See Commentary to Canon 3D(2).)

(2) Whenever a judge has personal knowledge,* or concludes in a judicial decision, that a lawyer has committed misconduct or has violated any provision of the Rules of Professional Conduct, the judge shall take appropriate corrective action, which may include reporting the violation to the appropriate authority.

Advisory Committee Commentary: Canons 3D(1) and 3D(2)

Appropriate corrective action could include direct communication with the judge or lawyer who has committed the violation, other direct action, such as a confidential referral to a judicial or lawyer assistance program, or a report of the violation to the presiding judge, appropriate authority, or other agency or body. Judges should note that in addition to the action required by

Canon 3D(2), California law imposes additional mandatory reporting requirements to the State Bar on judges regarding lawyer misconduct. See Business and Professions Code section 6086.7 and 6086.8, subdivision (a), and California Rules of Court, rules 10.609 and 10.1017.

"Appropriate authority" means the authority with responsibility for initiation of the disciplinary process with respect to a violation to be reported.

(3)   A judge shall promptly report in writing to the Commission on Judicial Performance when he or she is charged in court by misdemeanor citation, prosecutorial complaint, information, or indictment, with any crime in the United States as specified below. Crimes that must be reported are: (1) all crimes, other than those that would be considered misdemeanors not involving moral turpitude or infractions under California law; and (2) all misdemeanors involving violence (including assaults), the use or possession of controlled substances, the misuse of prescriptions, or the personal use or furnishing of alcohol. A judge also shall promptly report in writing upon conviction of such crimes.

If the judge is a retired judge serving in the Assigned Judges Program, he or she shall promptly report such information in writing to the Chief Justice rather than to the Commission on Judicial Performance. If the judge is a subordinate judicial officer,* he or she shall promptly report such information in writing to both the presiding judge of the court in which the subordinate judicial officer* sits and the Commission on Judicial Performance.

(4)   A judge shall cooperate with judicial and lawyer disciplinary agencies.

Advisory Committee Commentary: Canons 3D(3) and 3D(4)

See Government Code section 68725, which requires judges to cooperate with and give reasonable assistance and information to the Commission on Judicial Performance, and rule 104 of the Rules of the Commission on Judicial Performance, which requires a respondent judge to cooperate with the commission in all proceedings in accordance with section 68725.

(5)   A judge shall not retaliate, directly or indirectly, against a person known* or suspected to have assisted or cooperated with an investigation of a judge or a lawyer.

E. Disqualification and Disclosure

(1)   A judge shall disqualify himself or herself in any proceeding in which disqualification is required by law.*

(2)   In all trial court proceedings, a judge shall disclose on the record as follows:

    (a)   Information relevant to disqualification

A judge shall disclose information that is reasonably relevant to the question of disqualification under Code of Civil Procedure section 170.1, even if the judge believes there is no actual basis for disqualification.

    (b)   Campaign contributions in trial court elections

        (i)   Information required to be disclosed

In any matter before a judge who is or was a candidate for judicial office* in a trial court election, the judge shall disclose any contribution or loan of $100 or more from a party, individual lawyer, or law office or firm in that matter as required by this canon, even if the amount of the contribution or loan would not require disqualification. Such disclosure shall consist of the name of the contributor or lender, the amount of each contribution or loan, the cumulative amount of the contributor's contributions or lender's loans, and the date of each contribution or loan. The judge shall make reasonable efforts to obtain current information regarding contributions or loans received by his or her campaign and shall disclose the required information on the record.

(ii) Manner of disclosure

The judge shall ensure that the required information is conveyed on the record to the parties and lawyers appearing in the matter before the judge. The judge has discretion to select the manner of disclosure, but the manner used shall avoid the appearance that the judge is soliciting campaign contributions.

(iii) Timing of disclosure

Disclosure shall be made at the earliest reasonable opportunity after receiving each contribution or loan. The duty commences no later than one week after receipt of the first contribution or loan, and continues for a period of two years after the candidate takes the oath of office, or two years from the date of the contribution or loan, whichever event is later.

Advisory Committee Commentary: Canon 3E(2)(b)

Code of Civil Procedure section 170.1, subdivision (a)(9)(C) requires a judge to "disclose any contribution from a party or lawyer in a matter that is before the court that is required to be reported under subdivision (f) of Section 84211 of the Government Code, even if the amount would not require disqualification under this paragraph." This statute further provides that the "manner of disclosure shall be the same as that provided in Canon 3E of the Code of Judicial Ethics." Canon 3E(2)(b) sets forth the information the judge must disclose, the manner for making such disclosure, and the timing thereof.

"Contribution" includes monetary and in-kind contributions. See Cal. Code Regs., tit. 2, § 18215, subd. (b)(3). See generally Government Code section 84211 subdivision (f).

Disclosure of campaign contributions is intended to provide parties and lawyers appearing before a judge during and after a judicial campaign with easy access to information about campaign contributions that may not require disqualification but could be relevant to the question of disqualification of the judge. The judge is responsible for ensuring that the disclosure is conveyed to the parties and lawyers appearing in the matter. The canon provides that the judge has discretion to select the manner of making the disclosure. The appropriate manner of disclosure will depend on whether all of the parties and lawyers are present in court, whether it is more efficient or practicable given the court's calendar to make a written disclosure, and other relevant circumstances that may affect the ability of the parties and lawyers to access the required information. The following alternatives for disclosure are non-exclusive. If all parties are present in court, the judge may conclude that the most effective and efficient manner of providing disclosure is to state orally the required information on the record in open court. In the alternative, again if all parties are present in court, a judge may determine that it is more appropriate to state orally on the record in open court that parties and lawyers may obtain the required information at an easily accessible location in the courthouse, and provide an opportunity for the parties and lawyers to review the available information. Another alternative, particularly if all or some parties are not present in court, is that the judge may disclose the campaign contribution in a written minute order or in the official court minutes and notify the parties and the lawyers of the written disclosure. See California Supreme Court Committee on Judicial Ethics Opinions, CJEO Formal Opinion No. 2013–002, pp. 7–8. If a party appearing in a matter before the judge is represented by a lawyer, it is sufficient to make the disclosure to the lawyer.

In addition to the disclosure obligations set forth in Canon 3E(2)(b), a judge must, pursuant to Canon 3E(2)(a), disclose on the record any other information that may be relevant to the question of disqualification. As examples, such an obligation may arise as a result of contributions or loans of which the judge is aware made by a party, lawyer, or law office or firm appearing before the judge to a third party in support of the judge or in opposition to the judge's opponent; a party, lawyer, or law office or firm's relationship to the judge or role in the campaign; or the aggregate contributions or loans from lawyers in one law office or firm.

Canon 3E(2)(b) does not eliminate the obligation of the judge to recuse himself or herself where the nature of the contribution or loan, the extent of the contributor's or lender's involvement in the judicial campaign, the relationship of the contributor or lender, or other circumstance requires recusal under Code of Civil Procedure section 170.1, and particularly section 170.1, subdivision (a)(6)(A).

(3) A judge shall disqualify *himself or herself* in accordance with the following:

(a) Statements that commit the judge to a particular result. A judge is disqualified if the judge, while a judge or candidate for judicial office,* made a statement, other than in a court proceeding, judicial decision, or opinion, that a person aware of the facts might reasonably believe commits the judge to reach a particular result or rule in a particular way in a proceeding.

(b) Bond ownership. Ownership of a corporate bond issued by a party to a proceeding and having a fair market value exceeding $1,500 is disqualifying. Ownership of a government bond issued by a party to a proceeding is disqualifying only if the outcome of the proceeding could substantially affect the value of the judge's bond. Ownership in a mutual or common investment fund that holds bonds is not a disqualifying financial interest.

Advisory Committee Commentary: Canon 3E(3)(b)

The distinction between corporate and government bonds is consistent with the Political Reform Act (see Gov. Code, § 82034), which requires disclosure of corporate bonds, but not government bonds. Canon 3E(3) is intended to assist judges in complying with Code of Civil Procedure section 170.1, subdivision (a)(3) and Canon 3E(5)(d).

(4) An appellate justice shall disqualify himself or herself in any proceeding if for any reason:

(a) the justice believes his or her recusal would further the interests of justice; or

(b) the justice substantially doubts his or her capacity to be impartial;* or

(c) the circumstances are such that a reasonable person aware of the facts would doubt the justice's ability to be impartial.*

(5)   Disqualification of an appellate justice is also required in the following instances:

(a)   The appellate justice has served as a lawyer in the pending* proceeding, or has served as a lawyer in any other proceeding involving any of the same parties if that other proceeding related to the same contested issues of fact and law as the present proceeding, or has given advice to any party in the present proceeding upon any issue involved in the proceeding.

Advisory Committee Commentary: Canon 3E(5)(a)

Canon 3E(5)(a) is consistent with Code of Civil Procedure section 170.1, subdivision (a)(2), which addresses disqualification of trial court judges based on prior representation of a party in the proceeding.

(b)   Within the last two years, (i) a party to the proceeding, or an officer, director or trustee thereof, either was a client of the justice when the justice was engaged in the private practice of law or was a client of a lawyer with whom the justice was associated in the private practice of law; or (ii) a lawyer in the proceeding was associated with the justice in the private practice of law.

(c)   The appellate justice represented a public officer or entity and personally advised or in any way represented that officer or entity concerning the factual or legal issues in the present proceeding in which the public officer or entity now appears.

(d)   The appellate justice, his or her spouse or registered domestic partner,* or a minor child residing in the household, has a financial interest or is either a fiduciary* who has a financial interest in the proceeding, or is a director, advisor, or other active participant in the affairs of a party. A financial interest is defined as ownership of more than a 1 percent legal or equitable interest in a party, or a legal or equitable interest in a party of a fair market value exceeding $1,500. Ownership in a mutual or common investment fund that holds securities does not itself constitute a financial interest; holding office in an educational, religious, charitable, service,* or civic organization does not confer a financial interest in the organization's securities; and a proprietary interest of a policyholder in a mutual insurance company or mutual savings association or similar interest is not a financial interest unless the outcome of the proceeding could substantially affect the value of the interest. A justice shall make reasonable efforts to keep informed about his or her personal and fiduciary* interests and those of his or her spouse or registered domestic partner* and of minor children living in the household.

(e)   (i) The justice or his or her spouse or registered domestic partner,* or a person within the third degree of relationship* to either of them, or the spouse or registered domestic partner* thereof, is a party or an officer, director, or trustee of a party to the proceeding, or

(ii) a lawyer or spouse or registered domestic partner* of a lawyer in the proceeding is the spouse, registered domestic partner,* former spouse, former registered domestic partner,* child, sibling, or parent of the justice or of the justice's spouse or registered domestic partner,* or such a person is associated in the private practice of law with a lawyer in the proceeding.

(f)   The justice

    (i) served as the judge before whom the proceeding was tried or heard in the lower court,

    (ii) has personal knowledge* of disputed evidentiary facts concerning the proceeding, or

    (iii) has a personal bias or prejudice concerning a party or a party's lawyer.

(g)   A temporary or permanent physical impairment renders the justice unable properly to perceive the evidence or conduct the proceedings.

(h)   The justice has a current arrangement concerning prospective employment or other compensated service as a dispute resolution neutral or is participating in, or, within the last two years has participated in, discussions regarding prospective employment or service as a dispute resolution neutral, or has been engaged in such employment or service, and any of the following applies:

    (i)   The arrangement is, or the prior employment or discussion was, with a party to the proceeding;

    (ii)   The matter before the justice includes issues relating to the enforcement of either an agreement to submit a dispute to an alternative dispute resolution process or an award or other final decision by a dispute resolution neutral;

    (iii)   The justice directs the parties to participate in an alternative dispute resolution process in which the dispute resolution neutral will be an individual or entity with whom the justice has the arrangement, has previously been employed or served, or is discussing or has discussed the employment or service; or

    (iv)   The justice will select a dispute resolution neutral or entity to conduct an alternative dispute resolution process in the matter before the justice, and among those available for selection is an individual or entity with whom the justice has the arrangement, with whom the justice has previously been employed or served, or with whom the justice is discussing or has discussed the employment or service.

For purposes of Canon 3E(5)(h), "participating in discussions" or "has participated in discussions" means that the justice (i) solicited or otherwise indicated an interest in accepting or negotiating possible employment or service as an alternative dispute resolution neutral, or (ii) responded to an unsolicited statement regarding, or an offer of, such employment or service by expressing an interest in that employment or service, making any inquiry regarding the employment or service, or encouraging the person making the statement or offer to provide additional information about that possible employment or service. If a justice's response to an unsolicited statement regarding a question about, or offer of, prospective employment or other compensated service as a dispute resolution neutral is limited to responding negatively, declining the offer, or declining to discuss such employment or service, that response does not constitute participating in discussions.

For purposes of Canon 3E(5)(h), "party" includes the parent, subsidiary, or other legal affiliate of any entity that is a party and is involved in the transaction, contract, or facts that gave rise to the issues subject to the proceeding.

For purposes of Canon 3E(5)(h), "dispute resolution neutral" means an arbitrator, a mediator, a temporary judge* appointed under article VI, section 21 of the California Constitution, a referee appointed under Code of Civil Procedure section 638 or 639, a special master, a neutral evaluator, a settlement officer, or a settlement facilitator.

(i)   The justice's spouse or registered domestic partner* [or] a person within the third degree of relationship* to the justice or his or her spouse or registered domestic partner,* or the person's spouse or registered domestic partner,* was a witness in the proceeding.

(j)   The justice has received a campaign contribution of $5,000 or more from a party or lawyer in a matter that is before the court, and either of the following applies:

(i)   The contribution was received in support of the justice's last election, if the last election was within the last six years; or

(ii)   The contribution was received in anticipation of an upcoming election.

Notwithstanding Canon 3E(5)(j), a justice shall disqualify himself or herself based on a contribution of a lesser amount if required by Canon 3E(4).

The disqualification required under Canon 3E(5)(j) may be waived if all parties that did not make the contribution agree to waive the disqualification.

Advisory Committee Commentary: Canon 3E

Canon 3E(1) sets forth the general duty to disqualify applicable to a judge of any court. Sources for determining when recusal or disqualification is appropriate may include the applicable provisions of the Code of Civil Procedure, other provisions of the Code of Judicial Ethics, the Code of Conduct for United States Judges, the American Bar Association's Model Code of Judicial Conduct, and related case law.

The decision whether to disclose information under Canon 3E(2) is a decision based on the facts of the case before the judge. A judge is required to disclose only information that is related to the grounds for disqualification set forth in Code of Civil Procedure section 170.1.

Canon 3E(4) sets forth the general standards for recusal of an appellate justice. The term "appellate justice" includes justices of both the Courts of Appeal and the Supreme Court. Generally, the provisions concerning disqualification of an appellate justice are intended to assist justices in determining whether recusal is appropriate and to inform the public why recusal may occur.

The rule of necessity may override the rule of disqualification. For example, a judge might be required to participate in judicial review of a judicial salary statute, or might be the only judge available in a matter requiring judicial action, such as a hearing on probable cause or a temporary restraining order. In the latter case, the judge must promptly disclose on the record the basis for possible disqualification and use reasonable efforts to transfer the matter to another judge as soon as practicable.

In some instances, membership in certain organizations may have the potential to give an appearance of partiality, although membership in the organization generally may not be barred by Canon 2C, Canon 4, or any other specific canon. A judge holding membership in an organization should disqualify himself or herself whenever doing so would be appropriate in accordance with Canon 3E(1), 3E(4), or 3E(5) or statutory requirements. In addition, in some circumstances, the parties or their lawyers may consider a judge's membership in an organization relevant to the question of disqualification, even if the judge believes there is no actual basis for disqualification. In accordance with this canon, a judge should disclose to the parties his or her membership in an organization, in any proceeding in which that information is reasonably relevant to the question of disqualification under Code of Civil Procedure section 170.1, even if the judge concludes there is no actual basis for disqualification.

(6)   It shall not be grounds for disqualification that the justice:

     (a)   Is or is not a member of a racial, ethnic, religious, sexual, or similar group and the proceeding involves the rights of such a group;

     (b)   Has in any capacity expressed a view on a legal or factual issue presented in the proceeding, except as provided in Canon 3E(5)(a), (b), or (c);

     (c)   Has as a lawyer or public official participated in the drafting of laws* or in the effort to pass or defeat laws,* the meaning, effect, or application of which is in issue in the proceeding unless the judge believes that his or her prior involvement was so well known* as to raise a reasonable doubt in the public mind as to his or her capacity to be impartial.*

Advisory Committee Commentary: Cannon 3E(6)

Canon 3E(6) is substantively the same as Code of Civil Procedure section 170.2, which pertains to trial court judges.

CANON 4

A Judge Shall So Conduct the Judge's Quasi-Judicial and Extrajudicial Activities as to Minimize the Risk of Conflict With Judicial Obligations

A.   Extrajudicial Activities in General

A judge shall conduct all of the judge's extrajudicial activities so that they do not

     (1)   cast reasonable doubt on the judge's capacity to act impartially,*

     (2)   demean the judicial office,

     (3)   interfere with the proper performance of judicial duties, or

     (4)   lead to frequent disqualification of the judge.

Advisory Committee Commentary: Canon 4A

Complete separation of a judge from extrajudicial activities is neither possible nor wise; a judge should not become isolated from the community in which he or she lives. Expressions of bias or prejudice by a judge, even outside the judge's judicial activities, may cast reasonable doubt on the judge's capacity to act impartially as a judge. Expressions that may do so include inappropriate use of humor or the use of demeaning remarks. See Canon 2C and accompanying Commentary.*

Because a judge's judicial duties take precedence over all other activities (see Canon 3A), a judge must avoid extrajudicial activities that might reasonably result in the judge being disqualified.

B.   Quasi-Judicial and Avocational Activities

A judge may speak, write, lecture, teach, and participate in activities concerning legal and nonlegal subject matters, subject to the requirements of this code.

Advisory Committee Commentary: Canon 4B

As a judicial officer and person specially learned in the law,* a judge is in a unique position to contribute to the improvement of the law, the legal system, and the administration of justice,* including revision of substantive and procedural law* and improvement of criminal and juvenile justice. To the extent that time permits, a judge may do so, either independently or through a bar or judicial association or other group dedicated to the improvement of the law.* It may be necessary to promote legal education programs and materials by identifying authors and speakers by judicial title. This is permissible, provided such use of the judicial title does not contravene Canons 2A and 2B.

Judges are not precluded by their office from engaging in other social, community, and intellectual endeavors so long as they do not interfere with the obligations under Canons 2C and 4A.

C.   Governmental, Civic, or Charitable Activities

(1)   A judge shall not appear at a public hearing or officially consult with an executive or legislative body or public official except on matters concerning the law, the legal system, or the administration of justice* or in matters involving the judge's private economic or personal interests.

Advisory Committee Commentary: Canon 4C(1)

When deciding whether to appear at a public hearing or whether to consult with an executive or legislative body or public official on matters concerning the law, the legal system, or the administration of justice,* a judge should consider if that conduct would violate any other provisions of this code. For a list of factors to consider, see the explanation of "law, the legal system, or the administration of justice" in the Terminology section. See also Canon 2B regarding the obligation to avoid improper influence.

(2)   A judge shall not accept appointment to a governmental committee or commission or other governmental position that is concerned with issues of fact or policy on matters other than the improvement of the law, the legal system, or the administration of justice.* A judge may, however, serve in the military reserve or represent a national, state, or local government on ceremonial occasions or in connection with historical, educational, or cultural activities.

Advisory Committee Commentary: Canon 4C(2)

Canon 4C(2) prohibits a judge from accepting any governmental position except one relating to the law, legal system, or administration of justice* as authorized by Canon 4C(3). The appropriateness of accepting extrajudicial assignments must be assessed in light of the demands on judicial resources and the need to protect the courts from involvement in extrajudicial matters that may prove to be controversial. Judges shall not accept governmental appointments that are likely to interfere with the effectiveness and independence* of the judiciary, or that constitute a public *office within the meaning of article VI, section 17 of the California Constitution.*

Canon 4C(2) does not govern a judge's service in a nongovernmental position. See Canon 4C(3) permitting service by a judge with organizations devoted to the improvement of the law, the legal system, or the administration of justice* and with educational, religious, charitable, service,* or civic organizations not conducted for profit. For example, service on the board of a public educational institution, other than a law school, would be prohibited under Canon 4C(2), but service on the board of a public law school or any private educational institution would generally be permitted under Canon 4C(3).

(3)   Subject to the following limitations and the other requirements of this code,

     (a)   a judge may serve as an officer, director, trustee, or nonlegal advisor of an organization or governmental agency devoted to the improvement of the law, the legal system, or the administration of justice* provided that such position does not constitute a public office within the meaning of article VI, section 17 of the California Constitution;

     (b)   a judge may serve as an officer, director, trustee, or nonlegal advisor of an educational, religious, charitable, service,* or civic organization not conducted for profit;

Advisory Committee Commentary: Canon 4C(3)

Canon 4C(3) does not apply to a judge's service in a governmental position unconnected with the improvement of the law, the legal system, or the administration of justice.* See Canon 4C(2).

Canon 4C(3) uses the phrase, "Subject to the following limitations and the other requirements of this code." As an example of the meaning of the phrase, a judge permitted by Canon 4C(3) to serve on the board of a service organization* may be prohibited from such service by Canon 2C or 4A if the institution practices invidious discrimination or if service on the board otherwise casts reasonable doubt on the judge's capacity to act impartially* as a judge.

Service by a judge on behalf of a civic or charitable organization may be governed by other provisions of Canon 4 in addition to Canon 4C. For example, a judge is prohibited by Canon 4G from serving as a legal advisor to a civic or charitable organization.

Service on the board of a homeowners' association or a neighborhood protective group is proper if it is related to the protection of the judge's own economic interests. See Canons 4D(2) and 4D(4). See Canon 2B regarding the obligation to avoid improper use of the prestige of a judge's office.

     (c)   a judge shall not serve as an officer, director, trustee, or nonlegal advisor if it is likely that the organization

        (i)   will be engaged in judicial proceedings that would ordinarily come before the judge, or

        (ii)   will be engaged frequently in adversary proceedings in the court of which the judge is a member or in any court subject to the appellate jurisdiction of the court of which the judge is a member.

Advisory Committee Commentary; Canon 4C(3)(c)

The changing nature of some organizations and of their relationship to the law* makes it necessary for the judge regularly to reexamine the activities of each organization with which the judge is affiliated to determine if it is proper for the judge to continue the affiliation. Some organizations regularly engage in litigation to achieve their goals or fulfill their purposes. Judges should avoid a leadership role in such organizations as it could compromise the appearance of impartiality.*

(d)   a judge as an officer, director, trustee, or nonlegal advisor, or as a member or otherwise

      (i)   may assist such an organization in planning fundraising and may participate in the management and investment of the organization's funds. However, a judge shall not personally participate in the solicitation of funds or other fundraising activities, except that a judge may privately solicit funds for such an organization from members of the judge's family* or from other judges (excluding court commissioners, referees, retired judges, court-appointed arbitrators, hearing officers, and temporary judges*);

      (ii)   may make recommendations to public and private fund-granting organizations on projects and programs concerning the law, the legal system, or the administration of justice;*

      (iii) shall not personally participate in membership solicitation if the solicitation might reasonably be perceived as coercive or if the membership solicitation is essentially a fundraising mechanism, except as permitted in Canon 4C(3)(d)(i);

      (iv) shall not permit the use of the prestige of his or her judicial office for fundraising or membership solicitation but may be a speaker, guest of honor, or recipient of an award for public or charitable service provided the judge does not personally solicit funds and complies with Canons 4A(1) (2) (3), and (4).

Advisory Committee Commentary: Canon 4C(3)(d)

A judge may solicit membership or endorse or encourage membership efforts for an organization devoted to the improvement of the law, the legal system, or the administration of justice,* or a nonprofit educational, religious, charitable, service,* or civic organization as long as the solicitation cannot reasonably be perceived as coercive and is not essentially a fundraising mechanism. Solicitation of funds or memberships for an organization similarly involves the danger that the person solicited will feel obligated to respond favorably if the solicitor is in a position of influence or control. A judge must not engage in direct, individual solicitation of funds or memberships in person, in writing, or by telephone except in the following cases: (1) a judge may solicit other judges (excluding court commissioners, referees, retired judges, court-appointed arbitrators, hearing officers, and temporary judges*) for funds or memberships; (2) a judge may solicit other persons for membership in the organizations described above if neither those persons nor persons with whom they are affiliated are likely ever to appear before the court on which the judge serves; and (3) a judge who is an officer of such an organization may send a general membership solicitation mailing over the judge's signature.

When deciding whether to make recommendations to public and private fund-granting organizations on projects and programs concerning the law, the legal system, or the administration of justice,* a judge should consider *whether that conduct would violate any other provision of this code. For a list of factors to consider, see the explanation of "law, the legal system, or the administration of justice" in the Terminology section.*

Use of an organization's letterhead for fundraising or membership solicitation does not violate Canon 4C(3)(d), provided the letterhead lists only the judge's name and office or other position in the organization, and designates the judge's judicial title only if other persons whose names appear on the letterhead have comparable designations. In addition, a judge must also make reasonable efforts to ensure that the judge's staff, court officials, and others subject to the judge's direction and control do not solicit funds on the judge's behalf for any purpose, charitable or otherwise.

(e)   A judge may encourage lawyers to provide pro bono publico legal services.

Advisory Committee Commentary: Canon 4C(3)(e)

In addition to appointing lawyers to serve as counsel for indigent parties in individual cases, a judge may promote broader access to justice by encouraging lawyers to participate in pro bono publico legal services, as long as the judge does not employ coercion or abuse the prestige of judicial office.

D.   Financial Activities

(1)   A judge shall not engage in financial and business dealings that

(a)   may reasonably be perceived to exploit the judge's judicial position, or

(b)   involve the judge in frequent transactions or continuing business relationships with lawyers or other persons likely to appear before the court on which the judge serves.

Advisory Committee Commentary: Canon 4D(1)

The Time for Compliance provision of this code (Canon 6F) postpones the time for compliance with certain provisions of this canon in some cases.

A judge must avoid financial and business dealings that involve the judge in frequent transactions or continuing business relationships with persons likely to appear either before the judge personally or before other judges on the judge's court. A judge shall discourage members of the judge's family* from engaging in dealings that would reasonably appear to exploit the judge's judicial position or that involve family members in frequent transactions or continuing business relationships with persons likely to appear before the judge. This rule is necessary to avoid creating an appearance of exploitation of office or favoritism and to minimize the potential for disqualification.

Participation by a judge in financial and business dealings is subject to the general prohibitions in Canon 4A against activities that tend to reflect adversely on impartiality,* demean the judicial office, or interfere with the proper performance of judicial duties. Such participation is also subject to the general prohibition in Canon 2 against activities involving impropriety* or the appearance of impropriety* and the prohibition in Canon 2B against the misuse of the prestige of judicial office.

In addition, a judge must maintain high standards of conduct in all of the judge's activities, as set forth in Canon 1.

(2)   A judge may, subject to the requirements of this code, hold and manage investments of the judge and members of the judge's family,* including real estate, and engage in other remunerative activities. A judge shall not participate in, nor permit the judge's name to be used in connection

with, any business venture or commercial advertising that indicates the judge's title or affiliation with the judiciary or otherwise lend the power or prestige of his or her office to promote a business or any commercial venture.

(3)   A judge shall not serve as an officer, director, manager, or employee of a business affected with a public interest, including, without limitation, a financial institution, insurance company, or public utility.

Advisory Committee Commentary: Canon 4D(3)

Although participation by a judge in business activities might otherwise be permitted by Canon 4D, a judge may be prohibited from participation by other provisions of this code when, for example, the business entity frequently appears before the judge's court or the participation requires significant time away from judicial duties. Similarly, a judge must avoid participating in any business activity if the judge's participation would involve misuse of the prestige of judicial office. See Canon 2B.

(4)   A judge shall manage personal investments and financial activities so as to minimize the necessity for disqualification. As soon as reasonably possible, a judge shall divest himself or herself of investments and other financial interests that would require frequent disqualification.

(5)   Under no circumstance shall a judge accept a gift,* bequest, or favor if the donor is a party whose interests have come or are reasonably likely to come before the judge. A judge shall discourage members of the judge's family residing in the judge's household* from accepting similar benefits from parties who have come or are reasonably likely to come before the judge.

Advisory Committee Commentary: Canon 4D(5)

In addition to the prohibitions set forth in Canon 4D(5) regarding gifts, other laws* may be applicable to judges, including, for example, Code of Civil Procedure section 170.9 and the Political Reform Act of 1974 (Gov. Code, § 81000 et seq.).*

Canon 4D(5) does not apply to contributions to a judge's campaign for judicial office, a matter governed by Canon 5, although such contributions may give rise to an obligation by the judge to disqualify or disclose. See Canon 3E(2)(b) and accompanying Commentary and the Code of Civil Procedure section 170.1, subdivision (a)(9).

Because a gift, bequest, or favor to a member of the judge's family residing in the judge's household* might be viewed as intended to influence the judge, a judge must inform those family members of the relevant ethical constraints upon the judge in this regard and urge them to take these constraints into account when making decisions about accepting such gifts,* bequests, or favors. A judge cannot, however, reasonably be expected to know or control all of the financial or business activities of all family members residing in the judge's household.**

The application of Canon 4D(5) requires recognition that a judge cannot reasonably be expected to anticipate all persons or interests that may come before the court.

(6)   A judge shall not accept and shall discourage members of the judge's family residing in the judge's household* from accepting a gift,* bequest, favor, or loan from anyone except as hereinafter set forth, provided that acceptance would not reasonably be perceived as intended to influence the judge in the performance of judicial duties:

(a)   a gift,* bequest, favor, or loan from a person whose preexisting relationship with the judge would prevent the judge under Canon 3E from hearing a case involving that person;

Advisory Committee Commentary: Canon 4D(6)(a)

Upon appointment or election as a judge or within a reasonable period of time thereafter, a judge may attend an event honoring the judge's appointment or election as a judge provided that (1) the judge would otherwise be disqualified from hearing any matter involving the person or entity holding or funding the event, and (2) a reasonable person would not conclude that attendance at the event undermines the judge's integrity, impartiality,* or independence.**

(b)   a gift* for a special occasion from a relative or friend, if the gift* is fairly commensurate with the occasion and the relationship;

Advisory Committee Commentary: Canon 4D(6)(b)

A gift to a judge, or to a member of the judge's family residing in the judge's household,* that is excessive in value raises questions about the judge's impartiality* and the integrity* of the judicial office and might require disqualification of the judge where disqualification would not otherwise be required. See, however, Canon 4D(6)(a).*

(c)   commercial or financial opportunities and benefits, including special pricing and discounts, and loans from lending institutions in their regular course of business, if the same opportunities and benefits or loans are made available on the same terms to similarly situated persons who are not judges;

(d)   any gift* incidental to a public testimonial, or educational or resource materials supplied by publishers on a complimentary basis for official use, or an invitation to the judge and the judge's spouse or registered domestic partner* or guest to attend a bar-related function or an activity devoted to the improvement of the law, the legal system, or the administration of justice;*

(e)   advances or reimbursement for the reasonable cost of travel, transportation, lodging, and subsistence that is directly related to participation in any judicial, educational, civic, or governmental program or bar-related function or activity devoted to the improvement of the law, the legal system, or the administration of justice;*

Advisory Committee Commentary: Canon 4D(6)(e)

Acceptance of an invitation to a law-related function is governed by Canon 4D(6)(d); acceptance of an invitation paid for by an individual lawyer or group of lawyers is governed by Canon 4D(6)(g). See also Canon 4H(2) and accompanying Commentary.

(f)   a gift,* award, or benefit incident to the business, profession, or other separate activity of a spouse or registered domestic partner* or other member of the judge's family residing in the judge's household,* including gifts,* awards, and benefits for the use of both the spouse or registered domestic partner* or other family member and the judge;

(g)   ordinary social hospitality;

Advisory Committee Commentary: Canon 4D(6)(g)

Although Canon 4D(6)(g) does not preclude ordinary social hospitality, a judge should carefully weigh acceptance of such hospitality to avoid any appearance of impropriety or bias or any appearance that the judge is* *misusing the prestige of judicial office. See Canons 2 and 2B. A judge should also consider whether acceptance would affect the integrity,* impartiality,* or independence* of the judiciary. See Canon 2A.*

(h) an invitation to the judge and the judge's spouse, registered domestic partner,* or guest to attend an event sponsored by an educational, religious, charitable, service,* or civic organization with which the judge is associated or involved, if the same invitation is offered to persons who are not judges and who are similarly engaged with the organization.

(7) A judge may accept the following, provided that acceptance would not reasonably be perceived as intended to influence the judge in the performance of judicial duties:

(a) a scholarship or fellowship awarded on the same terms and based on the same criteria applied to other applicants;

(b) rewards and prizes given to competitors or participants in random drawings, contests, or other events that are open to persons who are not judges.

Advisory Committee Commentary: Canons 4D(6) and 4D(7)

The references to such scholarships, fellowships, rewards, and prizes were moved from Canon 4D(6) to Canon 4D(7) because they are not considered to be gifts* under this code, and a judge may accept them.

E.   Fiduciary* Activities

(1) A judge shall not serve as executor, administrator, or other personal representative, trustee, guardian, attorney in fact, or other fiduciary,* except for the estate, trust, or person of a member of the judge's family,* and then only if such service will not interfere with the proper performance of judicial duties.

(2) A judge shall not serve as a fiduciary* if it is likely that the judge as a fiduciary* will be engaged in proceedings that would ordinarily come before the judge, or if the estate, trust, or minor or conservatee will be engaged in contested proceedings in the court on which the judge serves or one under its appellate jurisdiction.

(3) The same restrictions on financial activities that apply to a judge personally also apply to the judge while acting in a fiduciary* capacity.

Advisory Committee Commentary: Canon 4E

The Time for Compliance provision of this code (Canon 6F) postpones the time for compliance with certain provisions of this canon in some cases.

The restrictions imposed by this canon may conflict with the judge's obligation as a fiduciary.* For example, a judge shall resign as trustee if detriment to the trust would result from divestiture of trust holdings the retention of which would place the judge in violation of Canon 4D(4).

F.   Service as Arbitrator or Mediator

A judge shall not act as an arbitrator or mediator or otherwise perform judicial functions in a private capacity unless expressly authorized by law.*

Advisory Committee Commentary: Canon 4F

Canon 4F does not prohibit a judge from participating in arbitration, mediation, or settlement conferences performed as part of his or her judicial duties.

G.   Practice of Law

A judge shall not practice law.

Advisory Committee Commentary: Canon 4G

This prohibition refers to the practice of law in a representative capacity and not in a pro se capacity. A judge may act for himself or herself in all legal matters, including matters involving litigation and matters involving appearances before or other dealings with legislative and other governmental bodies. However, in so doing, a judge must not abuse the prestige of office to advance the interests of the judge or member of the judge's family.* See Canon 2B.

This prohibition applies to subordinate judicial officers,* magistrates, special masters, and judges of the State Bar Court.

H.   Compensation, and Reimbursement, and Honoraria

A judge may receive compensation and reimbursement of expenses as provided by law* for the extrajudicial activities permitted by this code, if the source of such payments does not give the appearance of influencing the judge's performance of judicial duties or otherwise give the appearance of impropriety.*

(1)   Compensation shall not exceed a reasonable amount nor shall it exceed what a person who is not a judge would receive for the same activity.

(2)   Expense reimbursement shall be limited to the actual cost of travel, food, lodging, and other costs reasonably incurred by the judge and, where appropriate to the occasion, by the judge's spouse, or registered domestic partner,* or guest. Any payment in excess of such an amount is compensation.

(3)   No judge shall accept any honorarium. "Honorarium" means any payment made in consideration for a speech given, an article published, or attendance at any public or private conference, convention, meeting, social event, meal, or like gathering. "Honorarium" does not include earned income for personal services that are customarily provided in connection with the practice of a bona fide business, trade, or profession, such as teaching or writing for a publisher, and does not include fees or other things of value received pursuant to Penal Code section 94.5 for performance of a marriage. For purposes of this canon, "teaching" includes presentations to impart educational information to lawyers in events qualifying for credit under Mandatory Continuing Legal Education, to students in bona fide educational institutions, and to associations or groups of judges.

Advisory Committee Commentary: Canon 4H

Judges should not accept compensation or reimbursement of expenses if acceptance would appear to a reasonable person to undermine the judge's integrity,* impartiality,* or independence.*

A judge must assure himself or herself that acceptance of reimbursement or fee waivers would not appear to a reasonable person to undermine the judge's independence,* integrity,* or impartiality.* The factors a judge should consider when deciding whether to accept reimbursement or a fee waiver for attendance at a particular activity include whether:

(a)   the sponsor is an accredited educational institution or bar association rather than a trade association or a for-profit entity;

(b)   *the funding comes largely from numerous contributors rather than from a single entity, and whether the funding is earmarked for programs with specific content;*

(c)   *the content is related or unrelated to the subject matter of a pending* or impending* proceeding before the judge, or to matters that are likely to come before the judge;*

(d)   *the activity is primarily educational rather than recreational, and whether the costs of the event are reasonable and comparable to those associated with similar events sponsored by the judiciary, bar associations, or similar groups;*

(e)   *information concerning the activity and its funding sources is available upon inquiry;*

(f)   *the sponsor or source of funding is generally associated with particular parties or interests currently appearing or likely to appear in the judge's court, thus possibly requiring disqualification of the judge;*

(g)   *differing viewpoints are presented;*

(h)   *a broad range of judicial and nonjudicial participants are invited;* or

(i)   *the program is designed specifically for judges.*

Judges should be aware of the statutory limitations on accepting gifts.*

CANON 5

A Judge or Candidate for Judicial Office* Shall Not Engage In Political or Campaign Activity That Is Inconsistent With the Independence,* Integrity,* or Impartiality* of the Judiciary

Judges and candidates for judicial office* are entitled to entertain their personal views on political questions. They are not required to surrender their rights or opinions as citizens. They shall, however, not engage in political activity that may create the appearance of political bias or impropriety.* Judicial independence,* impartiality,* and integrity* shall dictate the conduct of judges and candidates for judicial office.*

Judges and candidates for judicial office* shall comply with all applicable election, election campaign, and election campaign fundraising laws* and regulations.

Advisory Committee Commentary: Canon 5

The term "political activity" should not be construed so narrowly as to prevent private comment.

A.   Political Organizations*

Judges and candidates for judicial office* shall not

(1)   act as leaders or hold any office in a political organization;*

(2)   make speeches for a political organization* or candidate for nonjudicial office or publicly endorse or publicly oppose a candidate for nonjudicial office; or

(3)   personally solicit funds for a political organization* or nonjudicial candidate; or make contributions to a political party or political organization* or to a nonjudicial candidate in excess of $500 in any calendar year per political party or political organization* or candidate, or in excess of an

aggregate of $1,000 in any calendar year for all political parties or political organizations* or nonjudicial candidates.

Advisory Committee Commentary: Canon 5A

This provision does not prohibit a judge or a candidate for judicial office* from signing a petition to qualify a measure for the ballot, provided the judge does not use his or her official title.

In judicial elections, judges are neither required to shield themselves from campaign contributions nor are they prohibited from soliciting contributions from anyone, including attorneys. Nevertheless, there are necessary limits on judges facing election if the appearance of impropriety* is to be avoided. In soliciting campaign contributions or endorsements, a judge shall not use the prestige of judicial office in a manner that would reasonably be perceived as coercive. See Canons 1, 2, 2A, and 2B. Although it is improper for a judge to receive a gift* from an attorney subject to exceptions noted in Canon 4D(6), a judge's campaign may receive attorney contributions.

Although attendance at political gatherings is not prohibited, any such attendance should be restricted so that it would not constitute an express public endorsement of a nonjudicial candidate or a measure not affecting the law, the legal system, or the administration of justice* otherwise prohibited by this canon.

Subject to the monetary limitation herein to political contributions, a judge or a candidate for judicial office* may purchase tickets for political dinners or other similar dinner functions. Any admission price to such a political dinner or function in excess of the actual cost of the meal will be considered a political contribution. The prohibition in Canon 5A(3) does not preclude judges from contributing to a campaign fund for distribution among judges who are candidates for reelection or retention, nor does it apply to contributions to any judge or candidate for judicial office.*

Under this canon, a judge may publicly endorse a candidate for judicial office.* Such endorsements are permitted because judicial officers have a special obligation to uphold the integrity,* impartiality,* and independence* of the judiciary and are in a unique position to know the qualifications necessary to serve as a competent judicial officer.

Although family members of the judge or candidate for judicial office* are not subject to the provisions of this code, a judge or candidate for judicial office* shall not avoid compliance with this code by making contributions through a spouse or registered domestic partner* or other family member.

B. Conduct During Judicial Campaigns and Appointment Process

(1) A candidate for judicial office* or an applicant seeking appointment to judicial office shall not:

(a) make statements to the electorate or the appointing authority that commit the candidate or the applicant with respect to cases, controversies, or issues that are likely to come before the courts, or

(b) knowingly,* or with reckless disregard for the truth, make false or misleading statements about the identity, qualifications, present position, or any other fact concerning himself or herself or his or her opponent or other applicants.

(2) A candidate for judicial office* shall review and approve the content of all campaign statements and materials produced by the candidate or his

or her campaign committee before its dissemination. A candidate shall take appropriate corrective action if the candidate learns of any misrepresentations made in his or her campaign statements or materials. A candidate shall take reasonable measures to prevent any misrepresentations being made in his or her support by third parties. A candidate shall take reasonable measures to ensure that appropriate corrective action is taken if the candidate learns of any misrepresentations being made in his or her support by third parties.

(3) Every candidate for judicial office* shall complete a judicial campaign ethics course approved by the Supreme Court no earlier than one year before or no later than 60 days after either the filing of a declaration of intention by the candidate, the formation of a campaign committee, or the receipt of any campaign contribution, whichever is earliest. If a judge appears on the ballot as a result of a petition indicating that a write-in campaign will be conducted for the office, the judge shall complete the course no later than 60 days after receiving notice of the filing of the petition, the formation of a campaign committee, or the receipt of any campaign contribution, whichever is earliest.

Unless a judge forms a campaign committee or solicits or receives campaign contributions, this requirement does not apply to judges who are unopposed for election and will not appear on the ballot.

Unless an appellate justice forms a campaign committee or solicits or receives campaign contributions, this requirement does not apply to appellate justices.

Advisory Committee Commentary: Canon 5B

The purpose of Canon 5B is to preserve the integrity* of the appointive and elective process for judicial office and to ensure that the public has accurate information about candidates for judicial office.* Compliance with these provisions will enhance the integrity,* impartiality,* and independence* of the judiciary and better inform the public about qualifications of candidates for judicial office.*

This code does not contain the "announce clause" that was the subject of the United States Supreme Court's decision in Republican Party of Minnesota v. White (2002) 536 U.S. 765. That opinion did not address the "commit clause," which is contained in Canon 5B(1)(a). The phrase "appear to commit" has been deleted because, although candidates for judicial office* cannot promise to take a particular position on cases, controversies, or issues prior to taking the bench and presiding over individual cases, the phrase may have been overinclusive.

Canon 5B(1)(b) prohibits knowingly making false or misleading during an election campaign because doing so would violate Canons 1 and 2A, and may violate other canons.

Candidates for judicial office* must disclose campaign contributions in accordance with Canon 3E(2)(b).

The time limit for completing a judicial campaign ethics course in Canon 5B(3) is triggered by the earliest of one of the following: the filing of a declaration of intention, the formation of a campaign committee, or the receipt of any campaign contribution. If a judge's name appears on the ballot as a result of a petition indicating that a write-in campaign will be conducted, the time limit for completing the course is triggered by the earliest of one of the following: the notice of the filing of the petition, the formation of a campaign committee, or the receipt of any campaign contribution. A *financial contribution by a candidate for judicial office* to his or her own campaign constitutes receipt of a campaign contribution.*

C.   Speaking at Political Gatherings

Candidates for judicial office* may speak to political gatherings only on their own behalf or on behalf of another candidate for judicial office.*

D.   Measures to Improve the Law

A judge or candidate for judicial office* may engage in activity in relation to measures concerning improvement of the law, the legal system, or the administration of justice,* only if the conduct is consistent with this code.

Advisory Committee Commentary: Canon 5D

When deciding whether to engage in activity relating to measures concerning the law, the legal system, or the administration of justice,* such as commenting publicly on ballot measures, a judge must consider whether the conduct would violate any other provisions of this code. See the explanation of "law, the legal system, or the administration of justice" in the Terminology section.

CANON 6

Compliance With the Code of Judicial Ethics

A.   Judges

Anyone who is an officer of the state judicial system and who performs judicial functions, including, but not limited to, a subordinate judicial officer,* a magistrate, a court-appointed arbitrator, a judge of the State Bar Court, a temporary judge,* or a special master, is a judge within the meaning of this code. All judges shall comply with this code except as provided below.

Advisory Committee Commentary: Canon 6A

For the purposes of this canon, if a retired judge is serving in the Assigned Judges Program, the judge is considered to "perform judicial functions." Because retired judges who are privately retained may perform judicial functions, their conduct while performing those functions should be guided by this code.

B.   Retired Judge Serving in the Assigned Judges Program

A retired judge who has filed an application to serve on assignment, meets the eligibility requirements set by the Chief Justice for service, and has received an acknowledgment of participation in the Assigned Judges Program shall comply with all provisions of this code, except for the following:

4C(2)—Appointment to governmental positions

4E—Fiduciary* activities

C.   Retired Judge as Arbitrator or Mediator

A retired judge serving in the Assigned Judges Program is not required to comply with Canon 4F of this code relating to serving as an arbitrator or mediator, or performing judicial functions in a private capacity, except as otherwise provided in the *Standards and Guidelines for Judicial Assignments* promulgated by the Chief Justice.

Advisory Committee Commentary: Canon 6C

Article VI, section 6 of the California Constitution provides that a "retired judge who consents may be assigned to any court" by the Chief Justice. Retired judges who are serving in the Assigned Judges Program *pursuant to the above provision are bound by Canon 6B, including the requirement of Canon 4G barring the practice of law. Other provisions of California law,* and standards and guidelines for eligibility and service set by the Chief Justice, further define the limitations on who may serve on assignment.*

D.   Temporary Judge,* Referee, or Court-Appointed Arbitrator[1]

A temporary judge,* a person serving as a referee pursuant to Code of Civil Procedure section 638 or 639, or a court-appointed arbitrator shall comply only with the following code provisions:

(1)   A temporary judge,* a referee, or a court-appointed arbitrator shall comply with Canons 1 [integrity* and independence* of the judiciary], 2A [promoting public confidence], 3B(3) [order and decorum], 3B(4) [patient, dignified, and courteous treatment], 3B(6) [require* lawyers to refrain from manifestations of any form of bias or prejudice], 3D(1) [action regarding misconduct by another judge], and 3D(2) [action regarding misconduct by a lawyer], when the temporary judge,* referee, or court-appointed arbitrator is actually presiding in a proceeding or communicating with the parties, counsel, or staff or court personnel while serving in the capacity of a temporary judge,* referee, or court-appointed arbitrator in the case.

(2)   A temporary judge,* referee, or court-appointed arbitrator shall, from the time of notice and acceptance of appointment until termination of the appointment:

(a)   Comply with Canons 2B(1) [not allow family or other relationships to influence judicial conduct], 3B(1) [hear and decide all matters unless disqualified], 3B(2) [be faithful to and maintain competence in the law*], 3B(5) [perform judicial duties without bias or prejudice], 3B(7) [accord full right to be heard to those entitled; avoid ex parte communications, except as specified], 3B(8) [dispose of matters fairly and promptly], 3B(12) [remain impartial* and not engage in coercive conduct during efforts to resolve disputes], 3C(1) [discharge administrative responsibilities without bias and with competence and cooperatively], 3C(3) [require* staff and court personnel to observe standards of conduct and refrain from bias and prejudice], and 3C(5) [make only fair, necessary, and appropriate appointments];

(b)   Not personally solicit memberships or donations for religious, service,* educational, civic, or charitable organizations from the parties and lawyers appearing before the temporary judge,* referee, or court-appointed arbitrator;

(c)   Under no circumstance accept a gift,* bequest, or favor if the donor is a party, person, or entity whose interests are reasonably likely to come before the temporary judge,* referee, or court-appointed arbitrator. A temporary judge,* referee, or court-appointed arbitrator shall discourage members of the judge's family residing in the judge's household* from accepting benefits from parties who are reasonably likely to come before the temporary judge,* referee, or court-appointed arbitrator.

(3)   A temporary judge* shall, from the time of notice and acceptance of appointment until termination of the appointment, disqualify himself or herself in any proceeding as follows:

---

[1]   Reference should be made to relevant commentary to analogous or individual canons cited or described in this canon and appearing elsewhere in this code.

(a) A temporary judge*other than a temporary judge solely conducting settlement conferences—is disqualified to serve in a proceeding if any one or more of the following are true:

(i) the temporary judge* has personal knowledge* (as defined in Code of Civil Procedure section 170.1, subdivision (a)(1)) of disputed evidentiary facts concerning the proceeding;

(ii) the temporary judge* has served as a lawyer (as defined in Code of Civil Procedure section 170.1, subdivision (a)(2)) in the proceeding;

(iii) the temporary judge,* within the past five years, has given legal advice to, or served as a lawyer (as defined in Code of Civil Procedure section 170.1, subdivision (a)(2), except that this provision requires disqualification if the temporary judge* represented a party in the past five years rather than the two-year period specified in section 170.1, subdivision (a)(2)) for a party in the present proceeding;

Advisory Committee Commentary: Canon 6D(3)(a)(iii)

The application of Canon 6D(3)(a)(iii), providing that a temporary judge* is disqualified if he or she has given legal advice or served as a lawyer for a party to the proceeding in the past five years, may depend on the type of assignment and the amount of time available to investigate whether the temporary judge* has previously represented a party. If time permits, the temporary judge* must 2 conduct such an investigation. Thus, if a temporary judge* is privately compensated by the parties or is presiding over a particular matter known* in advance of the hearing, the temporary judge* is presumed to have adequate time to investigate. If, however, a temporary judge* is assigned to a high volume calendar, such as traffic or small claims, and has not been provided with the names of the parties prior to the assignment, the temporary judge* may rely on his or her memory to determine whether he or she has previously represented a party.

(iv) the temporary judge* has a financial interest (as defined in Code of Civil Procedure sections 170.1, subdivision (a)(3) and 170.5) in the subject matter in the proceeding or in a party to the proceeding;

(v) the temporary judge,* or the spouse or registered domestic partner* of the temporary judge,* or a person within the third degree of relationship* to either of them, or the spouse or registered domestic partner* of such a person is a party to the proceeding or is an officer, director, or trustee of a party;

(vi) a lawyer or a spouse or registered domestic partner* of a lawyer in the proceeding is the spouse, former spouse, registered domestic partner,* former registered domestic partner,* child, sibling, or parent of the temporary judge* or the temporary judge's spouse or registered domestic partner,* or if such a person is associated in the private practice of law with a lawyer in the proceeding;

(vii) for any reason:

(A) the temporary judge* believes his or her recusal would further the interests of justice;

(B) the temporary judge* believes there is a substantial doubt as to his or her capacity to be impartial;* or

(C) a person aware of the facts might reasonably entertain a doubt that the temporary judge* would be able to be impartial.* Bias or prejudice toward an attorney in the proceeding may be grounds for disqualification; or

(viii) the temporary judge* has received a campaign contribution of $1,500 or more from a party or lawyer in a matter that is before the court and the contribution was received in anticipation of an upcoming election.

(b) A temporary judge* before whom a proceeding was tried or heard is disqualified from participating in any appellate review of that proceeding.

(c) If the temporary judge* has a current arrangement concerning prospective employment or other compensated service as a dispute resolution neutral or is participating in, or, within the last two years has participated in, discussions regarding prospective employment or service as a dispute resolution neutral, or has been engaged in such employment or service, and any of the following applies:

(i) The arrangement or current employment is, or the prior employment or discussion was, with a party to the proceeding;

(ii) The temporary judge* directs the parties to participate in an alternative dispute resolution process in which the dispute resolution neutral will be an individual or entity with whom the temporary judge* has the arrangement, is currently employed or serves, has previously been employed or served, or is discussing or has discussed the employment or service; or

(iii) The temporary judge* will select a dispute resolution neutral or entity to conduct an alternative dispute resolution process in the matter before the temporary judge,* and among those available for selection is an individual or entity with whom the temporary judge* has the arrangement, is currently employed or serves, has previously been employed or served, or is discussing or has discussed the employment or service.

For the purposes of Canon 6D(3)(c), the definitions of "participating in discussions," "has participated in discussions," "party," and "dispute resolution neutral" are set forth in Code of Civil Procedure section 170.1, subdivision (a)(8), except that the words "temporary judge" shall be substituted for the word "judge" in such definitions.

(d) A lawyer is disqualified from serving as a temporary judge* in a family law or unlawful detainer proceeding if in the same type of proceeding:

(i) the lawyer holds himself or herself out to the public as representing exclusively one side; or

(ii) the lawyer represents one side in 90 percent or more of the cases in which he or she appears.

Advisory Committee Commentary: Canon 6D(3)(d)

Under Canon 6D(3)(d), "one side" means a category of persons such as landlords, tenants, or litigants exclusively of one gender.

(4) After a temporary judge* who has determined himself or herself to be disqualified from serving under Canon 6D(3)(a)–(d) has disclosed the basis for his or her disqualification on the record, the parties and their lawyers may agree to waive the disqualification and the temporary judge* may accept the

waiver. The temporary judge* shall not seek to induce a waiver and shall avoid any effort to discover which lawyers or parties favored or opposed a waiver.

Advisory Committee Commentary: Canon 6D(4)

Provisions addressing waiver of mandatory disqualifications or limitations, late discovery of grounds for disqualification or limitation, notification of the court when a disqualification or limitation applies, and requests for disqualification by the parties are located in rule 2.818 of the California Rules of Court. Rule 2.818 states that the waiver must be in writing, must recite the basis for the disqualification or limitation, and must state that it was knowingly* made. It also states that the waiver is effective only when signed by all parties and their attorneys and filed in the record.

(5) A temporary judge,* referee, or court-appointed arbitrator shall, from the time of notice and acceptance of appointment until termination of the appointment:

(a) In all proceedings, disclose in writing or on the record information as required by law,* or information that is reasonably relevant to the question of disqualification under Canon 6D(3), including personal or professional relationships known* to the temporary judge,* referee, or court-appointed arbitrator, that he or she or his or her law firm has had with a party, lawyer, or law firm in the current proceeding, even though the temporary judge,* referee, or court-appointed arbitrator concludes that there is no actual basis for disqualification; and

(b) In all proceedings, disclose in writing or on the record membership of the temporary judge,* referee, or court-appointed arbitrator, in any organization that practices invidious discrimination on the basis of race, sex, gender, religion, national origin, ethnicity, or sexual orientation, except for membership in a religious organization.

(6) A temporary judge,* referee, or court-appointed arbitrator, from the time of notice and acceptance of appointment until the case is no longer pending in any court, shall not make any public comment about a pending* or impending* proceeding in which the temporary judge,* referee, or court-appointed arbitrator has been engaged, and shall not make any nonpublic comment that might substantially interfere with such proceeding. The temporary judge,* referee, or court-appointed arbitrator shall require* similar abstention on the part of staff and court personnel subject to his or her control. This canon does not prohibit the following:

(a) Statements made in the course of the official duties of the temporary judge,* referee, or court-appointed arbitrator; and

(b) Explanations about the procedures of the court.

(7) From the time of appointment and continuing for two years after the case is no longer pending* in any court, a temporary judge,* referee, or court-appointed arbitrator shall under no circumstances accept a gift,* bequest, or favor from a party, person, or entity whose interests have come before the temporary judge,* referee, or court-appointed arbitrator in the matter. The temporary judge,* referee, or court-appointed arbitrator shall discourage family members residing in the household of the temporary judge,* referee, or court-appointed arbitrator from accepting any benefits from such parties, persons or entities during the time period stated in this subdivision. The demand for or receipt by a temporary judge,* referee, or

court-appointed arbitrator of a fee for his or her services rendered or to be rendered would not be a violation of this canon.

(8) A temporary judge,* referee, or court-appointed arbitrator shall, from the time of notice and acceptance of appointment and continuing indefinitely after the termination of the appointment:

(a) Comply with Canon 3B(11) [no disclosure of nonpublic information* acquired in a judicial capacity] (except as required by law*);

(b) Not commend or criticize jurors sitting in a proceeding before the temporary judge,* referee, or court-appointed arbitrator for their verdict other than in a court order or opinion in such proceeding, but may express appreciation to jurors for their service to the judicial system and the community; and

(c) Not lend the prestige of judicial office to advance his, her, or another person's pecuniary or personal interests and not use his or her judicial title in any written communication intended to advance his, her, or another person's pecuniary or personal interests, except to show his, her, or another person's qualifications.

(9) (a) A temporary judge* appointed under rule 2.810 of the California Rules of Court, from the time of the appointment and continuing indefinitely after the termination of the appointment, shall not use his or her title or service as a temporary judge* (1) as a description of the lawyer's current or former principal profession, vocation, or occupation on a ballot designation for judicial or other elected office (2) in an advertisement about the lawyer's law firm or business, or (3) on a letterhead, business card, or other document that is distributed to the public identifying the lawyer or the lawyer's law firm.

(b) This canon does not prohibit a temporary judge* appointed under rule 2.810 of the California Rules of Court from using his or her title or service as a temporary judge* on an application to serve as a temporary judge,* including an application in other courts, on an application for employment or for an appointment to a judicial position, on an individual resume or a descriptive statement submitted in connection with an application for employment or for appointment or election to a judicial position, or in response to a request for information about the public service in which the lawyer has engaged.

(10) A temporary judge,* referee, or court-appointed arbitrator shall comply with Canon 6D(2) until the appointment has been terminated formally or until there is no reasonable probability that the temporary judge,* referee, or court-appointed arbitrator will further participate in the matter. A rebuttable presumption that the appointment has been formally terminated will arise if, within one year from the appointment or from the date of the last hearing scheduled in the matter, whichever is later, neither the appointing court nor counsel for any party in the matter has informed the temporary judge,* referee, or court-appointed arbitrator that the appointment remains in effect.

(11) A lawyer who has been a temporary judge,* referee, or court-appointed arbitrator in a matter shall not accept any representation relating to the matter without the informed written consent of all parties.

(12) When by reason of serving as a temporary judge,* referee, or court-appointed arbitrator in a matter, he or she has received confidential

information from a party, the person shall not, without the informed written consent of the party, accept employment in another matter in which the confidential information is material.

Advisory Committee Commentary: Canon 6D

Any exceptions to the canons do not excuse a judicial officer's separate statutory duty to disclose information that may result in the judicial officer's recusal or disqualification.

E.   Judicial Candidate

A candidate for judicial office* shall comply with the provisions of Canon 5.

F.   Time for Compliance

A person to whom this code becomes applicable shall comply immediately with all provisions of this code except Canons 4D(4) and 4E and shall comply with these Canons 4D(4) and 4E as soon as reasonably possible and shall do so in any event within a period of one year.

Advisory Committee Commentary: Canon 6F

If serving as a fiduciary when selected as a judge, a new judge may, notwithstanding the prohibitions in Canon 4E, continue to serve as a fiduciary* but only for that period of time necessary to avoid adverse consequences to the beneficiary of the fiduciary* relationship and in no event longer than one year.*

G.   (Repealed)

H.   Judges on Leave Running for Other Public Office

A judge who is on leave while running for other public office pursuant to article VI, section 17 of the California Constitution shall comply with all provisions of this code, except for the following, insofar as the conduct relates to the campaign for public office for which the judge is on leave:

2B(2)—Lending the prestige of judicial office to advance the judge's personal interest

4C(1)—Appearing at public hearings

5—Engaging in political activity (including soliciting and accepting campaign contributions for the other public office).

Advisory Committee Commentary: Canon 6H

These exceptions are applicable only during the time the judge is on leave while running for other public office. All of the provisions of this code will become applicable at the time a judge resumes his or her position as a judge. Conduct during elections for judicial office is governed by Canon 5.

CALIFORNIA RULE ON CONFIDENTIALITY OF PROCEEDINGS BEFORE THE COMMISSION ON JUDICIAL PERFORMANCE

(as amended effective 3/28/18)

RULE 102. Confidentiality and Disclosure

(a) (Scope of rule) Except as provided in this rule, all papers filed with and proceedings before the commission shall be confidential. Nothing in this rule prohibits the respondent judge or anyone other than a commission member or member of commission staff from making statements regarding the judge's conduct underlying a complaint or proceeding.

(b) (Disclosure after institution of formal proceedings) When the commission institutes formal proceedings, the following shall not be confidential:

(1) The notice of formal proceedings and all subsequent papers filed with the commission and the special masters, all stipulations entered, all findings of fact and conclusions of law made by the special masters and by the commission, and all determinations of removal, censure and public admonishment made by the commission;

(2) The formal hearing before the special masters and the appearance before the commission.

(c) (Explanatory statements) The commission may issue explanatory statements under article VI, section 18(k) of the California Constitution.

(d) (Submission of proposed statement of clarification and correction regarding commission proceedings by judge) Notwithstanding rule 102(a), if public reports concerning a commission proceeding result in substantial unfairness to the judge involved in the proceeding, including unfairness resulting from reports which are false or materially misleading or inaccurate, the involved judge may submit a proposed statement of clarification and correction to the commission and request its issuance. The commission shall either issue the requested statement, advise the judge in writing that it declines to issue the requested statement, or issue a modified statement.

(e) (Disclosure to complainant) Upon completion of an investigation or proceeding, the commission shall disclose to the person complaining against the judge that the commission (1) has found no basis for action against the judge or determined not to proceed further in this matter (2) has taken an appropriate corrective action, the nature of which shall not be disclosed, or (3) has publicly admonished, censured, removed, or retired the judge, or has found the person unfit to serve as a subordinate judicial officer. Where a matter is referred to the commission by a presiding judge or other public official in his or her official capacity, disclosure under this subdivision concerning that matter shall be made to the individual serving in that office at the time the matter is concluded. The name of the judge shall not be used in any written communication to the complainant, unless formal proceedings have been instituted or unless the complainant is a presiding judge or other public official in his or her official capacity. Written communications in which the judge's name is not used shall include the date of the complaint as a cross-reference.

(f) (Public safety) When the commission receives information concerning a threat to the safety of any person or persons, information concerning such a threat may be provided to the person threatened, to persons or organizations responsible for the safety of the person threatened, and to law enforcement and/or any appropriate prosecutorial agency.

(g) (Disclosure of information to prosecuting authorities) The commission may release to prosecuting authorities at any time information which reveals possible criminal conduct by the judge or former judge or by any other individual or entity.

(h) (Disclosure of records to public entity upon request or consent of judge) If a judge or former judge requests or consents to release of commission records to a public entity, the commission may release that judge's records.

(i) (Disclosure of records of disciplinary action to appointing authorities) The commission shall, upon request, provide to the Governor of any State of the Union, the President of the United States, or the Commission on Judicial Appointments the text of any private admonishment or advisory letter issued after March 1, 1995 or any other disciplinary action together with any information that the commission deems necessary to a full understanding of the commission's action, with respect to any applicant under consideration for any judicial appointment, provided that:

(1)   The request is in writing; and

(2)   Any information released to the appointing authority is simultaneously provided to the applicant.

All information disclosed to appointing authorities under this subdivision remains privileged and confidential. Private admonishments and advisory letters issued before March 1, 1995 shall only be disclosed under this section with the judge's written consent.

(j) (Disclosure of information regarding pending proceedings to appointing authorities) The commission may, upon request, in the interest of justice or to maintain public confidence in the administration of justice, provide to the Governor of any State of the Union, the President of the United States, the Commission on Judicial Appointments, or any other state or federal authorities responsible for judicial appointments information concerning any pending investigation or proceeding with respect to any applicant under consideration for any judicial appointment, provided that:

(1)   The request is in writing; and

(2)   Any information released to the appointing authority is simultaneously provided to the applicant.

If a disclosure about a pending matter is made and that matter subsequently is closed by the commission without discipline being imposed, disclosure of the latter fact shall be made promptly to the appointing authority and the judge.

All information disclosed to appointing authorities under this subdivision remains privileged and confidential.

(k) (Disclosure of information to regulatory agencies upon retirement or resignation) If a judge retires or resigns from office or if a subordinate judicial officer retires, resigns or is terminated from employment after a complaint is filed with the commission, or if a complaint is filed with the commission after the retirement, resignation or termination, the commission may, in the interest of justice or to maintain public confidence in the administration of justice, release information concerning the complaint, investigation and proceedings to the State Bar or to other regulatory agencies, provided that the commission has commenced a preliminary investigation or other proceeding and the judge or subordinate judicial officer has had an opportunity to respond to the commission's inquiry or preliminary investigation letter.

(l) (Disclosure of information about subordinate judicial officers to presiding judges) The commission may release to a presiding judge or his or her designee information concerning a complaint, investigation or disposition involving a subordinate judicial officer, including the name of the subordinate judicial officer, consistent with the commission's jurisdiction under article VI, section 18.1 of the California Constitution.

(m) (Disclosure of information regarding disciplinary action and pending proceedings to the Chief Justice) With respect to any judge who is under consideration for judicial assignment following retirement or resignation, or is sitting on assignment, the commission may, upon the request of the Chief Justice of California and with the consent of that judge, in the interest of justice or to maintain public confidence in the administration of justice, provide the Chief Justice information concerning any record of disciplinary action or any pending investigation or proceeding with respect to that judge, provided that:

(1) The request and consent are in writing;

(2) If the disclosure involves a pending investigation or proceeding, the judge has had an opportunity to respond to the pending investigation or proceeding; and

(3) Any information released to the Chief Justice is simultaneously provided to the judge seeking assignment.

If the disclosure involves disciplinary action, the commission may include any information the commission deems necessary to a full understanding of its action.

If a disclosure about a pending matter is made and that matter subsequently is closed by the commission without discipline being imposed, disclosure of the latter fact shall be made promptly to the Chief Justice and the judge.

All information disclosed to the Chief Justice under this subdivision remains privileged and confidential.

(n) (Disclosure of information to presiding judges about possible lack of capacity or other inability to perform) The commission may release to a presiding judge or his or her designee information concerning an investigation involving possible lack of capacity or other inability to perform judicial duties on the part of a judge of that court, except that no confidential medical information concerning the judge may be released.

(o) (Disclosure of closing to judge who provides information to the commission) Upon completion of the commission's review of a complaint or an investigation, the commission may notify a judge who is the subject of a complaint and has voluntarily provided information to the commission concerning the complaint, that the commission has found no basis for action against the judge or determined not to proceed further in the matter. The notification shall be in writing.

(p) (Disclosure of information to regulatory agencies) The commission may in the interest of justice, to protect the public, or to maintain public confidence in the administration of justice, release to a federal, state or local regulatory agency information which reveals a possible violation of a law or regulation within the agency's jurisdiction by a judge, former judge, subordinate judicial officer or former subordinate judicial officer, provided the commission has commenced a preliminary investigation.

In the event information is revealed under this subsection, the agency must be admonished that the fact that the commission has undertaken an investigation of the judge must remain confidential unless formal proceedings have been instituted.

(q) (Disclosure of information to mentor judge) When a judge has agreed to participate in a mentoring program, the commission may provide the mentor judge with the specifications of the allegations before the commission, any materials concerning the allegations the commission deems relevant and necessary for the mentor to perform his or her services, and any prior discipline, including private discipline, imposed on the judge for similar misconduct. The mentor judge will not be given the complaint or witness statements, but may be given a summary of information provided in the complaint and witness statements.

If a judge who participated in mentoring is found to have engaged in subsequent misconduct, any resulting discipline, including public discipline, on the subsequent matter may include a discussion of the prior matter that was the subject of the mentoring and that the judge participated in mentoring.

The provision of subsection (q) of rule 102 shall take effect June 29, 2016, and shall be operative until June 28, 2020, unless after review, it is reenacted by the commission.

CODE OF CONDUCT FOR UNITED STATES JUDGES

This Code of Conduct was initially adopted by the Judicial Conference of the United States on April 5, 1973. It was revised in 1987, 1992, 1996, 1999, 2000, 2009 and 2014. Federal judges are in the same line of work as state judges, so you will not be surprised that many of the standards are the same for each. Federal judges do not want to be bound by standards adopted by the states, however, so they created this separate document.

The Code of Conduct applies to United States Circuit judges, District judges, Court of International Trade judges, Court of Federal Claims judges, bankruptcy judges, and magistrate judges. Certain provisions apply to special masters and commissioners as indicated in the "Compliance" section. The Tax Court, Court of Appeals for Veterans Claims, and Court of Appeals for the Armed Forces have adopted this Code.

The Judicial Conference Committee on Codes of Conduct gives advisory opinions about the Code when asked by a judge to whom this Code applies.

CANON 1: A JUDGE SHOULD UPHOLD THE INTEGRITY AND INDEPENDENCE OF THE JUDICIARY

An independent and honorable judiciary is indispensable to justice in our society. A judge should maintain and enforce high standards of conduct and should personally observe those standards, so that the integrity and independence of the judiciary may be preserved. The provisions of this Code should be construed and applied to further that objective.

COMMENTARY

Deference to the judgments and rulings of courts depends on public confidence in the integrity and independence of judges. The integrity and independence of judges depend in turn on their acting without fear or favor. Although judges should be independent, they must comply with the law and should comply with this Code. Adherence to this responsibility helps to maintain public confidence in the impartiality of the judiciary. Conversely, violation of this Code diminishes public confidence in the judiciary and injures our system of government under law.

The Canons are rules of reason. They should be applied consistently with constitutional requirements, statutes, other court rules and decisional law, and in the context of all relevant circumstances. The Code is to be construed so it does not impinge on the essential independence of judges in making judicial decisions.

The Code is designed to provide guidance to judges and nominees for judicial office. It may also provide standards of conduct for application in proceedings under the Judicial Councils Reform and Judicial Conduct and Disability Act of 1980 (28 U.S.C. §§ 332(d)(1), 351–364). Not every violation of the Code should lead to disciplinary action. Whether disciplinary action is appropriate, and the degree of discipline, should be determined through a reasonable application of the text and should depend on such factors as the seriousness of the improper activity, the intent of the judge, whether there is a pattern of improper activity, and the effect of the improper activity on others or on the judicial system. Many of the restrictions in the Code are necessarily cast in general terms, and judges may reasonably differ in their interpretation. Furthermore, the Code is not designed or intended as a basis for civil liability or criminal prosecution. Finally, the Code is not intended to be used for tactical advantage.

CANON 2: A JUDGE SHOULD AVOID IMPROPRIETY AND THE APPEARANCE OF IMPROPRIETY IN ALL ACTIVITIES

A.   Respect for Law. A judge should respect and comply with the law and should act at all times in a manner that promotes public confidence in the integrity and impartiality of the judiciary.

B.   Outside Influence. A judge should not allow family, social, political, financial, or other relationships to influence judicial conduct or judgment. A judge should neither lend the prestige of the judicial office to advance the private interests of the judge or others nor convey or permit others to convey the impression that they are in a special position to influence the judge. A judge should not testify voluntarily as a character witness.

C.   Nondiscriminatory Membership. A judge should not hold membership in any organization that practices invidious discrimination on the basis of race, sex, religion, or national origin.

COMMENTARY

Canon 2A. An appearance of impropriety occurs when reasonable minds, with knowledge of all the relevant circumstances disclosed by a reasonable inquiry, would conclude that the judge's honesty, integrity, impartiality, temperament, or fitness to serve as a judge is impaired. Public confidence in the judiciary is eroded by irresponsible or improper conduct by judges. A judge must avoid all impropriety and appearance of impropriety. This prohibition applies to both professional and personal conduct. A judge must expect to be the subject of constant public scrutiny and accept freely and willingly restrictions that might be viewed as burdensome by the ordinary citizen. Because it is not practicable to list all prohibited acts, the prohibition is necessarily cast in general terms that extend to conduct by judges that is harmful although not specifically mentioned in the Code. Actual improprieties under this standard include violations of law, court rules, or other specific provisions of this Code.

Canon 2B. Testimony as a character witness injects the prestige of the judicial office into the proceeding in which the judge testifies and may be perceived as an official testimonial. A judge should discourage a party from requiring the judge to testify as a character witness except in unusual circumstances when the demands of justice require. This Canon does not create a privilege against testifying in response to an official summons.

A judge should avoid lending the prestige of judicial office to advance the private interests of the judge or others. For example, a judge should not use the judge's judicial position or title to gain advantage in litigation involving a friend or a member of the judge's family. In contracts for publication of a judge's writings, a judge should retain control over the advertising to avoid exploitation of the judge's office.

A judge should be sensitive to possible abuse of the prestige of office. A judge should not initiate communications to a sentencing judge or a probation or corrections officer but may provide information to such persons in response to a formal request. Judges may participate in the process of judicial selection by cooperating with appointing authorities and screening committees seeking names for consideration and by responding to official inquiries concerning a person being considered for a judgeship.

Canon 2C. Membership of a judge in an organization that practices invidious discrimination gives rise to perceptions that the judge's impartiality is impaired. Canon 2C refers to the current practices of the organization. Whether an organization practices invidious discrimination is often a complex question to which judges should be sensitive. The answer cannot be determined from a mere examination of an organization's current membership rolls but rather depends on how the organization selects members and other relevant factors, such as that the organization is dedicated to the preservation of religious, ethnic or cultural values of legitimate common interest to its members, or that it is in fact and effect an intimate, purely private organization whose membership limitations could not be constitutionally prohibited. *See New York State Club Ass'n. Inc. v. City of New York*, 487 U.S. 1, 108 S. Ct. 2225, 101 L. Ed. 2d 1 (1988); *Board of Directors of Rotary International v. Rotary Club of Duarte*, 481 U.S. 537, 107 S. Ct. 1940, 95 L. Ed. 2d 474 (1987); *Roberts v. United States Jaycees*, 468 U.S. 609, 104 S. Ct. 3244, 82 L. Ed. 2d 462 (1984). Other relevant factors include the size and nature of the organization and the diversity of persons in the locale who might reasonably be considered potential members. Thus the mere absence of diverse membership does not by itself demonstrate a violation unless reasonable persons with knowledge of all the relevant circumstances would expect that the membership would be diverse in the absence of invidious discrimination. Absent such factors, an organization is generally said to discriminate invidiously if it arbitrarily excludes from membership on the basis of race, religion, sex, or national origin persons who would otherwise be admitted to membership.

Although Canon 2C relates only to membership in organizations that invidiously discriminate on the basis of race, sex, religion or national origin, a judge's membership in an organization that engages in any invidiously discriminatory membership practices prohibited by applicable law violates Canons 2 and 2A and gives the appearance of impropriety. In addition, it would be a violation of Canons 2 and 2A for a judge to arrange a meeting at a club that the judge knows practices invidious discrimination on the basis of race, sex, religion, or national origin in its membership or other policies, or for the judge to use such a club regularly. Moreover, public manifestation by a judge of the judge's knowing approval of invidious discrimination on any basis gives the appearance of impropriety under Canon 2 and diminishes public confidence in the integrity and impartiality of the judiciary, in violation of Canon 2A.

When a judge determines that an organization to which the judge belongs engages in invidious discrimination that would preclude membership under Canon 2C or under Canons 2 and 2A, the judge is permitted, in lieu of resigning, to make immediate and continuous efforts to have the organization discontinue its invidiously discriminatory practices. If the organization fails to discontinue its invidiously discriminatory practices as promptly as possible (and in all events within two years of the judge's first learning of the practices), the judge should resign immediately from the organization.

CANON 3:   **A JUDGE SHOULD PERFORM THE DUTIES OF THE OFFICE FAIRLY, IMPARTIALLY AND DILIGENTLY**

The duties of judicial office take precedence over all other activities. In performing the duties prescribed by law, the judge should adhere to the following standards:

A. *Adjudicative Responsibilities.*

(1) A judge should be faithful to, and maintain professional competence in, the law and should not be swayed by partisan interests, public clamor, or fear of criticism.

(2) A judge should hear and decide matters assigned, unless disqualified, and should maintain order and decorum in all judicial proceedings.

(3) A judge should be patient, dignified, respectful, and courteous to litigants, jurors, witnesses, lawyers, and others with whom the judge deals in an official capacity. A judge should require similar conduct of those subject to the judge's control, including lawyers to the extent consistent with their role in the adversary process.

(4) A judge should accord to every person who has a legal interest in a proceeding, and that person's lawyer, the full right to be heard according to law. Except as set out below, a judge should not initiate, permit, or consider ex parte communications or consider other communications concerning a pending or impending matter that are made outside the presence of the parties or their lawyers. If a judge receives an unauthorized ex parte communication bearing on the substance of a matter, the judge should promptly notify the parties of the subject matter of the communication and allow the parties an opportunity to respond, if requested. A judge may:

    (a) initiate, permit, or consider ex parte communications as authorized by law;

    (b) when circumstances require it, permit ex parte communication for scheduling, administrative, or emergency purposes, but only if the ex parte communication does not address substantive matters and the judge reasonably believes that no party will gain a procedural, substantive, or tactical advantage as a result of the ex parte communication;

    (c) obtain the written advice of a disinterested expert on the law, but only after giving advance notice to the parties of the person to be consulted and the subject matter of the advice and affording the parties reasonable opportunity to object and respond to the notice and to the advice received; or

    (d) with the consent of the parties, confer separately with the parties and their counsel in an effort to mediate or settle pending matters.

(5) A judge should dispose promptly of the business of the court.

(6) A judge should not make public comment on the merits of a matter pending or impending in any court. A judge should require similar restraint by court personnel subject to the judge's direction and control. The prohibition on public comment on the merits does not extend to public statements made in the course of the judge's official duties, to explanations of court procedures, or to scholarly presentations made for purposes of legal education.

B. *Administrative Responsibilities.*

(1) A judge should diligently discharge administrative responsibilities, maintain professional competence in judicial

administration, and facilitate the performance of the administrative responsibilities of other judges and court personnel.

(2)   A judge should not direct court personnel to engage in conduct on the judge's behalf or as the judge's representative when that conduct would contravene the Code if undertaken by the judge.

(3)   A judge should exercise the power of appointment fairly and only on the basis of merit, avoiding unnecessary appointments, nepotism, and favoritism. A judge should not approve compensation of appointees beyond the fair value of services rendered.

(4)   A judge with supervisory authority over other judges should take reasonable measures to ensure that they perform their duties timely and effectively.

(5)   A judge should take appropriate action upon learning of reliable evidence indicating the likelihood that a judge's conduct contravened this Code or a lawyer violated applicable rules of professional conduct.

C.   Disqualification.

(1)   A judge shall disqualify himself or herself in a proceeding in which the judge's impartiality might reasonably be questioned, including but not limited to instances in which:

(a)   the judge has a personal bias or prejudice concerning a party, or personal knowledge of disputed evidentiary facts concerning the proceeding;

(b)   the judge served as a lawyer in the matter in controversy, or a lawyer with whom the judge previously practiced law served during such association as a lawyer concerning the matter, or the judge or lawyer has been a material witness;

(c)   the judge knows that the judge, individually or as a fiduciary, or the judge's spouse or minor child residing in the judge's household, has a financial interest in the subject matter in controversy or in a party to the proceeding, or any other interest that could be affected substantially by the outcome of the proceeding;

(d)   the judge or the judge's spouse, or a person related to either within the third degree of relationship, or the spouse of such a person is:

(i)   a party to the proceeding, or an officer, director, or trustee of a party;

(ii)   acting as a lawyer in the proceeding;

(iii)   known by the judge to have an interest that could be substantially affected by the outcome of the proceeding; or

(iv)   to the judge's knowledge likely to be a material witness in the proceeding;

(e)   the judge has served in governmental employment and in that capacity participated as a judge (in a previous judicial position), counsel, advisor, or material witness concerning the proceeding or has expressed an opinion concerning the merits of the particular case in controversy.

(2) A judge should keep informed about the judge's personal and fiduciary financial interests and make a reasonable effort to keep informed about the personal financial interests of the judge's spouse and minor children residing in the judge's household.

(3) For the purposes of this section:

(a) the degree of relationship is calculated according to the civil law system; the following relatives are within the third degree of relationship: parent, child, grandparent, grandchild, great grandparent, great grandchild, sister, brother, aunt, uncle, niece, and nephew; the listed relatives include whole and half blood relatives and most step relatives;

(b) "fiduciary" includes such relationships as executor, administrator, trustee, and guardian;

(c) "financial interest" means ownership of a legal or equitable interest, however small, or a relationship as director, advisor, or other active participant in the affairs of a party, except that:

(i) ownership in a mutual or common investment fund that holds securities is not a "financial interest" in such securities unless the judge participates in the management of the fund;

(ii) an office in an educational, religious, charitable, fraternal, or civic organization is not a "financial interest" in securities held by the organization;

(iii) the proprietary interest of a policyholder in a mutual insurance company, or a depositor in a mutual savings association, or a similar proprietary interest, is a "financial interest" in the organization only if the outcome of the proceeding could substantially affect the value of the interest;

(iv) ownership of government securities is a "financial interest" in the issuer only if the outcome of the proceeding could substantially affect the value of the securities;

(d) "proceeding" includes pretrial, trial, appellate review, or other stages of litigation.

(4) Notwithstanding the preceding provisions of this Canon, if a judge would be disqualified because of a financial interest in a party (other than an interest that could be substantially affected by the outcome), disqualification is not required if the judge (or the judge's spouse or minor child) divests the interest that provides the grounds for disqualification.

D. Remittal of Disqualification.

Instead of withdrawing from the proceeding, a judge disqualified by Canon 3C(1) may, except in the circumstances specifically set out in subsections (a) through (e), disclose on the record the basis of disqualification. The judge may participate in the proceeding if, after that disclosure, the parties and their lawyers have an opportunity to confer outside the presence of the judge, all agree in writing or on the record that the judge should not be disqualified, and the judge is then willing to participate. The agreement should be incorporated in the record of the proceeding.

COMMENTARY

Canon 3A(3). The duty to hear all proceedings fairly and with patience is not inconsistent with the duty to dispose promptly of the business of the court. Courts can be efficient and businesslike while being patient and deliberate.

The duty under Canon 2 to act in a manner that promotes public confidence in the integrity and impartiality of the judiciary applies to all the judge's activities, including the discharge of the judge's adjudicative and administrative responsibilities. The duty to be respectful includes the responsibility to avoid comment or behavior that could reasonably be interpreted as harassment, prejudice or bias.

Canon 3A(4). The restriction on ex parte communications concerning a proceeding includes communications from lawyers, law teachers, and others who are not participants in the proceeding. A judge may consult with other judges or with court personnel whose function is to aid the judge in carrying out adjudicative responsibilities. A judge should make reasonable efforts to ensure that law clerks and other court personnel comply with this provision.

A judge may encourage and seek to facilitate settlement but should not act in a manner that coerces any party into surrendering the right to have the controversy resolved by the courts.

Canon 3A(5). In disposing of matters promptly, efficiently, and fairly, a judge must demonstrate due regard for the rights of the parties to be heard and to have issues resolved without unnecessary cost or delay. A judge should monitor and supervise cases to reduce or eliminate dilatory practices, avoidable delays, and unnecessary costs.

Prompt disposition of the court's business requires a judge to devote adequate time to judicial duties, to be punctual in attending court and expeditious in determining matters under submission, and to take reasonable measures to ensure that court personnel, litigants, and their lawyers cooperate with the judge to that end.

Canon 3A(6). The admonition against public comment about the merits of a pending or impending matter continues until the appellate process is complete. If the public comment involves a case from the judge's own court, the judge should take particular care so that the comment does not denigrate public confidence in the judiciary's integrity and impartiality, which would violate Canon 2A. A judge may comment publicly on proceedings in which the judge is a litigant in a personal capacity, but not on mandamus proceedings when the judge is a litigant in an official capacity (but the judge may respond in accordance with Fed. R. App. P. 21(b)).

Canon 3B(3). A judge's appointees include assigned counsel, officials such as referees, commissioners, special masters, receivers, guardians, and personnel such as law clerks, secretaries, and judicial assistants. Consent by the parties to an appointment or an award of compensation does not relieve the judge of the obligation prescribed by this subsection.

Canon 3B(5). Appropriate action may include direct communication with the judge or lawyer, other direct action if available, reporting the conduct to the appropriate authorities, or, when the judge believes that a judge's or lawyer's conduct is caused by drugs, alcohol, or a medical condition, making a confidential referral to an assistance program. Appropriate action may also include responding to a subpoena to testify or otherwise participating in judicial or lawyer disciplinary proceedings; a judge should be candid and honest with disciplinary authorities.

Canon 3C. Recusal considerations applicable to a judge's spouse should also be considered with respect to a person other than a spouse with whom the judge maintains both a household and an intimate relationship.

Canon 3C(1)(c). In a criminal proceeding, a victim entitled to restitution is not, within the meaning of this Canon, a party to the proceeding or the subject matter in controversy. A judge who has a financial interest in the victim of a crime is not required by Canon 3C(1)(c) to disqualify from the criminal proceeding, but the judge must do so if the judge's impartiality might reasonably be questioned under Canon 3C(1) or if the judge has an interest that could be substantially affected by the outcome of the proceeding under Canon 3C(1)(d)(iii).

Canon 3C(1)(d)(ii). The fact that a lawyer in a proceeding is affiliated with a law firm with which a relative of the judge is affiliated does not of itself disqualify the judge. However, if "the judge's impartiality might reasonably be questioned" under Canon 3C(1), or the relative is known by the judge to have an interest in the law firm that could be "substantially affected by the outcome of the proceeding" under Canon 3C(1)(d)(iii), the judge's disqualification is required.

CANON 4: A JUDGE MAY ENGAGE IN EXTRAJUDICIAL ACTIVITIES THAT ARE CONSISTENT WITH THE OBLIGATIONS OF JUDICIAL OFFICE

A judge may engage in extrajudicial activities, including law-related pursuits and civic, charitable, educational, religious, social, financial, fiduciary, and governmental activities, and may speak, write, lecture, and teach on both law-related and nonlegal subjects. However, a judge should not participate in extrajudicial activities that detract from the dignity of the judge's office, interfere with the performance of the judge's official duties, reflect adversely on the judge's impartiality, lead to frequent disqualification, or violate the limitations set forth below.

A. *Law-related Activities.*

(1) *Speaking, Writing, and Teaching.* A judge may speak, write, lecture, teach, and participate in other activities concerning the law, the legal system, and the administration of justice.

(2) *Consultation.* A judge may consult with or appear at a public hearing before an executive or legislative body or official:

(a) on matters concerning the law, the legal system, or the administration of justice;

(b) to the extent that it would generally be perceived that a judge's judicial experience provides special expertise in the area; or

(c) when the judge is acting pro se in a matter involving the judge or the judge's interest.

(3) *Organizations.* A judge may participate in and serve as a member, officer, director, trustee, or nonlegal advisor of a nonprofit organization devoted to the law, the legal system, or the administration of justice and may assist such an organization in the management and investment of funds. A judge may make recommendations to public and private fund-granting agencies about projects and programs concerning the law, the legal system, and the administration of justice.

(4) *Arbitration and Mediation.* A judge should not act as an arbitrator or mediator or otherwise perform judicial functions apart from the judge's official duties unless expressly authorized by law.

(5) *Practice of Law.* A judge should not practice law and should not serve as a family member's lawyer in any forum. A judge may, however, act pro se and may, without compensation, give legal advice to and draft or review documents for a member of the judge's family.

B.   Civic and Charitable Activities. A judge may participate in and serve as an officer, director, trustee, or nonlegal advisor of a nonprofit civic, charitable, educational, religious, or social organization, subject to the following limitations:

(1) A judge should not serve if it is likely that the organization will either be engaged in proceedings that would ordinarily come before the judge or be regularly engaged in adversary proceedings in any court.

(2) A judge should not give investment advice to such an organization but may serve on its board of directors or trustees even though it has the responsibility for approving investment decisions.

C.   Fund Raising. A judge may assist nonprofit law-related, civic, charitable, educational, religious, or social organizations in planning fund-raising activities and may be listed as an officer, director, or trustee. A judge may solicit funds for such an organization from judges over whom the judge does not exercise supervisory or appellate authority and from members of the judge's family. Otherwise, a judge should not personally participate in fund-raising activities, solicit funds for any organization, or use or permit the use of the prestige of judicial office for that purpose. A judge should not personally participate in membership solicitation if the solicitation might reasonably be perceived as coercive or is essentially a fund-raising mechanism.

D.   Financial Activities.

(1) A judge may hold and manage investments, including real estate, and engage in other remunerative activity, but should refrain from financial and business dealings that exploit the judicial position or involve the judge in frequent transactions or continuing business relationships with lawyers or other persons likely to come before the court on which the judge serves.

(2) A judge may serve as an officer, director, active partner, manager, advisor, or employee of a business only if the business is closely held and controlled by members of the judge's family. For this purpose, "members of the judge's family" means persons related to the judge or the judge's spouse within the third degree of relationship as defined in Canon 3C(3)(a), any other relative with whom the judge or the judge's spouse maintains a close familial relationship, and the spouse of any of the foregoing.

(3) As soon as the judge can do so without serious financial detriment, the judge should divest investments and other financial interests that might require frequent disqualification.

(4) A judge should comply with the restrictions on acceptance of gifts and the prohibition on solicitation of gifts set forth in the Judicial Conference Gift Regulations. A judge should endeavor to prevent any member of the judge's family residing in the household from soliciting or accepting a gift except to the extent that a judge would be permitted to do so by the Judicial Conference Gift Regulations. A "member of the

CODE OF CONDUCT FOR UNITED STATES JUDGES

judge's family" means any relative of a judge by blood, adoption, or marriage, or any person treated by a judge as a member of the judge's family.

(5)   A judge should not disclose or use nonpublic information acquired in a judicial capacity for any purpose unrelated to the judge's official duties.

E.   Fiduciary Activities. A judge may serve as the executor, administrator, trustee, guardian, or other fiduciary only for the estate, trust, or person of a member of the judge's family as defined in Canon 4D(4). As a family fiduciary a judge is subject to the following restrictions:

(1)   The judge should not serve if it is likely that as a fiduciary the judge would be engaged in proceedings that would ordinarily come before the judge or if the estate, trust, or ward becomes involved in adversary proceedings in the court on which the judge serves or one under its appellate jurisdiction.

(2)   While acting as a fiduciary, a judge is subject to the same restrictions on financial activities that apply to the judge in a personal capacity.

F.   Governmental Appointments. A judge may accept appointment to a governmental committee, commission, or other position only if it is one that concerns the law, the legal system, or the administration of justice, or if appointment of a judge is required by federal statute. A judge should not, in any event, accept such an appointment if the judge's governmental duties would tend to undermine the public confidence in the integrity, impartiality, or independence of the judiciary. A judge may represent the judge's country, state, or locality on ceremonial occasions or in connection with historical, educational, and cultural activities.

G.   Chambers, Resources, and Staff. A judge should not to any substantial degree use judicial chambers, resources, or staff to engage in extrajudicial activities permitted by this Canon.

H.   Compensation, Reimbursement, and Financial Reporting. A judge may accept compensation and reimbursement of expenses for the law-related and extrajudicial activities permitted by this Code if the source of the payments does not give the appearance of influencing the judge in the judge's judicial duties or otherwise give the appearance of impropriety, subject to the following restrictions:

(1)   Compensation should not exceed a reasonable amount nor should it exceed what a person who is not a judge would receive for the same activity.

(2)   Expense reimbursement should be limited to the actual costs of travel, food, and lodging reasonably incurred by the judge and, where appropriate to the occasion, by the judge's spouse or relative. Any additional payment is compensation.

(3)   A judge should make required financial disclosures, including disclosures of gifts and other things of value, in compliance with applicable statutes and Judicial Conference regulations and directives.

COMMENTARY

Canon 4. Complete separation of a judge from extrajudicial activities is neither possible nor wise; a judge should not become isolated from the society in which the judge lives. As a judicial officer and a person specially learned in the law, a judge is in a unique position to contribute to the law, the legal system, and the administration of justice, including revising substantive and procedural law and improving criminal and juvenile justice. To the extent that the judge's time permits and impartiality is not compromised, the judge is encouraged to do so, either independently or through a bar association, judicial conference, or other organization dedicated to the law. Subject to the same limitations, judges may also engage in a wide range of non-law-related activities.

Within the boundaries of applicable law (*see, e.g.*, 18 U.S.C. § 953) a judge may express opposition to the persecution of lawyers and judges anywhere in the world if the judge has ascertained, after reasonable inquiry, that the persecution is occasioned by conflict between the professional responsibilities of the persecuted judge or lawyer and the policies or practices of the relevant government.

A person other than a spouse with whom the judge maintains both a household and an intimate relationship should be considered a member of the judge's family for purposes of legal assistance under Canon 4A(5), fund raising under Canon 4C, and family business activities under Canon 4D(2).

Canon 4A. Teaching and serving on the board of a law school are permissible, but in the case of a for-profit law school, board service is limited to a nongoverning advisory board.

Consistent with this Canon, a judge may encourage lawyers to provide pro bono legal services.

Canon 4A(4). This Canon generally prohibits a judge from mediating a state court matter, except in unusual circumstances (*e.g.*, when a judge is mediating a federal matter that cannot be resolved effectively without addressing the related state court matter).

Canon 4A(5). A judge may act pro se in all legal matters, including matters involving litigation and matters involving appearances before or other dealings with governmental bodies. In so doing, a judge must not abuse the prestige of office to advance the interests of the judge or the judge's family.

Canon 4B. The changing nature of some organizations and their exposure to litigation make it necessary for a judge regularly to reexamine the activities of each organization with which the judge is affiliated to determine if the judge's continued association is appropriate. For example, in many jurisdictions, charitable hospitals are in court more often now than in the past.

Canon 4C. A judge may attend fund-raising events of law-related and other organizations although the judge may not be a speaker, a guest of honor, or featured on the program of such an event. Use of a judge's name, position in the organization, and judicial designation on an organization's letterhead, including when used for fund raising or soliciting members, does not violate Canon 4C if comparable information and designations are listed for others.

Canon 4D(1), (2), and (3). Canon 3 requires disqualification of a judge in any proceeding in which the judge has a financial interest, however small. Canon 4D requires a judge to refrain from engaging in business and from financial activities that might interfere with the impartial performance of the judge's judicial duties. Canon 4H requires a judge to report compensation received for activities outside the judicial office. A judge has the rights of an ordinary citizen with respect to financial affairs, except for limitations required to safeguard the proper performance of the judge's duties. A judge's participation in a closely held family business, while generally permissible, may be prohibited if it takes too much time or involves misuse of judicial prestige or if the business is likely to come before the court on which the judge serves. Owning and receiving income from investments do not as such affect the performance of a judge's duties.

Canon 4D(5). The restriction on using nonpublic information is not intended to affect a judge's ability to act on information as necessary to protect the health or safety of the judge or a member of a judge's family, court personnel, or other judicial officers if consistent with other provisions of this Code.

Canon 4E. Mere residence in the judge's household does not by itself make a person a member of the judge's family for purposes of this Canon. The person must be treated by the judge as a member of the judge's family.

The Applicable Date of Compliance provision of this Code addresses continued service as a fiduciary.

A judge's obligation under this Code and the judge's obligation as a fiduciary may come into conflict. For example, a judge should resign as a trustee if it would result in detriment to the trust to divest holdings whose retention would require frequent disqualification of the judge in violation of Canon 4D(3).

Canon 4F. The appropriateness of accepting extrajudicial assignments must be assessed in light of the demands on judicial resources and the need to protect the courts from involvement in matters that may prove to be controversial. Judges should not accept governmental appointments that could interfere with the effectiveness and independence of the judiciary, interfere with the performance of the judge's judicial responsibilities, or tend to undermine public confidence in the judiciary.

Canon 4H. A judge is not required by this Code to disclose income, debts, or investments, except as provided in this Canon. The Ethics Reform Act of 1989 and implementing regulations promulgated by the Judicial Conference impose additional restrictions on judges' receipt of compensation. That Act and those regulations should be consulted before a judge enters into any arrangement involving the receipt of compensation. The restrictions so imposed include but are not limited to: (1) a prohibition against receiving "honoraria" (defined as anything of value received for a speech, appearance, or article), (2) a prohibition against receiving compensation for service as a director, trustee, or officer of a profit or nonprofit organization, (3) a requirement that compensated teaching activities receive prior approval, and (4) a limitation on the receipt of "outside earned income."

CANON 5:   A JUDGE SHOULD REFRAIN FROM POLITICAL ACTIVITY

A.   *General Prohibitions.* A judge should not:

(1)   act as a leader or hold any office in a political organization;

(2)   make speeches for a political organization or candidate, or publicly endorse or oppose a candidate for public office; or

(3)   solicit funds for, pay an assessment to, or make a contribution to a political organization or candidate, or attend or purchase a ticket

for a dinner or other event sponsored by a political organization or candidate.

B.   Resignation upon Candidacy. A judge should resign the judicial office if the judge becomes a candidate in a primary or general election for any office.

C.   Other Political Activity. A judge should not engage in any other political activity. This provision does not prevent a judge from engaging in activities described in Canon 4.

COMMENTARY

The term "political organization" refers to a political party, a group affiliated with a political party or candidate for public office, or an entity whose principal purpose is to advocate for or against political candidates or parties in connection with elections for public office.

Compliance with the Code of Conduct

Anyone who is an officer of the federal judicial system authorized to perform judicial functions is a judge for the purpose of this Code. All judges should comply with this Code except as provided below.

A.   Part-time Judge

A part-time judge is a judge who serves part-time, whether continuously or periodically, but is permitted by law to devote time to some other profession or occupation and whose compensation for that reason is less than that of a full-time judge. A part-time judge:

(1)   is not required to comply with Canons 4A(4), 4A(5), 4D(2), 4E, 4F, or 4H(3);

(2)   except as provided in the Conflict-of-Interest Rules for Part-time Magistrate Judges, should not practice law in the court on which the judge serves or in any court subject to that court's appellate jurisdiction, or act as a lawyer in a proceeding in which the judge has served as a judge or in any related proceeding.

B.   Judge Pro Tempore

A judge pro tempore is a person who is appointed to act temporarily as a judge or as a special master.

(1)   While acting in this capacity, a judge pro tempore is not required to comply with Canons 4A(4), 4A(5), 4D(2), 4D(3), 4E, 4F, or 4H(3); further, one who acts solely as a special master is not required to comply with Canons 4A(3), 4B, 4C, 4D(4), or 5.

(2)   A person who has been a judge pro tempore should not act as a lawyer in a proceeding in which the judge has served as a judge or in any related proceeding.

C.   Retired Judge

A judge who is retired under 28 U.S.C. § 371(b) or § 372(a) (applicable to Article III judges), or who is subject to recall under § 178(d) (applicable to judges on the Court of Federal Claims), or who is recalled to judicial service, should comply with all the provisions of this Code except Canon 4F, but the judge should refrain from judicial service during the period of extrajudicial appointment not sanctioned by Canon 4F. All other retired judges who are eligible for recall to judicial service (except those in U.S. territories and possessions) should comply with the provisions of this Code governing part-time judges. However, bankruptcy judges and magistrate judges who are eligible for recall but who have notified the Administrative Office of the United States Courts that they will not consent to recall are not obligated to comply with the provisions of this Code governing part-time judges. Such notification may be made at any time after retirement, and is irrevocable. A senior judge in the territories and possessions must comply with this Code as prescribed by 28 U.S.C. § 373(c)(5) and (d).

COMMENTARY

The 2014 amendment to the Compliance section, regarding retired bankruptcy judges and magistrate judges and exempting those judges from compliance with the Code as part-time judges if they notify the Administrative Office of the United States Courts that they will not consent to recall, was not intended to alter those judges' statutory entitlements to annuities, cost-of-living adjustments, or any other retirement benefits.

Applicable Date of Compliance

Persons to whom this Code applies should arrange their financial and fiduciary affairs as soon as reasonably possible to comply with it and should do so in any event within one year after appointment. If, however, the demands on the person's time and the possibility of conflicts of interest are not substantial, such a person may continue to act, without compensation, as an executor, administrator, trustee, or other fiduciary for the estate or person of one who is not a member of the person's family if terminating the relationship would unnecessarily jeopardize any substantial interest of the estate or person and if the judicial council of the circuit approves.

SELECTED FEDERAL STATUTES
APPLICABLE TO FEDERAL JUDGES

1.   28 U.S.C.A. § 47

§ 47.   Disqualification of trial judge to hear appeal

No judge shall hear or determine an appeal from the decision of a case or issue tried by him.

2.   28 U.S.C.A. § 144

§ 144.   Bias or prejudice of judge

Whenever a party to any proceeding in a district court makes and files a timely and sufficient affidavit that the judge before whom the matter is pending has a personal bias or prejudice either against him or in favor of any adverse party, such judge shall proceed no further therein, but another judge shall be assigned to hear such proceeding.

The affidavit shall state the facts and the reasons for the belief that bias or prejudice exists, and shall be filed not less than ten days before the beginning of the term at which the proceeding is to be heard, or good cause shall be shown for failure to file it within such time. A party may file only one such affidavit in any case. It shall be accompanied by a certificate of counsel of record stating that it is made in good faith.

3.   28 U.S.C.A. § 454

§ 454.   Practice of law by justices and judges

Any justice or judge appointed under the authority of the United States who engages in the practice of law is guilty of a high misdemeanor.

4.   28 U.S.C.A. § 455

§ 455.   Disqualification of justice, judge, or magistrate judge

(a)   Any justice, judge, or magistrate judge of the United States shall disqualify himself in any proceeding in which his impartiality might reasonably be questioned.

(b)   He shall also disqualify himself in the following circumstances:

(1)   Where he has a personal bias or prejudice concerning a party, or personal knowledge of disputed evidentiary facts concerning the proceeding;

(2)   Where in private practice he served as lawyer in the matter in controversy, or a lawyer with whom he previously practiced law served during such association as a lawyer concerning the matter, or the judge or such lawyer has been a material witness concerning it;

(3)   Where he has served in governmental employment and in such capacity participated as counsel, adviser or material witness concerning the proceeding or expressed an opinion concerning the merits of the particular case in controversy;

(4)   He knows that he, individually or as a fiduciary, or his spouse or minor child residing in his household, has a financial interest in the subject matter in controversy or in a party to the proceeding, or any other interest that could be substantially affected by the outcome of the proceeding;

(5)   He or his spouse, or a person within the third degree of relationship to either of them, or the spouse of such a person:

(i)   Is a party to the proceeding, or an officer, director, or trustee of a party;

(ii)   Is acting as a lawyer in the proceeding;

(iii) Is known by the judge to have an interest that could be substantially affected by the outcome of the proceeding;

(iv) Is to the judge's knowledge likely to be a material witness in the proceeding.

(c)   A judge should inform himself about his personal and fiduciary financial interests, and make a reasonable effort to inform himself about the personal financial interests of his spouse and minor children residing in his household.

(d)   For the purposes of this section the following words or phrases shall have the meaning indicated:

(1)   "proceeding" includes pretrial, trial, appellate review, or other stages of litigation;

(2)   the degree of relationship is calculated according to the civil law system;

(3)   "fiduciary" includes such relationships as executor, administrator, trustee, and guardian;

(4)   "financial interest" means ownership of a legal or equitable interest, however small, or a relationship as director, adviser, or other active participant in the affairs of a party, except that:

(i)   Ownership in a mutual or common investment fund that holds securities is not a "financial interest" in such securities unless the judge participates in the management of the fund;

(ii)   An office in an educational, religious, charitable, fraternal, or civic organization is not a "financial interest" in securities held by the organization;

(iii) The proprietary interest of a policyholder in a mutual insurance company, of a depositor in a mutual savings association, or a similar proprietary interest, is a "financial interest" in the organization only if the outcome of the proceeding could substantially affect the value of the interest;

(iv) Ownership of government securities is a "financial interest" in the issuer only if the outcome of the proceeding could substantially affect the value of the securities.

(e)   No justice, judge, or magistrate judge shall accept from the parties to the proceeding a waiver of any ground for disqualification enumerated in subsection (b). Where the ground for disqualification arises only under subsection (a), waiver may be accepted provided it is preceded by a full disclosure on the record of the basis for disqualification.

(f)   Notwithstanding the preceding provisions of this section, if any justice, judge, magistrate judge, or bankruptcy judge to whom a matter has been assigned would be disqualified, after substantial judicial time has been devoted to the matter, because of the appearance or discovery, after the matter was assigned to him or her, that he or she individually or as a fiduciary, or his or her spouse or minor child residing in his or her household, has a financial interest in a party (other than an interest that could be substantially affected by the outcome), disqualification is not required if the justice, judge, magistrate judge, bankruptcy judge, spouse or minor child, as the case may be, divests himself or herself of the interest that provides the grounds for the disqualification.

5. 5 U.S.C.A. APPENDIX 4, §§ 101–111 (Excerpts)

FINANCIAL DISCLOSURE REQUIREMENTS OF FEDERAL PERSONNEL

§ 101. Persons required to file

(a) Within thirty days of assuming the position of an officer or employee described in subsection (f), an individual shall file a report containing the information described in section 102(b) unless the individual has left another position described in subsection (f) within thirty days prior to assuming such new position or has already filed a report under this title with respect to nomination for the new position or as a candidate for the position.

. . .

(d) Any individual who is an officer or employee described in subsection (f) during any calendar year and performs the duties of his position or office for a period in excess of sixty days in that calendar year shall file on or before May 15 of the succeeding year a report containing the information described in section 102(a).

(e) Any individual who occupies a position described in subsection (f) shall, on or before the thirtieth day after termination of employment in such position, file a report containing the information described in section 102(a) covering the preceding calendar year if the report required by subsection (d) has not been filed and covering the portion of the calendar year in which such termination occurs up to the date the individual left such office or position, unless such individual has accepted employment in another position described in subsection (f).

(f) The officers and employees referred to in subsections (a) (d), and (e) are—

    (1) the President;

    (2) the Vice President;

    (3) each officer or employee in the executive branch, including a special Government employee as defined in section 202 of title 18, United States Code, who occupies a position classified above GS–15 of the General Schedule or, in the case of positions not under the General Schedule, for which the rate of basic pay is equal to or greater than 120 percent of the minimum rate of basic pay payable for GS–15 of the General Schedule; each member of a uniformed service whose pay grade is at or in excess of O–7 under section 201 of title 37, United States Code; and each officer or employee in any other position determined by the Director of the Office of Government Ethics to be of equal classification;

. . .

    (8) any civilian employee not described in paragraph (3), employed in the Executive Office of the President (other than a special government employee) who holds a commission of appointment from the President;

(9) a Member of Congress as defined under section 109(12);

(10) an officer or employee of the Congress as defined under section 109(13);

(11) a judicial officer as defined under section 109(10); and

(12) a judicial employee as defined under section 109(8).

(g)(1) Reasonable extensions of time for filing any report may be granted under procedures prescribed by the supervising ethics office for each branch, but the total of such extensions shall not exceed ninety days.

* * *

§ 102.   Contents of reports

(a) Each report filed pursuant to section 101(d) and (e) shall include a full and complete statement with respect to the following:

(1)(A) The source, type, and amount or value of income (other than income referred to in subparagraph (B)) from any source (other than from current employment by the United States Government), and the source, date, and amount of honoraria from any source, received during the preceding calendar year, aggregating $200 or more in value and, effective January 1, 1991, the source, date, and amount of payments made to charitable organizations in lieu of honoraria, and the reporting individual shall simultaneously file with the applicable supervising ethics office, on a confidential basis, a corresponding list of recipients of all such payments, together with the dates and amounts of such payments.

(B) The source and type of income which consists of dividends, rents, interest, and capital gains, received during the preceding calendar year which exceeds $200 in amount or value, and an indication of which of the following categories the amount or value of such item of income is within:

(i) not more than $1,000,

(ii) greater than $1,000 but not more than $2,500,

(iii) greater than $2,500 but not more than $5,000,

(iv) greater than $5,000 but not more than $15,000,

(v) greater than $15,000 but not more than $50,000,

(vi) greater than $50,000 but not more than $100,000,

(vii) greater than $100,000 but not more than $1,000,000,

(viii) greater than $1,000,000 but not more than $5,000,000, or

(ix) greater than $5,000,000.

(2)(A) The identity of the source, a brief description, and the value of all gifts aggregating more than the minimal value as established by section 7342(a)(5) of title 5, United States Code, or $250, whichever is greater, received from any source other than a relative of the reporting individual during the preceding calendar year, except that any food, lodging, or entertainment received as personal hospitality of an individual need not be reported, and any gift with a fair market value of $100 or less, as adjusted at the same time and by the same percentage as the minimal value is adjusted, need not be aggregated for purposes of this subparagraph.

(B) The identity of the source and a brief description (including a travel itinerary, dates, and nature of expenses provided) of reimbursements received from any source aggregating more than the minimal value as established by section 7342(a)(5) of title 5, United States Code, or $250, whichever is greater and received during the preceding calendar year.

(C) In an unusual case, a gift need not be aggregated under subparagraph (A) if a publicly available request for a waiver is granted.

(3) The identity and category of value of any interest in property held during the preceding calendar year in a trade or business, or for investment or the production of income, which has a fair market value which exceeds $1,000 as of the close of the preceding calendar year, excluding any personal liability owned to the reporting individual by a spouse, or by a parent, brother, sister, or child of the reporting individual or of the reporting individual's spouse, or any deposits aggregating $5,000 or less in a personal savings account. For purposes of this paragraph, a personal savings account shall include any certificate of deposit or any other form of deposit in a bank, savings and loan association, credit union, or similar financial institution.

(4) The identity and category of value of the total liabilities owed to any creditor other than a spouse, or a parent, brother, sister, or child of the reporting individual or of the reporting individual's spouse which exceed $10,000 at any time during the preceding calendar year, excluding—

(A) any mortgage secured by real property which is a personal residence of the reporting individual or his spouse . . . .

(B) any loan secured by a personal motor vehicle, household furniture, or appliances, which loan does not exceed the purchase price of the item which secures it.

With respect to revolving charge accounts, only those with an outstanding liability which exceeds $10,000 as of the close of the preceding calendar year need be reported under this paragraph.

(5) Except as provided in this paragraph, a brief description, the date, and category of value of any purchase, sale or exchange during the preceding calendar year which exceeds $1,000—

(A) in real property, other than property used solely as a personal residence of the reporting individual or his spouse; or

(B) in stocks, bonds, commodities futures, and other forms of securities.

Reporting is not required under this paragraph of any transaction solely by and between the reporting individual, his spouse, or dependent children.

(6)(A) The identity of all positions held on or before the date of filing during the current calendar year (and, for the first report filed by an individual, during the two-year period preceding such calendar year) as an officer, director, trustee, partner, proprietor, representative, employee, or consultant of any corporation, company, firm, partnership, or other business enterprise, any nonprofit organization, any labor organization, or any educational or other institution other than the United States. This subparagraph shall not require the reporting of positions held in any religious, social, fraternal, or political entity and positions solely of an honorary nature.

(B) If any person, other than the United States Government, paid a nonelected reporting individual compensation in excess of $5,000 in any of the two calendar years prior to the calendar year during which the individual files his first report under this title, the individual shall include in the report—

> **(i)** the identity of each source of such compensation; and

> **(ii)** a brief description of the nature of the duties performed or services rendered by the reporting individual for each such source.

The preceding sentence shall not require any individual to include in such report any information which is considered confidential as a result of a privileged relationship, established by law, between such individual and any person nor shall it require an individual to report any information with respect to any person for whom services were provided by any firm or association of which such individual was a member, partner, or employee unless such individual was directly involved in the provision of such services.

(7) A description of the date, parties to, and terms of any agreement or arrangement with respect to (A) future employment; (B) a leave of absence during the period of the reporting individual's Government service; (C) continuation of payments by a former employer other than the United States Government; and (D) continuing participation in an employee welfare or benefit plan maintained by a former employer.

(8) The category of the total cash value of any interest of the reporting individual in a qualified blind trust, unless the trust instrument was executed prior to July 24, 1995 and precludes the beneficiary from receiving information on the total cash value of any interest in the qualified blind trust.

. . .

(d)(1) The categories for reporting the amount or value of the items covered in paragraphs (3) (4) (5), and (8) of subsection (a) are as follows:

> **(A)** not more than $15,000;

> **(B)** greater than $15,000 but not more than $50,000;

> **(C)** greater than $50,000 but not more than $100,000;

> **(D)** greater than $100,000 but not more than $250,000;

> **(E)** greater than $250,000 but not more than $500,000;

> **(F)** greater than $500,000 but not more than $1,000,000;

> **(G)** greater than $1,000,000 but not more than $5,000,000;

> **(H)** greater than $5,000,000 but not more than $25,000,000;

> **(I)** greater than $25,000,000 but not more than $50,000,000; and

(J) greater than $50,000,000.

. . .

(e)(1) Except as provided in the last sentence of this paragraph, each report required by section 101 shall also contain information listed in paragraphs (1) through (5) of subsection (a) of this section respecting the spouse or dependent child of the reporting individual as follows:

(A) The source of items of earned income earned by a spouse from any person which exceed $1,000 and the source and amount of any honoraria received by a spouse, except that, with respect to earned income (other than honoraria), if the spouse is self-employed in business or a profession, only the nature of such business or profession need be reported.

(B) All information required to be reported in subsection (a)(1)(B) with respect to income derived by a spouse or dependent child from any asset held by the spouse or dependent child and reported pursuant to subsection (a)(3).

(C) In the case of any gifts received by a spouse or dependent child which are not received totally independent of the relationship of the spouse or dependent child to the reporting individual, the identity of the source and a brief description of gifts of transportation, lodging, food, or entertainment and a brief description and the value of other gifts.

(D) In the case of any reimbursements received by a spouse or dependent child which are not received totally independent of the relationship of the spouse or dependent child to the reporting individual, the identity of the source and a brief description of each such reimbursement.

(E) In the case of items described in paragraphs (3) through (5) of subsection (a), all information required to be reported under these paragraphs other than items (i) which the reporting individual certifies represent the spouse's or dependent child's sole financial interest or responsibility and which the reporting individual has no knowledge of (ii) which are not in any way, past or present, derived from the income, assets, or activities of the reporting individual, and (iii) from which the reporting individual neither derives, nor expects to derive, any financial or economic benefit.

(F) For purposes of this section, categories with amounts or values greater than $1,000,000 set forth in sections 102(a)(1)(B) and 102(d)(1) shall apply to the income, assets, or liabilities of spouses and dependent children only if the income, assets, or liabilities are held jointly with the reporting individual. All other income, assets, or liabilities of the spouse or dependent children required to be reported under this section in an amount or value greater than $1,000,000 shall be categorized only as an amount or value greater than $1,000,000.

Reports required by subsections (a) (b), and (c) of section 101 shall, with respect to the spouse and dependent child of the reporting individual, only contain information listed in paragraphs (1) (3), and (4) of subsection (a), as specified in this paragraph.

(2) No report shall be required with respect to a spouse living separate and apart from the reporting individual with the intention of terminating the marriage or providing for permanent separation; or with respect to any income or obligations of an individual arising from the dissolution of his marriage or the permanent separation from his spouse.

(f)(1) Except as provided in paragraph (2), each reporting individual shall report the information required to be reported pursuant to subsections (a) (b), and (c) of this section with respect to the holdings of and the income from a trust or other financial arrangement from which income is received by, or with respect to which a beneficial interest in principal or income is held by, such individual, his spouse, or any dependent child.

(2) A reporting individual need not report the holdings of or the source of income from any of the holdings of—

(A) any qualified blind trust (as defined in paragraph (3));

(B) a trust—

(i) which was not created directly by such individual, his spouse, or any dependent child, and

(ii) the holdings or sources of income of which such individual, his spouse, and any dependent child have no knowledge of; or

(C) an entity described under the provisions of paragraph (8),

but such individual shall report the category of the amount of income received by him, his spouse, or any dependent child from the trust or other entity under subsection (a)(1)(B) of this section.

(3) For purposes of this subsection, the term "qualified blind trust" includes any trust in which a reporting individual, his spouse, or any minor or dependent child has a beneficial interest in the principal or income, and which meets the following requirements:

(A)(i) The trustee of the trust and any other entity designated in the trust instrument to perform fiduciary duties is a financial institution, an attorney, a certified public accountant, a broker, or an investment advisor who—

(I) is independent of and not associated with any interested party so that the trustee or other person cannot be controlled or influenced in the administration of the trust by any interested party; and

(II) is not and has not been an employee of or affiliated with any interested party and is not a partner of, or involved in any joint venture or other investment with, any interested party; and

(III) is not a relative of any interested party.

(ii) Any officer or employee of a trustee or other entity who is involved in the management or control of the trust—

(I) is independent of and not associated with any interested party so that such officer or employee cannot be controlled or influenced in the administration of the trust by any interested party;

(II) is not a partner of, or involved in any joint venture or other investment with, any interested party; and

(III) is not a relative of any interested party.

(B) Any asset transferred to the trust by an interested party is free of any restriction with respect to its transfer or sale unless such restriction is expressly approved by the supervising ethics office of the reporting individual.

(C) The trust instrument which establishes the trust provides that—

(i) except to the extent provided in subparagraph (B) of this paragraph, the trustee in the exercise of his authority and discretion to manage and control the assets of the trust shall not consult or notify any interested party;

(ii) the trust shall not contain any asset the holding of which by an interested party is prohibited by any law or regulation;

(iii) the trustee shall promptly notify the reporting individual and his supervising ethics office when the holdings of any particular asset transferred to the trust by any interested party are disposed of or when the value of such holding is less than $1,000;

(iv) the trust tax return shall be prepared by the trustee or his designee, and such return and any information relating thereto (other than the trust income summarized in appropriate categories necessary to complete an interested party's tax return), shall not be disclosed to any interested party;

(v) an interested party shall not receive any report on the holdings and sources of income of the trust, except a report at the end of each calendar quarter with respect to the total cash value of the interest of the interested party in the trust or the net income or loss of the trust or any reports necessary to enable the interested party to complete an individual tax return required by law or to provide the information required by subsection (a)(1) of this section, but such report shall not identify any asset or holding;

(vi) except for communications which solely consist of requests for distributions of cash or other unspecified assets of the trust, there shall be no direct or indirect communication between the trustee and an interested party with respect to the trust unless such communication is in writing and unless it relates only (I) to the general financial interest and needs of the interested party (including, but not limited to, an interest in maximizing income or long-term capital gain) (II) to the notification of the trustee of a law or regulation subsequently applicable to the reporting individual which prohibits the interested party from holding an asset, which notification directs that the asset not be held by the trust, or (III) to directions to the trustee to sell all of an asset initially placed in the trust by an interested party which in the determination of the reporting individual creates a conflict of interest or the appearance thereof due to the subsequent assumption of duties by the reporting individual (but nothing herein shall require any such direction); and

(vii) the interested parties shall make no effort to obtain information with respect to the holdings of the trust, including obtaining a copy of any trust tax return filed or any information relating thereto except as otherwise provided in this subsection.

(D) The proposed trust instrument and the proposed trustee is approved by the reporting individual's supervising ethics office.

. . .

(4)(A) An asset placed in a trust by an interested party shall be considered a financial interest of the reporting individual, for the purposes of any applicable conflict of interest statutes, regulations, or rules of the Federal Government (including section 208 of title 18, United States Code), until such time as the reporting individual is notified by the trustee that such asset has been disposed of, or has a value of less than $1,000.

(B)(i) The provisions of subparagraph (A) shall not apply with respect to a trust created for the benefit of a reporting individual, or the spouse, dependent child, or minor child of such a person, if the supervising ethics office for such reporting individual finds that—

(I) the assets placed in the trust consist of a well-diversified portfolio of readily marketable securities;

(II) none of the assets consist of securities of entities having substantial activities in the area of the reporting individual's primary area of responsibility;

(III) the trust instrument prohibits the trustee, notwithstanding the provisions of paragraphs (3)(C)(iii) and (iv) of this subsection, from making public or informing any interested party of the sale of any securities;

(IV) the trustee is given power of attorney, notwithstanding the provisions of paragraph (3)(C)(v) of this subsection, to prepare on behalf of any interested party the personal income tax returns and similar returns which may contain information relating to the trust; and

(V) except as otherwise provided in this paragraph, the trust instrument provides (or in the case of a trust established prior to the effective date of this Act which by its terms does not permit amendment, the trustee, the reporting individual, and any other interested party agree in writing) that the trust shall be administered in accordance with the requirements of this subsection and the trustee of such trust meets the requirements of paragraph (3)(A).

. . .

(8) A reporting individual shall not be required to report the financial interests held by a widely held investment fund (whether such fund is a mutual fund, regulated investment company, pension or deferred compensation plan, or other investment fund), if—

(A)(i) the fund is publicly traded; or

(ii) the assets of the fund are widely diversified; and

(B) the reporting individual neither exercises control over nor has the ability to exercise control over the financial interests held by the fund.

(g) Political campaign funds, including campaign receipts and expenditures, need not be included in any report filed pursuant to this title.

. . .

§ 103. Filing of reports

(a) Except as otherwise provided in this section, the reports required under this title shall be filed by the reporting individual with the designated agency ethics official at the agency by which he is employed (or in the case of an individual described in section 101(e), was employed) or in which he will serve. The date any report is received (and the date of receipt of any supplemental report) shall be noted on such report by such official.

* * *

§ 104. Failure to file or filing false reports

(a)(1) The Attorney General may bring a civil action in any appropriate United States district court against any individual who knowingly and willfully falsifies or who knowingly and willfully fails to file or report any information that such individual is required to report pursuant to section 102. The court in which such action is brought may assess against such individual a civil penalty in any amount, not to exceed $50,000.

(2)(A) It shall be unlawful for any person to knowingly and willfully—

(i) falsify any information that such person is required to report under section 102; and

(ii) fail to file or report any information that such person is required to report under section 102.

(B) Any person who—

(i) violates subparagraph (A)(i) shall be fined under title 18, United States Code, imprisoned for not more than 1 year, or both; and

(ii) violates subparagraph (A)(ii) shall be fined under title 18, United States Code.

(b) The head of each agency, each Secretary concerned, the Director of the Office of Government Ethics, each congressional ethics committee, or the Judicial Conference, as the case may be, shall refer to the Attorney General the name of any individual which such official or committee has reasonable cause to believe has willfully failed to file a report or has willfully falsified or willfully failed to file information required to be reported. Whenever the Judicial Conference refers a name to the Attorney General under this subsection, the Judicial Conference also shall notify the judicial council of the circuit in which the named individual serves of the referral.

(c) The President, the Vice President, the Secretary concerned, the head of each agency, the Office of Personnel Management, a congressional ethics committee, and the Judicial Conference, may take any appropriate personnel or other action in accordance with applicable law or regulation against any individual failing to file a report or falsifying or failing to report information required to be reported.

(d)(1) Any individual who files a report required to be filed under this title more than 30 days after the later of—

(A) the date such report is required to be filed pursuant to the provisions of this title and the rules and regulations promulgated thereunder; or

(B) if a filing extension is granted to such individual under section 101(g), the last day of the filing extension period, shall * * * pay a filing fee of $200. All such fees shall be deposited in the miscellaneous receipts of the Treasury. The authority under this paragraph to direct the payment of a filing fee may be delegated by the supervising ethics office in the executive branch to other agencies in the executive branch.

(2) The supervising ethics office may waive the filing fee under this subsection in extraordinary circumstances.

§ 105. Custody of and public access to reports

(a) Each agency, each supervising ethics office in the executive or judicial branch, the Clerk of the House of Representatives, and the Secretary of the Senate shall make available to the public, in accordance with subsection (b), each report filed under this title with such agency or office or with the Clerk or the Secretary of the Senate . . . .

(b)(1) Except as provided in the second sentence of this subsection, each agency, each supervising ethics office in the executive or judicial branch, the Clerk of the House of Representatives, and the Secretary of the Senate shall, within thirty days after any report is received under this title by such agency or office or by the Clerk or the Secretary of the Senate, as the case may be, permit inspection of such report by or furnish a copy of such report to any person requesting such inspection or copy. With respect to any report required to be filed by May 15 of any year, such report shall be made available for public inspection within 30 calendar days after May 15 of such year or within 30 days of the date of filing of such a report for which an extension is granted pursuant to section 101(g). The agency, office, Clerk, or Secretary of the Senate, as the case may be, may require a reasonable fee to be paid in any amount which is found necessary to recover the cost of reproduction or mailing of such report excluding any salary of any employee involved in such reproduction or mailing. A copy of such report may be furnished without charge or at a reduced charge if it is determined that waiver or reduction of the fee is in the public interest.

(2) Notwithstanding paragraph (1), a report may not be made available under this section to any person nor may any copy thereof be provided under this section to any person except upon a written application by such person stating—

(A) that person's name, occupation and address;

(B) the name and address of any other person or organization on whose behalf the inspection or copy is requested; and

(C) that such person is aware of the prohibitions on the obtaining or use of the report.

Any such application shall be made available to the public throughout the period during which the report is made available to the public.

(3)(A) This section does not require the immediate and unconditional availability of reports filed by an individual described in section 109(8) or 109(10) of this Act if a finding is made by the Judicial Conference, in consultation with United States Marshals Service, that revealing personal and sensitive information could endanger that individual or a family member of that individual.

(B) A report may be redacted pursuant to this paragraph only—

(i) to the extent necessary to protect the individual who filed the report or a family member of that individual; and

(ii) for as long as the danger to such individual exists.

(C) The Administrative Office of the United States Courts shall submit to the Committees on the Judiciary of the House of Representatives and of the Senate and the Senate Committee on Homeland Security and Governmental Affairs and the House Committee on Oversight and Government Reform an annual report with respect to the operation of this paragraph including—

(i) the total number of reports redacted pursuant to this paragraph;

(ii) the total number of individuals whose reports have been redacted pursuant to this paragraph;

(iii) the types of threats against individuals whose reports are redacted, if appropriate;

(iv) the nature or type of information redacted;

(v) what steps or procedures are in place to ensure that sufficient information is available to litigants to determine if there is a conflict of interest;

(vi) principles used to guide implementation of redaction authority; and

(vii) any public complaints received relating to redaction.

(D) The Judicial Conference, in consultation with the Department of Justice, shall issue regulations setting forth the circumstances under which redaction is appropriate under this paragraph and the procedures for redaction.

(E) This paragraph shall expire on December 31, 2027, and apply to filings through calendar year 2027.

(c)(1) It shall be unlawful for any person to obtain or use a report—

(A) for any unlawful purpose;

(B) for any commercial purpose, other than by news and communications media for dissemination to the general public;

(C) for determining or establishing the credit rating of any individual; or

(D) for use, directly or indirectly, in the solicitation of money for any political, charitable, or other purpose.

(2) The Attorney General may bring a civil action against any person who obtains or uses a report for any purpose prohibited in paragraph (1) of this subsection. The court in which such action is brought may assess against such person a penalty in any amount not to exceed $10,000. Such remedy shall be in addition to any other remedy available under statutory or common law.

. . .

§ 106. Review of reports

(a)(1) Each designated agency ethics official or Secretary concerned shall make provisions to ensure that each report filed with him under this title is reviewed within sixty days after the date of such filing, except that the Director of the Office of Government Ethics shall review only those reports required to be transmitted to him under this title within sixty days after the date of transmittal.

(2) Each congressional ethics committee and the Judicial Conference shall make provisions to ensure that each report filed under this title is reviewed within sixty days after the date of such filing.

(b)(1) If after reviewing any report under subsection (a), the Director of the Office of Government Ethics, the Secretary concerned, the designated agency ethics official, a person designated by the congressional ethics committee, or a person designated by the Judicial Conference, as the case may be, is of the opinion that on the basis of information contained in such report the individual submitting such report is in compliance with applicable laws and regulations, he shall state such opinion on the report, and shall sign such report.

(2) If the Director of the Office of Government Ethics, the Secretary concerned, the designated agency ethics official, a person designated by the congressional ethics committee, or a person designated by the Judicial Conference, after reviewing any report under subsection (a)—

    (A) believes additional information is required to be submitted, he shall notify the individual submitting such report what additional information is required and the time by which it must be submitted, or

    (B) is of the opinion, on the basis of information submitted, that the individual is not in compliance with applicable laws and regulations, he shall notify the individual, afford a reasonable opportunity for a written or oral response, and after consideration of such response, reach an opinion as to whether or not, on the basis of information submitted, the individual is in compliance with such laws and regulations.

(3) If the Director of the Office of Government Ethics, the Secretary concerned, the designated agency ethics official, a person designated by a congressional ethics committee, or a person designated by the Judicial Conference, reaches an opinion under paragraph (2)(B) that an individual is not in compliance with applicable laws and regulations, the official or committee shall notify the individual of that opinion and, after an opportunity for personal consultation (if practicable), determine and notify the individual of which steps, if any, would in the opinion of such official or committee be appropriate for assuring compliance with such laws and regulations and the date by which such steps should be taken. Such steps may include, as appropriate—

    (A) divestiture,

    (B) restitution,

    (C) the establishment of a blind trust,

    (D) request for an exemption under section 208(b) of title 18, United States Code, or

    (E) voluntary request for transfer, reassignment, limitation of duties, or resignation.

The use of any such steps shall be in accordance with such rules or regulations as the supervising ethics office may prescribe.

(4) If steps for assuring compliance with applicable laws and regulations are not taken by the date set under paragraph (3) by an individual in a position in the executive branch (other than in the Foreign

Service or the uniformed services), appointment to which requires the advice and consent of the Senate, the matter shall be referred to the President for appropriate action.

(5) If steps for assuring compliance with applicable laws and regulations are not taken by the date set under paragraph (3) by a member of the Foreign Service or the uniformed services, the Secretary concerned shall take appropriate action.

(6) If steps for assuring compliance with applicable laws and regulations are not taken by the date set under paragraph (3) by any other officer or employee, the matter shall be referred to the head of the appropriate agency, the congressional ethics committee, or the Judicial Conference, for appropriate action; except that in the case of the Postmaster General or Deputy Postmaster General, the Director of the Office of Government Ethics shall recommend to the Governors of the Board of Governors of the United States Postal Service the action to be taken.

(7) Each supervising ethics office may render advisory opinions interpreting this title within its respective jurisdiction. Notwithstanding any other provision of law, the individual to whom a public advisory opinion is rendered in accordance with this paragraph, and any other individual covered by this title who is involved in a fact situation which is indistinguishable in all material aspects, and who acts in good faith in accordance with the provisions and findings of such advisory opinion shall not, as a result of such act, be subject to any penalty or sanction provided by this title.

. . .

§ 109.   Definitions

For the purposes of this title, the term—

(1) "congressional ethics committees" means the Select Committee on Ethics of the Senate and the Committee on Standards of Official Conduct of the House of Representatives;

(2) "dependent child" means, when used with respect to any reporting individual, any individual who is a son, daughter, stepson, or stepdaughter and who—

    (A) is unmarried and under age 21 and is living in the household of such reporting individual; or

    (B) is a dependent of such reporting individual within the meaning of section 152 of the Internal Revenue Code of 1986 [26 U.S.C.A. § 152];

(3) "designated agency ethics official" means an officer or employee who is designated to administer the provisions of this title within an agency;

(4) "executive branch" includes each Executive agency (as defined in section 105 of title 5, United States Code), other than the Government Accountability Office, and any other entity or administrative unit in the executive branch;

(5) "gift" means a payment, advance, forbearance, rendering, or deposit of money, or any thing of value, unless consideration of equal or greater value is received by the donor, but does not include—

    (A) bequest and other forms of inheritance;

(B) suitable mementos of a function honoring the reporting individual;

(C) food, lodging, transportation, and entertainment provided by a foreign government within a foreign country or by the United States Government, the District of Columbia, or a State or local government or political subdivision thereof;

(D) food and beverages which are not consumed in connection with a gift of overnight lodging;

(E) communications to the offices of a reporting individual, including subscriptions to newspapers and periodicals; or

(F) consumable products provided by home-State businesses to the offices of a reporting individual who is an elected official, if those products are intended for consumption by persons other than such reporting individual;

(6) "honoraria" has the meaning given such term in section 505 of this Act;

(7) "income" means all income from whatever source derived, including but not limited to the following items: compensation for services, including fees, commissions, and similar items; gross income derived from business (and net income if the individual elects to include it); gains derived from dealings in property; interest; rents; royalties; dividends; annuities; income from life insurance and endowment contracts; pensions; income from discharge of indebtedness; distributive share of partnership income; and income from an interest in an estate or trust;

(8) "judicial employee" means any employee of the judicial branch of the Government, of the United States Sentencing Commission, of the Tax Court, of the Court of Federal Claims, of the Court of Appeals for Veterans Claims, or of the United States Court of Appeals for the Armed Forces, who is not a judicial officer and who is authorized to perform adjudicatory functions with respect to proceedings in the judicial branch, or who occupies a position for which the rate of basic pay is equal to or greater than 120 percent of the minimum rate of basic pay payable for GS–15 of the General Schedule;

(9) "Judicial Conference" means the Judicial Conference of the United States;

(10) "judicial officer" means the Chief Justice of the United States, the Associate Justices of the Supreme Court, and the judges of the United States courts of appeals, United States district courts, including the district courts in Guam, the Northern Mariana Islands, and the Virgin Islands, Court of Appeals for the Federal Circuit, Court of International Trade, Tax Court, Court of Federal Claims, Court of Appeals for Veterans Claims, United States Court of Appeals for the Armed Forces, and any court created by Act of Congress, the judges of which are entitled to hold office during good behavior;

* * *

(14) "personal hospitality of any individual" means hospitality extended for a nonbusiness purpose by an individual, not a corporation or organization, at the personal residence of that individual or his family or on property or facilities owned by that individual or his family;

(15) "reimbursement" means any payment or other thing of value received by the reporting individual, other than gifts, to cover travel-related expenses of such individual other than those which are—

    (A) provided by the United States Government, the District of Columbia, or a State or local government or political subdivision thereof;

    (B) required to be reported by the reporting individual under section 7342 of title 5, United States Code; or

    (C) required to be reported under section 304 of the Federal Election Campaign Act of 1971 (2 U.S.C. 434);

(16) "relative" means an individual who is related to the reporting individual, as father, mother, son, daughter, brother, sister, uncle, aunt, great aunt, great uncle, first cousin, nephew, niece, husband, wife, grandfather, grandmother, grandson, granddaughter, father-in-law, mother-in-law, son-in-law, daughter-in-law, brother-in-law, sister-in-law, stepfather, stepmother, stepson, stepdaughter, stepbrother, stepsister, half brother, half sister, or who is the grandfather or grandmother of the spouse of the reporting individual, and shall be deemed to include the fiancé or fiancée of the reporting individual;

* * *

(18) "supervising ethics office" means—

    (A) the Select Committee on Ethics of the Senate, for Senators, officers and employees of the Senate, and other officers or employees of the legislative branch required to file financial disclosure reports with the Secretary of the Senate pursuant to section 103(h) of this title;

    (B) the Committee on Standards of Official Conduct of the House of Representatives, for Members, officers and employees of the House of Representatives and other officers or employees of the legislative branch required to file financial disclosure reports with the Clerk of the House of Representatives pursuant to section 103(h) of this title;

    (C) the Judicial Conference for judicial officers and judicial employees; and

    (D) the Office of Government Ethics for all executive branch officers and employees; and

(19) "value" means a good faith estimate of the dollar value if the exact value is neither known nor easily obtainable by the reporting individual.

§ 110. Notice of actions taken to comply with ethics agreements

(a) In any case in which an individual agrees with that individual's designated agency ethics official, the Office of Government Ethics, a Senate confirmation committee, a congressional ethics committee, or the Judicial Conference, to take any action to comply with this Act or any other law or regulation governing conflicts of interest of, or establishing standards of conduct applicable with respect to, officers or employees of the Government, that individual shall notify in writing the designated agency ethics official, the Office of Government Ethics, the appropriate committee of the Senate, the congressional ethics committee, or the Judicial Conference, as the case may be, of any action taken by the individual pursuant to that agreement. Such notification shall be made not later than the date specified in the agreement by which action by the individual must be taken, or not later than three months after the date of the agreement, if no date for action is so specified.

(b) If an agreement described in subsection (a) requires that the individual recuse himself or herself from particular categories of agency or other official action, the individual shall reduce to writing those subjects regarding which the recusal agreement will apply and the process by which it will be determined whether the individual must recuse himself or herself in a specific instance. An individual shall be considered to have complied with the requirements of subsection (a) with respect to such recusal agreement if such individual files a copy of the document setting forth the information described in the preceding sentence with such individual's designated agency ethics official or the appropriate supervising ethics office within the time prescribed in the last sentence of subsection (a).

§ 111.   Administration of provisions

The provisions of this title shall be administered by—

(1) the Director of the Office of Government Ethics, the designated agency ethics official, or the Secretary concerned, as appropriate, with regard to officers and employees described in paragraphs (1) through (8) of section 101(f);

(2) the Select Committee on Ethics of the Senate and the Committee on Standards of Official Conduct of the House of Representatives, as appropriate, with regard to officers and employees described in paragraphs (9) and (10) of section 101(f); and

(3) the Judicial Conference in the case of an officer or employee described in paragraphs (11) and (12) of section 101(f).

The Judicial Conference may delegate any authority it has under this title to an ethics committee established by the Judicial Conference.

AMERICAN BAR ASSOCIATION
CANONS OF PROFESSIONAL ETHICS*

Preamble

In America, where the stability of Courts and of all departments of government rests upon the approval of the people, it is peculiarly essential that the system for establishing and dispensing Justice be developed to a high point of efficiency and so maintained that the public shall have absolute confidence in the integrity and impartiality of its administration. The future of the Republic, to a great extent, depends upon our maintenance of Justice pure and unsullied. It cannot be so maintained unless the conduct and the motives of the members of our profession are such as to merit the approval of all just men.

No code or set of rules can be framed, which will particularize all the duties of the lawyer in the varying phases of litigation or in all the relations of professional life. The following canons of ethics are adopted by the American Bar Association as a general guide, yet the enumeration of particular duties should not be construed as a denial of the existence of others equally imperative, though not specifically mentioned.

1.   The Duty of the Lawyer to the Courts

It is the duty of the lawyer to maintain towards the Courts a respectful attitude, not for the sake of the temporary incumbent of the judicial office, but for the maintenance of its supreme importance. Judges, not being wholly free to defend themselves, are peculiarly entitled to receive the support of the Bar against unjust criticism and clamor. Whenever there is proper ground for serious complaint of a judicial officer, it is the right and duty of the lawyer to submit his grievances to the proper authorities. In such cases, but not otherwise, such charges should be encouraged and the person making them should be protected.

2.   The Selection of Judges

It is the duty of the Bar to endeavor to prevent political considerations from outweighing judicial fitness in the selections of Judges. It should protest earnestly and actively against the appointment or election of those who are unsuitable for the Bench; and it should strive to have elevated thereto only those willing to forego other employments, whether of a business, political or other character, which may embarrass their free and fair consideration of questions before them for decision. The aspiration of lawyers for judicial position should be governed by an impartial estimate of their ability to add honor to the office and not by a desire for the distinction the position may bring to themselves.

3.   Attempts to Exert Personal Influence on the Court

Marked attention and unusual hospitality on the part of a lawyer to a Judge, uncalled for by the personal relations of the parties, subject both the Judge and the lawyer to misconstructions of motive and should be avoided. A lawyer should not communicate or argue privately with the Judge as to the merits of a pending cause, and he deserves rebuke and denunciation for any

---

  *   These Canons, to and including Canon 32 and the recommended oath, were adopted by the American Bar Association at Its Thirty-First Annual Meeting at Seattle, Washington, on August 27, 1908. The Canons were applied, as amended, until the adoption of the Code in 1970. Reprinted with permission. Copyright © American Bar Association.

device or attempt to gain from a Judge special personal consideration or favor. A self-respecting independence in the discharge of professional duty, without denial or diminution of the courtesy and respect due the Judge's station, is the only proper foundation for cordial personal and official relations between Bench and Bar.

4. When Counsel for an Indigent Prisoner

A lawyer assigned as counsel for an indigent prisoner ought not to ask to be excused for any trivial reason, and should always exert his best efforts in his behalf.

5. The Defense or Prosecution of Those Accused of Crime

It is the right of the lawyer to undertake the defense of a person accused of crime, regardless of his personal opinion as to the guilt of the accused; otherwise innocent persons, victims only of suspicious circumstances, might be denied proper defense. Having undertaken such defense, the lawyer is bound, by all fair and honorable means, to present every defense that the law of the land permits, to the end that no person may be deprived of life or liberty, but by due process of law.

The primary duty of a lawyer engaged in public prosecution is not to convict, but to see that justice is done. The suppression of facts or the secreting of witnesses capable of establishing the innocence of the accused is highly reprehensible.

6. Adverse Influences and Conflicting Interests

It is the duty of a lawyer at the time of retainer to disclose to the client all the circumstances of his relations to the parties, and any interest in or connection with the controversy, which might influence the client in the selection of counsel.

It is unprofessional to represent conflicting interests, except by express consent of all concerned given after a full disclosure of the facts. Within the meaning of this canon, a lawyer represents conflicting interests when, in behalf of one client, it is his duty to contend for that which duty to another client requires him to oppose.

The obligation to represent the client with undivided fidelity and not to divulge his secrets or confidences forbids also the subsequent acceptance of retainers or employment from others in matters adversely affecting any interest of the client with respect to which confidence has been reposed.

7. Professional Colleagues and Conflicts of Opinion

A client's proffer of assistance of additional counsel should not be regarded as evidence of want of confidence, but the matter should be left to the determination of the client. A lawyer should decline association as colleague if it is objectionable to the original counsel, but if the lawyer first retained is relieved, another may come into the case.

When lawyers jointly associated in a cause cannot agree as to any matter vital to the interest of the client, the conflict of opinion should be frankly stated to him for his final determination. His decision should be accepted unless the nature of the difference makes it impracticable for the lawyer whose judgment has been overruled to co-operate effectively. In this event it is his duty to ask the client to relieve him.

Efforts, direct or indirect, in any way to encroach upon the professional employment of another lawyer, are unworthy of those who should be brethren at the Bar; but, nevertheless, it is the right of any lawyer, without fear or favor, to give proper advice to those seeking relief against unfaithful or neglectful counsel, generally after communication with the lawyer of whom the complaint is made.

8.   Advising Upon the Merits of a Client's Cause

A lawyer should endeavor to obtain full knowledge of his client's cause before advising thereon, and he is bound to give a candid opinion of the merits and probable result of pending or contemplated litigation. The miscarriages to which justice is subject, by reason of surprises and disappointments in evidence and witnesses, and through mistakes of juries and errors of Courts, even though only occasional, admonish lawyers to beware of bold and confident assurances to clients, especially where the employment may depend upon such assurance. Whenever the controversy will admit of fair adjustment, the client should be advised to avoid or to end the litigation.

9.   Negotiations With Opposite Party

A lawyer should not in any way communicate upon the subject of controversy with a party represented by counsel; much less should he undertake to negotiate or compromise the matter with him, but should deal only with his counsel. It is incumbent upon the lawyer most particularly to avoid everything that may tend to mislead a party not represented by counsel, and he should not undertake to advise him as to the law.

10.   Acquiring Interest in Litigation

The lawyer should not purchase any interest in the subject matter of the litigation which he is conducting.

11.   Dealing With Trust Property

The lawyer should refrain from any action whereby for his personal benefit or gain he abuses or takes advantage of the confidence reposed in him by his client.

Money of the client or collected for the client or other trust property coming into the possession of the lawyer should be reported and accounted for promptly, and should not under any circumstances be commingled with his own or be used by him.

12.   Fixing the Amount of the Fee

In fixing fees, lawyers should avoid charges which overestimate their advice and services, as well as those which undervalue them. A client's ability to pay cannot justify a charge in excess of the value of the service, though his poverty may require a less charge, or even none at all. The reasonable requests of brother lawyers, and of their widows and orphans without ample means, should receive special and kindly consideration.

In determining the amount of the fee, it is proper to consider: (1) the time and labor required, the novelty and difficulty of the questions involved and the skill requisite properly to conduct the cause; (2) whether the acceptance of employment in the particular case will preclude the lawyer's appearance for others in cases likely to arise out of the transaction, and in which there is a reasonable expectation that otherwise he would be employed, or will involve the loss of other employment while employed in the particular case or antagonisms with other clients; (3) the customary charges of the Bar for similar services; (4) the amount involved in the controversy and the benefits resulting to the client from the services; (5) the contingency or the certainty of the compensation; and (6) the character of the employment, whether casual or for an established and constant client. No one of these considerations in itself is controlling. They are mere guides in ascertaining the real value of the service.

In determining the customary charges of the Bar for similar services, it is proper for a lawyer to consider a schedule of minimum fees adopted by a Bar Association, but no lawyer should permit himself to be controlled thereby or to follow it as his sole guide in determining the amount of his fee.

In fixing fees it should never be forgotten that the profession is a branch of the administration of justice and not a mere money-getting trade.

13. Contingent Fees

A contract for a contingent fee, where sanctioned by law, should be reasonable under all the circumstances of the case, including the risk and uncertainty of the compensation, but should always be subject to the supervision of a court, as to its reasonableness.

14. Suing a Client for a Fee

Controversies with clients concerning compensation are to be avoided by the lawyer so far as shall be compatible with his self-respect and with his right to receive reasonable recompense for his services; and lawsuits with clients should be resorted to only to prevent injustice, imposition or fraud.

15. How Far a Lawyer May Go in Supporting a Client's Cause

Nothing operates more certainly to create or to foster popular prejudice against lawyers as a class, and to deprive the profession of that full measure of public esteem and confidence which belongs to the proper discharge of its duties than does the false claim, often set up by the unscrupulous in defense of questionable transactions, that it is the duty of the lawyer to do whatever may enable him to succeed in winning his client's cause.

It is improper for a lawyer to assert in argument his personal belief in his client's innocence or in the justice of his cause.

The lawyer owes "entire devotion to the interest of the client, warm zeal in the maintenance and defense of his rights and the exertion of his utmost learning and ability," to the end that nothing be taken or be withheld from him, save by the rules of law, legally applied. No fear of judicial disfavor or public unpopularity should restrain him from the full discharge of his duty. In the judicial forum the client is entitled to the benefit of any and every remedy and defense that is authorized by the law of the land, and he may expect his lawyer to assert every such remedy or defense. But it is steadfastly to be borne in mind that the great trust of the lawyer is to be performed within and not without the bounds of the law. The office of attorney does not permit, much less does it demand of him for any client, violation of law or any manner of fraud or chicane. He must obey his own conscience and not that of his client.

16. Restraining Clients from Improprieties

A lawyer should use his best efforts to restrain and to prevent his clients from doing those things which the lawyer himself ought not to do, particularly with reference to their conduct towards Courts, judicial officers, jurors, witnesses and suitors. If a client persists in such wrongdoing the lawyer should terminate their relation.

17. Ill-Feeling and Personalities Between Advocates

Clients, not lawyers, are the litigants. Whatever may be the ill-feeling existing between clients, it should not be allowed to influence counsel in their conduct and demeanor toward each other or toward suitors in the case. All personalities between counsel should be scrupulously avoided. In the trial of a cause it is indecent to allude to the personal history or the personal peculiarities and idiosyncrasies of counsel on the other side. Personal colloquies between counsel which cause delay and promote unseemly wrangling should also be carefully avoided.

18. Treatment of Witnesses and Litigants

A lawyer should always treat adverse witnesses and suitors with fairness and due consideration, and he should never minister to the malevolence or prejudices of a client in the trial or conduct of a cause. The client cannot be made the keeper of the lawyer's conscience in professional matters. He has no right to demand that his counsel shall abuse the opposite party or indulge in offensive personalities. Improper speech is not excusable on the ground that it is what the client would say if speaking in his own behalf.

19. Appearance of Lawyer as Witness for His Client

When a lawyer is a witness for his client, except as to merely formal matters, such as the attestation or custody of an instrument and the like, he should leave the trial of the case to other counsel. Except when essential to the ends of justice, a lawyer should avoid testifying in court in behalf of his client.

20. Newspaper Discussion of Pending Litigation

Newspaper publications by a lawyer as to pending or anticipated litigation may interfere with a fair trial in the Courts and otherwise prejudice the due administration of justice. Generally they are to be condemned. If the extreme circumstances of a particular case justify a statement to the public, it is unprofessional to make it anonymously. An *ex parte* reference to the facts should not go beyond quotation from the records and papers on file in the court; but even in extreme cases it is better to avoid any *ex parte* statement.

21. Punctuality and Expedition

It is the duty of the lawyer not only to his client, but also to the Courts and to the public to be punctual in attendance, and to be concise and direct in the trial and disposition of causes.

22. Candor and Fairness

The conduct of the lawyer before the Court and with other lawyers should be characterized by candor and fairness.

It is not candid or fair for the lawyer knowingly to misquote the contents of a paper, the testimony of a witness, the language or the argument of opposing counsel, or the language of a decision or a textbook; or with knowledge of its invalidity, to cite as authority a decision that has been overruled, or a statute that has been repealed; or in argument to assert as a fact that which has not been proved, or in those jurisdictions where a side has the opening and closing arguments to mislead his opponent by concealing or withholding positions in his opening argument upon which his side then intends to rely.

It is unprofessional and dishonorable to deal other than candidly with the facts in taking the statements of witnesses, in drawing affidavits and other documents, and in the presentation of causes.

A lawyer should not offer evidence which he knows the Court should reject, in order to get the same before the jury by argument for its admissibility, nor should he address to the Judge arguments upon any point not properly calling for determination by him. Neither should he introduce into an argument, addressed to the court, remarks or statements intended to influence the jury or bystanders.

These and all kindred practices are unprofessional and unworthy of an officer of the law charged, as is the lawyer, with the duty of aiding in the administration of justice.

23. Attitude Toward Jury

All attempts to curry favor with juries by fawning, flattery or pretended solicitude for their personal comfort are unprofessional. Suggestions of counsel, looking to the comfort or convenience of jurors, and propositions to dispense with argument, should be made to the Court out of the jury's hearing. A lawyer must never converse privately with jurors about the case; and both before and during the trial he should avoid communicating with them, even as to matters foreign to the cause.

24. Right of Lawyer to Control the Incidents of the Trial

As to incidental matters pending the trial, not affecting the merits of the cause, or working substantial prejudice to the rights of the client, such as forcing the opposite lawyer to trial when he is under affliction or bereavement; forcing the trial on a particular day to the injury of the opposite lawyer when no harm will result from a trial at a different time; agreeing to an extension of time for signing a bill of exceptions, cross interrogatories and the like, the lawyer must be allowed to judge. In such matters no client has a right to demand that his counsel shall be illiberal, or that he do anything therein repugnant to his own sense of honor and propriety.

25. Taking Technical Advantage of Opposite Counsel; Agreements With Him

A lawyer should not ignore known customs or practice of the Bar or of a particular Court, even when the law permits, without giving timely notice to the opposing counsel. As far as possible, important agreements, affecting the rights of clients, should be reduced to writing; but it is dishonorable to avoid performance of an agreement fairly made because it is not reduced to writing, as required by rules of Court.

26. Professional Advocacy Other Than Before Courts

A lawyer openly, and in his true character may render professional services before legislative or other bodies, regarding proposed legislation and in advocacy of claims before departments of government, upon the same principles of ethics which justify his appearance before the Courts; but it is unprofessional for a lawyer so engaged to conceal his attorneyship, or to employ secret personal solicitations, or to use means other than those addressed to the reason and understanding, to influence action.

27. Advertising, Direct or Indirect

It is unprofessional to solicit professional employment by circulars, advertisements, through touters or by personal communications or interviews not warranted by personal relations. Indirect advertisements for professional employment such as furnishing or inspiring newspaper comments, or procuring his photograph to be published in connection with causes in which the lawyer has been or is engaged or concerning the manner of their conduct, the magnitude of the interest involved, the importance of the lawyer's position, and all other like self-laudation, offend the traditions and lower the tone of our profession and are reprehensible; but the customary use of simple professional cards is not improper.

Publication in reputable law lists in a manner consistent with the standards of conduct imposed by these canons of brief biographical and informative data is permissible. Such data must not be misleading and may include only a statement of the lawyer's name and the names of his professional associates; addresses, telephone numbers, cable addresses; branches of the profession practiced; date and place of birth and admission to the bar; schools attended; with dates of graduation, degrees and other educational distinctions; public or quasi-public offices; posts of honor; legal authorships; legal teaching positions; memberships and offices in bar associations and committees thereof, in legal and scientific societies and legal fraternities; foreign language ability; the fact of listings in other reputable law lists; the names and addresses of references; and, with their written consent, the names of clients regularly represented. A certificate of compliance with the Rules and Standards issued by the Standing Committee on Law Lists may be treated as evidence that such list is reputable.

It is not improper for a lawyer who is admitted to practice as a proctor in admiralty to use that designation on his letterhead or shingle or for a lawyer who has complied with the statutory requirements of admission to practice before the patent office, to so use the designation "patent attorney" or "patent lawyer" or "trademark attorney" or "trademark lawyer" or any combination of those terms.

28. Stirring Up Litigation, Directly or Through Agents

It is unprofessional for a lawyer to volunteer advice to bring a lawsuit, except in rare cases where ties of blood, relationship or trust make it his duty to do so. Stirring up strife and litigation is not only unprofessional, but it is indictable at common law. It is disreputable to hunt up defects in titles or other causes of action and inform thereof in order to be employed to bring suit or collect judgment, or to breed litigation by seeking out those with claims for personal injuries or those having any other grounds of action in order to secure them as clients, or to employ agents or runners for like purposes, or to pay or reward, directly or indirectly, those who bring or influence the bringing of such cases to his office, or to remunerate policemen, court or prison officials, physicians, hospital *attachés* or others who may succeed, under the guise of giving disinterested friendly advice, in influencing the criminal, the sick and the injured, the ignorant or others, to seek his professional services. A duty to the public and to the profession devolves upon every member of the Bar having knowledge of such practices upon the part of any practitioner immediately to inform thereof, to the end that the offender may be disbarred.

29. Upholding the Honor of the Profession

Lawyers should expose without fear or favor before the proper tribunals corrupt or dishonest conduct in the profession, and should accept without hesitation employment against a member of the Bar who has wronged his client. The counsel upon the trial of a cause in which perjury has been committed owe it to the profession and to the public to bring the matter to the knowledge of the prosecuting authorities. The lawyer should aid in guarding the Bar against the admission to the profession of candidates unfit or unqualified because deficient in either moral character or education. He should strive at all times to uphold the honor and to maintain the dignity of the profession and to improve not only the law but the administration of justice.

30. Justifiable and Unjustifiable Litigations

The lawyer must decline to conduct a civil cause or to make a defense when convinced that it is intended merely to harass or to injure the opposite party or to work oppression or wrong. But otherwise it is his right, and, having accepted retainer, it becomes his duty to insist upon the judgment of the Court as to the legal merits of his client's claim. His appearance in Court should be deemed equivalent to an assertion on his honor that in his opinion his client's case is one proper for judicial determination.

31. Responsibility for Litigation

No lawyer is obliged to act either as adviser or advocate for every person who may wish to become his client. He has the right to decline employment. Every lawyer upon his own responsibility must decide what employment he will accept as counsel, what causes he will bring into Court for plaintiffs, what cases he will contest in Court for defendants. The responsibility for advising as to questionable transactions, for bringing questionable suits, for urging questionable defenses, is the lawyer's responsibility. He cannot escape it by urging as an excuse that he is only following his client's instructions.

32. The Lawyer's Duty in Its Last Analysis

No client, corporate or individual, however powerful, nor any cause, civil or political, however important, is entitled to receive nor should any lawyer render any service or advice involving disloyalty to the law whose ministers we are, or disrespect of the judicial office, which we are bound to uphold, or corruption of any person or persons exercising a public office or private trust, or deception or betrayal of the public. When rendering any such improper service or advice, the lawyer invites and merits stern and just condemnation. Correspondingly, he advances the honor of his profession and the best interests of his client when he renders service or gives advice tending to impress upon the client and his undertaking exact compliance with the strictest principles of moral law. He must also observe and advise his client to observe the statute law, though until a statute shall have been construed and interpreted by competent adjudication, he is free and is entitled to advise as to its validity and as to what he conscientiously believes to be its just meaning and extent. But above all a lawyer will find his highest honor in a deserved reputation for fidelity to private trust and to public duty, as an honest man and as a patriotic and loyal citizen.

33. Partnerships—Names

Partnerships among lawyers for the practice of their profession are very common and are not to be condemned. In the formation of partnerships and the use of partnership names care should be taken not to violate any law, custom, or rule of court locally applicable. Where partnerships are formed between lawyers who are not all admitted to practice in the courts of the state, care should be taken to avoid any misleading name or representation which would create a false impression as to the professional position or privileges of the member not locally admitted. In the formation of partnerships for the practice of law, no person should be admitted or held out as a practitioner or member who is not a member of the legal profession duly authorized to practice, and amenable to professional discipline. In the selection and use of a firm name, no false, misleading, assumed or trade name should be used. The continued use of the name of a deceased or former partner, when permissible by local custom, is not unethical, but care should be taken that no imposition or deception is practiced through this use. When a member of the firm, on becoming a judge, is precluded from practicing law, his name should not be continued in the firm name.

Partnerships between lawyers and members of other professions or non-professional persons should not be formed or permitted where any part of the partnership's employment consists of the practice of law.

34. Division of Fees

No division of fees for legal services is proper, except with another lawyer, based upon a division of service or responsibility.

35. Intermediaries

The professional services of a lawyer should not be controlled or exploited by any lay agency, personal or corporate, which intervenes between client and lawyer. A lawyer's responsibilities and qualifications are individual. He should avoid all relations which direct the performance of his duties by or in the interest of such intermediary. A lawyer's relation to his client should be personal, and the responsibility should be direct to the client. Charitable societies rendering aid to the indigents are not deemed such intermediaries.

A lawyer may accept employment from any organization, such as an association, club or trade organization, to render legal services in any matter in which the organization, as an entity, is interested, but this employment should not include the rendering of legal services to the members of such an organization in respect to their individual affairs.

36. Retirement From Judicial Position or Public Employment

A lawyer should not accept employment as an advocate in any matter upon the merits of which he has previously acted in a judicial capacity.

A lawyer, having once held public office or having been in the public employ, should not after his retirement accept employment in connection with any matter which he has investigated or passed upon while in such office or employ.

37. Confidences of a Client

It is the duty of a lawyer to preserve his client's confidences. This duty outlasts the lawyer's employment, and extends as well to his employees; and neither of them should accept employment which involves or may involve the disclosure or use of these confidences, either for the private advantage of the lawyer or his employees or to the disadvantage of the client, without his knowledge and consent, and even though there are other available sources of such information. A lawyer should not continue employment when he discovers that this obligation prevents the performance of his full duty to his former or to his new client.

If a lawyer is accused by his client, he is not precluded from disclosing the truth in respect to the accusation. The announced intention of a client to commit a crime is not included within the confidences which he is bound to respect. He may properly make such disclosures as may be necessary to prevent the act or protect those against whom it is threatened.

38. Compensation, Commissions and Rebates

A lawyer should accept no compensation, commissions, rebates or other advantages from others without the knowledge and consent of his client after full disclosure.

39. Witnesses

A lawyer may properly interview any witness or prospective witness for the opposing side in any civil or criminal action without the consent of opposing counsel or party. In doing so, however, he should scrupulously avoid any suggestion calculated to induce the witness to suppress or deviate from the truth, or in any degree to affect his free and untrammeled conduct when appearing at the trial or on the witness stand.

40. Newspapers

A lawyer may with propriety write articles for publications in which he gives information upon the law; but he should not accept employment from such publications to advise inquirers in respect to their individual rights.

41. Discovery of Imposition and Deception

When a lawyer discovers that some fraud or deception has been practiced, which has unjustly imposed upon the court or a party, he should endeavor to rectify it; at first by advising his client, and if his client refuses to forego the advantage thus unjustly gained, he should promptly inform the injured person or his counsel, so that they may take appropriate steps.

42. Expenses of Litigation

A lawyer may not properly agree with a client that the lawyer shall pay or bear the expenses of litigation; he may in good faith advance expenses as a matter of convenience, but subject to reimbursement.

43. Approved Law Lists

It shall be improper for a lawyer to permit his name to be published in a law list the conduct, management or contents of which are calculated or likely to deceive or injure the public or the profession, or to lower the dignity or standing of the profession.

44. Withdrawal From Employment as Attorney or Counsel

The right of an attorney or counsel to withdraw from employment, once assumed, arises only from good cause. Even the desire or consent of the client is not always sufficient. The lawyer should not throw up the unfinished task to the detriment of his client except for reasons of honor or self-respect. If the client insists upon an unjust or immoral course in the conduct of his case, or if he persists over the attorney's remonstrance in presenting frivolous defenses, or if he deliberately disregards an agreement or obligation as to fees or expenses, the lawyer may be warranted in withdrawing on due notice to the client, allowing him time to employ another lawyer. So also when a lawyer discovers that his client has no case and the client is determined to continue it; or even if the lawyer finds himself incapable of conducting the case effectively. Sundry other instances may arise in which withdrawal is to be justified. Upon withdrawing from a case after a retainer has been paid, the attorney should refund such part of the retainer as has not been clearly earned.

45. Specialists

The canons of the American Bar Association apply to all branches of the legal profession; specialists in particular branches are not to be considered as exempt from the application of these principles.

46. Notice to Local Lawyers

A lawyer available to act as an associate of other lawyers in a particular branch of the law or legal service may send to local lawyers only and publish in his local legal journal, a brief and dignified announcement of his availability to serve other lawyers in connection therewith. The announcement should be in a form which does not constitute a statement or representation of special experience or expertness.

47. Aiding the Unauthorized Practice of Law

No lawyer shall permit his professional services, or his name, to be used in aid of, or to make possible, the unauthorized practice of law by any lay agency, personal or corporate.

MODEL COURT RULE ON
INSURANCE DISCLOSURE (2004)

In August 2004, the ABA House of Delegates voted to adopt the following as a "Model Court Rule" but not as part of the Model Rules of Professional Conduct.

Rule ___. Insurance Disclosure

A.   Each lawyer admitted to the active practice of law shall certify to the [highest court of the jurisdiction] on or before [December 31 of each year]: 1) whether the lawyer is engaged in the private practice of law; 2) if engaged in the private practice of law, whether the lawyer is currently covered by professional liability insurance; 3) whether the lawyer intends to maintain insurance during the period of time the lawyer is engaged in the private practice of law; and 4) whether the lawyer is exempt from the provisions of this Rule because the lawyer is engaged in the practice of law as a full-time government lawyer or is counsel employed by an organizational client and does not represent clients outside that capacity. Each lawyer admitted to the active practice of law in this jurisdiction who reports being covered by professional liability insurance shall notify [the highest court in the jurisdiction] in writing within 30 days if the insurance policy providing coverage lapses, is no longer in effect or terminates for any reason.

B.   The foregoing shall be certified by each lawyer admitted to the active practice of law in this jurisdiction in such form as may be prescribed by the [highest court of the jurisdiction]. The information submitted pursuant to this Rule will be made available to the public by such means as may be designated by the [highest court of the jurisdiction].

C.   Any lawyer admitted to the active practice of law who fails to comply with this Rule in a timely fashion, as defined by the [highest court in the jurisdiction], may be suspended from the practice of law until such time as the lawyer complies. Supplying false information in response to this Rule shall subject the lawyer to appropriate disciplinary action.

ABA MODEL COURT RULE ON PROVISION OF LEGAL SERVICES FOLLOWING DETERMINATION OF MAJOR DISASTER (2007)

RULE ___. PROVISION OF LEGAL SERVICES FOLLOWING DETERMINATION OF MAJOR DISASTER

(a) DETERMINATION OF EXISTENCE OF MAJOR DISASTER. Solely for purposes of this Rule, this Court shall determine when an emergency affecting the justice system, as a result of a natural or other major disaster has occurred in:

(1) this jurisdiction and whether the emergency caused by the major disaster affects the entirety or only a part of this jurisdiction, or

(2) another jurisdiction but only after such a determination and its geographical scope have been made by the highest court of that jurisdiction. The authority to engage in the temporary practice of law in this jurisdiction pursuant to paragraph (c) shall extend only to lawyers who principally practice in the area of such other jurisdiction determined to have suffered a major disaster causing an emergency affecting the justice system and the provision of legal services.

(b) TEMPORARY PRACTICE IN THIS JURISDICTION FOLLOWING MAJOR DISASTER. Following the determination of an emergency affecting the justice system in this jurisdiction pursuant to paragraph (a) of this Rule, or a determination that persons displaced by a major disaster in another jurisdiction and residing in this jurisdiction are in need of pro bono services and the assistance of lawyers from outside of this jurisdiction is required to help provide such assistance, a lawyer authorized to practice law in another United States jurisdiction, and not disbarred, suspended from practice or otherwise restricted from practice in any jurisdiction, may provide legal services in this jurisdiction on a temporary basis. Such legal services must be provided on a pro bono basis without compensation, expectation of compensation or other direct or indirect pecuniary gain to the lawyer. Such legal services shall be assigned and supervised through an established not-for-profit bar association, pro bono program or legal services program or through such organization(s) specifically designated by this Court.

(c) TEMPORARY PRACTICE IN THIS JURISDICTION FOLLOWING MAJOR DISASTER IN ANOTHER JURISDICTION. Following the determination of a major disaster in another United States jurisdiction, a lawyer who is authorized to practice law and who principally practices in that affected jurisdiction, and who is not disbarred, suspended from practice or otherwise restricted from practice in any jurisdiction, may provide legal services in this jurisdiction on a temporary basis. Those legal services must arise out of and be reasonably related to that lawyer's practice of law in the jurisdiction, or area of such other jurisdiction, where the major disaster occurred.

(d) DURATION OF AUTHORITY FOR TEMPORARY PRACTICE. The authority to practice law in this jurisdiction granted by paragraph (b) of this Rule shall end when this Court determines that the conditions caused by the major disaster in this jurisdiction have ended except that a lawyer then representing clients in this jurisdiction pursuant to paragraph (b) is authorized to continue the provision of legal services for such time as is reasonably necessary to complete the representation, but the lawyer shall not thereafter accept new clients. The authority to practice law in this jurisdiction granted by paragraph (c) of this Rule shall end [60] days after this Court declares that the conditions caused by the major disaster in the affected jurisdiction have ended.

(e) **COURT APPEARANCES.** The authority granted by this Rule does not include appearances in court except:

(1) pursuant to that court's pro hac vice admission rule and, if such authority is granted, any fees for such admission shall be waived; or

(2) if this Court, in any determination made under paragraph (a), grants blanket permission to appear in all or designated courts of this jurisdiction to lawyers providing legal services pursuant to paragraph (b). If such an authorization is included, any pro hac vice admission fees shall be waived.

(f) **DISCIPLINARY AUTHORITY AND REGISTRATION REQUIREMENT.** Lawyers providing legal services in this jurisdiction pursuant to paragraphs (b) or (c) are subject to this Court's disciplinary authority and the Rules of Professional Conduct of this jurisdiction as provided in Rule 8.5 of the Rules of Professional Conduct. Lawyers providing legal services in this jurisdiction under paragraphs (b) or (c) shall, within 30 days from the commencement of the provision of legal services, file a registration statement with the Clerk of this Court. The registration statement shall be in a form prescribed by this Court. Any lawyer who provides legal services pursuant to this Rule shall not be considered to be engaged in the unlawful practice of law in this jurisdiction.

(g) **NOTIFICATION TO CLIENTS.** Lawyers authorized to practice law in another United States jurisdiction who provide legal services pursuant to this Rule shall inform clients in this jurisdiction of the jurisdiction in which they are authorized to practice law, any limits of that authorization, and that they are not authorized to practice law in this jurisdiction except as permitted by this Rule. They shall not state or imply to any person that they are otherwise authorized to practice law in this jurisdiction.

Comment

[1] A major disaster in this or another jurisdiction may cause an emergency affecting the justice system with respect to the provision of legal services for a sustained period of time interfering with the ability of lawyers admitted and practicing in the affected jurisdiction to continue to represent clients until the disaster has ended. When this happens, lawyers from the affected jurisdiction may need to provide legal services to their clients, on a temporary basis, from an office outside their home jurisdiction. In addition, lawyers in an unaffected jurisdiction may be willing to serve residents of the affected jurisdiction who have unmet legal needs as a result of the disaster or, though independent of the disaster, whose legal needs temporarily are unmet because of disruption to the practices of local lawyers. Lawyers from unaffected jurisdictions may offer to provide these legal services either by traveling to the affected jurisdiction or from their own offices or both, provided the legal services are provided on a pro bono basis through an authorized not-for-profit entity or such other organization(s) specifically designated by this Court. A major disaster includes, for example, a hurricane, earthquake, flood, wildfire, tornado, public health emergency or an event caused by terrorists or acts of war.

[2]   Under paragraph (a)(1), this Court shall determine whether a major disaster causing an emergency affecting the justice system has occurred in this jurisdiction, or in a part of this jurisdiction, for purposes of triggering paragraph (b) of this Rule. This Court may, for example, determine that the entirety of this jurisdiction has suffered a disruption in the provision of legal services or that only certain areas have suffered such an event. The authority granted by paragraph (b) shall extend only to lawyers authorized to practice law and not disbarred, suspended from practice or otherwise restricted from practice in any other manner in any other jurisdiction.

[3]   Paragraph (b) permits lawyers authorized to practice law in an unaffected jurisdiction, and not disbarred, suspended from practice or otherwise restricted from practicing law in any other manner in any other jurisdiction, to provide pro bono legal services to residents of the affected jurisdiction following determination of an emergency caused by a major disaster; notwithstanding that they are not otherwise authorized to practice law in the affected jurisdiction. Other restrictions on a lawyer's license to practice law that would prohibit that lawyer from providing legal services pursuant to this Rule include, but are not limited to, probation, inactive status, disability inactive status or a non-disciplinary administrative suspension for failure to complete continuing legal education or other requirements. Lawyers on probation may be subject to monitoring and specific limitations on their practices. Lawyers on inactive status, despite being characterized in many jurisdictions as being "in good standing," and lawyers on disability inactive status are not permitted to practice law. Public protection warrants exclusion of these lawyers from the authority to provide legal services as defined in this Rule. Lawyers permitted to provide legal services pursuant to this Rule must do so without fee or other compensation, or expectation thereof. Their service must be provided through an established not-for-profit organization that is authorized to provide legal services either in its own name or that provides representation of clients through employed or cooperating lawyers. Alternatively, this court may instead designate other specific organization(s) through which these legal services may be rendered. Under paragraph (b), an emeritus lawyer from another United State jurisdiction may provide pro bono legal services on a temporary basis in this jurisdiction provided that the emeritus lawyer is authorized to provide pro bono legal services in that jurisdiction pursuant to that jurisdiction's emeritus or pro bono practice rule. Lawyers may also be authorized to provide legal services in this jurisdiction on a temporary basis under Rule 5.5(c) of the Rules of Professional Conduct.

[4]   Lawyers authorized to practice law in another jurisdiction, who principally practice in the area of such other jurisdiction determined by this Court to have suffered a major disaster, and whose practices are disrupted by a major disaster there, and who are not disbarred, suspended from practice or otherwise restricted from practicing law in any other manner in any other jurisdiction, are authorized under paragraph (c) to provide legal services on a temporary basis in this jurisdiction. Those legal services must arise out of and be reasonably related to the lawyer's practice of law in the affected jurisdiction. For purposes of this Rule, the determination of a major disaster in another jurisdiction should first be made by the highest court of appellate jurisdiction in that jurisdiction. For the meaning of "arise out of and reasonably related to," see Rule 5.5 Comment [14], Rules of Professional Conduct.

[5]   Emergency conditions created by major disasters end, and when they do, the authority created by paragraphs (b) and (c) also ends with

appropriate notice to enable lawyers to plan and to complete pending legal matters. Under paragraph (d), this Court determines when those conditions end only for purposes of this Rule. The authority granted under paragraph (b) shall end upon such determination except that lawyers assisting residents of this jurisdiction under paragraph (b) may continue to do so for such longer period as is reasonably necessary to complete the representation. The authority created by paragraph (c) will end [60] days after this Court makes such a determination with regard to an affected jurisdiction.

[6]   Paragraphs (b) and (c) do not authorize lawyers to appear in the courts of this jurisdiction. Court appearances are subject to the pro hac vice admission rules of the particular court. This Court may, in a determination made under paragraph (e)(2), include authorization for lawyers who provide legal services in this jurisdiction under paragraph (b) to appear in all or designated courts of this jurisdiction without need for such pro hac vice admission. If such an authorization is included, any pro hac vice admission fees shall be waived. A lawyer who has appeared in the courts of this jurisdiction pursuant to paragraph (e) may continue to appear in any such matter notwithstanding a declaration under paragraph (d) that the conditions created by major disaster have ended. Furthermore, withdrawal from a court appearance is subject to Rule 1.16 of the Rules of Professional Conduct.

[7]   Authorization to practice law as a foreign legal consultant or in-house counsel in a United States jurisdiction offers lawyers a limited scope of permitted practice and may therefore restrict that person's ability to provide legal services under this Rule.

[8]   The ABA National Lawyer Regulatory Data Bank is available to help determine whether any lawyer seeking to practice in this jurisdiction pursuant to paragraphs (b) or (c) of this Rule is disbarred, suspended from practice or otherwise subject to a public disciplinary sanction that would restrict the lawyer's ability to practice law in any other jurisdiction.

LAWYER'S CREED OF PROFESSIONALISM*

The ABA House of Delegates, at its August 1988 meeting, adopted as ABA policy a recommendation that state and local bar associations "encourage their members to accept as a guide for their individual conduct, and to comply with, a lawyers' creed of professionalism." The ABA Torts and Insurance Practice Section, which had sought and won the ABA's approval of such a policy, also set forth an example of such a "Lawyer's Creed of Professionalism." This document is published below in full text. The House of Delegates made clear that "nothing in such a creed shall be deemed to supersede or in any way amend the Model Rules of Professional Conduct or other disciplinary codes, alter existing standards of conduct against which lawyer negligence might be judged or become a basis for the imposition of civil liability of any kind."

At the same meeting, the House of Delegates authorized the dissemination to the profession of a "Lawyer's Pledge of Professionalism," which the ABA Young Lawyer's Section had proposed. This document is also published below in full text, and reprinted with permission.

Preamble

As a lawyer I must strive to make our system of justice work fairly and efficiently. In order to carry out that responsibility, not only will I comply with the letter and spirit of the disciplinary standards applicable to all lawyers, but I will also conduct myself in accordance with the following Creed of Professionalism when dealing with my client, opposing parties, their counsel, the courts and the general public.

A. With respect to my client:

1. I will be loyal and committed to my client's cause, but I will not permit that loyalty and commitment to interfere with my ability to provide my client with objective and independent advice;

2. I will endeavor to achieve my client's lawful objectives in business transactions and in litigation as expeditiously and economically as possible;

3. In appropriate cases, I will counsel my client with respect to mediation, arbitration and other alternative methods of resolving disputes;

4. I will advise my client against pursuing litigation (or any other course of action) that is without merit and against insisting on tactics which are intended to delay resolution of the matter or to harass or drain the financial resources of the opposing party;

5. I will advise my client that civility and courtesy are not to be equated with weakness;

6. While I must abide by my client's decision concerning the objectives of the representation, I nevertheless will counsel my client that a willingness to initiate or engage in settlement discussions is consistent with zealous and effective representation.

---

*   Not adopted by the ABA House of Delegates. Not American Bar Association Policy. Reprinted with permission. Copyrighted by the A.B.A.

B. With respect to opposing parties and their counsel:

1. I will endeavor to be courteous and civil, both in oral and in written communications;

2. I will not knowingly make statements of fact or of law that are untrue;

3. In litigation proceedings I will agree to reasonable requests for extensions of time or for waiver of procedural formalities when the legitimate interests of my client will not be adversely affected;

4. I will endeavor to consult with opposing counsel before scheduling depositions and meetings and before re-scheduling hearings, and I will cooperate with opposing counsel when scheduling changes are requested;

5. I will refrain from utilizing litigation or any other course of conduct to harass the opposing party;

6. I will refrain from engaging in excessive and abusive discovery, and I will comply with all reasonable discovery requests;

7. I will refrain from utilizing delaying tactics;

8. In depositions and other proceedings, and in negotiations, I will conduct myself with dignity, avoid making groundless objections and refrain from engaging in acts of rudeness or disrespect;

9. I will not serve motions and pleadings on the other party, or his counsel, at such a time or in such a manner as will unfairly limit the other party's opportunity to respond;

10. In business transactions I will not quarrel over matters of form or style, but will concentrate on matters of substance and content;

11. I will clearly identify, for other counsel or parties, all changes that I have made in documents submitted to me for review.

C. With respect to the courts and other tribunals:

1. I will be a vigorous and zealous advocate on behalf of my client, while recognizing, as an officer of the court, that excessive zeal may be detrimental to my client's interests as well as to the proper functioning of our system of justice;

2. Where consistent with my client's interests, I will communicate with opposing counsel in an effort to avoid litigation and to resolve litigation that has actually commenced;

3. I will voluntarily withdraw claims or defenses when it becomes apparent that they do not have merit or are superfluous;

4. I will refrain from filing frivolous motions;

5. I will make every effort to agree with other counsel, as early as possible, on a voluntary exchange of information and on a plan for discovery;

6. I will attempt to resolve, by agreement, my objections to matters contained in my opponent's pleadings and discovery requests;

7. When scheduling hearings or depositions have to be canceled, I will notify opposing counsel, and, if appropriate, the court (or other tribunal) as early as possible;

8. Before dates for hearings or trials are set—or if that is not feasible, immediately after such dates have been set—I will attempt to verify the

availability of key participants and witnesses so that I can promptly notify the court (or other tribunal) and opposing counsel of any likely problem in that regard;

9.   In civil matters, I will stipulate to facts as to which there is no genuine dispute;

10.   I will endeavor to be punctual in attending court hearings, conferences and depositions;

11.   I will at all times be candid with the court.

D.   With respect to the public and to our system of justice:

1.   I will remember that, in addition to commitment to my client's cause, my responsibilities as a lawyer include a devotion to the public good;

2.   I will endeavor to keep myself current in the areas in which I practice and, when necessary, will associate with, or refer my client to, counsel knowledgeable in another field of practice;

3.   I will be mindful of the fact that, as a member of a self-regulating profession, it is incumbent on me to report violations by fellow lawyers of any disciplinary rule;

4.   I will be mindful of the need to protect the image of the legal profession in the eyes of the public and will be so guided when considering methods and content of advertising;

5.   I will be mindful that the law is a learned profession and that among its desirable goals are devotion to public service, improvement of administration of justice, and the contribution of uncompensated time and civic influence on behalf of those persons who cannot afford adequate legal assistance.

CIVILITY CODE
THE NORTHAMPTON COUNTY BAR ASSOCIATION GUIDE TO CONDUCT AND ETIQUETTE AT THE BAR

These guiding principles comprise the considered opinion of the Bench and Bar of Northampton County concerning professional etiquette and are a result of suggestions made by the Bench at the request of the Bar.

1. Lawyers should dress in a fashion consistent with the respect they expect the public to have for their profession. Lawyers should not appear before the Court in overcoats or other wearing apparel designed for outdoor wear. Lawyers who are at the courthouse for reasons other than a Court appearance should nonetheless recognize the courthouse as the center and focus of their professional activity and dress accordingly. The same formality of dress that is appropriate for the courtroom is appropriate for an appearance before a Judge at the Judge's office or in the Judge's chambers.

2. Lawyers should ask permission to address the Court rather than just jumping up and starting to talk. The proper method of requesting such permission is to preface one's remark by the phrase: "May it please the Court . . . "

3. Lawyers should request permission to approach the bench prior to doing so. While at sidebar, lawyers should not rest upon nor "drape themselves" over the bench.

4. Lawyers should first address the Court and opposing counsel before addressing the jury. The proper form of doing this is to first address the Court: "May it please the Court." The Court then acknowledges counsel. Counsel then addresses opposing counsel first: "Mr., Ms., Mrs., _____," and then "Ladies and Gentlemen of the Jury."

5. Lawyers should always stand when addressing the court. This should be done even at the call of the hearing list and the various trial lists.

6. Lawyers when making objections should stand and state a brief (one word if possible) reason for the objection, such as "Objection: Hearsay." If it is necessary to enlarge the record after an objection, lawyers should approach the bench and quietly, out of the hearing of the jury, state their reasons. They should not present their arguments to the jury but only to the Court.

7. In addressing a witness lawyers should stand behind their desk and if for any reason they want to approach the witness, they should only do so after obtaining the court's permission.

8. When marking exhibits for identification, it is suggested that the courteous way of doing this is to give the exhibit to the court reporter to have the exhibit marked, and to then exhibit it to the court and to opposing counsel. All of these actions should be performed before questions are again directed to the witness. The court reporter cannot possibly mark an exhibit and record testimony at the same time. Where there are a multitude of exhibits, they should be marked in advance by the court reporter or the lawyers. When possible and not too

cumbersome, separate copies of exhibits should be provided for the Court. This permits the original to remain with the court reporter and avoids the problem of lawyers having to search for them on the bench or elsewhere.

9. Lawyers should always keep their voices up and remind their witnesses to do the same.

10. Lawyers should never directly address opposing counsel in Court. Lawyers should directly address only the Court, the jury, and the witnesses.

11. A lawyer should not call any witness, even his or her client, by the witness' first name.

12. Lawyers should limit voir dire questions to the proper purpose of voir dire and should not attempt to instruct the jury as to the law or to argue their case to the jury by means of voir dire questions.

13. As a tactical point, there is a great weight of authority to the effect that cases are won or lost on direct examination. Young lawyers uniformly have a tendency to overdo the cross-examination of witnesses.

14. Motion Court convenes at 9:00 A.M. every day except weekends and holidays. Except for rules to show cause, lawyers should supply to all opposing counsel a copy of the proposed motion and notice of the date the motion is to be presented at least three days prior to presenting the motion. A motion should not be presented to any Judge other than the Motion Judge, nor at any time other than during Motion Court, unless emergency relief is required.

15. Lawyers should be on time for all court appearances, including all calls of the list.

16. Lawyers who have cases on a miscellaneous hearing list should remain immediately available, so that when their case is called they are ready to begin promptly.

17. Lawyers should not initiate conversation with jurors who have served on a jury in a case they were trying.

18. If a lawyer has an uncontested motion or rule to show cause and cannot get to Motion Court, he or she may leave it with the Court Administrator who will present it to the Motion Judge and return it to the lawyer.

19. All lawyers, in accordance with the Court Rules and Rule 1.1 of the Rules of Professional Conduct, should be prepared at all times when they appear before the Court.

20. Lawyers should exhibit courtesy in the courtroom toward opposing counsel as well as to the court and to witnesses.

21. Lawyers should at all times deal with each other honestly and with respect. It is suggested that communication between counsel in the presence of clients and before the court shall be with respect and courtesy—"Treat others as you would have them treat you."

22. Lawyers should be cognizant of the effect of use of gender specific terms when addressing another lawyer. Such language tends to degrade the recipient in the eyes of clients and others.

23. By the very nature of our profession, heated exchanges occur. Threats of physical violence, however, cannot and should not be tolerated or condoned under any circumstances.

24. Whenever possible, trial counsel should include the authority relied upon in points for charge and refrain from unduly repetitious points.

25. Lawyers should wait until all of the assignments have been announced on a miscellaneous hearing or argument list before engaging others in conversation or gathering their briefcases, charts, and other paraphernalia and leaving the courtroom.

26. Lawyers should be available in their offices or at the Courthouse to respond to telephone civil status calls at least one-half hour prior to the designated time.

27. Trials or hearings may not be continued without Court approval. Discovery deadlines fixed by court order may not be extended without Court approval. The mere agreement of counsel to a continuance or to an extension is insufficient.

28. The Court's overall view is that it is pleased with the courtroom demeanor of the Northampton County Bar.

29. These guidelines should not be construed as being a criticism of the Bar in general, or of any lawyers in particular, but merely as suggestions to all members of the Bar who are perhaps not aware of these matters.

30. The Court has particularly expressed its satisfaction with the preparedness of counsel at pretrial conferences and will continue to insist that this level of preparedness be maintained.

Revised January 1994.

DADE COUNTY BAR ASSOCIATION, FLORIDA CODE OF PROFESSIONALISM AND CIVILITY

PREAMBLE: Honor and integrity are the essence and an indispensable part of our profession. It is not enough to speak of honor or profess integrity. In the end, a personal commitment to honor and integrity must be established. Professionalism may no longer be relegated to a secondary topic and/or study that is then summarily filed away. We must acknowledge the responsibilities we have to society and each other. We as attorneys pledge to practice law in an honorable manner and devote ourselves to this Code of Professionalism and Civility.

AS A PROFESSIONAL, I WILL ALWAYS:

- Remember that my responsibilities include a devotion to the public good, respect for the civil rights and sensibilities of others, and a willingness to provide pro bono or reduced fee services where appropriate.

- Exercise courtesy and civility in all communications and avoid rudeness and other acts of disrespect.

- Avoid personal criticism of another lawyer.

- Set a good example for and assist newer members of the bar.

- Consider the effect of my conduct and deportment on the image of lawyers and the system of justice.

- Counsel clients about alternative forms of dispute resolution where appropriate and available.

- Avoid non-essential litigation and non-essential pleadings in litigation.

- Communicate with opposing counsel in an effort to avoid litigation and to attempt to resolve litigation that has commenced.

- Attempt to resolve by non-coerced agreement my objections to matters contained in my opponent's pleadings and discovery requests.

- Prevent misuses of court time by verifying the availability of key participants for scheduled appearances before the court.

- Stipulate to facts in civil matters as to which there is no genuine dispute.

- Speak or write courteously and respectfully in all communications with the court or tribunal and show my respect by my attire and demeanor.

- Exercise candor with the court at all times and act with complete honesty.

- Attempt to determine compatible dates with opposing counsel before scheduling motions, meetings, and depositions.

- Avoid serving motions and pleadings in such a manner or at such a time as to harass opposing counsel or preclude an opportunity for a competent response.

- Attempt to resolve any dispute with opposing counsel prior to filing any notice or scheduling any hearing.

- Identify clearly all changes made in documents submitted to opposing counsel for review.

- Respect the commitments of others by striving to always be punctual.

- Remember that the conflict is between the clients and not the lawyers.

- Respond promptly to all requests by opposing counsel.

- Counsel clients about the value of cooperation and compromise in the resolution of disputes.

- Advise clients against pursuing litigation or other actions that are without merit or intended merely to harass, delay, or exhaust the financial resources of the opposing party.

- Reach clear agreements, preferably in writing, with clients concerning the nature of the representation and the fees to be charged.

- Keep clients advised as to the progress of their matter and communicate promptly and clearly with clients.

- Strive to achieve my client's goals expeditiously, and at a reasonable fee.

- Recognize that uncivil conduct does not advance and may compromise the rights of my clients.

https://www.dadecountybar.org/page/code